THE**GREEN**GUIDE
Sicily

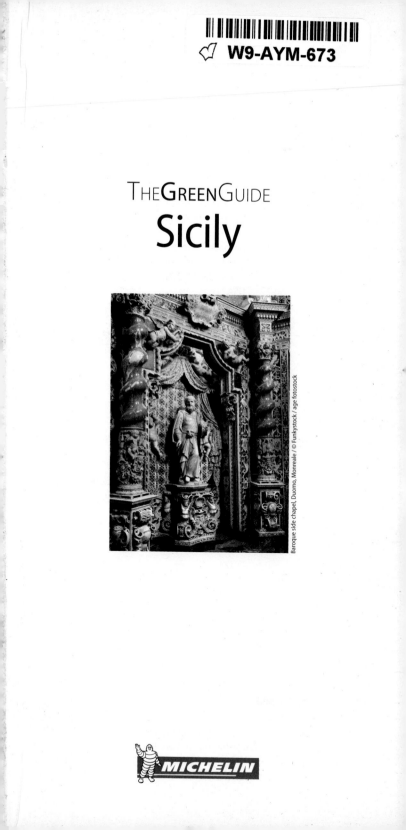

Baroque side chapel, Duomo, Monreale / © Funkystock / age fotostock

MICHELIN

THEGREENGUIDE SICILY

Editorial Director	Cynthia Ochterbeck
Edited & Produced by	Jonathan P. Gilbert
Contributing Writer	Steven Durose
Production Manager	Natasha G. George
Cartography	Peter Wrenn
Interior Design	Chris Bell
Layout	Chris Bell
Cover Design	Chris Bell, Christelle Le Déan
Cover Layout	Michelin Travel Partner, Natasha G. George

Contact Us	Michelin Travel and Lifestyle North America One Parkway South Greenville, SC 29615 USA travel.lifestyle@us.michelin.com www.michelintravel.com
	Michelin Travel Partner Hannay House 39 Clarendon Road Watford, Herts WD17 1JA UK ✆01923 205240 travelpubsales@uk.michelin.com www.ViaMichelin.com
Special Sales	For information regarding bulk sales, customized editions and premium sales, please contact us at: travel.lifestyle@us.michelin.com www.michelintravel.com

HOW TO USE THIS GUIDE

PLANNING YOUR TRIP

The blue-tabbed PLANNING YOUR TRIP section at the front of the guide gives you. **ideas for your trip** and **practical information** to organise it. You'll find tours, practical information, a host of outdoor activities, a calendar of events, information on shopping, sightseeing, children's activities and more.

INTRODUCTION

The orange-tabbed INTRODUCTION section explores the **Nature**, geography and geology of Sicily. The **History** section explores pre-Hellenistic archaeological evidence through to present day Sicily. The **Art and Culture** section covers architecture, art, literature and music, while **Sicily Today** delves into modern Sicilian lifestyle, people and cuisine.

DISCOVERING

The green-tabbed DISCOVERING section features Principal Sights by region, featuring the most interesting local **Sights**, **Walking Tours**, nearby **Excursions**, and detailed **Driving Tours**. Admission prices shown are normally for a single adult.

ADDRESSES

We've selected the best hotels, restaurants, cafés, shops, nightlife and entertainment to fit all budgets. See the Legend on the cover flap for an explanation of the price categories. See the back of the guide for an index of where to find hotels and restaurants.

Sidebars

Throughout the guide you will find blue, orange and green-coloured text boxes with lively anecdotes, detailed history and background information.

😊 A Bit of Advice 😊

Green advice boxes found in this guide contain practical tips and handy information relevant to your visit or to a sight in the Discovering section.

STAR RATINGS★★★

Michelin has given star ratings for more than 100 years. If you're pressed for time, we recommend you visit the ★★★, or ★★ sights first:

★★★　**Highly recommended**

★★　　**Recommended**

★　　　**Interesting**

MAPS

- 🗺 Country map
- 🗺 Principal Sights map
- 🗺 Region maps
- 🗺 Maps for major cities and villages
- 🗺 Local tour maps

All maps in this guide are oriented north, unless otherwise indicated by a directional arrow. The term "Local Map" refers to a map within the chapter or Tourism Region. A complete list of the maps found in the guide appears at the back of this book.

PLANNING YOUR TRIP

INTRODUCTION TO SICILY

CONTENTS

© Ian Murray / age fotostock

DISCOVERING SICILY

Welcome to Sicily

Strategically positioned between Europe and North Africa, Sicily was a prized possession of both the Greek and Roman Empires. Coveted by successive waves of Arab and Norman invaders, with a pivotal role to play in the European theatre of war, the Mediterranean's largest island reads like a cultural primer. Sicily has had a huge impact on world civilisation, inspiring everything from Homer and the Greek legends to modern-day artists and filmmakers. For today's traveller, it has something to suit all tastes and interests – archaeology, Ancient architecture, history and magnificent works of art, perfectly-preserved marine environments and dramatic landscapes – and, of course, one of Italy's great cuisines.

PALERMO AND ITS SURROUNDINGS *(pp118–177)*

The capital of Sicily, nestled between hills and sea, Palermo is an essential stop on any Sicilian sojourn with its Arabo-Norman palaces, deliciously ornamented Baroque churches, intriguing medieval old town, Liberty-style architecture, lush botanical gardens and bustling street markets. Monreale, with its magnificent duomo and other lovely hill towns, merits at least a day trip, as does the beautiful coastline of the Golfo di Castellammare.

WESTERN SICILY *(pp178–211)*

The medieval fishing town of Trapani is an up-and-coming seaside resort to rival Taormina on the other side of the island. An excursion along the coast to the famous wine town of

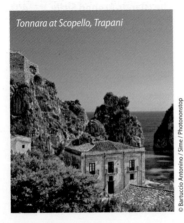

Tonnara at Scopello, Trapani

© Bartuccio Antonino / Sime / Photononstop

Marsala takes visitors past dazzling saltpans. Other must-see sites include the unforgettable perched site of Erice and the Greek temple at Segesta.

AGRIGENTO AND THE SOUTH COAST *(pp212–238)*

Agrigento's Valley of the Temples with its collection of sacred Doric buildings is one of the world's most important monuments to Greek art and culture. The coast towards Sciacca and its surrounding hills offer some of the island's most beautiful natural sites.

Temple of Heracles, Agrigento

© M. Guillot / MICHELIN

CENTRAL SICILY *(pp239–265)*

The heartland of Sicily is ideal for road trips across a dramatic landscape of rolling hills that changes with the seasons. Essential stops include Enna (prized by Norman kings as the "lookout of Sicily"), the great Roman mosaics at the Villa Romana del

Casale, and Caltagirone – a centre of ancient ceramic and majolica traditions.

THE BAROQUE TRIANGLE: SIRACUSA, NOTO AND RAGUSA *(pp266–p317)*

The southeastern corner of Sicily, whose towns were rebuilt in an enthusiastic spurt of Baroque construction following the devastating earthquake of 1693, is perfect for lovers of architecture, history and beautiful mountain views. The setting for Siracusa and several remarkable civilisations, from prehistory to the present day, and crossed by the fertile, peaceful Iblei mountains, this region is prized for its olive oil, honey and almonds.

THE IONIAN COAST: CATANIA, ETNA AND TAORMINA *(pp318–360)*

One of the most popular tourist spots in Sicily, the Ionian Coast is home to Taormina, a coastal resort perched above a dramatic bay at the foot of the island's iconic active volcano, Mount Etna. Explore the beautiful city of Catania and its monuments, and the citrus-, pistachio- and wine-producing towns around Etna before making the ascent. A corner of Sicily where the wilderness and opportunities for outdoor sports meet sophistication, music and culture.

Duomo, Catania

© Sandro Bedessi / Fototeca ENIT

THE TYRRHENIAN COAST FROM MILAZZO TO CEFALÙ *(pp361–402)*

Mountains rise out of the sea on this exceptional stretch of coastline backed by two ranges – the Madonie and the Nebrodi - where you'll find Sicily's largest forests and two regional nature parks. Age-old traditions, history and nature blend seamlessly in this area ideal for lovers of the outdoors and anyone who likes travelling off the beaten track.

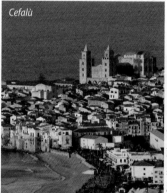

Cefalù

© Bruno Morandi / hemis.fr

THE ISLANDS AROUND SICILY *(pp403–439)*

Sicily's satellite islands vary from chic to isolated, flat to mountainous, fertile to barren and dormant to actively volcanic. A ferry ride away from the main island, the Aeolian islands, Egadi Islands, Pelagie Islands, Pantelleria and Ustica offer an ideal retreat for anyone who wants to leave modern civilisation behind. Remarkably, each island has a different feel, natural environment, tradition and local cuisine. They also provide excellent diving opportunities.

Piazza Duomo, island of Ortygia, Siracusa
© White Star Monica G / age fotostock

Michelin Driving Tours

LOCAL DRIVES

👣*The following is a selection of the Driving Tours from the Discovering section. Allow ample time to enjoy the scenery and make unexpected stops.*

INLAND FROM PALERMO

👣*See Palermo. 120km/75mi. Allow a day.* Circuit includes mountain views, archaeological sites and the magnificent duomo at Monreale.

PALERMO TO CASTELLAMMARE DEL GOLFO

👣*See Golfo di Castellammare. 100km/62mi. Allow a day.* A drive along the beautiful coast to archaeological sites and the Zingaro nature reserve.

TRAPANI–MARSALA (LA VIA DEL SALE)

👣*See Trapani. 30km/19mi. Allow a half-day.* This excursion skirting the coastal salt flats includes a visit to the Island of Mozia.

Scala dei Turchi along the southern coast

© Ripani Massimo / Sime / Photononstop

FROM AGRIGENTO TO ERACLEA MINOA ALONG STUNNING BEACHES

👣*See Agrigento and La Valle dei Templi. 90km/56mi. Allow a day.* An evocative tour through Antique vestiges to a nature reserve on the southern coast.

NATURAL HISTORY, ARCHAEOLOGY AND SULPHUR ROUTE

👣*See Enna. 130km/81mi. Allow a day.* From the "lookout of Sicily" to a legend-inspiring landscape of hills and ancient sulphur mining towns.

ARCHAEOLOGY AROUND SIRACUSA

👣*See Siracusa. 80km/50mi. Allow a day.* Go back in time to some of Sicily's oldest settlements dating to the 15C BC.

GLI IBLEI

👣*See The Iblei Mountains. 160km/100mi. Allow two days with an overnight in Vizzini.* Explore the rolling mountains and beautiful terraced landscapes of olive and almond trees.

ETNA'S NORTHEAST FLANK

👣*See Etna. 60km/37mi. Allow a half-day.* Discover the towns and natural environment of Etna's north face. Add another half-day to ascend the summit with the four-wheel drive tour.

THE ALCANTARA VALLEY

👣*See Taormina. 60k/37mi. Allow a day.* Explore the river gorges created by ancient lava flows with waterfalls, ponds and a kaleidoscope of colours.

LA FIUMARA D'ARTE

👣*See Madonie. 80km/50mi. Allow a half-day.* The "river of art" from the coast inland features original contemporary sculpture integrated into the landscape.

A DAY IN THE NEBRODI

👣*See The Nebrodi Mountains. 200km/125mi. Allow a full day.* A drive through Sicily's largest expanse of forests, with ancient castles, traditional mountain villages and stunning views.

PANTELLERIA ISLAND CIRCUIT

👣*See Pantelleria. 40km/25mi. Allow a half-day.* A drive on the coastal roads along cliffs with dramatic views.

When and Where to Go

WHEN TO GO
CLIMATE

In Giuseppe Lampedusa's 1958 novel *The Leopard,* the Prince describes the Sicilian climate as "six months of 40°C (104°F) temperatures". Although the writer exaggerated, the southern coast and its immediate hinterland do indeed bake in summer. The northern and eastern shores, and the islands off Sicily enjoy milder climates, thanks to the coastal mountains that shield them from hot African winds. The inland area has cooler summers and harsh winters. Catania is an exceptionally hot city, made more unpleasant by smog. July and August are the most uncomfortable months, while April, May, June, September and October offer pleasantly warm temperatures. Rainfall is scarce, but the centuries-old water shortage does not usually affect visitors as most hotels have cisterns.

SEASONS

In **spring**, the weather is mild, crowds are smaller and rates lower. However, Etna is usually covered in snow and therefore inaccessible until early May, the sea is a little cool for swimming, and the offshore islands only welcome tourists from April or May to October. Most major festivals take place during the **Easter** holidays so book months in advance. **Summer** is the most popular period: all tourist facilities are open, and museums and monuments extend their hours. Disadvantages include the hordes and the heat, which is almost unbearable in some areas: the central inland region, the southern coast, Catania and Palermo.
Autumn is a more pleasant time, offering similar conditions to spring.
Winter is perfect for anyone planning a purely cultural trip, just check opening hours carefully in advance. Be cautious driving inland, as the mountains can be wet and snowy.

THEMED TOURS
SICILIAN WINE ROUTES

Explore the island's major vineyards on itineraries put together by the Istituto Regionale della Vite e del Vino (*www.vitevino.it*).

The Alcamo Route

Alcamo is a dry and fresh white table wine. This tour wends between Castellammare del Golfo, Scopello, Alcamo, Segesta and Calatafimi.

The Dessert Wine Routes

The Moscato *passito* is a rich, sweet, amber wine made from *zibibbo* grapes; Marsala is a darker and more famous blend (See Marsala).
The Marsala route passes through Erice, Trapani, Marsala, Salemi and Gibellina, while the Moscato trip covers the island of Pantelleria.

The Insolia Route

The Insolia (or Ansonica) grape variety – present in almost all Sicilian DOC (*Dominazione di Origine Controllata*) wines – adds a pleasant, fresh palate and floral aromas to the more robust white wines. This tour covers the wine-producing areas of the southern coast, stretching from Mazara del Vallo to Agrigento. It then crosses inland to Palermo's outskirts, passing through Sambuca di Sicilia, Santa Margherita Belice and Monreale en route.

The Nero d'Avola/ Cerasuolo di Vittoria Route

The popular Nero d'Avola grape variety is the basis of rich Sicilian reds. The best territory for the grape is Eloro and its surroundings in southeastern Sicily near the town of Avola, which gives the grape its name. Blended with the Frappato grape, it produces the Cerasuolo di Vittoria (*near Vittoria*), an elegant wine with warm tones and the only Sicilian DOCG wine.

The Moscato di Noto and Moscato di Siracusa Route

These two *moscati* wines have a sweet and harmonious palate and a delicate floral aroma. This tour explores the extreme southeast corner of Sicily, including Siracusa, Noto, Palazzolo Acreide and Pantalica.

The Etna Wine Route

The lower slopes of Mount Etna (1 000 metres/3 280 feet) provide a dramatic backdrop to Sicily's most dynamic wine scene, which attracts winemakers from across Italy and the world. These high-altitude vineyards produce elegant reds dominated by the Nerello Mascalese grape, while mineral-rich whites are made from Carricante. The vines stretch along the sea-facing side of the mountain above Riposto and over the north side from Linguaglossa to Randazzo.

The Malvasia delle Lipari

This ancient method of drying grapes on reed mats produces a delicate, fragrant wine. The tour explores the islands of the Aeolian archipelago.

IDEAS FOR YOUR VISIT

Given Sicily's size and rich heritage, it's best to spend at least one week there, although a two-week stay will allow you to explore the offshore islands. However, below are a few suggestions for shorter breaks.

SHORT BREAKS (3–4 DAYS)
HIGHLIGHTS OF CATANIA

One of the region's highlights is **Mount Etna**, combined with a stop at the delightful town of **Taormina**, before watching the sun set on a beautiful beach. Spend another day at **Siracusa** (*Ortygia and the archaeological site*), followed by a dusk excursion to **Noto** or **Ragusa Ibla**. Your third day's sightseeing should focus on the Valle dei Templi in **Agrigento**, easily combined with the magnificent **Villa Romana del Casale**, near Piazza Armerina.

HIGHLIGHTS OF PALERMO

After arriving at **Palermo airport**, start by exploring the capital city. On Day 2, admire the mosaic masterpieces in the cathedral at **Monreale**, followed by those in **Cefalù**, then retire to a beach in the late afternoon. Possible excursions for Day 3 include a day trip to the Valle dei Templi in **Agrigento**, or to the delightful town of **Erice**, stopping to admire the splendid Doric temple at **Segesta**.

THE IONIAN COAST

In addition to **Taormina** and its neighbouring seaside resorts, highlights include **Mount Etna**, the **Alcantara Valley**, **Catania** and **Siracusa**. Allow 1hr 30min to travel from Taormina to Siracusa (*100km/62mi*).

OUTSKIRTS OF PALERMO

Palermo is an excellent base. Spend one day exploring **Scopello** and the **Riserva dello Zingaro**, another visiting **Erice** and the **Via del Sale** between Trapani and Marsala, and a third following the suggested tour **inland from Palermo** (*⟲See Palermo*).

A FEW DAYS IN THE MOUNTAINS

Visitors based on the north coast at **Cefalù** or **Capo d'Orlando** can discover an unusual facet of Sicily by exploring the Alpine landscapes of the **Madonie e Nebrodi** (*⟲See Madonie, Nebrodi Mountains*).

LONGER BREAK (1–2 WEEKS)

This week-long introduction to the island includes two days in **Palermo**, **Monreale** and **Cefalù**, one day at **Segesta** and **Erice**, and one at the Valle dei Templi in **Agrigento**. Spend one day at the **Villa Romana del Casale** and the **Baroque towns** of Ragusa Ibla, Noto and Modica; the next in **Siracusa**; and the last visiting **Etna** and **Taormina**… with maybe even some time to relax on the beach.

Greek theatre and the Ionian sea, Taormina

© Sime / Photononstop

THE TYRRHENIAN COAST

Start in the island's capital and chief sea port, **Palermo**. Take a day to explore the city. Don't miss the **Historic Quarter** and vibrant **Kalsa** district. Beat the midday heat with visits to the Galleria regionale di Sicilia, Museo Archeologico Regionale or the fascinating, if macabre, 16C–20C interred friars at the *Catacombe dei Cappuccini* just outside the city. The next day, branch out from your Palermo base to **Monreale** and **Cefalù** to admire splendid cathedral frescoes and mosaics.

Start Day three with a morning visit to the ancient splendour of **Segesta** and its Doric temple. In the afternoon, lose yourself in the shady maze of **Erice**'s cobbled streets, dotted with churches and monasteries.

MEDITERRANEAN AND IONIAN COASTS

Head down to the Mediterranean coast and **Agrigento** on Day 4 to stroll through the **Valle dei Templi**. Sense the onward march of the ancient Romans the following day at the **Villa Imperiale del Casale**, with its superb mosaic floors. Arrive early to avoid the crowds and high temperatures, then retire to the shady town squares of **Noto**, **Modica** or **Ragusa Ibla** in the afternoon to soak up their Baroque beauty. Spend the next day

in **Siracusa** exploring the immense Teatro Greco, before heading to **Taormina**. There, either admire the views of **Mount Etna** from the Greek Theatre before relaxing on the beach, or take an early-morning trip to climb the volcano itself.

ISLAND HOPPING
THE AEOLIAN ISLANDS

The seven Aeolian islands are linked to each other, and to the mainland, by regular hydrofoil and ferry services. Highlights include the active volcanoes on **Stromboli** and **Vulcano**, the latter with its dramatic black lava beaches and healing mud. **Lipari**, the largest of the Aeolian islands, is fringed with spectacular beaches, such as the white pumice stretch at **Canneto**. On **Salina** the panoramic coastal road leads to beautiful coves such as Pollara. On **Filicudi** visit the Bronze Age village at **Capo Graziano**, while isolated **Alicudi** and tiny **Panarea** offer secluded traditional charm.

THE EGADI ISLANDS

Renowned for their wild coastal beauty, all three Egadi islands are easily reached from Trapani in under an hour. On Favignana, the tufa caves (once quarries), are now secret gardens. Offshore, take a boat trip out to the Grotta Azzurra and Grotta dei Sospiri. Divers and sunbathers will love the pristine bays of Cala Rotonda and Cala Grande. The tiny, hilly island of Levanzo is a peaceful haven, with a single road and hamlet, Cala Dogana. The island's highlight is the Grotta del Genovese, a two-hour walk away, with its Palaeolithic wall paintings. Marettimo has no hotels on it, although you can rent rooms. Visitors come here for the seclusion and beautiful walks, including those winding up the Punta Troia, topped with the ruins of a 17C Spanish castle.

PANTELLERIA

Start your day in Nika with its cubic Arab-style houses, dammuso and traditional walled Pantelleria gardens filled with citrus trees. Inland, La Montagna Grande and Monte Gibele offer lovely walks and spectacular views. Other highlights include the ancient rock-hewn tombs at Ghirlanda and the natural cave sauna at Grotta Benikula.

USTICA

Surrounded by a Marine National Park, the small volcanic island of Ustica is popular with scuba divers. Highlights include the **Grotta dei Gamberi** and Roman artefacts, to admire in situ along the sub-aqua archaeological trail off the **Punta Gavazzi** headland. Above water, boat trips around the coast offer popular excursions.

THE PELAGIE ISLANDS

The archipelago of Isole Pelagie comprises the large island of Lampedusa and two smaller ones, Linosa and uninhabited Lampione. With their rocky volcanic coastlines and desert interiors, the islands are primarily of interest for the superb diving and snorkelling around their shores.

LITERARY ROUTES

These itineraries celebrate the life and works of authors.

LUIGI PIRANDELLO

This route links the towns between Agrigento and Porto Empedocle which both have a connection with the Nobel Prize-winning playwright. **Contact** Il Cerchio, Via Ugo La Malfa a Monte 1, Agrigento; ℘0922 40 28 62; www.parcopirandello.it.

SALVATORE QUASIMODO

Towns such as Modica (Salvatore Quasimodo's birthplace) and Roccalumera (between Messina and Taormina), whose Saracen tower inspired one of the poet's works, are included on this route. **Contact** Via Posteria, Modica; ℘0932 75 38 64; www.salvatore-quasimodo.it.

LEONARDO SCIASCIA

This journey focuses on Racalmuto, Leonardo Sciascia's birthplace, and Caltanissetta, where he studied. **Contact** the Fondazione Leonardo Sciascia, Viale della Vittoria 3, Racalmuto; ℘0922 94 19 93; www.fondazioneleonardosciascia.it.

PARCO CULTRALE DEL GATTOPARDO

This route links Palermo, the birthplace of **Giuseppe Tomasi di Lampedusa**; Santa Margherita Belice, where he spent much of his childhood and adolescence; and Palma di Montechiaro, the family's fief. **Contact** Foro Umberto 1, Palermo; ℘091 62 54 011; www.parcotomasi.it.

GIOVANNI VERGA

This route wends its way between Catania, Aci Castello and Aci Trezza, home to the author Giovanni Verga and many of his characters. **Visit** www.parchiletterari.com/parchi/giovanniverga.

ELIO VITTORINI

This literary park in Siracusa is dedicated to the writer Elio Vittorini. **Visit** www.sicilyontour.com/eng/park_elio_vittorini_literary_park.htm.

What to See and Do

OUTDOOR FUN

Sicily is the ideal destination for outdoor activity enthusiasts, with plenty of opportunities for hiking, horse-riding, scuba-diving, canoeing, sailing, cycling and mountain biking. Explore other options with *La Guida del Turismo in Sicilia*, available in bookshops or from the publisher, **Krea** *(Piazza Scannaserpe, Palermo; ℘091 54 35 06; www.sikania.it).* The same company produces a guide to nature reserves, *Le Riserve Naturali Orientate (Italian only).*

BIKING

Several bike tour companies organise themed outings in different areas of Sicily. **Sciclando Active holidays** *(US and Canada: ℘1 800 881 0484; UK: ℘203 355 4186, www.siciclando. com)* organises cycling tours of the island for individuals and groups. Themes include mountains, sea, Baroque art and hills, and cooking. *For general information about cycling in Italy, contact the Federazione Ciclistica Italiana: www.federciclismo.it.*

CANYONING

Information on canyoning in Sicily is available from the **Associazione Italiana Canyoning**, **Sezione Sicilia** *(Signor Diego Leonardi, ℘095 70 81 995; www.aic-canyoning.it), and from* **Etna Adventure** *(E. Longo 8, Zafferana Etnea, ℘329 91 88 187; www.etnaadventure.it).*

CAVING

Some of Sicily's cave-systems are classed as nature reserves and maintained by the **Club Alpino Italiani** (CAI) *(Via Petrella, 19, Milano, ℘02 20 57 231, www.cai.it);* and by **Legambiente**, *(Via Genoa 7, Palermo, ℘091 61 11 735; www.legambiente. com).* The main caving options are listed opposite:

Riserva Grotta di Carburangeli

at Carini *(Province of Palermo).* Guided tours of the cave are organised by Legambiente *(Corso Umberto I 64, Carini; ℘091 86 69797; www.parks.it/ riserva.grotta.carburangeli).*

Riserva Grotta di Santa Ninfa

(Province of Trapani). Contact the local Legambiente office for tour details *(Via S. Anna 101, Santa Ninfa; ℘0924 62 376; www.parks.it/riserva.grotta.santa. ninfa).*

Riserva Naturale Grotta Conza

(Province of Palermo). Contact the central reservation desk: ℘*091 61 18 805; www.caisicilia.it/riserve/riserva-naturale-grotta-conza.*

Riserva Naturale Monte Conca

(Province of Caltanissetta). More information from the central reservation desk: ℘*091 61 18 805; www.caisicilia.it/riserve/riserva-naturale-grotta-conca.*

Riserva Naturale Grotta di Entella

at Contessa Entellina *(Province of Palermo).* The cave is often closed due to accidents. Contact the town of Contessa Entellina: ℘*091 83 02 152; www.comunedicontessaentellina.it.*

CIRCUMETNEA TOURIST TRAIN

Loop the volcano on the **Circumetnea train**, which starts in Catania and arrives in Riposto some five hours later. The return trip to Catania is by bus or train operated by Italian State Railways. Return €5/10 depending on journey. Closed Sun and holidays. *(For further information, contact Ferrovia Circumetnea, Via Caronda 352; ℘095 54 12 50; www.circumetnea.it).*

ECOTOURISM

Both the WWF and Legambiente run **wildlife reserves** in Sicily. The WWF has reserves *(Centri Recupero Animali Selvatici)* at Enna, Messina and Alcamo, where it also breeds endangered domestic animals (such as local strains of hen, goat and donkey). The group has marine turtle rescue centres at various locations.

Visitors are welcome during annual field trips. *Contact the Sicilian branch of the WWF (Delegazione Sicilia del WWF) at Via E. Albanese 98, Palermo; ℘091 58 30 40; www.wwf.it/sicilia.* Legambiente also organises excursions to various wildlife reserves, including one at Lampedusa (for the protection and monitoring of marine turtles) and another at Pantelleria *(Contact the tourist offices of Lampedusa and Pantelleria for more information).*

GOLF

Golf courses on the island include Il Picciolo Golf Club on the side of Mount Etna *(Via Picciolo S, Castiglione di Sicilia; ℘0942 986 252; www.ilpicciologolf.com).*

HANG-GLIDING

Contact the **Accademia Siciliana Volo Libero** *(Corso Calatafimi 326; ℘091 77 90 312; www.asvl.it)* for information on hang-gliding sites.

HORSE-RIDING

Several *agriturismi* organise pony trekking and horse-riding around the island. *(For general information on*

Windsurfing at Mondello, near Palermo

© Sandro Bedessi / Fototeca ENIT

equestrian activities in Sicily, contact the Federazione Italiana Turismo Equestre, www.fitetrec-ante.it)

SCUBA-DIVING

Much of the Sicilian coastline is fringed by fascinating underwater seascapes. The water is particularly clear and the sea-life especially varied around Sicily's offshore islands. On Ustica, the **Riserva Naturale Marina** organises sea-watching and diving trips, special scuba-diving courses and an opportunity to explore underwater archaeology and photography. *(For further information, contact the Federazione Italiana Pesca Sportiva Attivita Subacquea, www.fipsas.it.)*

SKIING

The best place for skiing in Sicily is obviously Etna. The two main resorts are at **Nicolosi** and **Piano Provenzana (Linguaglossa)**. *(See www.etnasci.it.)*

Skiing is also possible at **Piano Battaglia** (1,600m/5,248ft) in the Madonie.

WATER SPORTS

For details of **yacht charters**, contact specialist tour operators in your home country or the Federazione Italiana Vela (*℘010 544 541; www.federvela.it).* Information on **canoeing** and **kayaking** is available from the Federazione Italiana Canoa e Kayak *(Viale Tiziano 70 - 000196 Roma; www.federcanoa.it).* The most popular areas for **windsurfing** are Mondello, Cefalù, Capo d'Orlando, Marinello-Oliveri, Tremestieri *(south of Messina),* Scaletta, Catania, Portopalo, Marina di Ragusa, Agrigento, Pozziteddu *(Capo Granitola, south of Campobello di Mazara)* and Lo Stagnone. **Surfing** enthusiasts should make for Mondello, Aspra and Termini Imerese, while the best **kitesurfing** zones include Marina di Ragusa, Pozzallo and Scoglitti.

Parco Fluviale dell'Alcantara

© Sandro Bedessi / Fototeca ENIT

PARKS AND NATURE RESERVES
REGIONAL PARKS

Sicily has four regional parks. The **Parco delle Madonìe** and **Parco dei Nebrodi** lie inland between Palermo and Messina, and provide the perfect setting for excursions of varying length and difficulty (*See Madonie, Nebrodi Mountains*). Another popular area for **walking** is the **Parco dell'Etna**, which has a number of hiking routes and nature trails (*contact the park authorities for information on Etna, especially if you are planning to climb to the craters. We also recommend you book an authorised guide*). The fourth park, the **Parco Fluviale dell'Alcantara**, home to the impressive gorges of the same name, is located in the same area. (*Contact the Ente Parco Fluviale dell'Alcantara; ℘0942 98 99; www.parcoalcantara.it and www.parks.it*).

REGIONAL NATURE RESERVES

Sicily has a number of regional nature reserves, including:

- **Cava Grande del Cassibile**
  Spectacular natural canyon, stretching across the Hyblaean plateau to the coast and cradling a necropolis of 11–9 BC cave tombs.
  See Noto

- **Fiume Ciane**
  Habitat of lush vegetation that includes ancient ash trees, eucalyptus and a papyrus grove.
  See Siracusa

- **Riserva Naturale di Fiumefreddo**
  This river reserve supports an unusual variety of water-loving plants, including papyrus.
  See Etna

- **Foce del Fiume Belice e Dune Limitrofe**
  The wind-sculpted dunes and marshy terrain of this nature reserve on the River Belice attract species such as the Caretta-Caretta turtle.
  See Castelvetrano

- **Riserva Naturale della Foce dell'Irminio,**
  One of the last scrub forests in Sicily, full of interesting foliage shaped by high winds.
  Near Marina di Ragusa. *Contact ℘0932 67 51 11 (Provincia Regionale di Ragusa, Viale delFante 2, 97100 Ragusa).*

- **Riserva Naturale Macalube di Aragona**
  A volcanic hillside dotted

with mud cones, a volcanic phenomenon known as *vulcanelli*.
See Agrigento and la Valle dei Templi

♦ **Riserva Naturale Oasi del Simeto**
Sand dune, marshland and wetland reserve for birds located at the mouth of the River Simeto.

♦ **Riserva Naturale di Vendicari**
Marshy coastline that provides a rare and completely protected habitat for migratory species.
See Noto

♦ **Riserva della Valle dell'Anapo**
Stunning stretch of gorges and cliffs that combine natural and archaeological points of interest.
See Siracusa

♦ **Riserva Naturale dello Zingaro**
A variety of ecosystems set in 1,600 hectares, from the ravines and caves of its calcerous coastline to the peak of Mt Speziale.
See Golfo di Castellammare

♦ **Riserva Naturale Orientata Monte Pellegrino**
Reserve on the slopes of Monte Pellegrino, renowned for its birds of prey *(Run by Rangers d'Italia, Viale Diana, loc. Giusino, Palermo; ℘091 67 16 066).*

WWF NATURE RESERVES
The World Wildlife Fund manages the following reserves:

♦ **Riserva Naturale Orientata Capo Rama**
Birdwatching hotspot, 2km/1.2mi from Terrasini, with species such as kingfishers, kestrels, peregrine falcons and blackbirds.
(For more information on the site, visit www.wwfcamporama.it).

♦ **Saline di Trapani e Paceco**
A large saltwater nature reserve habitat supporting many different species of bird.
See Trapani

♦ **Riserva Naturale Integrale del Lago Preola e dei Gorghi Tondi**
This lake and wetland habitat is a couple of miles southeast of Mazara del Vallo. *(For more information on the site, visit www.wwfpreola.it).*

♦ **Riserva Naturale Orientata di Torre Salsa**
Variety of habitats – dunes, cliffs, marshland and Mediterranean *maquis* – inhabited by porcupines, birds of prey, waders, crows and sea birds.
See Agrigento and La Valle dei Templi

♦ **Riserva Regionale di Isola Bella**
Protected island nature reserve linked to the main shore by a narrow strip of land.
See Taormina

🛈 *For further information, contact WWF Sezione Regionale Sicilia, Via Malaspina, Palermo; ℘091 58 30 40; www.wwf.it/regioni.*

PARKS ORGANISATIONS
For a complete list of parks and reserves, log onto www.parks.it/regione.sicilia/index.html; or contact the **Assessorato Regionale Territorio e Ambiente** *(Via La Malfa 169, Palermo; ℘091 70 77 870)* or local CAI *(Club Alpino Italiano)* groups *(www.cai.it).* The main offices of this group in Sicily are:
♦ Piazza Scammacca 1, Catania; ℘095 71 53 515
♦ Via Natoli 20, Messina; ℘090 65 10 126
♦ Via N. Garzilli 59, Palermo; ℘091 32 94 07
♦ Via Maestranza 33, Siracusa; ℘0931 64 751

SPAS

Sicily is renowned for its hot springs. The following resorts are listed by province:

- **Agrigento:**
  The biggest thermal town in this region is **Sciacca**, famous for its sulphurous waters for centuries. **Terme di Sciacca** (*See Sciacca*) **Terme di Acqua Pia**, loc. AcqueCalde, **Montevago**; *0925 39 026; www.termeacquapia.it.

- **Catania:**
  The baths of Santa Caterina in Terme di Santa Venera are noted for their radioactive, sulphurous composition and traces of sodium bromide (*See Catania*)

- **Messina:**
  There are a number of spas in the area, most with a focus on thermal water and mud treatments (*Fonte di Venere, Viale Stabilimento 85*); **Terme Vigliatore** (*090 97 81 078); **Terme di Giuseppe Marino** (*Via Roma 25; www.termemarino. it; *0942 71 50 31*) and **Terme di Granata Cassibile** (*Via Crispi 1/13; *0942 71 50 29*), both at **Alì Terme**; **Terme di Vulcano** (*Aeolian Islands, *See Isole Eolie*);

- **Palermo:**
  Built on the ruins of a previous 17C baths, this spa offers inhalation, mud therapies, massage and thermal water treatments. **Terme di Termini Imerese** (*Piazza delle Terme 2; *091 81 13 557 www.grandhoteldelleterme.it*)

- **Trapani:**
  The thermal waters at this spa have an alkaline and sulphurous composition said to aid dermatological and rheumatic ailments. **Terme di Gorga, contr. Gorga, Calatafimi** (*0924 23 842 www.termegorga.com*).

FAMILY HOLIDAYS

Italians love children, which makes Sicily a wonderful place for a family holiday. Sicilians will go out of their way to make families comfortable and your *bambini* will have a fuss made of them wherever they go. Family dining in restaurants is the norm and children generally stay up as late as everyone else – or fall asleep on a parent's lap. It's rare to find special children's menus, but restaurants will provide smaller versions of meals on request. It's not unusual to see kids in bars either, usually running around happily outside, while parents have an al fresco drink. Hotels will put an extra cot in your room for a small charge.

Take the fierce Sicilian heat into account on holiday: cover children in sunblock at all times and make sure they drink plenty of water.

- **Take The Family** – www.takethefamily.com
- **Baby Goes 2** – *01273 230669; www.babygoes2.com
- **Eurocamp** – Fully-equipped camping sites in Italy. (*0844 273 8633; www.eurocamp.co.uk.*)
- **Tots to Italy** – *0800 014 2770; www.totstotravel.co.uk.
- **Ciao Bambino!** – *(510) 763 8484; www.ciaobambino.com.

ACTIVITIES FOR KIDS 👪

Sights in the Discovering section of particular interest for children are marked by the 👪 symbol.

A good time for families to visit is undoubtedly during Carnival or over the Easter holidays, when many of the island's towns and villages hold colourful, traditional festivals. *See Calendar of Events*. The following also hold special appeal for younger visitors:

- **Museo dei Pupi dell'Opra** (puppet museum) in Acireale (*See Catania*);

- **Museo del Giocattolo** *(Piazzale Asia, Le Ciminiere, Catania)*, with its collection of antique toys. ⊙*Open Tue–Sun 9am–1pm.* ⊛*€2.* ☏*095 40 11 928.*
- **Etnaland**, at the foot of Etna, with its exciting water park and prehistory theme park. ⊙*Park open Apr–Oct, facilities open 9.30am–6pm (summer 7.30pm–1am).* ⊛*Prices vary with the season and activities. www.etnaland.eu.*
- **Centro Studi sulle Tartarughe Marine** at Linosa *(⌖See Lampedusa)*;
- The **saltpans**, Museo del Sale *(salt museum)* and windmill in Nubia *(⌖See Trapani)*;
- **Museo Internazionale delle Marionette** in Palermo *(⌖See Palermo).*

SHOPPING
FOOD AND WINE

The area around **Trapani** and the **Egadi Islands** (especially Favignana) is well known for **tuna** specialities, as well as fish roe and smoked swordfish. **Pantelleria** and **Salina** produce excellent **capers**, while the **herbs** and **spices** that form such an important part of Sicilian cuisine can be found in markets and grocery stores all over the island. The most common include oregano, wild fennel, pistachios *(near Bronte)* and Sicilian saffron.

The **Palermo** region is famed for its delicious *paste reali* (colourful marzipan delicacies, which come in all shapes and sizes). Sweet specialities on the Ionian coast include the local *paste di mandorla* (almond pastries). The famous Sicilian crushed *ice granite* might be difficult to take home, but you can export a key ingredient: packets of almond paste (also used to make almond milk).

Numerous **table wines** stand out, especially Nero d'Avola, as well as Sicily's sweet wines: Moscato di Noto, Moscato Passito di Pantelleria, Marsala and Malvasia delle Lipari.

SOUVENIRS

One of the most typical crafts is **ceramic work**. The most important centres are Caltagirone, Santo Stefano di Camastra, Erice and Sciacca. The shops of these small towns display a fine array of vases, statuettes, crockery, ornaments and knick-knacks, as well as traditional containers for Sicilian *mostarda* (a caramel-like substance made from prickly-pear juice) and quince jam.

Apart from ceramics, plenty of other natural products and handicrafts are evocative of the island. These include **carpets** from the area around Erice;

Detail of a Sicilian cart – carretto

© René Mattes / hemis.fr

Cathédrale San Giorgio, Raguse Ibla

© Jon Arnold / hemis.fr

natural sponges from Lampedusa; and **papyrus work** (paper and cloth) from the Siracusa region. Finally, Sicilian puppets and traditional carts can be bought in antique and second-hand shops or, in Palermo, from the few remaining artisans.

SIGHTSEEING

Information on admission times and charges for museums and monuments is given in the *Discovering Sicily* section of the guide. Admission times and charges are liable to alteration without prior notice. Due to fluctuations in the cost of living and constant changes in opening times – as well as possible closures for restoration work – our information should merely serve as a guideline. Visitors are advised to confirm details. The admission prices are for single adults with no concession; there are reductions for children, students, those over 60 years old and large groups *(requested on site with proof of ID)*. Special conditions often exist for groups, but arrangements should be made in advance. For EU citizens, many institutions provide free admission to visitors under 18 and over 65, and a 50% reduction for visitors under 25 years of age.

During **National Heritage Week** *(Settimana dei Beni Culturali)*, which takes place at a different time each year, many sights don't charge admission. When custodians specially open museums, churches or other sites – or guide visitors – it is customary to leave a donation.
In summer, many museums and monuments close from 1 to 4pm.

MUSEUMS, GARDENS AND ARCHAEOLOGICAL SITES

Museums generally don't open on Mondays; otherwise ticket offices shut 30–60min before closing.
As this rule is strictly applied, it is almost impossible to enter a museum after this time. Many require use of the luggage deposit.
Taking photos with a flash is usually forbidden.
Archaeological sites generally close 1hr before dusk.

CHURCHES

Churches are usually open 8.30am–noon and 4–6pm, except during services. Exceptions are listed in the *Discovering Sicily* section of this guide. Notices outside a number of churches formally request visitors to dress in a manner deemed appropriate when entering a place of worship – this excludes sleeveless and low-cut tops, short miniskirts or skimpy shorts and bare feet.

Visitors are advised to visit churches in the morning, when the natural light provides better illumination of the works of art; also note that churches are occasionally forced to close in the afternoons due to a lack of staff. Works of art are often illuminated by coin-operated lighting, so take change.

BOOKS

This island has long been a source of fascination for both Italian and foreign authors. The suggestions below include translated works by famous Sicilians, as well as history books, mythology, biography and travel literature.
For a wide selection of English and Italian books written about Sicily, log on to www.sicilybooks.it.

FICTION

The Leopard – Giuseppe Lampedusa (Harvill Press 1996)
Little Novels of Sicily – Giovanni Verga, D.H. Lawrence (Steerforth Press 2000)
Sometimes the Soul: Two Novellas of Sicily – Gioia Timpanelli (W.W. Norton & Co. 1998)
"Cavalleria Rusticana" and Other Stories – Giovanni Verga, H. McWilliam (Penguin Books 1999)
Short Sicilian Novels – Giovanni Verga (Dedalus Ltd. 1994)
The House by the Medlar Tree – Giovanni Verga (University of California Press 1983)
Il Giorno Della Civetta – Leonardo Sciascia, G. Slowey (Ed) (St Martin's Press 1998)

BIOGRAPHY

Italian Journey – J.W. von Goethe (Penguin Books 1970)
The Sicilian – M. Puzo (Arrow 2000)
The Happy Ant-heap – Norman Lewis (Jonathan Cape 1998)
The Dark Princes of Palermo – Norman Lewis (Jonathan Cape 2000)
I Came, I Saw: An Autobiography – Norman Lewis (Picador 1996)
On Persephone's Island: A Sicilian Journal (Vintage Departures) –
Mary Taylor Simeti (Vintage Books 1995)
Sicilian Lives – D. Dolci (Writers and Readers 1982)

REFERENCE

The Greek Myths – R. Graves (Penguin Books 1984)
Metamorphoses – Ovid, E.J. Kenney (Ed), A.D. Melville (Trans) (Oxford Paperbacks 1998)
Odes – Pindar (Penguin Books 1901)
The Odyssey – Homer, R. Fagles (Trans.), B. Knox (Intro.) (Penguin Books 1997)
The Aeneid – Virgil, D. West (Trans.) (Penguin Books 1991)
The Normans in Sicily – John Julius Norwich (Penguin Books 1992)
The Sicilian Vespers – S. Runciman (Cambridge University Press 1992)
The Norman Kingdom of Sicily – D. Matthew (Cambridge University Press 1992)
The Golden Honeycomb – V. Cronin, W. Forman (Harvill Press 1992)
Walking in Sicily – Gillian Price (Cicerone Press 2000)
In Sicily – Norman Lewis (Jonathan Cape 2000)
The Honoured Society – Norman Lewis (Eland Books 1984)
Palmento: A Sicilian Wine Odyssey – Robert V. Camuto (University of Nebraska 2010)
Sicily: A Literary Guide for Travellers – Andrew and Suzanne Edwards (Tauris 2014)
Sicilian Mafia: A True Crime Travel Guide – Carl Russo (Strategic Media 2014)

FILMS

L'Avventura – Michelangelo Antonioni (*1960*). A portrait of three characters, set against the harsh Sicilian landscape.
Divorzio all'italiana – Pietro Germi (*1962*). A superb performance by Marcello Mastroianni that met with international acclaim.
Il Mafioso – Alberto Lattuada (*1962*). A story of great cruelty, starring the masterful Alberto Sordi.

UNESCO

"Our cultural and natural heritage are both irreplaceable sources of life and inspiration", insists the United Nations Educational, Scientific and Cultural Organization (UNESCO). This non-profit group has helped preserve locations since 1972.

More than 180 State Parties have joined in protecting over 800 sites "of outstanding universal value" on the World Heritage List. Representatives from 21 countries, assisted by technical organisations, annually evaluate proposals. A site must be nominated by its home country. The protected cultural heritage may be monuments (buildings, sculptures, archaeological structures, etc.) with unique historic, artistic or scientific features; groups of buildings (such as religious communities and ancient cities); or sites (human settlements and exceptional landscapes), which are the combined works of man and the earth's beauty. Sites may celebrate the stages of geological history or the development of human cultures and creative genius. They may also honour significant ecological processes, superlative natural phenomena or provide a habitat for threatened species.

Well-known sites include: Australia's Great Barrier Reef (1981), India's Taj Mahal and Peru's Macchu Pichu (1983), the Vatican City and the United States' Statue of Liberty (1984), Canada's Rocky Mountain Parks (1984), Jordan's Petra (1985), The Great Wall of China and Greece's Acropolis (1987), Russia's Kremlin and Red Square (1990), England's Stonehenge (1986), Indonesia's Komodo National Park and France's Banks of the Seine (1991), Cambodia's Angor Wat (1992) and Japan's Hiroshima Peace Memorial (1996).

Italy's latest UNESCO sites are Tivoli's Villa Adriana (1999), Assisi's Basilica of San Francesco and Other Franciscan Sites (2000), the City of Verona (2000), the Aeolian Islands (2000), Tivoli's Villa d'Este (2001), Southeastern Sicily's late-Baroque towns of the Val di Noto (2002), the Sacri Monti of Piedmont and Lombardy (2003), Etruscan Necropolises of Cerveteri and Tarquinia (2004), Val d'Orcia (2004), and Syracuse and the Rocky Necropolis of Pantalica (2005), Genoa: Le Strade Nuove and the Palazzi dei Rolli (2006), the Rhaetian Railway in the Albula / Bernina Landscapes (2008) and The Dolomites (2009).

A ciascuno il suo – Elio Petri (1967). Based on Sciascia's novel, this film tells the tale of an academic captured by the Mafia.

The Godfather – Francis Ford Coppola (1972). The first of the Oscar-winning classic trilogy starring Marlon Brando and Al Pacino.

Cadaveri eccellenti – Francesco Rosi (1976). Obscure political plots are uncovered in this film, based on Sciascia's *Contesto*.

Il siciliano – Michael Cimino (1987). The story of the bandit Giuliano, based on Mario Puzo's novel.

Mery per sempre – Marco Risi (1989), set in Palermo Prison; and its sequel, *Ragazzi fuori* (1990).

Porte aperte – Gianni Amelio (1990). Based on a novel by Sciascia and inspired by a real-life event, this film explores the themes of crime and punishment.

Johnny Stecchino – Roberto Benigni (1991). Comedy about a naïve bus driver mistaken for a Mafia boss.

Il giudice ragazzino – Alessandro di Robiland (1993). Last days of Assistant Public Prosecutor Livatino, killed by the Mafia in 1990.

Lo zio di Brooklyn – Ciprì and Maresco (1995). The first feature film by these two controversial directors, set in the Palermo suburbs.

UNESCO
Cultural World Heritage Sites in Italy

18C Royal Palace at Caserta with the Park, the Aqueduct of Vanvitelli, and the San Leucio Complex (1997)

Sacri Monti of Piedmont and Lombardy (2003)

Archaeological Area and the Patriarchal Basilica of Aquileia (1998)

Archaeological Area of Agrigento (1997)

Archaeological Areas of Pompei, Herculaneum and Torre Annunziata (1997)

Assisi, the Basilica of San Francesco and Other Franciscan Sites (2000)

Botanical Garden (Orto Botanico), Padua (1997)

Castel del Monte (1996)

Cathedral, Torre Civica and Piazza Grande, Modena (1997)

Church and Dominican Convent of Santa Maria delle Grazie (1980)

Cilento and Vallo di Diano National Park (1998)

City of Verona (2000)

City of Vicenza and the Palladian Villas of the Veneto (1994)

Costiera Amalfitana (1997)

Crespi d'Adda (1995)

Early Christian Monuments of Ravenna (1996)

Etruscan Necropolises of Cerveteri and Tarquinia (2004)

Ferrara, City of the Renaissance and its Po Delta (1995)

Genoa: Le Strade Nuove and the system of the Palazzi dei Rolli (2006)

Historic Centre of Florence (1982)

Historic Centre of Naples (1995)

Historic Centre of Rome, the Properties of the Holy See in that City

Enjoying Extraterritorial Rights and San Paolo Fuori le Mura (1980)

Historic Centre of San Gimignano (1990)

Historic Centre of Siena (1995)

Historic Centre of the City of Pienza (1996)

Historic Centre of Urbino (1998)

Late-Baroque towns of the Val di Noto *(Southeastern Sicily)* (2002)

Longobards, Places of Power (2011)

Mantua and Sabbioneta (2008)

Medici Villas and Gardens in Tuscany (2013)

Piazza del Duomo, Pisa (1987)

Portovenere, Cinque Terre and the Islands *(Palmaria, Tino and Tinetto)* (1997)

Residences of the Royal House of Savoy (1997)

Rhaetian Railway in the Albula / Bernina Landscapes (2008)

Rock Drawings in Valcamonica (1979)

Su Nuraxi di Barumini (1997)

Syracuse and the Rocky Necropolis of Pantalica (2005)

The Trulli of Alberobello (1996)

The Sassi and the Park of the Rupestrian Churches of Matera (1993)

Val d'Orcia (2004)

Venice and its Lagoon (1987)

Villa Adriana (Tivoli) (1999)

Villa d'Este, Tivoli (2001)

Villa Romana del Casale (1997)

Natural:

Isole Eolie *(Aeolian Islands)* (2000)

Monte San Giorgio (2003)

The Dolomites (2009)

La lupa – Gabriele Lavia (1997). Based on the play by Verga.

Sicilia! – Danèle Huillet and Jean-Marie Straub (1999). Based on *Conversazione in Sicilia* by Elio Vittorini, this black-and-white film follows a man returning to Sicily in search of his childhood.

I giudici – Ricky Tognazzi (1999). The story of Giovanni Falcone and Paolo Borsellino.

Malèna – Giuseppe Tornatore (2000). A young boy in provincial Sicily falls in love with Monica Bellucci at the beginning of WWII.

Placido Rizzotto – Pasquale Scimeca (2000). The story of the trade unionist Placido Rizzotto, killed in Corleone in 1948.

Il manoscritto del principe – Roberto Andò (2000). The experiences of Prince Giuseppe Tomasi di Lampedusa, recounted against the backdrop of 1950s Palermo.

Prime luci dell'alba – Lucio Gaudino (2000). Family problems force the main character of this film to examine his relationship with Sicily.

Respiro – Emanuele Crialese (2002). This film, set amid the stunning scenery of Lampedusa, examines the breakdown of a young woman's sanity.

Angela – Roberta Torre (2002). This intense movie, quite unlike the early work of the director, examines the life of a woman in the Mafia.

Calendar of Events

The following are just a few highlights of Sicily's social events. For a complete list, contact the APT *(tourist information office)* in the relevant area.

♻ *Festivals in towns marked * are also mentioned in the Discovering Sicily section of the guide.*

Processione dei Misteri, Trapani

© Saffo Alessandro / Sime / Photononstop

EASTER FESTIVALS

Easter Week is one of the most evocative times to visit Sicily, with passion plays and dramatic processions throughout the island recalling the crucifixion and resurrection of Christ. These *via crucis* parades often involve floats held aloft by hooded members of local *confraternities* and are watched by huge crowds. Book accommodation well in advance if you plan to visit at this time.

Alcamo
Good Friday procession.

Caltanissetta*
Good Friday procession of the Ancient Black Christ, with 16 groups of statues.

Castelvetrano
Good Friday procession. Easter Sunday morning: Festa dell'Aurora, held here since 1860.

Enna*
Procession of floats carried by hooded members of the Confraternities on Good Friday. www.enna-sicilia.it

Erice*
Processione dei Misteri held on Good Friday. www.trapani-sicilia.it

Acireale Carnival

© Giuseppe Famoso / Dreamstime.com

Marsala*

Large Medieval Holy Week procession of the *Misteri,* accompanied by local musicians.

Messina*

Processione delle Barette: procession of wooden sculptures following the Stations of the Cross on Good Friday.

Piana degli Albanesi

During Holy Week, the inhabitants wear costumes embroidered with gold and silver thread. On Good Friday, choral concert and the Enkomia procession. On Easter Sunday, white doves are released, sprigs of rosemary tossed about and red-painted eggs exchanged.

Prizzi

Easter Sunday morning: *U n'contru – U ballu di diavula.* Villagers dance through the streets sporting terrifying iron masks and pretending to be the devil collecting souls.

Ragusa*

Good Friday: *Processione e fiaccolata dei Misteri.* Statues of Christ and the Sorrowful Virgin from the city's churches are brought together in the Cathedral square and paraded through the streets. www.comune.ragusa.it

Scicli*

Procession of the Resurrected Christ on Easter Sunday. www.comune.scicli.rg.it

Trapani* *Processione dei Misteri* held on Good Friday afternoon and Saturday morning is one of the island's most famous – involving 17C and 18C religious statues. www.comune.trapani.it/turismo

OTHER FESTIVALS

6 JANUARY
Piana degli Albanesi

Festa della Teofania –Greek-Orthodox Epiphany.
☞*See Palermo*

20 JANUARY
Acireale*

Festa di San Sebastiano (St Sebastian). Annual parade of the float of San Sebastian through the streets.
☞*See Catania*

FIRST WEEK IN FEBRUARY (5 FEB)
Catania*

Festa di Sant'Agata. Procession of wooden floats, decorated with tableaux from the saint's life.
☞*See Catania*

3 FEBRUARY
Salemi

Festa dei Pani di San Biagio – Festival of St Blaise held in the Rabato district. Small decorative loaves of bread are baked.
☞*See Castelvetrano*

CARNIVAL WEEK, CULMINATING IN MARTEDÌ GRASSO (SHROVE TUESDAY)

Acireale*
Sciacca*
Termini Imerese*
Carnival with a parade of allegorical parade floats.
See Catania, Sciacca and Cefalù

SATURDAY PRECEDING 19 MARCH
Scicli*
Cavalcata di San Giuseppe.
Festival commemorating the flight of Joseph and Mary into Egypt.
See Modica

19 MARCH
Salemi
Festa di San Giuseppe (St Joseph's day) – *Cene di San Giuseppe,* with special dinners and votive loaves of bread baked.
See Castelvetrano

END OF MAY
Scicli*
Festa della Battaglia delle Milizie.
A statue of the Madonna on horseback is carried in colourful procession through the town.
See Modica

LAST SUNDAY IN MAY
Ragusa*
Re-enactment of the martyrdom of St George that ends with a giant firework display.
See Ragusa

14–15 JULY
Palermo*
"U festinu", a festival for the city's patron saint, Santa Rosalia, with costumed parades, processions and grand firework displays.
See Palermo

24–25 JULY
Caltagirone*
Festa di San Giacomo with the *Luminaria.* Festival in honour of the town's patron saint. The steps of Santa Maria del Monte are decorated with small oil lamps.
See Caltagirone

2–6 AUGUST
Cefalù*
Festa di San Salvatore:
Festival of the town's patron saint includes a competition to balance on a horizontal pole and reach a statue of San Salvatore.
See Cefalù

14 AUGUST
Cefalù*
Madonna della Luce. Procession of boats make their way from Kalura to the old harbour and back.
See Cefalù

21–24 AUGUST
Lipari*
Festa di San Bartolomeo:
Lively festival that ends with a spectacular offshore firework display.
See Isole Eolie

2 SEPTEMBER
Piana degli Albanesi
Festa della Madonna Odigitria.
Festival of Piana's patron saint, with horse races and a brightly costumed parade.
See Palermo

7–8 SEPTEMBER
Mistretta*
Madonna della Luce: the Madonna of Light festival centres on a solemn procession of the Madonna, flanked by the two giants, Kronos and Mytia.
See Madonie

NOVEMBER–JANUARY
Caltagirone*
Festa del Presepe: exhibition of terracotta Nativity figures and cribs at different locations throughout the town, celebrating the art and tradition of the Nativity sculptors that flourished here in the 18C.
See Caltagirone

2 NOVEMBER
Palermo*

Festa dei Morti.
Children receive gifts and sweets
from their departed loved ones in
celebration of All Souls' Day.
&See Palermo

CULTURAL EVENTS
1–15 FEBRUARY
Agrigento*

Sagra del Mandorlo in fiore
(Almond-blossom Festival) and
International Folklore Festival.
&See Agrigento and La Valle
dei Templi

MAY–JUNE
Siracusa*

Performances of classical drama
at the Greek theatre.
&See Siracusa

JUNE–DECEMBER
Gibellina*

Orestiadi: theatre, music and
film festival held in the ruins of
Gibellina.
www.fondazioneorestiadi.it
&See Castelvetrano

JULY–SEPTEMBER
Segesta*

Concerts and classical drama
at the Greek theatre.
&See Segesta
Taormina*

Taormina Arte: theatre, music,
film and dance festival.
&See Taormina
Tindari*

Tindari Estate: readings, music
and dance in the Greek theatre.
&See Milazzo

END OF JULY
Marsala*

Marsala Jazz Festival.
&See Marsala

AUTUMN (VARIES ANNUALLY)
Monreale*

Settimana di Musica Sacra:
Festival of sacred music.
&See Monreale

**LATE-NOVEMBER TO
MID-DECEMBER**
Palermo*

Festival di Morgana.
Performances by puppeteers
from around the world.
&See Palermo

OTHER TRADITIONAL EVENTS
APRIL–MAY
Taormina*

*Festa del Costume e del Carretto
Siciliano.* Festival of traditional
Sicilian carts and local costume.
&See Taormina

25 APRIL
Vizzini

Sagra della Ricotta.
Ricotta cheese festival.
&See Caltagirone

THIRD SUNDAY IN MAY
Noto*

Primavera Barocca and the
Infiorata. Spring festival,
culminating in a fragrant flower
festival.
&See Noto

12–14 AUGUST
Piazza Armerina*

Palio dei Normanni.
Re-enactment of the arrival of
Roger de Hauteville in the town,
followed by jousting competitions.
&See Piazza Armerina

14 AUGUST
Messina*

Passeggiata dei Giganti. Procession
of the Moor Grifone and Mata,
legendary founder of the city.
&See Messina

Know Before You Go

USEFUL WEBSITES

The following sites offer information on Italian history and art, as well as trip-planning suggestions.

ITALY

www.enit.it
Italian tourist office
www.museionline.info
Italian museums
www.beniculturali.it
Government site exploring archaeology and culture.
www.trenitalia.com
State Railway

SICILY

www.pti.regione.sicilia.it
Official regional portal
www.coloridisicilia.it
Photographs and culture
www.bestofsicily.com
English magazine on Sicily
www.parks.it
Natural parks and reserves.
www.wwf.it/sicilia
World Wildlife Fund, Sicily
www.festedisicilia.it
Festivals and events
www.insicilia.it
Tourism in Sicily
www.siciliano.it
Sicily search engine

SICILIAN PROVINCES

Agrigento:
www.agrigentoweb.it and
www.lampedusa.to (Lampedusa)
Catania:
www.turismo.provincia.catania.it,
www.parcoetna.ct.it
(Etna National Park)
Enna: www.provincia.enna.it
Isole Eolie: www.portaledelleolie.it
Palermo: www.aapit.pa.it,
www.arcidiocesi.palermo.it *(churches)*,
Ragusa: www.ragusaturismo.it
Siracusa: www.comune.siracusa.it
Taormina: www.comune.taormina.
me.it

Trapani: www.apt.trapani.it,
www.welcometoegadi.it
(Egadi Islands)

TOURIST OFFICES
INTERNATIONAL

◆ **Canada**
110 Younge Street,
Suite 503,
Toronto M5C 1T4 ℰ(416) 925 4882
www.italiantourism.com

◆ **UK**
1 Princes Street,
London W1B 2AY
℘0207 408 1254
www.italiantouristboard.co.uk

◆ **US – New York**
630 Fifth Avenue,
Suite 1565, New York, NY, 10111
℘(212) 245 5618
www.italiantourism.com

◆ **US – (LA)**
12400 Wilshire Blvd., Suite 550,
Los Angeles, CA 90025
℘(310) 820 1898
www.italiantourism.com

◆ **US – Chicago**
500 North Michigan Avenue 506,
Chicago, IL 60611
℘(312) 644 0996
www.italiantourism.com

LOCAL TOURIST OFFICES
ITALIAN STATE TOURIST OFFICE

Contact your country's ENIT bureau (Ente Nazionale Italiano per il Turismo) or visit www.enit.it.

REGIONAL TOURIST OFFICES

Local offices are listed near attractions, where applicable. Regional tourist information on Sicily is available from:

◆ **Assessorato Regionale del Turismo**, delle Comunicazioni e dei Trasporti Via Notarbartolo 9, 90141 Palermo. ℘091 70 78 201; www.regione.sicilia.it/turismo/web_turismo

INTERNATIONAL VISITORS
ITALIAN EMBASSIES ABROAD

For entry requirements and visas, ask the nearest Italian outpost.

Canada

275 Slater Street, 21st Floor, Ottawa, Ontario K1P 5H9
&(613) 232 2401
Fax (613) 233 1484
www.ambottawa.esteri.it

UK

14 Three Kings Yard, London W1K 4EH
&0207 312 2200
Fax 0207 312 2230
www.amblondra.esteri.it

US

3000 Whitehaven Street, NW Washington, DC 20008
&(202) 612 4400
Fax (202) 518 2151
www.ambwashingtondc.esteri.it

ITALIAN CONSULATES ABROAD

For language classes, cultural and tourist information, contact:

Canada

3489 Drummond Street, Montreal, Quebec H3G 1X6
&(514) 849 8351
Fax (514) 499 9471
www.consmontreal.esteri.it;
136 Beverley Street, Toronto, Ontario M5T 1Y5
&(416) 977 1566
Fax (416) 977 1119
www.constoronto.esteri.it

UK – Edinburgh

32 Melville Street, Edinburgh EH3 7HW
&(0131) 226 3631
Fax (0131) 226 6260
www.consedimburgo.esteri.it

UK – Manchester

20 Dale Street (4th Floor), Manchester M1 1EZ
&(0161) 236 9024
Fax (0161) 236 5574
www.consmanchester.esteri.it

US

500 N Michigan Ave, Suite 1850, Chicago, IL, 60611
&(312) 467 1550 Fax (312) 467 1335
www.conschicago.esteri.it

FOREIGN EMBASSIES AND CONSULATES IN ITALY

Australia

Via Antonio Bosio 5, 00161 Rome
&06 85 27 21; Fax 06 85 27 23 00
www.italy.embassy.gov.au

Canada

Via Salaria 243, 00199 Rome
&06 85 44 41; Fax 06 85 44 42 912
www.canada.it

Ireland

Villa Spada, Via Giamcomo Medici 1-00153 Rome
&06 5852381; Fax 06 581 3336
www.ambasciata-irlanda.it

UK (Rome)

Via XX Settembre 80A, Rome 00187
&06 42 20 00 01
www.gov.uk/government/world/italy

USA (Palermo)

Via Vaccarini 1, 90143 Palermo
&091 30 58 57; Fax 091 62 56 026

USA (Rome)

Via Veneto 119A, 00187 Rome
&06 46 741; Fax 06 46 742 356
italy.usembassy.gov

ENTRY REQUIREMENTS
PASSPORTS

British citizens and people from outside of the EU must must carry a valid passport. Other EU citizens only need a national identity card. In case of loss or theft, report to the embassy or consulate and the police.

VISAS

Entry visas are required for Australian, New Zealand, Canadian and US citizens *(for a visit of more than three months)*. Apply to the Italian Consulate *(visa issued same day; delay if submitted by mail)*.
The US booklet **Your Trip Abroad** supplies information on visa requirements, customs regulations, medical care, etc. – available from the Superintendent of Documents, PO Box 37954; Pittsburgh, PA 15250-7954; &(202) 512 1800; Fax (202) 512 2104; www.access.gpo.gov.

CUSTOMS REGULATIONS

Since 1999, those travelling between European Union countries can no longer purchase "duty-free" goods. Visitors arriving from another EU country may import unlimited duty-paid goods for personal use. For more detailed information, request a free leaflet, **Duty Paid**, from:

> HMRC National Advice Service (written enquiries section),
> Alexander House,
> Victoria Ave, Southend,
> Essex SS99 1BD
> ℘0845 010 9000
> www.hmrc.gov.uk.

The US Customs Service offers a free publication **Know Before You Go** for US citizens: www.cbp.gov/travel

PETS (CATS AND DOGS)

Pets entering Italy from another country must have an Export Health Certificate and proof of rabies vaccination from a local veterinarian. To return to the UK, cats and dogs must have a "pet passport" under The Pet Travel Scheme: www.direct.gov.uk.

HEALTH

Medical facilities are excellent and most have English-speaking doctors. Pharmacists can sometimes supply oral contraception and medicines for straightforward ailments like conjunctivitis (pink eye).

More serious complaints and injuries may be treated at local hospital casualty departments *(pronto soccorso)*. UK citizens should obtain an **EHIC (European Health Insurance Card)** before leaving home: www.nhs.uk/ehic; ℘0191 218 1999.

This entitles the bearer to free or reduced-cost medical treatment in the state healthcare system when temporarily visiting an EU country. Separate travel and medical insurance is highly recommended.

North Americans can contact the **International Association for Medical Assistance to Travelers (IAMAT)** ℘(716) 754 4883 or, in Canada, ℘(416) 652 0137; www.iamat.org for tips on travel and lists of local, English-speaking doctors.

The **US Center for Disease Control and Prevention** also advises on health hazards and food safety: ℘(800) 232 4636; www.cdc.gov.

ACCESSIBILITY

Many historic monuments do not have elevators, ramps or other facilities. Contact:

> **CO.IN** *(Consorzio Cooperative Integrate)*,
> Via Enrico Giglioni 54,
> Roma
> ℘06 23 26 9231
> Fax 06 232 69 231
> www.coinsociale.it.

English-language advice is also available at www.disability-europe.net/countries/italy. Sights in the guide marked with the symbols ♿ have full or partial access for wheelchairs.

In the UK

♦ **Holiday Care Service**
℘0845 124 9971;
www.holidaycare.org.uk

♦ **RADAR (Royal Association for Disability and Rehabilitation)**
℘020 7250 3222;
www.radar.org.uk

In Italy

♦ **Accessible Italy**
℘(378) 941 111;
www.accessibleitaly.com

In the US

♦ **SATH (Society for the Advancement of Travel for the Handicapped)**
℘(212) 447 7284;
www.sath.org

♦ **Alternative Leisure Co**
℘(781) 275 0023;
www.alctrips.com

Getting There and Getting Around

BY PLANE

As airport security and baggage regulations change frequently, it is always advisable to check the rules before you fly. For more information about what to carry, visit www.dft. gov.uk/hand-luggage-restrictions/ overview.

Several international carriers serve Palermo, Catania and Reggio Calabria on the mainland. Flights are more frequent in summer.

ALITALIA

Alitalia is Italy's national airline. It operates services to 27 domestic destinations, including Catania and Palermo, and 74 international destinations, including the UK, US and Canada.

♦ **UK**
℘0871 424 1424;
www.alitalia.com/gb_en

♦ **Ireland**
℘(00) 39 06 65649; www.alitalia. com/en_en

♦ **USA**
℘001 800 223 5730 (toll-free);
www.alitalia.com/us_en

♦ **Italy**
Viale Marchetti 111, 00148 Rome;
℘(00) 39 06 65649; www.alitalia.it

OTHER CARRIERS

♦ **Airone:** serves Mediterranean and Italian destinations. ℘892 444 (from Italy), ℘09 12 551 047 (elsewhere); www.flyairone.it

♦ **Meridiana:** links to Italian and European cities. ℘892 928 (from Italy), ℘0845 355 55 88 (from UK), ℘0789 52 682 (elsewhere); www.meridiana.it

♦ **Ryanair:** flies Palermo to London Stansted and Trapani to Dublin ℘895 895 8989 (from Italy), ℘0871 246 0000 (from UK),

℘+44 871 246 0002 (elsewhere); www.ryanair.com

♦ **easyJet:** flies Catania-Milan and Palermo-London Gatwick. ℘0845 104 5000 (from UK); www.easyjet.com

DIRECT FROM THE USA

♦ **American Airlines**
www.aa.com
♦ **Delta Airlines**
www.delta.com
♦ **Northwest Airlines**
www.nwa.com
♦ **Meridiana**
www.meridiana.it
♦ **United Airlines**
www.united.com
♦ **USAirways**
www.usairways.com

TOUR OPERATORS

♦ **Citalia**
℘0843 770 6528;
www.citalia.com
♦ **Italian Journeys**
℘0207 434 7492;
www.italianjourneys.com
♦ **Page and Moy Ltd**
℘01858 415407;
www.page-moy.co.uk

AIRPORTS

Sicily's two main airports are **Falcone e Borsellino** (www.gesap.it), which is also referred to as **Punta Raisi**, in Palermo, and **Fontanarossa** – close to Catania; the latter is best for Taormina and Siracusa (www.aeroporto.catania. it). Tiny airports at **Trapani Birgi** (www.airgest.it) and on the islands of **Pantelleria** and **Lampedusa** connect to the mainland and a few European hubs. Finally, consider flying into **Aeroporto dello Stretto** at Reggio di Calabria on the "boot's toe" (www. aeroportodellostretto.it).

AIRPORT TRANSFERS

Falcoe e Borsellino is 35km/22mi from Palermo on the A 29 motorway. There is a taxi rank outside the arrivals terminal or call ℘091 225 455.

By train, the Trinacria Express links the terminal directly with Palermo; www.trenitalia.it.
Tickets €5.50. Airport buses to Palermo run every half hour and cost €5.30. Regular airport buses also run every 20 minutes between Catania and **Fontanarossa**.

BY SHIP

Ferries operate to Palermo from Genoa *(20hr)*, Livorno *(19hr)*, Civitavecchia *(12hr)*, Naples *(11hr)* and Cagliari *(13hr)*. Other routes include Trapani–Cagliari *(10hr)*, Catania–Naples *(10hr)* and Messina–Salerno *(8hr)*.
See Catania, Messina, Palermo and Trapani

Ferry crossing the Strait of Messina
© Francesco Alessi/Dreamstime.com

BY TRAIN

The rail network is limited in Sicily and doesn't cover the whole island. The main services operate along the coast, linking **Messina–Siracusa** *(3hr)*, **Messina–Palermo** *(3hr)*, **Palermo–Agrigento** *(2hr)* and **Palermo–Trapani** *(2hr 30min)*. Services to the mountainous area inland are infrequent, ✆89 20 21 *(from Italy)*; www.trenitalia.com. The train operates via the **Straits of Messina**, with coaches loaded directly onto the ferry at Villa San Giovanni.

Ticket prices are all-inclusive. For information, apply to the **Ferrovie dello Stato** (Italian State Railways), ✆89 20 21 *(from Italy)*; www.trenitalia.com.

BY COACH/BUS

The coach network offers the best way to explore the island for visitors without their own transport, with regular services to many towns and cities. Contact the local tourist office *(See the chapter headings in the* **Discovering Sicily** *section)*.

Eurolines connects London's Victoria Coach Station and Italy: ✆08717 818178; www.eurolines.co.uk or www.nationalexpress.com. **Segesta Internazionale** runs buses between Rome, Palermo and Trapani. Journey time between Rome and Palermo is 12hr. ✆0935 565111; www.interbus.it *(See PALERMO)*

BY CAR

The link between Sicily and the rest of Italy is provided by ferries and hydrofoils between Reggio Calabria or Villa San Giovanni and Messina. Ferrovie dello Stato (Italian State Railways) provide a car-ferry service from Villa San Giovanni *(✆89 20 21; www.trenitalia.com)*.
The crossing time depends on the ferry type *(car-only or auto-train)*, and varies between 25–45min. Società Caronte also operates a service: ✆800 62 74 14 *(toll-free in Italy)*; www.carontetourist.it.
Because of the frequent service *(every 20min)*, booking is not necessary. From Reggio Calabria, foot passengers can board the ferry *(✆89 20 21; www.trenitalia.it)* or hydrofoil *(Ustica Lines, ✆0923 87 38 13, www.usticalines.it)*.

DRIVING IN SICILY

A car makes the island's remote stretches accessible. However, Palermo traffic is so chaotic that most visitors rely on shoe leather and public transport. Narrow, medieval streets in villages also make driving difficult. The **motorways** (autostrade) in Sicily do not cover the whole island. Stretches include Messina-Palermo (A 20), Palermo-Trapani-Mazara del Vallo (A 29) and Palermo-Enna-Catania (A 19).

Most major routes are free of charge. Roads to mountain settlements are usually stunning, but tend to be winding and therefore slower.

DRIVING LICENCE

EU citizens need a valid **national driving licence**. Visitors from other countries may want an **international driving licence**, which translates details. In the US, the American Automobile Association issues these ($18 for members and $20 for non-members. AAA National Headquarters ℰ(407) 444 7000; www.aaa.com). Other documents required include the vehicle's **current log book** and a **green card** for insurance.

ROAD REGULATIONS

- ♦ Traffic drives on the right and the **minimum age** is 18 years.
- ♦ **Seat belts** are mandatory in the front and back of the vehicle.
- ♦ Drivers must wear **shoes**, carry **spare lights** and an **emergency red triangle** sign and a **valid driving licence**.
- ♦ Motorways (autostrade) and dual carriageways (superstrade) are indicated by green signs; ordinary roads by blue signs; tourist sights by yellow signs.
- ♦ Pay **motorway tolls** with cash, credit or **Viacard**, sold at motorway entrances and exits, in Autogrill restaurants and through ACI (Automobile Club Italiano): ℰ803 116; www.aci.it.

Speed Restrictions

- ♦ 50kph/31mph in built-up areas;
- ♦ 90–110kph/55–68mph on open country roads;
- ♦ 90/56 (600cc) – 130kph/ 80mph (excess of 1,000cc) on motorways, depending on engine capacity.

PARKING

The symbol 🅿 denotes car parks on the city maps and in this guide.
☞Do not leave valuable items in your car and pack all luggage out of sight.

MAPS AND PLANS

♿A list of Michelin maps helpful for navigating to and around Sicily appears in Maps and Plans at the back of this guide.

ROADSIDE ASSISTANCE

- ♦ **ACI (Automobile Club Italia)** ℰ803 116 (24-hr emergency service); www.aci.it

PETROL/GAS

Fuel is sold as super (4-star), senza piombo (unleaded 95 octane), super plus or Euro plus (unleaded 98 octane) or gazolio (diesel).
Manned petrol stations usually close noon–4pm and at night. Petrol can be bought 24 hours a day and on Sundays from automatic petrol pumps.

CAR RENTAL

The main car hire agencies have offices in cities and at airports. Some tour operators offer "fly-drive" packages. Call (from Italy only):

- ♦ **Avis:** ℰ199 100 133; www.avis.co.uk
- ♦ **Hertz:** ℰ199 112 211, 0248 233 662 (from a mobile/cell); www.hertz.co.uk
- ♦ **Europcar:** ℰ0870 607 5000 (UK), +44 1132 422 233 (international reservations); www.europcar.co.uk
- ♦ **Maggiore:** ℰ199 151 120; www.maggiore.it

Where to Stay and Eat

Hotel and **Restaurant** recommendations are located in the Address Books throughout the **Discovering Sicily** section of the guide.
For coin ranges and a description of the symbols used in the Addresses, see the Legend on the cover flap.

WHERE TO STAY

For popular destinations, book well in advance, especially for trips in April to October. In general, prices dip from November to March, and many hotels offer discounts or weekend deals.
Check the rates before booking and ask for written confirmation.

HOTELS AND PENSIONI

Generally, the word **pensione** describes a small family-run hotel. Sometimes within a residential building, it offers simple, basic rooms, often without a private bathroom. Some *pensioni* do not accept credit cards.

RURAL ACCOMMODATION

Rural guesthouses – *agriturismi* – house visitors on farms and feed them the bounty of the land: olive oil, wine, honey, vegetables and meat. Extremely popular in Sicily, some properties rival the elegance of the best hotels – with prices to match. Catering options vary from breakfast to full board or an apartment kitchenette.
We've selected *agriturismi* that sometimes accept one-night reservations. However, during high season, expect a minimum stay *(3–7 nights)*. Prices are only given when this formula is compulsory.
Also, bear in mind that the rates are for double rooms (the only sort available in this genre). Solo travellers may request – but should never expect – discounts.

Take a look at the following guides: *Turismo Verde in Sicilia,* published by the Consorzio Villaggio Globale, part of the Confederazione Italiana Agricoltiori di Palerme (*091 30 81 51*); *Vacanze e Natura,* published by Associazione Terranostra (*06 48 28 862; www.terranostra.it,* with a selection of addresses); Agriturismi (again by Terranostra and published by De Agostini, *06 99 32 09), Guida all'Agriturismo,* published by Demetra; *Agriturismo e Vacanze Verdi,* published by Associazione Agriturist (*Corso Vittorio Emanuele 101, Rome; *06 68 52 342; www.agriturist.it); Agriturismo e vacanze in campagna*, published by Touring Club (*www.touring club.com*).
You'll also find some interesting addresses in the *Guida del Turismo alternativo* (Sicilia occidentale and Sicilia orientale), which you can buy from book stalls and book shops, or free from the Sicilian Tourist Service (piazzetta Scannaserpe 3, Palermo; *091 36 15 67; www.stsitalia.it*), which can provide you with information and book your accommodation. For more information, you can also contact *Turismo Verde* (Via Caio Mario 27, Rome; *06 36 11 051; www.turisoverde.it*) which also lists a number of addresses.

BED AND BREAKFAST

In this varied category, the lines between hotel and B&B blur. Typically, hosts rent out their apartment, home or a few rooms. Minimum-stay requirements are common, credit cards are not. However, prices are competitive, especially given their cosiness and authenticity.
Contact **Bed & Breakfast Italia**, *Palazzo Sforza Cesarini, Corso Vittorio Emanuele II 282, 00186 Rome; *06 68 78 618; www.bbitalia.it*, or **Caffelletto** *Via Rogati 1, 35122 Padova; *04 9 66 39 80; www.caffelletto.it*

See also:
www.bedandbreakfast.it
www.primitaly.it/bb
www.bedebreakfast.it

CAMPSITES

A good option for travellers on a budget, a campsite usually has a restaurant, bar and food shop, sometimes even a disco or swimming pool. Some sites also rent bungalows and caravans. Prices shown are daily rates for two people, one tent and a single car.

An **International Camping Carnet** for caravans is useful, but not compulsory; buy one from motoring organisations or the **Camping and Caravanning Club** (℘0845 130 7633; www.campingandcaravanningclub. co.uk). Request further details from the **Confederazione Italiana Campeggiatori** (℘055 88 23 91; fax 055 88 25 918; www.federcampeggio.it). The organisation offers a map of campsites and highlights those with special rates for cardholders. It also publishes an annual guide, *Campeggi e Villagi Turistici in Italia,* in collaboration with the Touring Club Italiano (TCI). Local tourist boards will also supply information on campsites.

YOUTH HOSTELS AND RELIGIOUS BOARDING HOUSES

Hostel accommodation is only available to members of the Youth Hostel Association. Join at any of the YHA hostels and renew your membership annually.
Despite the name, all ages are welcome. In Italy, hostels are run by the **Associazione Italiana Alberghi per la Gioventù** (Via Cavour 44, 00184 Rome; ℘06 48 71 152; www. ostellionline.org).
Case per ferie (holiday homes), generally found in the big cities, offer simple but clean and reasonably priced accommodation. The disadvantage is the curfew: visitors are expected to be back by 10.30pm.
Contact the tourist offices and CITS (Centro Italiano Turismo Sociale,

Associazione dell'Ospitalità Religiosa, viale del Monte Oppio 20, 00184 Rome; ℘06 48 73 145; www.citsnet.it).

🔆The Discovering section outlines places to stay and recommends establishments for different kinds of trips.

WHERE TO EAT

🔆see INTRODUCTION: The Island Today, Food and Wine.
In Sicily, lunch is usually served from 1 to 2.30pm and dinner from 8.30pm. Booking is recommended, especially in high season. Dining out in Sicily is about enjoying the food, plain and simple. Nobody will mind if you just order a salad and a pasta dish, or ask for a first course as a main course. However, a traditional Sicilian feast starts with an antipasto, a pre-meal nibble that can be anything from stuffed artichoke hearts to sardines, followed by a first course, *il primo* – usually a soup. A meat or fish dish comes next for *il secondo,* with salads and vegetables ordered separately. The meal is rounded off with a desert, either teeth-jangling sweet Sicilian concoctions, or more commonly fruit salad or ice cream. It's customary for a small cover charge per person to be added to the bill (il conto) for bread.

DINING OUT

Ristorante – The distinction between different restaurant types is not as obvious as it once was but in general, a *ristorante* offers elegant cuisine and service in a relatively formal atmosphere. However, as this is Sicily, in many cases "formal" simply means extras such as tablecloths, waiters and a written menu. *Ristorante* are usually open for both lunch and dinner.
Trattoria or osteria – Dining is a more relaxed, informal affair in a *trattoria,* many of which are family-run. Those in smaller towns and villages will often only open for lunch. Here the emphasis is on hearty, unpretentious home cooking (cucina casalinga). Written menus are often

Sardines dish

© Jacques Sierpinski / hemis.fr

not available – instead, a waiter will describe the dishes of the day for you to choose from. When ordering these, check the price to avoid nasty shocks when the bill arrives. Be wary of tourist menus, which limit choices. *Trattorias* used to almost exclusively serve house wine (by the carafe), but many now offer extensive wine lists.

SNACKS

Bars, *pasticcerie* (pastry shops) and cafeterias offer a range of snacks and local specialities such as *arancini* (rice balls), *panelle* (fried chickpea pancakes) and slices of pizza. Alternatively, lunch on a dollop of sweet crushed ice *granita* or ice cream *(gelato)* traditionally eaten in a brioche. Sandwiches *(panini)* are a more filling option on the run. Most large towns will have sandwich bars, but in smaller villages, grocery shops *(alimentari)* will usually make you one up on request.

TAKING A BREAK

Cafés and bars are ideal for a quick break in between sightseeing. In Italy, bars are used more as a pit stop for a morning espresso and *cornetto* (custard, jam or chocolate croissant) or a beer, than a place to sit all afternoon.

Pay at the cash desk first, then present your receipt to the barman. In both bars and cafés it's always cheaper to drink standing up at the counter, as the Sicilians do. The island's best cafés and bars are listed under **Taking a Break** in some of the Address Books.

SPECIALITIES

Gelateria – Sicilian ice cream *(gelato)* is renowned and locals like nothing better than an evening stroll while enjoying a cone *(un cono)*. Bars often sell ice cream, but for the widest choice of flavours head for the gelateria. A sign saying *produzione propria* means the shop makes its own ice cream on site.

Pizzeria – Sicilian pizza is some of the best in Italy; the authentic wafer-thin crust is topped with tomato sauce and a variety of ingredients. Slices are readily available from takeaway counters and bars. The best pizzas, however, are those in sit-down pizzerias. These are cooked to a bubbling, slightly charcoaled perfection in traditional wood-burning ovens *(forno a legna)*. Classic Sicilian flavours to try include oregano, capers, pecorino cheese and lots of anchovies.

Gelati

© Lisa Kyle Young/iStockphoto.com

AND DON'T FORGET THE MICHELIN GUIDE ITALIA

For a more exhaustive list of suggestions, please consult the *Michelin Guide Italia*. Establishments that offer particularly good dining value for money are marked with the **Bib Gourmand** symbols.

GASTRONOMIC TERMS

Caffè corretto: *espresso* laced with brandy or *grappa*

Caffè decaffeinato (caffè "Hag"): decaffeinated coffee

Caffè latte: mainly hot milk, with a splash of coffee

Caffè lungo: coffee not quite as strong as *espresso*

Caffè macchiato: *espresso* with a splash of milk

Cannelloni: large pasta tubes filled with a meat or other sauce

Cappellini: very thin spaghetti

Cappuccino (or *cappuccio*): coffee topped with frothy milk and a dusting of cocoa

Cassata: ice cream containing chopped nuts and mixed dried fruit (similar to tutti-frutti)

Crema: vanilla (ice cream)

Farfalle: pasta bows

Fettuccine: slightly narrower, Roman version of tagliatelle

Fior di latte: very creamy variety of ice cream

Fusilli: small pasta spirals

Gnocchi: tiny potato dumplings

Lasagne: sheets of pasta arranged in layers with tomato and meat sauce (or other) and cheese sauce, topped with Parmesan and baked

Maccheroni: small pasta tubes

Panino: type of sandwich (bread roll)

Panna: cream; similar to *fior di latte*

Prosciutto: cured ham

Ravioli: little pasta cushions, enclosing meat or spinach

Schiacciata: type of sandwich (on a pizza-type base)

Spaghetti: the great classic

Stracciatella: chocolate chip (ice cream)

Tagliatelle: long narrow pasta ribbons

Tiramisù: coffee-flavoured frozen gâteau *(semifreddo)*

Tortellini: small crescent-shaped pasta rolls filled with a meat or cheese stuffing, often served in a clear meat broth

Tramezzino: type of sandwich (on slices of bread)

Zabaglione: dessert made from egg yolks and Marsala wine

Zuppa inglese: trifle

Basic Information

BUSINESS HOURS

Shops – Most shops open Monday–Saturday from 8am–1pm and 3.30–7.30 or 8pm. Many supermarkets are closed on Wednesday afternoons.

Museums and galleries – Opening times in Sicily are dependent on the time of year, local and national holidays and closures for restoration work. If there's something you are particularly set on seeing, it's worth telephoning ahead, either to the venue or the local tourist office, to check that it is open. Smaller museums open from 9am to 1pm, and some larger ones also open for a few hours in the afternoon. Open-air sites usually open between 8–9am and close one hour before sunset.

Churches – Most Sicilian churches are open in the mornings between 8am and midday, which is the best time for sightseeing. Churches will usually open around 6–7pm as well, when evening Mass is held.

COMMUNICATIONS

All forms of communication are widely available in Sicily, so you'll have no trouble keeping in touch. After many years in the cyber dark ages, Italy has now fully embraced the internet and you'll find Internet cafés in larger towns and cities (hourly costs vary between €0.50 and €2), modem points in the rooms of many larger hotels and even Wi-Fi connections. Check cafe.ecs.net for a list of internet points across Italy. The Sicilian telephone service is organised by TELECOM ITALIA (formerly SIP), and public telephones are common, even though practically everyone owns a mobile (cell) phone in Italy. Telecom Italia offices also have public booths, where the customer pays for units used (*scatti*) at the counter after the call. Italy has some of the highest phone tariffs in Europe, so save telephone calls until after 6.30pm to take advantage of cheaper rates. Rates are even lower between 10pm and 8am.

PHONE CARDS

Phone cards (*schede telefoniche*) are sold in denominations of €1, €2.50, €5 and €8 and are supplied by CIT offices and post offices, as well as tobacconists. These prefixes quickly drain any phone card: 0338, 0335, 0339, 0349, 0347 and 0368.

AREA CODES

When making a call within Italy, the area code (e.g. 091 for Palermo) is always used, both from outside and from within the city you are calling.

INTERNATIONAL CALLS

For international calls, dial 00 plus the following country codes:
- **61** for Australia
- **1** for Canada
- **64** for New Zealand
- **44** for the UK
- **1** for the USA

If calling from outside the country, the international code for Italy is 39. Dial the full area code, even when making an international call; for example, when calling Palermo from the UK, dial 00 39 091 followed by the correspondent's number. If you're on a budget, it's worth bearing in mind that international calls from Italy are markedly cheaper after 11pm.

USEFUL NUMBERS

(*See also Emergencies*)
- **176:** International Directory Enquiries. Provides phone numbers outside of Italy in English and Italian. Calls to this number are subject to a charge.
- **170:** Operator-assisted International Calls. This number is not toll-free either.

ELECTRICITY

The voltage is 220v, 50Hz; the sockets are for two-pin plugs. Most laptops and digital camera chargers have built-in convertors and only require an adaptor. Check carefully before trying hair dryers or shavers, however.

EMERGENCIES

- ℘**113:** General emergency services (*soccorso pubblico di emergenza*). Calls are free.
- ℘**112:** Police (*carabinieri*); truly an emergency hotline. Calls are free.
- ℘**115:** Fire Brigade (*vigili del fuoco*). Calls are free.
- ℘**118:** Emergency Health Services (*emergenza sanitaria*). Calls are free.
- ℘**1515:** Forest Fire Service. Environmental emergencies. Calls are free.
- ℘**803 116:** Automobile Club d'Italia Emergency Breakdown Service. Calls are free.

MAIL/POST
OPENING HOURS

Post offices are open 8am–2pm on weekdays and 8.30am–noon on Saturday. In cities and large towns opening hours may extend to 6 or 7pm, while those in smaller towns and villages will often close at the weekend. All post offices are closed on public holidays. Stamps are also sold at tobacconists (*tabacchi*), where queues are usually shorter. *Tabacchi* are identified by either a blue or black sign with a white T hanging outside.

STAMPS

The Italian postal service is notoriously slow and unreliable, so if a letter is urgent consider sending it by express service. Stamps cost €0.65 for postage within the EU, €1 outside (*posta prioritaria*).

MONEY

The unit of currency is the euro, which is issued in notes (€5, €10, €20, €50, €100, €200 and €500) and in coins (*1 cent, 2 cents, 5 cents, 10 cents, 20 cents, 50 cents, €1 and €2*). Correct change is something of a commodity in Sicily. Many bars, for example, are unable to break a €20 or €50 note. Keep a supply of small notes.

BANKS

Banks usually operate Monday to Friday, 8.30am–1.30pm and 3–4pm. Some are open downtown and in shopping centres on Saturday mornings; almost all close on Saturday afternoons, Sundays and holidays. Exchange bureaux in Sicily include post offices (*except traveller's cheques*), money-changers at railway stations and airports, and some hotel receptions (always on a rather stinging commission).

CREDIT CARDS

Payment by credit card is widespread in shops, hotels and restaurants and also some petrol stations. *The Michelin Guide Italia* and *The Michelin Guide Main Cities of Europe* indicate which ones are welcome at hotels and restaurants. Money may also be withdrawn from a bank, but could incur steep interest charges.

TAXES

In most cases VAT (**IVA**) in Italy is 20%. EU non-resident travellers can get a VAT refund for goods purchased for personal use. For information on how to claim a refund, go to www.agenziadogane.it.

NEWSPAPERS

The main regional newspapers are *La Gazzetta del Sud* (www.gazzetta delsud.it) for the area around Messina, *La Sicilia* (*www.lasicilia.it*) for Catania and the *Giornale di Sicilia* (*www.gds.it*) for Palermo. Foreign newspapers are available in major cities and large towns.

PHARMACIES

These are identified by a red and white or green neon cross. When closed, each pharmacy advertises on-duty competitors and a list of doctors on call.

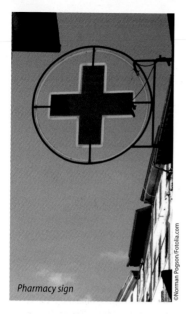

©Norman Pogson/Fotolia.com

Pharmacy sign

REDUCED RATES

Visitors trying to keep costs down will find information on budget accommodation (*pensioni,* youth hostels, campsites, convents and monasteries) in the **Addresses** located in the *Discovering Sicily* sections of the guide (⏱ *See also Where to Stay*).

BY AIR

Several airlines offer budget fares to Italy, although only Ryanair flies into Palermo from London Stansted. Prices vary according to how far in advance the booking is made.
Virgin Express: www.virgin-express.com;
BMI (British Midland): www.flybmi.com;
Ryanair: www.ryanair.com;
easyJet: www.easyjet.com

PUBLIC HOLIDAYS

A working day is *un giorno feriale; giorni festivi* and these include Saturdays, Sundays and 11 holidays. Public holidays are reverently observed in Sicily, so plan ahead and brace yourself for closed banks and shops, limited public transportation, and throngs on the roads and rails.

Alitalia has various special offers for passengers buying their ticket one, two or three weeks before departure. The airline also offers special weekend rates for travellers departing on a Saturday and returning on a Sunday of the same weekend (*tipo corto*) and for the same type of ticket, but valid for a month (*tipo lungo*).

BY TRAIN
Inter-Rail

The rail network does not cover the whole island. The main lines run along the coast, between Messina and Syracuse, Messina and Palermo, and Palermo and Trapani.
The island is linked from north to south between Termini Imerese and Agrigente. The countryside inland is poorly served.

Discounts

The Inter-Rail card and Euro Domino vouchers are valid for travel in 28 European and North African countries for a limited period only.
For more information, contact Trenitalia on ✆ 89 20 21 (national number) or visit www.trenitalia.it.

1 January	New Year
6 January	Epiphany
Easter Sunday and Monday	*lunedì dell'Angelo*
25 April	St Mark's Day and liberation in 1945
1 May	*Festa dei Lavoratori*
Sunday nearest 2 June	Anniversary of the Republic
15 August	The Assumption – *Ferragosto*
1 November	All Saints – *Tutti i Santi*
8 December	Immaculate Conception
25 and 26 December	Christmas and St Stephen's Day

Taormina Station

© Stanley Rippel/Dreamstime.com

DISCOUNTS FOR UNDER-26
BY TRAIN

The **Carta Verde Railplus** (€40, valid for a year; www.trenitalia.it) gives a 25% discount for people aged 12–25 on first- or second-class international ticket prices on routes connecting any two of the countries taking part in the RAILPLUS scheme (www.railplus.com). The ticket is non-transferable.

DISCOUNTS FOR SENIOR CITIZENS
BY TRAIN

For travellers over 60 years of age, the **Carta d'Argento** (€30, valid for a year) offers the same discounts and conditions as the Carta Verde (👆see above).

DISCOUNTS FOR FAMILIES AND SMALL GROUPS
BY TRAIN

Children aged 4–12 travel half-price. Those younger travel free, but must share a seat with a family member. Easter, Christmas and summer holidays may invalidate these offers. Limited availability (www.trenitalia.it.)

BY AIR

Some airlines offer discounts for families as long as they meet certain criteria. Check with your airline before booking flights in order not to miss out on any potential discount.

👆See Getting There and Getting Around for details of airlines flying to Sicily.

SMOKING

Since 2005 it has been illegal to light up inside any hotel, bar, restaurant or public building or on public transport throughout Italy. On-the-spot fines of up to €270 can be imposed. All Sicilian hotel rooms are non-smoking. However, Italy is still a nation with a smoker's psyche, and those wanting an after-dinner cigarette can find solace at tables in the outdoor dining areas of restaurants. These areas are common and open for much of the year thanks to Sicily's warm climate.

TOBACCONISTS

Besides smoking products, *tabacchi* sell postcards, stamps, confectionery, phone cards, public transport tickets, lottery tickets and such like. The shops – sometimes inside bars – are instantly recognisable by the white "T" on a blue or black sign.

TIME

The time in Italy is usually the same as in the rest of mainland Europe (one hour ahead of the UK) and changes during the last weekends of March and October, between summer time (ora legale) and winter time (ora solare).

TIPPING

Leaving a token of your gratitude for good service is welcome in Sicily. Service is generally included on restaurant bills, but a couple of coins in the dish over this is appreciated. If no service charge has been included in your bill it's customary to leave 10%. If you're having a drink standing at the bar it's a nice gesture to leave the copper-coloured change from your order. Seated drinkers should put 40–50 cents in the saucer if the service has been friendly. Tipping for taxi drivers ranges from rounding up your fare to 10% on top, depending on how you feel about the journey.

CONVERSION TABLES

Weights and Measures

EU	US	UK	
1 kilogram (kg)	**2.2 pounds (lb)**	**2.2 pounds**	*To convert*
6.35 kilograms	14 pounds	1 stone (st)	*kilograms*
0.45 kilograms	16 ounces (oz)	16 ounces	*to pounds,*
1 metric ton (tn)	**1.1 tons**	**1.1 tons**	*multiply by 2.2*
1 litre (l)	**2.11 pints (pt)**	**1.76 pints**	*To convert litres*
3.79 litres	1 gallon (gal)	0.83 gallon	*to gallons, multiply*
4.55 litres	1.20 gallon	1 gallon	*by 0.26 (US)*
			or 0.22 (UK)
1 hectare (ha)	**2.47 acres**	**2.47 acres**	*To convert*
1 sq kilometre	**0.38 sq. miles**	**0.38 sq. miles**	*hectares to*
(km²)	**(sq mi)**		*acres, multiply*
			by 2.4
1 centimetre (cm)	**0.39 inches (in)**	**0.39 inches**	*To convert metres*
1 metre (m)	**3.28 feet (ft) or 39.37 inches**		*to feet, multiply*
	or 1.09 yards (yd)		*by 3.28; for*
			kilometres to miles,
1 kilometre (km)	**0.62 miles (mi)**	**0.62 miles**	*multiply by 0.6*

Clothing

Women	EU	US	UK
	35	4	2½
	36	5	3½
	37	6	4½
Shoes	38	7	5½
	39	8	6½
	40	9	7½
	41	10	8½
	36	6	8
	38	8	10
Dresses	40	10	12
& suits	42	12	14
	44	14	16
	46	16	18
	36	6	30
	38	8	32
Blouses &	40	10	34
sweaters	42	12	36
	44	14	38
	46	16	40

Men	EU	US	UK
	40	7½	7
	41	8½	8
	42	9½	9
Shoes	43	10½	10
	44	11½	11
	45	12½	12
	46	13½	13
	46	36	36
	48	38	38
Suits	50	40	40
	52	42	42
	54	44	44
	56	46	48
	37	14½	14½
	38	15	15
Shirts	39	15½	15½
	40	15¾	15¾
	41	16	16
	42	16½	16½

Sizes often vary depending on the designer. These equivalents are given for guidance only.

Speed

KPH	10	30	50	70	80	90	100	110	120	130
MPH	6	19	31	43	50	56	62	68	75	81

Temperature

Celsius (°C)	0°	5°	10°	15°	20°	25°	30°	40°	60°	80°	100°
Fahrenheit (°F)	32°	41°	50°	59°	68°	77°	86°	104°	140°	176°	212°

To convert Celsius into Fahrenheit, multiply °C by 9, divide by 5, and add 32.
To convert Fahrenheit into Celsius, subtract 32 from °F, multiply by 5, and divide by 9.
NB: Conversion factors on this page are approximate.

Useful Words and Phrases

	Translation
Avenue	Viale
Boulevard	Corso
(bus-) Stop	Fermata
Customs	Dogana
Danger	Pericolo
Descent	Discesa
Entrance	Ingresso
Esplanade	Piazzale
Exit, Way out	Uscita
Level crossing	Passaggio a livello
Pass	Passo
Prohibited	Vietato
Men at work	Lavori in corso
Motorway	Autostrada
Open	Aperto
Narrow	Stretto
Pavement	Banchina
(railway) Platform	Binario
River	Fiume
Snow	Neve
Square, Place	Piazza, Largo
Station	Stazione
To the left	A sinistra
To the right	A destra

Places and Things to See

	Translation
Abbey, Monastery	Abbazia, Convento
Arch	Arco
Beach	Spiaggia
Cable Car	Funivia
Castle	Castello
Cathedral	Duomo
Chairlift	Seggiovia
Chapel	Cappella
Church	Chiesa
Cloisters	Chiostro
Closed	Chiuso
Courtyard	Cortile
Environs	Dintorni
Excavations	Scavi
Façade	Facciata
Feudal Castle	Rocca
Floor, Storey	Piano
Frescoes	Affreschi
Gardens	Giardini
Gorges	Gole
House	Casa
Library	Biblioteca
Picture Gallery	Pinacoteca
Pulpit	Pulpito
Picture	Quadro
Ruins	Rovine, Ruderi
Sacristy	Sagrestia
Stairway	Scala
Tapestries	Arazzi
Treasure	Tesoro
Tower	Torre, Torazzo
Town	Città
View	Vista
Walk, Promenade	Passeggiata
Waterfall	Cascata

Common Words

	Translation
All	Tutto, Tutti
Dear	Caro
Excuse me	Mi scusi
Enough	Basta
Good morning	Buon giorno
Goodbye	Arrivederci
How much?	Quanto?
Large	Grande
Madam	Signora
Miss	Signorina
More, Less	Più, Meno
Much, Little	Molto, Poco
Please	Per favore
Sir	Signore
Small	Piccolo
Thank you very much	Grazie tante
Where? When?	Dove? Quando?
Where is?	Dov'è?
Yes, No	Si, No

Numbers

	Translation
0	zero
1	uno
2	due
3	tre
4	quattro
5	cinque
6	sei
7	sette
8	otto
9	nove
10	dieci
11	undici
12	dodici
13	tredici
14	quattordici
15	quindici
16	sedici
17	diciassette
18	diciotto
19	diciannove
20	venti
30	trenta
40	quaranta
50	cinquanta
60	sessanta
70	settanta
80	ottanta
90	novanta
100	cento
1,000	mille
5,000	cinquemila
10,000	diecimila
1.00	l'una
1.15	l'una e un quarto
1.30	un ora e mezzo
1.45	l'una e quaranta cinque

Time, days of the week and seasons

	Translation
Morning	Mattina
Afternoon	Pomeriggio
Evening	Sera
Yesterday	Ieri
Today	Oggi
Tomorrow	Domani
A Week	Una Settimana
Monday	Lunedì
Tuesday	Martedì
Wednesday	Mercoledì
Thursday	Giovedì
Friday	Venerdì
Saturday	Sabato
Sunday	Domenica
Winter	Inverno
Spring	Primavera
Summer	Estate
Autumn/Fall	Autunno

USEFUL PHRASES

Do you speak English?
Parla inglese?
I don't understand
Non capisco
Please speak slowly
Parli piano per favore
Where are the toilets?
Dove sono i bagni?
At what time does the train/ bus/plane leave?
A che ora parte il treno/ l'autobus/ l'aereo?
At what time does the train arrive?
A che ora arriva il treno ...?
What does it cost?
Quanto costa?
Where is the post office?
Dove è l'ufficio postale?
Where can I buy an English newspaper?
Dove posso comprare un giornale inglese?
Where can I change my money?
Dove posso cambiare i miei soldi?
May I pay with a credit card?
Posso pagare con una carta di credito?
the road to ...?
Si può visitare?
what time is it?
Che ora è?
I would like...
Desidero/vorrei...

Tempio di Hera Lacinia,
La Valle dei Templi, Agrigento
Kevin Galvin / age-fotostock

Sicily Today

A constant feature of the island's clear seas, blue sky and grandiose mountains framing the coast, beauty is the first element to strike visitors to Sicily. The scenery here is far from subtle: the island's stunning natural landscapes offer bright colours, fragrant scents and unforgettable views.

The region has been inhabited by many different people over the centuries: the Greeks established colonies here that were later developed by the Romans; the Arabs created magnificent buildings and gardens, subsequently converted into splendid palaces by the Normans; and the French and Spanish introduced the severe Gothic and exuberant Baroque styles. Sicily was dominated by foreign rulers until 1860, when Garibaldi and his troops landed near Marsala, paving the way for the unification of Italy.

Three thousand years of tumultuous history have endowed Sicily with its complex character, best expressed through the island's varied and fascinating art. The human and social mosaic here is even more challenging. Media coverage focuses all too often on Mafia-related crime and Sicilians are often frustrated by the portrayal of their homeland.

And yet Sicily has many facets, as the title *La luce e il lutto* (The Light and the Struggle), a collection of essays by the Sicilian writer Gesualdo Bufalino, suggests. The traditional images are of sunshine, blue skies, warm seas, Greek temples, the Mafia and southern Mediterranean vegetation. Visitors willing to look beyond, however, will discover a proud, hospitable people and a rich, vibrant culture.

POPULATION

Historically, Sicily has been one of the more populated of Italy's regions and today it has the fourth highest regional population in the country. However, the relatively extensive size of the region – which includes the Aeolian islands – means the population density is only slightly higher than the national average. Population density is highest around the coastal areas, where the bulk of tourism and industry are also concentrated, while the inland zone, dominated by agriculture, is relatively uninhabited. This is also partly due to a trend in migration of workers from the countryside to the cities, where earning potential is higher. The most densely populated

Tuna fishing in Favignana, Isole Egadi

© Paola Ghirotti/Fototeca ENIT

Trinacria

A legend tells of three nymphs who travelled the world to collect its best produce. Coming across a sea of extraordinary beauty, they dropped their flowers and fruit into it.

From the waters rose the land mass of Sicily – with its three headlands of Capo Peloro, Capo Passero and Capo Lilibeo – the jewel-casket of the world's beauty. This myth attempts to explain the origins of the harmoniously shaped triangular island, known as Triskeles (three legs) to the Greeks and Triquetra (three peaks) to the Romans. The island's symbol is the Trinacria, a figure with three legs running around a Medusa's head.

© eldorado/Fotolia.com

areas are around Palermo and Catania, along the coastal areas between Catania and Messina, Siracusa and around Agrigento. The high grounds of the island – Etna, the Iblei, Erei mountains and the Sicilian Apennines – have the lowest population density of all, so much so that a few hours' drive may offer almost complete solitude out of season.

ECONOMY

Sicily's economy is relatively underdeveloped compared to the rest of Italy and its unemployment rate is the highest in the country. Agriculture is the primary economic activity on the island, which has historically been coveted for its fertile land and long, hot growing season.

However, the land is divided between a large number of smallholdings, with the result that incomes are relatively low across the board. The main crops are oranges and lemons, peaches, pears, figs, almonds, salt from Trapani and grapes, as well as barley, corn and wheat, particularly around Enna where durum wheat is grown for pasta and bread. Sicily's farms also produce and export a significant amount of dairy products including ricotta and Pecorino cheeses. Other agricultural industries are wine (from Malvasia, Marsala, Donna Fugata and Regaleali), balsalmic vinegar, olive oil, bottled water from Geraci and honey. On the coast, the fishing industry still flourishes, providing important tuna and sardine fisheries, as well as catches of swordfish, octopus, squid, prawns and sea bream for domestic consumption. Away from the farms and orchards, industrial development on the island plays an increasingly prominent part in the Sicilian economy.

This has been immeasurably aided by the growth of transport companies and vast improvements to the road system over the past decade. Refined petroleum, from petroleum fields in the southeast, natural gas and sulphur (traditionally a Sicilian industry at the sulphur mines in Caltanissetta) make up the bulk of the island's modern industries. Sicily's other major industry is tourism, which brings an important influx of foreign currency to the island through the summer months.

"Climb aboard this triangular ark of stone floating upon the waves of millennia… And keep a smattering of Greek to hand, lest you encounter Aphrodite, the goddess of love, emerging from the sea and eager to exchange a few words…"

– Gesualdo Bufalino, *La luce e il lutto (The Light and the Struggle)*

GOVERNMENT

Sicily became an autonomous region in 1946 under the new Italian constitution, with its own parliament and elected President. Sicilian politics is hung on the framework of a presidential representative democracy in which the President of Regional Government *(Presidente della Regione)* is the head of government *(Giunta Regionale)* and also of a multi-party system. The Sicilian Regional Assembly *(Assemblea Regionale Siciliana, ARS)* is elected for a five-year term and, along with the President, has legislative power. However, if a vote of no confidence is registered in the President, or he or she resigns or dies, this triggers a new election.

A regional election was held on 13–14 April 2008, following the resignation of President Salavatore Cuffaro as a result of his conviction on charges of aiding the Mafia, to which he pleaded not guilty. Investigations into Cuffaro, whose first presidential term was in 1991, had been running since 2003. Despite this shadow, he managed to be re-elected President of Sicily in the 2006 regional election, beating Rita Borsellino, sister of the Mafia-executed judge, Paolo Borsellino. The subsequent election was fought by Anna Finocchiaro for the centre-left and Raffaele Lombardo (centre-right). Lombardo won by a landslide, 65.3 per cent. A new election was held on 28 October 2012 after Lombardo was forced to resign over allegations of Mafia collaboration. The election was won by the centre-left candidate, Rosario Crocetta, who obtained 30.5 per cent of the votes and became the first openly gay mayor in Italy.

FOOD AND DRINK

Talk of food in Sicily is like talking about the weather in England – it is fundamental to life itself. Every region has its own dishes and each community sings the praises of their home-grown vegetables and fragrant herbs, which impart flavour, texture and colour to the local cuisine. The island's eternal links with the sea are also clearly evident, with myriad fish dishes.

Sicilian cuisine relies on an abundance of strongly flavoured basic ingredients

Arancine di Riso (Deep-Fried Rice Balls)

400g/1lb rice, ½ small packet of saffron, six eggs, 100g/4oz butter, 100g/4oz shelled peas, ½ chopped onion, 150g/6oz minced veal, ½ peeled tomato, 75g/3oz sliced fresh caciocavallo cheese, 300g/12oz flour, 300g/12oz breadcrumbs. Serves four.

© msheldrake/iStockphoto.com

Boil the rice until it has a crunchy, *al dente* texture and then mix it with the saffron, three eggs and half the butter. Leave to cool. Parboil the peas, drain and brown in the remaining butter. In a separate pan, gently fry the chopped onion. Add the meat, peeled tomato, salt and pepper. Cover and cook over a low heat. Once the meat sauce is ready, mix with the peas. To make the *arancini* balls, shape the rice mixture into shell shapes with your hands, add to a dish, then pour in some of the meat sauce. Add a slice of cheese and cover with more of the rice, making a ball. Whisk the remaining eggs and add a little salt. Roll the rice balls in flour, then in the egg mixture and finally the breadcrumbs. Fry in plenty of sunflower oil and serve hot.

Dried cherry tomatoes for sale in the market on Corso Vittorio Emanuele, Lipari

© Jean-Pierre Degas/hemis.fr

(fennel, for example), which are blended and fused with tasty sun-blush tomatoes, the most gleaming rich aubergines (eggplants), delicate courgettes (zucchini) and the freshest tuna. The food is a natural extension of the local landscape. It forms an integral part of the gastronomic culture of the Mediterranean, halfway between Greece and North Africa, Spain and Ancient Phoenicia (the Middle East). Just as the landscapes of the coast and the hinterland are radically different, so too is their cuisine quite distinctive. Imagine, therefore, Sicily's gastronomy as a palette of paints, with strong colours and subtle hints.

See food terms in *Useful Words and Phrases.*

TYPICAL MEDITERRANEAN CUISINE

As with all simple culinary traditions, the most popular single-course meal is often the tastiest. Pasta, prepared with seasonal vegetables and local olive oil, is the main staple. *Pasta con le sarde,* originally a Palermo dish using freshly caught sardines, is now common across the whole island. Pasta cooked predominantly with vegetables is more typically served with meat ragout and peas, or ham and cheese), and is symbolic of the island's traditional cuisine.

Fish abounds, as do the different ways of cooking it. Tuna has always occupied a prime position; sardines and anchovies appear everywhere, while *pesce spada* (swordfish) is more common around Messina. Fish prepared with onions, olives, capers and tomatoes *(alla ghiotta)* is an unusual speciality. Around Trapani, the *cuscusu* is the island's version of the Moroccan dish, where fish replaces meat.

SWEET DELICACIES

Sicily has a long cake- and pastrymaking tradition. Crushed herbs (rosemary, wild fennel, oregano, basil, thyme) grow throughout the countryside. Convent sweetmeats, like the brightly coloured *frutta martorana,* named after

Cannoli

© Jonatha Borzicchi/Dreamstime.com

51

the convent in Palermo where they originated, have become popular throughout the island.

Cannoli, cassate, pignoccata, biancomangiare and the traditional *gelo di mellone* (watermelon jelly) are the most common, but each province has its own particular specialities.

The area produces *gelato* and *granite*, which are not merely products of great craftsmanship and culinary pride but smack of the habits and rituals of another era.

In summer, it is almost compulsory to offer guests a coffee-, lemon- or almond-flavoured *granita* when they arrive. Literature even mentions such sophisticated delights as a jasmine *granita*, consumed by the Piccolo barons.

WINES

Sicily's wines were once regarded as *vini da taglio,* padding to boost other blends. Today, Sicilian table wines and DOC *(Denominazione di Origine Controllata)* wines – such as Eloro Nero d'Avola, Etna Rosso and Bianco, Cerasuolo di Vittoria (DOCG) and Contea di Sclafani – are absolute delights.

Festivals and Traditions

By combining pagan rites, holy days allowed by the Christian Church and local festivals, the Sicilians ensure that lavish celebrations are high points in their social calendars. The most important festivals are Easter, Carnival and the feast days of local saints. Other highlights include the *Palio dei Normanni*, which commemorates Roger II's delivery of Piazza Armerina; events derived from pagan rites, such as Gangi's *Sagra della Spiga* with a procession dedicated to the ancient goddess Demeter (Ceres); and festivals linked to a celebration of nature, such as Agrigento's *Sagra del Mandorlo in fiore* (celebrating the blossoming of the almond trees) and Vizzini's *Sagra della Ricotta*, both of which fête the advent of spring.

Patron saints

The most spectacular festivals in honour of patron saints are those held in the large towns. In Palermo, *U fistinu*, dedicated to Santa Rosalia, lasts for six whole action-packed days.

Sagra del Mandorlo in fiore, Agrigento

© M. Magni/MICHELIN

Popular Sicilian Music

At the very mention of this island's name, anyone with a keen ear for music recalls the *siciliana*, an ancient shepherds' dance. This was transcribed in pieces of the 17C and 18C. Traditional dance music features the straight reed pipe (*fiscalettu or friscaleddu*), and the *marranzanu*, a mouth harp.

Popular music includes songs *alla carrittera* – literally "of the cart-driver" and those sung by the *cantastorie* – modern equivalents of minstrels who travel with a guitar and a board illustrating their story. The most famous of these was Ciccio Busacca (1926–84).

In addition to the famous **Marsala**, dessert wines made here include Moscato di Noto, Passito di Pantelleria and Malvasia di Lipari. *For a description of wine routes in Sicily, see Planning Your Trip: Themed Tours.*

In Catania, the citizens honour St Agatha, whose relics, contained in a precious silver bust of the saint set with enamels and jewels, are processed for three days by the *nudi* – men dressed in simple jute sacks to commemorate the night in 1126 when citizens poured onto the streets as the relics were brought back to the city from Constantinople.

In Siracusa, eyes of wax, silver and bronze are fixed to the litter of St Lucy in grateful acknowledgement of grace received from the Saint, protector of all things optical. In Messina, the most spectacular festival is held on 15 August, when thousands pull an enormous statue representing the Assumption of the Virgin Mary to the cathedral, where it remains for two days, guarded by 14 young girls dressed in white.

This Festa della Vergine is celebrated alongside the anniversary of the arrival of Count Roger: the sacred mixes with the profane in an inseparable cocktail of religious devotion, high spirits, social occasion and entertainment.

Easter

Easter is certainly the most eagerly awaited festival. In almost every town and small village enormous effort is invested in preparing for the processions and the celebrations of a rite that has changed little through the centuries. Processions move the sacred element – a representation of a holy figure – through the streets of the town, stopping here and there to re-enact the Madonna's desperate search for her son, the Crucifixion and the events of the Passion. The most poignant elements fall between the Thursday before Easter and Easter Sunday (the discovery of the empty tomb as evidence of the Resurrection), although these can be more protracted, as is the case with celebrations held at **Trapani**. There, the evenings leading up to the Good Friday grand procession are devoted to the *discese delle Vergini*.

At sunset, representatives of each and every *ceto* of the town (associations roughly comparable to the medieval trade guilds) bear on their shoulders the image of their patron Madonna *(Madre dei Massari, Madre Pietà del Popolo)* and carry her down to the old part of town by candlelight. Men compete to be chosen as bearers. The icon sways along, stopping at wayside crosses, shrines and churches, but also outside the houses and workplaces of those who have offered a donation.

Good Friday procession, Trapani

© Patrick Frilet/hemis.fr

In so doing, it is almost as though the Madonna herself is paying homage to those who worship her. The elegant *palazzi* open their doors and gracious inner courtyards to visitors, to the crowd, and to the band – who at intervals interrupt the silence with a burst of music. On Good Friday, 20 figurative groups are continuously borne aloft round the town over a period of 20 hours: in a meaningful and symbolic succession of day, night and day *(from early afternoon on the Friday through the night to Saturday morning)*, the faithful are reminded of, and share in, the emotional endurance and physical pain suffered by the Madonna and by Christ in His Passion. An equally evocative occasion is the procession through Caltanissetta of 16 groups of statues.

In **Marsala** the re-enactment of the Passion is assigned to local men and women. At **Enna**, the celebrations reach their climax on Good Friday, when hooded members of the confraternities progress through the streets to the town centre carrying two heavy statues of the dead Christ and the *Addolorata* (Our Lady of Sorrows). The processions meet at the cathedral and together undertake an exhausting journey that lasts throughout the night. The whole event is then repeated on the Sunday, but with one fundamental difference: this time, the meeting between the Madonna and the Resurrected Christ takes place in a happy, festive atmosphere. A rather unusual rite takes place in **Prizzi** on the Sunday morning. It is called the **Uballu di diavula**: devils – dressed in red, with goatskins slung across their shoulders, their faces covered by horrible tin masks – run through the streets of the town rattling iron chains. Another masked figure, dressed in yellow and armed with a wooden crossbow, represents Death. Anyone struck is carried off to the bar (identified as hell), where he pays for a whole round of drinks. The devils jump around, uttering threats and trying to avert the Madonna from meeting the Resurrected Christ. This scene is repeated several times until at last the two angels accompanying the Madonna strike them to the ground. Only Death cannot be touched, partly spared in recognition of human mortality and partly because Christ has already overcome it. At **Terrasini**, the festival of **li schietti** (eligible bachelors) is more profane: young men prove their virility by lifting orange trees.

In addition to staging elaborate re-enactments, some areas bedeck the streets with spectacular decorations. At San Biagio Platani, for example, locals build grand triumphal arches and ornament them with sculptures made of bread.

Religion

Like mainland Italy, Sicily is almost exclusively Catholic, but the island has developed a more exuberant brand of Catholicism than elsewhere and religion is often mixed with ancient superstitious rituals.

CHRISTIANITY

"We landed at Syracuse and stayed there for three days." This extract from the Acts of the Apostles, which describes the travels of St Paul and his companions after their shipwreck on the island of Malta, is the only mention of Sicily in the Bible. Assuming the account is historically accurate, the Apostle Paul would barely have had time to evangelise the population of Syracuse.

A LATE START

Whereas Christianity began to take hold in southern Italy in the 2C, most likely Sicily was a late convert to Christianity. However, according to a legend quoted by the Eastern Churches, the young St Pancras, a native of Antioch, was sent by the Apostle Paul to evangelise Sicily in the 1C. St Pancras is said to have been the first bishop of Taormina before being stoned to death for his faith. A Catholic legend also tells of Saint Lucy (Lucia), who was a virgin martyr in Syracuse in the early 4C during Diocletian's persecutions of the Christians. So it seems likely that Christianity did not really become established on the island until it gained favour under the reign of the Emperor Constantine (306–337).

THE ORTHODOX INFLUENCE

Until the 9C the island's Greek heritage and Byzantine domination had a profound influence on the development of Christianity in Sicily. During the iconoclastic period (8C–9C), Sicily remained faithful to image worship. Later, the Catholic and the Orthodox churches split permanently in the Great Schism of 1054, after the Pope and the Patriarch of Constantinople, who had both understood the need to need to unify their rites after the coming of the Arabs and the Normans, were unable to come to an agreement. Areas of disagreement included the issue of whether baptism should be by total or partial immersion, the use of unleavened bread, celibacy for priests and the dogma of the Trinity. This last issue was the focus of a long-standing debate known as the "Filioque dispute", which related to the status of the Holy Spirit, and whether it proceeded from the Father *(ex Patre)* or from the Father and the Son *(ex Patre Filio*

Easter celebrations of the Albanian community in Piana degli Albanesi, near Palermo

© WpN/Photoshot

Arab-Norman decoration of the cathedral, Palermo

© Franck Guiziou/hemis.fr

que). In Sicily, history decided in favour of Roman Catholicism and today the Byzantine rite is only celebrated in the community of Piana degli Albanesi, near Palermo, which is composed of Albanian members of the Italo-Greek Catholic church who arrived as refugees in the 18C. Although Catholic, their priests are able to marry. The Eastern traditions also continue in the churches of Mezzojuso and La Martorana in Palermo. Protestant evangelical groups, meanwhile, gain increasing numbers of followers and the Jehovah's Witnesses are now Italy's second-largest religion by number.

ISLAM

When Sicily was conquered by the Arabs, the Christian church was organised into dioceses, with several monasteries, some of them under the direct authority of the Pope. Pilgrimages were organised, and it appears Sicily had venerated the Virgin Mary from the 3C, as attested by the sites of Tindari and Brucoli. Given this background, the island's Muslim conquest was only ever partial. Helped by Byzantium, the Christians staged resistance in the mountains of Valdemone, between Cefalù, Messina and Taormina, based around the stronghold of Demenna *(modern-day San Marco d'Alunzio)*. So, a Christian principality subsisted in the region during the period of Arab domination and some Muslim opponents of the Emir of Palermo even took refuge there and converted to Christianity.

A TOLERANT REGIME

The Muslim regime took a tolerant approach, allowing Christian institutions to remain in regions under Islamic control. A bishop worked with the Emir of Palermo and monasteries continued to operate in Vicari and San Filipo d'Argirò. Christian officials of Greek background protected their fellow Christians while serving their Arab rulers. Following the Norman conquest, the new rulers took an open-minded approach towards Arab culture *(see History)*, but also had to follow the rules set down by the Papacy, which was in conflict with Islam.

As a result, some Muslims converted to Christianity, while others chose to go into exile. Under Spanish rule, Muslims and Jews were mercilessly persecuted by the Inquisition. Today, Sicily has a small Muslim community of a few thousand, most of them immigrant workers from Tunisia or Morocco.

JUDAISM

We have evidence from a tombstone in Catania that the Jews have been present in Sicily from as early as the 4C. They arrived in large numbers during the Muslim period and accounted for nearly 5% of the Sicilian population in the Middle Ages. Sicily's Jews were Arab-speaking, mainly craftsmen, fishermen, doctors or small-scale merchants, and lived freely on the island without being confined to ghettos. This same spirit of tolerance continued under the Normans, but vanished without trace in the late 13C, when the Aragonese Dominicans arrived with the forces of the Inquisition. The repression culminated with the 1374 massacre of 400 innocent Jews in Modica, before the Spanish Inquisition left the Jews with a choice between forced conversion or exile in northern Italy, the Maghreb or the Balkans. By the end of the 15C, Sicily's Jewish community had disappeared.

To this day, there is still a small synagogue in Rome known as the "Sicilian" synagogue. The Jewish tradition also survives in the food rituals followed by Catholics at Easter, when they eat unleavened bread and artichokes, just as people do in the Jewish tradition at Passover.

THE TRIUMPH OF CATHOLICISM

It was not until the 15C and the reign of King Alphonso V of Aragon that Sicily became permanently bound to Roman Catholicism. The introduction of the courts of the Inquisition in 1497 was aimed as much at pursuing Jews and Muslims as controlling the population, with the intention of turning Sicily into a bastion of Christianity in the face of the Turkish threat. It was also from Sicily that a Christian fleet bringing together ships from Venice, Spain, Tuscany and the Papal States set out on an expedition against the Turks, who were defeated at the Battle of Lepanto in 1571.

Sicily and its Baroque churches avoided the Reformation and became the showcase of the Counter-Reformation. An uncompromising brand of Catholicism developed on the island, supported by the Inquisition and its methods of terror. Even after the Inquisition was suppressed in 1786, the Sicilian church remained extremely conservative in both religious and political terms, and the same is true to this day.

RELIGION, TRADITION, SUPERSTITION

The exuberance of Sicilian Catholicism is something that goes beyond the Christian faith. Along with the family, the Church is the institution that safeguards morality, tradition and the social order. It is through the Church, and with its blessing, that the milestones in people's lives are celebrated, from birth until death. Sicilian fervour emerges most strongly in the veneration of the island's saints, particularly the female saints Lucia, Rosalia and Agata. They are constantly invoked to ward off anything from disease and volcanic eruptions to misfortune and death. Sicilians also venerate supernatural phenomena, as illustrated by the example of Padre Pio. This popular devotion goes hand in hand with Sunday masses that are attended in great numbers and can be seen in the veneration of altars erected at crossroads, with their wealth of votive offerings and candles.

At the same time, typically Mediterranean superstitious practices are alive and well, such as a belief in the Evil Eye and the protective power of the horn. It is not unusual for people to visit *jettatori* (bearers of the Evil Eye), and *gabbera* (sorcery) has not completely disappeared either. It is also common to ask for the priest for a blessing (in return for payment) to protect a house, to help you pass an exam, when playing the lottery, to treat an illness or to win back a loved one's affection. Curious rites, such as implanting scissors into the wall of a house to ward off enemy spirits, are also alive and well.

Temple of Heracles (Hercules) La Valle dei Templi, Agrigento
© Herbert Spichtinger/age fotostock

History

In the 14C BC, the Mediterranean was crucial to the history of mankind: in the words of Plato, people flocked to its coasts "like frogs around a pond". Sicily lies at the centre of this sea and consequently became a natural intersection of many cultures and civilisations. The island attracted navigators from the East and over the centuries its coastline was transfigured by myth and poetry.

ANCIENT GREEKS

Legends about the Greeks in Sicily date back to the 8C BC. Furious at a failed sacrifice in his honour, Neptune caused a shipwreck off the eastern coast of Sicily. The sole survivor took refuge in the vast bay that extends between Capo Taormina and Capo Schisò. Struck by the island's beauty, he persuaded others to found a colony there.

HISTORY AND SOCIAL PHENOMENA

Contacts between Sicily and the Hellenistic world go back to the dawn of Greek civilisation: numerous archaeological artefacts testify to thriving maritime centres along the eastern and southern Sicilian coast trading with Crete and Mycenae from the middle of the 2nd millennium BC. Colonisation only began when living conditions within Ancient Greece became untenable: famine followed civil war and unrest from the new "social class", drawn from restless second sons, who could not inherit land.

Foundations

Various small groups of Hellenes took part in colonising Sicily. The pioneers were the Ionians: in 735 BC, they settled near Capo Schis and founded Naxos, then Leontinoi, Catane and Zancle (now Messina).

Almost simultaneously, Dorians founded Syracuse; meanwhile, colonists from Megara settled at Megara Hyblaea.

At the beginning of the 7C BC, Rhodians and Cretans arrived and founded Gela on the south coast. This first phase of expansion involved sites with abundant fresh water that were easily accessible from the sea, yet with space to expand inland.

Founders

Each expedition, comprised predominantly – but not exclusively – of men. Before scouting sites, the leader (*oikistes*) would travel to Delphi to ask the gods where to found the colony. This role had great power and prestige. He transferred the holy flame and the lifeblood of the religious cult from the metropolis to the satellite colonies. Advised by surveyors,

engineers and soothsayers, he presided over the construction of the citadel and the public buildings, and over the administration of justice. The leader was also responsible for ensuring fair practice when the draw for plots of land took place: his decisions were considered sacred. On his death, he was honoured almost like a deity.

Colony

The founder would establish the new city's institutions. Each colony (*apoikia*, meaning "new family" in Greek) was completely independent. Despite Corinth's vain attempts to maintain control, its satellites embraced autonomy as independent entities. In this way, Akragas (Agrigento) was able to develop excellent trading relations with Carthage, which was officially hostile to Greece. Zancle and Reggio blockaded the Straits of Messina and demanded Greek ships pay harbour taxes. The colonists duly lost rights of citizenship in their city of origin and acquired the equivalent status in their new home. Restrictions on religious practices were kept in place, as was the option of "exchanging" citizenship of one city with the residency of another by mutual consent. The colonies were not only independent from their motherland, but also from each other. All grew quickly, thanks to flourishing trade links and fertile territories. A sharp increase in population, partly from births and partly from immigration, sparked secondary settlement farther inland.

The Greeks and Indigenous Populations

Relations with the indigenous peoples were extremely varied. In some cases, the rapport inspired commercial and religious exchanges. These coastal Hellenic settlements barely disturbed the pre-existing communities yet when the Greeks spread inland, strife began. Eventually, open conflict led to the systematic extermination of villages as happened during the great revolt by the indigenous population that gripped the eastern part of the island sometime in the mid-5C. With defeat came obligations to pay tributes and, in some cases, enforced conditions of slavery. In Syracuse, the descendants of the indigenous people (the Cilliri) were constrained to cultivating the land of their overlords (Gamòroi), who were descended from the ancient colonists.

The Greek settlers were known as the **Siceliots**. These people, armed and endowed with sophisticated technology, rapidly imposed their civilisation upon Sicily: between the 6C BC and the 5C BC, they managed to completely hellenise the territories they held.

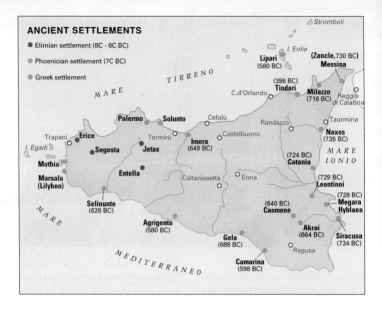

ANCIENT SETTLEMENTS

● Elimian settlement (8C - 6C BC)
● Phoenician settlement (7C BC)
● Greek settlement

⌀ *Stromboli*

I. Eolie

Lipari
(580 BC)

(Zancle,730 BC)
Messina

TIRRENO

(396 BC)
Tindari

Milazzo
(716 BC)

Reggio
di Calabria

MARE

C.d'Orlando

Palermo   **Solunto**

Cefalú

Randazzo

Taormina

Trapani   **Erice**

Termini

Castelbuono

Naxos
(735 BC)

I. Egadi

Segesta   **Jetas**

Imera
(649 BC)

MARE

Mothia

(724 BC)
Catania

IONIO

Marsala
(Lilybeo)

Entella

Caltanissetta

Enna

(729 BC)
Leontinoi

Selinunte
(628 BC)

(640 BC)
Casmene

(728 BC)
**Megara
Hyblaea**

MARE

Agrigento
(580 BC)

Akrai
(664 BC)

Siracusa
(734 BC)

Gela
(688 BC)

Ragusa

MEDITERRANEO

Camarina
(598 BC)

Economy

Prosperity depended not only on the natural fertility of the Sicilian land, but also on good farming practices. Grafts improved the yields of wild plants. Colonists adapted common wheat for intensive cultivation, planted almond trees and pomegranates, and selectively bred animals. The cities reclaimed land where possible, most notably at Camarina and Selinus, under the direction of Empedocles. Besides their success at arable farming and careful husbandry, the Western Greeks amassed fortunes through commerce, trading with the motherland as well as Spain, southern Italy and North Africa. They imported fine ceramics, perfumes and metals against timber, wheat and wool. Soon the Siceliot cities needed their own currencies. The earliest coins were of silver – later gold and bronze were introduced.

POLITICAL EVOLUTION

To qualify for citizenship, individuals were required to own a piece of land and have a fixed abode. In reality, many of the Greeks would have earned their living as skilled craftsmen, fishermen, traders and collectors of customs duties. At least one-third of the population must have worked on large-scale construction projects, be it as a woodcutter or a painter. Many more lived from one day to the next without a roof over their heads or permanent employment. In the space of a few years, therefore, the very inequalities that the colonists thought they had escaped in leaving Greece had become issues of contention. The aristocracy, together with the owners of the best land, hoarded power. They repressed the new moneyed classes of businessmen and those who owned no land. To deal with the continual crises provoked by economic rivalry and internal social pressures, some cities tried to correct the balance by replacing the oral legal system of oaths with a written constitution. The first codex, transcribed by **Charondas of Catane** (6C BC), was copied by many other cities, including Athens. It established duties and rights within the family; prescribed punishments for violence and perjury, and the death penalty for anyone entering a political meeting armed; and instituted a sort of citizens' jury, decreeing that a fine – proportional to earnings – be paid by anyone who refused to participate.

TYRANNICAL RULE

Tyranny was the other way of averting economic and social crises. The **tyrant**, who was generally a member of the new moneyed class or the army, held most of the power and delegated the rest to his most loyal supporters. Syracuse achieved its greatest splendour and managed to impose its authority throughout the island first under **Gelon** and then **Hieron I**. The other Siceliot cities, desperate to salvage their independence, sought assistance from Carthage or Athens, but to no avail. Meanwhile, the civil strife continued to split the Greek communities and the Carthaginian threat was growing.

After a period of anarchy, **Timoleon**, who had arrived from Corinth to assist the colonies, succeeded in restoring democracy and peace to Sicily. Upon his death, the Greeks once more began to quarrel among themselves and with the Carthaginians. Finally, in the second half of the 3C BC, the citizens of Messina (Zancle) turned to Rome for help, opening their gates to the Imperial city and precipitating her conquest of Sicily.

CULTURE

Legend relates how **Alpheus**, a river god, was wandering across the Greek region of Arcadia when he came across Arethusa, one of Artemis' water nymphs. He fell in love with the nymph but as he tried to seize her, she changed into a stream, slipping from him into the Ionian Sea only to re-emerge as a spring in Siracusa. Alpheus pursued her, mingling their waters. This myth, diffused among the Greek population of Sicily, symbolises the transference of the Greek civilisation from the motherland to Sicily. Far from being marginal, the island attracted some of the culture's most illustrious figures. It also succoured native geniuses, who became famous throughout the Hellenic world.

According to some scholars, Greek culture should be indebted to Sicily for one of its fundamental masterpieces, the *Odyssey*. Many of Ulysses' adventures were unequivocally set in the Island of the Sun, the name used by **Homer** to describe Sicily, so obviously that Apollodorus defined the *Odyssey* as a kind of "journey around Sicily".

Many of the places can be identified with Sicily *(see map)*: the Aeolian Islands are the kingdom of Aeolus and the "errant rocks" mentioned by Circe in Book XII are the Faraglioni rocks between Lipari and Vulcano; Scylla and Charybdis personify the impetuous currents in the Straits of Messina; the port at which Ulysses' companions steal the flocks of the Sun is Messina; the Sirens (according to the Sicilian interpretation of the work) waited for sailors in the seas around Capo Peloro; the Cyclops' cave was inside Mount Etna; and the rocks thrown by Polyphemus landed in the sea in front of Aci Trezza.

ULYSSES IN SICILY

Lastly, the Lestrigoni, the giant cannibals of Book X, lived near Lentini, while the Lotus Eaters (Book IX) lived between Agrigento and Camarina.

TYRANNICAL PATRONS

According to Aristotle, comedy in its classical form was invented by the Megareans of Greece and Sicily. Undoubtedly both **Epicharmus** and **Phormis**, the two earliest identifiable authors of comedies engaged at the court of Gelon were Sicilian. Interestingly, the tyrants were noted for being generous patrons, summoning to their courts the best poets of the time.

Among the illustrious guests was the poet **Simonides**, famous as a writer of epigrams and funeral laments. He dedicated many verses to Sicily, telling how Hephaestus and Demeter disputed possession of the island because of its fire and abundant wheat harvests. The simultaneous presence of poets of a certain renown also generated bitter rivalries: for years, **Bacchylides** and **Pindar** contested Hieron's favours as they exalted his success at the games. At the height of his achievement, the great tragedian **Aeschylus** was based at the court of Hieron.

To celebrate the conquest and re-naming of the city of Aetna (later Catania), he arranged performances of *The Women of Etna* (now lost) and *The Persians*. Pindar marked the occasion by composing his Pythian Odes. **Theocritus** (c. 300–260 BC), meanwhile, was a native of Syracuse; he is attributed with inventing pastoral poetry.

PHILOSOPHY

Two of the most interesting pre-Socratic thinkers were born in Sicily: **Empedocles** came from Agrigento and **Gorgias** from Leontinoi. Empedocles (c. 500–c. 430 BC) is a complex figure: a mystic, miracle worker, doctor and student of natural philosophy. He also founded a school of medicine that regarded the heart as the seat of life, an idea taken up by Aristotle. He taught that all matter was composed of four elements (earth, water, air and fire).

These – regulated by the two universal forces harmony and discord (love and hate) – gave rise to the whole cosmos. According to legend, he jumped into one of the fiery craters of Mount Etna to persuade his fellow citizens that he had been summoned by the gods. Gorgias (483–375 BC) responded to a different cultural climate, one of sophism (false argument), that aimed to satisfy the requirements of the emerging democracy with particular emphasis on moral and political issues. He became an orator of considerable renown, especially in Athens, where he was acclaimed a "master of wisdom."

The first great philosopher of mathematical harmony was Pythagoras. His doctrines were widespread in Sicily, particularly in Agrigento and Catania. The **School of Pythagoras** was established at Croton in the 6C–5C BC. This group had much political clout and suggested a new aristocracy be drawn from businessmen and tradesmen.

Sicily was also the setting envisaged by **Plato** for his Utopian state, ruled by philosophers, as contemplated in the *Republic*.

The philosopher visited Syracuse in 388–387 BC; when the tyrant became suspicious of the Athenian, he incarcerated Plato as a slave on the island of Aegina. He later returned to Sicily after Dionysius II had succeeded his father; to begin with, Plato appears to have found Dionysius II the better disciple – that is, until Dion was sent into exile and Plato detained as a prisoner.

SCIENCE AND HISTORY

Archimedes (first half of the 3C BC) was the one person in the Greek world capable of consolidating the theoretical and practical aspects of scientific knowledge at that time. Besides his important discoveries in the fields of mathematics, geometry and naval engineering, his name is associated with the invention of war machines. His weapons of mass destruction convinced the Romans that they battled gods.

Diodorus Siculus, born at Agyrion in the 1C BC, was the author of a universal history of 40 volumes entitled *Biblioteca*. He traced Greek history from the mythical era to contemporary times; this still constitutes a valuable source for scholars.

PAINTING AND POTTERY

Greeks considered painting the most noble and eloquent form of artistic expression, described by the poet Simonides (5C BC) as "mute poetry". Unfortunately, examples are rare because of the pigments' fragility and vulnerability to weather conditions. Large easel paintings, extolled by original sources, can be partially reconstructed from vase painting renditions.

Styles – Vases with **black figures** on a red or pale yellow background date from the Archaic and early Classic phase. The artists scratched away the black paint with a steel-tipped instrument. The most common subjects were from mythology or everyday life; but sometimes geometric or abstract motifs appeared, especially on the early vases.

Red-figure vases appear in southern Italy towards the latter half of the 5C BC, earlier than in Greece, where this style became prevalent from 480 BC. In this case, the black paint forms a background, with the figures in brick red colour with touches of black and white. This inverted technique, allowing greater freedom of expression, was a revolutionary discovery; designs acquired softer lines and contours than those graffitied with a sharp steel point. The choice of subjects, however, does not change a great deal. Among the most beautiful examples of imported Attic vases are the magnificent two-handled craters from Agrigento (5C BC).

TIME LINE
PRE-HELLENISTIC SICILY

The Greek historian Dionysius of Halicarnassus chronicled how ancient expeditions embarked in the East, setting sail for the Italian peninsula and Sicily. Archaeology provides more concrete proof. Evidence of Mycenaean visits has been found at Thapsos and Panarea (pottery incised with Linear B script: the Mycenaean syllabic alphabet).

1270–650 BC – Late Bronze Age: the Greeks seem to have brought iron and a higher level of material civilisation. Athenian historian Thucydides recorded this colonisation and described the island's indigenous peoples: the **Siculi** and the **Sicani**. The former resided in eastern and central southern Sicily, inland from Syracuse. The origins of the western Siculi should, perhaps, be traced back to the Italian peninsula, given commonalities with the mainland's Apennine culture. The Sicani seem not to conform with Indo-European people, but rather to be of Iberian origin.

The **Elimi**, founders of Erice (Eryx) and Segesta, seem to belong to the ancient family of Mediterranean and pre-Indo-European peoples. Various evidence suggests contact with the East (like the cult of Aphrodite Ericina) and a rapid Hellenisation of this people (the Doric temple at Segesta).

Phoenicians from Carthage settled at Solunto, Panormus (modern Palermo) and Mozia (Motya) in the northwestern part of the island, where the foundations of Lilybaeum (modern Marsala) – an impregnable stronghold and the fulcrum of Carthaginian military power – were later laid.

Archaeological Museum, Syracuse/SCALA Syracuse/SCALA

Syracusan coins

Statue of a goddess restored as Demeter (Museo Pio-Clementino, Vatican)

The Greek Gods in Sicily

Acis: god of the river of the same name and lover of Galatea (🔊 *see Catania*).

Aeolus: son of Poseidon, god of the winds and lord of the Aeolian Islands.

Alpheus: god of the river of the same name in the Peloponnese. He fell in love with the water-nymph, Arethusa, and followed her to Sicily (🔊 *see Siracusa*).

Aphrodite (Venus): goddess of love and wife of Hephaestus, much worshipped in Erice.

Charybdis: a monster who inhabited the Sicilian shore of the Straits of Messina. Three times a day the creature swallowed huge amounts of water, creating dangerous whirlpools, including one which trapped Ulysses' ship.

Cocalus: Sicilian king who offered refuge to Dedalus; the latter was pursued by Minos after helping Theseus to escape from Minos' labyrinth.

Demeter (Ceres): goddess of the harvest who fought with Hephaestus for control of Sicily.

Eryx: son of Aphrodite and Butes (or Poseidon). He challenged Heracles and was killed by him.

Etna: a Sicilian nymph who intervened in the dispute between Demeter and Hephaestus over the possession of Sicily. One legend recounts that the Palici were born from her union with Hephaestus.

Galatea: a nymph who was loved by the monster Polyphemus while she herself was in love with Acis (🔊 *see Catania*).

Giants: son of Gaia (the Earth) and Uranus, enemies of the Olympic gods and particularly of Zeus and Athena.

Hades (Pluto): brother of Zeus; lord of the kingdom of the dead. He abducted Demeter's daughter, Proserpina, on the banks of Lake Pergusa.

Helios: god of the sun. He owned a herd of cattle in Sicily, some of which were eaten by Ulysses' companions, thus incurring the wrath of the god.

Hephaestus: god of fire and lord of the volcanoes, in which he worked with his helpers, the Cyclops.

Heracles: a hero during his earthly life and a god after his death. One of his 12 Labours, that of the cattle of Geryon, took place in Sicily.

Palici: twin sons of Zeus and the muse Thalia or, according to another tradition, of Hephaestus and Etna, born in the waters of Lake Naftia, near Palagonia.

Persephone (Proserpina): goddess of the Underworld and wife of Hades.

Typhon: a giant who fought with Zeus and Athena. He escaped by crossing the Sicilian sea, but was then crushed when Zeus hurled Sicily on top of him.

Remains of the walls at Megara Hyblaea

© DEA/G COZZI/age fotostock

SIKELÍA: SICILY UNDER THE GREEKS

775 BC Establishment of the trading colony of Pithecusa on Ischia; the first Hellenistic settlement near mainland Italy.

735 The first Hellenistic settlement, Naxos, is created in Sicily, securing trade routes through the Straits of Messina. The Corinthians found Syracuse (Siracusa) in 734.

730–700 The Chalcidians found Catana, Leontinoi and Zancle (now Messina); the Megarians found Megara Hyblaea.

688 Colonists from Rhodes and Crete found Gela, the same city that seized Akragas (Agrigento) in 580.

598 Foundation of Camarina.

491 Gelon becomes the tyrant of Gela. In 488, he wins the chariot race at Olympia – and thus great prestige.

480–479 The Greeks in Sicily face hostility from the Carthaginians and the Etruscans.

485 Gelon becomes Syracuse's tyrant.

480 Battle of Himera: the Syracusans defeat the Carthaginians.

474 Hieron, tyrant of Syracuse, wins a decisive naval victory at Cumae over the Etruscans. Catania, on the Ionian coast, is occupied by Dorian colonists and subjugated to the rule of Hieron's son.

465 The tyrant Thrasybulus is expelled and Syracuse ruled by a moderate democracy.

453 Rebellion of Ducetius: the Siculi towns form a confederation. The uprising ceases in 450.

414 Athenians besiege Syracuse. The Spartan Gylippus comes to the town's rescue.

413 The Athenian hold over Sicily is broken. During the war, Athens loses 50,000 men (including 12,000 ordinary citizens) and more than 200 triremes.

409 Carthaginians attack and destroy Selinunte and Himera.

406 The general Dionysius I seizes power in Syracuse. Over the ensuing years, he secures a vast dominion, including a large portion of southern Italy and the Adriatic coast (he conquers Croton and founds Ancona).

392 Peace between the Carthaginians and Dionysius I.

The Codex Astensis: Frederick II granting privileges to the town of Asti

Frederick II

The Life of Frederick II

On 27 January 1186, Costanza d'Altavilla, heiress to the throne of Sicily, married Henry VI of Swabia, son of Frederick I Barbarossa and heir to the Holy Roman Empire, with great pomp and ceremony in Milan. Aged 31, she had long passed the usual age for matrimony and was 11 years older than her husband. The couple were married for eight years before producing an heir. On 26 December 1194, Costanza went into labour at Jesi and decided to birth the infant under a canvas in the city's main square, possibly to dispel aspersions cast on her fertility at such an advanced age. In 1197, aged 32, Henry died of a fever caught while hunting on Mount Etna. His wife died the following year, but before doing so entrusted their son Frederick to Pope Innocent III, who had the child crowned king of Sicily in 1198. For political and dynastic reasons, Frederick had a difficult, lonely childhood in Palermo. Left to his own devices, he would frequent the poorer districts of the city, mixing with people of all religions and walks of life.

367	Death of Dionysius I.
347	Dionysius II, exiled previously by Dion – a family relative and fellow adherent of Plato – returns to Syracuse.
344	The mother city of Corinth sends 700

soldiers to Syracuse led by Timoleon, who defeats the Carthaginians at the battle of River Crimisus (341).

316 Agathocles, a man of modest origins, heads a revolt against the barons and seizes power in Syracuse.

Archivio Municipale di Asti/SCALA

These cosmopolitan experiences influenced the future emperor's broad view of life and grand political projects. Back in the court, Frederick's education was worthy of his lineage: he possessed an enquiring mind, loved nature and culture, studied Latin and the natural sciences and deepened his knowledge of the Arab classics and Islamic culture.

In 1215, Pope Innocent III excommunicated Otto IV, Emperor of the Holy Roman Empire, crowning Frederick II emperor in his place.

Frederick travelled to Germany and only returned to Sicily in 1220. In 1227, he was excommunicated by Pope Honorius III and in 1229, having completed the "Crusade of the Excommunicants", declared himself king of Jerusalem. The following year the Pope withdrew the excommunication.

After years of conflict with the Pope and two excommunications, Frederick died in the Castello di Fiorentino on 13 December 1250. He was buried in Palermo Cathedral.

A Prodigious Talent

Frederick II was a man of many talents. A skilful statesman, commander and legislator, he loved the arts and sciences and was the author of a famous treatise on falconry entitled *De arte venandi cum avibus*. His character combined the medieval holiness of his imperial role and a remarkably modern eclecticism. Frederick's court was a meeting place for scholars from all fields, including writers, mathematicians, astronomers, doctors and musicians. He was responsible for the foundation of the University of Naples, the development of the Salerno Medical School (where a Chair of Anatomy was created) and the birth of the School of Sicilian Poetry.

Dante affirms Frederick's fame as a man of culture, describing the emperor as "a great logician and scholar". Credited as a lover of wisdom and patron of the arts, Frederick II showed considerable open-mindedness in his political dealings. His greatest wish was to be regarded as the "emperor of recent times", summoned with a mission to restore the Golden Age of justice on earth. This legendary vision conflicts with the accusations made by the papal curia, which tended to regard him as the Antichrist mentioned in the Bible.

The Four Wives of Frederick II

1209: Constance of Aragon, mother of Henry VII, who rebelled against his father. She died in 1222.

1225: Isabella of Brienne, heiress to the throne of Jerusalem. She bore Frederick two children: Conrad IV and Margherita. Isabella died in 1228.

1235: Elizabeth of England, sister of Henry III of England and mother of Henry. She died in 1241.

1250: Bianca Lancia. Just before his death, Frederick II married the woman with whom he had enjoyed a relationship for many years. She was the mother of his favourite son, Manfred; also of Costanza and possibly, Violante.

310	The Carthaginians defeat Agathocles at Ecnomus. Soon after, he lands in Africa at the head of 14,000 men bent on wreaking vengeance on Carthage.	**289**	Death of Agathocles. In the same year, the Mamertini, mercenaries of Campanian origin, seize Messina.
		280	Pyrrhus, king of Epirus in Greece, tries in vain to unite Sicily between 278 and 275.

269   Hieron II, formerly one of Pyrrhus' officers, declares himself *basileus* (king) of Syracuse after a victory over the Mamertini.

264–241   First Punic War.

SICILY UNDER THE ROMANS

Ruled by a praetor and two quaestors, Sicily was of prime importance to Rome (not least for the large tributes it paid). The island continued to be of economic importance despite two devastating slave rebellions and Syracuse's disastrous revolt (and subsequent sacking).

Sicily possessed many large estates, which, in turn, provided the Roman aristocracy with elegant residences. In many cases, these villas became centres of literary patronage and recreation for the ennobled Romans.

227 BC   Sicily is made a province.

218–201   Second Punic War. In 211, after a long siege, Consul Marcellus sacks Syracuse for rebelling against Rome.

149–146   Third Punic War and final destruction of Carthage.

138–131   First slave revolt in Sicily led by the Syrian slave, Eunus.

104–99   Second slave revolt led by the slave Trifon.

70   Several towns accuse Verres, Sicily's praetor, of embezzlement. The great orator Cicero leads their legal defence.

48   Battle of Pharsalus: Caesar's troops defeat Pompey's.

44   Pompey's son, Sextus Pompeius, controls Sardinia, Corsica and Sicily with his fleets. In 36 BC, he is defeated by Vipsanius Agrippa, one of Octavian's admirals.

31   Battle of Actium: Octavian (later Augustus) becomes sole ruler of Rome.

2C AD   Spread of Christianity on the island.

468   Gaiseric, King of the Vandals in Africa, conquers the island.

ARABIC SICILY

Sicily benefited from almost two centuries of Muslim domination. A magnificent and highly original Arab-Norman style of architecture evolved, along with a unique literary tradition and a predilection for scholarship (here Plato's *Dialogues* were first translated in the 11C). This autonomous culture has proved vital to all European history.

AD 491   Theodoric's Ostrogoths assume control of the island: its administration is re-organised according to Imperial standards. The Roman Church extends its land holding.

535   The Eastern Roman Empire annexes Sicily at the start of the Gothic-Byzantine war.

652   First Arab incursions.

663   For political reasons, the Byzantine basileus Constans II takes up residence in Sicily.

725   Iconoclastic crisis: Sicily remains faithful to the cult of images.

827   The Arabs land at Mazara. Invaders (mostly Berbers and Persians) conquer Palermo and make it their capital.

842-59   Messina, Modica, Ragusa and Enna fall. Only the northeast resists effectively, with Byzantine assistance.

878   Syracuse, the ancient capital, is stormed and destroyed.

902   Fall of Taormina, the last Byzantine stronghold in Sicily.

948–1040   Sicily is ruled by the Emirs of the Kalbite dynasty.

The arrival of the Arabs split the political and economic status quo. The indigenous people and invaders collaborated profitably in the west. However, the area around Syracuse never fully accepted Arab dominion, even if their arrival sealed the demise of the decadent ancient metropolis and of eastern Sicily, where the Greek language and culture still prevailed. The northeast, which maintained its Christian solidarity, offered fierce resistance. Palermo came to symbolise Arab-Sicilian civilisation. It was densely populated (estimated at 300,000 inhabitants) and wealthy, with bands of sprawling suburbs and small farms. Some 300 mosques and as many *madrasa* (Koranic schools) were instituted. The Emir was advised by an assembly *(giama'a),* drawn from the local aristocracy. Land was divided into small plots, thus benefiting the new rulers; intensive and more sophisticated farming methods were imposed (including irrigation channels known as *qanat*) and new cash crops introduced, such as cotton, flax, sugar cane, rice, citrus fruits, henna, nuts and dates. Culture also flourished, encouraged by links with Islam from around the Mediterranean (Andalucia in the case of literature; the Maghreb and Egypt in the case of science).

The perfect expression of this cross-fertilisation is the splendid Arabic literature from the court at Palermo. In his melancholy farewell to Sicily, Ibn Hamdis wrote: *"a land to which the dove lent its collar, clothed by the peacock from its many-coloured mantle of feathers".*

1061	The Normans land in Sicily. During the next 30 years, Christianity struggles to reaffirm itself across the island and drive out Islamic culture.

SICILY UNDER THE NORMANS

By 911, the "men of the north", having set out from their homes in Scandinavia, had settled in what is now Normandy. Some of these fierce warriors fought as mercenaries in Italy's south, where disputes raged among Roman popes, Lombard dukes of Benevento and Salerno, Arabs in Sicily and Byzantines in Apulia and Calabria.

Through the Treaty of Melfi (1059), the Normans not only became vassals of the Pope, they also secured feudal rights over southern Italy. One, a certain Robert Guiscard ("the Sly"), acquired the title of Duke of Apulia and promptly subdued Bari and Salerno.

His brother **Count Roger** (1031–1101) set about conquering Sicily, marching into Palermo in 1072. The last Arab stronghold, Noto, did not capitulate until 1091, when Roger won the coveted title of Papal Legate, making him the Holy See's representative on the island.

1130	Roger II (1095–1154) succeeds his father Roger I in 1101; the title of King of Sicily and Duke of Campania is conferred on him by the Antipope Anacletus II; nine years later this position is sanctioned by Pope Innocent II.

Roger II extended his kingdom as far as Tronto, adding Capua, Amalfi and Naples; he maintained his capital at Palermo. The feudal system spread through Sicily, though the government's administration remained complex, reflecting its Byzantine origins.

In ecclesiastical circles, special prerogatives were given to the Norman sovereigns nominated as Papal Legates by Pope Urban II: their prime objective was to eradicate Islam and to resist corruption from the (Greco-Byzantine) Eastern Church. Meanwhile, the Arab influence persisted at Roger II's court at Palermo: there, the geographer **al-Idrisi** constructed a large silver planisphere and wrote his geographical treatise, entitled *Kitab-Rugiar,* or *The Book of Roger.*

1147	Incursions by the Norman fleet in the Byzantine Empire: Corfu, Thessalonika and Thebes are sacked; numerous craftsmen skilled in working with silk are deported to Sicily.
1154	**William I** (1120–66) succeeds his father Roger II. While engaged in conflict with Frederick Barbarossa, he must also confront a rebellion from his barons, which he succeeds in quelling in 1156.

Sclàfani Bagni, Madonie mountains

© Sandro Bedessi / Fototeca ENIT

1166 **William II** (1153–89), William I's son, is crowned king. By supporting the Pope and the northern towns in their struggle against Barbarossa, he is also able to attack the declining Byzantine Empire. He is hailed a champion of the Third Crusade against Saladin: in fact, Norman troops were committed to rescuing Tripoli.

He designates his aunt Costanza as heir; she is betrothed to Henry, eldest son of Barbarossa; thus the Swabian dynasty can claim legitimate rights to the throne of Sicily.

SWABIANS AND ANGEVINS

1186 The marriage of the future Emperor Henry VI (Barbarossa's son) to Costanza d'Altavilla is celebrated.

> "This is the light of the great Constance, who, from the second gale of Swabia, produced the third, which was also the last."
>
> – Dante Alighieri,
> *The Divine Comedy, Paradise III*
> *(Oxford University Press)*

1190–97 Henry VI of Swabia (1165–97) is made Emperor and King of Sicily. 1198 – Innocent III is elected Pope. Costanza has her young son Frederick crowned king of Sicily.

1209 Frederick marries Costanza of Aragon.

1214 Innocent III excommunicates Emperor Otto of Brunswick and nominates Frederick II in his place. Frederick arrives in Germany; he does not return to Sicily until 1220.

1228 Exhorted by Pope Gregory IX, Frederick leaves for the Holy Land, where he reaches a peaceful agreement with the Sultan. In 1229, he is crowned king of Jerusalem.

1231 Frederick II issues the *Constitutions of Melfi,* a code of law designed for a centralised state that is operational outside the jurisdiction of the feudal lords.

1250 Death of Frederick II.

1250–54 Conradin IV (1228–54) succeeds his father Frederick II and is crowned Emperor, despite the rivalry with **Manfred** (1232–66), Frederick's son and heir, who was "fair and well-made and of gentle aspect" *(The Divine Comedy)*.

1265 Pope Clement IV summons the Christian princes to rally against Manfred; the French, led by Charles of Anjou, rise.

1266 Battle of Benevento during which Manfred is defeated and killed.

1268 Defeat of the Ghibellines (supporters of the Empire) at Tagliacozzo; Conradin, the 15-year-old Swabian heir, is beheaded in Naples. The **Guelphs**

Detail of The Sicilian Vespers, Domenico Morelli, 1843–1901, oil on canvas

© Museo di Capodimonte, Naples / SCALA

of Anjou secure rule of southern Italy.

SICILIAN VESPERS AND THE ARAGONESE (1282–1416)

1282 A revolt against the ruling Angevins by the **Sicilian Vespers** breaks out in Palermo. Corleone and Messina, seat of the Angevin viceroy at that time, also rise to join the cause. Nobles appeal to **Peter III of Aragon** (1239–85) for help.

1285 Charles dies in 1285, before he is able to return to Sicily.

1296 **Frederick of Aragon** concedes the right for an annual assembly of the barons.

1302 Peace of Caltabellotta ends the war: Frederick of Aragon, Peter's son, is declared King of Trinacria (avoiding the name "Sicily") provided that, on his death, the kingdom returns to Robert of Anjou. The pact was broken and the Norman kingdom split.

1425–42 **Alfonso V of Aragon** (1396–1458) intervenes against the Angevins in Naples. The island and the mainland are once again united under one king.

15C TO THE 20C

1492 Sicily expels Jews from Salemi and Palermo.

1497 The *Tribunale di Sant'Uffizio*, the Spanish Inquisition, is introduced to Sicily.

1556 Parliament – which only has advisory power – is nonetheless revered. Three *Brazos* or Chambers host the clergy, the 72 barons, military leaders and town representatives.

1570 A great Christian fleet rallies at Messina and recruits crews from Calabria and Sicily. In 1571, it famously triumphs over the Turks at Lepanto.

1624 Plague ravages Palermo. The miraculous discovery of Santa Rosalia's bones helps, according to popular belief, to assuage the epidemic. Henceforth, the saint is acclaimed a patron of the city.

1647 Revolt in Palermo, coinciding with the insurrection in Naples. The anti-Spanish uprising is spearheaded by two commoners, Nino de la Pelosa and Giuseppe d'Alessi, but the rebellion is quickly suppressed. In 1674, Messina also rises up against the Spanish, with help from the king of France. The town is brutally recaptured in 1678.

1693 A terrible earthquake shakes southeastern Sicily.

1713 The Treaty of Utrecht assigns Sicily to Savoy; **Victor Amadeus**, the new king, visits.

1718–20 Spain recaptures Sardinia and threatens Naples and Palermo. The British sink the Spanish fleet at Capo Passero. The Habsburg emperor trades Sardinia to Savoy and assumes control of Sicily.

1733 Scottish writer Patrick Brydone publishes his *Tour through Sicily and Malta*.

1735 The coronation of **Charles Bourbon** (1716–88) in Palermo.

1781–86 Caracciolo is viceroy of the island: a number of reforms are promised with the aim of increasing his powerbase. The Inquisition is abolished.

1794 Leblanc's discovery of how to isolate sodium carbonate (soda or soda ash) revolutionises several industrial processes; the price of sulphur becomes competitive. From 1790, Sicilian citrus fruits are exported on a large scale across Europe. In 1814, English-owned distilleries in Marsala begin producing a sherry-like wine.

1806 British troops are stationed in Sicily to provide

The Thousand's landing at Marsala in 1860

© Museo del Risorgimento, Roma / SCALA

House in Messina severely damaged by the earthquake of 28 December 1908

© UPPA / Photoshot

protection from the armies of Napoleon Bonaparte. These contribute to the economic prosperity.

1812 With help from Britain's representative in Sicily, Lord Bentinck, reforms are implemented for a more liberal constitution that abolishes feudal rights.

1816 Creation of the Kingdom of Two Sicilies: the kingdoms of Naples and Palermo are unified and the Sicilian flag is abolished.

1840 The issue of water and its illegally controlled distribution comes to a head. Smuggling also get out of hand.

1847 An investigation reveals that half of the island's woodland has been destroyed over the past 100 years, resulting in the climate becoming drier. Francesco Ferrara's *Letter from Malta* proposes Sicilian autonomy within a federation of Italian states.

1848–49 Insurrections in Palermo and across Sicily.

1860 In April, there is rioting in Palermo, provoked by agents from the north. The Thousand are sent to Sicily, headed by Garibaldi (ⓒ *see Trapani*). On 21 October, a plebiscite sanctions the island's union with the Kingdom of Italy.

1866 Revolt in Palermo as a result of the acute economic situation (15,000 unemployed). In the end, the Italian fleet bombards the city, while 4,000 soldiers quash the riots.

1886 The Jacini report on the state of Italian agriculture reveals the island is heading towards a food shortage, aggravated by a rise in population. Between 1880 and 1914, about 1.5 million Sicilians leave, with the majority heading for the United States.

1893 The Notarbartolo scandal surrounding the director of the Banca d'Italia breaks out; he is assassinated after denouncing political and financial malpractice.

1894 A poor harvest, coupled with inequalities in the distribution of ecclesiastical land, causes disorder and insurrection rallied by the supporters of the *Fasci di Lavoratori*. Sicilian Francesco Crispi forms a new

Linguistic Traces of the Arabs in Sicily

Traces of the Arab presence in Sicily can be found in the language of the island, especially in place names. Names of towns and villages that have evolved from Arabic include Calascibetta, Calatafimi, Caltabellotta, Caltagirone, Caltanissetta and Caltavuturo, all of which derive from the word *kalat,* meaning castle; Marsala from *marsa* (port); Mongibello, Gibellina and Gibilmanna from *gebel* (mountain); Modica from *mudiqah* (narrowing in the road); Racalmuto and Regalbuto from *rahal* (hamlet); and Sciacca from shaqqah (fissure, referring to the caves at Monte Kronio). The most common Italian words to have derived from Arabic are *albicocca* (apricot), *alcohol, algebra* (from *al giabr,* meaning transport), *arancia* (orange), *bizzeffe* (galore, from *bizzef,* meaning many), *calibro* (gauge, from *qalib,* the measurement used for shoes), *carciofo* (artichoke), *cifra* (figure) and *zero* (both from *sifr,* meaning empty), *cotone* (cotton), *dogana* (customs), *limone* (lemon), *magazzino* (warehouse), *melanzana* (aubergine), *ragazzo* (boy, from *raqqas,* meaning messenger), *taccuino* (notebook, from *taquim,* meaning proper order), *tazza* (cup), *tariffa* (tariff), *zafferano* (saffron), *zecca* (mint, from *sikka,* meaning coin) and *zucchero* (sugar).

government and imposes martial law.

1908 An earthquake in Messina causes over 60,000 fatalities.

1911 Population census: 58% of Sicilians are illiterate.

1925 Fascist government extends the "battle of wheat" to Sicily. **Mori**, nicknamed the "Iron Chief of Police" because of his anti-Mafia efforts, becomes Palermo's Chief of Police.

SICILY IN THE 20C

1940 The government announces a series of agricultural reforms, impeded by outbreak of war.

1943 American and British troops – **Operation Husky** under Eisenhower's command – seize Licata and Augusta. On 22 July, Palermo falls, then Messina. On 3 September, at Cassibile, near Siracusa, emissaries of the Badoglio government sign the armistice.

1947 In elections, separatists receive less than 10 per cent of the vote and seek to take up arms. **Salvatore Giuliano**, in hiding since 1943, is nominated colonel of EVIS (the Voluntary Army for Sicilian Independence). On 1 May 1947, his men fire on a group of farmers demonstrating at Portella delle Ginestre, killing 12. Giuliano is found dead on 5 July 1950, at Castelvetrano. The separatists dissolve with the 1951 election.

1950 Agricultural reforms are implemented: 115 000ha/ 284 000 acres are now reallocated to over 18,000 farmers.

1951–75 A million Sicilians emigrate to northern Italy and Europe.

1953 Crude oil is discovered at Ragusa and Gela; in 1966, eight million barrels are extracted.

1958 A terrorist bomb shatters the headquarters of the Palermo daily newspaper, *L'Ora,* following its allusion to the power of the Mafia.

1968 A disastrous earthquake affects the Belice Valley.

1973–76 The Parliamentary Anti-Mafia Commission begins.

27 June 1980 An Italvia DC9, flying from Bologna to Palermo, crashes off the coast of Ustica, killing 81.

3 September 1982
The Palermo Chief of Police, General Carlo Alberto Dalla Chiesa, his wife and a police escort are killed in a terrorist attack.

1986 During the American–Libyan crisis, the Libyans launch missiles at Lampedusa.

1987 End of the major court case held in Palermo against the Mafia, with 19 sentenced to life imprisonment.

1992 12 March: the politician Salvo Lima is murdered in Palermo. 23 May: Giovanni Falcone, Director of Penal Affairs at the Ministry of Justice, is killed by an explosive device placed at a motorway crossing near Capaci. 19 July: in Via D'Amelio in Palermo a car bomb kills Judge Paolo Borsellino and four police. In September, Mafia boss Giovanni Madonìa is arrested.

1993 Mafia boss Salvatore Riina, head of the Corleonesi, is arrested in Palermo.

1996 The dome and a large section of the nave of the cathedral of Noto collapse.

1997 The Teatro Massimo in Palermo reopens after 20+ years.

Eruption of the Stromboli

© Hervé Hughes / hemis.fr

THE NEW MILLENNIUM

2001–2002 Etna continues to make its presence felt, with eruptions destroying the cable car and part of the base station at Rifugio Sapienza.

2002 March: 1,000 migrants, mainly Kurds, land in Sicily – the largest group yet.

2003 January: Stromboli evacuates, as the threat of eruption increases. March: police arrest crime boss Salvatore Rinella in Palermo.

2004 June: Sicily rehabilitates property seized in Mafia raids as tourist accommodation.

2005 Immigration issues continue, as do anti-Mafia raids. Salvatore Cuffaro, head of Sicily's regional

---

The super-trials or "Maxiprocessi"

In 1982, Tommaso Buscetta, a disillusioned Mafioso, broke the Mafia's sacred code of silence (the *omerta*) and turned police informant, sparking the so-called super-trials. The biggest of these trials, in 1986, lasted 18 months and dealt a devastating blow to organised crime syndicates. Buscetta's information on the inner workings and hierarchies of the Cosa Nostra and his testimony helped judges Giovanni Falcone and Paolo Borsellino convict 357 Mafiosi. Nineteen were given life sentences, the sentences of the other 338 totalled 2,065 years. Both judges were later assassinated by Mafia car bombs in the early 1990s.

Town of Corleone

© DEA A VERGANI / age fotostock

The Changing Face of the Mafia

The roots of the organised crime structure synonymous with Italy's deep south rest in its rural landscapes. Once considered feudal folk heroes standing against Sicily's tyrannical overlords, the Mafia tide took a less "righteous" turn in the early 20C with the emergence of organised crime nurtured through traditions and values inextricable from Sicilian society. These principles were mafia with a small "m" – a perverted shorthand for family, honour, solidarity, silence.

The biggest Sicilian Mafia boss at this time was Don Vito Cascio Ferro, who had links with the Black Hand, a growing immigrant Mafiosi organisation in America. Mussolini's anti-Mafia campaigns in WWII responded to the power that organised crime was beginning to exhibit. Il Duce wanted to clear a path for unchallenged Facist leadership, and employed Cesare Mori as prefect of Palermo to put some 11,000 Mafiosi in prison (often on little or no evidence) – but the triumph was short-lived.

Following the end of the war, they were set free by an Anglo-American administration. The flood of Mafiosi back onto the scene, coupled with the general municipal upheaval of Italy's reconstruction, led to an explosion of crime in the south. Key Mafia figures such as Don Calogero Vizzini and Lucky Luciano were part of a vanguard of Mafiosi who now took organised crime away from its rural roots and into the cities – real estate, protection money (**known as** *pizzo*)

government, stands trial for leaking police secrets to organised crime.

2006 Cuffaro re-elected as his trial continues. Scientists identify a giant underwater volcano, off Sicily's southern coast. October: plans scrapped to build the world's longest single-span suspension bridge across the Messina Straits.

2008 Centre-right candidate Raffaele Lombardo is elected mayor by a landslide after Cuffaro

The Sicilian Statute

On 15 May 1946, a royal decree promulgated a law on Sicilian autonomy. Then, on 26 February 1948, the Constituent Assembly turned the Statute of Sicily into law in accordance with provisions under Article 116 of the Italian Constitution listing the specifications and conditions for autonomous rule as granted to five Italian regions. The regional statute provides for a regional council (known as the Parliament) composed of 90 members. Parliament elects a regional committee *(Giunta Regionale)* and a president from among its members by a majority consensus. The President has the right to sit in with the Council of Ministers in Rome during debates on issues affecting Sicily. Parliament can approve legislation for the island – its powers, sanctioned by Article 117 of the Italian Constitution, being fairly extensive. Special delegations from the Council of State and the State Audit Court sit permanently in Palermo so as to ensure a certain degree of administrative decentralisation.

and construction – and even transatlantically, as abilities to control the growing heroin trade began to determine power within the Mafia structure. Government investigations in the 1960s prompted a new wave of activity, the targeting of state officials – and indeed anyone threatening the Cosa Nostra in any way – in a sustained campaign of intimidation. In 1982, police General Dalla Chiesa began to investigate Sicily's construction industry, his intense scrutiny threatening to expose the full extent of corruption in high-ranking political circles – the so-called "Third Level". He was gunned down three months later in Palermo. The onset of the super-trials or *Maxiprocessi,* in the 1980s used information from former Mafia member Tommaso Buscetta to convict over 350 Mafiosi. Layers of social infiltration by the Cosa Nostra continued to peel away as further testimonies from *pentiti,* Mafiosi turned police informants, began implicating the highest levels of government. Those called into question included former prime minister Guilio Andreotti, who was acquitted in 1999. Silvio Berlusconi also faced allegations of Mafia money laundering in 1998, but was also acquitted. Even though high-profile arrests continue to be made, Giovanni Brusca of the Corleone famly (1996) and most recently, former Sicilian President Salvatore Cuffaro in 2008 (see Government), violence and corruption continue. *Pizzo* continues to be paid by a high proportion of small businesses in Sicily.

The bloodbath of the 80s and 90s has declined for now, though, thanks in part to popular culture and media such as television destroying the stranglehold of silence around the Mafia and, some might say, a softening of the fierce, fearless approach that previous anti-Mafia crusaders took – and paid the price for.

resigns over allegations of aiding the Mafia.

2012 Lombardo resigns over allegations of Mafia collaboration. Centre-left candidate Rosario Crocetta wins the snap election with 30.5 per cent of the vote.

2013 Almost 40,000 illegal migrants land in Sicily by boat from Africa.

2014 19 March: 2 000 migrants are rescued off the coast of Sicily within 48 hours.

Art and Architecture

ANCIENT GREEK

The **Palici** rank among Sicily's own ancient divinities, whom the Greeks later appropriated by adopting them as the twin sons of Zeus and the muse, Thalia. The cult's centre was Naftia, a small lake with bubbling sulphurous waters in the Plain of Catania, near Palagonia. The myth relates how Thalia, fearing the wrath of Hera, hid underground. The birth of the divine twins caused the waters of the lake to bubble and steam. Beside the sanctuary dedicated to the Palici, the Greeks swore solemn oaths and enacted a ritual in the lake.

If tablets bearing written agreements sank, this was interpreted as a sign of perjury, which the Palici punished with blinding. According to another tradition, the Palici were the children of Hephaestus, god of fire, and Etna, the nymph who intervened in the struggle between the god and Demeter for control of Sicily.

In general, the Siceliots were hugely sensitive to the indigenous cults, especially the worship of the dead and of the chthonic gods of the Underworld.

MYSTERIES

Mystery rites were also particularly widespread in Sicily. These religious practices provided answers to the inexplicable and soothed concerns about facing death. The Mysteries promised to purify celebrants through an initiation and thus ensure happiness in the afterlife. One of the most famous cults, the Eleusinian Mysteries, revolved around Demeter and Persephone.

ARCHITECTURE: CIVIL AND MILITARY

The oldest ruins date to the end of the 6C BC. Presumably, military emplacements existed here from the 8C, when the various cities rivalled one another before the rise of tyrants.

Fortresses and Fortifications – Under the tyrants, buildings were fortified with local materials: in the east, lava was common, as at **Naxos** and **Lipari**. In the absence of suitable stone, walls were sun-dried brick with a base of broken stones, or pebbles and clay.

Only a few forts have survived. These citadels ensured the defence of a city, its roads and other means of access.

Urban planning – Almost on arrival, the Greek settlers organised the area into a rational system. They designated some places of worship, other parts for public buildings and as residential quarters. Generally Sicilian cities conformed to the urban planning theories outlined by **Hippodamus of Miletus,** the 5C BC Greek philosopher and surveyor. He advocated a city on a rectangular street plan, centred around two axes: the *cardo* (or *stenopos,* in Greek) that ran from north to south and the *decumanus maximus* (*plateia* in Greek) bisecting it from east

The Siceliot House

The Archaic houses were fairly simplistic affairs: rectangular sun-dried brick buildings with bases of dry pebbles stood inside a walled plot. Flat tiles covered the sloping gable roof. In the courtyard tools were stored and great terra-cotta jars for provisions; it also served as a communal area where the family gathered, ate and received visitors. The terrace was used for drying fruit, as a place to sit and talk, pray and sleep. Among the foundations a talisman, sometimes a bone or a votive object, was hidden to ensure the house remained sturdy and solid. Often it was sprinkled with the blood of a young animal, as were the threshold, the architrave and the door-jambs. In time, the houses became more sophisticated: a raised floor was added, complete with a stairway supported by a portico. The largest of the rooms – facing onto the portico and connected to the kitchen – hosted gatherings, for it was here that the men met for their *symposia*.

Metope of Temple C at Selinunte showing Heracles dragging the thieving Cercopes, National Archaeological Museum, Palermo

© 1990 Photo Scala, Florence / National Archaeological Museum, Palermo

to west. Smaller streets ran parallel to both. A precise set of buildings and zones was then constructed, such as the *agora*, the main square and the centre of public life; the *pritaneo*, which stood beside the *agora* and was the setting for a range of civic activities; the *ekklesiasterion*, a secular public building reserved for the people's assembly *(ekklesia)*, the most famous example of which can be seen at Agrigento; and the *bouleutérion*, where the citizen's council *(boulé)* met. The temples, sometimes outside the city limits, were often surrounded by other sacred buildings, which could include porticoes, votive monuments, gymnasia and theatres.

Walls usually fortified the urban area; beyond lay the agricultural land, subdivided into family plots, and a burial ground.

All the Greek cities and, sometimes even the villages, were supplied with reservoirs for water and aqueducts, the most famous being that built by the architect Phaeax at Akragas (Agrigento), and the extremely complex one at Syracuse.

ARCHITECTURE: SACRED AND RELIGIOUS

There are two forms of sacred building: the **temple** and the **theatre**. Usually located outside the city, they were designed to be visible from a distance.

Temples – From the 8C BC, Greek colonists brought cults and gods to Sicily, transforming the island into what is now regarded as one of the most extraordinary open-air museums of "severe style" Doric temples. The heart of the building comprised the **naos** *(cella)*, an oblong chamber housing a statue of the god. Temples normally faced east so that the statue could be illuminated by the rising sun, the source of all life. Before the *naos* was the **pronaos** (a kind of antechamber), while behind stood the **opisthodomos**, which served as a treasury. A **peristyle**, or **colonnade**, surrounded the building.

The temple was founded on a stepped base; onto the last step (**stylobate**) were erected the **columns**, which rose to support the **architrave**. A sloping roof covered the building.

First conceived in the Peloponnese, the **Doric style** spread to mainland Greece and subsequently to its colonies, including Sicily.

The Doric order, which combines majesty with sobriety, comprises a baseless column shaft indented with 20 vertical grooves or flutes (as from the 5C) that sits directly on the stylobate. The entablature consists of a plain architrave, the upper section of which comprises a frieze articulated by **metopes** (generally panels sculpted with shallow relief) and

The discovery of the **bronze ram** at Castello Maniace (on display at the Palermo Archaeological Museum) betrays the major impact of Greek aesthetics, notably their canons of beauty, on a city such as Syracuse.

of the façades were slightly inclined inwards, thereby countering the natural tendency to lean outwards. Finally, they cut a slight bulge into columns so they wouldn't appear to taper absurdly (particularly in large buildings, such as the Temple of Concord at Agrigento and the temples at Selinunte and Segesta). When compared to the architecture of mainland Greece, the temples of Magna Graecia and Sicily are more monumental, pay more attention to spatial effect and have abundant decoration. Sculptures crown the prominent features, in some cases those elements with no structural function – on the **tympanum** of a pediment, for example, or above the **metopes** of the architrave and on the edges of roofs.

triglyphs (rectangular projections ornamented with two deep vertical grooves in the centre flanked by a narrower one at each edge).
In the 6C BC almost all the temples built in Sicily were peripteral (that is, surrounded by a line of columns) and hexastyle (six-columned front elevation) although some examples have more than six front columns, such as Temple G at Selinunte. As a result of its simplicity of structure and perfect harmony of proportion, the temple was long considered to be the architectural prototype of ideal beauty. Building designers corrected for the human eye's distortion: the central section of the architrave (which appeared to sag slightly) was fractionally raised to restore an impression of perfect balance. The outer columns

Theatres – Beside most of the Greek sanctuaries, there was a theatre where Dionysian celebrations were held (in honour of Dionysus, the god of wine) with hymns called "dithyrambs," from which Greek tragedy later derived.
Built first of wood and then from the 4C BC in stone, a theatre would comprise a **cavea** *(koilon)* – a series of tiered ledges arranged in a semicircle, the first row being reserved for priests and dignitaries. Access was from the base by means of side entrances *(parodos)*; one passage *(diazoma)* led through to the central section, another up to the top rows of seating. The **orchestra** consisted of a circular area where the chorus and actors, wearing masks corresponding to their roles, took their places around the

Pithos: used for storing grain

Amphora: stored and transported oil and wine

Pelike: container for oil

Crater: container for wine

Hydria: container for water.

altar of Dionysus. Behind the orchestra stood the **proscenium**, a construction similar to a portico, which served as backdrop scenery, and the **skéné** which at once fulfilled three functions, namely stage scenery, backstage and a storage area. During the Hellenistic period, the *skéné* came to be reserved for actors. Given these complexes are generally set in the most splendid landscape, on the slope of a hill or a mountain, the natural scenery (particularly spectacular at Taormina and Segesta) provided the perfect background for productions. The *skéné*, almost always raised onto a platform, dominated the circular orchestra, where sacrifices were also sometimes made.

SCULPTURE

According to authors such as Diodorus Siculus (1C BC historian) and Pausanias (Greek traveller of the 2C AD), Sicily had established an artistic heritage even before it was colonised.

During colonisation, indigenous artistic taste and aesthetics were affected by Greek influences, leading to the gradual erosion and eventual extinction of a purely "Sicilian" style. In such a way, the island succumbed to the three chronological phases of Greek art: the Archaic, Classic and Hellenistic eras.

The scarcity of marble – and the particular Sicilian taste for pictorial and chiaroscuro effects – resulted predominantly in limestone and sandstone constructions. Clay was widely used in the pediments and acroteri of the temples, as well as for votive statues.

Ephebus

The white marble Ephebus of Motya, now on display in the Joseph Whitaker Museum near where it was found, clearly demonstrates the evolution of the Ionic style. The 1.81m/5.93ft youth is dressed in a long tunic of soft, figure-hugging linen, which flatters the athlete's muscular body. *See Agrigento and La Valle dei Templi, Trapani.*

Archaic (8C–5C BC) – This phase coincides with the production of the first large, rather wooden, hieratic figures which, in the 6C BC, gave rise to two distinctive forms: the *kouros* – the young male nude – and the *koré* – the young female equivalent, though modestly dressed in a tunic.

The statue of the **Ephebus of Agrigento** is one excellent example of Late-Archaic sculpture: it suggests the sculptor was striving to conform to a predetermined aesthetic type, although the basic sense of balance has yet to be perfected (the right leg appears extremely rigid, while the outstretched arms seem set too far away from the body).

As far as Archaic sculptural ornament used to adorn temples is concerned, two examples are to be found in Sicily: the polychrome winged **Gorgon** that once graced the pediment of the Athenaion in Syracuse and the six **metopes of**

Oinochoe: a jug for wine | Kantharos: a tall goblet | Kylix: drinking cup | Rhyton: a cup shaped like a horn or an animal's head | Lekythos: a vase for ointment

MICHELIN

Selinunte, now displayed in the archaeological museum at Palermo.

Classic (5C–3C BC) – The Ionic style of sculpture, which appeared in Sicily from the 6C BC onwards, is characterised by a better portrayal of individual features and a greater sense of realism and sensitivity, now free of the severe rigidity of the earlier phase, as shown in the famous **Ephebus of Motya**.

Hellenistic (3C–1C BC) – During this phase, sculpture becomes yet more expressive and oriental. Deities are portrayed with more realism, with human – rather than ideal – features and in a less formal state of dress (Aphrodite, goddess of beauty and love, is often shown in a pleated, flowing shift nonchalantly revealing her glorious nudity). Sculpture from this period is highly expressive in emotion, physical strength and movement.

The terra-cotta **theatrical masks** in the Archaeological Museum on Lipari (*over 250 examples*) portray a great range and subtlety of expression. Mainly they were inspired by Greek tragedy, which became widespread in Sicily from the 3C BC. ♿*see Isole Eolie: Limari.*

ARCHITECTURAL TERMS

Altarpiece (or ancona): a large painting or sculpture adorning an altar.

Ambulatory: extension of the aisles around the chancel for processions.

Antefix: a carved ornament at the end of the eaves of a roof used to hide the joints between tiles.

Antependium: a covering hung over the front of an altar.

Apse: a semicircular or polygonal end of a church behind the altar; the outer section is known as the "chevet".

Apsidiole: small chapel opening onto the ambulatory of a Romanesque or Gothic church.

Architrave: the lowermost horizontal division of a Classical entablature sitting directly on the column capital and supporting the frieze.

Archivolt: arch moulding over an arcade or upper section of a doorway.

Arcosolium: a tomb found in numerous catacombs, which was built in the wall and surmounted by a niche.

Atlas figure or telamon: a sculpted figure of a man used as a column (the female equivalent is called a **caryatid**). In Sicily, the most famous are the telamons of the Temple of Olympian Zeus at Agrigento.

Bay: any of a number of principal divisions or spatial units of a building (or part of a building like an aisle of a church) contained within two or four vertical supports (piers, columns, pilasters).

Bouleuterion: meeting place for the town council *(boulé)*.

Buttress: external support of a wall, which counterbalances the thrust of the vaults and arches.

Capital: the upper end of a column, pillar or pier crowning the shaft and taking the weight of the entablature or architrave. There are three Classical orders: Doric (♿*see illustration in the section on Greek Art)*; Ionic, with a scroll-like ornament – the Composite has the Ionic scrolls and acanthus leaf ornament; and the Corinthian, ringed with burgeoning acanthus leaves, especially popular in the 16C and 17C for Baroque buildings. The **abacus** sits between the capital and the architrave; the structure beneath the abacus is the **echinus**.

Cardo: one of the main axes of the town plan as recommended by the Classical surveyor Hippodamus of Miletus, normally orientated north–south; the Greek equivalent is the stenopos.

Cathedra: the high-backed throne of a bishop, in Gothic style.

Chiaramonte: an architectural style characterised by two- or three-light windows surmounted

Thermal baths

VILLA DEL CASALE
Plan of the thermal baths (3C-4C AD) and hypocaust

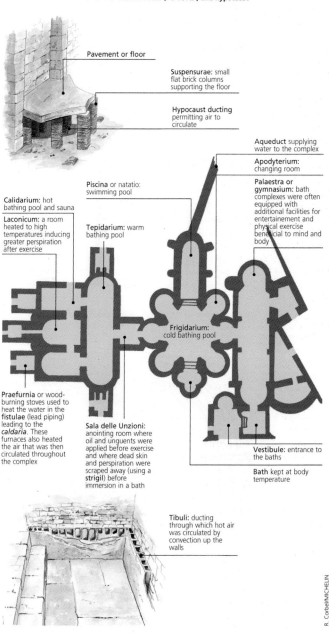

Pavement or floor

Suspensurae: small flat brick columns supporting the floor

Hypocaust ducting permitting air to circulate

Aqueduct supplying water to the complex

Apodyterium: changing room

Palaestra or gymnasium: bath complexes were often equipped with additional facilities for entertainment and physical exercise beneficial to mind and body

Piscina or natatio: swimming pool

Calidarium: hot bathing pool and sauna

Laconicum: a room heated to high temperatures inducing greater perspiration after exercise

Tepidarium: warm bathing pool

Frigidarium: cold bathing pool

Praefurnia or wood-burning stoves used to heat the water in the **fistulae** (lead piping) leading to the *caldaria*. These furnaces also heated the air that was then circulated throughout the complex

Sala delle Unzioni: anointing room where oil and unguents were applied before exercise and where dead skin and perspiration were scraped away (using a **strigil**) before immersion in a bath

Vestibule: entrance to the baths

Bath kept at body temperature

Tibuli: ducting through which hot air was circulated by convection up the walls

R. Corbel/MICHELIN

Religious architecture

RAGUSA IBLA – Duomo di San Giorgio (18C)

Latin cross floor plan with transepts

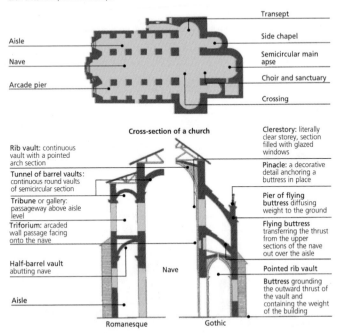

Transept

Aisle

Side chapel

Semicircular main apse

Nave

Choir and sanctuary

Arcade pier

Crossing

Cross-section of a church

Rib vault: continuous vault with a pointed arch section

Tunnel of barrel vaults: continuous round vaults of semicircular section

Tribune or gallery: passageway above aisle level

Triforium: arcaded wall passage facing onto the nave

Half-barrel vault abutting nave

Aisle

Nave

Romanesque

Gothic

Clerestory: literally clear storey, section filled with glazed windows

Pinacle: a decorative detail anchoring a buttress in place

Pier of flying buttress diffusing weight to the ground

Flying buttress transferring the thrust from the upper sections of the nave out over the aisle

Pointed rib vault

Buttress grounding the outward thrust of the vault and containing the weight of the building

NICOSIA – Cattedrale di San Nicolò: main doorway (14C)

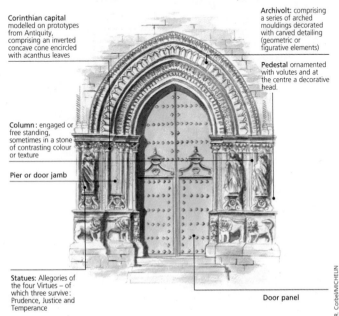

Corinthian capital modelled on prototypes from Antiquity, comprising an inverted concave cone encircled with acanthus leaves

Column: engaged or free standing, sometimes in a stone of contrasting colour or texture

Pier or door jamb

Statues: Allegories of the four Virtues – of which three survive: Prudence, Justice and Temperance

Archivolt: comprising a series of arched mouldings decorated with carved detailing (geometric or figurative elements)

Pedestal ornamented with volutes and at the centre a decorative head.

Door panel

R. Corbel/MICHELIN

PALERMO – Cappella Palatina: ceiling detail (12C)

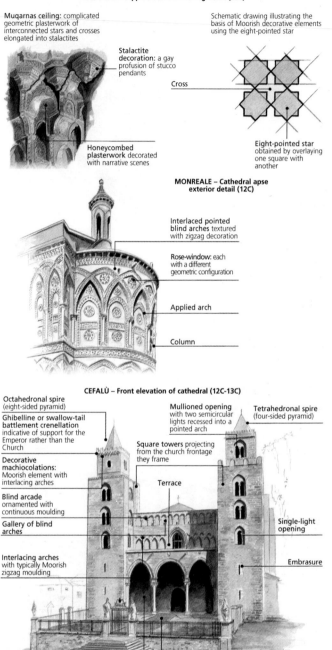

Muqarnas ceiling: complicated geometric plasterwork of interconnected stars and crosses elongated into stalactites

Stalactite decoration: a gay profusion of stucco pendants

Honeycombed plasterwork decorated with narrative scenes

Schematic drawing illustrating the basis of Moorish decorative elements using the eight-pointed star

Cross

Eight-pointed star obtained by overlaying one square with another

MONREALE – Cathedral apse exterior detail (12C)

Interlaced pointed blind arches textured with zigzag decoration

Rose-window: each with a different geometric configuration

Applied arch

Column

CEFALÙ – Front elevation of cathedral (12C-13C)

Octahedronal spire (eight-sided pyramid)

Ghibelline or swallow-tail battlement crenellation indicative of support for the Emperor rather than the Church

Decorative machiocolations: Moorish element with interlacing arches

Blind arcade ornamented with continuous moulding

Gallery of blind arches

Interlacing arches with typically Moorish zigzag moulding

Mullioned opening with two semicircular lights recessed into a pointed arch

Square towers projecting from the church frontage they frame

Terrace

Tetrahedronal spire (four-sided pyramid)

Single-light opening

Embrasure

Spacious square terrace before the church known as the *Turniale*

Portico

R. Corbel/MICHELIN

85

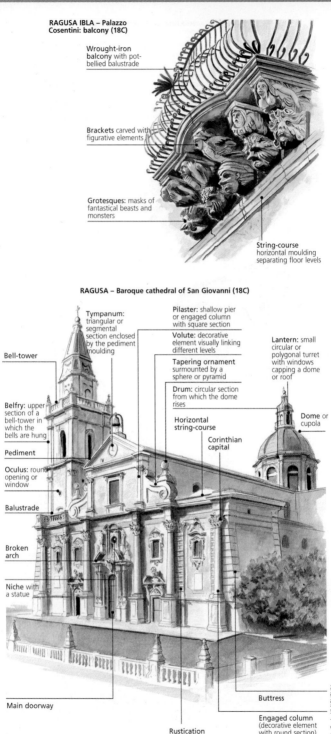

RAGUSA IBLA – Palazzo Cosentini: balcony (18C)

Wrought-iron balcony with pot-bellied balustrade

Brackets carved with figurative elements

Grotesques: masks of fantastical beasts and monsters

String-course horizontal moulding separating floor levels

RAGUSA – Baroque cathedral of San Giovanni (18C)

Tympanum: triangular or segmental section enclosed by the pediment moulding

Pilaster: shallow pier or engaged column with square section

Volute: decorative element visually linking different levels

Lantern: small circular or polygonal turret with windows capping a dome or roof

Bell-tower

Tapering ornament surmounted by a sphere or pyramid

Drum: circular section from which the dome rises

Dome or cupola

Belfry: upper section of a bell-tower in which the bells are hung

Horizontal string-course

Pediment

Corinthian capital

Oculus: round opening or window

Balustrade

Broken arch

Niche with a statue

Main doorway

Buttress

Rustication

Engaged column (decorative element with round section)

R. Corbel/MICHELIN

CASTELBUONO – Cappella di Sant'Anna (Castello dei Ventimiglia) (1683)

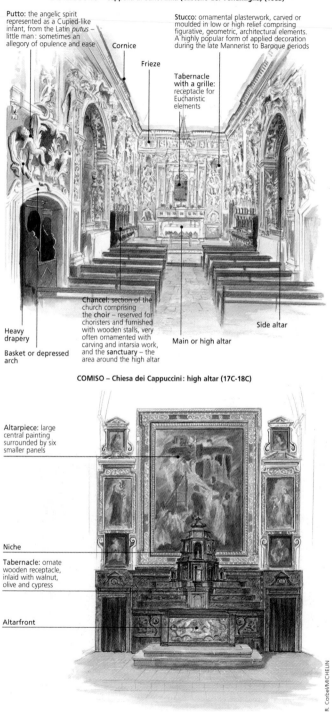

Putto: the angelic spirit represented as a Cupied-like infant, from the Latin *putus* – little man: sometimes an allegory of opulence and ease

Cornice

Frieze

Stucco: ornamental plasterwork, carved or moulded in low or high relief comprising figurative, geometric, architectural elements. A highly popular form of applied decoration during the late Mannerist to Baroque periods

Tabernacle with a grille: receptacle for Eucharistic elements

Side altar

Chancel: section of the church comprising the **choir** – reserved for choristers and furnished with wooden stalls, very often ornamented with carving and intarsia work, and the **sanctuary** – the area around the high altar

Main or high altar

Heavy drapery

Basket or depressed arch

COMISO – Chiesa dei Cappuccini: high altar (17C-18C)

Altarpiece: large central painting surrounded by six smaller panels

Niche

Tabernacle: ornate wooden receptacle, inlaid with walnut, olive and cypress

Altarfront

R. Corbel/MICHELIN

87

Civil and military buildings

Sicilian stronghold or *baglio*

Complex of buildings arranged around a central courtyard, including living quarters and workshops. In some cases the complex includes a small private chapel. Fortifications are integrated for defensive purposes. Examples located in rural positions were often used as grain depositories and for storing farm equipment; those located by the sea were inhabited by fishing communities (especially tuna fishermen) and included areas reserved for processing the fish and for repairing boats. At Marsala these *bagli* served as wineries (hence by implication, an actual cellar). Today most of these complexes have been transformed into museums or hotels.

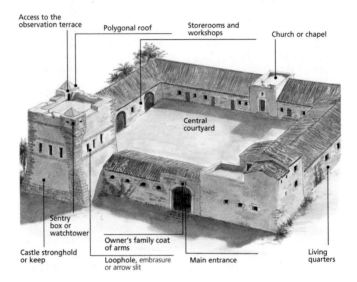

Access to the observation terrace

Polygonal roof

Storerooms and workshops

Church or chapel

Central courtyard

Sentry box or watchtower

Owner's family coat of arms

Castle stronghold or keep

Loophole, embrasure or arrow slit

Main entrance

Living quarters

CATANIA – Castello Ursino (1239-50)

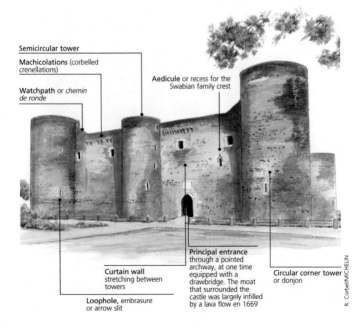

Semicircular tower

Machicolations (corbelled crenellations)

Watchpath or *chemin de ronde*

Aedicule or recess for the Swabian family crest

Curtain wall stretching between towers

Loophole, embrasure or arrow slit

Principal entrance through a pointed archway, at one time equipped with a drawbridge. The moat that surrounded the castle was largely infilled by a lava flow en 1669

Circular corner tower or donjon

R. Corbel/MICHELIN

by arches with tracery or polychrome geometric decoration.

Ciborium: a canopy (baldaquin) over an altar.

Corbel (or truss): a triangular bracket, usually made of wood, supporting a roof.

Counter-façade: the internal wall of church façade.

Cross (church plan): churches are usually built in the plan of a Greek cross, with four arms of equal length, or a Latin cross, with one arm longer than the other three.

Crypt: an underground chamber or vault usually beneath a church, often used as a mortuary, burial place or for displaying holy relics. Sometimes it was a small chapel or church in its own right.

Decumanus: a major thoroughfare bisecting a Classical town plan, running on a complementary axis to the cardo, orientated east–west; the Greek equivalent is the plateia.

Dosseret: supplementary capital in the shape of the base of an upturned pyramid, often decorated, set above a column capital to receive the thrust of the arch.

Ekklesiasterion: a meeting place for popular assemblies (ekklesia).

Entablature: in certain buildings, the section at the top of a colonnade consisting of three parts: the architrave (flat section resting on the capitals of a colonnade), the frieze (decorated with carvings) and the cornice (projecting top section).

Exedra: the section in the back of Roman basilicas containing seats; by extension, curved niche or semicircular recess outside.

Fresco: a wall painting applied to wet plaster.

Ghimberga: a triangular Gothic pediment adorning a portal.

Hypocaust: an underground heating system used in Antiquity, whereby floors were raised on a series of small brick columns, enabling hot air to circulate underneath.

Intrados: the inner surface of an arch or vault.

Jamb or pier: a pillar flanking a doorway or window and supporting the arch above.

Keep: the tower stronghold of a castle, usually situated in the centre of a well-protected area.

Keystone: the topmost stone in an arch or vault.

Lantern: a turret with windows on top of a dome.

Lesene (or Lombard strips): a decorative band of pilasters joined at the top by an arched frieze.

Matroneo: the gallery reserved for women in palaeo-Christian and Romanesque churches.

Merlon: part of a crowning parapet between two crenellations. There are two types of merlon: Ghibelline (swallow-tailed), symbolising civil, Imperial power and Guelf (rectangular), symbolising religious, Papal power.

Modillion: a small console supporting a cornice.

Moulding: an ornamental shaped band, which projects from the wall.

Ogive: a pointed arch.

Opus signinum: floor covering obtained by mixing fragments of terra-cotta and other small pieces of rubble with lime. It is sometimes decorated with marble or stone cobbles.

Overhang: an overhanging or corbelled upper storey.

Ovolo moulding: an egg-shaped ornament incorporated into the entablature.

Palazzo: Italian for town house or square building (housing commercial offices, for example) subtly different in connotation to the word "palace". In the Renaissance, the ground floor was usually reserved for storage or commercial activities, the first floor or *piano nobile* comprised the main apartments, while the second floor *(alto piano)* was allocated to children and domestic staff.

Pantocrator: a hieratic figure of Christ with his hand raised in blessing, often depicted in the apse of palaeo-Christian churches.

Pendentive: the spherical triangular panel that provides the transition from a square or polygonal base (at a crossing) to a circular dome.

Peristyle: the range of columns surrounding a Classical building or courtyard.

Pilaster strip: a structural column partially set into a wall.

Pluteus: a decorated balustrade made from various materials, separating the chancel from the rest of the church.

Polyptych: a painted or carved work consisting of more than three folding leaves or panels (diptych: two panels; triptych: three panels).

Predella: the base of an altar-piece, divided into small panels.

Pulpit: an elevated dais from which sermons are preached in the nave of a church.

Pyx: a cylindrical box made of ivory or glazed copper for jewels or the Eucharistic host.

Raceme: ornamental vine motif with tendrils, leaves and stylised fruits.

Relief: high relief *(altorilievo)* is a sculptural term describing the modelled forms that project from the background by at least half their depth (halfway between shallow relief and sculpture in the round). Low relief *(bassorilievo)* projects only very slightly from the background (also known as bas relief).

Retable: a large and ornate altar-piece divided into several painted or carved panels, especially common in Spain after the 14C.

Rib: a projecting moulding or band on the underside of a dome or vault, which may be structural or ornamental.

Rustication: the facing of a building that exaggeratedly replicates dressed stonework, raised or otherwise from the mortar joints. Rustication was used in the Renaissance to consolidate the impression of impregnability on the ground floor of a palazzo.

Splay: a surface of a wall that forms an oblique angle to the main surface of a doorway or window opening.

Squinch: an alternative to a pendentive comprising a compound number of miniature strainer arches, often intricately decorated with Moorish plasterwork.

Tambour: a circular or polygonal structure supporting a dome.

Trompe l'oeil: two-dimensional painted decoration giving the three-dimensional illusion of relief and perspective.

Vault: an arched structure of stone or brick forming a ceiling or roof over a hall, room, bay or other wholly or partly enclosed space.

> **Barrel vault** – a vault with a semicircular cross section.
> **Groin vault** (or cross vault) – formed by the perpendicular intersection of two vaults.
> **Bowl-shaped vault** – a spherical vault enclosing a semicircular apse.
> **Vaulting cell:** one of the four segments of the cross vault.
> **Window cross:** a stone or wooden post which divides the opening of a window or door. The vertical posts are known as **mullions**.

ART

From the period of Greek colonisation to the present day, Sicilian creativity has never been idle. The complex history of this island – fashioned and formed by a number of foreign peoples and cultures, isolated by the sea – in part explains the unique and varied nature of Sicilian expression over the centuries.

ROMAN ART

Vestiges from Roman times are fewer and less impressive than those of the Greek period, largely because the Romans showed comparatively little interest in Sicily. Once the threat of a Carthaginian invasion receded, the island lost its strategic importance and was exclusively prized as a "Roman granary". This allowed the enriched native land owners to build splendid villas by the sea – as the ruins at Patti, near Tyndaris, testify. Not until the end of the 3C AD, during the reign of Diocletian, did Sicily become sought-after by the Roman aristocracy, who acquired large tracts of land on the island.

During seven centuries of occupation (3C BC–5C AD), Rome did not endow Sicily with any prestigious monuments other than the odd functional public building (amphitheatres, public baths) and the foundations for a comprehensive road system.

Architecture

Unlike the Greeks, the Romans knew about cement and how to use it effectively. They erected walls, vaults and columns using casements filled with small bricks, and then poured concrete into them. Finishing touches were added in the form of marble facings (or high-quality stone) or, for the interiors, ably applied stucco that suggested splendid stone walls.

Civil architecture – During this period, **Greek theatres**, like the ones at **Taormina** and **Catania**, underwent considerable transformation. The circular orchestra (reserved for the chorus) was reduced to a semicircle, while a stage wall was added for the special effects machinery. The theatre provided a venue both for circus entertainment and combat with wild animals; to protect the spectators, a wall was constructed along the bottom of the cavea *(part of which can still be seen at Taormina)*. Roman monuments of special interest include the amphitheatres at **Siracusa** and **Catania**; the odeons at **Taormina** and **Catania**, and, finally, the

Naumachie of Taormina *(now badly damaged)*, which consists of a large-scale brick-built gymnasium *(122m/400ft long)* ornamented with niches. Besides these complexes dedicated to sport and entertainment, the Romans left nothing of value in terms of civic architecture. The fine basilica at Tyndaris suggests the Romans introduced the art of vaulting to Sicily (for it was unknown to the Greek civil engineers) and more significantly, to settlements removed from the major urban centres. Vestiges of **public baths complexes** *(terme)*, largely dating from the Imperial period, are preserved at **Catania**, **Taormina**, **Comiso**, **Solunto** and **Tindari**. Traces of *fora* have been found at **Taormina**, **Catania**, **Siracusa** and **Tindari**.

Domestic architecture – The Romano-Sicilian house closely resembles its Hellenistic counterpart. The peristyle town house was introduced towards the close of the 3C–2C BC (Morgantina). The most elegant homes, however, were the country villas, the most typical example being the magnificent **Villa Imperiale del Casale** near Piazza Armerina. Here, private bath facilities indicate this was a highly sophisticated and luxurious house; it is particularly renowned for its splendid floor mosaics.

BYZANTINE ART

Archaeological excavation undertaken in Palermo and Siracusa has uncovered complete cemeteries on the outskirts dating from Late Antiquity, when the Romans imposed Christianity on Sicily. The **catacombs** preserve traces of painted decoration – most particularly those at Siracusa (4C–5C AD) – and provide the earliest examples of Christian art in Sicily. Gradually islanders were coerced into erecting churches, modelled on the Roman **prototype basilica**: this consisted of a simple rectangular building, articulated by columns into three aisles, with a central nave terminated by a single apse. The other, more striking solution, was to incorporate a church around a pagan Antique temple – as with the **Temple of**

Concord at Agrigento and the **Temple of Athena** at Siracusa. The walls of the cella were cut away to make arcades and the outer colonnade infilled with masonry.

In AD 535, as a result of the Byzantine conquest links between the Church of Sicily and the Exarchate of Ravenna were reinforced. In 751, when Ravenna fell to the Lombards, this allegiance was transferred to Constantinople. Interestingly enough, the rift dividing the Roman and Byzantine Churches as a result of Pope Gregory II's opposition to Emperor Leo III's Iconoclast movement in 725–26 had serious repercussions in Sicily.

The ban on the cult of holy icons imposed by the Byzantine Emperor prompted crowds of refugees to seek asylum in Sicily, where the icon continued to be venerated. Whole monastic communities and groups of skilled craftsmen found sanctuary and set about applying their trades, notably in the art of mosaic.

This prosperous period gave rise to the building of numerous shrines (including the ones at Cava d'Ispica and Pantalica) and the institution of troglodyte settlements hewn into the bedrock (almost all now destroyed). Small, centrally planned, square (typically Byzantine) churches appeared. A few examples survive in the eastern part of the island, north and east of Etna (*see Taormina: Castiglione di Sicilia*), in the vicinity of Noto and around Siracusa. Other Byzantine monuments were completely transformed, dismembered or converted to another use through the ensuing centuries.

ARABO-NORMAN ART
Arab Occupation
The Muslim conquest began in 827 in the area of Trapani. During their two-and-a-half centuries of sovereignty, the Arabs transformed the appearance of Sicily. They shifted their power base from Siracusa to Palermo, altering the countryside with irrigation and eastern crops. Most dramatically, they introduced new architectural forms. They were prolific builders and sensitive planners, ever conscious of a building's relationship with its natural setting: palaces, mosques and minarets stood among gardens and fountains. In terms of design, their acute sense of line and elegance was applied to sophisticated decorative schemes. Human figures gave way to geometric and arabesque forms, house interiors were transformed with coloured ceramic tiles, while ceilings were encrusted with rich plaster decoration *(muqarnas)*.

Alas, no important monument survives intact from the Arab occupation. Indeed, most of their splendid buildings disappeared with the arrival of the Normans, who appropriated, rebuilt and redecorated them.

A few examples of Arab craftsmanship survive, as do a number of intricate networks of irregular streets tucked away in cities like Palermo.

Norman Eclecticism
The Arabo-Norman style combines elements from Islamic, Romanesque (introduced by Franco-Norman Benedictine monks) and Byzantine art. Much of its wealth is rooted in the Norman sovereigns' desire to copy the splendour of Byzantium, a city they yearned to conquer. The new Sicilian master builders channelled their creative power into monuments of incomparable beauty. From the end of the 11C and throughout the next century, large churches were conceived by architect-monks, mainly from the Benedictine and Augustinian orders, whether Greek, French or Latin (from mainland Italy).

Designs were modelled on Classical prototypes: a transept was incorporated in a basilica, giving it a Latin- or Greek-cross plan, towers were erected to house bells, a doorway inserted in the front elevation, the presbytery was often crowned with a dome. At the same time, these edifices were given the latest contemporary decoration: Byzantine mosaics laid by Orthodox (Greek) artists and Moorish features (horseshoe arches, arabesque and honeycomb ornament). The mixture of these three styles is quite unique.

Byzantine influence – The Eastern elements incorporated into religious architecture include the square centralised plan, adapted in turn to the Greek cross, roofed with intersecting barrel vaults *(Church of the Martorana, San Nicolò at Mazara del Vallo, or Santissima Trinita di Delia at Castelvetrano)*. Elsewhere, the intersection is vaulted with the typical Sicilian Byzantine dome rising from a polygonal drum. Even the capitals reflect an Arabo-Norman style adapted from the Byzantine by incorporating a dosseret between the capital and the impost of the arch *(Monreale Cathedral)*.

The reason for the lack of Byzantine sculptures of humans is threefold: firstly, the Christians wished to distance themselves from pagan statuary; secondly, the Iconoclastic movement forbade the veneration of anything that might be construed as an idol; and, lastly, the Islamic influence. They also adapted the techniques; stone was no longer worked just on the surface, but in the round, drilling tiny holes and fretting effects that resembled stone lace.

The Byzantine artists' richest and most effective medium was the mosaic. This they applied to immense areas, animating them with figures and decorative motifs, upgrading the art form to monumental proportions. Apart from the Martorana, which fully conforms to Byzantine canons, the iconography and presentation of subject matter were adapted in Sicilian churches. At Cefalù, Monreale and the Cappella Palatina in Palermo, Christ Pantocrator fills the top of the vault above the apse; in Greek Byzantine churches, he would always be in the dome. Finally, the Norman kings had themselves depicted in areas traditionally reserved for saints, with the symbols of the basilei (Byzantine emperors), as a way of asserting their power.

Islamic influence – The Arabs brought new building methods and decorative know-how that enabled them to create masterpieces. In architecture, they introduced the horseshoe (or Moorish) arch: the upper part of this arch is semicircular, although it can be pointed at the apex, but comes in at the base to form a horseshoe shape. The interiors of Arab buildings were often encrusted with stalactite plasterwork decoration called **muqarnas**; this in turn was painted, carved and textured into overhanging honeycombs. The interior decoration of Monreale Cathedral, the Palatine Chapel, the Zisa and Cuba *palazzi* are splendid testimonies to the influence of Islam. The Arab predilection for elaborate ornament featured in the serrated edge to the cornice with merlons of San Cataldo in Palermo – an elegant base for the three pink domes. They also brought an alternative view of proportion and volume, as indicated by the squat domes of San Giovanni degli Eremiti.

Romanesque influence – The most typical elements of the Romanesque style are the Latin-cross plan and the façade framed by massive towers, features devised by the Benedictine monks, most notably at Cluny, for the buildings they planned on a massive and monumental scale. On the whole, the religious buildings did not allocate much space to Norman sculpture (primarily geometric motifs on small arches and other decorative details – like strips of small leaves and ovolo moulding – applied to the dosserets of capitals). Their inclination towards stylisation touched representations of animals and plants which are reduced to simple palmettes or rather thin, flat, rigid-looking flowerless species (reeds and rushes). A handful of monuments, including the cloisters at Monreale, preserve some most splendid figurative capitals relating historical and biblical scenes, founded in the Romanesque tradition.

Arabo-Norman Creativity

Although many buildings conformed to a clearly defined influence, some combinations of styles became models and prototypes for other art forms promoted during the rule of the Altavilla (de Hauteville) dynasty.

Duomo, Siracusa

© Sandro Bedessi / Fototeca ENIT

Religious buildings – The undisputed masterpiece of this Sicilian Norman School is the Palatine Chapel *(Cappella Palatina)* in Palermo. Here elements of Romanesque art – an extended plan comprising nave, side aisles and narrow windows through which light suffuses – are married with the Moorish love for sumptuous decoration *(notable in the ceiling)*, calligraphy *(various Arabic inscriptions)* and structural design *(pointed arches)*. All this merges with the monumental splendour of Byzantine art *(dome pendentives, gold-background mosaics, marble wall facing, and inlaid floors)*. The chapel demonstrates how the centrally planned Byzantine choir is superimposed onto the wooden-vaulted Latin basilica nave *(set at a lower level)*. This became a new prototype, subsequently used at Monreale.

Secular buildings – Besides the odd large castle in a strategic position – Palermo, Castellammare and Messina – the Norman kings built various palaces for rest and recreation. At the end of the Altavilla (de Hauteville) rule, there were nine such residences in Sicily; today only the **Zisa** and **Cuba** *palazzi* in Palermo survive. These splendid houses are surrounded by large gardens ornamented with expanses of water.

The interior space divided into two main areas: the *iwan* (a room with three exedras) and an open courtyard containing one or more fountains and surrounded by porticoes. The first of these two distinctive areas originated in Abbasid Persia, the second in Fatimid Egypt. Together, they appear in Sicily sometime in the 12C, imported via the Maghreb (North Africa), which then extended as far as the coasts of modern Tunisia and was under Sicilian rule.

The decoration is also largely drawn from Islamic art: herringboned marble or brick cover the floors, Moorish-motif mosaics face the walls. Finally, the ceilings and arches are encrusted with carved and painted muqarnas.

GOTHIC ART

For two centuries, between the 13C and the 15C, Sicily suffered political instability under a succession of sovereigns: the Swabians (1189–1266), Angevins (1266–82), and the House of Aragon. All appreciated the Gothic style on a grand scale – not the case on the mainland.

Swabian military constructions – Henry VI, and more particularly **Frederick II**, who enjoyed a longer reign (1208–50), preserved the numerous religious and civil buildings erected by the Normans. They also built fortresses designed by northern master masons, who introduced the Gothic style. From this era date the castles at Siracusa (Castello Maniace), Catania (Castello Ursino) and Augusta, as well as the fortifications of the castle at Enna (eight imposing towers survive). These buildings conform to a highly geometric ground plan (square centrepiece defended with angle, and sometimes lateral, towers), doorways and windows set into pointed arches, austerely bare walls pierced with embrasures, that rise to battlements and finally, quadripartite vaulted casements.

14C: Chiaramonte style – The great feudal dynasties in power during the 14C, most especially the Chiaramonte, demonstrated a real talent for the construction of town houses and churches. The Palermo residence, Palazzo Chiaramonte, provided a model for future *palazzi*: the façade is extremely refined, the windows set into decorative pointed arches are unique and quite wonderful, the roof line crested with merlons. The Chiaramonte style is characterised by two-or three-light windows surmounted by arches with tracery or polychrome geometric decoration. The Chiaramonte, who maintained their supremacy throughout the 14C as the royal power base declined, sponsored many new buildings and restored others: from Mussomeli to Racalmuto, Montechiaro to Favara, they are responsible for at least 10 castles and palazzi.

15C: Catalan Gothic – Catalan Gothic flourished easily in Sicily because of the Spanish viceroys' influence from the late 14C, under the rule of the House of Aragon. This more sober form of Gothic is characterised by elongated forms, a marked tendency towards breadth of space over height (particularly in the religious context), and ample windows alternating with bare flat wall surfaces. Typical examples include the Palazzo Santo Stefano and Palazzo Corvaja at Taormina and the main doorway of Palermo Cathedral.
At the end of the 15C, **Matteo Carnelivari** probably best epitomises the new influence, mixing Catalan features with Byzantine, Arab and Norman elements.

Carnelivari designed Palazzo Abatellis and Palazzo Ajutamicristo, and probably the Church of Santa Maria della Catena in Palermo.

Sculpture and painting – Only non-Sicilian artists achieved any renown in these two fields at this time: sculptors were summoned from Tuscany, particularly from Pisa. **Nino Pisano** completed a graceful Annunziata for the cathedral in Trapani, a place that attracted a large number of sculptors to its marble quarries from the 14C. Bonaiuto Pisano carved the eagle that stands above the gateway of Palazzo Sclafani in Palermo. In painting, **Antonio Veneziano** (trained in Venice, worked in Florence), **Gera da Pisa**, and various Spanish artists such as **Guerau Janer** also worked in Sicily for a time. At the end of the 15C, some painters became so successful that they settled in Sicily, among them **Nicolò di Maggio** (from Siena), who worked particularly in Palermo.

RENAISSANCE AND MANNERISM

Because the Aragonese court favoured the Spanish Gothic style, the Renaissance and Mannerism that spread from Italy to the rest of Europe did not have a great impact on Sicily. It fell to artists trained by the great Tuscan masters to introduce the principles to Sicily.

Painting – In the 15C, Sicily started to show an interest in the new Renaissance movement, prompted by the work of **Antonello da Messina**. Although his life and career have long been a mystery, this artist remains the most famous Sicilian painter. Born in Messina in 1430; he was in Naples, possibly engaged as a pupil to the workshop of Colantonio, in 1450. There he would most certainly have seen Flemish painting. In 1475–76, Antonello was in Venice, where he must have encountered Giovanni Bellini and Piero della Francesca.
Antonello's supreme reputation, however, is founded on his mastery of the Van Eycks' exacting oil-painting techniques. His mature style combines detail so typical of Flemish art with the

Courtyard, Palazzo Abatellis

© Photo Scala, Florence / Luciano Romano

breadth of form upheld by the Italian Schools. Indeed, his works are static in composition, explore texture and demonstrate an almost-perfect tonal unity in terms of colour.

His works found in Sicily include an *Annunciation* in Siracusa's Palazzo Bellomo, *Polyptych of St Gregory* in the Messina's Museo Regionale, and the *Portrait of an Unknown Man* in Cefalù's Museo Mandralisca. These are among the most notable works of the Renaissance to be preserved in Sicily.

During the first half of the 16C, the painters **Cesare da Sesto, Polidoro da Caravaggio** and Vincenzo da Pavia played their part in spreading the Mannerist style prevalent in Tuscany and Rome.

Simone de Wobreck, meanwhile, who lived in Sicily until 1557, introduced the basic elements of Flemish Mannerism.

Sculpture – In the second half of the 15C, sculpture was completely revitalised by a range of Italian artists, notably **Francesco Laurana** and **Domenico Gagini**. The sculptor and engraver **Laurana** spent five years in Sicily (1466–71). He worked at the Cappella Mastrantonio in the Church of San Francesco and produced the bust of Eleonora of Aragon in Palermo's Palazzo Abatellis. Other paintings include a *Madonna and Child*

in Noto's Church of the Crocifisso, another in the Church of the Immacolata in Palazzolo Acreide and a third in the museum at Messina.

Gagini, who was born into a family of Italian sculptors and architects from Lake Lugano, moved south and settled in Sicily. There he practised his art in association with his son **Antonello**, who was born in Palermo in 1478. Their workshop flourished in the capital, producing works that satisfied the contemporary

© Museo Mandralisca, Cefalù / SCALA

Portrait of an Unknown Man by Antonello da Messina, 1470

predilection for elegant, refined forms in Carrara marble, rather than travertine. Domenico's style and technique were continued by his descendants (including his son Giandomenico), sculptors and goldsmiths who achieved fame up to the mid-17C. Numerous Sicilian churches preserve splendid statues executed by the Gagini, although the very proliferation has aroused accusations of their work being repetitive and therefore considered of a lesser value.

Mannerism exercised its influence on sculpture in the 16C largely thanks to artists such as the Florentine **Angelo Montorsoli** (1505–63), who was working in Messina around 1547–57. The fact that he had collaborated with Michelangelo in Florence and Rome gave Montorsoli a certain cachet. His work demonstrates a shift from the Renaissance style to a Michelangelesque Mannerism. The works that survive include the **Fontana di Orione** (1547–50) in Messina, which is regarded as one of the greatest masterpieces of the 16C.

BAROQUE

During the 16C, the Spanish authorities asserted their influence in the arts. They imposed the values promoted by the Counter-Reformation (resulting from the Council of Trent, 1545), before choosing to sponsor an elaborate, exuberant form of the Baroque that was more typically Spanish than Italian.

Counter-Reformation – Sicily soon succumbed to the power and influence of the Society of Jesus (later known as the Jesuits), founded in 1540 by the Spaniard St Ignatius Loyola (1491–1556). Modelled on the Chiesa del Gesù in Rome, the **Jesuit** churches in Sicily were designed with the same features. The one broad nave is devoid of any element that might restrict the congregation's view of the main altar or obstruct or deflect the words of the preacher from reaching the faithful. The solemnity, authority, opulence and luminosity of the internal space is in keeping with the exterior: the main body of the church, so tall and wide, is screened by a cen-

tral bay; the lateral chapels which open directly off the nave are screened by a lower bay. The bare surfaces that lent a dignity to the Renaissance buildings are here textured with features that vary in weight and depth: engaged columns at ground level give way to superficial pilasters above as sharp contrasts effectively dissolve into lightness *(the Church of Sant'Ignazio all'Olivella in Palermo is a good example of this style)*.

The painting of the **Counter-Reformation** revives a predilection for those images rejected by Protestantism, subjects such as the Virgin Mary, the dogma of the Eucharist and the veneration of saints. Painting follows the examples of Michelangelo and Raphael, although in Sicily the practitioners of this style, such as Vincenzo degli Azani, are few and lesser known.

Politics and style – The Baroque style, which in Spain reached its apogee in the second half of the 17C, was quickly assimilated by the Sicilians, for they had enjoyed and appreciated the opulent use of marble and gilding since Arab and Byzantine tastes prevailed in previous centuries. This movement placed great importance on detail, producing finely worked wrought-iron railings and gates, balcony brackets carved with the most original grotesques and imagina-

Baroque façade, Chiesa Madre, Palma di Montechiaro, Naro

© Daniele La Monaca / Tips Images

Baroque balcony details, Ragusa

© Christophe Boisvieux / hemis.fr

tive designs interpreted in polychrome panels of *pietra dura*.

At the beginning of the 17C, the Spanish viceroy's administration launched an ambitious building programme. They founded some 100 new towns to reorganise and then develop their extensive territories. The earthquake of 1669, followed by a more devastating one in 1693, destroyed almost all the southeastern part of the island. The rebuilding of the towns was immediately initiated under the combined direction of the local authorities, the aristocracy, town planners (Fra' Michele la Ferla, Fra' Angelo Italia) and architects (Vaccarini, Ittar, Vermexio, Palma and Gagliardi). The earthquake laid bare a great expanse of land stretching from Catania to Siracusa, damaging Avola, Noto, Scicli, Modica, Ragusa, Vittoria, Lentini and Grammichele. As a result, Sicilian Baroque is concentrated in this swathe and around Palermo *(Bagheria, Trapani)*, being the seat of power.

Architecture – The majority of the Baroque architects had trained in Rome. They therefore modelled their own ideas on Roman interpretations of the Baroque, sometimes exaggerating their iconographic forms, volumes and subject matter for sculptural effect. The delicate relationship between the fragility of life and the forces of nature was translated into an art form far removed from any quest for beauty. The grotesque, excess, death, suffering and even ugliness (decrepitude of old age, poverty and physical deformity) underlie the expressions of exuberance ornamenting every surface at this time. Contorted form proved an ideal vehicle for expressing movement through façades or an internal decorative scheme.

Giovanni Battista Vaccarini (1702–69) served his apprenticeship in Rome under Carlo Fontana, through whom he absorbed the ingenuity of the tormented Borromini. On his return to Sicily around 1730, Vaccarini settled in Catania and devoted the next 30 years of his life to rebuilding the city. His undoubted masterpiece is the Church of St Agatha, which is elliptical in shape and has a restless and undulating façade inspired by Borromini's oval Church of San Carlo alle Quattro Fontane in Rome.

Even **Palermo** bristles with buildings modelled on prototypes in Rome. Most of these were built by one of the city's most highly regarded architects, **Giacomo Amato** (1643–1732), who came from Palermo and was trained in Rome. He uses decorative elements borrowed from 16C Roman architecture; characteristic examples include the Church of Santa Teresa alla Kalsa (1686), the Church of the Pietà that rises through two imposing storeys articulated with columns (1689), the Church of the Santissimo Salvatore with its oval dome, as well as numerous private *palazzi*. The monument that best epitomises the urban Baroque style in Palermo is the Quattro Canti junction faced with four interacting façades and fountains.

Noto had to be completely rebuilt following the 1693 earthquake. Thus it exemplifies the Baroque homogeneity in Sicilian cities, largely as a result of being conceived as a vast theatre.

The author of this exceptional ensemble is presumed to be the enigmatic **Rosario Gagliardi**, about whom little is known other than his year and place of birth (Siracusa, 1680) and death (Noto, 1726). The greatest Baroque architect of Sicily exerted his considerable impact on this small area around Noto and its two neighbouring towns: Ragusa and Modica. In **Ragusa**, he is responsible for the churches of San Giuseppe and San Giorgio; in **Modica**, he designed the magnificent Church of San Giorgio with its distinctive slender bell tower.

The most evocative Sicilian Baroque villas are to be found at **Bagheria**, about 18km/11mi east of Palermo. One of the most remarkable of these refined residential buildings, endowed with luxuriously furnished halls and gardens populated with statuary, is the *Villa Palagonia*, famous for its wildly extravagant interior decoration. The villa became a symbol of the absurd, renowned throughout Europe during the Age of Enlightenment, long before Goethe's famous visit in 1787.

Sculpture and applied decoration – Baroque sculpture and decoration is characterised by rich ornamentation. Altarpieces are provided with carved marble panels and contained among twisted columns; cornices and pediments are crested with figures of angels. Ranking high among his many fellow artist-craftsmen, **Giacomo Serpotta** (1652–1732) excelled at using marble, stucco and polychrome decoration.

After training in Rome, Serpotta returned to his home town of Palermo to work on an equestrian statue of Charles II of Spain. He then embarked on a long career as a decorator specialising in stucco. The Oratory of San Lorenzo, the Oratory of Santa Cita and the Oratory of the Rosary at San Domenico are encrusted throughout with figures and swirling curlicues in bold relief, executed with an exquisite attention to detail. The other church interiors on which Serpotta worked include La Gancia, and Il Carmine. Later in life, he was engaged on the decoration of the Church of San Francesco d'Assisi and that of Sant'Agostino (with pupils), which contains a number of narrative panels in shallow relief that illustrate a rare degree of virtuosity. While Serpotta is regarded as the greatest exponent of Sicilian Baroque sculpture, he is also considered to be a precursor of the characteristic forms of Rococo.

Baroque painting – Baroque painters were predominantly engaged in experimentation with perspective and *trompe l'oeil*, constructing complex compositions on diagonal axes around swirling gestures. Their most common subjects were narrative scenes from the Bible or mythology. The most representative adherent of this movement was Caravaggio. Michelangelo Merisi (1573–1610), known as **Caravaggio** after his birthplace near Bergamo, began his career in Rome alongside Cavaliere

Hall of Mirrors, Villa Palagonia, Bagheria

© Sandro Bedessi / Fototeca ENIT

d'Arpino in 1588. Thanks to his temper and bad behaviour, Caravaggio was forced to flee the city in 1605, making for Naples, Malta and then Sicily. Venturing to the extremes of every artistic convention, he perfected a highly personal style using low-life figures to animate his pictures. He heightened the drama with bold contrasts of light and shadow, a technique known as "chiaroscuro". While in Sicily, he executed a number of important works, notably the *Burial of St Lucy (1609, in Palazzo Bellomo in Siracusa)*, *The Adoration of the Shepherds* and *The Resurrection of Lazarus (in the Messina museum)*.

These paintings fired the imagination of many subsequent artists, namely Alfonso Rodriguez (1578–1648) and **Pietro Novelli** (1603–47). Novelli was also influenced by the Dutch painter **Anthony Van Dyck**, who, during a sojourn in Palermo in 1624, painted *The Madonna of the Rosary* for the oratory in the Church of San Domenico.

18C TO THE PRESENT DAY

Neoclassicism – The Classical revival started in the mid-18C and was fed by the passion for Ancient Greek and Roman architecture following the discovery and excavation of Herculaneum, Pompeii and Paestum. In the graphic arts, this movement was translated into depictions of Romantic ruins and topographical views that met with great success. One of the most successful of the neoclassical sculptors was **Ignazio Marabitti** (Palermo, 1719–97), who trained in Rome under Filippo della Valle. Works by this artist include the altarpiece of St Ignatius commissioned for the Church of Sant'Agata al Collegio in Caltanissetta. In Palermo, the native-born **Venanzio Marvuglia** (1729–1814) met with moderate success: a pupil of Vanvitelli in Rome, he was responsible for enlarging the Church of San Martino delle Scale, the Oratory of Sant'Ignazio dell'Olivella *(Palermo)* and the villa for the Prince of Belmonte. Marvuglia's predominantly Classical style is sometimes touched with the exotic, as the **Chinese pavilion** in the park of La Favorita in Palermo testifies.

Naturalism – Although sharing with many other contemporary Italian artists a keenness to portray reality, the sculptor **Domenico Trentacoste** (b. Palermo, 1859, d. Florence, 1933) still cannot be regarded as a true exponent of Naturalism. Fascinated first by 15C exponents, Trentacoste then turned to **Rodin**, whom he encountered in Paris in around 1880, before gradually concentrating on popular painting, mythological subjects, portraiture and nude painting (*Little Faun* in the Galleria E. Restivo in Palermo). **Ettore Ximenes** (b. Palermo, 1855, d. Rome, 1926) trained first in Palermo and then in Naples under Domenico Morelli.

Stile Liberty – The Art Nouveau style, already well established in Europe, appeared in Italy at the turn of the 20C. Its main impact was on the decorative arts; its most distinctive feature, the serpentine line, insinuated itself into figurative depictions, wrought-iron work, and furniture. The best exponent in Sicily is the architect **Ernesto Basile** (b. Palermo, 1857, d. 1932), son of **Giovanni Basile** (designer of the Teatro Massimo in Palermo), who turned to the Art Nouveau style after studying

Sculpture by Ignazio Marabitti in Villa Giulia, Palermo

© Photo Scala, Florence

Façade of Palazz
Biscari, Catania

© Emilio Suetone / hemis.fr

forms of Arabo-Norman and Renaissance design. Examples of his work from this period include the decoration of Villa Igiea (today the five-star *Hilton Hotel Villa Igiea Palermo*), notably the wonderful floral decoration of the dining room, Caffè Ferraglia in Rome, and various villas in Palermo, such as **Villino Florio**. He also worked on designing soft furnishings, fabrics and furniture.

Palermo's **Villa Malfitano**, once owned by the Whitakers, a prominent English family, epitomises the success and effectiveness of the Stile Liberty in Sicily.

Contemporary art – Although Sicily has not given rise to an international movement, it has nurtured several interesting personalities.

The painter **Fausto Pirandello** (1889–1975), son of the famous writer, was mainly interested in Cubist painting (Braque, in particular). Later, he balanced the abstract and figurative.

The Neo-Realist painter **Renato Guttuso** (1912–87) studied Classics in Palermo before moving to Rome and then Milan. There, he affirmed his political position as clearly anti-Fascist. During these years he turned to Realist art. His paintings are characterised by a flattened perspective and by form refracted into geometric shapes –

reminiscent of Picasso. Yet his subjects always reflect his social predicament. From 1958 onwards, Guttuso was influenced by Expressionism. The result is a new painting style: the realism that pervaded his subject matter is now imbued with emotion, movement is suggested by the use of strong colour and boldly decisive line.

Among contemporary Sicilian artists, mention should be made of various sculptors. **Pietro Consagra**, who came from Mazara del Vallo (1920–2005), studied in Palermo before going to Rome, where he came into contact with abstract art. He experimented with different materials, honing them to produce the finest end result.

The sculptor **Emilio Greco** (b. Catania, 1913, d. Rome, 1995) sought that elusive harmony and equilibrium, drawing inspiration from Greek, Etruscan, Roman and Renaissance art. One of his favourite subjects was the female body; other concepts and ideas explored are associated with religion (the bronze doors of Orvieto Cathedral and the monument

> *Without Sicily, Italy leaves no image in the soul: it is the key to everything.*
>
> – *Italian Journey*, J.W. von Goethe

101

The Grand Tour

During the reign of the English Queen Elizabeth I (1533–1603), the concept of a "Grand Tour" of the Continent first became popular. The medieval style pilgrimages by noblemen had been decried by the likes of Erasmus. Now, excursions were for education and pleasure *(utilitas et verits):* Venice, Milan, Verona, Florence and Rome, of course, were the compulsory ports of call.

But after Elizabeth I's excommunication and aggressive actions against Spain, Protestant travellers would have been wary of journeying south to Naples and Sicily, then under the dominion of the Spaniards and their Catholic Inquisition. Slowly the Papacy endeavoured to woo the English. Aristocrats sojourned at leisure in Italy (the Earl of Leicester's son, Sir Robert Dudley, was in Florence; Earl Arundel spent time in Padua); Inigo Jones (1573–1652) reported on the delights of Classical and Palladian architecture. Finally, after the Restoration of Charles II (1660), the frontiers were opened once more.

The **Age of Sensibility** exalted Italy as the cradle of civilisation. Instructive journeys completed the education of young intellectuals. They travelled to the Continent, visiting places endowed with rich artistic heritage and cultural fervour. Richard Boyle, then Lord Burlington (1684–1753), and Robert Adam (1728–92) followed in the wake of Jones to study the antique monuments.

As the **Age of Reason** dawned, still Rome and its academic institutions attracted ambitious young artists to study, muse and enjoy life without responsibility.

to Pope John XXIII for St Peter's Basilica in Rome).

Finally, **Salvatore Fiume** (1915–97), also known as Giocondo, was active in various media, including sculpture, film and painting. The latter range from ideal depictions of nature to flat portrayals of everyday life (such as women at a market). Clearly, he was influenced by the various cultures and civilisations that history imprinted on Sicily. In later life, Fiume devoted himself to religious art, illustrating biblical texts for the Catholic publisher Edizioni Paoline.

ENGLISHMEN ABROAD

The first English traveller to compile a journal of his travels abroad is **Sir Thomas Hoby** (1530–66), who set out from England in June 1549 and travelled to Padua, Florence, Rome, Naples, Calabria and Sicily. **John Dryden, Jr.** travelled the Mediterranean in the early 18C (*A Voyage to Sicily and Malta* was published in 1776).

In 1770, the Scotsman **Patrick Brydone** visited the island: his impressions are contained in the entertaining letters that form his *Journey to Sicily and Malta* (published 1773), which library records prove to be the most popular book of the late 18C. The first thing that strikes him is the port of Messina, a harbour enclosed by a sickle-shaped tongue of land protecting it from all the winds. Here, reality combines immediately with myth, in which the terrible monsters of Scylla and Charybdis lurk in the underground caves on either side of the Straits of Messina.

The luxuriant vegetation also catches the traveller's eye, alongside the more everyday crops of vines, olives and wheat, which alternate with flowers, bushes and prickly pears. Ever present in the background stands the menacing form of Etna, smouldering benignly – the ultimate "curiosity" in this southern region. Then Taormina, and the first leap into the classical past, and Etna looms up again – a sleeping giant, but ever-vigilant and ready to prove its great power: "in the centre we could just see the summit of the mountain raising its proud head, vomiting clouds of smoke."

After the Seven Years' War (1756–63), the Grand Tour became institutionalised: now not only the British **(Sir William Hamilton**, **Gavin Hamilton**, **Benjamin West)** came, but also the French, the Germans and the Dutch. Visitors extended their tours to Naples and the south following the exciting discovery and excavation of Pompeii (1740s) and the neighbouring Herculaneum (1750s). This provided a genuine and "scientific" view of Roman life, buried intact beneath layers of volcanic debris since the eruption of Vesuvius in AD 79, as had been described by Pliny the Younger. Scholars and tourists alike extended their travels to take in Paestum (documented by two other Englishmen, **John Berkenhout** and **Thomas Major**, in 1767–68). Before long, Sicily was also included in the itinerary but these discoveries not only encouraged interest in things Roman relevant to Neoclassicism and the Greek Revival, they also precipitated an ever-greater fascination for the latent power of volcanoes. This is encapsulated by Sir William Hamilton (Plenipotentiary at the Court of Naples 1764–1800) in his book *Observations on Mount Vesuvius, Mount Etna and other Volcanos* (1773).

Napoleon's invasion of Italy (1796) interrupted all forms of travel across the Continent. When peace was restored, the grandness of the tours evaporated. After 1815, Thomas Cook began operating his package tours and visitors urged the Italians to rise against their Austrian occupiers. Yet all the while, Italy provided a safe haven for those fleeing trouble at home, most especially those young and of a Romantic disposition (Byron, Shelley, Browning).

For travellers, Etna acts as a powerful magnet: the very antithesis of the peace and serenity of the past inspired by the Greek ruins of Girgenti (Agrigento). It symbolises life in the form of fire and heat, an uncontrollable, unpredictable phenomenon.

The fact that it is visible from a long way off seems almost to endow it with the inevitability of something that man cannot control, similarly to life and death. Brydone journeys on towards the larger towns on the island: Catania, Siracusa, Agrigento and the "beautiful, elegant" Palermo, to which pages and pages of description are devoted.

In Brydone's footsteps followed **Henry Swinburne**, urged on by the other writer's "lies" and "nonsensical froth"; he published his travels in four volumes entitled *Travels in the Two Sicilies in the Years 1777, 1778, 1779 and 1780*.

These, along with the Brydone account, were soon translated into French and German. **Johann Wolfgang von Goethe** (1749–1832) used Brydone and J.H. Von Riedesel's *Reise* (1771) when he undertook his Italian journey, writing his own *Italienische Reise* (1786-88).

As descriptions were penned, draughtsmen and painters flocked to the island, eager to depict the natural landscape, the topography of the cities and views, the ruins and the people. Towards the end of the century, Sicily became the key destination for anyone undertaking the Grand Tour: it was the gateway of all things classical, but also a natural treasure trove of rare features that could not be found elsewhere.

TRAVELLING DIARY

The diary was the traveller's faithful companion. In it, he would transcribe impressions, musings, pleasures and discomforts (Goethe's descriptions of seasickness, for example) in an informal letter to himself or a close friend.

What is remarkable is how perceptive these observations are, touching upon technical and scientific details, curious facts, encounters, and images of a Sicily that has since changed profoundly. Yet the portraits of the people, their kindness and hospitality are true for all time.

Literature

Sicilian literature has evolved in a curious way: nowhere has dialect been used as a literary language for such a long time and in such an uncompromising way as on this island. In fact, it has given rise to two linguistically different parallel streams, often present in the same author: one form being written in Italian, the other in the Sicilian dialect. The Sicilian School of Poetry's Golden Age came to an end with the decline of the Magna Curia of Frederick II. During the 14C–15C, poetry was modelled on Tuscan literature; it then faded gradually, overshadowed by a more popular genre in local dialect.

HUMANISM AND THE RENAISSANCE

The discovery of Classical texts, in particular the understanding of Ancient Greek which underpinned the emergence of Humanism, resounded strongly in Sicily. Noto, Palermo, Siracusa, Catania and Messina became leading cultural centres. The latter instituted a school for Greek, which achieved international acclaim, largely thanks to the teachings of **Costantino Lascaris**.

The 16C saw a resurgence in the use of Sicilian. Local patriotism and pride swelled as publishers debuted the first Sicilian-Latin dictionaries and a grammar for the regional dialect. As far as poetry is concerned, the preponderance of the Petrarchan style found expression in dialect through **Antonio Veneziano** (1543–93). He was imprisoned in Algiers with **Cervantes** and was the author of two volumes of poems entitled *Celia*.

17C–18C

In keeping with the general mood of the Baroque, the 17C witnessed an upsurge of interest and development in the theatre, largely generated by the tragedies of **Ortensio Scammacca** and by comedies, both in Italian and in dialect.

In the course of the 18C, the Age of Enlightenment made its presence felt, as expressed in the *History of Sicily* written by the abbot **G. Battista Caruso** (1673–1724) and the *History of Sicilian Literature* edited by **Antonio Mongitore** (1663–1743).

Philosophical reflection inspired various other literary genres: Cartesian thought was voiced by **Tommaso Campailla** (1668–1740), who wrote a poem entitled *Adamo, ovvero il mondo é creato (Adam, or How the World was Created)*. Leibniz, meanwhile, was exalted by **Tommaso Natale** in *La filosofia Leibniziana (The Philosophy of Leibniz)*. Rousseau's precepts on the Noble Savage and the relationship between morality and the environment were promoted by the great poet, **Giovanni Meli** (1740–1815), in his contemplations *La bucolica* and philosophical satires clearly influenced by the Enlightenment: *L'origini du lu munnu, Don Chisciotti e Sanciu Panza*.

19C

Romanticism encouraged the writing of lengthy histories and research into the origins of regional culture and tradition. **Michele Amari** (1806–89) initiated a new period of historical criticism with his *La guerra del Vespro siciliano (War of the Sicilian Vespers)* and *Storia dei Musulmani di Sicilia (History of the Muslims in Sicily)*. **Giuseppe Pitré** (1841–1916) studied folklore, thereby raising the life and traditions of Sicilians to a level worthy of historical consideration.

Realism was formulated as a reaction to Romanticism and became widespread in Sicily towards the close of the 19C. Early foundations were laid by the Positivist poetry of **Mario Rapisardi** (1844–1912); reinforcements came from the accomplished theorist **Luigi Capuana** (1839–1915). He argued that art should embrace a sense of real life and examine the contemporary world and the laws of nature so as to document human life. His masterpieces – *Giacinta* and *Il Marchese di Roccaverdina* – reflect these values; furthermore they portray reality in an impersonal way. Even **Giovanni Verga** (1830–1922), after the Late-Romantic tone of his earlier work, demonstrates a move towards Realist

Sicilian School of Poetry

Literature developed in Frederick's court, the *Magna Curia,* as an elegant pastime for aristocrats, princes and high officials. The Sicilian poets modelled their subject matter and style on the Provençal troubadour poetry of courtly love: the sort of loving service that man, as a servant, dedicates to a Madonna. The language was a refined Sicilian, stripped of any colloquialisms, enriched instead with Latin and Provençal phraseology. Strictly literary, it excluded any form of realism, which influenced Italian lyric poetry as a whole.

Among the Sicilian School poets ranked several sovereigns: Frederick II and his sons Henry, Frederick, Manfred and Enzo king of Sardinia all wrote poetry. Other exponents of the genre include the court notary **Giacomo da Lentini**, who is regarded as the inventor of the sonnet, **Pier della Vigna** (mentioned by Dante in Inferno, Canto XIII v 25) and **Cielo d'Alcamo**, author of the famous dialogue-poem *Rosa Fresca Aulentissima*. With the decline of the *Magna Curia*, the Sicilian School's golden age came to an end.

poetry. His masterpiece – *I Malavoglia*, intended as the first part of a cycle of novels entitled *I Vinti (The Conquered)* – was followed by just one sequel *(Mastro Don Gesualdo)*. Verga's main theme concentrates on the description of the real Sicily, with the destiny of the humble folk portrayed objectively, yet compassionately. He uses a sombre writing style and a language which, when compared to the Italian mainstream, succeeds in mimicking the cadences and rhythms of the spoken vernacular. Other followers of the Realist School include **Federico de Roberto** (1861–1927) – author of *I Viceré (The Viceroys)* and *L'Illusione (The illusion)* – and the poets **Giuseppe Aurelio Costanzo** (1843–1913) and **Giovanni Alfredo Cesareo** (1861–1937).

20C

Modern Italian literature is indebted to Sicily for one of its greatest protagonists: the 1934 Nobel Prize winner **Luigi Pirandello** (1867–1946). His early work as a poet and novelist lies in the Realist vein. Later works explore the theme of isolation, painting the individual at sea in a society that is foreign to him *(Il fu Mattia Pascal, Novelle per un anno)*. This idea found its most poignant expression on stage; Pirandello's masterpieces include *Liolà, Pensaci Giacomino! (Think about it, Giacomino), Così é (se vi pare) – That's How It Is (If You Like)* and *Sei personaggi in cerca di autore (Six Characters in Search of an Author)*.

Another figure central to the history of Italian culture is the philosopher **Giovanni Gentile** (1875–1944), who, as Minister for Education in the Fascist government, promoted the reform of the Italian education system. On the opposing political front, **Concetto Marchesi** (1878–1957) published studies of the history of Latin literature still regarded as classics today.

The decadence of the Sicilian aristocracy during the Risorgimento is poignantly, if bitterly, portrayed in *Il Gattopardo (The Leopard)*, the novel by **Prince Giuseppe Tomasi di Lampedusa** (1896–1957), published posthumously. The satirical and grotesque storyteller **Vitaliano Brancati** attacked myths of eroticism and sexual conceit in his novels *(Don Giovanni in Sicilia, Il bell'Antonio* and *Paolo il Caldo)*. **Elio Vittorini** (1908–66) played a fundamental role in spreading awareness of contemporary American literature and in revitalising the Italian narrative tradition in the neo-Realist convention *(Conversazione in Sicilia, Uomini e no)*. The rough-and-ready style more often associated with police inquiries animates the novels of **Leonardo Sciascia** (1921–89), which include *Il giorno della civetta (The Day of the Owl), Todo modo* and *Candido ovvero un sogno fatto in Sicilia (Candido, or a Sicilian Dream)*. **Gesualdo Bufalino** (1920–96) is a huge literary personality, having emerged at the age of 60 with *Diceria dell'untore*. Both critics and the

© John Frumm / hemis.fr

Sicilian Puppets

The fate of puppets and marionettes in Italy took an upward turn in the 16C, when the aristocracy took an interest in marionettes. The spread to a wider audience came about in the 18C, but it was not until the mid-19C that the puppet show became a genre, complete with shiny armour, swords and agile fight scenes.

Sicilian puppet masters weave their stories around bandits, saints and Shakespearean heroes, as well as local vignettes. The favourite source of subject matter is the popular **picaresque stories of chivalry**, from the **Carolingian cycle**, in particular. The puppeteers prepare a text that follows the basic lines of the plot, and then exaggerate clashes between the paladins and infidels, as the fight is always the culmination of the show.

The puppet master also prepared various boards with panels summarising the salient elements of the story. The board, displayed outside the theatre, would act as an advertisement for the evening and also summarise for the public the story so far. In 2001, Sicilian puppet theatre was declared a masterpiece of oral tradition by UNESCO.

Principal characters

The most famous protagonists were the paladins (courtly peers) of France who, under the leadership of Charlemagne, spent their lives fighting the infidels. The show hinged on predetermined values and sentiments: there were "goodies" (the paladins), "baddies" (the infidels) and traitors, such as **Gano di Magonza**. The audience participates in the show and takes the side of one character or another. At one time puppet performances were followed so closely that the audience would immediately recognise the characters. The easiest markers are the shields: Orlando's shield has a cross, while Rinaldo and Bradamante carry shields bearing a lion.

public alike acclaimed his prose, poetry, memoirs and criticism *(Argo il cieco, Il Guerrin Meschino)*. The baroque prose of **Vincenzo Consolo** (b. 1933) is full of precise reflections on history.

The detective novels of **Andrea Camilleri** (1925), based on the fictitious character of police superintendent Montalbano, have enjoyed great suc-

cess, both in Italy and abroad. His novels are infused with musical language, rich with Sicilian expressions and vocabulary. Other works in this genre include the novels of Santo Piazzese (Palermo, 1948), which are based on Sicily's capital city.

As far as poetry is concerned, **Salvatore Quasimodo** (1901–68), awarded the

Performance

The show has three main elements: the puppet who acts on stage, the master who remains off-stage, pulls the strings and voices several characters at a time and the music. The latter emphasises the most dramatic moments, particularly when there is a duel. Stunt puppets even pull off special effects: one might lose its head or be torn asunder, another might need a disguise, turning from a pretty, angelic face to a death mask.

Two traditions

Puppets are made of wood and are jointed with metal hinges (the warriors, at least); their manipulation is controlled by lengths of wire connected to the head and right hand. There are two main schools: Palermo and Catania, which build puppets to different criteria.

The Palermo puppet is around 80cm–1m/2.5–3.25ft in height, weighs 8kg/18lb, has flexible knees and can draw and sheathe its sword. Its relative lightness makes it easy to manoeuvre: the puppet moves with agility, reacting quickly to provocation.

Palermo puppets are moved from the side and the puppet master has to stretch out his arm to reach the centre of the stage. The Catania puppet measures 1.4m/4.6ft in height and weighs between 16 and 20kg/35–44lb. Its knees are rigid and its sword is always drawn, ready to parry blows. The Acireale puppet has the same features as the Catania puppet, but the height (1.2m/4ft) and the weight (15–18kg/33–40lb) are different again.

©Photo Scala, Florence/Museo Etnografico Siciliano Pitre', Palermo

Nobel Prize for Literature in 1959, occupies a position of prime importance. His later work sought to draw attention to political and social issues (*Ed é subito sera, La terra impareggiabile, Dare e avere*). Less well known, but nevertheless of interest, is the metaphorical poetry of **Lucio Piccolo** (1903–69), cousin of Tomasi di Lampedusa and author of *Canti Barocchi and Plumelia*. A great sense of social commitment is voiced in the poetry of **Ignazio Buttitta** (1899–1997), who demonstrated once again that dialect was the best vehicle for expressing the thoughts and emotions of the Sicilian people (*Lu pani si chiama pani, La peddi nova*).

Cinema

Many famous directors have attempted to create a portrait of Sicily on film. This complex, stunningly beautiful island is inhabited by a proud, hospitable people who, despite a certain reserve, are happy to extend warmth and generosity in equal measure. Here, the conspiracy of silence known as "omertà" exists alongside an equally ardent will to fight it. Transcribing all these characteristic traits into art is no simple task.

The first great masterpieces were based on the classics: **Luchino Visconti** turned to Verga to make such films as *La Terra Trema (The Ground Trembles)* in 1948, based on his book *I Malavoglia*, and to Tomasi di Lampedusa for **Il Gattopardo** *(The Leopard)* in 1963 from the book of the same name. He was determined to capture reality in all its guises, while peppering it with local colour and poetry. Visconti therefore selected his main cast from amateur actors living in a typical community, such as Aci Trezza, who spoke in dialect. He also chose a historical epic that was respected and established in its own right, set in the magnificent, yet already decadent Palermo of the late 19C. This he then illuminated with sparkling performances by Claudia Cardinale, Burt Lancaster and Alain Delon.

In the same vein is the sad and agonising tale recounted in **Stromboli terra**

Nuovo Cinema Paradiso

© Photos 12 / Alamy / Cristaldifilm / Films Ariane

di Dio (1949). This strong portrait of a woman, filmed against a background of untamed nature, was directed by **Roberto Rossellini** and starred Ingrid Bergmann. Films about the Mafia are a case apart. Since the making of the films-cum-denunciations – **In nome della legge** *(In the Name of the Law)*, directed by Pietro Germi (1949), and **Salvatore Giuliano**, directed by Francesco Rosi (1961), the subject matter and circumstances quickly transformed into an entire genre, which for Italian viewers compares well with the popular Spaghetti Western elsewhere. This in turn generated a veritable industry of Mafia family epics with the inevitable shoot-outs, clashes and use of broad Sicilian dialect.

These films were distributed all over the world, giving a somewhat negative impression of the island. However, also belonging to this genre are works of social importance, such as **I cento passi** *(One Hundred Steps)* directed by Tullio Giordana (best screenplay in the 2000 Venice Film Festival), which skilfully recounts the story of the journalist Peppino Impastato, who was killed in 1978 after many years of opposing the Mafia.

A very different Sicily appears on the cinema screen: one that is mournful, but veined with humour emerges in the magnificent tales retold in **Kaos** *(Chaos)*, made in 1984 by the **Taviani brothers**, based on novels by Pirandello (with brilliant performances by Franco Franchi and Ciccio Ingrassia in *La Giara)*. A poetic view is portrayed in Michael Radford's **Il Postino** *(The Postman),* made in 1994 and starring Massimo Troisi, and in Giuseppe Tornatore's **Nuovo Cinema Paradiso** (1989), which received an Oscar for Best Foreign Film in 1990. An ironic Sicily – "in search of its lost tranquillity" – is shown in the Isole episode (about the Aeolian Islands) in *Caro Diario* (1993) by Nanni Moretti and in the very funny *Tano da Morire* (1997), a musical about the Mafia by Roberta Torre. In 2000, Bagheria-born director Giuseppe Tornatore scored a European hit with *Malèna* starring Monica Bellucci.

Nature

Emerald pastures unfold above the sparkling Mediterranean, while prickly pears cling to slopes scorched by volcanic lava. White almond blossom dots the terrain like snowflakes. Of all Italy's provinces, Sicily, with its wild beauty, lives closest to nature. Seasons bring myriad colours and changes to the landscape: the yellow broom, mimosa and sweetly scented orange blossom of spring; the red poppies, bougainvillea and green meadows of early summer and the ochre-coloured earth of early autumn burned by a relentless sun. On this island of beaches and mountains, in just a few miles you can travel from the heights of magnificent Mount Etna *(Sicily's highest peak at over 3,000m/10,000ft and the highest volcano in Europe)* to a secluded, sandy bay on the coast. Best of all, the wild scenery is tempered with all the *dolce vita* comforts at which Italians excel.

LANDSCAPE

Sicily is the largest island of the Mediterranean (25,709sqkm/9,926sqmi).

It is separated from the Italian peninsula by the Straits of Messina – a mere 3km/1.8mi at the widest point – and from Africa, about 140km/87mi away, by the Sicily Canal. The island is more or less triangular in shape, its long sides fronting the Tyrrhenian Sea in the north and the Sicily Canal to the south. The short side fringes the Ionian Sea to the east. Under Muslim occupation, the island was divided into three large "valleys" or provinces: the **Val di Mazara** to the west, **Val Demone** in the northeast and the **Val di Noto** to the southeast.

AN ISLAND AMONG ISLANDS

The region of Sicily includes many minor islands: off the northern coast, in the Tyrrhenian Sea, are the Aeolian or Lipari Islands (northeast) and Ustica (northwest); the Egadi lie to the west, close to the Trapanese Coast. To the south, in the Sicily Canal, lie Pantelleria and the Pelagian Islands, including Lampedusa (113km/70mi from Tunisia and 205km/128mi from the Sicilian coast). **Ferdinandea Island** (originally claimed by the British as "Graham Island" and by the French as "Ile de Giulia") is a tiny outcrop that surfaced off Sciacca's coast in 1831, only to sink again a few months later. It now lies 7m/22ft below sea level.

Marina Corta, Lipari, Isole Eolie

© Jean-Pierre Degas / hemis.fr

© Sabrina Dvihally/Dreamstime.com

Beach of Capo Bianco on the south coast

SANDY BEACHES AND ROCKY CLIFFS

The Sicilian coastline stretches over some 1,000km/621mi. The northern or Tyrrhenian flank extends from Cape Peloro, near Messina, to Cape Lilibeo in the vicinity of Marsala: here, the rocks are uniformly high and protrude jaggedly out into the sea.

In contrast, the short western coast between Trapani and Marsala is flat and dotted with saltpans. The southern shoreline remains flat and mainly sandy all the way out to Capo Passero, the far southwestern spur of the island. Resorts such as Mazzara del Vallo, Sciacca and Gela dominate the broad bay that lies between Licata and Marina di Ragusa. The eastern coast facing the Ionian Sea is low-lying at first, shaped into a succession of three broad sweeps: the Gulf of Noto, the Gulf of Augusta and the great Gulf of Catania, which provides Sicily's largest plain with a sea front. North of Catania, the shoreline to Messina consists once more of high cliffs broken by a series of craggy inlets. As Etna's tall black lava flows give way to the Peloritani Mountain limestone *(an extension of the Calabrian Apennines)*, a number of huge, steep cliffs plunge down to the sea, bestowing a matchless beauty on the landscape, especially at Taormina and Acireale.

MOUNTAINS AND VALLEYS

The Sicilian land mass is predominantly hilly (62% of the surface area); 24% is mountainous, with the remainder classified as plain or lowland. The highest outcrop is Etna, with an altitude of 3,323m/10,902ft. This mountain dominates the skyline from almost every viewpoint on the island. North of Etna, separated from the Alcantara Valley, rise the precipitous heights of Sicily's principal mountain range, which runs some 200km/124mi parallel to the Tyrrhenian Coast. The **Appennino Siculo** fall into three distinctive sections: the western portion constitutes the **Monti Peloritani**, which lie between Messina and Patti; the highest peak is Montagna Grande *(1,374m/4,507ft)*. This relief does not rise to any great altitude; in contrast with a steeply angular and craggy profile, its lower slopes have been eroded by powerful streams. The range extends westward with the **Monti Nebrodi**; these have gentler slopes and rounded, densely wooded summits, which culminate in Monte Soro *(1,847m/6,060ft)*. West of the Nebrodi come the **Madonie**; these include several high peaks, such as Carbonara *(1,979m/6,491ft)*, the second-highest summit on the island. The vast area between Termini Imerese and the Trapanese consists of gently undulating hills and broad valleys. This is rudely broken by three minor massifs: the **Monti Termini Imerese**, **Monti di Palermo** and **Monti di Trapani**.

The south is a vast open region of arid upland (often called the *solfiferi* or *solfataras* after the high levels of sulphur deposits in the area), which stretches from Marsala to Caltanissetta. The only mountains in the area are the **Sicani Mountains** behind Agrigento and the **Monti Erei** to the east of Caltanissetta. In the southwestern corner of the island are the massive calcareous (limestone) Monti Iblei, rising to 1,000m/3,300ft.

Sicily's largest expanse of lowland plain is the **Piana di Catania**, which extends from the southern lower slopes of Etna to the foothills of the Iblei range. Crisscrossed by large rivers, the plain is renowned for being especially fertile and is intensively farmed (citrus, fruit and market gardening).

RIVERS AND LAKES

Sicily's lack of water has been a major problem throughout its history. The land here has limited permeability, rainfall is erratic and water distribution poorly managed. Although numerous, the rivers that run into the Tyrrhenian Sea are short and flow quickly to the sea. The aquifer of the southern slopes feeds a more extensive system of sunken wells, natural springs and sluggish rivers. The rivers **Gornalunga**, **Dittaino** and **Simeto** irrigate the fertile plain of Catania before flowing into the Ionian. Sicily has almost no natural lakes (except **Lago di Pergusa**); however, man-made reservoirs nestle among the mountains. Brackish ponds – known as **bivieri** or **pantani** – form behind the dunes along the shore. A few survive on the southeastern coast of the island and near Capo Peloro.

VOLCANOES

According to mythology, Sicily's underworld was inhabited by the god of fire, Hephaestus, and his team of giant blacksmiths, who worked the forge to make the weapons of the gods.

The Ancient Greeks attributed the volcanic rumblings to the underground anvil and forge, while eruptions from Mount Etna were furnace sparks.

VOLCANOLOGY
Volcanic Activity

Traditionally, there are four types of volcanic explosion: Plinian, Hawaiian, Strombolian and Vulcanian. The last two take their name from the volcanoes on the Aeolian Islands, where the phenomena were first observed.

The **Strombolian**, peculiar to the volcano on Stromboli, has phases of

Sulfur vapor at the top of Vulcano, Lipari Island

© R.Gerth / age fotostock

persistent, moderate explosions, followed by periods of idleness. Large gas build-ups suddenly release, like a pressure cooker and these eruptions can project tall fountains of lava up to several hundred metres.

First observed on the island of Vulcano in 1888, **hydrovolcanic**, or Vulcanian, eruptions expel lava and pyroclastics (solid fragments suspended in clouds of dense gas that reach exceptionally high temperatures) down the volcano's slopes at speeds that can reach up to 300m/330yd per second.

Volcanic Fallout

Volcanoes belch three types of matter: lava, pyroclastics and gas (including smoke, steam and chemical vapours). **Lava** consists of magma, which flows and folds around any obstacles, quickly cooling into glassy smooth stone like obsidian. In contrast, viscous lava sludges overground with difficulty, breaking into blocks. Both types appear on Etna, as well as lava tunnels in the gorges of the Alcantara and at the Faraglioni dei Ciclopi.

By-products of explosive eruption are generally classified as **pyroclastics**. The blast lifts rock fragments from the immediate environment, crystals (solidified particles in the magma or granite) and **juvenile** formations or tuff (consolidated volcanic fragments and solidified magma), which include various types of ash, lapilli and volcanic bombs, depending on size. Should the discharge cool rapidly, it

Zeus and Typhon

In his *Metamorphoses*, Ovid recounts the struggle between Zeus and the giant Typhon (or Typhoeus), in which the god overcomes the giant by crushing him with the island of Sicily: "Because Typhon dared to covet the divine throne, his gigantic limbs were crushed under the vast land mass of Sicily. The giant often fights and struggles to release himself, but his right hand is held down by Peloro, his left by Pachino, his legs are weighed down by Lilibeo and his head by Etna. Typhon lies helpless under this great weight, furiously kicking sand and vomiting flames from his mouth."

Isole Eolie o Lipari
I. di Stromboli 924
I. di Basiluzzo
I. di Panarea
I. di Salina 962
I. di Filicudi
I. di Lipari
I. di Alicudi
I. di Vulcano

TIRRENO

Capo Peloro
MESSINA
Capo di Milazzo
Reggio di Calabria

Capo Calavà
G. di Patti
M. PELORITANI

Golfo di Palermo
Golfo di Termini Imerese
Capo d'Orlando
Patti
Montagna Grande 1374
Taormina

Capo Zafferano
Cefalù
VAL DEMONE
NEBRODI
M.Soro 1847
Alcantara
MARE

Termini
P.zo Carbonara 1979
M. ETNA

Rocca Busambra 1613
MADONIE
Torto
MONTI EREI
Lago di Pozzillo
SIMETO
Acireale
IONIO

1578
M. Cammarata
Caltanissetta
Enna
Dittaino
Piana di Catania
Gornalunga
CATANIA
Golfo di Catania

Salso
L. di Pergusa

Platani
Agrigento
Piana
di
VAL DI
M.Lauro 986
MONTI IBLEI
Anapo
Siracusa
C. Murro di Porco

Gela
Gela
NOTO
Noto
Golfo di Noto

MEDITERRANEO
Golfo di Gela
Ragusa
Capo Scaramia
Capo Passero

solidifies into a dense formation such as obsidian or lava glass; should it cool slowly, trapped gases can bubble out, imparting a distinct sponge-like appearance, as in the case of pumice and scoria.

Eruptions also release great quantities of volcanic vapour – indeed, sometimes only this material spouts. Both Etna and Vulcano have intensively active vents or fumeroles that expel **hot gases** like carbon, hydrogen and sulphur.

VOLCANIC AREAS OF SICILY
Aeolian Islands

A volcanic fault, a result of the collision between ocean and continental crust, arcs some 200km/124mi in a semicircle and comprises eight separate islands *(the seven Aeolians, plus Ustica)* and many submerged volcanoes. The still-active **Stromboli**, was in fact created by 100,000 years of volcanic layers. According to classical mythology, the Aeolian islands were the home of Aeolus, ruler of the winds, who forecast the weather by interpreting the shape of the cloud rising from Stromboli. A more prosaic explanation for the cloud's shape is found in the influence of atmospheric pressure on it. Today the active craters, which vary in number and position, emerge at about 700m/2,300ft up the Sciara del Fuoco. At a distance

Bocca Nova crater, Mount Etna

© Henri Faure / iStockphoto.com

of 1.5km/1mi off the northeastern coast of Stromboli sits **Strombolicchio:** the outcrop is over 40m/130ft high and is all that remains of the volcano's original core.

Mount Etna

Mount Etna (also known as *Muncibeddu* in Sicilian dialect and *Mongibello* in Italian) is Europe's largest active volcano and one of the most active in the world, being in an almost constant state of eruption. It rises to a height of over 3,300m/10,900ft from a base diameter of about 40km/25mi, with rich, fertile volcanic soils on its lower slopes supporting vineyards and extensive agricultural production. The volcano's activity started 600,000 years ago, following movement between the tectonic plates: this released magma through the ocean floor into the Aci Castello area, and caused surges of lava that settled near present-day Patern. During the past 100,000 years, the activity has shifted westward. The mountain's present profile is largely the result of an explosion about 14,000 years ago, when the Cratere Ellittico (or elliptical crater) came into being. Etna's summit comprises four active craters: (Cratere di Sud-Est, Bocca Nuova, Voragine, Cratere di Nord-Est). Eruptions also occur periodically on the flanks of the volcano, due to some 300 vents ranging in diameter from small holes to larger craters.

Sicily Canal

The Sicily Canal harbours two volcanic islands, Pantelleria and Linosa, and many submarine outcrops (also known as seamounts). A rift between the continental shelves of Sicily and Tunisia is the genesis of all this excitement. Its most recent landscaping efforts include the emergence of the small island of Ferdinandea, some 50km/31mi northeast of Pantelleria, in 1831. This was the fifth time the island mass had risen above the waves since volcanic activity was first documented here, around the time of the First Punic War. Its reappearance sparked a territorial dispute over sovereignty. However, before the issue of ownership could be resolved, the island disappeared again, slipping below the water just five months later, where it remains today, lying some 7m/22ft below the surface. There was also significant activity in 1891, on the sea bed approximately 7km/4mi northwest of Pantelleria. In 2006, scientists identified these fissures as one giant underwater volcano. Named in honour of the Greek philosopher Empedocles, it has a base larger than the city of Rome.

FLORA AND FAUNA

The mild climate of Sicily nurtures a fairly typical range of Mediterranean flora. The most common species found include **myrtle** *(Myrtus)*, **strawberry tree** *(Arbutus)*, **lentisk** *(Pistacia len-*

tiscus) and **tree spurge** (Euphorbia dendroides) – a bush that grows to a height of 1.5m/5ft. In springtime, sun-drenched hillsides are set ablaze with yellow-flowering, sweet-smelling broom bushes (Ginestra cinera). These species alternate with such imports as the evergreen, river-bed loving **olender** (Nerium); the **carob tree** (Ceratonia) that produces toffee-brown bean pods, populating the landscape around Ragusa; the more formal **gum** or **eucalyptus** with its weeping branches and aromatic leaves; the tall pyramidal **maritime pine** (Pinus pinaster); and the majestic **stone or umbrella pine** (Pinus pinea). The **wild olive** (Olea oleaster) grows everywhere: this spiny shrub produces rather mean, less fleshy fruits than its cultivated cousin.

Large tracts of land are devoted to **vineyards**, groves of **olive trees** (Olea) that twist with age and **citrus trees** (lemons; sweet, blood and Seville oranges; mandarins. Note: here "giardino" describes a citrus grove and not an ornamental garden, as elsewhere in Italy).

In the more arid areas thorny plants are common, such as varieties of thistle (Silybum), **palms** and **dwarf palms** – a perennial typical of the Zingaro area (so much so that it has been chosen as the symbol of the nature reserve). A broad range of succulent plants encompass the huge **agave** or **century plant**, **cactuses** and the ubiquitous **prickly pears** (Opuntia – known locally as Fico d'India).

The first signs of spring, heralded by meadows of wild garlic and oxalis, stir the **almond trees** (especially around Agrigento) into clouds of white blossom. Next comes the fluffy yellow mimosa and the sweet-smelling, crisp white **orange blossom**, from which bees produce a particularly fragrant honey. Soon the pinks and reds of the **oleanders** and **hibiscus** mark the advent of summer. They are joined by garishly purple, puce and magenta **bougainvilleas** and the intensely perfumed **jasmine**, which blinks open its starry flowers all over the main island – but most especially in Pantelleria and the Aeolian Islands. Throughout the summer, stone walls sprout cascades of round-leafed **caper plants**. Chefs steal the buds long before the exquisite, pinkish white flowers can flourish.

Each region has its local flora, such as the **cork plantations** near Niscemi (inland from Gela), **papyrus** plants along the River Ciane (just outside Siracusa) and the **ash tree manna** grown in the Castelbuono area of the Madonie.

Agave

After a long period of vegetation – lasting up to 50 years – the agave plant produces a lengthy stem. Shaped like a candelabra, it can grow to a height of 6–8m/20–26ft.

Highly scented flowers blossom along this stem, just before the plant dies. Legend compares the agave plant with a young girl, who having waited years to get married, dies a year after her wedding.

© M. Magni / MICHELIN

Castellammare del Golfo, Golfo di Castellammare, near Palermo
© Ian Murray / age fotostock

PALERMO AND ITS SURROUNDINGS

The capital of Sicily and its surrounding area are an almost overwhelming tableaux of contrasts, where history meets infamy, splendour meets squalor, and the stillness of the local hill towns clashes with the riot of traffic in the city centre. You can spend the morning in one of Palermo's raucous street markets, the afternoon marvelling at the ornate mosaics of Monreale's 12C cathedral and return to town for an evening stroll past Palermo's evocative Arabo-Norman palaces, its Liberty-style villas, Baroque churches and piazzas. Palermo is, in many ways, a microcosm of Sicily, occupied by many – Phoenicians, Greeks, Romans, Byzantines, Arabs, Normans, Aragonese, French, Bourbons (and the Piemontese of Northern Italy when the country was unified in 1861) – but never exactly conquered. It seems to have taken something from every successive civilisation while discarding what it had no use for. This melting pot is visible in the customs and way of life of its people, architecture and cuisine. One of Palermo's most popular dishes is *pasta con le sarde* - sardines tossed with tomatoes, wild fennel, pine nuts, raisins and saffron - which mixes historic influences, sweet and savoury flavours and the fruits of sea and earth with compelling results.

Highlights

A safe city

For a city with such a grand aristocratic tradition, Palermo is surprisingly down-to-earth. It also has a more provincial, safer feel compared to the largest southern Italian cities. Women can be seen walking alone late at night, for example, and the *Palermitani* can be very frank on all subjects, whether talking about food, politics or the Mafia.

Mafia links

This region is perhaps best known for the organised crime groups that took Palermo hostage for decades after World War II. In the late 1950s–early 1960s, during the "Sack of Palermo", the city's green belt was flattened by corrupt city officials to make way for cheap concrete structures built by Mafia interests. Two Mafia wars in the early 1960s and early 1980s turned Palermo into a near war zone, and it was only the 1992 assassinations of two popular anti-Mafia judges, Giovanni Falcone and Paolo Borsellino, that led the Italian state to act by arresting Mafia boss Salvatore Riina in 1993 in Palermo, where he had spent decades living as a fugitive. After many years, the anti-Mafia movement has taken hold with the backing of the mayor and anti-crime organisations. **Libera Terra** (*see p164*) was founded with the idea of taking seized Mafia lands and turning them over to wine and olive production.

Culture of cuisine

If you want to understand this region, you need to spend a certain amount of time at its dinner tables or exploring

Piazza Pretoria, Palermo

© Giacomo Costa / Fotolia.com

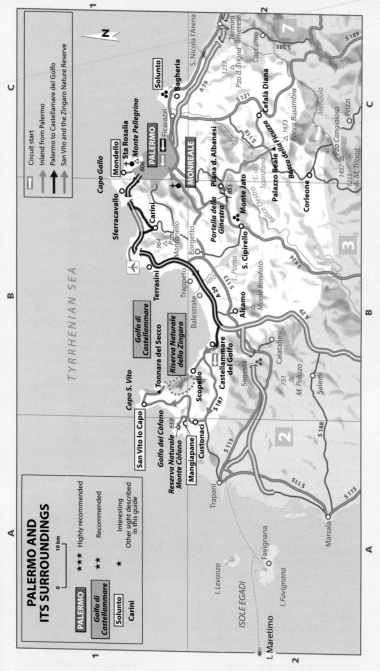

PALERMO AND ITS SURROUNDINGS

0	10 km

PALERMO	Highly recommended
Golfo di Castellammare	★★★
Soluto	Recommended
Carini	★★
	Interesting
	★
	Other sight described in this guide

Circuit start

Inland from Palermo

Palermo to Castellammare del Golfo

San Vito and the Zingaro Nature Reserve

TYRRHENIAN SEA

ISOLE EGADI

its public markets. Palermo's markets are an exotic mix of southern Italian and North African influences, and are popular with everyone from youths on scooters to elegant grandmothers, offering a window into Sicily's cultural and historic roots extending back over millennia.

Palermo★★★

Palermo, the capital and chief seaport of Sicily, is nestled in a delightful **setting★★** at the head of a wide bay enclosed to the north by Monte Pelligrino and to the south by Capo Zafferano. It lies on the edge of a wonderfully fertile plain, bounded by hills and nicknamed the Conca d'Oro (Golden Basin or horn of plenty), where lush citrus plantations, palm trees and olive groves flourish.

A BIT OF HISTORY

The Phoenicians, who laid the foundations of the city in the 7C BC, called it "Ziz", meaning flower. In time, it was conquered by the Romans, who gave it the name "Panormus" (from the Greek meaning "large port or rock") from which "Palermo" (corrupted by the introduction of the Arabic name *Balharm*) was eventually derived. The city's Golden Age began under Arab domination (9C), when it was established as one of the main Islamic centres in the West. The town expanded as new quarters were developed beyond the old centre, known as the "Cassaro" (from the Arabic *Qasr* meaning castle); the Kalsa (from *al Halisah* – the chosen one), in particular, flourished by the seafront and provided a residence for the Emir.

In 1072, the city fell to the Norman **Count Roger**, but the transfer was peaceful as merchants, artisans and Muslims were permitted to continue to live and practise their chosen professions. Indeed, it was precisely this magnanimity that made it possible for the Arabo-Norman decorative and structural style to develop. **Roger II**, son of Count Roger, who harboured a predilection for luxury, built Oriental-style gardens to complement his palaces (La Zisa and La Cuba). After a short period of disorder and decadence, Palermo and Sicily passed into the hands of Frederick II of Swabia (1212), under whom the city regained its importance and vigour. The Swabians were succeeded by the Angevins, in turn driven out by the Spaniards at the end of

▶ **Population:** 659 433

Michelin Map: p119; C1; 365 AO-AP 55.

Info: Piazza Castelnuovo 34 ☏091 60 58 351, www.comune.palermo.it.

▶ **Location:** The Viale Regione Siciliana, an extension of the A19 motorway, runs through the outskirts of the city. The historical centre is clustered around the crossroads of the two main streets, Corso Vittorio Emanuele and Via Maqueda; from the Viale Regione Siciliana, take the Corso Calatafimi exit (this street runs into Corso Vittorio Emanuele).

P **Parking:** Parking can be difficult. Visitors are advised to park in a car park on the outskirts of the city *(marked by a P on the map).*

Don't Miss: The vibrant renaissance of the **Kalsa** district, Baroque splendour at the **Oratorio del Rosario di Santa Cita**, fine frescoes at the **Galleria Regionale di Sicilia** and Sicilian artefacts at the **Museo Archeologico Regionale**. Outside the city, take in the macabre **Catacombe dei Cappuccini** with its 8 000 interred friars and the sulphurous Turkish baths at **Cefala Diana**.

Kids: International Puppet Museum and puppet collections and theatres at Teatro di Mimmo Cuticchio, Teatro Ippogrifo and Teatroarte-Cuticchio.

Timing: Most churches are open in the morning and late afternoon. Allow one day for an inland driving tour from Palermo, taking in Monreale, Bosco della Ficuzza and Cefala Diana.

Death by tongue-twister

Sicilian Vespers – Charles of Anjou arrived in Palermo in 1266, supported by the Pope. The Sicilians held the French in scorn and nicknamed them *tartaglioni* (stutterers) because of their inability to pronounce Italian. In 1282, on Easter Monday, in front of the Church of Santo Spirito, just as the bell was calling the faithful to Vespers, a French soldier directed an insult at a Sicilian woman, thereby sparking off indignation in the crowd. The situation deteriorated and with the help of the local aristocracy, the quarrel was transformed into a revolt which then spread throughout Sicily. Any Frenchmen unable to correctly pronounce the word *cicero* were massacred, while the others were driven out. Eventually Peter of Aragon, husband of Costanza d'Altavilla, the daughter of Manfred (the Swabian king ousted by the Angevins), was called upon to rule the island.

the War of the Sicilian Vespers. In the 18C the city fell to the Bourbons of Naples, who embellished it with Baroque palaces.

The 19C heralded the opening of the city to trade and relations with Europe, and the entrepreneurial bourgeoisie became the new economic driving force. Soon the city outgrew its boundaries. The Viale della Libertà, an extension of Via Maqueda, was inaugurated; the surrounding district mushroomed, populated with elegant Liberty-style buildings. Sadly, this was to be the final flurry before a period of stagnation. The bombing raids of 1943 badly damaged the historical centre, destruction that was followed by an earthquake in 1968. The construction of large and modern – now crumbling – buildings in the suburbs did nothing to improve its image. Today, this trend is being reversed as a new sense of determination prompts a re-evaluation and restoration of its magnificent monuments in an attempt to stir the wonderful giant of the East from its protracted slumber.

The Mandamenti – Palermo is centred on the intersection of two main streets: Corso Vittorio Emanuele and Via Maqueda.

View of the street in the historic centre

© John Frumm / hemis.fr

GETTING THERE

BY AIR – This is certainly the easiest and quickest way to get to Palermo. **Falcone-Borsellino** airport *(once known as Punta-Raisi airport; www.gesap.it)* is 30km/19mi north of Palermo, on the A29 motorway. It is served by a number of airlines operating both domestic and international flights.

There are a number of **car rental** agencies at the airport:
Avis ℘091 59 16 84
Europcar ℘091 59 16 88
Hertz ℘091 21 31 12
Holiday ℘091 59 16 87
Maggiore ℘091 59 16 81
Sicily by Car ℘091 59 12 50
Connections with the city centre – A bus links the airport with the city centre every 30min from 5am until the arrival of the last flight of the day, stopping in via Libertà, via Amari, piazza Ruggero-Settimo, gare centrale. The journey takes 50 minutes and costs €6.10. Contact **Prestia e Commandè, Stazione Centrale**; ℘091 58 04 57. The cost of a **taxi** from the airport to the city is about €45. Beware of individuals who offer transport at lower prices.

BY CAR – Close to Palermo the motorway joins the ring road around the city *(the Viale Regione Siciliana)*, from where various exits lead to most of the major sites of interest. The **Corso Calatafimi** exit is the most convenient for the historical centre, as this road eventually continues into **Corso Vittorio Emanuele**, one of the main streets through the old town.

Car Parks The difficulty in finding somewhere to park in Palermo discourages many visitors from driving. Large car parks are found on the outskirts of the city *(marked P on the map)*. The following guarded car parks are situated in the old town: **Piazza Giulio Cesare 43** *(railway station)*; **Via Guardione 81** *(running parallel with Via Cavour to the north,* *in the port area)*; **Via Archimede 88** *(north of Politeama)*; **Via Sammartino 24** *(northwest of Teatro Massimo)*. These car parks cost about €20 for 24hr but often have special arrangements with hotels nearby.
☺ *Do not leave luggage or valuables in your car.*

BY BOAT – Ferries leave for Palermo from **Genova** *(Grandi Navi Veloci, 20hr)*; **Livorno** *(Grandi Navi Veloci, three times a week, 19hr)*; Naples *(Tirrenia, 10hr and SNAV, 11hr, plus a fast service, Apr–Oct, 5hr 30min)*; Cagliari *(Tirrenia, once a week, 13hr 30min)*.
For information and reservations, contact: **Grandi Navi Veloci** ℘010 55 091 or 899 199 069; www1.gnv.it.
SNAV, Stazione Marittima, Napoli; ℘081 42 85 555; www.snav.it.
Tirrenia, Molo Angioino, Napoli; ℘199 123 199; www.tirrenia.it.
BY BUS – There is a direct daily service between **Rome** *(Stazione Tiburtina)* and **Palermo** *(Via P. Balsamo 26)*, operated by Sais Trasporti (℘091 617 11 41; www.saistrasporti.it)*; departs from Rome at 9pm and arrives in Palermo at 5.30pm the next day, €47 single journey. Palermo can also be reached from all other major towns in Sicily: SAIS operates services to Messina, Enna, Gela and Piazza Amerina; ℘091 61 66 028; www.saisautolinee.it.
BY TRAIN – Travelling to Sicily by train from mainland Italy involves crossing the **Straits of Messina**; the train drives directly onto the ferry *(crossing is included in the price)*. For information, contact the **Italian State Railways** *(Ferrovie dello Stato), www.trenitalia. com)*. For visitors travelling within Sicily, Palermo has connections with Messina *(approx. 3hr)*, Caltanissetta *(approx. 2hr)* and Catania *(over 3hr, infrequent service)*. Palermo's **main railway station** is situated in Piazza Giulio Cesare.

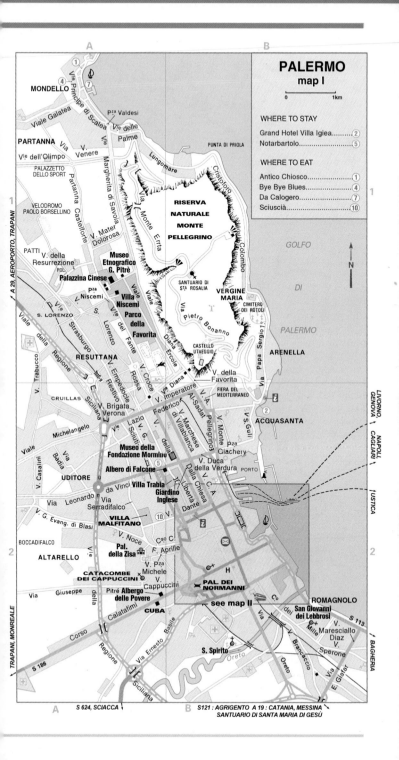

PALERMO
map I

0   1km

WHERE TO STAY

Grand Hotel Villa Igiea..........②
Notarbartolo........................⑤

WHERE TO EAT

Antico Chiosco....................①
Bye Bye Blues.....................④
Da Calogero........................⑦
Sciuscià............................⑩

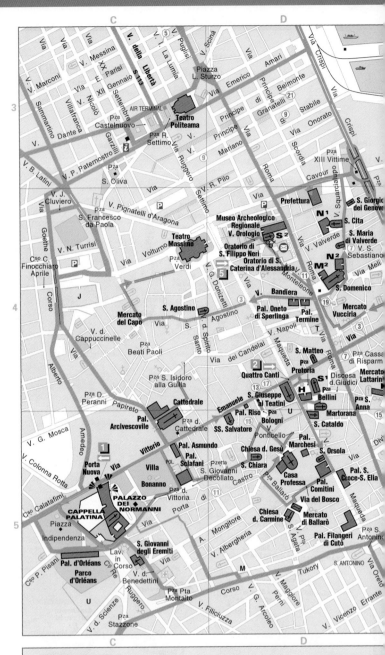

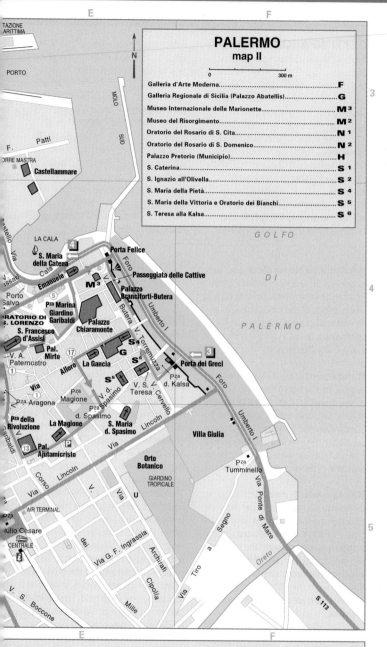

PALERMO
map II

0   300 m

Galleria d'Arte Moderna..**F**
Galleria Regionale di Sicilia (Palazzo Abatellis)...................**G**
Museo Internazionale delle Marionette.............................**M³**
Museo del Risorgimento..**M²**
Oratorio del Rosario di S. Cita..**N¹**
Oratorio del Rosario di S. Domenico...................................**N²**
Palazzo Pretorio (Municipio)...**H**
S. Caterina..**S¹**
S. Ignazio all'Olivella..**S²**
S. Maria della Pietà...**S⁴**
S. Maria della Vittoria e Oratorio dei Bianchi.....................**S⁵**
S. Teresa alla Kalsa...**S⁶**

GETTING AROUND

It is best to avoid driving in Palermo because of the traffic congestion and the difficulty of parking. The best way to see the city is on foot or using public transport or taxis for longer distances. An enjoyable alternative is one of the horse-drawn carriages available for hire outside the central station or elsewhere in the city. It is advisable to agree a price in advance.

BY BUS – Palermo's city bus services are operated by AMAT, (℘091 35 01 11 or 848 800 817; www.amat.pa.it.), which offers two types of bus ticket: one valid for up to 90 minutes (€1.30) or a 12-hour ticket (€3.50); 20 single tickets €23.50) can be bought from tobacconists or newsagents.

RADIO TAXIS – Two main taxi firms are Autoradio Taxi (℘091 51 31 11); Radio Taxi Trinacria (℘091 22 68 78).

BY CAR – Leave your car parked while in Palermo, either at a hotel garage or in a car park on the edge of town. After 7am traffic can be intense and parking places are rare. To park on public streets, buy a ticket in a *tabaccaio* (tobacconist shop).

Mandamento Monte di Pietà or Capo, to the northwest, was an area mostly inhabited by the Islamic population and where much of the city's artisanal and commercial activity took place. This is still the case today, as revealed by a visit to the lively Capo market.

Mandamento Castellammare or Loggia, to the northeast, was spoiled by the opening of Via Roma at the end of the 19C and badly damaged by bombing in 1943. Formerly a port, it once bustled with merchants from Amalfi, Pisa and Genoa, whose legacy can be explored in the historic Vucciria market.

Mandamento Tribunali or Kalsa, to the southeast, takes its name from the Court of the Inquisition, whose head-quarters were in the Palazzo Chiara-monte. It grew up around the Kalsa, the fortified citadel, and Via Alloro, along which noble mansions were built in the 15C. From the 18C onwards, *palazzi* with wide terraces were built along the seafront.

🐾 WALKING TOURS

Unless otherwise stated, churches are open in the morning and late afternoon.

1 THE HISTORIC QUARTER

Circuit in green on the map on p124. Allow 4hr.

Palazzo Dei Normanni, Cappella Palatina★★★

Open Mon–Sat 8.15am–5.45pm, Sun and hols 8.15am–1pm. ⊛€8.50 (Fri–Mon), €7 (Tue–Sat). ℘091 62 62 833. www.federicosecondo.org.

The **Norman Palace** is located at the heart of the original town, probably on a site occupied in Punic times by a fortress. The earliest documents, however, date from the Arab occupation and confirm this to be where the Emir's palace was once situated.

The castle was eventually abandoned and the Emir's residence transferred to the Kalsa. The area returned to favour when the Normans re-established a royal seat here, having extended and embellished the palace. Life in the palace revolved around the green hall, in which regal ceremonies, assemblies and banquets were held. The building comprised various wings assigned to different people and functions, interconnected by a terrace or garden ornamented with fountains. Four towers punctuated the corners: the Greek, the Pisan, the Joaria (from the Arabic for airy) and the Kirimbi. Sadly, only the central part of the original complex survives today, together with the Pisan Tower. The palace was then abandoned

Mosaics in Cappella Palatina

© Franck Guiziou / hemis.fr

and fell into disrepair until the 17C, when the Spanish viceroys restored it and added the impressive south front and courtyard with its loggias.

Today, the *palazzo* serves as the seat of the Sicilian Parliament.

Cappella Palatina

On the first floor (take the staircase on the left).

Before entering the Palatine Chapel, take a moment to admire the superb **courtyard** enclosed by three superimposed loggias. The chapel was built by Roger II between 1130 – the year of his coronation – and 1140. It initially stood alone, but was gradually incorporated into a complex of other buildings so that it is now completely concealed. What can still be seen is the exterior of the side wall *(corresponding to the north aisle)* with its two-tier decoration. The lower section echoes the decorative arrangement at the same level inside: slabs of white marble surrounded by *pietra dura* decoration (an inlay of semi-precious stones). The upper tier comprises 19C composite panels depicting scenes from the life of David. At the rear, Roger II is depicted handing a decree to the *ciantro* (literally a singer, but in this case, the person in charge of the chapel).

The Arabo-Norman interior decor of blazing gold offset by the marble is particularly notable.

Structure – The internal space, with its rectangular ground plan, is divided into two parts: the first section is split into three aisles by 10 granite columns; the second comprises the chancel, which is contained within a marble balustrade. On the right, near the division of the two halves, is the double **ambo** (a raised stand for reading the Gospel), supported by four columns and two small pilasters, with integrated lecterns borne by the eagle of St John and the lion of St Mark. To one side is the richly-decorated Paschal **candlestick** (12C). Above, Christ sits in a mandorla supported by angels holding the Gospels in his hand, while below, a figure in bishop's clothing kneels before him (possibly Roger II himself). Two tiers of birds (vultures pecking the tails of slender storks) support three figures representing the three ages of man.

Set against the back wall of the chapel is the majestic **royal throne**, which also forms an integral part of the mosaic above depicting Christ seated, attended by the Archangels St Michael and St Gabriel (representing death and birth respectively) and by the Apostles St Peter and St Paul. The actual throne is inlaid with mosaic and porphyry; a coat-of-arms in the centre is that of the House of Aragon.

The remarkable **wooden muqarnas ceiling★★** in the central nave is a masterpiece by North African artists and depicts a number of scenes from daily life: courtly and hunting scenes, drinking, dancing, games of chess, animals, etc. This exceptional work of art comprises the most extensive cycle of Fatimid painting to have survived to the present day.

Mosaics – The exquisite mosaics comprise tesserae of coloured paste (cement and pigment) and glass with delicate gold-leaf application. They recount the story of the Old Testament *(nave)* and the lives of Christ *(chancel)*, St Peter and St Paul *(aisles)*.

The mosaics were executed in different phases: the oldest ones date from the 1140s, the ones in the nave are from 1160–1170, and the sequence of scenes in the nave is didactic. Of particular note is the illustration of the earth being separated from the sea: the terrestrial globe is shown as a sphere of water in which there are three areas of land (America and Oceania had not yet been discovered). These are divided by the sea, which takes the form of a "Y" – the symbol of the Holy Trinity; the firmament is not yet illuminated by stars. Look out for the **Creation of Adam**: note the striking resemblance of the face of Adam to that of God, thereby underlining the inscription in Latin: *"creavit ds ominem at imaginem sua"* (And God created Man in His own image). The scene recounting the story of **Original Sin** is unusual since both Adam and Eve are shown with the forbidden fruit in their mouths. The section following on from the second half of the panel illustrating the **Sacrifice of Cain and Abel** up to the scene showing Noah and his family was substantially remodelled in the 19C: this is evident from the radical change in style.

To read the Old Testament scenes in the nave, begin from the top of the right-hand side of the nave and follow the length of the top register along the left-hand side; continue with the second register, starting again on the right-hand side (*for an explanation of the lesser-known biblical stories, see the description of the mosaics in Monreale).*

In contrast, the iconography of the scenes in the **chancel** is modified for contemplation by the clergy and therefore conducive to reflection. Thus scenes from the life of Christ are not arranged sequentially but in order of importance *(note especially above the right-hand apse).* The **cupola** above the choir contains the figure of Christ Pantocrator, flanked by the three Archangels (St Gabriel, St Michael and St Raphael), Tobit and four angels.

The Annunciation is represented above the graceful arch of the apse, placed there as a reminder of the Word of God, which foretold Christ in Benediction *(in the vault)* and the enthroned Madonna, Queen of Heaven.

In the **south transept**, pride of place is given to the figure of St Paul *(apse vault)* surrounded by scenes from the life of Christ. The story of the Nativity is particularly well related: the three kings are represented on their journey towards Bethlehem and the Christ Child. The Magi on the left wear Phrygian caps, a pointed hat with the top folded forward, to denote the fact that they come from the East.

Dominating the **north transept** is St Andrew *(apse vault)*, who replaced the original mosaics of St Peter in the 14C; beside him is the Hodegetria Madonna and Child (Guide or Instructress pointing to the Way of Redemption based on an icon said to have been painted by St Luke). To one side, St John the Baptist preaches in the desert.

Royal Apartments★★

Guided tours only (30min), Mon, Fri and Sat, 8.15am–6.15pm, Sun and public holidays 8.15am–12.15pm. Groups by appointment only.
091 62 62 833.
www.federicosecondo.org.

The visit begins in the Salone d'Ercole (1560), now the chamber of the Sicilian Parliament and so-called after the large frescoes by Giuseppe Velasquez (19C) depicting the Twelve Labours of Heracles. Today, only six panels are visible, namely *(starting from the far end of the hall)* Heracles and the giants, the slaying

CAPPELLA PALATINA

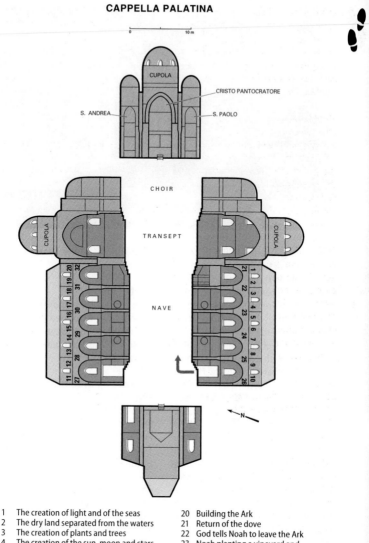

1	The creation of light and of the seas
2	The dry land separated from the waters
3	The creation of plants and trees
4	The creation of the sun, moon and stars
5	The creation of fish and birds
6	The creation of land animals
7	The creation of Adam
8	God resting from his labours
9	God pointing out the tree to Adam
10	The creation of Eve
11	Original sin
12	The shame of Adam and Eve
13	Paradise lost
14	Adam and Eve at work
15	The sacrifice of Cain and Abel
16	Cain kills Abel and lies to God
17	Lamech confesses to his two wives that he has killed two men
18	Enoch taken up to heaven on account of his deep faith
19	Noah with his wife and three sons
20	Building the Ark
21	Return of the dove
22	God tells Noah to leave the Ark
23	Noah planting a vineyard and getting drunk
24	Noah's descendants build the city of Babel
25	Abraham meets three angels and offers them hospitality
26	Lot on the threshold of his house tries to restrain the Sodomites
27	Destruction of Sodom and Lot leaving the city
28	God tells Abraham to sacrifice Isaac, but an angel intervenes
29	Rebecca at the well and departure for Canaan
30	Isaac blessing Jacob
31	Jacob's dream
32	Jacob wrestling with the angel

San Giovanni degli Eremiti

© Vito Arcomano / Fototeca ENIT

of the many-headed Hydra of Lerna, the capture of the Ceryneian hind, the taming of the three-headed dog Cerberus, the capture of the Erymanthean boar and the Cretan Bull. The frescoed ceiling illustrates the birth, triumph and death of the hero.

Across the hall of the viceroys is a small entrance room that once constituted the heart of the **Joaria**, one of the Norman palace's original towers, now incorporated into other buildings. On the left is the **Sala di Ruggero II**, with decoration reminiscent of the Palatine Chapel. From the marble panelling, framed within friezes of mosaic, springs the golden mantle that covers the upper sections of the wall and ceiling. Hunting scenes alternate with symbolic animals such as the peacock (for eternity, as it was alleged that its flesh did not decompose) and the lion (for royalty and strength); all are portrayed in pairs, in accordance with Eastern iconography. A number of other 18C and 19C rooms follow, including the Yellow Hall (or Hall of Mirrors).

Osservatorio Astronomico

Top floor of the Pisan Tower.
Closed for renovation. Call for reopening dates. ℘091 233 111. *www.astropa.unipa.it.*

The **astronomical observatory** houses a collection of historic instruments used in astronomy, meteorology, seismology and topography. From the top, there is a fabulous bird's-eye **view★★★** over Palermo.

Porta Nuova

Built under the Emperor Charles V, the gateway is topped by a Renaissance-style loggia. Beyond the gate, **Corso Vittorio Emanuele** stretches to **Porta Felice**.

Palazzo e Parco d'Orléans

This elegant house and garden, with its magnificent banyan tree, is where Louis Philippe d'Orléans, the future King of France, lived in exile from 1810–14. Today, it is used as a municipal building by the Sicilian regional authorities.

▷ Cross the Corso Ruggero and turn right down Via dei Benedettini.

San Giovanni degli Eremiti★★

○*Open 9am–7pm; Sun and public hols 9am–1.30pm (last admission 30min before closing).* ✆€6. ℘091 65 15 019.

The **Church of St John of the Hermits** stands in a luxuriant garden of palm trees, agaves, bougainvillea and orange trees. Built around the middle of the 12C at the request of **King Roger II**, this is one of the most famous Arabo-Norman monuments in Palermo. Its simple, square forms enclose spaces consisting of perfect cubes and rise to a red roof with five squat domes (echoing the profile of San Cataldo, not far away), all clearly the work of Moorish crafts-men. The simple interior is shaped into a Latin-cross plan.

At one time, the church was flanked by its monastery. Today, only the delicate 13C **cloisters★** with their paired columns remain.

▷ Return towards the Palazzo dei Normanni and head down Via del Bastione.

Villa Bonanno★

These public gardens lie behind the Palazzo Reale. Extensive excavations have revealed the remains of **Roman patrician houses** containing colourful mosaics that feature the seasons and Orpheus, now housed in the Museo Archeologico Regionale (& see Historic Centre, p144). The upper part of the park features a 17C monument to Phillip V.

▷ Cross the square to the Palazzo Sclafani.

Palazzo Sclafani

The front of the building (1330) overlooking Piazzetta San Giovanni Decollato is ornamented with fine Gothic two-light windows within interlacing arches and an elegant, cusped doorway. It is from this *palazzo* that the famous fresco *The Triumph of Death* was transferred to the Galleria Regionale di Sicilia.

▷ Cross Via Vittorio Emanuele.

Cattedrale★★

🕓Open 7am–7pm; Sun 7am–1pm and 4–7pm. ℘091 33 43 75. www.cattedrale.palermo.it.
Palermo's cathedral is an imposing edifice built in the late-12C in the Sicilian-Norman style with considerable alteration over the centuries. A notable addition from the 15C is the Catalan Gothic south porch: on the outermost wall are the symbols of the four Evangelists *(St Mark's lion and St Matthew's angel on the right, St Luke's ox and St John's eagle, left)*. The neo-Classical dome was added in the 18C when the interior was also completely refurbished. The original fabric of the building, however, can still be seen in the **apses★**, which retain their distinctive geometric decoration.

Sarcophaguses, treasury and crypt

🕓Opening times same as cathedral (visit in the morning to see the treasury and crypt). ☞€1.50/3. Access from the south transept.
The first chapel on the right contains the tombs of members of the Swabian and Norman royal families: Frederick II, his wife Costanza of Aragon, Henry VI and at the rear, Roger II and his daughter, Costanza d'Altavillhe. To the right

Cattedrale

© Vito Arcomano / Fototeca ENIT

© Nicolas Thibaut / Photononstop

I "Quattro Canti" (Piazza Vigliena)

of the transept is the entrance leading to the **treasury**, which contains a fine carved ivory staff made in Sicily in the 17C and jewels belonging to Queen Costanza of Aragon, including the magnificent **Imperial gold crown★** set with precious stones, pearls and enamels. Among the tombs in the crypt is a Classical Roman **sarcophagus** featuring the nine Muses, Apollo, and a seated man wearing a toga.

As you walk down Via Vittorio Emanuele, on the right at no. 452, don't miss the Castrone Santa Ninfa, an impressive Renaissance palace.

▶ Continue down Via Vittorio Emanuele.

Chiesa del Santissimo Salvatore★
℘091 32 33 92. Only open for marriages.

The present oval-shaped Church of the Holy Saviour was designed in the late-17C by **Paolo Amato**. The interior is richly decorated in the Baroque style, and contains fragments of a fresco of the *Triumph of St Basil* (1763).

Further along Corso Vittorio Emanuele is **Piazza Bologni**: among a series of 18C buildings sits the **Palazzo Alliata di Villafranca**.

② THE QUATTRO CANTI TO THE ALBERGHERIA
Circuit in green on the map on p124. Allow 1.5hr.

I "Quattro Canti"★★ (Piazza Vigliena)

At the intersection of Palermo's two main thoroughfares, Via Vittorio Emanuele and Via Maqueda, is a spacious octagon: the infilled corners of the square feature four elegant 18C Baroque *palazzo* façades, their elevations subdivided into sections with Classical columns *(Doric, Ionic and Corinthian)*. At the centre of each one is an elaborate fountain dedicated to the four seasons. The niches of the middle storey contain statues of the four Spanish kings of Sicily, those in the upper level contain effigies representing the patron saints of Palermo, who protected the districts lying behind them: St Christina, St Ninfa, St Oliva and St Agatha (who was subsequently replaced by St Rosalia).

▶ Walk down Via Vittorio Emanuele, staying to the left.

San Matteo

The Church of St Matthew was built in the mid-17C. Its façade consists of three orders, the niches and projecting surfaces of which contrast to produce striking *chiaroscuro* effects. The richly decorated interior reflects the church's ties with the Unione dei Miseremini, founded with the aim of hearing masses for souls suffering in Purgatory. Works of art here include two canvases by Pietro Novelli (*The Presentation at the Temple* and *The Marriage of the Virgin*, fourth chapel in the side aisle), the 18C frescoes in the vault and dome by Vito d'Anna, and the statue of *Faith and Justice* to the side of the presbytery and the lunette portraying *Christ Freeing Souls from the Flames of Purgatory* opposite by **Giacomo Serpotta**. Serpotta himself is buried in the crypt of the church *(access from the left aisle)*.

▷ Cross the street and walk up the steps to Piazza Pretoria.

Piazza Pretoria★★

At the centre of this lovely piazza is a spectacular **fountain★★** by the 16C Florentine sculptor Francesco Camilliani, originally intended as a garden ornament for a Tuscan villa and comprising concentric circles of gods and goddesses, nymphs, monsters, animal heads, allegories, ornamental stairways and balustrades.

The top basin is divided into four sections; below each is a smaller basin, which in turn is overlooked by one of the four allegories of the rivers of Palermo: Gabriele, Maredolce, Papireto and Oreto. Among the statuettes guarding the ramps is Ceres, the Classical patroness of Sicily, who holds a sheaf of wheat and a horn of plenty. The piazza is bounded by fine buildings: to one side the dome of **Santa Caterina;** on the south axis the **Palazzo Pretorio** (Palazzo Senatorio or Palazzo delle Aquile). Across the road is the church of San Giuseppe ai Teatini.

Palazzo Pretorio

🕒*Open Tue–Sat, 9.30am–1pm.* 📞*091 84 31 605. www.palermocultura.it.* Concealed by the present austere exterior, the result of 19C renovations, lie the vestiges of a succession of earlier façades in various styles, the oldest of which dates from the 1300s. Since then, it has been the seat of the City Council.

La Martorana's Fruitful Nuns

Frutta martorana is also known as *pasta reale* (one of the most typical kinds of Sicilian *pasticcerie*) after the church of the same name. According to tradition, the origins of this delicacy can be traced back to medieval times when every convent specialised in a different confection. The sweets made by the Benedictine convent of la Martorana for the feast of All Saints were of marzipan, shaped and coloured to resemble various fruits. This tradition continues today: during the Fiera dei Morti at the beginning of November the district between Via Spicuzza and Piazza Olivella is packed with brightly coloured stalls selling *frutta martorana*, along with children's toys.

© S. Sauvignier / MICHELIN

Marzipan is of medieval origin: the term is derived from the Arabic *mauthaban*, which originally denoted a coin, then a unit of measurement and finally the container used to store the paste made of almonds, sugar and egg whites.

Occultist and Traveller

Giuseppe Balsamo was born in Palermo in 1743. He became fascinated by occult science and founded a Masonic lodge; assuming the name **Count of Cagliostro**, he embarked on his travels around Europe practising the arts of healing and magic with his miraculous "water of eternal youth". In France, he became involved in court intrigues, which led to him being imprisoned in the Bastille. Following his return to Italy, fortune still refused to smile on him and he was again arrested. This time, accused of belonging to the sect of the *Illuminati*, he was incarcerated in the fortress of San Leo in the Montefeltro, near Urbino. There, he died in poverty and his body was taken to the cemetery in Palermo. His house is located off Piazza Ballarò, in Via Cagliostro.

Rooms open to the public include the **Sala dei Lapidi**, lined with marble tablets bearing inscriptions and now used for Council meetings *(note the magnificent central 17C chandelier carved from a single piece of wood)*, and **Sala Garibaldi**, named after the Italian hero who addressed the assembled crowds from the balcony in 1860. A glass case on the right contains a collection of weapons and scabbards inlaid with gold and mother-of-pearl that once belonged to Napoleon Bonaparte.

Piazza Bellinia★★

This small square is contained by three churches: **Santa Caterina** *(dating from the end of the 16C, with an 18C dome)*, La Martorana and San Cataldo, which lends an Eastern flavour with its three red domes.

La Martorana★★

This church is named after Eloisa Martorana, who founded the nearby Benedictine convent in 1194, to which the church served as a chapel. Dedicated to **Santa Maria dell'Ammiraglio** (St Mary of the Admiral), the church was founded in 1143 at the request of George of Antioch, an admiral in the fleet of Roger II. Mass is celebrated here according to the Greek Orthodox liturgy. The **interior** is divided into two parts: the first two bays, added in the 16C, were frescoed in the 17C; the older church features glorious **mosaics★★** of Byzantine iconography. The wall, which once constituted the main façade, has two mosaic panels representing George

of Antioch at the feet of the Virgin *(on the left)* and Roger II receiving the crown from Christ *(right)*. Filling the nave dome is Christ Pantocrator surrounded by four Archangels. In the register below are eight Prophets and in the pendentives, the four Evangelists.

The nave vault holds the Nativity *(on the left)* and the Death (Dormition) of the Virgin *(right)*.

San Cataldo★★

🕐 *Open 9.30am–1pm, 3.30–6.30pm; Sun 9.30am–1pm.* 🕐 *Closed public hols.* 𝄞 *091 61 61 692.*

The church, the main seat of the Knights of the Holy Sepulchre, was built during the Norman period (12C).

A distinctive Moorish quality is imparted by the combination of its severe square forms, crenellated walls, perforated window screens and characteristic bulbous red domes (resembling a eunuch's hat, according to the Italians).

▷ Cross Via Maqueda to San Giuseppe ai Teatini.

San Giuseppe ai Teatini

Piazza Pretoria is bordered by the side of this striking Baroque church. The most eye-catching element is the original campanile, which rises to an octagonal section with spiral columns at the top. The theatrical **interior★** in the form of a Latin cross is endowed with a majestic ceiling, white and gold stucco decoration and frescoes. To either side of the entrance is one of a pair of impressive 18C **stoups★**, each consi-

Ballarò food market

© Franck Guiziou / hemis.fr

sting of an angel in flight with a basin in its arms.

▶ Continue along Via Maqueda to San Cataldo, on the same side of the road.

Sant'Orsola

This 17C church was once the headquarters of the Compagnia dell'Orazione della Morte, an organisation that was responsible for burying the deceased of the district.

In the last chapel to the right, decorated by Serpotta, the usual rejoicing *putti* are replaced by skeletons and dangling bones.

▶ Return to Via Maqueda. Palazzo Comitini stands on the left at the corner of the street.

Palazzo Comitini

Via Maqueda 100. ⊙*Open 9.30am– 12.30pm, 3.30–4.30pm.* ⊙*Closed Sat– Sun and public hols.* ♿ ✆*091 66 28 260.* The *palazzo* (1768–71), built for the Prince of Gravina, incorporates two older palaces belonging to the Roccafiorita -Bonanno and Gravina di Palagonia families.

The front has two large entrances and nine openings *(now windows)* on the ground floor and a series of bulbous balconies (evocatively described in Italian as a *petto d'oca*, which translates

as "goose breasted") on the first floor. The building was radically altered in 1931 with the addition of another floor for use as administrative offices for the Province of Palermo. A wide staircase leads up from the internal courtyard to the loggia on the first floor and the Sala delle Armi *(Armoury)*, now the Salone dei Commessi – the two masks flanking the doorway served as torch extinguishers. To the left is the Green Room, furnished with a fine 18C Murano glass lamp. **Sala Martorana★**, now the seat of the Provincial Council, is lined throughout with 18C wood panelling inlaid with mirrors; these add luminosity to the room and enhance the impact of the ceiling, which is frescoed with *The Triumph of True Love*.

▶ Return to the Palazzo Comitini and take Via del Bosco, bordered with elegant palaces.

Chiesa del Carmine

Piazza del Carmine is brought to life each day by the **Ballarò food market**. Before entering the church, admire the splendid tile-covered **dome** supported by four giant Atlas figures. Inside, two sumptuous **altars★** in the transepts are decorated with pairs of golden twisting columns on which spirals of stucco tell the story of the life of the Virgin Mary *(on the left)* and of Christ *(right)*. They are the work of Giacomo and Giuseppe

Serpotta. Above the left-hand altar is a 15C canvas of *La Madonna del Carmine*.

◗ Take Via Ballaro and turn right down Via Casa Professa.

Chiesa del Gesù di Casa Professa

When the Jesuits arrived in Sicily in the mid-16C, the Spanish government gave them its generous support. Here, they founded their first church, which was later damaged during the Allied bombing of 1943. The sober façade contrasts with the Baroque exuberance of the interior, which is encrusted with stucco and *pietra dura* decoration. The **chancel decor★** shows a euphoric display of cherubs holding flowers, torches, musical instruments, set squares and lances with which they pierce devils. The second chapel on the right has two paintings by **Pietro Novelli**: *St Philip of Agira* and **St Paul the Hermit★**; the last figure on the left is a self-portrait of the artist. Next to the church stands **Casa Professa**, housing the **municipal library**, which contains a large number of incunabula and manuscripts.

◗ Walk around the church along Via Casa Professa and Vicolo Averna to Piazza Santissimi Quaranta Martiri.

Camera dello Scirocco di Palazzo Marchesi

From Piazza SS Quaranta Martiri, enter passageway no 14 (left of the tower), and from the courtyard, take the staircase on the left.

One of the oldest of the Palermo *scirocco* rooms is under the cloisters of the 15C **Palazzo Marchesi**, at a depth of 8m/26ft. An enormous Arabic cistern, once used for the city's water supply, has been found next to this room.

◗ Return to the Chiesa del Gesu and Piazza Casa Professa to Via Nino Basile and Salita Raffadali, then turn left along Via Puglia.

Walk past the 15C **Palazzo Speciale** on the left and enter a delightful square

dominated by the church of **Santa Chiara**. Built in the 14C and transformed in the 17C, it has retained its interior.

◗ Continue along Via Puglia and turn right into Via Matteo Sclafani.

Palazzo Asmundo

Via Pietro Novelli 3. ◷*Open Mon–Fri 9.30am–11am, 1–2pm.* ⬤€4. ✆*091 65 19 022.*

Behind the fine façade of this palazzo facing the cathedral lies a lavishly decorated interior, including frescoes by G. Martorana.

◗ Cross Via Vittorio Emanuele and turn into Via Matteo Bonello, then right into Via dell'Incoronazione.

Behind the Loggia dell'Incoronazione, the **chapel of Santa Maria** Incoronata was built in the 12C and contains the remains of a 9C mosque. In the same street, the church of **Santa Maria di Monte Oliveto** (known as the church of the Badia Nuova) boasts elegant architecture and a richly-decorated Interior. Not far away, the church of **Sant'Agata alla Guilla** was founded by the Normans and restored in the 15–16C. The area is known as La Guilla, from the Arabic *wadi* (river), which became *guidda*, then *guilla*. Moving on, you come to the church of San Paolino dei Giardinieri (16C), which was destroyed by bombing and has since been turned into a mosque.

③ LA KALSA AND VIA ALLORO

Circuit in green on the map on p125. Allow 4hr.

The Kalsa district behind the port was razed by Allied bombing raids in 1943, during which many lives were lost and countless buildings destroyed. The ruins were thrown into the sea and as a result, the **Foro Italico** now stands a little way from the seafront. This fascinating district is currently undergoing major reconstruction, with the creation of new squares such as **Piazza**

Magione, *palazzi* and monuments, and the opening of cultural centres such as the **Chiesa dello Spasimo** and **Teatro Garibaldi** breathing new life into the historic heart of Arabo-Norman Palermo.

The focal point is **Piazza della Kalsa**, although the district itself stretches all the way to **Corso Vittorio Emanuele** and contains a high proportion of the city's most interesting monuments.

The main entrance to the quarter is the **Porta dei Greci**, beyond which lies the piazza and the church of **Santa Teresa alla Kalsa**, a monumental Baroque place of worship built by **Paolo Amato** between 1686 and 1706.

Turning onto Via Torremuzza, note the beautiful stone-framed Noviziato dei Crociferi at number 20 and farther along on the opposite side of the street, **Santa Maria della Pietà** designed by Giacomo Amata.

Via Alloro

Throughout the Middle Ages, this served as the quarter's main street. Today, most of the elegant *palazzi* that once lined its thoroughfare have been destroyed or have fallen into disrepair. The few remaining buildings include Palazzo Abatellis and, next to it, the lovely **Chiesa della Gancia**.

Palazzo Abatellis★

This magnificent *palazzo*, built in Catalan-Gothic style with some Renaissance features, was designed by Matteo Carnelivari, who worked in Palermo towards the end of the 15C. Its elegant front has a great square central doorway ornamented with fasces (bundles of rods, an Ancient symbol of authority) and a series of two-and three-light windows. The *palazzo* is arranged around an attractive square courtyard and now houses the Galleria Regionale di Sicilia (◖*see Historic Centre*).

La Gancia

The church dedicated to **Santa Maria degli Angeli** was originally built by the Franciscans in the late-15C. The exterior retains its original square profile and

rustication. On the side of the church flanking Via Alloro, note the *Buca della Salvezza:* this "Hole of Salvation" was made by two patriots who hid in the crypt during the anti-Bourbon rebellion of 1860.

The **interior★** gives the impression of being Baroque although elements date from several different periods. The wooden ceiling painted with stars, a magnificent **organ★★** by Raffaele della Valle, the marble **pulpit** and Antonello Gagini's relief tondi of the *Annunciation (either side of the altar)* date from the 16C. Most of the superficial decoration is from the 17C and fine original details survive, including a **novice monk★** peeping out over a cornice in the chapel to the left of the altar.

◖ Cross Piazza della Magione.

Santa Maria dello Spasimo★

The church and convent were built inside the walls of the Kalsa in 1506 and to mark the occasion, **Raphael** was commissioned to paint a picture of the anguish of the Madonna before the Cross *(now in the Prado in Madrid)*. Building work on the church was not complete when the Turkish threat made it necessary to build a new bastion just behind the church. In turn, the complex

Santa Maria dello Spasimo

© SIME/Giovanni Simeone/Simeone/Photononstop

was transformed into a fortress, a theatre, a hospice for plague victims (1624) and later for the poor (1835) and, finally, a hospital. It was eventually abandoned in 1986. The church and former hospital have been transformed into venues for cultural events *(the church houses the Scuola Europea di Music Jazz)*. The section around the 16C cloisters is accessible to the public.

The **church★** beyond is the only example of Northern Gothic architecture in Sicily; its slender nave reaches up towards the open sky without a roof and ends with a polygonal **apse**, while the original entrance is given prominence by a *pronaos* with two side chapels. This, in turn, provides access to the old Spanish bastion, now laid out as a garden. The area is particularly impressive as the sun sets.

▷ Walk along Piazza della Magione

La Magione

An attractive little avenue of palm trees leads up to the Romanesque church, which was founded in the 12C by Matteo d'Ajello, a prominent official in the service of the Norman sovereigns. In 1193, it was given to the Order of Teutonic Knights by Emperor Henry VI, in whose hands it remained for more than 300 years. The **front elevation★** rises through three tiers of pointed arches, elegantly ornamented at the lower levels. The church has fine **cloisters** from the original Cistercian monastery. The remains of pre-existing constructions, including a 10C Arab tower, are visible from the cloisters.

Via della Magione runs along the side of **Palazzo Ajutamicristo**, an imposing building that was designed by **Matteo Carnelivari** in the 15C.

▷ Turn down via Garbaldi.

Piazza della Rivoluzione

This little square is where the anti-Bourbon rebellion of 1848 was ignited. In the centre is a fountain depicting a king feeding a serpent and symbolising the city.

▷ Follow via Aragona. At piazza Aragona, head left and follow via Sant'Anna.

Piazza Sant'Anna

In the heart of the ancient Lattarini market, this lively square is home to the church of Sant'Anna (17C–18C) and the adjoining **Galleria d'Arte Moderna**, which is housed in a former monastery (*see Historic Centre tour, p145*). On the adjacent **Piazza Croce dei Vespri**, the **Palazzo Valguarnera-Gangi**, provided the opulent setting for Luchino Visconti's film, *The Leopard*.

▷ Retrace your steps to via Alloro. The tour continues to the north of the street.

San Francesco d'Assisi★

Little of the original 13C church survives and its appearance owes much to careful restoration of the original design. The front elevation includes the rose window and Gothic **portal★** from the original 13C structure. Of note are eight statues by Giovanni Serpotta and the **entrance doorway★** to the Mastrantonio Chapel by **Francesco Laurana** and **Pietro di Bonitate** *(fourth chapel on the left)*.

Oratorio di San Lorenzo★★★

Open 10am–6pm. €2.50.
339 23 76 652.

This late masterpiece by **Giacomo Serpotta** has been described as a "cave of white coral". On the walls, paintings alternating with statues of the Virtues illustrate scenes from the life of St Francis *(to the right)* and St Lawrence *(left)*; the martyrdom of the latter is depicted opposite these works. Nude thinkers on the upper sections of the wall are reminiscent of Michelangelo. The lofty detachment of the Virtues and the veiled sadness of the nudes contrast with the triumph of the delightful rejoicing *putti*, depicted in the most imaginative poses *(note the figure making a soap bubble and two characters tenderly kissing)*. However, the innocent vitality is in contrast to the church's

Palermo's Markets

Mercato del Capo

Palermo has some of Europe's oldest and most colourful street markets, which have been set in the same backstreets for centuries. The most colourful are, without doubt, the food markets. Makeshift vibrant awnings cover stands and resemble a lively Arab souk, with the calls of fruit sellers, fishmongers, street food vendors and butchers – usually in Sicilian dialect not heard elsewhere.

La Vucciria – This is Palermo's biggest and most historic market. Constantly filled with colour and noise, it is the most celebrated food market in the city. It is set back from the waterfront in Via Cassari-Argenteria and the surrounding area *(stretching as far as Piazza San Domenico)*. The origin of the name is controversial: some maintain that it comes from the French-Norman term *boucherie* (meat), others are of the opinion that it refers to the deafening clamour of the traders' voices drawing attention to their wares.

Ballarò – Ballarò market is held in the area stretching from Piazza Casa Professa to Corso Tukory. The food stalls are clustered around Piazza del Carmine, while clothing and second-hand items are near **Casa Professa**. A lively atmosphere, especially in the morning.

Il Capo – The first and most picturesque food section is along Via Carini and Via Beati Paoli; the clothing and shoe stalls are packed into Via Sant'Agostino and Via Bandiera. In addition to the brightly coloured stalls, it is worth noting the interestingly named streets in this area, such as Sedie Volanti (flying chairs) and Gioia Mia (my love).

Mercato delle Pulci – A range of antique and modern bric-a-brac can be found in the lively fleamarket *(located between Piazza Peranni and Corso Amedeo)*, where intense haggling over prices is mandatory!

I Lattarini – The name derives from the Arabic *suk-el-attarin* (grocery market). Once a food market, its stalls now sell clothing, work tools and ironmongery.

Mercato della Vucciria

Oratorio del Rosario di San Domenico

most notorious event, the 1969 theft of Caravaggio's *Nativity*, which once hung above the altar.

▶ Keeping the Chiesa di San Francesco to your left, continue to Palazzo Mirto *(see Historic Centre below)*.

Piazza Marina

In the centre of this piazza at the heart of medieval Palermo is an attractive garden, the **Giardino Garibaldi**, planted with magnificent **banyan trees★★**.
The piazza is enclosed by fine buildings: Palazzo Galletti (no. 46), Palazzo Notarbartolo (no. 51) and Palazzo Chiaramonte. Diametrically opposite sits the lovely **Fontana del Garraffo** (from the Arabic *gharraf* meaning abundant water) which was constructed at the close of the 17C by G. Vitaliano to designs by Paolo Amato.

Palazzo Chiaramonte★

⊙*Open Tue–Sat, 9am–1pm, 2.30–6.30pm; Sun 10am–2pm.* €5.
𝒫*091 60 75 306.*

This splendid *palazzo* was built in 1307 for the Chiaramonte family, one of the wealthiest and most powerful dynasties of the Aragonese period. The building also came to be known as **Lo Steri** from *Hosterium*, a fortified residence. It passed into the hands of the Spanish

viceroys and served as the headquarters of the Court of the Inquisition from the 17C until 1782, when the institution was abolished in Sicily.
The main front is ornamented by elegant two- and three-light **windows★★** *(note the fabulous stone inlays to the underside of the arches on the first floor).* The style is so distinctive as to be described simply as "Chiaramonte" and may be discerned in many other Sicilian civic buildings of the same period. The **Museo Internazionale delle Marionette** is nearby *(see Historic Centre).*
Also nearby stands the monumental **Porta Felice** (1582), marking the eastern end of Via Vittorio Emanuele. The 17C **Loggiato di San Bartolomeo** can be seen close to the gate and is now a venue for exhibitions and cultural events.
The Foro Italica, the old **Passeggiata alla Marina**, starts at Porta Felice. From the 16C onwards this promenade, with its esplanade overlooking the sea, was a popular area for Palermo's elegant aristocracy to stroll, as well as the site of festivals and parades.
A number of fine *palazzi* were built here, including the 18C **Palazzo Branciforti-Butera**. Don't miss the neo-Classical bandstand *(immediately after the crossroads with Via Alloro).*

© Christophe Boisvieux / age fotostock

Passeggiata delle Cattive

Built in 1823 along the wall that marked the end of the Passeggiata alla Marina, this promenade owes its unusual name to the popular expression *"mura delle cattive"*, which translates as the "wall of the wayward women". The walkway provided widows with more privacy (as well as a better view) than the promenade below. The splendid seafront façade of the Palazzo Branciforti-Butera can be admired from here.

④ THE OLD HARBOUR TO THE VUCCIRIA

Circuit in green on the map on p125. Allow 3hr.

The *cala*, the city's ancient harbour, was once protected by the **Castellammare**, built by the Arabs and later transformed into a fortress, prison and private residence. The massive construction was, however, damaged in 1922 when the jetty was extended. Any visit to the Cala quarter, which extends behind the old harbour, should begin with the church as this was where the chains used to close off the area were kept through the centuries, hence its dedication to Santa Maria della Catena.

Santa Maria della Catena★

The design of the church is attributed to Matteo Carnelivari. Its elevation is dominated by the broad square portico with three arches; behind these are doorways set with low reliefs by Vincenzo Gagini. The overall style is transitional Gothic-Renaissance (1490), with a lovely interior brought to life by blind arcading into square bays with pointed cross-arches. The second chapel on the right contains fragments of a frescoed Madonna and on the altar are symbolic chains.

The church is especially magical at sunset when its façade is dramatically lit by the glowing colours of the setting sun. Farther along the curve of the harbour lies Piazza Fonderia, with the historic **Vucciria** market *(between Via Cassari and Piazza San Domenico)* behind it.

▷ Take Via Meli to San Domenico.

San Domenico

🕐 *Hours vary.* 🕿 *091 58 48 72.*

An attractive **piazza** stretches out before the church with a statue of the Madonna raised on a column at the centre of it.

The church was initiated in the 17C and completed a century later. Its Baroque

Stucco decoration in Oratorio del Rosario di Santa Cita: cherubs and the Battle of Lepanto

© SCALA

front elevation rises in three ordered tiers of Doric and Corinthian columns and square pilasters framing a statue of St Dominic. The spacious interior is divided into nave and aisles, with a side chapel off each bay.

A fine arrangement of inlaid *pietra dura* decoration ornaments the fourth chapel on the right and the Chapel of the Rosary in the north transept. Adjacent to the church are lovely 14C **cloisters** with paired columns.

Neighbouring buildings accommodate the **Sicilian Historical Society** (*Società Siciliana per la Storia Patria*) which in turn has its own small **Museo del Risorgimento** containing mementoes of Garibaldi. From the windows of the museum is a splendid **view** of the cloisters of San Domenico.

▶ Turn right down Via dei Bambinai.

Oratorio del Rosario di San Domenico★★★

🕐 *Open Mon–Sat 9am–1pm.* 🕐 *Closed Sundays.* ♿ €5. 📞 *091 33 27 79.*

The oratory is a treasure trove of stucco decoration by **Giacomo Serpotta**, who conferred a spontaneous playfulness to the antics of his sculpted cherubs.

The stucco provides frames for a series of paintings relating to the Joyful Mysteries of the Rosary *(left and rear walls)*, some of which are by **Pietro Novelli**, and the *Sorrowful Mysteries of the Rosary (right wall)*, which include a *Flagellation* by Matthias Stomer. Niches alternate with the paintings, containing allegories of the Virtues, a series of female figures remarkable for their poise. In some instances they are attended by *putti*; the statue of Meekness, for example, holding a dove, is flanked by a *putto* in monk's attire stretching a podgy little hand out towards her.

In the large ovals above the paintings, Serpotta has depicted scenes from the Apocalypse of St John: note how the figure of the Devil writhes as he falls from heaven.

Above the altar dome, still more cherubs hold up a great sheet. On the high altar itself sits the splendid painting of the *Madonna of the Rosary* (1628) by Anthony Van Dyck. The ceiling, frescoed by **Pietro Novelli**, illustrates the *Coronation of the Virgin*.

Grand Dame of Fame, Aristocracy and Intrigue

Grand Hotel et Des Palmes – This building first came to prominence in the mid-1800s when used as a residence by **Ben Ingham**, an Englishman who played a key role in the history of Marsala. Soon converted into a hotel *(Via Roma 398, 📞 091 58 39 33)*, it has provided hospitality to Wagner, who finished *Parsifal* here, Guttuso and Fiume, whose sketches furnish one of the salons, politicians past and present (President Andreotti for one), great names from the world of theatre and countless aristocrats, who have all passed through its corridors over the years. It has been the scene of important political occasions, newsworthy events, mysterious incidents linked to *omertà* (tacit complicity demanded by the Mafia) and intrigue. It was here, in 1957, that a private dinner was held for the top henchmen of the Italian and American Mafia. It was also here that a secret agent disappeared in mysterious circumstances, having fallen from the seventh floor straight through the skylight of the great hall of mirrors (before being immediately rushed "to hospital" by two equally mysterious figures on standby). In 1933, the French writer Raymond Roussel ended his dissolute and tragic life in the hotel either by committing suicide or overdosing on hallucinogenic drugs. Another strange tale involves the Baron of Castelvetrano, who lived hidden away in his suite on the first floor for more than half a century. This enforced exile was allegedly levied upon him for having killed a boy guilty of petty theft; the sentence was pronounced by the father of the victim.

Liberty-Style – The Città Nuova and Beyond

Besides those described under Città Nuova (👣 *see Historic Centre p144*), Palermo's best Liberty-style residences include **Palazzo Dato** with its pink external detailing on the corner of Via XX Settembre and Via XII Gennaio; Ernesto Basile's **Villa Favaloro Di Stefano** in Piazza Virgilio and the **Villino Ida** at 15 Via Siracusa, with its fine wrought-iron balcony and tiled frieze.

Another must, albeit in a completely different part of the city, is the **Villa Igiea** *(Salita Belmonte 43, 𝒫091 63 12 111)*. This large building is attractively positioned on the slopes of Monte Pellegrino. It began life as a nursing home for Igiea Florio (who suffered from tuberculosis) and was adapted from a pre-existing neo-Gothic building to designs for an exotically luxurious home by Ernesto Basile. The dining room in particular, now the **Sala Basile★** *(accessible by request and subsequent permission from the hotel staff, who are always very helpful)*, was completely renovated: wooden panelling was installed and the interior decoration with beautiful female figures surrounded by delicate, long-stalked flowers commissioned from **Ettore de Maria Bergler**, a well-known Liberty-style painter. On the walls of the corridor are photographs depicting illustrious guests who have stayed here in the past, including many European kings and queens.

▶ Continue to Via Squarcialupo.

Santa Maria di Valverde

🕐 *Open Mon–Sat 9am–1pm.* 🕐 *Closed Sundays.* 👛 €5. 𝒫091 33 27 79.
An elegant marble portal by Pietro Amato (1691) leads into this small church. The **interior** is extravagantly decorated in the Baroque style using different types of marble, sculpted into soft drapery on the side altars.

Santa Cita

🕐 *Open 9am–1pm. Afternoon hours vary. If the chapel crypt is closed, contact nuns in the nearby Istituto del Sacro Cuore.*
This church was badly damaged by the bombing raids of 1943, which destroyed its side aisles. Note the beautiful **marble chancel arch★** by Antonello Gagini in the presbytery: the Nativity and Dormition of the Virgin are represented inside the arch; Dominican saints can be seen in the pilaster panels, and portraits of St Thomas Aquinas and St Peter the Martyr grace the two medallion tondi on the corners. In the eight coffers of the arch intrados are scenes from the life of St Zita. Also worthy of note is the beautiful **Cappella del Rosario** *(to the right of the presbytery)*, with its delicate stuccowork and polychrome marquetry. Access to the **crypt** *(cripta della Cappella Lanza)*, decorated with different types of marble, is from the chapel *(to the left of the presbytery)*.

Oratorio del Rosario di Santa Cita★★★

Access from Via Valverde or Via da S. Cita.
🕐 *Open Mon–Sat, 9am–1pm.*
𝒫091 84 31 605.
The oratory is a remarkable work by the leading Baroque decorator **Giacomo Serpotta**, who worked here between 1686 and 1718. A host of angels and cherubs are bestowed with carefree expressions and realistic attitudes, intent on playing among themselves, climbing up onto the window frames, larking about with garlands of flowers, crying, sleeping and hugging their knees deep in thought.
On the wall at the back of the nave a great drape hangs across the entire wall, supported by a struggling crowd of cherubs. A central panel depicts in relief the Battle of Lepanto; this is flanked by two emaciated youths symbolising the horrors of war. All around the oratory, even below the side windows, are panels depicting the Mysteries of the Rosary. On the left wall begins the

series relating to the Joyful Mysteries: the Annunciation, Visitation, Nativity and Presentation at the Temple. On the right are the Sorrowful Mysteries: Jesus in the Garden at Gethsemane, the Flagellation, Crowning of Thorns and Calvary. At the far end is a second series of Joyful Mysteries *(starting bottom left)*: the Resurrection, Ascension, Descent of the Holy Spirit and the Assumption of Mary. At the top, in the centre, is the Crowning of Mary.

A little farther on sits **San Giorgio dei Genovesi** (🕐 *open during exhibitions only)* overlooking its own piazza: this is one of the rare expressions of the late Renaissance. Now de-consecrated, the former church houses various temporary exhibitions.

In Via Cavour is the **Prefettura**: a Venetian neo-Gothic building that was once known as Villa Whitaker, having been built by an heir to the Ingham-Whitaker Marsala fortune.

5 FROM VIA ROMA TO THE CAPO QUARTER

Circuit in green on the map on p125. Allow 3hr.

Via dell'Orologio, on the right just before Teatro Massimo on Via Maqueda, offers an unusual view of one of Sant'Ignazio's two bell towers.

Bust of Eleonora of Aragon, Galleria Regionale di Sicilia

SCALA

Sant'Ignazio all'Olivella

🕐 *Access to the Oratorio di San Filippo Neri (or Sant'Ignazio) is from the south transept only.*

This fine Baroque church was initiated in the late 16C on the site where, according to tradition, the villa of the family of Santa Rosalia once stood. The possible origin of the name Olivella – *Olim villa,* once a villa (stood here) – would confirm this. Inside, an eye-catching inscription in bright red proclaims *jahvé* in the centre of the Gloria behind the altar.

The first chapel on the right contains a wealth of decorative inlay in the form of polychrome *pietra dura*.

The small **Museo Archeologico Regionale** stands next door to the church (👉 *see Historic Centre, p146).*

Oratorio di San Filippo Neri

Access from the piazza or from Sant'Ignazio. 🕐*Opening times vary.* 📞*091 58 68 67. www.oratoriosan filipponeripalermo.org*

This building was designed by the architect **Venanzio Marvuglia**. Inside, stuccowork illustrates the Gloria: the attractive composition with the angel surrounded by groups of joyful cherubs in twos and threes is recognised as the work of **Ignazio Marabitti**.

Oratorio di Santa Caterina d'Alessandria

Via Monteleone 50. Ring bell to enter.

Although more static and less lively than work by his father **Giacomo**, this stuccowork by **Procopio Serpotta** elegantly portrays various scenes from the life of St Catherine, protector of scholars, alongside allegories of the sciences: Rhetoric, Ethics, Geography and Astrology *(right)*; Dialectics, Physics, Geometry and Theology *(left)* and under the beautiful triple-arched tribune of the entrance wall, Knowledge and Science. The ceiling is decorated with delicate foliage patterns.

▶ Continue along Via Monteleone as far as the intersection with Via Roma.

Palermo's botanical charms

In the time of the Arabs and Normans, the parks around Palermo covered large swathes of land. The one lying to the west of the city, known as the **Genoard** or the "Paradise on Earth", was chosen by the sovereigns as an apt place for a summer residence or a pleasure palace in the Oriental sense of the word: a peaceful haven set among gardens of exotic plants, with pools containing fish, watercourses and even wild animals from distant lands. Such were the dreams that inspired the building of the city's many parks, which included **La Zisa** and the much-restored **Scibene Castle**, which is still visible from Viale Tasca Lanza *(from Via Pitrè, the continuation of Via Cappuccini, turn right after passing Viale Regione Siciliana)*. Also of importance were the **Cuba Sottana** and **Cuba Soprana**, now part of the crumbling Villa Napoli complex *(a few arches are just visible; entrance at Corso Calatafimi 575)*. In the latter stands **La Cubola**, a small, square pavilion surmounted by the characteristic bulbous red dome, which is accessible from Via Zancla *(heading towards the centre, cross Corso Calatafimi to your left and Viale Regione Siciliana shortly thereafter)*.

This passion for gardens has continued over the centuries and the city now houses many peaceful oases filled with exotic plants and trees. Veritable corners of paradise, they are ideal for relaxing or strolling amid the greenery: the exotic garden of San Giovanni degli Eremiti, Villa Bonanno, Villa Giulia, the Botanical Gardens, Villa Malfitano, Villa Trabia, Giardino Garibaldi in Piazza Marina, and the beautiful **English Garden** are extremely well kept, with an enormous number of palms, cactuses, parasol (maritime) pines and banyans.

Sant'Agostino

The splendid 13C St Augustine's was built at the request of the Chiaramonte and Sclafani families. The **front★** is graced with an entranceway decorated with duotone geometric and flower motifs, and a lovely rose window.

The Gaginiesque side entrance in Via Sant'Agostino is also worthy of note. The interior is dominated by Baroque alterations, including stuccoes by followers of the **Serpotta School**, signed on the shelf under the second statue on the right with Serpotta's mark, a lizard. The heart of the quarter, which lies farther along Via Sant'Agostino, is brought to life every morning by the busy market, the **mercato di Capo**.

▶ To continue, take Via Porta Carini and then turn right onto Via Mura di San Vito to Piazza Verdi.

CITTÀ NUOVA

At the beginning of the 19C, the city underwent a period of expansion. The wealthy merchant bourgeoisie chose the northwest side of the city to build fine residences lavishly decorated with wrought-iron work, glass and floral panels.

The hub of high society shifted from Via Maqueda to its extension, which took the name of Via Ruggero Settimo and a little farther on, **Via della Libertà**. Here, they built great temples of opera, two theatres – the Massimo and the Politeama – and a large number of modern *palazzi* scattered through the neighbouring streets. Even today, a walk along Via XX Settembre, Via Dante and Via Siracusa gives a flavour of the splendour promoted by the wealthy upper-middle classes in the late 19C.

Teatro Massimo★

Guided tours of the theatre are available from 10am–3pm. ⊙*Closed Mondays.* ⊚€8. ℘091 60 53 267. www.teatromassimo.it.

This opera house is one of the largest in Europe. The front of the imposing neo-Classical structure is composed of six columns and a broad, triangular pediment modelled on the *pronaos* of an ancient temple. Set back, a great dome rises from its high drum.

The initial design was completed by Giovan Battista Basile in 1875; building work was concluded by his son Ernesto, who took it upon himself to add the two small, distinctive Liberty-style kiosks in front of the theatre. (The exterior of the theatre was the setting for the final killing scene in *The Godfather Part III*). The **interior** is highly elegant: the ceiling of the auditorium is adorned with a magnificent gilded wheel, decorated with a representation of the Triumph of Opera.

Politeama Garibaldi

The Politeama Theatre, built in the same neo-Classical style, faces onto the Piazza Castelnuovo. Its façade is dominated by a quadriga of bronze horses.

The delightful **Villa Malfitano** (*see Modern City, below*) stands right at the end of Via Dante, which heads west, starting from Piazza Castelnuovo.

At no. 36 Viale Regina Margherita *(the street running across Via Dante near Villa Malfitano)* stands **Villino Florio★**, a magnificent house built for one of the most powerful families in 19C Sicily: the Florios. One of the finest examples of the Palermo Liberty style, it was designed by **Ernesto Basile** and originally surrounded by a garden.

HISTORIC CENTRE
Galleria Regionale di Sicilia★★

Via Alloro 4. ◐*Open Tue–Sat 9am–6pm; Sat–Sun and public holidays 9am–1pm.* ◐*Closed Mon.* ◈*€8.* ☏*091 62 30 011.*

The gallery's internal layout was completed in the 1950s by Carlo Scarpa, one of Italy's foremost contemporary interior designers. For each important work of art, the designer has created a tailor-made solution in terms of support and background, using different materials and colours to display it in the best possible manner.

The gallery brings together sculptures and paintings from the medieval period. One of the main points of interest on the ground floor is the magnificent fresco of the **Triumph of Death★★★** (**Room II**), from the Palazzo Sclafani. Its title probably refers to the 13th card of Tarot, which was popular in the Middle Ages and also known as *Trionfi* (Triumphs). The painting shows Death astride a skeletal horse and armed with a bow and arrows in the act of striking down men and women in the full flush of youth. On the left, a figure gazes out from the picture *(top)*; the brush in his right hand

Museo Archeologico Regionale Salinas

© luiginifosi.it/Bigstockphoto.com

denoting a self-portrait of the unknown painter of the picture.

The admirable **bust of Eleonora of Aragon**★★*(Room IV)*, with its gentle expression and delicate features, together with the bust of a young woman, are by the sculptor **Francesco Laurana**, who worked in Sicily during the 15C. The gallery also has a fine **Madonna and Child**★ by **Antonello da Messina**. The first floor is entirely devoted to painting *(with many works from the Sicilian School)*. Note the lovely portable Byzantine icon *(first room opposite the entrance)* with scenes from the life of Christ, and Antonello da Messina's gloriously peaceful **Annunciation**★★★. In the room devoted to Flemish painting is the **Malvagna Triptych**★★(1510) by **Mabuse**, which shows the Virgin and Child surrounded by angels singing and playing instruments in a lavishly decorated frame set against an equally fabulous landscape background.

Galleria d'Arte Moderna★★

Via Sant'Anna 21. ◷*Tue–Sun.* €*7.*
♿ ℘*091 64 31 605. www.galleriadarte-modernapalermo.it .*

The buildings adjoining the church of Sant'Anna were originally a mansion built in 1480 for the Catalan merchant Gaspare Bonet. The house was later sold to the Jesuits, then to the Franciscans, who transformed it into a monastery. This very attractive space now houses a major collection of 19C and 20C Italian *and* Sicilian paintings, displayed in an instructive and enjoyable context, arranged in chronological order over three floors.

The **19C Sicilian** section covers a range of trends that began and simultaneously developed in several genres. The major subject areas are drawn from history (in particular Garibaldi's expedition to Sicily and the unification of Italy), the landscape, rural living conditions – a subject that corresponds to the literary movement led by Giovanni Verga *(see p. 120)* – and exotic themes relating to Italy's foreign colonies. Major figures of Sicilian painting are well represented here, including **Francesco Lojacono** (1838–1915), an artist with a strong realist bent, whose **Veduta di Monte Catalfano**★ parallels the technique of Corot's classic landscapes. Later, his work developed towards impressionism, for example in the sumptuous **Studio di Palude**★★. In the work of **Michele Catti** (1855–1914), we can detect the influence of the Parisian views painted by the French artist Gustave Caillebotte: with great precision and a sometimes highly innovative approach to framing his subjects, Catti captures early 20C Palermo entering the industrial era. There are some particularly spectacular examples of how painters have captured Sicily's landscape and light in the ruins painted by **Gennaro Pardo** (1865–1927), the view of Taormina by **Ettore De Maria Bergler** (1850–1938) and above all in the work of **Antonino Leto** (1844–1913), which occupies a room of its own. His **Case bianche**★★★ is a particularly moving piece, as are scenes of life in the fields. Moving on to the 20C, we find the work of **Giovanni Boldini** (1842–1931), the Ferrara-born painter who became the great portraitist of the declining aristocracy.

Sculpture is also represented, including **Gli Iracondi**★★ by **Mario Rutelli** (c. 1910), while the expressive **Self-Portrait**★★★ and **Nude Reading the Newspaper**★★ by **Renato Guttuso** (1912–1987) are among the highlights of the collections. **Mattino d'Estate**★ by **Aleardo Terzi** (1870–1945) shows the Influence of the Pointillist movement and forms a gentle counterpart to the more symbolist vision of **Franz Von Stuck's Il Peccato**.

Museo Archeologico Regionale Salinas ★★

Piazza Olivella. ◷*Tue–Fri 8.30am–1.30pm, 3–6.30pm. Sat–Mon and public holidays 8.30am–1.30pm.*♿€*4 Palazzo.* ♿ ℘*091 61 16 805. www.regione.sicilia.it/beniculturali/salinas.*

The Regional Archaeological Museum is situated in the Olivella monastery, which, with the adjoining Baroque church of **Sant'Ignazio all'Olivella** (*see above*), was founded in the 17C by the fathers of St Philip Neri. The museum contains a magnificent collection of artefacts recovered from Sicilian sites, in particular those from Selinunte.

Ground floor

The visit begins with a set of **small cloisters**★ with a hexagonal fountain in the centre. At the back is a beautiful single-light window with a decorative surround. The portico shelters an assortment of Punic and Roman anchors. One small room, devoted to Phoenician art, features two sarcophagi from the 6C BC; another is dedicated to Egyptian and Punic finds, including the hieroglyphic inscription known as the **Palermo Stone** (the other three parts are in Cairo and London), which narrates 700 years of Egyptian history; a Punic inscription recovered near Marsala harbour bears the figure of a priest before a perfume burner, worshipping the god Tanit.

Beyond are a series of rooms devoted to artefacts from **Selinunte**. The first displays the twin stelae formed by pairs of busts representing the gods of the Underworld, both in shallow relief and in the round. This leads into the Sala Gabrici (*interactive information terminals*), which contains a reconstruction of the front elevation of Temple C and a selection of the original triglyphs. Sala Marconi has various lion masks with waterspouts from the Temple of Victory at Himera.

The exhibits in the following, larger room are principally from Selinunte, including the range of marvellous **metopes**★★ dating from 575 BC.

As these are the only sculptures of their kind to have been discovered in the region, experts believe that there may have been a sculpture school in the city. Some of the metopes represent the gods worshipped in Selinunte, such as the Apollonian triad (Apollo, Artemis and their mother, Latona), Demeter and Persephone. The oldest (smaller) artefacts, notably from a 6C BC Archaic temple, are displayed below the window on the right: one fragment depicts the Rape of Europa by Zeus disguised as a bull. On the left are three more marvellous metopes from Temple C (6C BC), with traces of colour on the bodies and clothes. The high relief, which in places verges on being in the round, shows Perseus severing the head of Medusa, while Pegasus, the winged horse, springs from her breast; above is Athena, with the four-horse chariot of Apollo to the left and Heracles capturing the Cercopi.

Against the back wall are four metopes from Temple E: these are considered to be the finest in terms of their expressiveness. Starting from the left, they show Heracles fighting with an Amazon, Hera before Zeus, Actaeon being transformed into a stag and Athena fighting the giant Enceladus. The four rooms filled with Etruscan finds contain some fine cinerary urns and *bucchero* ware.

First floor

Among the various **bronzes** from the Greek, Roman and Punic periods are **Heracles catching the stag**★ and the lifelike bronze **Ram**★★, a Hellenistic work from Syracuse. This masterpiece, dating from the 3C BC, was originally part of a pair that adorned the tyrants' palace on the island of Ortygia.

The following room displays a number of small marble statues that include a fine **Satyr**★, a Roman copy of an original by the sculptor Praxiteles.

Second floor

On this floor are the museum's prehistoric collections and a selection of its finest Greek vases, Roman mosaics and frescoes.

The room with the mosaics includes panels illustrating **Orpheus with the animals**★ (3C AD), the seasons, and representations of allegories and myths associated with the cult of Dionysus.

Museo Internazionale delle Marionette ★★

Piazzetta Antonio Pasqualino 5 (Via Butera). ⏱*Open daily Mon–Sat 9am–1pm, 2.30–6.30pm, Sun 10am–1pm.* ⏱*Closed Sun Jun–Aug.* €5.

📞091 32 80 60.www.museomarionette palermo.it.

The International Puppet Museum contains a rich collection of pupi (articulated puppets operated with strings), shadow puppets, scenery and panels from all over the world. The first rooms are devoted to Sicilian puppets, many presented "on stage". Notice in particular the delicate facial features of Gaspare Canino's theatre puppets (19C). The second section presents the European tradition, including such renowned figures as the English *Punch and Judy,* and a vast Oriental collection: Chinese glove-puppets; string-puppets from India, Burma, Vietnam, Thailand and Africa; shadow puppets from Turkey, India and Malaysia (made of leather).

All the caricatures are displayed in semi-darkness (for preservation purposes). The final section is dedicated to special puppets destined for a violent, spectacular death. The museum also has a theatre *(performance details available from the museum).* The walls are hung with decorative puppeteers' posters.

Palazzo Mirto★

Via Merlo 2. 🕐*Open Tue–Fri 9am–6pm, Sat–Sun and public holidays 9am–1pm.* ✸€4. 📞091 61 64 751. *www.regione.sicilia.it/beniculturali/palazzomirto.*

The *palazzo* of the princes Lanzi Filangeri was altered several times to meet the noble family's needs. Its current form dates from the late 18C.

Just inside, on the left, are the magnificent **stables★** (19C), complete with stalls and ornamental bronze horseheads. A red marble staircase leads up to the first floor, which is still mostly furnished with original pieces.

Among the rooms open to the public is the **Chinese sitting room★** with its leather-covered floor, painted silk walls depicting scenes from everyday life and fine *trompe l'oeil* ceiling: this was used as an intimate smoking room or for playing cards. The next room, a small vestibule, contains a good set of

19C Neapolitan plates decorated with people in costume; it is said that the service was used for masked balls and each guest would sit in front of the plate featuring their particular costume.

Another unusual **smoking room★** leads from the vestibule; it is panelled with painted and embossed leather, a suitable material as it does not become impregnated with smoke.

The most striking features of the **Pompadour sitting room★** are the beautiful wall silks embroidered with flowers. The mosaic floor is the only original one in the entire palace.

The dining room contains a **Meissen** service (18C), exquisitely painted with flowers and birds.

MODERN CITY
Villa Malfitano★★

Via Dante. 🔍*Guided tours (30min), 9am–1pm.* 🕐*Closed Sun, public holidays.* ✸€6. 📞091 68 20 522.

The Liberty-style Villa Malfitano, contained within its glorious **garden★★**, was begun in 1886 by **Joseph Whitaker**, grand nephew of **Benjamin Ingham**, the English merchant who came to live in Sicily in 1806 and built himself a commercial empire founded on Marsala wine. In contrast to Ingham, Whitaker was fascinated by ornithology and archaeology and to satisfy his interests he travelled to Tunisia, where he

Garden, Villa Malfitano

© M.Magni / MICHELIN

studied birds and initiated a programme of excavation on the island of Mozia *(see MOZIA)*. Another of his passions was botany: these gardens soon comprised rare and exotic species: palm trees, Dragon's Blood trees, the only example in Europe of *Araucaria Rouler* and an enormous banyan tree. Lavish parties were held there and important guests, such as the reigning monarchs of Great Britain and Italy, were received and entertained.

The internal furnishings are exquisite: a profusion of Oriental items include a pair of *cloisonné* elephants from the Royal Palace in Beijing and a pair of wading-birds riding on the back of a turtle. Also notable is the *Safari in Tunisia* by Lo Jacono and the pastel portrait of Joseph's daughters by Ettore de Maria Bergler above the lovely spiral staircase leading up to the first floor.

The real highlight of the Whitaker house, however, is the **decoration** conceived by the same artist for the **Sala d'Estate** (Summer Room): this consists of a *trompe l'oeil* covering the walls and ceiling, transforming the space into a cool veranda surrounded by vegetation.

Orto Botanico★★

Via Lincoln 2. ⏲*Open daily May–Aug 9am–8pm, Apr and Sept 9am–7pm, Mar and Oct 9am–6pm, Nov–Feb 9am–5pm.*⊛*€5.* ☏*091 23 89 12 36. www.ortobotanico.unipa.it.*

The Botanical Gardens have occupied their present site since 1789 and contain a huge range of species, including Oriental and exotic plants, such as the majestic *Dendrocalamus giganteus* or the incredible **banyan tree★★** *(Ficus magnoloides).*

Villa Giulia

Via Lincoln 12.
This vast garden was designed in the 18C and contains a fine **fountain** by Ignazio Marabitti (1780) surrounded by four exedrae (large niches). The same sculptor was responsible for the fountain topped by the Genio di Palermo (spirit of Palermo) that you can see on the way to the nearby botanical garden.

Albero di Falcone

Via Notarbartolo 23 (which intersects with Viale della Libertà) on the right heading towards the ring road.
"Falcone's Tree" stands outside the house of **Giovanni Falcone**, the judge who was killed by a Mafia bomb in 1992. Since his death, the tree appears to have become a shrine in its own right: messages, photographs and offerings bear witness to the people's esteem and affection for Falcone and for **Paolo Borsellino**, another popular anti-Mafia judge assassinated in 1992.

Teatro Massimo

© Vito Arcomano / Fototeca ENIT

Museo della Fondazione Mormino - Villa Zito

Viale della Libertà 52. ⚬➡*Closed for renovations. Reopening May/June 2014.* ✆*091 77 92 724. www.fondazionesicilia. it. The collections are temporarily on display at the Palazzo Branciforte, Via Bara all'Olivella 2.* ⚬*€7.* ✆*091 88 87 767.*

The private Mormino Museum is housed on the first floor of the Banco di Sicilia and displays art work, original creations and recovered artefacts acquired over the years by the Bank. The first rooms are devoted to pieces recovered during the excavations of Selinunte, Himera, Solunto and Terravecchia di Cuti, a small town farther inland.

A second section displays **majolica** from Sicily and Italy (with a few examples from Turkey and China). The third section is devoted to 13C–19C coins and medals.

On the ground floor is the Bank's philatelic collection, with stamps dating from the era of the Kingdom of the Two Sicilies.

Villa Trabia

Via Salinas. Take Via Latini, then Via Cusmano to Piazza D. Siculo; Via Salinas leads off this square.

A wonderful **garden** surrounds the villa, built in the 18C and purchased the following year by Giuseppe Lanza Branciforte, prince of Trabia and Butera. Now used as municipal offices, it has a splendid entrance reached by a monumental staircase.

BEYOND THE CITY GATES
Catacombe dei Cappuccini★★

Via Cappuccini. 🕐*Open 9am–1pm, 3–6pm.* ⚬*€3.* ✆*091 65 24 156.*

The Capuchin Catacombs consist of a maze of corridors containing thousands of mummified bodies, perfectly dressed, in niches and appended to, or propped up against walls. The catacombs contain the remains of almost 8,000 Capuchin friars *(the oldest corpses date from the late 16C)*, as well as those of illustrious or wealthy Palermitani, children and virgins. The condition of the corpses, preserved intact by the special environmental conditions, is extraordinary. The body of a two-year old girl who died in 1920 is so well preserved that she seems merely asleep. This particular visit is not recommended for those with small children.

In the cemetery adjacent to the Capuchin monastery is the tomb of **Giuseppe Tomasi di Lampedusa**, author of *The Leopard,* who died in 1957 *(third avenue on the left).*

La Cuba★

Corso Calatafimi 100. 🕐*Open summer, 9am–6.30pm; Sun and public hols, 9am–1pm.* ⚬*€2.* ♿ ✆*091 59 02 99.*

The last Norman era monument built in Palermo, the cube-shaped Cuba Sottana palace, was erected in 1180 on the instruction of William II. Now incorporated into a military barracks, it was probably surrounded by a vast artificial lake known as the Pescheria (fishpond). In the old stables *(just inside the entrance on the right)* is a reconstruction of how the palace must have originally looked. The decoration is exquisitely simple: above a series of tall pointed arches of differing widths are various other smaller openings. The internal space was divided into three parts; in the central section is a star-shaped pool from which water would gently trickle into the Pescheria without breaking the surface and disturbing the reflections.

La Zisa★

Piazza Guglielmo il Buono. 🕐*Open Tue–Sat 9am–1pm, 2–6.30pm, Sun–Mon 9am–1pm.* ⚬*€6.* ♿ ✆*091 65 20269.*

The name of this 12C palazzo is derived from El Aziz, meaning the splendid or noble one. Today, only the shell of the palace remains, yet it retains an undeniable aura. It was initiated by William I and completed by his son William II between 1166 and 1175; work on the building was entrusted entirely to Moorish craftsmen. After a period of neglect in the 14C, it was transformed into a fortress and then a depository for objects contaminated by the plague (16C), before being converted into a *palazzo* for a noble family. Recent restoration has attempted to return it to its original state.

Tour

The main attraction on the ground floor is the room with the fountain: built on a cruciform plan, it has two square pools that collect water from the main channel in the centre of the room, fed from a waterspout. The upper section of wall has a **mosaic frieze** of peacocks and arches. From here runs a succession of rooms, each with a ventilation system so carefully calculated that air can circulate through the gaps in the walls.

The niches and windows have *muqarnas*, a honeycomb of miniature vaults and stalactite pendants characteristic of Islamic architecture. The *palazzo* houses a collection of objects mainly from Egypt (from the Mameluke and Ottoman periods), typifying the style of furnishings that might once have adorned the original palace.

Albergo delle Povere

Corso Calatafimi 217. Open to the public during exhibitions and conferences.
This complex was originally intended at the end of the 18C as a hospice for the poor; in the 19C, it was reserved for spinsters, who set up a weaving workshop

there. It is now used to house temporary exhibitions.

The left wing still shelters Opera Pia, a charity providing assistance to the poor; the right wing serves as the operational headquarters for the *carabinieri* unit charged with protecting Sicily's artistic heritage.

Ponte dell'Ammiraglio

Corso dei Mille.
The picturesque medieval bridge once straddled the River Oreto (which has since been diverted). It was built in 1113 by George of Antioch, an admiral serving under **Roger II**.

San Giovanni dei Lebbrosi★

Via Cappello 38 (a road left off Corso dei Mille, beyond the Ponte dell'Ammiraglio).
Supposedly founded in 1070 (some say it may have been a century later), St John of the Lepers may be the oldest Norman church in Sicily.

Santo Spirito (Chiesa dei Vespri)

Inside the cemetery of Sant'Orsola: on Piazza di Sant'Orsola (from Piazzetta Montalto, take Via Colomba and turn right into Via dei Vespri).
The Church of the Holy Spirit, or of the Vespers, was built in 1178 in the reign

Rock engravings, Grotte dell'Addaura

© Werner Forman Archive/Photolibrary

Beach at Mondello

© Sandro Bedessi / Fototeca ENIT

of Roger II. It came to fame on 31 March 1282, when during Evensong (Vespers), a French soldier insulted a Sicilian woman, causing bystanders to leap to her defence and so providing a pretext for an outburst of growing resentment towards the invaders.

The incident sparked off the War of the Sicilian Vespers, which in turn led to the eviction of the French.

Santuario di Santa Maria di Gesù

Follow Viale della Regione Siciliana to the intersection with Via Oreto (the southern extension of Via Maqueda). Turn right along Via Santa Maria di Gesù (look out for the green sign above the shoe shop on the corner). ○*Open daily, 8am–12.30pm.*

The 15C Sanctuary of St Mary of Jesus occupies a serene and cool spot on the slopes of **Monte Grifone**. The way to it leads through a cemetery, where traditionally aristocratic families kept their mausoleums.

The area in front of the church is surrounded by fine patrician tombs, including the Liberty-style chapel belonging to the princes of Lanza di Scalea.

Inside, the chancel has two bays articulated by pointed arches; Antonio Alliata's marble sarcophagus is attributed to Antonello Gagini *(in the chan-*

cel, high up on the right); there is a rare **wooden statue of the Virgin**★(1470) and a fine coffered **wooden ceiling**, painted with flowers and angels *(early 16C)*, which spans the church entrance and the organ above it, painted with scenes from the life of St Francis (1932).

Parco della Favorita★

3km/1.8mi N. Follow Viale della Libertà to Piazza Vittorio Veneto. Turn right into Piazza dei Leoni; Viale del Fante runs by the park as far as the Chinese palace.

The parkland at the foot of Monte Pellegrino was created in 1799 by Ferdinand III of Bourbon when the Napoleonic troops drove him out of Naples (where he had reigned as Ferdinand IV). It was given to the King by noble Palermo families and became his private hunting estate; he had a house built there, the **Chinese palace**. The servants' quarters lay in the building next door, arranged around a courtyard facing the kitchens (connected to the palace by an underground passageway); now the **Museo Etnografico Pitré**.

Museo Etnografico Pitré

Viale Duca degli Abruzzi 1, Parco della Favorita. ○*Open 9am–8pm.* ○*Closed Fri and public hols. Temporarily transferred to the Palazzo Tarallo, Via delle*

Pergole 74. ℘091 616 6621. Library only open to visitors.

The Pitré Ethnographic Museum houses artefacts associated with local folklore; reconstructions of houses containing tools, needlework and embroidery, fabrics, a 17C wrought-iron bedhead, pottery, "Sunday-best" clothes, splendid engraved horn goblets and gourd containers for water or wine. Amulets and trinkets linked with magic and superstition, together with handmade votive objects, testify to the faith of the country people. The museum also has a **library** (◷*open mornings only*).

Villa Niscemi★

Piazza Niscemi, at the end of Viale del Fante. ◷Open Mon–Sat 9am–dusk (gardens); Sun 9am–12.30pm (villa). ☞Free. ℘091 74 04 822.

Next to the **Parco della Favorita** stand the gardens and beautiful country villa that once belonged to the princes Valguarnera di Niscemi. Purchased by the city in 1987, the villa has several frescoed rooms decorated with 18C furnishings. One of the most attractive is the Salone delle Quattro Stagioni with a fresco of Charlemagne depicted on the Valguarnera coat-of-arms.

EXCURSIONS
Monte Pellegrino

14km/9mi N. From Viale della Libertà, turn right into Via Imperatore Federico and then head along Via Bonanno.

The road up Monte Pellegrino offers magnificent **views★★★** over Palermo and the Conca d'Oro; in places it is crossed by a much steeper, paved path dating from the 17C.

As the road climbs, it passes **Castello Utveggio**, a massive pink building that can also be seen from the city, then continues on to the **Santuario di Santa Rosalia** (17C), a sanctuary built around the cave where, legend has it, St Rosalia lived, and where her bones were found in 1624.

The bones were carried through the streets and credited with freeing the city from the Plague. Following this, St Rosalia became the patron saint of Palermo. The cave has guttering to collect dripping water from the walls, which is considered by locals to possess miraculous properties.

Farther on up, the road reaches a lookout point with breathtaking sea **views★**.

Mondello★

*11km/7mi NW of Palermo.
Continue along the seafront.*

The road passes below the slopes of **Monte Pellegrino**. This area, now an

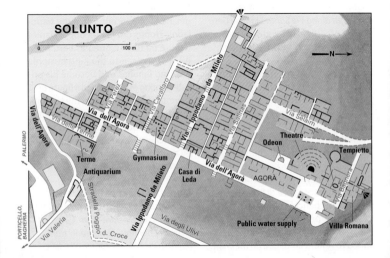

Tufa statues, Villa Palagonia
© Schütze / Rodemann / age fotostock

elegant holiday resort, was discovered at the beginning of the century by rich Palermitani, who were looking for a short break to enjoy the benefits of the warm sea air on their health and well-being.

There's little to see in this quiet town, other than the ruins of a **medieval tower** and a small harbour, with a lively jetty populated by amateur fishermen in summer.

Mondello's main attraction, its sweep of **sandy beach**, runs between nearby Valdesi to the resort. In the evenings, join locals and visitors alike in Piazza Mondello for the *passeggiata* and enjoy a relaxed drink at one of the many bars in the square.

Grotte dell'Addaura★

Between Mondello and Arenella. Take Via Crispi and follow the Lungomare Cristoforo Colombo to Punta di Priola. From Monte Pellegrino, travel along Via Bonanno, turn right into Viale Regina Margherita, then right again along the seafront.
o━┓*No longer open to visitors.*
www.palermoweb.com/cefaladiana.
A series of caves among the lower slopes of Monte Pellegrino were inhabited during Palaeolithic times (5th millennium BC) and **rock engravings**, possibly associated with an initiation

ceremony or a ritual, have been found in one of them.

Bagheria

Bagheria, around 15km/9mi from Palermo, can be reached along the A 19 motorway (Bagheria exit), the S 113 or by train (the station is close to Villa Cattolica). The easiest way to access these villas is by driving to the town via the S 113, then taking the Corso Butera to the Corso Umberto.
Bagheria is known for its numerous Baroque villas built from the 17C onwards by wealthy Palermo aristocrats as their summer residences.

Villa Palagonìa★

The entrance is located to the rear, although the façade gives onto the small Garibaldi square, at the end of Corso Umberto. ◷*Open Apr–Oct 9am– 1pm, 4pm–7pm; Nov–Mar 9am–1pm, 3.30pm–5.30pm.* ⊛€5. ℘091 93 20 88. *www.villapalagonia.it.*
This most celebrated of the Bagheria villas, built in 1715, Palagonia has a concave façade and convex rear. The house was constructed by Prince Gravina's father, but it was the Prince's idea to add the exuberant **sculptural decoration★**. Goethe considered it a monstrosity but this arrangement, consisting of 60 crude, often monstrous tufa statues,

155

Ruins of Solunto

© Richard Ashworth/age fotostock

has provoked various esoteric interpretations. They include mythological figures, musicians, soldiers, dragons and grotesque beasts, which create a surreal atmosphere.

This eccentricity runs through the rooms of the villa. The great oval entrance hall, painted with **trompe l'oeil frescoes** illustrating four of the twelve Labours of Heracles, leads into the distorted **Hall of Mirrors**.

Villa Butera

This stands at the southern end of Corso Butera.

The villa was built in the second half of the 17C by Prince Branciforti di Raccuia. Although now in a sad state of repair, it preserves an imposing **tufa doorway** to the piano nobile.

Villa Cattolica

Via Consolare 9 (S 113). From the motorway, cross Bagheria, following the signs to Aspra. &. ⊙*Open Tue–Sun 9.30am–2pm, 3pm–7.30pm* ⊙*Closed Mon, national hols.* ⊜€5. ℘091 94 39 02. www.museoguttuso.it.

This massive square building, built in 1736 by Giuseppe Bonanni Filangeri, Prince of Cattolica, houses the **Civica Galleria d'Arte Moderna e Contemporanea Renato Guttuso**. This modern art gallery exhibits works by Sicily's native son **Guttoso** and other artists close to him. The villa gardens harbour the **tomb** of the painter, designed by his friend, Giacomo Manzù.

Rovine di Solunto★

From Bagheria, cross the level crossing near the station and turn down S 113 towards Porticello. A minor road forks left towards the hill. ⊙*Open Tue–Sun 9am–6.30pm, Sun 9am–1pm.* ⊙*Closed Mon.* ⊜€2. ℘091 94 39 02.

Solunto, one of Sicily's three Punic cities with Mozia and Palermo, occupies a delightful position on a promontory of Monte Catalfano. The magnificent ruins include a **frescoed patrician house** and agora.

Solunto was founded by the Carthaginians in the 4C BC and succumbed to Roman rule in the 5C BC. The name has two origins: the legend of the evil creature **Soluntus** and the Carthaginian word *Selaim*, meaning "crag".

The urban layout conforms to Classical principles upheld by Hippodamus of Miletus, arranged orthogonally with a *decumanus maximus* and perpendicular side streets. The steep site required terracing and tall houses.

The way up to the ruins passes the **Antiquarium** *(just inside the gate)* displaying artefacts from the site.

Baths

The thermal baths preserve underfloor brick supports that enabled hot air to flow from below and a bathing room with **mosaics**.

Via dell'Agorà

The *decumanus maximus* is partly paved in stone and, unusually, in terra-cotta. It bisects the town on a southwest to northeast axis, extending to the forum or agora.

Gymnasium

This is the name commonly given to the patrician house with an atrium and a peristyle, from which there remain three Doric columns and part of the entablature, complete with architrave, frieze of metopes and triglyphs and cornice.

Via Ippodamo da Mileto

The view from the bottom of this former *cardo* (secondary road) offers a magnificent **view★★** over the bay of Palermo and Monte Pellegrino.

Casa di Leda

This large patrician house gets its name from its **fresco** of Leda and the Swan. The house is arranged around a peristyle (as indicated by the stump of a corner column and cavities for the other columns) with an *impluvium* designed for rainwater collection. One of the rooms facing the peristyle is frescoed in **Pompeiian** style.

Agora

The square was originally enclosed on all sides by public buildings and lined with shops (*at the far end*). On the east side was a large **public cistern**: note the bases of the 26 columns that supported the roof.

Odeon

The small theatre was intended for musical performances or council meetings: the orchestra and a few rows of seating are still visible.

The Albanian Community

In the 16C, an Albanian *condottiere* (group of mercenaries) put down a revolt in southern Italy, where the soldiers stayed before trickling to Sicily. They were welcomed and allowed to practise their Greek Orthodox faith and to maintain their traditions, language and literature. One of their most important communities is in Piana degli Albanesi, and although now integrated into the local population, the Albanians retain their own traditions, especially during religious festivals, two of the most important being Epiphany (12 days after Christmas) and Easter, when the locals don splendid costumes, typically embroidered with gold and silver, before rallying at the churches of Santa Maria Odigitria, nearby San Giorgio and San Demetrio, the town's main church. Even the road signs and street names are inscribed in two languages.

Villa Romana

From this villa, once a vast residence with two floors and a peristyle, there is a good **view** of Capo Zafferano and **Sant'Elia**. At the far end of the bay on the headland what is left of the **medieval castle** of Solunto sits looking out to sea.

Corleone

55km/34mi S of Palermo towards Agrigento. Leave Palermo on the E 90, then follow the SS 121 and SS 118.

For decades this quiet town nestled in a pastoral mountain cirque was home to Palermo's Mafia bosses. Corleone's infamous reputation is based both on fact (it was the home of the now-imprisoned **Salvatore Riina** and **Bernardo Provenzano**) and fiction (author Mario Puzo's *The Godfather* Don Corleone was introduced to screen by director Francis Ford Coppola decades before the rise of

Chiesa Madre, Corleone

© Mike Cumberbatch / age fotostock

the real Corleone clans in the Mafia wars of the 1980s).

Today Corleone is an important centre for the anti-Mafia movement with a museum documenting the Mafia's rise and fall in Sicily through photographs and newsclips: the **Centro Internazionale di Documentazione sulle Mafie e del Movimento AntiMafia** (*Via Giovanni Valenti 7;* ✆*guided 1hr visits by appointment. 10am–5pm;* ℘*340 402 5601*).

Local bars still play up the notoriety by displaying pictures of film versions of the Corleone family and serve a bitter digestivo, Amaro Don Corleone. (Note: in *The Godfather* films Coppola actually shot scenes representing old Corleone on the other side of island in the hills above Taormina.)

Do not miss the other charms of Corleone. The leafy park, where locals gather in the evenings, is home to 40 churches including the majestic **Chiesa Madre** from the early 14C.

🚗 DRIVING TOUR

INLAND FROM PALERMO
120km/75mi. Allow one day.

This day trip, combining archaeology, art and natural landscapes, passes through verdant scenery with splendid views.

▷ From Viale Regione Siciliana take the Calatafimi-Monreale exit and follow S 186 to Monreale *(8km/5mi)*.

Monreale★★★
♿*See Monreale.*

▷ Return to S 186.

After Pioppo and the turning off to San Giuseppe Jato, there is a magnificent **view★** of Palermo and the sea.

▷ After Giacalone, turn left onto S 624 (the Palermo–Sciacca road). Turn off at San Cipirello *(25km/16mi)* and take the road to Corleone and Tagliavia. Turn left at the yellow signs for Scavi del Monte Jato. The road winds uphill for 5km/3mi. The final dirt-track section must be undertaken on foot.

Scavi del Monte Jato
🕐*Open sunrise to sunset; closes at 12pm public holidays. Info at Pro Loco.* ⊜*Free.* ℘*091 85 73 083.*
Founded by the Elimi (or the Sicani) as early as the 1st millennium BC, Jetae enjoyed its period of greatest splendour in the 3C BC.

On the west side of the **agora** or market place (300 BC) stand a portico and *bouleuterion* – a council chamber, where the orator would stand between the two doorways to address the assembly. West of the agora is the **theatre** (late 4C–early 3C BC), which held an audience of up to 4,400. The **house** with the peristyle was built over two storeys, around a porticoed courtyard.

The **Temple of Aphrodite** (opposite the south side of the house), erected in c. 550 BC in Greek style, bears witness to the earliest cultural exchanges between the indigenous population and the Greek world.

Museo Civico di San Cipirello

Antiquarium Case d'Alia, Via Roma 320. ◷Open daily, 8.30am–1.30pm; Mon, Wed and Fri 3–6pm. ⊗Free ♿ ℘091 85 81 014.

This municipal museum displays artefacts recovered from the archaeological excavations at **Monte Jato**, including **sculptures** from the theatre: maenads and satyrs, followers of Dionysus, god of the theatre (and wine), and a crouching lion.

▷ Follow the S 624 towards Palermo and take the turning for Piana degli Albanesi.

The road affords magnificent **views** of the valley as it climbs up to **Portella della Ginestra**, where a monument marks a massacre perpetrated by the bandit Salvatore Giuliano in 1947. The road then descends to **Piana degli Albanesi** (12km/7.5mi).

▷ From Piana degli Albanesi, follow signs to Ficuzza (20km/12.5mi S). The winding road leads upward and offers splendid views of the town and man-made lake.

Palazzo Reale and Bosco della Ficuzza

The village of Ficuzza is arranged around the piazza in front of this **hunting lodge** built for Ferdinando III of Bourbon in the 19C. The limestone walls of Rocca Busambra (1,613m/5,290ft) are an impressive backdrop to the striking neo-Classical building.

To the right, the **Centro di Recupero della Fauna selvatica di Ficuzza** (Ficuzza Wildlife Protection Centre) provides information on local fauna.

▷ A road to the left of the palace leads into the woods and is the starting-point for a number of excursions.

The **Bosco della Ficuzza**, once a royal hunting ground, is a plateau covering approximately 7,000ha/17,300 acres of land dominated by Rocca Busambra. The forest comprises mainly holm oak, maple, oak and cork oak, while its rich fauna includes porcupines, martens, hedgehogs, tortoises, **golden eagles** and **peregrine falcons**.

▷ From Ficuzza, return to the main road and head towards Godrano and Cefala Diana (17km/10.5mi E).

Cefalà Diana

The town deserves a visit for its 10C **Turkish baths**, the only example of its kind in Sicily, and the remains of its 13C **castle**.

Also notable are the expressive bronze sculptures in the main piazza by a contemporary artist from Corleone, Biagio Governali.

The baths

◷Open daily, 9.30am–12.45pm. ◷Closed public holidays. ⊗Free. ℘091 82 01 184.

The baths are located just over 1km/ 0.6mi outside the town by the River Cefala, within a restored complex. The original complex of baths, built sometime pre-1570, was used to relieve rheumatism by locals, who bathed in the hot, sulphurous springs.

▷ Return to the main road and continue as far as the junction with S 121. Follow the signs back to Palermo (87km/54mi).

ADDRESSES

🛏 STAY

Notarbartolo – *Via E. Notarbartolo 35. ℘091 73 08 333 or 346 53 65 197. www. notarbartolo.com. 6 rooms.* ⌓. Located in a quiet residential area, near a busy shopping street, Via Libertà, this B&B is on the 4th floor (no lift) of a Liberty building. Spacious, comfortable rooms. Good breakfast with home-made pastries.

Palazzo Speciale – *Via Giuseppe Mario Puglia 2. ℘091 33 21 73. www. palazzospecialepalermo.it.* At the heart of the old town, these unfussy, elegant apartments (sleeping 2 to 5 people, with equipped kitchenette) are located in a 15C palazzo. The best apartments have terraces with views over the roofs of Palermo.

Il Giardino di Ballaro – *Via Porta di Castro 75-77. ℘091 21 22 15 or 339 18 34 950. www.ilgiardinodiballaro.it. 4 rooms.* ⌓. Right in the heart of the historic Ballaró market district, this B&B was recently renovated in sand and cream hues. Breakfast is served in the courtyard in summer.

Al Giardino dell'Alloro – *Vicolo San Carlo 8. ℘091 617 69 04 or 338 224 35 41. www.giardinodellalloro.it. 4 rooms* ⌓. Located in an alley in the Kalsa district, this guesthouse offers comfortable rooms with a mixture of contemporary style and traditional decor. Upstairs rooms can accommodate three people for € 110. Copious breakfast and a friendly welcome.

Alla Kala – *Via Vittorio Emanuele 71. ℘091 743 47 63. www.allakala.it. 5 rooms.* This pleasant B&B on the first floor of a modern building with views over the port of Cala, a short walk from Piazza Marina, is decorated in a marine style.

Abali Gran Sultanato – *Via S. Agostino 5. ℘338 335 29 97. www.abali.it. 5 rooms.* Guests enjoy a warm welcome in this one-of-a-kind B&B where One Thousand and One Nights meets Pop Art.

B&B 22 – *Largo Cavalieri di Malta 22. ℘091 611 16 10 or 335 790 87 33. 4 rooms.* ⌓. Located in a narrow street in the historic centre, this charming, impeccably renovated house has bright rooms mixing modern design and tradition, plus luxurious suites from €170–200 facing onto a garden.

Palazzo Ajutamicristo – *Via G. Garibaldi 23. ℘091 61 61 894. www. palazzoajutamicritsto.it. 3 rooms* ⌓. Tucked away in one of the most beautiful palaces in Palermo, these Visconti-esque rooms have been lovingly decorated down to the last detail. Sicilian-style breakfast served on the terrace in summer.

Quintocanto Hotel & Spa – *Via Vittorio Emanule 310. ℘091 58 49 13. www.quintocantohotel.com. 20 rooms.* A stone's throw from the Piazza Quattrocanti, this quality, designer hotel is housed in a former palace. Spa and gastronomic restaurant. Excellent deals.

Grand Hotel Federico II – *Via Principe di Granatelli 60. ℘091 749 50 52. www.grandhotelfedericoii.it. 60 rooms* ⌓. This hotel with a solid reputation is located in a quiet street. The spacious, comfortable bedrooms offer real value for money.

Grand Hotel Villa Igiea – *Salita Belmonte 43. ℘091 63 12 111. www.hoteligieapalermo.com. 123 rooms* ⌓. An historic building located in a residential area on the coast, with views over the bay. Sophisticated décor, quality restaurant and excellent level of service.

Santa Cristina di Gela

Agrirelais Baglio di Pianetto – *Via Francia, Contrada Pianetto, 22km/13mi from Palermo. SS624 dir. Sciacca. From Altofonte take the SP5 to Piana degli Albanesi, then follow the signs to Santa Cristina di Gela et Baglio. ℘091 85 71 230.www.agrirelais.com.* ⌇.*13 rooms.* This tastefully-restored *baglio* surrounded by vineyards a few miles from Piana degli Albanesi has everything you need for a relaxing, pleasurable stay: comfortable, charming rooms, swimming pool with turquoise water, and Sicilian cuisine served with vintage wines.

🍴EAT

SICILIAN FAST FOOD

Local specialities include snacks such as *u sfinciuni* or *sfincione* (a type of pizza topped with tomato, anchovies, onion and breadcrumbs), *pani ca' meusa* or *panino con la milza* (roll filled with charcoal-grilled pork offal), *panelle* (fried chickpea flour pancakes) and *babbaluci* (tiny marinated snails served in paper cornets), which are often sold from stalls in the local markets.

⊖ **Sciuscià** – *Via Dante 212. ☎091 68 22 700. Closed Sun.* By far the best pizza in Palermo. Its secret? Deliciously stuffed crusts. The pleasant, relaxed dining room is too small to accommodate its many fans. Booking advised.

⊖ **Antica Focacceria San Francesco** – *Via A. Paternostro 58, Palermo. ☎091 32 02 64. www.afsf.it.* Situated in the heart of the old town opposite San Francesco church, this historic family café (founded in 1834) has marble tables and serves traditional *foccacia con la milza* from an antique cast-iron stove. It offers a selection of *focaccia farcita* (flat, heavy pizza dough baked with various fillings) as well as *arancini di riso* (a Sicilian staple – deep-fried rice balls stuffed with various fillings from vegetables to meat sauce, cheese and nuts), *torte salate* (Sicilian savoury "cakes"), fried ricotta cheese and *sfincione*. The focacceria also has an elegant full-service restaurant upstairs and terrace dining in season.

⊖⊜ **Casa del Brodo** – *Via Vittorio Emanuele 175. ☎091 32 16 55. www. casadelbrodo.it. Closed Sun in summer and Tues in winter.* This former soup kitchen, founded one hundred years ago, is now one of the best places to sample traditional Sicilian cuisine. Diners enjoy a large antipasti buffet in the corridor between two rooms, and a menu of fish, olive oil and vegetables. Specialities include seafood risotto and sardine pasta. Booking recommended.

⊖⊜ **Obikà** – *c/o La Rinascente, Piazza S. Domenico 18. ☎091 60 17 861. Open daily 9am–midnight.* A "mozzarella bar" with a contemporary design located on the top floor of the department store on Via Roma. A great place for lunch or a glass of wine as you look out over Palermo.

⊖⊜ **Santandrea** – *Piazza Sant'Andrea 4. ☎091 33 49 99. Closed Sun.* Tucked away in the Vucciria district, at the foot of the church of San Domenico, this cosy restaurant is renowned for its freshly-made dishes. One of the best fish couscous in Palermo.

⊖⊜ **Il Maestro del Brodo** – *Via Pannieri 7. ☎091 32 95 23. Closed Mon.* This is one of the rare restaurants good enough for the locals. This cool, well-kept establishment on a Via Vittorio Emanuele side street has built its reputation on its meat stew (*brodo*). Its other specialities include aubergines rolls, grilled tuna steak with mint sauce and its delicious *cassata dessert*.

⊖⊜ **Il Mirto e la rosa** – *Via Principe di Granatelli 30. ☎091 32 43 53. www.ilmirto elarosa.com. Closed Sun.* The food here is essentially vegetarian, with dishes such as caponatina di melanzane – a sweet and sour aubergine stew – served with pistachio couscous. Very welcoming.

⊖⊜ **Sapori Perduti** – *Via Principe di Belmonte 32. ☎091 32 73 87. Closed Sun eve. and Mon.* Giving onto Via Principe di Belmonte, a leafy pedestrian street, this small restaurant with a modern, refined décor revisits the classics of Sicilian cuisine and specialises in raw, marinated or lightly-cooked fish. Helpful, attentive service.

⊖⊜ **Osteria dei Vespri** – *Piazza Croce dei Vespri 6. ☎091 61 71 631. www. osteriacrocedeivespri.it. Closed Sun.* Located inside the Palazzo Gangi, the backdrop to several scenes from the *Leopard*, this restaurant enjoys the perfect setting for its quality cuisine. Tradition and innovation are the watchwords of chef Alberto Rizzo. His cellar includes 700 vintages, making it one of the best restaurants in Palermo.

⊖⊜ **Ristorantino Palazzo Sambuca** – *Via Alloro 26. ☎091 50 76 794. Closed Sun.* Offering the decadent charm of an ancient palace in the historic centre combined with a modern, chic and streamlined décor, this restaurant specialises in fish. Don't miss the swordfish rolls with citrus fruits and mussel and clam soup.

⊖⊜ **Officina del Gusto Bye Bye Blues** – *Via Vittorio Emanuele 316. ☎091 61 16 678. www.officinabyebyeblues.com.* This "taste laboratory" comes hot on the heels of its star-spangled brother, Bye Bye Blues in Mondello. In the courtyard of the highly central Quintocanto hotel, the palace surroundings do nothing to dampen the lively atmosphere. Fish and seafood take pride of place on the menu.

⊖⊜ **Cucina Papoff** – *Via Isidoro La Lumia 32. ☎091 58 64 60. www. cucinapapoff.com. Closed Mon and Aug.* Although this restaurant's name might sound Russian, it has been serving genuine Sicilian cuisine for thirty years. Rustic-chic atmosphere and a select menu of traditional dishes, such as tuna carpaccio and stuffed squid.

MONDELLO

◉ **Antico Chiosco** – *Piazza Mondello 4.* *℘091 450 667.* On the central square, a stone's throw from the beach, this large café, pasticceria and gelateria offers snacks or self-service meals at lunchtime.

◉◉ **Da Calogero** – *Via Torre 22. ℘091 684 13 33.* Facing the beach, this trattoria, with its colourful tiled interior, is the best place in the area to try pasta with sea urchins or other seafood dishes.

◉◉◉ **Bye bye blues** – *Via del Garofalo 23. ℘091 68 41 415. www.byebyeblues. it. Closed Tue, lunch Mon–Fri and Nov.* ⤳. *Booking recommended.* This restaurant is well worth a visit for its original atmosphere and inventive cuisine, with a good balance of meat and fish dishes. It also has an excellent wine list.

BAGHERIA

◉◉ **Don Ciccio** – *Via del Cavaliere 87/c. ℘091 93 24 42. www.trattoriadonciccio. net. Closed Wed.* Close to the Villa Palagonia, this family-run trattoria has been a favourite with locals for 50 years. Each meal begins with a hard boiled egg accompanied by a small glass of marsala.

TAKING A BREAK
POLITEAMA DISTRICT

Antico Caffè Spinnato – *Via Principe di Belmonte 107–115. ℘091 74 95 104. www. spinnato.it.* One of the oldest cafés in Palermo (founded 1860), the elegant Antico Caffè enjoys a splendid setting on the chic Via Principe Belmonte. Since 1860, it has served excellent cakes and pastries on the attractive terrace, which features a jazz pianist on summer evenings.

Pasticceria Mazzara – *Via Mag-liocco 15. ℘091 32 14 43.* An historic bar once frequented by Giuseppe Tomasi di Lampedusa, started as a *pasticceria* (the cassata, *cannoli*, other pastries, and ice cream are excellent), then extended to include a rosticceria, self-service restaurant and pizzeria.

Cappello – *Via Colonna Rossa 68. ℘091 48 96 01. www.pasticceriacappello.it.* Near the Zisa palace, this artful pasticceria is run by a master pastry chef and specialist in Sicilian-style chocolate. Specialities

include the Volo, a chocolate mousse with pistachio cream.

Gelateria Ilardo – *Foro Umberto I 12.* One of Palermo's historic *gelaterie*, where the ice cream is entirely handmade.

Magrì – *Via Isidoro Carini 42. ℘091 61 61537.* Near the Politeama theatre, this is an excellent place for lovers of almond-paste sweets.

Stancampiano – *Via E. Notarbartolo 51, Palermo. ℘091 62 54 099. www.gelateria stancampiano.it.* This gelateria has the largest selection of ice creams in Palermo. Do as the Sicilians and enjoy your ice cream accompanied by a brioche.

SIGHTSEEING

The tourist office publishes a monthly magazine, *Un Ospite a Palermo (online at www.unospiteapalermo.it)* featuring events and opening times for museums, churches and various palazzi.

Combined tickets – There are combined tickets for the Zisa, Galleria Regionale di Palazzo Abatellis, Chiostro di San Giovanni degli Eremit, Chiostro di Monreale, and Palazzo d'Aumale in Terrasini *(€24; valid for five days)*; the Zisa, Galleria Regionale di Palazzo Abatelli, and a choice of Galleria Chiostro di San Giovanni degli Eremit, Chiostro di Monreale or Palazzo d'Aumale *(€10.50; valid for three days)*; the choice of two sites from Zisa, Galleria Chiostro di San Giovanni degli Eremit, Chiostro di Monreale, and Palazzo d'Aumale *(€9; valid for three days)*; and the Galleria Regionale di Palazzo Abatelli, and Palazzo Mirto *(€10; valid for one day)*.

City Sightseeing Palermo offers two hop-on, hop-off routes in the city *(€20 for both)* as well as an additional guided visit to the Cathedral in Monreale *(€25)*; English spoken. Buses leave from the Teatro Politeama. *℘091 58 94 29. www.palermo.city-sightseeing.it.*

The **tourist train** *(trenino)* organises city tours with commentaries starting from Via Francesco Crispi, in the port *(€8).* *℘095 82 042 81.*

SHOWTIME

◉ Palermo has come alive in recent years and the city now offers a wealth of cultural events. To find out what's on, try the weekly cultural listings in the free newspaper *Lapis*, the free bi-monthly magazine *Balarm* (www.balarm.it) or *visitPalermo* (www.visitpalermo.it).

Albergo delle Povere – *Corso Calatafimi 217.* This former hospice founded in the late 18C now regularly hosts exhibitions and lectures (♿*see also p152*).

Cantieri culturali alla Zisa – *Via Gili 4, Palermo.* ☎*091 65 24 942.* The old Ducrot warehouses, near Castello della Zisa, were once home to a well-known furniture factory. Nowadays, they have been transformed into public rooms hosting a broad range of exhibitions, concerts and plays.

Ex Magazzini Ferroviari ai Lolli – *Piazza Lolli.* Concerts and other cultural events are held in this fine late-19C building.

Ex Stazione Sant'Erasmo – *Via Messina Marine.* This late-19C building at the mouth of the River Oreto was formerly a station and has now become a venue for interesting exhibitions.

Kursaal Kalhesa – *Foro Umberto I 21.* ☎*091 61 62 828. www.kursaalkalhesa. it.* The Palazzo Forcella *(19C)* contains an art gallery, exhibition space, bookshop, restaurant and wine bar with terrace.

Kursaal Tonnara – *Via Bordonaro 9, Vergine Maria Arenella.* ☎*091 63 72 267. www.kursaaltonnara.it.* This former *tonnara* on the seafront hosts performances and dance nights in the summer.

Parco letterario Giuseppe Tomasi di Lampedusa – *Vicolo della Neve all'Alloro 2/5.* ☎*091 60 93 150.www.parcotomasi. it.* A cultural centre offering informative tours that will immerse you in the atmosphere of Luchino Visconti's film version of *The Leopard*.

Lo Spasimo – *Via Spasimo (Piazza Magione), Palermo.* ☎*091 61 61 486.* The Santa Maria dello Spasimo complex, home to the Scuola Europea di Musica Jazz, provides an atmospheric setting for a range of cultural events.

👥 IL TEATRO DEI PUPI

The Cuticchio family is synonymous with the ancient tradition of the puppet theatre in Palermo. For generations not only have these highly skilled puppeteers put on performances, they make puppets too. At one time puppet shows were the talk of the day and provided work not only for puppeteers but also for skilled craftsman, who specialised in giving form to their fabulous creations. A simple suit

of armour, for example, might comprise some 35–36 individual parts.

Figli d'arte Cuticchio – *Via Bara all'Olivella 95.* ☎*091 32 34 00. www.figli dartecuticchio.com.* The venue for performances by Mimmo Cuticchio's company. Opposite is the workshop where puppets and accessories are kept.

Teatro Ippogrifo – *Vicolo Ragusi 6 (near the Quattro Canti), Palermo.* ☎*091 32 91 94. Performances at 6pm (for a minimum audience of 20 people).* This theatre belongs to Nino and Pina Cuticchio.

SHOPPING

👀 **Good to know:** Most shops are closed on Monday morning *(food shops close on Wednesday afternoon)*. Shops generally open between 9am and 1pm, and from 3.30pm–7.30pm (4pm–8pm on Saturday).

LOCAL MARKETS

A must for any trip to Palermo is a morning walk through one of the city's street markets – some of the oldest and most colourful in Europe. ♿*See p139.*

SHOPS

The city's most elegant shops are concentrated in the new development along Via della Libertà, Via Roma and Via Maqueda. The pedestrianised **Via Principe di Belmonte** is also lined with elegant shops; the central section of the street has been planted with trees to provide shade for tables spilling onto the pavement from its many bars. In the bustling **Via Calderai** *(which crosses Via Maqueda south of Piazza Bellini)* there are arts and crafts shops selling firedogs for fireplaces, chairs, china and crockery. The small **Via Bara all'Olivella** *(opposite Teatro Massimo)* is lined with handicraft shops for ceramics, woodwork and puppets.

Enoteca Picone – *Via G. Marconi 36, Palermo.* ☎*091 33 13 00. www.enotecapi cone.it. Closed Sun. See Taking a Break.*

Enoteca Sicilia Museo del Vino – *Palazzo Palagoni, Via del IV Aprile.* ☎*091 61 62 288. www.enotecasicilia.it. Open 9am–12pm. Closed Sun and public hols. €5.* This exhibition of Sicilian wine labels is housed in the beautiful Palazzo Ramacca. Wine tasting is included in the price of the guided tour *(two wines)*.

Confezionando – *Via Vittorio Emanuele 299.* ☎*091 61 24 654. Closed Sun.* A small high-quality food shop by the Quattro Canti with a wide range of Sicilian products (preserves, sauces, wines, etc.) as well as decorative objects.

Franco Bertolino – *Salita Ramires 8, Palermo. ✆0347 05 76 923. Closed Sun.* Bertolino is one of the last remaining artists to specialise in the production of the traditional, colourful Sicilian carts. His workshop, boutique and small museum are housed near the cathedral.

Il Laboratorio Italiano – *Via Principe di Villafranca 2, Palermo. ✆091 62 69 785. www.laboratorioitaliano.it. Closed Sun.* A range of fine, hand-crafted ceramics are sold in the three rooms of this small workshop. A reputable address renowned for its unusual and original items.

La Bottega d'Arte di Angela Tripi – *Corso Vittorio Emanuele 450, Palermo. ✆091 65 12 787. www.angelatripi.it. Open Mon–Sat, 9.30am–7.30pm.* Situated near the cathedral in Palazzo Santa Ninfa, this workshop specialising in small terracotta statues for cribs is famous throughout the world. A superb showcase of high-quality craftwork.

Vincenzo Argento e Figli – *Corso Vittorio Emanuele 445, Palermo. ✆091 61 13 680. Open Mon–Sat from 10am (shop); performance at 6pm.* The art of traditional puppet-making has been handed down through generations in this century-old family business.

THE ANTI-MAFIA SHOPS

The campaign to end corruption in Sicilian cities and italian society is aided by two organisations **Addio Pizzo** *(www.addiopizzo.org)* and **Libera Terra** *(www.liberaterra.it)*. These shops can provide you with information on items produced on land confiscated from the Mafia. In Palermo, the products are sold in two outlets:

Libera - Bottega della Legalità – *Piazza Castelnuovo 13. ✆091 322 023.* Libera Terra's Palermo boutique sells olive oil, wines, tomato sauce, pasta, honey and other products from former Mafia bosses' lands.

AddioPizzo – *Via Vittorio Emmanuele 35.* The association also provides lists of businesses that refuse to pay *pizzo* (protection money.)

FESTIVALS

U' Fistino – This festival, held in honour of the city's patron saint, Santa Rosalia, takes place on 14–15 July, with processions, costumed parades and grand fireworks.

Festa dei Morti – On 2 November, in celebration of All Souls' Day, children receive gifts and sweets from their departed loved ones.

Festival di Morgana – This gathering of puppeteers and performers from around the world is held at the Museo Internazionale delle Marionette (*end of Nov–mid-Dec*).

Le Terrazze alla Kalsa – From April to May, this festival in the courtyard of the Palazzo Bonagia presents a mix of jazz, traditional and electronic music under the stars. Information from the Teatro Massimo: ✆091 60 53 111. *www.teatromassimo.it.*

Festival dello Spasimo – From late May to early September, an excellent open-air jazz festival is held at the historic church of Lo Spasimo. ✆091 61 66 480. *www.thebrassgroup.it.*

Festival di Verdura – *Viale del Fante70/b. ✆091 60 53 35. www.teatromassimo. it.* This festival organised in July by the Teatro Massimo presents international musicians, singers and dancers in a particularly friendly atmosphere.

Monreale★★★

Commanding spectacular views down the Conca d'Oro valley, the small hill town of Monreale grew up around the palace built by William II and its majestic cathedral, the Duomo. Today, life in Monreale is centred on the Piazza Monreale, which feeds into a maze of narrow lanes lined with cafés and small restaurants.

A BIT OF HISTORY

In Norman times, Monte Reale was a royal hunting ground and hunting lodge. In addition to the cathedral, this splendid complex including a Benedictine abbey and royal palace (converted in the late-16C into the Archbishop's Seminary) was initiated by the grandson of Roger II, **William II**, around 1172. Legend relates how the Madonna appeared to him in a dream to suggest that he build a church with money concealed by his father in a hiding place that she would reveal.

The building should be so grandiose as to rival the greatest cathedrals in other European cities and should outshine the beauty of the Palatine Chapel in Palermo, built by his grandfather, Roger. And so the most highly skilled craftsmen were employed to work on the project, with no expense spared.

The church was flanked by the royal palace and the Benedictine monastery, whose magnificent cloisters can still be admired today.

DUOMO★★★ (SANTA MARIA LA NUOVA)

◔Duomo open daily 8.30am–1pm and 2.30–5.30pm; Mon–Sat 9am–1pm, 2.30–5.30pm (treasury in the Cappella del Crocifisso), ⊛€4; ascent to the terraces 8.30am–noon, 3.30pm–6pm additional ⊛€2. ℘091 64 02 424.

The left side of the Duomo overlooks Piazza Vittorio Emanuele with its Fontana del Tritone. The main front overlooks a smaller piazza that provides access to the cloisters and a small **public garden** (last doorway on the right facing

- ▶ **Population:** 36 895
- ⚷ **Michelin Map:** p119: C2; 365: A0 55.
- ▯ **Info:** Tourist Office, Piazza Castelnuovo 34, ℘091 60 58 35, www.palermotourism.com.
- ◖ **Location:** The historical centre of the town stretches across the slopes of Monte Reale, with the cathedral visible to the east.
- Ⓟ **Parking:** Visitors are advised to park in the lower town car parks.
- ⊛ **Don't Miss:** Mosaics and cloisters at the Duomo, views over the town from Colle della Croce and Colle di San Matteo.
- ◔ **Timing:** Head for the cool climate of San Martino delle Scale in the hot summer months.

the cloisters, entrance across a large courtyard), offering a magnificent **view**★★ over the Conca d'Oro.

Exterior

The work of several generations of craftsmen, this impressive church reveals a variety of artistic styles. The two great towers on either side of the main front are quintessentially Norman, as are the apses, the basilica plan and, therefore, the fundamental arrangement of the cathedral. The superficial decoration applied to the **apses**, on the other hand, is clearly Arab in origin: this can best be **viewed**★★ from Via dell'Arcivescovado. From the same street, it is possible to make out the remains of the original royal palace, which is now incorporated into the Archbishop's Palace.

The apses are denoted by three tiers of intersecting blind arcading: the pointed arches, of varying heights, rise from tall bases through slender columns. The decorative effect is heightened by the use of two different kinds of stone

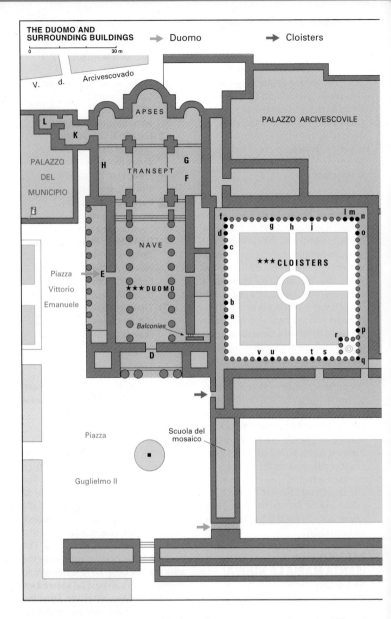

THE DUOMO AND
SURROUNDING BUILDINGS → Duomo → Cloisters

0 ——— 30 m

V. d. Arcivescovado

APSES

PALAZZO ARCIVESCOVILE

L

K

PALAZZO
DEL
MUNICIPIO

H

G

TRANSEPT

F

NAVE

★★★ CLOISTERS

f e d c g h j l m n o

Piazza
Vittorio
Emanuele

E

★★★ DUOMO

b a

Balconies

r p

D

v u t s q

Piazza

Scuola del
mosaico

Guglielmo II

(gold-coloured limestone and black lava). The same elements are repeated on the façade, although the full impact is marred by the portico, rebuilt in the 18C. This shelters the magnificent **bronze doors★★(D)**, designed in 1185 by **Bonanno Pisano** – the architect and sculptor responsible for the Leaning Tower of Pisa. It comprises 46 panels illustrating scenes from the Old and New Testaments. The two doors are hung within an elaborately moulded stone door frame, in which panels of geometric motifs alternate with animals and human figures in shallow relief and narrow strips of mosaic. The entrance from Piazza Vittorio Emanuele, beneath a 16C portico, also consists of bronze

CLOISTERS

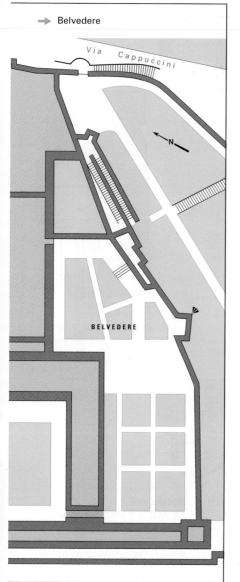

Belvedere

Via Cappuccini

N

BELVEDERE

a   The parable of dives and lazarus

b   Corinthian capital with windswept leaves

c   The story of Samson

d   The Massacre of the Innocents

e   The Four Evangelists dominated by a mermaid

f   The Annunciation

g   Owls, symbols of vigilance formerly placed above a monk's cell

h   Birds pecking the volutes of the capital

j   Joseph sold into slavery in Egypt

l   The Resurrection

m   Telamons

n   Constatine and Helen present the cross of Christ rediscovered on Calvary, symbol of the Church's victory over the Synagogue

o   Acrobat

p   The cult of Mithras

q   The Apostles' mission to evangelise the world: they are depicted in groups of three, in tabernacles protected by a flying angle

r   The 12 months of the year

s   William II offering Monreale cathedral to the Virgin

t   Men of oriental appearance

u   Cherubs feeding animals

v   The story of Noah

doors★(E) with several narrative panels, this time by Barisano da Trani.

Interior

Entrance from the west end.

Take small change for the coin-operated lighting of the mosaics.

The wide nave is separated from two, much smaller side aisles by columns with splendid capitals, some Corinthian, others of a composite order with acanthus leaves below and representations of Demeter and Persephone *(Ceres and Proserpine)* above. The capitals and the intrados *(curved inner surface of the springer arches)* sandwich dosserets decorated with Arab mosaics. Just beyond the halfway mark, the nave is interrupted by a monumental triumphal arch preceding the spacious area contained by the transept and apses that rise up and above the level of the nave and aisles. This section of floor is inlaid marble, as are the skirting and lower part of the walls, echoing

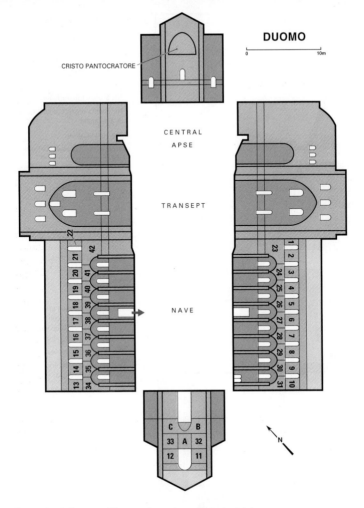

DUOMO

0   10m

CRISTO PANTOCRATORE

CENTRAL
APSE

TRANSEPT

NAVE

N

Byzantine influences. The wooden ceiling above the choir is 19C.

The church contains the tombs of William I (**F**) and William II (**G**); the altar in the north transept (**H**) encloses the heart of Louis IX (St Louis), King of France, who died in Tunis in 1270, while his brother Charles I ruled Sicily.

The **Cappella del Crocifisso★(K)**, situated in the north apse, is elaborately decked with marble Baroque decoration; inlay work, shallow- and high-relief carving, figurative statues and volutes. The wooden Crucifix dates from the 1400s. The **treasury (L)**, set to one side of the chapel, houses various reliquaries and other cult objects.

Mosaics★★★

Against a gold background, the characters of the Bible re-enact their stories. The colours are not so bright as those of the contemporary mosaics in the Palatine Chapel, but the figures are represented with greater realism and more expressive personality. These mosaics were completed during the late 12C and early 13C by craftsmen from Venice and Sicily and tell the story of Divine Redemption, beginning with the Creation of the Earth and Man.

The individual scenes are full of realistically portrayed incidental detail: the ropes that bind the scaffolding erected around the Tower of Babel (**29**); the knives on the table at the Wedding at Cana *(high up on the left-hand side of the crossing)*; the coins falling from the table upset by Christ when he chased the moneylenders from the temple *(about halfway along the north aisle)*; the astonishing variety of fish depicted in the Creation (**6**) and caught in the fishermen's nets illustrating the Miraculous Draft of Fishes *(north transept)*.

Many iconographic symbols are used, such as the cloud *(to denote transportation to another world)* that wraps itself around the figures that have fallen asleep, as in the scene of the angel appearing to Joseph *(crossing, on the right)*, or the little dark figure that appears in several scenes, representing the devil. Note also how the soul of Abel is depicted as a small red figure of spilt blood (**20**).

Christ Pantocrator majestically fills the **central apse**, with the Virgin and Child below, pictured among angels and Apostles. The lowest tier is populated with saints. Below the arch, in the middle, is the Throne of Judgement.

The vaults of the **lateral apses** accommodate the figures of St Peter *(right)* and St Paul *(left)* with scenes from their lives.

The life of Christ is depicted in the **chancel**, starting at the crossing where a series of stories from his childhood are related. Christ's adult life is represented in the transept *(starting south side)* until the descent of the Holy Spirit. The aisles illustrate Christ's miracles.

Below the **triumphal arch**, across the far side of the transept, sit two thrones with mosaic scenes above: the one on the right, above the archbishop's throne, shows William II's symbolic tribute to the church (the King offers up a model of the cathedral to the Madonna); on the left, the royal throne stands as confirmation of the Divine Protection conferred upon the King (Christ Himself is depicted crowning William).

The **nave** is devoted entirely to the Old Testament: (**1**) The spirit of God moving upon the face of the waters. (**2**) God dividing the light from the darkness in the presence of seven angels (one designated for each day of the Creation). (**3**) The making of the firmament (Heaven) to divide the waters above the heavens from those below.

(**4**) Separation of the waters into the seas from the land that was Earth. (**5**) Creation of the sun, the moon and the stars. (**6**) Creation of the birds of the air and the fish of the oceans. (**7**) Creation of Man. (**8**) God resting. (**9**) God leads Adam into the Garden of Eden. (**10**) Adam in the Garden of Eden. (**11**) Creation of Eve. (**12**) Eve is presented to Adam. (**13**) Eve is tempted by the Serpent. (**14**) Original Sin. (**15**) God discovers that Adam

Mosaics, Duomo

and Eve are ashamed of their nudity. (**16**) Adam and Eve are expelled from Earthly Paradise. (**17**) Adam working. Eve is seated with a spindle in her hand. (**18**) Sacrifice of Cain and Abel. *Only the sacrifice of Abel pleases God, symbolised by the ray of light shining straight from the Lord's hand.* (**19**) Cain slays Abel.

(**20**) God discovers Cain's crime and curses him. (**21**) Cain is slain by Lamech *(a story from the Jewish tradition and not mentioned in Genesis).* (**22**) God commands Noah to build an Ark. (**23**) Noah builds the Ark. (**24**) The animals board the Ark. (**25**) Noah welcomes the dove carrying the olive sprig, the sign that the waters have abated. (**26**) The animals come out of the Ark.

(**27**) Noah's sacrifice as a sign of thanks to God. Behind him is the rainbow, the symbol of God's covenant with Man. (**28**) The grape harvest *(on the left).* On the right, Noah, drunk and half-naked, is discovered by his son, Ham, who calls his brothers to deride him. They are more respectful of their father's dignity and cover his nudity. *Hence Noah's curse on Ham and his descendants, the Canaanites.* (**29**) Noah's descendants unite and build the Tower of Babel in an attempt to reach heaven; this results in chaos. Fearing that the force of Man might overthrow Him, God caused the people to quarrel with each other, to confound their language and scatter them abroad: this story is often taken to be a parable for upholding Church authority in the face of Man's litigiousness. (**30**) Abraham, having settled in the land of Sodom and Gomorrah, encounters three angels sent by God and invites them to his house. *The angels represent the Trinity.* (**31**) The hospitality of Abraham. (**32**) God sends two angels to destroy Sodom. Lot, Abraham's nephew, shows them hospitality. Lot tries to prevent the inhabitants of Sodom from entering the house where the two angels are.

The three following scenes do not come from the Old Testament but relate to the story of St Cassius, St Castus and St Castrense (patron saint of Monreale).
(**A**) Cassius and Castus, condemned to being thrown to the lions because they refused to renounce their faith in Christ, are saved when the lions are suddenly tamed and lick their feet.

(**B**) Cassius and Castus are taken to a pagan temple causing it to collapse onto the infidels. (**C**) St Castrense cures a man possessed of the Devil, who throws himself into the sea and causes a storm. (**33**) Sodom in flames while Lot flees with his daughters; his wife, turning round to look back, is transformed into a pillar of salt. (**34**) God appears to Abraham and bids him sacrifice his only son, Isaac.

(**35**) The angel of the Lord stops Abraham from sacrificing his son.

(**36**) Abraham sends a servant to seek a wife for Isaac. At the well, Rebecca offers up water to Abraham's servant and his camels to drink. (**37**) Rebecca sets out on the journey to her chosen bridegroom, Isaac. (**38**) Isaac with his favourite son Esau, and his second son Jacob.

(**39**) Isaac blesses Jacob, mistakenly believing he is Esau *(depicted on the right, as he returns from hunting).* Isaac, who is almost blind in his old age, is deceived by the goatskins covering the arms of Jacob who, unlike his brother, is smooth-skinned. (**40**) Jacob flees from the vengeful anger of his brother, from whom he has stolen his father Isaac's blessing. (**41**) On his journey, Jacob dreams of a ladder leading from earth up to heaven being ascended by angels. God, at the top, grants him the land on which he has fallen asleep; on waking, Jacob takes the stones he has been using as pillows and lays them down as a foundation for his city. (**42**) Jacob wrestles with the angel. On his journey back to his brother Esau's, Jacob sent forth his sheep and goats as offerings to him. That night, having made his family ford the stream, an angel approaches and wrestles with him until dawn, when the angel blessed Jacob and bestows on him a new name: Israel *(meaning the one who has fought with God and with Man, and has prevailed).*

Ascent to the terraces★★★
Access from the end of the south aisle: an arduous climb.

The first outlook provides a **view** down over the cloisters. Farther round, there is a wonderful **view** of the **apses★★**.

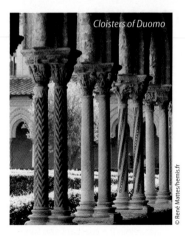

Cloisters of Duomo

© René Mattes/hemis.fr

The highest section has magnificent **views★★** of the Conca d'Oro.

Cloisters★★★

🕐Open Mon–Sat, 9am–1.30pm, 2–7.30pm, Sun–Mon 9am–1.30pm. ☜€6. ♿ ♪091 64 04 403.

The cloisters consist of a series of pointed arches supported by sets of small paired columns, many decorated with polychrome mosaic that is Eastern in inspiration. Those columns are sculpted with animals and human figures interwoven among luxuriant vegetation. The highlights, though, are the **Romanesque capitals★★**, each distinctively and imaginatively carved. The subject matter is drawn from both medieval and Classical iconography. Even the Classical subjects betray a certain inventiveness: the acanthus leaves of the Corinthian capitals, for example, appear ruffled by the wind (**b**). To these are added a variety of other subjects: birds stretching down to peck the plant volutes of the capital (**h**), Atlas figures reaching up to support the weight of the arch (**m**), cherubs feeding animals (**u**), exotic characters wearing turbans with snakes (**t**). Perhaps the most remarkable capital is the one in which William II offers up the church to the Madonna (**s**): note the detail with which the south side of the church has been carved. One capital depicts a man killing a bull, the sacred symbol of the cult of Mithras (**p**). Another features an acrobat (**o**): his position, his weight supported by his arms, his back

arched so that his feet rest on the back of his head *(his head in the centre)*, recalls the Trinacria, the ancient symbol of Sicily. The tiny cloisters in the southwest corner include a **fountain**. The column in the circular basin is sculpted with banding and crested with animals.

ADDRESSES

🛏STAY

🍴🍴 **Palazzo Ducale Suites** – *Via Duca degli Abruzzi 8*. ♪*091 64 04 298*. *www.palazzoducalesuites.it*. 🅿. *7 rooms*. ☕. This B&B near the Duomo is tucked away in the alleyways of Monreale. Its biggest asset is its private car park. The rooms are spacious and comfortable and some are almost suites. Pretty terrace.

🍴EAT

Several snack bars around the Duomo serve focaccia and light meals. On the left, opposite the entrance to the church, you will find reasonable prices at **Baby Bar**.

🍴🍴 **Antica Forneria Tusa Nazareno** – *Via Via Odigitria 39*. ♪*091 64 04 034*. *Mon-Sat 2am-2.30pm* A traditional bakery famous for its wood-fired oven and rustic loaves, sesame buns and cakes made from almonds.

🍴🍴🍴 **Taverna del Pavone** – *Vicolo Pensato 18*. ♪*091 64 06 209*. *www.tavernadelpavone.it*. *Closed Mon.* A pleasant terrace on a pedestrianised street and a kitchen serving up some of the classics of Sicilian cuisine.

EVENT

Holy music week – Generally held in November, with concerts taking place in various churches. For more information, contact the tourist office.

Golfo di Castellammare★★

This gulf is encircled by gently-rolling hills dominated to the west by the imposing mass of Mount Còfano, best seen from the promontory on Capo San Vito. As well as its coastal landscape, this region is famed for castles, tuna fisheries and archaeological sites.

DRIVING TOURS

FROM PALERMO TO CASTELLAMMARE DEL GOLFO

This tour of about 100km/62mi takes you from Palermo to the Zingaro nature reserve.

Carini

25km/15mi to the W of Palermo on the A 29, heading towards Trapani. Leave the road after 16km/9mi and follow the signs.

The road curves up to this graceful town, poised between a hill and gulf. Legend holds that the town was originally built by Daedalus, who called it "Hyccara" in memory of his son Icarus, while history shows it was razed by the Athenians and rebuilt by the Phoenicians. Later, its imposing medieval castle was the setting for the tragic fate of Baroness Laura Lanza and her lover.

Corso Umberto I, Carini's main street, begins just beyond a belvedere presenting sweeping **views** over the coast. From here, a horseshoe-shaped flight of shallow steps makes its way up past the town's medieval water fountain to a 12C archway and beyond to the old part of the town, threaded by narrow streets, and the castle.

Castle

⊙*Open Tue–Sun 9am–1pm, 4–8pm.*
⊙*Closed Mon.* ⊙€3. ℘*091 88 15 666.*
www.comune.carini.pa.it.
This ancient Norman fortress-cum-castle has foundations dating back to the 10C and is the setting for a famous

- 🔖 **Michelin Map:** p119: B1; 365 AL-AM-AN 54–55.
- 🔳 **Info:** Tourist office, Piazza Castello 7. ℘0924 30 217. www.sanvitoweb.com.
- ▶ **Location:** The Golfo di Castellammare stretches from Capo San Vito to Capo Rama. A scenic road follows the coast as far as Scopello, then heads inland at the Riserva dello Zingaro to rejoin the coast at Capo San Vito.
- 👁 **Don't Miss:** Scopello's tuna fishery, the reserve of Zingaro, the Grotta Mangiapane.
- 🕐 **Timing:** Summer months, avoiding August.
- 👥 **Kids:** Boat tours at the Zingaro Reserve and the Grotta Mangiapane.

and dramatic Sicilian story of thwarted love. Here, in 1563, **Baronessa di Carini** was killed by her father for having an affair while betrothed. The episode was later immortalised in an anonymous contemporary poem, now one of the most famous verses in Sicily's lyrical canon and a favourite of traditional ballad singers.

The building has now decayed but still houses some worthwhile sights. On the ground floor is the **Salone delle Derrate** (*Victuals Hall*), this was later transformed into a library, with its two elegant 15C stone arches springing from a single solid pier. On the floor above, the **Salone delle Feste** has a wonderful 15C coffered wooden **ceiling**, heavy with Catalan Gothic decorative pendentives.

Return to the Corso Umberto I where, opposite the fountain, stands the **Chiesa di San Vincenzo**. The space is bisected by a wrought-iron grille (*segregating the* *area reserved for the nuns from the adjacent convent)* and decorated with white and gold neo-Classical stucco festoons, cherubs and grotesques.

Corso Umberto I opens out into **Piazza del Duomo**, overlooked by two churches: San Vito *(on the right)* and the **Chiesa Madre** *(left).*

Chiesa Madre

Although subject to considerable alteration in the 18C, the church retains a loggia on its right side and a series of interesting majolica panels depicting the *Crucifixion, Assumption, St Rosalia* and *St Vitus* (1715).

Inside, it houses a prized *Adoration of the Magi* by Alessandro Allori (1578), an eminent Tuscan painter who came to prominence at the Medici court.

In the chapel dedicated to the Crucifixion sits an exquisite 17C wooden Christ with a crown of silver on a cross of agate. The statue is set above a grandiose altar, which is flanked by stucco statues by Procopio Serpotta.

Oratorio del Santissimo Sacramento

The oratory beside the Chiesa Madre dates from the mid-16C. Its interior is a glorious profusion of **stucco decoration★★** (18C) by the Trapani artist Vincenzo Messina depicting allegories (Faith, Charity, Strength, Penitence, Hope, Justice, Divine Grace and the Roman Catholic Church).

Elsewhere, surfaces are encrusted with Serpotta-like elements: cherubs, flower garlands and fruit, heraldic coats-of-arms and grotesques.

Chiesa di Santa Maria degli Angeli

Behind the Chiesa Madre, in Via Curreri.
This church once belonged to the Capuchin monastery; a ring of side chapels radiate from the nave, each one embellished with intricate intarsia. In the elaborate Rococo chapel of the Crucifixion, among the various small reliquaries is a lovely wooden **Crucifix** by the Capuchin Fra' Benedetto Valenza (1737), who also worked on the overall decor.

Chiesa degli Agonizzanti

Via Roma.
This church, completed in 1643, is richly decorated inside with white and gold **stucco★**: playful cherubs, eagles, garlands of flowers and fruit encircle a number of frescoed panels about Mary, which culminate in the ceiling *(Apotheosis of the Virgin).*

About halfway along the side walls are frescoes depicting the Death of Joseph and the Madonna.

▷ Take the S 113 towards the airport. When the coast comes into view near to the A 29 sliproad, carry on along the same secondary road, following the signs for Terrasini, which is 35km/21mi W of Palermo.

Terrasini

The main area of this seaside resort comprises a nice sandy strip, edged by small trattoria with outdoor tables and upmarket hotels.

The bay curls before a lofty red **cliff★**, which intermittently shelters little beaches and delightful creeks well worth exploring on a hot day.

The Palazzo D'Aumale

Lungomare Peppino Impastato.
🕐*Open Mon–Sat 9am–1.30pm, 2pm–6.45pm, Sun 9am–1pm.* 🎫€6. 📞091 88 10 989. www.regione.sicilia.it/beniculturali/museodaumale.

Terrasini has an interesting local **museum**, although the presentation doesn't match the quality of the collections.

The most significant of three departments is **natural history★** *(Via Cala Rossa 8)*, including the rich Orlando collection of birds with species ranging from crows, nocturnal birds, storks and raptors to those approaching extinction. In the archaeological department *(in Piazza Falcone e Borsellino)* are displays of artefacts retrieved from shipwrecks off Terrasini.

▷ From Terrasini take the A29 along the coast for 30km/18mi. Exit at Castellammare del Golfo.

Castellammare del Golfo

Set in the beautiful bay of the same name, this town, now a popular seaside resort, was once the main port and principal trading post for the ancient cities of Segesta and Erice.

In the centre of the town stands the **medieval castle**. After Castellammare del Golfo, the road winds its way up a ruggedly bleak mountainside, providing glorious **views★**.

SAN VITO AND THE ZINGARO NATURE RESERVE

From Castellammare del Golfo, a road leads to the charming village of Scopello.

♠♣ Riserva Naturale dello Zingaro★★

Accessible from Scopello and San Vito lo Capo. ⊕€3. ✆0924 35 108. www.riservazingaro.it.

Sicily's first nature reserve measures 7km/4mi in length and covers approximately 1,650ha/4,076 acres. The main track follows the coastline high above the sea, offering spectacular **views★** of an unspoilt Sicily over successive creeks, bays, beaches *(many of which are accessible)*, sheer cliffs and rocky headlands.

The lush Mediterranean vegetation *(some 700 species)* occasionally shows patches of red bedrock beneath.

Other equally attractive paths meander inland. As the scenery changes, so too does the vegetation until at last it is largely dominated by tumbling capers and flowering ash.

The reserve maintains a number of nooks and crannies that provide sheltered burrows and nesting sites for a variety of animals and, more particularly, birds (with 39 different species documented including Peregrine falcons, Bonelli's eagles and **kestrels**).

Neolithic and Mesolithic settlements have been uncovered near the **Grotta dell'Uzzo**, while the remains of rural settlements, consisting of some 20 well-preserved houses, have been discovered at **Borgo Cusenza**. Other settlements have been found at **Tonnarella dell'Uzzo**.

Scopello

The road leads to Scopello, a small hamlet on the sea dominated by its 18C *baglio* (a large, fortified building), which faces onto the central piazza. After a bend, a dirt road on the right leads down to the old tuna fishery *(accessible on foot)*.

Riserva Naturale dello Zingaro

© Sandro Bedessi / Fototeca ENIT

San Vito lo Capo

© Sandro Bedessi / Fototeca ENIT

La Tonnara

The tuna fishery, now disused, testifies to an activity that once flourished in these fish-rich waters. Out of season, silence reigns among the abandoned buildings and the net weights sit waiting for the return of the fishermen. In the summer, the place bustles with sun-seekers and bathers. There is a good sea **view★** of monolithic rocks (*i faraglioni*), that recall their famous cousins off the island of Capri.

▷ There is no coast road from Scopello to San Vito lo Capo, so retrace your journey for a couple of kilometres, then turn right to Castelluzzo.

As the road climbs towards **Custonaci** enjoy the splendid **views★** of the Golfo del Cofano. To the left, note one of the many 16C watchtowers that punctuate this area. The road then continues past an attractive, characteristically cube-like, little chapel, dedicated to **Santa Crescenzia** (16C).

San Vito lo Capo★

San Vito is a well-known resort, noted in particular for its beautiful coastline and bay lined with pretty beaches lapped by clear blue and green waters.

The small whitewashed town, which developed in the 18C, clusters around the **Chiesa Madre**, which is square and massive in profile. It's a constant reminder of its early beginnings as a Saracen fortress. The site was once occupied by a small church dedicated to San Vito, but this became too small to accommodate the pilgrims who visited it so it was enlarged until it incorporated the very building which once harboured it.

Capo San Vito and the Golfo del Còfano

Leaving San Vito to the east and heading beyond the Punta di Solanto, a scenic road provides **views** to the left of the old, and now abandoned, tuna fishery **(Tonnara del Secco)**, and continues as far as the solitary **Torre dell'Impiso** *(visible on the return trip)*. The Riserva dello Zingaro starts at the end of the road.

▷ Return to San Vito and take the road to Castelluzzo. Once past Castelluzzo, turn right to Custonaci and head up the hill on the road to the right.

Riserva Naturale Monte Còfano

The towering limestone peak and the bay that surrounds it, now a nature reserve, make for a magnificent **sight★**, as the steep pinky-red cliffs extending skywards are mirrored in the calm sea.

A number of quarries are gouged into the rocky flank, from which is extracted the startlingly white marble known as *Perlato di Sicilia*. The **Grotta Mangiapane cave★** *(near Scurati)* nestles not far from the quarries *(follow the signs)*. Inside, it shelters a tiny rural hamlet, which is enchantingly complete with chapel and cobbled street. The charm of this abandoned village, with its vaguely Mexican air, is especially poignant at Christmas when it stages a live Nativity.

EXCURSION
Alcamo
About 11km/6.5mi S of Castellammare del Golfo.

The town name is suggestive of the 13C poet **Cielo d'Alcamo**, author of *Rosa Fresca Aulentissima (The Fresh Fragrant Rose)*, one of the earliest texts written in Italian. The name also denotes the local dry white wine from the surrounding vineyards. Its churches contain works by members of the **Gagini** family (16C) and by Giacomo Serpotta, one of the Sicilian masters of Baroque.

The main works are to be found in Santa Oliva, San Francesco d'Assisi, San Salvatore and the imposing **Chiesa Madre**, which also has a fine 15C chapel. Overlooking Piazza Repubblica – laid out with gardens – is the **Castello dei Conti di Modica**. The castle, built for the Counts of Modica in the 14C, is a rhomboid shape with two rectangular and two round towers. Inside is a regional *enoteca* and **wine museum**.

ADDRESSES

🛏STAY
CASTELLAMMARE DEL GOLFO

🍽🍽 **Cala Marina** – *Via Don L. Zangara 1, on the marina.* ✆*0924 53 18 41. www.hotel calamarina.it. 14 rooms* ⬜. The nicest rooms in this modest hotel have balconies overlooking the marina. The others, at the back, offer mountain **views**.

🍽🍽🍽 **Cetarium** – *Via Don L. Zangara 45.* ✆*0924 53 34 01. www.hotelcetarium.it. 26 rooms.* ⬜. This former tuna fishery has been transformed into a hotel. Cool, pleasant rooms decorated in contemporary style.

SCOPELLO

🍽🍽🍽 **Tonnara di Scopello** – *Largo Tonnara Scopello 1, 2.3km/1.7mi from the centre of Scopello.* ✆*339 67 41 046. www. tonnaradiscopello.com -* 🚭 *- 15 apart.* Set in the most enchanting spot in the north of Sicily, this former tuna fishery still sports its fishing boats and net weights. The simply-furnished apartments have bathrooms, kitchenettes and some have terraces.

SAN VITO LO CAPO

🍽 **El Bahira** – *Contrada Salinella, Bahira, 4km/2.5mi S of San Vito Lo Capo.* ✆*0923 97 25 77. www.elbahira.it.* 🚭 This campsite offers a good range of sports and leisure facilities. The site is divided into separate sections for tents, campervans and caravans, and also has chalets and small apartments for rent.

🍽🍽 **L'Agave** – *Via Nino Bixio 35, San Vito Lo Capo.* ✆*0923 92 10 88. www.lagave.net. Closed Nov. 10 rooms* ⬜. Although this small hotel has only 10 rooms, it has plans to grow. Enjoy a quiet, relaxing stay in this modern establishment with good service.

🍽🍽 **Piccolo Mondo** – *Via N. Bixio 7.* ✆*0923 97 20 32. www.piccolomondo hotel.net. 10 rooms.* ⬜. A neat, pretty, family-run hotel close to the beach.

🍽🍽 **Locanda Pocho** – *Località Isulidda - Makari.* ✆*0923 97 25 25. www.pocho.it.* ✕*12 rooms.* ⬜. Enjoying a huge terrace that's perfect at sunset, this distinctive hotel, 200m/218yds from the beach in the hamlet of Isulidda is also home to an excellent restaurant.

ALCAMO

🍽🍽 **Sirignano Wine Resort** – *Contrada Sirignano, 12 km to W of Alcamo.* ✆*0924 21 664. www.sirignanowineresort.it. 12 rooms.* ⬜. Surrounded by vineyards and olive trees as far as the eye can see, this *baglio* has retained the authentic feel of rural Sicily. Run by the same family since 1730, it's an essential stop for wine lovers.

♈/EAT

CASTELLAMMARE DEL GOLFO

😑😑 **Ristorantino del Monsù** –
Piazza Pisani angle via Pisani 2.
☎0924 53 10 31. Served in a rustic room
decorated in yellow tones or on the
terrace, this restaurant's dishes include
cuttlefish couscous and pasta with
pistachio *pesto*.

😑😑 **Egesta Mare** – *Via Fiume angle*
Piazza Petrolo. *☎0924 30 409.* Healthy,
tasty cooking made from the day's catch:
seafood antipasto, hot and cold, and
fried fish. Good value for money.

SCOPELLO

😑 **Pan cunzato** – *Via Galluppi. Closed*
Thu. Tucked away in the backstreets,
this traditional bakery has a wood-fired
oven producing *pan cunzato* – two slices
of warm bread stuffed with tomatoes,
anchovies and cheese sprinkled with
olive oil.

SAN VITO LO CAPO

😑😑🍽 **Gnà Sara** – *Via Duca degli Abruzzi*
8. *☎0923 9743 08. www.gnasara.com.*
Closed Nov and Mon, Oct–Jun. On a street
parallel to the town's main thoroughfare,
this restaurant serves generous portions
of good-quality fish. Meals are served at
tables dressed with linen tablecloths in
the dining room or summer veranda.

😑😑🍽 **Da Alfredo** – *Contrada Valanga*
3.1km/6mi S of San Vito Lo Capo. *☎0923 97*
23 66. Closed 20 Oct–20 Nov and Mon Nov–
mid-Jun. A splendid terrace-cum-garden,
friendly atmosphere, a delightful shady
arbour and a menu full of traditional
Sicilian cuisine.

SPORTS AND LEISURE

BOAT TRIPS

Riserva dello Zingaro – Two boats
from San Vito Lo Capo *(in summer).*
From Castellammare *(all year round),*
you can choose from the *Leonardo*
da Vinci and the *Primero 6* (*☎0924 34*
222). Destinations include the Riserva
dello Zingaro, San Vito lo Capo and the
faraglioni de Scopello with a break for
swimming and lunch onboard.

DIVING

The Nautic Club Poseidon – *Via Roma 86.*
Castellammare del Golfo. *☎338 250 11 10.*
www.clubposeidon.it. The only diving club
in the area organises dives around the
gulf of Castellammare and the Zingaro
nature reserve. *(€40 per dive or €50 if you*
hire full equipment.)

Cetaria – *Via Marco Polo 3. Scopello.* *☎0924*
54 11 77 or 368 386 48 08. www.cetaria.com.
Organises dives around the Zingaro
reserve, with an interesting archaeological
tour on which you can admire ancient
remains at depths of 18–20m (62–65ft).
(€55/dive, including equipment.)

Nautisub – *Via Faro 24. San Vito Lo Capo.*
☎348 294 06 10 or 328 818 07 48. www.
nautisub.it. Nautisub offers dives around
the Zingaro reserve. *(Prices from €40.)*

BICYCLE HIRE

San Vito Charter – *Via Savoia 20. San*
Vito Lo Capo. *☎0923 97 21 57. www.sanvi-*
tocharter.it. Standard bicycles, mountain
bikes or electric bikes. *(€5/day for stand-*
ard bikes or €30/day for electric bikes.)

FESTIVALS

Festa di Maria Santissima del
Soccorso – The festival of the patron
saint of Castellammare del Golfo is
celebrated from 19–21 August with
thousands of candles floating on the sea.

Couscous Fest – In September a festival
celebrating Mediterranean food and
wine is held at San Vito Lo Capo, along
with concerts of world music and other
cultural events. *www.couscousfest.it.*

The Festa di li Schietti – On the Saturday
before Easter in Carini, all the town's
bachelors (known as *schietti* or "pure
men") cut down a bitter orange tree,
trim it into a ball shape then decorate it
with coloured ribbons and *ciancianieddi*
– strings of little bells. On the Sunday
morning, they are blessed on the square
in front of the *chiesa madre*. Next, with
his friends cheering him on, each *schietto*
goes to the house of his fiancée and
demonstrates his strength by lifting
the tree. These days, the event is just a
colourful festival, but in days gone by, it
was a genuine test of virility.

WESTERN SICILY

Carpeted with rolling hills and fertile plains, western Sicily looks like any other Italian Mediterranean destination. But scratch the surface and you'll find a region that's closer to North Africa than it is to the Italian mainland, with a culture, architecture and cuisine influenced as much by the arrival of the Phoenicians and Arabs as the Ancient Greeks and Romans.

Highlights

Colourful Trapani and Erice

The landscape to the west of this region is dotted with fascinating towns. Erice, a medieval *comune* perched high on a mountain top, is often shrouded in mist, giving it a fairytale appearance. On a clear day, it commands spectacular views over the Egadi Islands. The lively town of Trapani was once a prosperous trading centre, with bustling tuna and salt industries. As both have gone into decline, the town has been reborn as a top tourist destination to rival Taormina on the island's eastern coast.

Trapanese cuisine has a distinctive North African twist, with dishes based around fish and couscous, making it a favourite for gastronomes eager to try *bottarga* (cured fish roe), handmade *busiate* pasta and jasmine-flavoured granite (flavoured ices).

Coastal Trade and Culture

South of Trapani, white saltpans stretch along the coast almost as far as Marsala. Some of the original windmills used in salt production are still in operation. The saltpans are a striking sight in summer, when their white and pink hues glisten in the sunshine. The Phoenicians were the first to produce salt there, and the remains of their colony at Mozia in the Stagnone di Marsala are still clearly visible and are especially attractive in the spring, when the area is awash with flowers.

World-famous for its amber-coloured fortified wine, Marsala and its quiet, narrow streets and elegant buildings make a good starting point from which to explore the surrounding area.

From Marsala, the coastline becomes a series of sandy beaches, where locals flee to escape the scorching heat during July and August, and which stretch beyond the bustling fishing port of Mazara del Vallo. This is where western Sicily's links with North Africa are most obvious, and many Tunisians and Moroccans still work here, servicing one of Italy's largest fishing fleets. The town's historic centre is an eclectic mix of Baroque churches set in small squares, while the Casbah's maze of narrow, winding streets are home to the local North African community and filled with the scent of spicy cooking.

A museum here houses an exquisite Ancient Greek bronze satyr discovered by local fishermen and subsequently painstakingly restored.

Along the coast at Selinunte is one of Sicily's best archaeological sites. Scattered across a large area, this Ancient Greek colony features several dramatic temples and breathtaking **views** out to sea.

The nearby Cava di Cusa provides an insight into how the ancients quarried the stone used to create their places of worship.

To the north, the archaeological park of Segesta is equally fascinating, with its lonely Doric temple on a hill - one of the best preserved from antiquity.

Inland Contrasts

The countryside around Castelvetrano and the Valle del Belice is one of gentle slopes packed with vineyards and olive

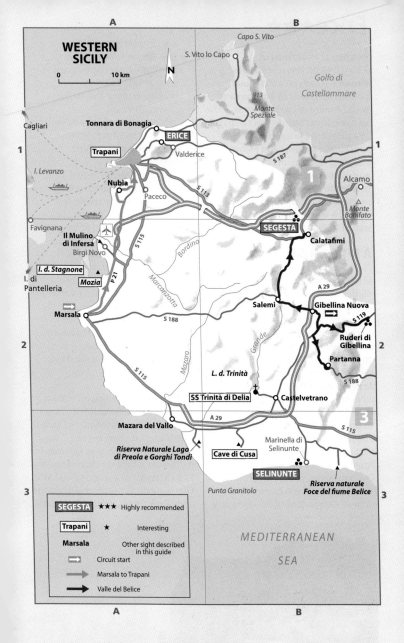

WESTERN SICILY

Map labels:

Capo S. Vito
S. Vito lo Capo
Golfo di Castellammare
913 Monte Speziale
S 187
Cagliari
Tonnara di Bonagia
ERICE
Trapani
Valderice
Alcamo
I. Levanzo
Nubia
Paceco
S 113
Monte Bonifato
Favignana
Il Mulino di Infersa
Birgi Novo
S 115
Bordino
SEGESTA
Calatafimi
I. d. Stagnone
Mozia
Marcanzotta
A 29
I. di Pantelleria
Salemi
Gibellina Nuova
S 119
Marsala
S 188
Grande
Ruderi di Gibellina
Partanna
Mazaro
L. d. Trinità
S 188
SS Trinità di Delia
Castelvetrano
Mazara del Vallo
A 29
S 115
Riserva Naturale Lago di Preola e Gorghi Tondi
Cave di Cusa
Marinella di Selinunte
SELINUNTE
Riserva naturale Foce del fiume Belice
Punta Granitolo
MEDITERRANEAN SEA

0   10 km

N

Legend:

SEGESTA	★★★	Highly recommended
Trapani	★	Interesting
Marsala		Other sight described in this guide
⇨		Circuit start
→		Marsala to Trapani
→		Valle del Belice

---

groves that produce some of Sicily's best wine and olive oil.

Yet this area suffered a devastating earthquake in 1968 that wiped out many of its oldest villages, some of which were relocated to accommodate a new highway.

The tragedy has been commemorated at the Ruderi di Gibellina and, where the village of Gibellina once stood, there is now a haunting piece of concrete land art, the Cretto, which delineates where homes and churches once stood and people lost their lives.

Erice★★★

Perched at an altitude of 751m/2,463ft, this remarkable site★★★ stands on a triangular plateau defended by bastions and walls. A maze of cobbled lanes, some so narrow just one person can pass at a time, Erice brims with bright sunshine in summer and enjoys stunning views across the plain and out to sea. Come winter, clouds muffle the city and it returns to its medieval roots, standing silently behind a seemingly impenetrable wall of wood and stone.

- **Population:** 28,534
- **Michelin Map:** 177 A-1.
- **Info:** Tommaso Guarrasi 1. ℘0923 869388, www.regione.sicilia.it/turismo.
- **Location:** 120km/74.5mi southwest of Palermo.
- **Parking:** Near Porta Trapani.
- **Don't Miss:** The two roads that climb up to the town offer good views across the plain and out to sea (the road to the north, overlooking Monte Cofano is the easier of the two); walking the narrow alleys in the centre; cakes at Pasticceria Maria Grammatico.
- **Kids:** The Giardino del Balio gardens at the base of Castello di Venere.
- **Timing:** Allow half a day.

A BIT OF HISTORY

The history of Erice is lost in the mists of folklore and superstition. It supposedly derives its name from the mountain upon which the mythical hero and king of the Elimi, Eryx, built a temple to his mother, Venus Erycina, later associated with the cult of Aphrodite.

The origins of the town are also linked with Aeneas. In Virgil's narrative, Aeneas came ashore at the foot of the mountain to perform the funeral of his father Anchises. Having lost several ships in a fire, he was forced to abandon a number of companions, who founded the town. Another major mythological figure associated with Erice is Heracles. The hero landed in this part of Sicily on his way back to Greece, having stolen the cattle of Geryon (one of the legendary Twelve Labours). During his sojourn, he killed the Elimian king. He left, warning that one of his descendants, Dorieus, would later take over as ruler.

In antiquity, Erice was famous for its temple where, in succession, the Phoenicians worshipped Astarte, the Greeks venerated Aphrodite and the Romans celebrated Venus.

Castello di Venere

© J.-L. Gallo / MICHELIN

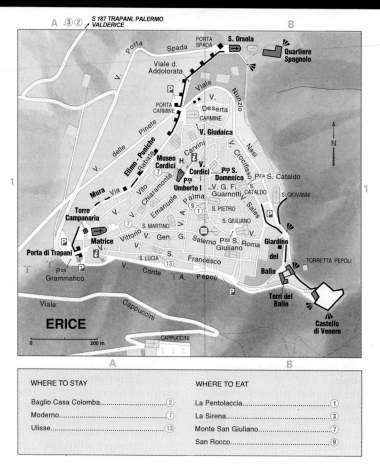

WHERE TO STAY	
Baglio Casa Colomba	②
Moderno	⑦
Ulisse	⑬

WHERE TO EAT	
La Pentolaccia	①
La Sirena	③
Monte San Giuliano	⑦
San Rocco	⑨

Mount Eryx served as a point of reference for sailors because at night a large fire would be lit in the sacred precinct, turning it into a guiding beacon.

WALKING TOUR

This small walled mountain town takes the shape of a perfect equilateral triangle, whose symbolism has provoked endless argument; it is bounded by the Castello di Venere (southeastern axis) and the Chiesa Madre (southwestern side).

Exactly in the centre of the triangle is the Chiesa di San Pietro. Around it lies an intricate maze of narrow streets, each cobbled with polished, rectangular stones, including some alleys so narrow that only one person can pass at a time. A wander through this atmospheric web provides unexpected glimpses of Erice's churches and monasteries, of which there are over 60 scattered through the town.

As you walk, explore the small shops tucked down side streets, selling some of the local handicrafts that still flourish here, including colourful ceramics, tapestries and almond-paste sweets (*dolci di badia*).

GETTING THERE AND AROUND

A.S.T. buses (*℘0923 23222*) run between Trapani (*Piazza Malta*) and Erice. Journey time is approx 50min.

Chiesa Matrice★

℘0923 86 91 23.

The town's main church is situated near **Porta di Trapani**, built by the Normans over 8C fortifications like most of the town's other gates and walls. The Chiesa Matrice itself was built in the 14C, again reusing stone, this time from the Temple of Venus. Its massive form and merlon-topped walls suggest it was a church-fortress. The façade is graced with a fine rose window (replicating the original), now partly concealed by the Gothic porch that was added a century later. Inside, the rather austere, gloomy interior was extensively remodelled in the 19C; its main draw is a lovely *Madonna and Child*, said to have been painted by Francesco Laurana.

Bell tower

The lone tower that remains of the church was originally a watchtower. Its first level has simple narrow slits, while the upper section is graced with fine two-light Chiaramonte-style windows.

The town hall on Piazza Umberto I houses the Museo Antonio Cordici. Further along, to the right of the piazza, is Via Antonio Cordici, leading into the picturesque Piazza San Domenico, a harmonious confection of elegant palazzi.

SIGHTS
Museo Cordici

Piazza Umberto I, 1. ◷Open Mon–Fri, 8.30am–1.30pm (2.30–5.15pm Mon and Thu). ◷Closed national holidays. ℘0923 502148.

Inside the town hall is the local museum, which houses finds from Neolithic, Punic, Greek and Roman archaeological sites. The museum has an interesting and varied collection for its size, which includes jewellery, bronze statues, terra cotta and marble sculptures. Notable exhibits include **Antonello Gagini**'s sculpture of the Annunciation (1525) from the Chiesa del Carmine, a fine **head of Aphrodite** dating from the 4C and a small marble head of a woman modelled on a Greek original.

Elimo-Punic Walls★

The Elimini built a mighty wall (8C–6C BC) around the northeastern flank of the town – the only section open to possible attack. Massive blocks characterise the most ancient stone courses. The skyline was punctuated with lookout towers, steep stairways provided access to the *chemin-de-ronde*, while small openings allowed residents to freely come and go and supplies to be imported.

The best-preserved walls run along Via dell'Addolorata, from Porta Carmine to Porta Spada.

Town centre

Santa Orsola

This church, built in 1413, preserves its original Gothic rib-vaulting down the nave. The 18C Mystery figures, representing the Stations of the Cross, are kept here when not being processed around the town on Good Friday.

Quartiere Spagnolo

From the top of the so-called Spanish Quarter building, initiated in the 17C but never completed, there is a marvellous **view** over the bay of Monte Cofano and the area beyond, then down towards the tuna fishery at Bonagìa.

Giardino del Balio

The public gardens centre around the **Castello di Venere** and the **Torri di Balio** – the Norman defences.

The glorious **view★★★** embraces Monte Cofano, Trapani, the Egadi Islands, and on a clear day it's even possible to catch a distant watercolour glimpse of Cap Bon, some 170km/106mi away in Tunisia.

Castello di Venere

Via Castello di Venere. ○*Open 10am–7pm (4pm in winter).*

Covered in a veil of ivy, the 12C Castle of Venus crowns the mountain that sits at the easternmost corner of the town. This was originally the site of an ancient temple to Venus Erycina, goddess of fertility, and large enough for sailors to use as a landmark. Erycina eventually became associated with the goddess of love, Aphrodite – especially after Rome dedicated a temple to her (217 BC).

The temple subsequently fell into decay and centuries later, when Count Roger conquered Erice, the Normans were ordered to clear all traces of the pagan ruins. In its place they built a fortress surrounded by great walls incorporating chunks of stone from the temple.

The towers **(Torri del Balio),** once accessible from the castle by a drawbridge, offer a perfect **viewpoint★★★** over the Egadi Islands.

ADDRESSES

🏠 STAY

🛏🛏 **Ulisse** – *Via Santa Lucia 2.* ℘*0923 86 01 55 or 389 985 60 89. www.sitodiulisse.it. 15 rooms* ⌂. Unassuming pensione offering very good value for Erice. Turn-of-the-century style rooms with pretty embroidered curtains and exposed beams, some of them with balconies.

🛏🛏 **Moderno** – *Via Vittorio Emanuele 63.* ℘*0923 86 93 00. www. hotelmodernoerice.it. 40 rooms.* ⌂. This family hotel with a popular restaurant serving hearty cuisine enjoys a central location. Stunning views from the sun terrace.

🛏🛏 **Baglio Casa Colomba** – *20 km/12mi E of Erice, Via Toselli 165/183,*

View from Giardino del Balio

© Sandro Bedessi / Fototeca ENIT

Erice and bay of Monte Cofano

© Sandro Bedessi / Fototeca ENIT

Buseto Palizzolo. ☏ *0923 85 27 29.*
www.casecolomba.com. 10 rooms. ☐.
Surrounded by orchards, this 19C
residence with pleasantly decorated
rooms is an ideal base from which to
explore the surrounding area.

☺/EAT

☕☕ **San Rocco** – *Via G. F. Guarnotti 23.*
☏ *0923 869 337.* A traditional restaurant
with a calm atmosphere in which to
savour Sicilian produce, nestling on the
corner of a backstreet and the bustling Via
Guarnotti.

☕☕☕ **La Pentolaccia** – *Via G. F.*
Guarnotti 17. ☏ *0923 86 90 99. www.*
ristorantelapentolaccia.it. Closed Tue and
Jan–Feb. On arrival at this 17C convent
converted into a restaurant, you are
greeted by an antique Sicilian cart.
Upstairs, enjoy high-quality Sicilian
cuisine in the two dining rooms. Wide
selection of antipasti. An institution.

☕☕☕ **Monte San Giuliano** *–Vicolo*
San Rocco 7. ☏ *0923 869595. www.monte*
sangiuliano.it. Closed Mon, 6–25 Jan and
2–17 Nov. Booking recommended. This fine
restaurant located in the heart of Erice
specialises in local cuisine. Wide-ranging
menu, meals served in pleasant, rustic
dining rooms or under a pretty arbour
in a cool inner courtyard.

BONAGIA

☕☕ **La Sirena** – *Via Lungomare 45,*
12km/7.4mi north of Erice via Valderice.
☏ *0923 57 31 76. Closed Tue in summer.*
Facing the harbour, next to the Saracen

tower of the tonnara, this huge, popular
restaurant is patronised by families who
come for the fresh fish. One of the best
restaurants in town.

TAKING A BREAK

Pasticceria Maria Grammatico – *Via*
Vittorio Emanuele 14. ☏ *0923 869390. Via*
Guarnotta 1. Signora Maria's 15 years
spent in a convent introduced her to
the secrets of delicious pastries. Her
specialities include almond and marzipan
cakes, *buccellati* (stuffed with dried figs,
almonds, walnuts and sultanas), *genovesi*,
and orange and chocolate *palline*.

SHOPPING

Bazar del Miele – *Via Cordici 16.*
☏ *0923 86 91 81. www.bazardelmiele.com.*
An attractive shop, where you can taste
and buy the whole range of traditional
Sicilian products.

FESTIVALS

Good Friday – 18C wooden figures are
borne aloft in procession through the
town during the traditional Good Friday
Processione dei Misteri.

**Settimana di Musica Medievale e
Rinascimentale** – Concerts are held in
Erice's churches during the Medieval and
Renaissance Music Festival, which takes
place annually at the end of the summer.

Trapani ★

Located on a spur of land that juts into the Tyrrhenian Sea, Trapani is home to a sheltered port brought to life by a daily fish market.

👣 WALKING TOUR

CENTRO STORICO★

The medieval districts of the old town are situated on the headland, while the tip was developed by the Spanish in the 14C *(quartiere Palazzo)*. The oldest section, built in Moorish fashion around a network of interconnecting narrow streets, stretches back along the peninsula; originally this would have been enclosed by walls.

Rua Nova

Now named Via Garibaldi, the "New Road" was laid in the 13C by the Aragonese. Today, it is lined with fine 18C *palazzi* and churches, including the statue-crested **Palazzo Riccio di Morana**, **Palazzo Milo** and **Badia Nuova** *(Santa Maria del Soccorso;* 🕐*no set opening hours)* – the flamboyant interior of which is decorated with Baroque polychrome marble and two elaborate **galleries★**, which are supported by angels.

▶ Palazzo Burgio opposite is graced with a fine 16C doorway.

▶ **Population:** 70 654

Michelin Map: 177: A-1.

Info: Via S. Francesco d'Assis 27, ☎0923 806804; www.comune.trapani.it/turismo.

Location: 110km/68.4mi southwest of Palermo. Most visitors will drive along the central Via G. B. Fardella, which crosses the modern town and leads to the medieval district at the end of the headland.
Trapani is the main port for the Egadi Islands and Pantelleria. Most monuments of interest are located in the old town.

Don't Miss: Sculpture by the Gagni family and **majolica ceramics** at the Museo Pepoli; the medieval district, the **Centro Storico**.

Via Torrearsa is lined with elegant shops to the left and leads down to the Piazza Mercato del Pesce *(fish market)* on the right. Beyond the intersection, Via Garibaldi continues as Via Libertà, past **Palazzo Fardello di Mokarta** and Palazzo Melilli with its 16C doorway.

View of Trapani from the fishing port

© Franck Guiziou/hemis.fr

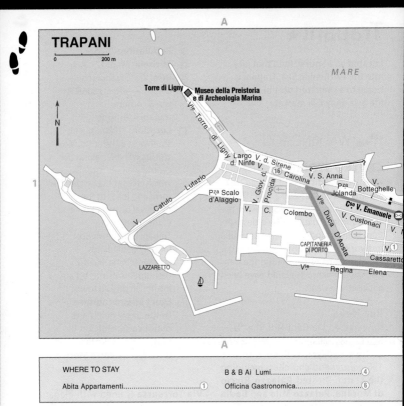

TRAPANI

0   200 m

MARE

Torre di Ligny

**Museo della Preistoria
e di Archeologia Marina**

N

Largo
d. Ninfe

V. d. Sirene

V. Carolina

V. S. Anna

Pza
Jolanda

V.
Botteghelle

Pza Scalo
d'Alaggio

V. Giov. d. Procida

C.

Colombo

Cso V. Emanuele

V. Duca D'Aosta

V. Custonaci

V.

CAPITANERIA
DI PORTO

Cassaretto

Regina   Elena

V.

LAZZARETTO

Catulo

Lutazio

Vle Torre di Ligny

WHERE TO STAY		
Abita Appartamenti		①
B & B Ai Lumi		④
Officina Gastronomica		⑤

GETTING THERE AND AROUND

Trapani is approximately 150km/ 95mi from Agrigento and 100km/ 60mi from Palermo, to which it is connected by both bus and train *(3hr 30min and 5hr 30min, and 1hr 30min and 3hr respectively)*. The bus and train stations are both situated in Piazza Umberto I.

For further information and time-tables, contact the tourist office.

Birgi airport *(15km/9mi to the south of the town; ℘0923 842502; www.airgest. it)* operates services from Trapani to Pantelleria *(www.aeroportotrapani. com)* and mainland cities. Ferry services to the Egadi Islands and Pantelleria leave from Trapani, operated by **Siremar** (*℘091 74 93 11; www.siremar.it*) and Ustica Lines (*℘0923 87 38 13; www.usticalines.it*).

▷ Turn left into Corso Vittorio Emanuele.

Rua Grande

The second principal thoroughfare constructed in the 13C *(the modern Corso Vittorio Emanuele)* stretches between elegant Baroque buildings such as the Palazzo Berardo Ferro *(no. 86)* and the Sede del Vescovado *(Bishop's Palace)*.

Cattedrale

ⓞ*Open Mon–Fri 8am–12am, 4–7.30pm, Sun 8am–12.30am, 4–8pm. ℘0923 23362. www.parrocchie.it/trapani/ cattedrale.*

The cathedral dedicated to St Lawrence was erected in the 17C on the site of an earlier 14C building.

Inside, it contains a number of paintings by Flemish artists: a **Nativity** *(third chapel on the right)*, a crucifixion and a **Deposition** *(fourth chapel on the left)*.

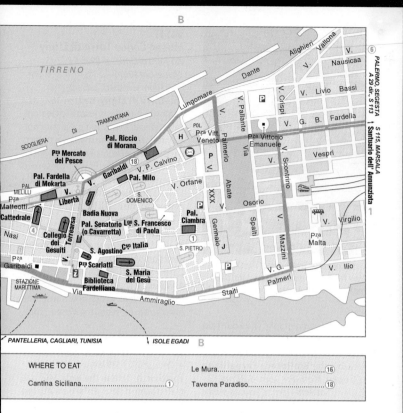

Chiesa del Collegio dei Gesuiti

The 17–18C church has an imposing Mannerist façade, ornamented by pediments, columns, pilasters, grotesque masks and caryatid figures.

Palazzo Senatorio (Cavaretta)

The elaborate façade of this lovely *palazzo* rises through two orders of columns and statues up to a pair of large clocks. Alongside stands a 13C bell tower.

▶ Turn right into Via Torrearsa, then take a left into Piazza Scarlatti.

Sant'Agostino

This church, built in the 14C, was badly damaged during the Second World War. Built by the Knights Templar, it is one of the only buildings associated with the order still in existence on the island. The **rose window★** with its Islamic geometric arabesque pattern and Gothic

Cathedral and Corso Vittorio Emanuele

Detail of an 18C reliquary of the Old and New Testament made of ivory coral and mother of pearl, Museo Pepoli

© Christophe Boisvieux / age fotostock

doorway, is memorable. The **Fountain of Saturn** in front of the church commemorates the building of an aqueduct. Nearby, the **Biblioteca Fardelliana** (🕐 open Mon–Fri 9am–1.30pm, 3–7.30pm, Sat 9am–1pm; 🕐 closed public hols and 7 Aug; 📞0923 21 540/506) displays engravings from the **Gatto** collection.

Santa Maria del Gesù

This church, founded by Emperor Charles V, dates from the 16C. Inside, through its lovely Catalan Renaissance doorway, the Cappella Staiti *(in the right aisle at the back of the church)* houses the terracotta **Madonna degli Angeli★** by **Andrea della Robbia**, underneath a magnificent marble tribune by Antonello Gagini (1521).

▶ Head along Corso Italia.
Turn left by the church of San Pietro, then immediately right.

Palazzo Ciambra (della Giudecca)

This fine example of the 16C Plateresque *(Spanish renaissance)* style has heavy rustication to emphasise the doors, windows and front of the tower.

VISIT
Museo Civico Torre di Ligny

Via Torre di Ligny. 📞0923 54 72 75. 🕐Tue–Sat 10am–12.30pm, 4–6.30pm *(5–7.30pm summer).* ☞Free.

The **Torre di Ligny**, built in 1671 as a defensive bastion, houses archaeological artefacts, fossils and palaeontological finds. Most of the medieval objects were recovered from nearby shipwrecks, including a display of well-preserved Spanish amphorae. At the top of the tower, a fine **view** extends over the town and out to the Egadi islands.

L'Annunziata

At the far eastern end of town *(in the direction of Palermo)* stands the large Carmelite institution known as the Annunziata. The church itself adjoins the former convent, which now houses the town's main museum, the Museo Pepoli.

Santuario dell'Annunziata★

Via Conte A. Pepoli. 🕐Open 7am–noon, 4–7pm. 📞0923 539184.

The church, built in the early 14C, was transformed and enlarged during the 18C. The original front elevation is ornamented with a Chiaramonte Gothic portal, surmounted by an elaborate **rose window** above.

The **Cappella dei Marinai** (16C) is a lovely Renaissance tufa building surmounted by a dome. Inside, a fusion of styles are drawn from Eastern and Renaissance sources.

The **Cappella della Madonna** extends from behind the main altar of the church. Access is through a Renaissance arch with bronze gates dating from 1591. On the altar is the delicate marble figure of the **Madonna of Trapani** (14C), attributed to Nino Pisano.

Museo Pepoli★

Via Conte A. Pepoli 200. 🕐Open Mon–Sat 9am–1pm, 3-7.30pm, Sun 9am–12.30am. ☞€6. 📞0923 553269. 🖐Poor lighting in the museum means that it is best to visit early in the day.

The ex-Carmelite convent beside the Santuario dell'Annunziata is entered through the Villa Pepoli. Inside, the museum, which is named after the benefactor and obsessive collector Count Pepoli, houses a wide-ranging collection of artefacts and artworks from prehistoric times to the 19C.

The ground floor is devoted to sculpture and the Gagini family is well represented, the star exhibit being four statues of saints, including *St James the Greater* by **Antonello Gagini**.

A sumptuous polychrome marble staircase leads up to the first-floor **art gallery**: the most arresting paintings are the **Trapani polyptych★**(15C) and a **Pietà★** by the Neapolitan Roberto di Oderisio (14C). Also notable are a *St Francis Receiving the Stigmata* by Titian and *Madonna and Child with Angels* by Pastura (1478–1509). Works from the Neapolitan School include *St Bartholomew* by Ribera.

The medium favoured by local artists and craftsmen of the 16C–19C was Mediterranean red coral, found on the reefs off the Trapani and San Vito Lo Capo coasts. The coral is now virtually extinct in the region – the spread of liturgical objects and jewellery represented here give an indication as to why. Elsewhere in the museum is a wonderful series of 16 small wooden figurative groups depicting the *Slaughter of the Innocents* (17C).

Local **pottery** is represented by a pair of maiolica panels depicting the **mattanza** *(the ritual killing of tuna fish)* and a 17C **view** of Trapani.

ADDRESSES

⌂ STAY

⌂ **Abita Appartamenti** – *Via S Francesco 53. ℘0923 437 595. www. abita-appartamenti.com. 20 rooms .* Apartment complex around a patio. Annexe in the former sailors' residence offers studios.

⌂⌂⌂ **Ai Lumi** – *Corso V. Emanuele 71. ℘0923 87 24 18. www.ailumi.it. 5 rooms , restaurant ⌂⌂(closed Sun).* On the 1st floor of the attractive 18C Palazzo Ferro, this guesthouse is right in the heart of the historic centre. Some rooms have a

corner kitchen, but you might as well eat in the restaurant of the same name just downstairs, which is very popular for its generous portions.

⌂⌂⌂ **Officina Gastronomica** – *Via G. Ricevuto 14. ℘0923 53 25 94. www. officinagastronomica.com. 8 rooms ⌂ ✗ €40/60.* A small hotel opened by Sicilian chef Peppe Giuffré, who has transformed this former baglio into a haven of peace close to Trapani. Charming rooms and artfully prepared cuisine.

⍩/ EAT

One of Trapani's more typical dishes is *cuscus di pesce,* which originates from North Africa and has been adapted by the addition of locally-caught fish.

⌂⌂ **Cantina Siciliana** – *Via Giudecca 36 ℘0923 28673, www.cantinasiciliana.it. Eve.booking recommended.* Located near the church of San Pietro, the cantina has been serving up local specialities since the 1950s, such as *busiate* (a type of pasta) and fish dishes. Charming service and a rustic atmosphere.

⌂⌂ **Taverna Paradiso** – *Lungomare Dante Alighieri 22. ℘0923 22 303. Closed Sun.* If you like tuna this seafront restaurant is for you.

⌂⌂⌂ **Le Mura** – *Viale delle Sirene 15. ℘0923 872 622. Closed Mon.* In elegant surroundings with a terrace under the old port ramparts, Le Mura prepares fish and seafood dishes such as *pappardelle* with cuttlefish ink and sea urchins.

TAKING A BREAK

Gelateria Gino – *Piazza Generale Dalla Chiesa 4. ℘0923 21104.* On a little bench in front of the shop, you can enjoy Gino's delicious hand-made ice creams.

Pasticceria Colicchia – *Via delle Arti 6. ℘0923 54 76 12. Closed Sun pm.* A long-standing purveyor of the city's best *cannoli* and *granite.*

FESTIVAL

Settimana Santa – Holy Week celebrations culminate in the **Processione dei Misteri** on Good Friday as 20 groups of sculpted figures are carried through the streets all day and the following night. At other times, the statues are kept in the **Chiesa del Purgatorio** *(in the town centre, in Via San Francesco)*; made of wood, cloth and glue by local craftsmen. They date from between 1650 and 1720.

Segesta★★★

Set amid gently rolling ochre and red-brown hills, the Segesta archaeological park is dominated by an elegant Doric temple, one of the best preserved in the world, which stands in magnificent isolation on a small hillock surrounded by a deep valley. Apart from its theatre, now a venue for concerts and plays, this temple is all that's left of the ancient city of Segesta.

A BIT OF HISTORY

Ancient Segesta was probably founded in the 12C BC on the slopes of Monte Barbaro by the Elimi, under Greek patronage. Like Erice (Eryx) it soon ranked among the leading towns of the Mediterranean basin.

In the 5C BC, it was pitched against its great rival Selinunte (Selinus).

In an attempt to rally its defences against this threat, Segesta appealed for help from Athens in 415 BC, but these reinforcements were subsequently defeated by Syracuse, whose forces were allied to Selinunte. In 409 BC, Segesta turned to Carthage for support; on landing in Sicily, these troops destroyed both Selinus and Himera in vast and bloody battles. In turn, Segesta was destroyed by the Syracusan tyrant **Agathocles** in 307 BC, but rose again under the Romans. Subsequent developments are not well documented, although it is thought that the city probably succumbed to further damage at the hand of the Vandals in the 5C AD.

What is certain is that the area was inhabited in medieval times as the excavated ruins of a Norman castle and a small three-apsed basilica situated in the northern part of the ancient acropolis testify.

This part of the site extended over two areas separated by a hollow. The south-eastern section was predominantly residential, whereas the north mainly served as the location for public buildings, including the theatre.

Michelin Map: 177: B-2.

Info: Servizio Parco Archeologico di Segesta; ℘0924 952356; www.regione.sicilia.it/beniculturali.

Location: 40km/24.8mi east of Trapani, Segesta occupies a splendid **position★★** in a small, deep valley, framed by Monte Bernardo and Monte Barbaro. Segesta is accessible by train from Palermo but connecting at Alcamo can be time consuming, so travellers may prefer to take the bus (Autoservizi Tarantola, ℘0924 310 20), which leaves from the central train station in Palermo twice a day and takes around an hour and twenty minutes.

Don't Miss: In July and August, the **city** theatre stages concerts and plays. Performances of music, poetry and literature, known as albe (dawns), take place at 5am.

Parking: Park at the site's car park and take the shuttle bus to the theatre.

Timing: There is no shade at the site of Segesta, so visit early morning, preferably when it opens at 9am, or late afternoon in summer when the light is at its most evocative for some quiet contemplation.

ARCHAEOLOGICAL SITE

Open Oct–Mar 9am–4pm, Apr–Sep 9am–6pm. €6. A regular shuttle bus service operates to the theatre (€1.50). Bar and restaurant. ℘0924 952356.

Tempio★★★

Built in 430 BC, this amazingly well-preserved temple is a Doric building with the 36 limestone columns of its peri-

Tempio

© René Mattes/hemis.fr

style, plus entablature and pediment almost completely intact. The shafts are unfluted: no holes were left in the architrave for roof beams and, coupled with the absence of a *cella*, this arrangement has prompted the suggestion that the temple was abandoned before completion. Some scholars dismiss this theory, claiming the lack of a *cella* (usually the first part of the sanctuary to be undertaken) might indicate that the building was intended to consist merely of a peristyle, making it a pseudo-temple. Other recent academic theories and exploration suggest that the Egestans stopped work around 420 BC, which would put paid to the idea of the structure serving as some sort of outdoor temple for a Elymian cult. The mystery of whether the temple was used for worship or not is compounded by the lack of any indication as to which, if any, deity it might have been dedicated to.

The road up to the theatre *(approx 2km/1.2mi: take the regular minibus service from the car park)* winds through overgrown wild fennel and provides fabulous **views★★** back over the temple. Before the theatre *(on the right)* other layers of history have been peeled back, further illustrating the importance of this strategic site. These include the remains of the Hermitage of San Leone, with a single apse built over the foundation of an earlier, three-apsed church and, behind it, the ruins of the Norman castle.

Teatro★

The white stone theatre was built in the 3C BC during the Hellenistic period, while the area was under Roman domination. It consists of a perfect semicircle with a diameter of 63m/207ft slotted into a rocky slope. The 20 tiers of seats face west towards the hills, beyond which *(to the right)* you can glimpse the broad bay of Golfo di Castellammare.

Sanctuary of the Elymians

The third of Segesta's sites is only accessible by a strenuous hike eastwards uphill towards Contrado Magno. Now just a large, overgrown and partially excavated area, probably dating from around the 6C BC, it was once a site of some religious significance to the Elymians. There's not much to see here compared to the impressively intact remains of the temple and theatre, but it is still of interest, if only to appreciate the poetic isolation and natural splendour of the site with few or no other visitors.

Marsala

Although the city continues to produce the fortified wine for which it is famed, the area's intoxicating charms extend beyond a glass of Marsala. With its large Tunisian population, lively port and maze of alleyways criss-crossing the centre, Marsala has a uniquely North African atmosphere.

A BIT OF HISTORY

Marsala is situated on the headland that continues to bear the town's ancient name, Lilybaeum (from *lily* meaning water and *beum* referring to the Eubei, its pre-Phoenician inhabitants). The settlement is presumed to have been founded in 397 BC by the Phoenicians, who fled Motya following their defeat by the Syracusans. The name "Marsala" probably derives from the Arabic *Marsah el Ali,* meaning port of Ali, indicating its role as a important maritime town since early history, including witnessing one of Sicily's most momentous events: the landing of Garibaldi's Thousand.

Grazie... mille – In early May 1860, accompanied by 1,000 volunteers, Garibaldi set sail from Quarto *(near Genoa)* bound for Sicily to overthrow the Bourbon government and liberate the Kingdom of the Two Sicilies. On 11 May, the two ships – the *Lombardo* and the *Piemonte* – moored at Marsala. The Mille (one thousand) made their way inland, winning their first battle at Calatafimi, opening up the way to Palermo. As the campaign progressed, the band was swollen by new volunteers so that by the time they reached the Straits of Messina, their number exceeded 20,000. In less than two months, Sicily had been liberated from Bourbon rule. The expedition swept through the rest of the kingdom until on 21 October, following a plebiscite, the island was admitted to the northern states (Piedmont, Lombardy, Liguria, Emilia Romagna, Tuscany and Sardinia) that were later to form the Kingdom of Italy.

▶ **Population:** 82 765
⏱ **Michelin Map:** 177: A-2.
Info: Via XI Maggio 100; ℘0923 714097; www.comune.marsala.tp.it.
Location: 33km/19mi south of Trapani, Marsala sits on the western tip of Sicily and is closer to Africa than to the rest of Europe. Situated on the headland of Capo Lilibeo *(also known as Capo Boeo),* behind the Lungomare Boeo and Piazza Vittoria, its historical centre is a maze of narrow streets. Marsala is a good base for excursions.
Don't Miss: Exploring the centre from Piazza Vittoria, Via XI Maggio leads to the hub of the city, **Piazza della Repubblica** *(see Walking Tour);* sample **Marsala wine** at local wineries *(appts necessary);* the Flemish tapestries at the **Museo degli Arazzi**.
Kids: Punic ship remains at the Museo Archeologico di Baglio Anselmi.
🕐 **Timing:** Allow half a day.

MARSALA WINE

History – In 1770, a storm forced a British ship to take shelter in Marsala harbour. A merchant, John Woodhouse, disembarked and went into town to sample the Marsala wine in one of the taverns. Although more accustomed to the liqueur wines of Spain and Portugal, his palate immediately detected their similarity, prompting him to dispatch a consignment of wine (blended with alcohol so as to withstand the journey) to his native land to sound out the market. The response was positive and the merchant set up his own company in Marsala. A little later, a second English merchant landed in Marsala: Ben Ingham, a connoisseur of fortified wines.

Ingham helped to improve the quality of the wine using blends of different grape varieties. His business passed to his nephews, the Whitakers. In 1833, the entrepreneur Vincenzo Florio, Calabrese by birth and Palermitano by adoption, bought land between the two largest established Marsala producers and set to making his own vintage with an even more specialised range of grapes. By the end of the 19C, several more winemakers had joined the competition, including Pellegrino (1880). After the turn of the century, Florio bought out Ingham and Woodhouse, and retained the two labels before succumbing in turn to a takeover by a conglomeration of other producers.

The wine – Marsala is registered as a DOC wine (a state-designated label of controlled quality); this means production is restricted to an exclusive area around Trapani and a collection of additional vineyards in the provinces of Agrigento and Palermo. Only grape varieties with a high natural sugar content are used to make Marsala. After fermentation, the wine is traditionally barrel-aged and then fortified with a sweet alcohol blend called mistella to produce the different types and flavours of Marsala. Relative to the sugar content, Marsala may be categorised as dry, semi-dry or sweet. Its main denomination, however, is relative to the length of time it is left to mature: Marsala Fine *(1 year)*, Superiore *(2 years)*, Superiore Riserva *(4 years)*, Vergine *(5 years)* and Vergine Riserva *(10 years)*. Dry Marsala is usually served as a refreshing aperitif, while the sweeter forms are drunk as a dessert wine.

WALKING TOUR

The most impressive way to enter Marsala is through the **Porta Nuova**, a grand entrance restored in the time of Mussolini. Inside the gate, Via XI Maggio, the city's main street, leads to the **Piazza della Repubblica**.

The literal and spiritual heart of Marsala, the square sits in the centre of a network of quiet narrow streets radiating out from it. Garibaldi ignited the unification of Italy here in 1860, with a stirring nationalist speech. Today, this elegant square is defined by two 18C buildings, the Chiesa Madre and the arcaded Palazzo Senatorio.

Chiesa Madre

The main church, dedicated to San Tommaso di Canterbury, the patron saint of Marsala, was built during the Norman

Marsala wine cellar

© Giovanni Rinaldi / iStockphoto.com

occupation. Its exterior was extensively remodelled in the 18C; inside it contains a fine icon by **Antonello Gagini** and Berrettaro (north apse), and a delicate Madonna by **Domenico Gagini** from 1490 (south transept). Above this, a Renaissance painting by Antonello Riggio depicts the Presentation of the Virgin at the Temple.

The main thoroughfare leading from Piazza della Repubblica is Via XI Maggio, the old Decumanus Maximus of the Roman town, lined with splendid buildings. Perpendicular to the principal axis, **Via Garibaldi** leads southwards to **Porta Garibaldi** on the edge of town, running past the town hall, a former Spanish military barracks.

Behind the Chiesa Madre is the Museo degli Arazzi.

Museo degli Arazzi

Via Garraffa 57. ©Open Tue–Sat 9.30am–1pm, 4pm–6pm, Sun 9.30am–1pm. €4. 0923 711327.
The collection comprises eight enormous 16C Flemish **tapestries** (arazzi)★ depicting scenes from the war waged by Emperor Vespasian and his son Titus against the Jews and the capture of Jerusalem. Hand-stitched and woven in rich red, gold and green wool and silk, they were originally a gift to the city from King Philip II of Spain via the Spanish ambassador, who was also the archbishop of Messina.

Museo Archeologico di Baglio Anselmi

Lungomare Boeo (turn left at the end of Viale Vittorio Veneto and follow the road along the headland). ©Open Tue–Sun 9am–8pm, Mon 9am–1.30pm. €4. 0923 95 25 35.
Pride of place at this archaeological museum, located in a stone-vaulted warehouse, is given to the remains of a **Punic ship**★ (3C BC) recovered in 1971 near the island of Motya. This was probably a liburna, a type of fast warship (35m/115ft long) used and lost at the end of the First Punic War, in the Battle of the Egadi (241 BC).

Today less than 5 percent of the ship, which was originally around 32m (105ft) long, remains, but the reconstruction is impressive nevertheless. Analysis of the ship has provided detailed information on Phoenician life – including the crew's diet – and shipbuilding methods, including the use of prefabricated units and remarkable metal alloy nails that show no deterioration, even after 2,000 years submerged underwater.

Elsewhere in the museum, the displays include items found in or around the ship, such as anchors and amphorae, as well as photographs and a detailed explanation of how the ship was raised from the sea and restored.

Parco Archeologico di Lilibeo (Capo Boeo)

At the end of Viale Vittorio Veneto turn right and follow the headland.
On the tip of the headland sit the remains of three **Roman insulae** (blocks of buildings). One is taken up by a large **villa** (3C BC), complete with a set of baths. Look out for fragments of the **mosaic floors** and small pillars (suspensurae) that were used to support the floor and enable hot air to circulate through the cavity. The perfectly preserved paving stones of the **Decumanus Maximus**, a Roman ceremonial road, are also visible.

A little farther on stands the **church of San Giovanni al Boeo**, built around the grotto of the Sibyl of Lilybaeum, one of the three legendary prophetesses of antiquity reputed by some legends to have foreseen the coming of Christ.
For information on the guided tours, contact the museum.

WINE PRODUCERS
Florio

Via Vincenzo Florio 1 (between Marsala to Mazara) Guided tours Mon–Fri at 11am and 3.30pm, Sat 11.30am (arrive 10 minutes before the tour starts). ©Closed Sun and public holidays. €10. 0923 781111. www.cantineflorio.it.
A tour of this **winery** and its small museum allows visitors to compare

old and new wine-making techniques and equipment. The 19C wine cellars *(cantine),* built by Vincenzo Florio, are somewhat close and stuffy: the environment is maintained at a constant temperature by tufa walls *(insulation),* a tiled roof *(aeration)* and sand on the floor *(temperature control and humidity).* The most interesting part of the process, however, is the **Soleras Method** by which the wine is conditioned through a pyramid of oak barrels.

Pellegrino

Via del Fante 39. 🗣 *Guided tours by reservation only.* ⏰ *Closed Sun pm.* ⌨ *€5.* 🚻 📞 *0923 719911/28.* *www.carlopellegrino.it.*

Another of the large producers, fortifying a wine full of tangy raisin and citrus zest flavours. This winery also produces the superlative sweet wines of Passito and Moscato di Pantelleria.

Marco De Bartoli

Contrada Samperi 292. 🗣 *Guided tours by appointment only.* ⏰ *Open Mon–Sat 9am–1pm, 3pm–6.30pm.* ⌨ *€20.* 📞 *0923 962093. www.marcodebartoli.com.*

This producer, situated in the Samperi district, is responsible for one of the best Marsalas, a feat achieved by traditional production methods.

Donna fugata

Via S. Lipari 18. 📞 *0923 724 245/263. www.donnafugata.it.* ⏰ *Open Mon–Sat.* 🗣 *Guided tours by appointment only.*

Located in one of Marsala's historic vineyards, these wine cellars are open throughout the year.

🚗 DRIVING TOUR

FROM MARSALA TO TRAPANI
La Via del Sale★

This 30km/18mi route displayed on the regional map p179, runs from Marsala to Trapani via the SP 21. You will need a full day, especially if you include a visit to the Mozia peninsula. Take the SP 21 coastal road to Trapani.

A succession of fine **views★★** over the saltpans of Trapani, Paceco and Stagnone.

Mozia★

♿ *Access to the island and museum, Apr–Oct 9.30am–6.30pm, Nov–Mar 9am–3pm.* ⌨ *€5(ferry); €9 (museum).* 📞 *0923 712598.* *www.fondazionewhitaker.it.*

One of the four islands of the Stagnone di Marsala, Motya was once a prosperous Phoenician colony. The Carthaginians laid siege to it in the 6C BC and when its inhabitants fled to the mainland, the colony was forgotten. Its renaissance came in the 1800s, when Englishman Joseph Whitaker, a member of a family of Marsala wine exporters, built a house here. Today the island greets visitors with a profusion of scents and colours: the Mediterranean vegetation is especially beautiful in spring and worth a visit in itself.

As recently as 1971, it was possible to take a horse-drawn cart across the old Phoenician causeway linking the island to the mainland. With the causeway just below the water's surface, passengers got the impression that they were "walking on water" (🗣 *See Porta Nord, below*). This was also how Grillo grapes, used for making Marsala, were transported. In the centre, the 19C house built by the Whitakers is now a museum.

Excavations

Footpaths run along the island perimeter among the remains of the Phoenician town *(allow 90min; visitors are advised to follow the path in an anticlockwise direction).*

Fortifications

The island lies in the lee of what was once a peninsula – modern-day Isola Grande – naturally protected from attack by the mainland and the Stagnone di Marsala's shallow waters. Motya was also enveloped by a 6C BC wall with watchtowers.

The footpath skirts the remains, notably those of the **east tower** with its staircase up to the ramparts.

Mozia★

The Island– The ancient Phoenician colony was founded in the 8C BC on one of the four islands of the Stagnone di Marsala lagoon, now known as the island of **San Pantaleo**. Motya, the Phoenician name by which it was once known, translates loosely as "spinning centre", a reference to the wool carding and spinning cottage industries on the island. Like most other Phoenician colonies, the island became a commercial trade centre and staging post for Phoenician ships plying the Mediterranean.

The 8C BC also saw the beginning of the Greek colonisation of Sicily, mainly concentrated on the east side of the island. The Phoenicians consolidated their activities in the west, enabling **Motya** to grow in importance. In the 6C BC, the struggle for Greek or Carthaginian supremacy over Sicily gained momentum and Motya was forced into taking sides. In 397 BC, the tyrant of Syracuse Dionysius the Elder laid siege to the town until it capitulated. Its surviving inhabitants sought refuge on the mainland and integrated themselves among the people of Lilybaeum, present-day Marsala.

The rediscovery of Motya is associated with the name of **Joseph Whitaker**, an English nobleman living in the 1880s related to the family who owned a well-established and flourishing business producing and exporting Marsala wines. Today the house on the island built for Whitaker accommodates a small museum.

The Lagoon – Since 1984, the **Stagnone di Marsala**, Sicily's largest lagoon (*2,000ha/5,000 acres*), has been designated a nature reserve of special interest – the **Riserva Naturale Orientata**. This area extends into the sea and includes the coastline between Punta Alga and Capo San Teodoro. The water here is shallow and very salty, providing ideal conditions for **salt works**, which were set up all along the coast and on Isola Grande, where it soon became the main industry; many of these have since dwindled into disuse.

The lagoon harbours four islands: Isola Grande – the largest, Santa Maria – the greenest, San Pantaleo and Schola – a tiny islet with roofless houses that give it an eerie air.

The most common plant species to thrive here include the Aleppo pine, dwarf palm, bamboo (*Isola Grande*), **sea marigold** (*Calendula maritima*) which, in Europe, grows only here and in Spain, glasswort or sea samphire (with fleshy branches), sea scilla with its star-like white flowers, the sea lily and the sea rush. The islands are also populated with a multitude of bird species, including the lark, goldfinch, Kentish plover, tawny pipit and Sardinian warbler. The waters of the Stagnone (*large pool*) provide a fertile habitat for underwater flora and fauna: sea anemones, murex – collected by the Phoenicians for its valuable purple dye – and over 40 kinds of fish, including sea bass, white bream and sole.

The seabed also supports the **Poseidonia oceanica**, a ribbon-leafed seaweed that produces a flower like an ear of wheat from its centre. This plant is fast becoming a menace, spreading like wildfire through the Mediterranean: its contribution, however, is to thrive in polluted and stagnant conditions. It stabilises the sea bed, oxygenates the water and provides nutrients for other species, thereby playing a role similar to that of a forest on land.

Porta Nord

The North Gate is the better preserved of the town's two entrances. Inside, a section of the original main street shows wear, its surface deeply rutted by ancient cart wheels. On the seaward side, just below the surface of the water, a paved causeway once linked Motya to Birgi on the mainland *(7km/4.5mi)*. Today, it is marked above the surface allowing visitors to walk the causeway *(⊘wear flip-flops or plastic sandals as the surface is rough)*.

▶ Enter through the gate and proceed along the main street.

Cappiddazzu

This area covers the streets just inside the North Gate. One of the buildings is divided into three aisles and may have once served some sort of religious function.

▶ Make your way back towards the shore.

Necropolis

A series of stelae and urns indicate the area used for Archaic cremations and burials. A second necropolis was located on the mainland at Birgi, at the far end of the submerged causeway directly opposite.

Tophet

The sacred area consists of an open-air sanctuary where urns containing the remains of human sacrifices to the goddess Tanit and the god Baal Hammon were deposited.

At that time, the immolation of first-born male children was widespread. Farther along the track is Schola – recognisable by its three pink, roofless houses.

Cothon

The rectangular man-made harbour is linked to the sea by a narrow channel. The **Porta Sud** *(South Gate)* is situated immediately beyond the harbour: like the North Gate, it too is framed by towers. Farther on, the **Casermetta**,

Ephebus of Motya

© Bartuccio Antonino/Sime/Photononstop

reserved for the military, has typical Phoenician vertical stone shafts.

The last monument is the **Casa dei Mosaici**, with two black and white pebble panels that depict a griffin chasing a deer and a lion attacking a bull.

Museum

The museum has a display of artefacts recovered from the island itself, from Lilybaeum *(Marsala)* and the necropolis at Birgi, on the shore opposite Motya. The front courtyard features a series of stelae from the Tophet.

The Phoenician and Punic pottery is simple in shape and devoid of decoration; imported Corinthian, Attic and Italiot vases are decorated with black or red figures. Sculpture includes allegorical statuettes of motherhood such as the figurine of the *Great Mother*; terracotta heads betraying a Greek influence and the **Ephebus of Motya**★★ *(⊘see Introduction: Art and Architecture)*.

Casa delle Anfore

The House of the Amphorae is behind the museum. Its name derives from the considerable number of amphorae found here. The coast road winds to

Salt flats, Marsala

© Sandro Bedessi / Fototeca ENIT

La Via del Sale

Ancient origins – The Phoenicians began exploiting the coastal area between Trapani and Marsala when, realising its shallow water, searing temperatures and arid winds were ideal for producing salt, they set about building basins in which to collect it. This valuable commodity was then exported all over the Mediterranean to treat perishable food for the lean winter months. After the Phoenicians, however, there are no reliable references to the saltpans around Trapani until the Norman era, when Frederick II himself alludes to them in the Constitutions of Melfi. From this date on, the rise in status of the port of Trapani can be fairly easily tracked. The economic success of the saltpans shows that major fluctuations in output shadowed the rise and fall in fortune of the territory as it succumbed to wars, epidemics and transitions of government. On the whole, the area and its commercial activity were profitable and that is why it has continued, albeit in fits and starts, until the present day. The salt is still being extracted, although the methods used have changed and the windmills that dot the landscape are no longer in use.

Automating the saltworks

Mechanisation – The most important individual pieces of machinery used in the cultivation and processing of salt – in the past, at least – were the classic Dutch windmill, the American windmill (introduced in the early 1950s) and the Archimedes screw.

The Dutch windmill comprises a conical building and roof, and six trapezoidal vanes consisting of cloth sails attached to wooden frames that catch the wind and propel a system of mechanical gears. Inside the building, a complex system of interconnected cogs and wheels, shafts and stays allow the circular roof (and hence, the sails) to be orientated according to the wind direction and so exploit the natural resource to grind the salt or to pump water.

Should the mill be required to pump water, the gearing is harnessed to an Archimedes screw.

The main difference between the American windmill and its smaller Dutch counterpart is its sophistication: it has a greater degree of automation (including a gearing system allowing the roof to regulate itself automatically to catch the wind).

The Archimedes screw can be activated in a few centimetres of liquid and is powered by hand or by means of a windmill. It consists of a rotating shaft with small wooden blades attached to form a continuous spiral.

Manpower – Few people were fully employed to work the saltpans all year round other than the curatolo, the overseer and the miller. In July, a team of seasonal labourers would begin breaking up the crust of salt. Next, the salt was shovelled into piles in rows, thereby allowing any damp residue to dry out.

A band of 20 men (or *venna*) were charged with filling baskets with the salt and emptying them onto the dike in larger piles. In the autumn, the heaps were covered with tiles by the *curatolo*.

Marsala along a particularly spectacular route at sunset.

▷ Return along the coast to Trapani.

Working windmill

Contrada Ettore Infersa. ◐*Open 9.30am–7.30pm.* ⬤*€6.* ☎*0923 733003. www.salineettoreinfersa.com.*
This 16C windmill, once indispensable for grinding salt, survives today in working order because of the loving attention of its owners *(Saline Ettore e Infersa).*
The sails can rotate at 20kph/12.5mph and generate up to 120 horsepower.

▷ Continue to Nubia.

Nubia is home to the offices of the WWF which manages the **Riserva naturale integrale Saline di Trapani e Paceco** *(via Garibaldi 138;* ☎*0923 86 77 00; www. wwfsalineditrapani.it;* ♿ ☞*guided tours by reservation only),* a naturally rich expanse of brackish water that provides a habitat for around 170 species of birds (flamingoes, storks, cranes and herons).

Museo del Sale

Via Chiusa - Nubia Paceco. ◐*Open daily 9.30am–7pm.* ☞*Guided tours available (30 minutes).* ⬤*€2.50.* ♿
☎*0923 867061. www. museodelsale.it.*
A small salt museum has been set up in a 300-year-old salt worker's house: it recounts the different stages involved in collecting salt from the saltpans and displays tools adapted for its extraction and harvest.

▷ Return towards Trapani on the SP21.

Le Saline di Nubia

The saltworks in front of the museum provides an example of the "cultivation" and extraction of the crystallised salt.
A canal supplements the two large basins on the outer edge of the complex known as the **fridde** (a corruption of *freddo* meaning "cold" because of the temperature of the incoming water). The **mulino Americano** (literally, the "American mill") located between these two basins uses an

Windmill in the saltworks

© M. Magni / MICHELIN

Archimedes screw contraption to transfer water into the **vasu cultivu**, a reservoir where it blends with the yeast-like residue of the previous crop.
The greater the saline concentration (measured in Baum), the warmer the water. From here, the water is drained to the **ruffiana**, an intermediary stage between the **vasu** and the **caure**, where the water temperature is considerably warmer and the salinity attains 23 Baum. Next in line comes the **sintine**, where the high concentration of salt and the high temperature combine to lend a pinkish tinge to the solution and so begin the last stages in the process.
The water now passes into the salting pans or **caseddri**, where layers of pure salt crystals are allowed to form (27–28 Baum) in preparation for harvest twice a year, usually around mid-July and mid-August. The conical piles of sand, aligned the length of the **arione**, are left open to the elements to be rinsed through by the rain before being covered with "Roman" tiles for protection from heavy downpours and dirt.

▷ Return to Trapani, stopping to admire the Trapani, Paceco and Stagnone saltpans.

ADDRESSES

🛏 STAY

TOWN CENTRE

🛏🛏 **Centrale** – *Via Salinisti 19.* ☎*0923 951777. www.hotelcentralemarsala.it.* 🅿. *7 rooms* ⌷. Good value for money in the downtown area, this hotel has nice rooms on two floors, each with refrigerators. Central patio.

🛏🛏 **Carmine** – *Piazza Carmine 16.* ☎*0923 711907. www.hotelcarmine.it.* *28 rooms* ⌷. This quiet and comfortable hotel in an old convent is tastefully decorated. All the rooms are different and furnished in a traditional style. Good breakfast served in the courtyard garden.

OUTSIDE THE CENTRE

🛏🛏 **Tenuta Volpara** – *Contrada Digerbato, 7km/4.3mi E of Marsala.* ☎*0923 98 45 88. www.tenutavolpara.it.* *18 rooms* ⌷, *restaurant* 🛏🛏. Situated in the countryside outside Marsala, this farm guesthouse offers genuine Sicilian hospitality. The restaurant specialises in local cuisine, including a special warm ricotta cheese with whey, known as *zabbina*, traditionally served at breakfast.

🛏🛏🛏 **Villa Sparta** – *Contrada Amabilina 3, on the way out of town.* ☎*0923 980000. www.villasparta.com. Closed Nov–Mar. 4 rooms* ⌷. In Marsala's old residential district, this elegant villa offers all the comforts required for a pleasant stay. Italian-style breakfast.

LA VIA DEL SALE

🛏🛏🛏 **La Finestra sul sale** – *Contrada Ettore Infersa.* ☎*0923 73 30 03. www. salineettoreinfersa.com. 3 rooms.* ⌷ ✗ €*25.* If you've ever dreamed of drifting to sleep as you watch the sun set over pink-tinged saltpans, this B&B housed in buildings once used by the Salines Ettore Infersa is for you. Restaurant with veranda.

🍴 EAT

🍴🍴 **Divino Rosso** – *Via XI Maggio (Largo Andrea di Girolamo).* ☎*0923 711770. Closed Mon. Booking recommended.* This restaurant-cum-wine bar, situated in the historical centre of Marsala, serves typical Sicilian cuisine and excellent fresh fish dishes. In summer, the tables outside on the main street are shaded beneath large parasols.

🍴🍴 **Il Gallo et l'Innamorata** – *Via Stefano Bilardello 18.* ☎*0923 1954446. www.osteriailgalloelinnamorata.com. Closed Tue.* In the dining room decorated with strings of garlic hung from the vaulted ceiling, enjoy cuisine made from fresh market produce. Seafood antipasti, pasta with bottarga and a good selection of wines. The bottles are stored on shelves and staff use a special pincer tool to get them down. Evening entertainment provided by the owner who likes to sing.

TAKING A BREAK

You will find several lively cafés for an aperitif around **Piazza del Popolo**.

ICE CREAM

E & N – *Via XI Maggio 130.* ☎*0923 951969.* Choose from a range of Sicilian patisseries, cannoli, cassata and lunchtime dishes.

WINE

La Sirena Ubrica – *Via Garibaldi 39.* ☎*0923 020500.* Near the fish market, this enoteca offers tasty home-made antipasti served up on wine-barrel tables. The very knowledgeable owner will guide you through countless marsalas to find the right wine for you. Wines sold to take away.

Enoteca Morsi e Sorsi – *Via Diaz 66. Open 6pm-1am. Closed Tues.* ☎*0923 713 598.* Good choice of fine wines recommended by an experienced wine connoisseur.

Russurisira – *Antico Mercaro Porta di Mare.* ☎*340 21 20419. www.russurisira.it.* Lively cocktail bar located in the former fish market.

FESTIVALS

Settimana Santa – Marsala becomes progressively more animated in the period leading up to Easter: celebrations begin with a Maundy Thursday procession (*the eve of Good Friday*) when the Stations of the Cross are re-enacted in the streets.

Marsalestate – In summer there are concerts and shows at various locations throughout the town, including a fashion show, and food and wine tasting.

Marsala Jazz Festival – *End of July.* This festival, sponsored by local wine companies, attracts many major jazz musicians.

Mazara del Vallo

A natural haven close to Africa, the ancient Phoenician city of Mazara was already a major port in Antiquity. Valued as a trading post by the Greeks, the city rose to great heights under its Arab and Norman masters. Still home to a large North African population and a leading hub of Italy's deep sea fishing industry, Mazara is a hive of activity, energy and life.

● WALKING TOUR

Harbour and shipping canal

The heart of the town is the harbour, which teems with life early in the morning when the fishing fleet returns with its catch and the quays bustle with activity. Overlooking the scene with benign approval, set back from the actual harbour front, is the restored Norman church, San Nicolò Regale, with a simple interior that rises to a single cupola.

San Nicolò Regale

This evocative building, erected under William I, has a square plan with the three apses that are contained by a bulbous dome, a characteristic of Arabo-Norman architecture.
Below the floor inside, fragments of mosaic have been discovered. Dating from palaeo-Christian times, these probably form part of a Roman floor.
Among the streets to the rear is Piazza Plebiscito and elegant façade of Sant'Ignazio (18C) and the former Jesuit College (17C), now the library, local museum and the Sala Consagra (*See Sights*).

Chiesa di S. Egidio – Museo del Satiro★★

Piazza Plebiscito. ○*Open 9am–6.30pm.* ⊜€6. ℘*0923 933917.*
The former church of San Egidio now houses this small museum entirely dedicated to the extraordinary **Greek**

- ▶ **Population:** 51 491
- **Michelin Map:** 177: A-3.
- **Info:** Via XX Settembre 5 ℘0923 944610.
- **Location:** 23km/14.3mi southeast of Marsala, the town is centred on the harbour and shipping canal of the River Mazara, where its fishing industry is based. The main monuments lie to the east of the harbour, behind Lungomare Mazzini.
- **Parking:** Car parking is available around the Piazza della Repubblica.
- **Don't Miss:** Passeggiata at Lungomare Mazzini; the Museo Civico and Sala Consagra; the beautiful Greek statue at the Museo del Satiro; wandering the narrow streets of the Kasbah.
- **Timing:** Start the day early at the harbour and watch the bustling scene as the catch comes in. As dusk falls, stroll along Lungomare Giuseppe Mazzini.

satyr★ statue dating from the 4C BC that was discovered in 1998 by a group of fisherman from Mazara in the Strait of Sicily.

Museo Civico and Sala Consagra

Piazza Plebiscito 2. ⚬*Closed for restoration at the time of going to press.* ℘*0923 942776.*
This compact museum, housed in the Collegio dei Gesuiti, contains a small selection of artefacts predominantly representing the Neolithic, Roman and late-Byzantine eras. The **Sala Consagra** is devoted to the etchings, acquatints and relief panels of Pietro Consagra, a contemporary artist born in Mazara.

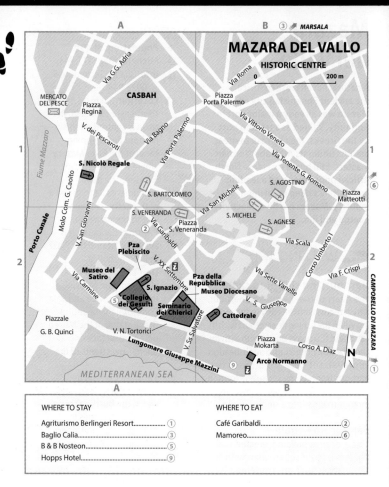

MAZARA DEL VALLO
HISTORIC CENTRE
0   200 m

Museo Diocesano

Entrance at Via dell'Orologio 3.
Open Tue–Sat, 10am–12.30pm (also
4.30–6pm Wed, Fri, Sat). Closed
Mon and Sun, public hols. Donations
welcome. 0923 909431.
www.museodiocesanomazara.it.
The most important section of this
collection, comprising silverware,
church furnishings and vestments
(14C–19C), is a display containing items
belonging to the cathedral treasury.

Cathedral

The main building dates from the 11C,
although it was considerably remodelled in the 17C. The façade, completed
in 1906, is ornamented with a highly
decorative doorway and a 16C shal-

low relief panel that depicts Roger I on
horseback, felling a fleeing Saracen.

Interior★

The overall theatrical effect is achieved
by interspersing gilded stucco decoration among frescoed *trompe l'oeil* stucco
volutes, curlicues and cherubs. The most
complex group is in the central apse,
where a large drape is drawn aside by
angels to reveal the **Transfiguration★**.
The composition of seven marble statues by Antonello Gagini sits upon a
majestic Renaissance altar.
Nestled in the niche to the right of the
altar is a fragment of 13C Byzantine
fresco depicting Christ Pantocrator. In
the first chapel on the right is an ancient
ciborium, possibly used at the christen-

ing of Frederick II's son. The Chapel of the Crucifix *(also right of centre)*, takes its name from the wooden Crucifix (13C) found in the adjoining room. A glass plate in the floor reveals ancient Norman foundations. Through a marble doorway on the right of the nave are some fine Roman sarcophagi bearing interesting reliefs of a hunting scene and a battle.

Piazza della Repubblica

This piazza laid out in the Baroque period dominates the old town. The statue (1771) in the centre is by **Ignazio Marabitti** and represents San Vito, patron saint of Mazara.

A harmonious collection of sandstone and white stucco *palazzi* from the 18C rise up on all sides: at the far end, the cathedral is overshadowed by an elegant Baroque campanile.

Along the left side stands the Bishop's Palace; to the right extends the **Seminario dei Chierici** complete with its neo-Classical portico and round-headed arched loggia. The former seminary now houses a small **Museo Diocesano**.

Lungomare Mazzini

South of Piazza della Repubblica.
The seafront is flanked by gardens shaded by magnolias and palm trees, perfect for the *passeggiata*.

Kasbah

Take the time to wander around the Kasbah, with its narrow winding alleys *(around Via Bagno)* leading to tiny little squares. This corner is home to a significant Tunisian community, since the town's fishing fleet employs a lot of Tunisian and Moroccan fishermen.

EXCURSION
Riserva Naturale Lago di Preola e Gorghi Tondhi

10km/6mi southeast of Mazara towards Torretta Granitola. ℰ0923 934055. www.wwfpreola.it.
In the heart of a huge valley surrounded by hills, several small lakes form a cool oasis of fresh water. Springtime provides the best opportunities for wildlife-watching.

ADDRESSES

🛌 STAY

🛏 **B&B Nosteon** – *Via Plebiscito 9. ℰ0923 651619. www.nosteon.it.🚭. 2 rooms ⬜*. This renovated old building in Mazara's old town is comfortable and well-kept.

🛏 **Hopps Hotel** – *Via Glacomo Hopps 29 ℰ0923 946133. www.hoppshotel.it.🏊. 187 rooms ⬜, restaurant ⬜⬜🍽*. Large hotel near the centre with a nice swimming pool. Most rooms have sea **views**.

🛏⬜🍽 **Baglio Calia** – *Contrada Serroni, N of Mazara, close to motorway junction (ask for directions). ℰ0923 909390. www.bagliocalia.it. 3 rooms ⬜, restaurant ⬜⬜🍽*. This former baglio is part of the agriturismo farm-stay network. Traditionally furnished rooms and a decent restaurant.

🛏⬜🍽🍽 **Agriturismo Berlingeri Resort** – *Contrada Berlingeri. ℰ0923 18 77 292. www.berlingeriresort.it. ✕🛏12 rooms.* This agritourismo, devoted to organic farming, offers a high standard of service.

🍴 EAT

🍴🍴 **Café Garibaldi** – *Via Garibaldi 53/55. ℰ347 4440170. www.cafegaribaldi.it. Closed Mon–Weds out of season.* The café stands on a nice little square and serves up modern takes on Sicilian dishes such as *peccato di gola* (sinful indulgence).

🍴⬜🍽 **Marmoreo** – *Lungocanale Ducezio 30. ℰ0923 93 16 19. Closed Sun eve.* This Mazara institution benefits from the culinary expertise of a family of fishermen, the Marmoreos. The varied set menu changes according to the catch of the day.

TAKING A BREAK

Trinca e Rocca – *Piazza Matteotti 26. ℰ0923 941250. www.trincaerocca.it.* Excellent choice of ice creams and traditional pastries. Delicious almond-paste specialities.

Selinunte★★★

Founded in the mid-7C BC and destroyed twice – in 409 and 250 BC – by the Carthaginians and the Romans, the town and port of Selinunte has a fascinating history that can still be explored among the scattered ruins of its temples.

A BIT OF HISTORY

The most westerly, and one of the most important of all the Greek colonies, ancient Selinus was founded by settlers from Megara Hyblaea during the 7C BC. Situated on a fertile plain, carpeted in wild celery (the city's name is derived from the Greek name – *selinon*), it occupied a much-coveted stretch of land that unsurprisingly drew constant territorial attention from bitter rivals, the Segestans and the Carthaginians in the west and northwest of the island.

Despite this, from the 6C BC Selinunte itself enjoyed a short but intensive period of prosperity over two centuries, thanks to prudent government by its successive tyrants.

However, in 409 BC Segesta allied itself to Carthage to beat its rival. As a result, Selinunte was destroyed by the Carthaginian general Hannibal in a surprise attack that sent 100,000 men into the city to capture it over a bloody period of nine days. His ferocious methods to win supremacy resulted in the death of 16,000 Selinuntini and the capture of 5,000 as prisoners, most of whom were sold into slavery.

The survivors begged him to spare the city's many temples in return for a substantial payment. Hannibal consented but once he had the money, he sacked the temples and pulled down the walls.

Selinunte invested every last effort in repairing the damage, but the city never managed to regain its former prosperity and eventually reverted to Carthaginian rule once more, serving as a garrison town until the First Punic War. Against all the odds, it survived largely intact until the Second Punic War, when it was razed to the ground by earthquakes.

⚭ **Michelin Map:** 177: B-3.
🛈 **Info:** Via Caboto Giovanni. ℘0924 46 251. www.selinunte.net.
▸ **Location:** 35km/21.7mi southeast of Mazara del Vallo. Take the Castelvetrano motorway exit and follow S 115d to Marinella di Selinunte. Buses run from Agrigento, Castelvetrano, Marsala, Mazara del Vallo and Trapani. It's possible to drive from the Tempi orientali *(eastern temples)* to the Acropoli *(acropolis)*.
⊗ **Don't Miss:** The Cave di Cusa, where the temple's stone blocks were quarried.
🕑 **Timing:** The ruins are scattered over a deserted area with little shade, therefore sightseeing in summer is best done in the early morning or late afternoon when the heat is not so fierce.
🅿 **Parking:** Parking is available by the Visitors Centre at the Tempi eastern temples and at the acropolis.

Parts of the city that remained, however, were still occupied all the way up to 250 BC, when the last inhabitants moved to Marsala prior to the Roman invasion. Fleetingly occupied by the Arabs and then again in the 13C, Selinunte fell into decay and lay forgotten until it was rediscovered in the 16C and painstakingly excavated in the 18C by two Englishmen, Samuel Angeli and Walter Harris.

ARCHAEOLOGICAL SITE

🕑*Open 9am–6pm.* ⚭€6.
⚭.℘0924 46251.
The archaeological site is divided into four areas: the first, spread across the hill

Breaking Stone with Wood and Water

Once the dimensions and profile of a stone building block had been marked out in the quarry, a double groove about half a metre deep was dug around it to enable the stonemasons to work and cut the block in situ. The tools used included picks, bronze saws and wedges. To split the harder layers, wooden wedges were inserted into cracks and then dampened with water so that as they swelled, the stone would crack open. The block was then severed at the base and removed by means of winches or slid down ramps. The deep U-shaped grooves visible in some of the square blocks were made so that a rope could be fed through them for lifting. Many blocks have a square hole at either end. Into these sockets were fitted special shafts that enabled the blocks to be moved and set in place. The blocks were transported on wooden frames with wheels and pulled by oxen and slaves. A wide, rocky track led from the quarries to Selinunte on the harbour and the shipping canal of the River Mazara, where the town's fishing industry is based. The main monuments of the town lie to the east of the harbour behind Lungomare Mazzini.

on the eastern side, contains three large temples, one having been re-erected in 1957; the second, on the hill to the west and surrounded by walls, comprises the acropolis, south of the third area, where the ancient town ruins can be seen; the fourth, west of the acropolis, also consisted of a sacred precinct of temples and sanctuaries.

The ruins are scattered over a deserted area, abandoned since Selinunte's downfall: the ruined temples continue to point great columns to the sky; other buildings, reduced to monumental rubble, probably by an earthquake, lend a tragic air of desolation.

The nearby quarries that provided the tufa stone used in the temples' construction lie a short distance away and are also worth a visit, if you have time. Huge, roughly-hewn blocks that still litter the quarries put the incredible architectural feats of the Selinunte temples into perspective.

Templi orientali

The first of the eastern temples to come into view is **Temple E**, dedicated to Hera and the only reconstruction on the site, having been re-erected in 1957. A fine example of Doric peripteral elegance, it dates from the 5C BC and is built on a complex ground plan. The entrance to the *pronaos* was from the east-facing side, through the colonnade. Only the

capitals from the doorway remain, lying on the ground. Beyond lay the *cella* with a secret chamber (the *adytum*), where the statue of the deity was kept. Behind that lay the *opisthodomus*, which was identical to the pronaos. On the right lie the ruins of **Temple F**, on a smaller scale than Temple E and belonging to the mid-6C BC. This graceful temple is made up of unusually slender columns topped by widely protruding capitals, arranged in a pattern of six at the end and 14 along the sides. The temple is comparable in size to Temple C, and was probably dedicated to the goddess Athena.

Lastly, **Temple G**, one of the four largest **Greek temples** in the world – and the second-largest Greek temple in Sicily after the Temple of Olympian Zeus at Agrigento – would have been the most impressive. Conceived on gigantic proportions – 17 columns long and eight wide, each with a diameter of almost 3.5m/11.5ft and a height of more than 16m/53ft – it was probably dedicated to the god Apollo. The temple, the only octastyle one found on the site *(the rest are all hexastyle)* was never finished: work was interrupted by the attack on the city by Carthage, led by Hannibal in 409BC. In the nearby quarries of Cusa, huge columns intended for it can still be seen, gouged from the tufa rock.

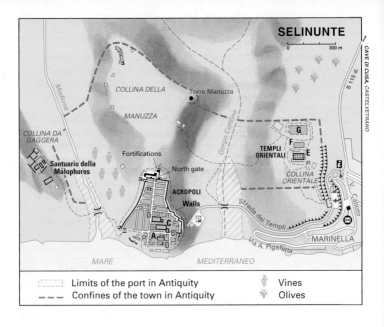

Limits of the port in Antiquity
Confines of the town in Antiquity

Vines
Olives

Acropoli

Drive from the eastern temples car park to the next one.

The acropolis stretched across a hill on the far side of the dip called Gorgo di Cottone, through which the River Cottone flowed down to the sea, where the town's **harbour** *(now overgrown)* was situated. The site was levelled off by the first settlers here, allowing them to build on it, starting with sacred buildings, and followed later by residential and commercial structures. The acropoli itself was enclosed within defensive walls built in the 6C–5C BC. The streets were laid out according to the Classical town plan proposed by Hippodamus of Miletus, with three main arteries bisected by a grid of smaller streets.

This area contained public and religious buildings and houses that accommodated all the highest-ranking members of society. Today, the agora *(market-place)* and two main streets have been fully excavated and help provide a picture of ancient life here.

The path skirts the graduated walls that run all the way around the eastern side of the acropolis.

Temples

As the track climbs uphill, you will see the ruin of **Temple A**. Within the wall are two spiral staircases, the most ancient examples known to date. This precinct, however, is dominated by 14 of the 17 monolithic columns of **Temple C**, which were re-erected in 1925. This, the earliest surviving temple at Selinus *(initiated early 6C BC)*, was probably dedicated to Apollo or Heracles, and would have originally been decorated with terracotta and polychrome elements.

It is hard to imagine the impact of the pediment *(an imposing Gorgon's head in shallow relief, whose function was to look over and protect the city)* as it lies broken on the ground.

The finest metopes, depicting scenes from Greek mythology recovered from this site, are now displayed in pride of place at the archaeological museum in **Palermo**. Also found in the museum is a reconstruction of the pediment.

Fortifications

At the far end of the *decumanus maximus* rises a curtain wall, which once surrounded the acropolis. What you see now are the fortifications built using stone recycled from the previous site, which was destroyed in 409 BC.

A second, smaller circle of walls was built around 305 BC. Beyond the north gate, the grand **Porta Nord** is a three-storey structure of two superimposed galleries surmounted by arches, allowing soldiers and equipment to move quickly and easily through them.

Ancient town

The residential part of the town was situated on the hill of Manuzza: over the period following the 4C BC, this area was gradually abandoned and used as a necropolis for burials.

Santuario della Malophoros

The sanctuary may be reached by following the track that extends from the first cardo to the left of the decumanus maximus (from the acropolis); allow 20min there and back.
The sanctuary was built in honour of Demeter, also known as Malophoros *(she who bears the pomegranate)*, the goddess of plants and protector of farmers and growers. It was built around 575 BC inside a sacred precinct *(temenos)* on the opposite side of the River Modione. Beyond the propylaeum is a sacrificial altar. A channel bearing water from the Gaggera mountain spring separates it from the temple. The latter, without columns, comprised a *pronaos*, a *cella*

and an *adytum* containing a statue of the deity. Over 12,000 votive statues of Demeter were found outside the sanctuary, giving some indication as to the importance and power of the cult of Demeter at the time of Selinute's power. Around the sanctuary also lies a large necropolis, with tombs stretching up the nearby coastline.

EXCURSION
Cave di Cusa★

20km/12mi northwest of Selinunte. Head towards Campobello di Mazara, then follow signs to Cave di Cusa.
🕐*Open 9am–dusk.* ⊛€2.
The Cusa quarries were the main source of building stone for the temples of Selinunte. The stone, a fine-grained and resistant tufa, was quarried for more than 150 years, from the first half of the 6C BC. The huge blocks were hewn straight from the base rock, worked here in situ and moved from the quarry to the site on wheeled wooden frames, pulled by oxen and slaves. However, work at the quarry ground to a halt in 409 BC following the outbreak of war, when Selinunte was forced to confront the Carthaginian onslaught (resulting in the town's eventual destruction). The quarries and houses of those who worked here were abandoned suddenly, as shown by the enormous blocks of rock that remain here, half-quarried.

Temple E, Selinunte

© Bruno Morandi/hemis.fr

From the considerable number of such unfinished blocks, scholars have calculated that there may have been anything up to 150 stone masons working at the Cave di Cusa, using a lengthy and complex technique to work the stone to make it fit for construction.

In the first section of the quarry, blocks sit cut and ready for transporting; others barely sketched out are ready for the stonecutter. At the far end of the quarry is a capital in the making. Its cylindrical mass tapers from a square base; the cracks still show pick marks.

ADDRESSES

☞ STAY

⊜⊜ **Sicilia Cuore Mio** – *Via della Cittadella 44, Marinella di Selinunte. ℰ0924 46077. www.siciliacuoremio.it. Closed Dec–Feb. 5 rooms▭.* In this peaceful house set in a pretty garden, the impeccable rooms are decorated in a restrained, typically Mediterranean style.

⊜⊜⊟ **Hotel Miramare** – *Via Pigafetta 2, Marinella di Selinunte. ℰ0924 46045. www.hotelmiramareselinunte.com. Closed Dec–Feb. 19 rooms▭, restaurant⊜⊟.* You will be well looked after in this hotel. The rooms are spotless and bright, most with a balcony overlooking the sea. The restaurant serves food on a large terrace with **views** over the sea. Small, private beach.

�‖EAT

⊜ **Pierrot** – *Via Marco Polo 108, Marinella di Selinunte. ℰ0924 46205. www.ristorante pierrotselinunte.it. Closed Jan–mid-Feb.* Family-style cuisine in a restaurant with panoramic **views**.

Castelvetrano

Home to the famous bronze statue, the Ephebus of Selinunte, this pleasant agricultural area is renowned for its olives. Elegant churches and architecture grace the town's centre.

●●◗ WALKING TOUR

The focal centre of Castelvetrano hinges on three adjacent squares, **Piazza d'Aragona e Tagliava**, **Piazza Umberto I** and **Piazza Garibaldi**. The town's major monuments are found in this area.

Piazza Garibaldi

The square is lined with fine buildings such as the town's main church and the **Chiesa del Purgatorio** *(now an auditorium)*. The latter has elaborate details, drawn from a transitional late-Mannerist-Baroque style. The Neoclassical **Teatro Selinus** (19C) has its original stage.

▸ **Population:** 30 516

◔ **Michelin Map:** 177: B-3.

▤ **Info:** Piazza Carlo d'Aragona e Tagliavia. ℰ0924 902004.

◗ **Location:** 20km/12.4mi east of Mazara del Vallo, the first sight of the town is the hospital and, beyond, the old town.

⊛ **Don't Miss:** The Santissima Trinità di Delia Anglo-Norman church; the Ephebus of Selinunte at the Museo Civico.

≗ **Kids:** The lake at the Trinità estate; dunes and turtles at the Riserva Naturale Orientata Foce del Fiume Belice e Dune Limitrofe.

◷ **Timing:** The nature reserve is at its most beautiful in the spring.

Chiesa Madre

Castelvetrano's principal church dates in its present form from the 16C. The front elevation rises through two storeys; a pair of pilasters ornamented with garlands flank the entrance at ground level, the upper section is pierced by a **rose window**.

The glorious stucco **decoration**★ adorning the triumphal arch is attributed to **Gaspare Serpotta** (17C, father of the more famous Giacomo): a host of angels bearing festoons and garlands interact with others brandishing musical instruments. The same elements are applied to the transept arch, albeit in a more restrained fashion.

Piazza Umberto I

This delightful little piazza lies to the left of the church, providing a clear view of the bell tower, which is hidden from the front. Gracing the square is a lovely fountain, the 17C **Fontana della Ninfa**, erected to celebrate the restitution of an aqueduct. In the nearby Piazza Regina Margherita, overlooking a pleasant municipal garden, is the stark façade of **San Domenico** (15C). Next to it is a secondary school, which was once a convent attached to the church and thus contains cloisters (entrance to the right of the church). Opposite sits the 16C **church of San Giovanni** and its massive bell tower.

Museo Civico

Via Garibaldi 50. Open Mon–Sat 9am–1pm, 3–6.30pm, Sun 9am–1pm. €2.50. 0924 909605.

The 16C palazzo, once home to the Majo family, now accommodates a museum for artefacts recovered from Selinunte. The well-presented displays are arranged around the prize exhibit: an elegant bronze statue of a young man (c. 460 BC), known as the **Ephebus of Selinunte**★ (see Introduction: Art and Architecture).

In a side niche nestles a lovely Madonna and Child by **Francesco Laurana** and his workshop, from the Church of the Annunziata. The museum also includes displays of religious objects and reliefs by the contemporary artist **Giuseppe Lo Sciuto**.

EXCURSIONS

Santissima Trinità di Delia★

4km/2.4mi west: follow directions from Piazza Umberto I. The church is part of the Baglio Trinità farm complex.

Guided tours by appointment only. 0924 902004.

This enchanting Arabo-Norman church (12C) conforms to a Greek-cross plan with three apses projecting on one side; it is capped by a pink dome. The exterior walls are pierced by single-light windows screened with perforated stone panels. Inside, the dome hovers above **pendentives** – a typically Moor-

Inside Santissima Trinità di Delia

© DEA PICTURE LIBRARY/age fotostock

ish element – supported by four marble columns with Corinthian capitals. A few metres from the church *(on the opposite side of the road)* extends the Trinità forestry estate, a lush area of eucalyptus, palm trees and pines. This idyllic picnic spot overlooks an attractive **man-made lake**.

Riserva Naturale Foce del Fiume Belice e Dune Limitrofe

12km/7.5mi south, between Marinella di Selinunte and Porto Palo di Menfi.
For guided tours, contact tourist office. ℘0924 902004. www.parks.it/ riserva.foce.fiume.belice/.
Crisply sculpted by the wind, the dunes make this natural reserve at the mouth of the River Belice particularly evocative. The marsh-like terrain attracts a number of species of bird, as well as the Caretta-Caretta turtle *(See Lampedusa).*

🚗 DRIVING TOUR

VALLE DEL BELICE
70km/43mi. Allow at least half a day.

On the afternoon of 14 January 1968, an earthquake shattered western Sicily. Many of the villages in the Belice region were destroyed and rebuilt away from their original locations. Some have yet to be completely rebuilt.

Gibellina Nuova
The town has been reconstructed 18km/ 11mi from the original and part of it is called Nuova Gibellina. The former mayor enlisted the aid of writers and artists to help create artworks in the new town. The 50-plus works of art include the imposing **Stella del Belice** at the

town entrance by Pietro Consagra, Alessandro Mendini's **Torre Civico** musical clock tower on the square by the town hall and the white spherical **Chiesa Madre** by Ludovico Quaroni.

▷ S 188 heading S. Turn left on S 119 following signs to Ruderi di Gibellina.

Ruderi di Gibellina
The ruins of Gibellina are still visible, although many are concealed by a work of art called the Cretto *(Crack)*. The Tuscan sculptor **Alberto Burri** covered much of the old town in a concrete blanket furrowed by cracks.

▷ Return to Santa Ninfa and take S 188 to Partanna.

Partanna
This small town was badly affected by the earthquake of 1968. Its distinguishing feature, a castle with battlements, was rebuilt in the 17C by the princes of Graffeo (or Grifeo) on the foundations of an earlier, Norman, construction.
The flat area behind the castle provides a good **view★** of the valley. The churches have been reduced to shells and all that remains of San Francesco on Via Vittorio Emanuele is a bell tower (16C–17C). Higher up, the church of the Madonna delle Grazie preserves its original tower.

▷ Take S 188 to Salemi.

Salemi
The small town of Salemi enjoys a lovely position surrounded by vineyards. The older parts bear the indelible imprint of Arab influences.
Narrow cobbled streets wind up to the inevitable hilltop castle. Salemi was declared the capital of Italy following the arrival of Garibaldi in Sicily.

Castello Normanno
The Norman castle was erected at the request of Roger d'Altavilla on the foundations of a fortress: the castle has two square towers and one high round one. On its right stand the remains of

Narrow street of Salemi

© Peeter Viisimaa/iStockphoto.com

the **Chiesa Madre**, destroyed by the 1968 quake.

▷ Turn down Via D'Aguirre and along past the church.

Chiesa e Collegio dei Gesuiti

🕐*Open Tue–Sun 9.30am–1pm, 4–7pm;* 🕐*Closed Mon.* 🎫€6. 📞*0924 98 2376.*
The elegant façade of the church is Baroque, with a portal flanked with spiral columns of tufa. The Collegio houses the Museo Civico, which contains various religious works of art rescued from the churches destroyed in the earthquake of 1968: a highlight is the Madonna della Candelora (Candlemas) by Domenico Gagini. Beyond the last room of the museum sits an 18C chapel that replicates the Casa Santa of Loreto. Downhill lies the picturesque Rabato quarter. The outside streets provide wonderful **views**a of the valley. Here, on 3 February each year, residents distribute tiny loaves of bread for the feast day of San Biago.

Museo della Mafia Leonardo Sciascia

Via D'Aguirre. 🕐*Open Tue–Sat 10am–1pm, 4–7pm.* 🎫€6. 📞*0924 98 23 76.*
Opened in 2010, this museum reveals the true story of the Mafia in Sicily

and Italy through a particularly striking display exploring Mafia-related themes – murder, political corruption, blackmail, imprisonment, the church and spirituality, the sanitary system and the *famiglia* – through videos, contemporary artworks and various documents.

▷ Take S 188A north, then follow S 113 to Calatafimi.

Calatafimi

This little town was once well defended by its **Castello Eufemio**, a Byzantine fortress rebuilt in the 13C and now in ruins. A fine **view★** stretches over valley and town. On the hill opposite stands the **Pianto Romano**, a monument commemorating the followers of Garibaldi, who died there in battle. A marvellous **view★★** extends from here.
Every five years, during the first three days of May, the **Festa del Santissimo Crocifisso** procession winds through the streets with representations from various town *ceti (ranks)*.

▷ From Calatafimi, it is possible to continue to Segesta (4km/2.5mi).

ADDRESSES

🍽 STAY / 🍴/EAT

🛏🛏🛏 **Baglio San Vincenzo** –
Via Leopardi 11, contrada San Vincenzo, Menfi, 10km/6.2mi from Porto Palo di Menfi. 📞*0925 75065. www.bagliosanvincenzo.it. Closed mid-Jan to mid-Feb. 12 rooms, restaurant*🍴🛏🛏. A truly unique place to stay. The owners of this carefully restored 17C building produce and sell their own oil and wine.

SHOPPING

Olive oil – The area surrounding Mazara del Vallo produces **Valle del Belice DOC** extra virgin olive oil from a local cultivar, the *nocellara del beli*. The Peruzza brand has a good reputation (*Via Maffei, Castelvetrano, in the southeast of the town.* 📞*0924 905133. www.peruzzaolio.com. Sold direct Mon–Fri, 8am–1pm, 2–6pm*).

AGRIGENTO *and the South Coast*

Agrigento is not just a city, it is also home to Sicily's largest archaeological treasure trove. The Valle dei Templi (Valley of the Temples) is not actually a valley at all, but a high plateau facing Africa over the Mediterranean Sea, on which rests probably the most important inventory of Greek architecture outside Greece. The seven monumental temples in this sacred area make it one of the world's most evocative places to experience the powerful aura and culture of Ancient Greece.

Highlights

1 Walking among **Ancient Greece's sacred temples** (p214)

2 Nobel Prize-winning author **Pirandello's birthplace** (p224)

3 The fine **Mediterranean beaches** of **Capo Bianco** (p225)

4 Sciacca's **thermal treatments** (p230)

5 The **spectacular views** from the summit of **Monte Kronio** (p230)

A Conquered City

Akragas, as it was known, was founded relatively late by Greek settlers but quickly grew to become one of the most important cities of Greece's Golden Age in the 5C and 6C BC. Though the ancient city was huge, its glory was short-lived. It suffered a crushing defeat to the Carthaginians in 406 BC that nearly razed it.

The city was rebuilt in successive stages by Carthage and the list of subsequent conquerors includes Romans, Arabs and Normans. The exposed nature of the coast with few inlets is thought to have prevented the development of Agrigento's ports, which in turn left it isolated and an easy target for hostile armies.

The Shift in Trade

For millennia, the local economy was fuelled by the mining of sulphur. Wheat was also an important staple. But the reduction in demand for wheat, as well as the closing of sulphur mines in the 1970s, forced the area to develop other forms of local agriculture as well as tourism.

An Inspirational Landscape

The southern coast has some stunningly beautiful coastlines, which include the dramatic Scala dei Turchi *(p222)*, where limestone-rich cliffs have been carved into a series of smooth sunbathing beaches by the wind and sea.

Also not to be missed is the Riserva Naturale Orientata di Torre Salsa *(p223)*, a seaside reserve of protected habitats (dune, maquis, cliff and marshland) with a rich selection of wildlife and birds.

Sciacca, to the northwest, is a restful port famous for its colourful majolica and natural thermal baths.

The hills along the coast have long had a mysterious allure. Outside Agrigento in Aragona curious *vulcanelli* (p225) mud cones emit cool, volcanic slime. On Sciacca's periphery are the Stufe di San Calogero, natural caves which have been prized since Antiquity for the medicinal quality of the steam that rises from the rock.

This region was the birthplace to two of Sicily's literary giants. Luigi Pirandello was born in Agrigento's Contrada Caos (p222), where his ashes are also buried. The home where he was born now features exhibits on the 1934 Nobel Prize-winning poet, novelist and playwright and his work.

In the hills of Racalmuto, birthplace of the Sicilian writer and commentator Leonardo Sciascia (p234), you will also find a "literary park", where you can learn about the man and his poignant commentaries written while still growing up in an area dominated by sulphur mines.

At the furthest eastern stretches of the coastline lies Gela, an ancient city whose massive petrochemical plant have made it unpopular with tourists, but which is still well worth a visit.

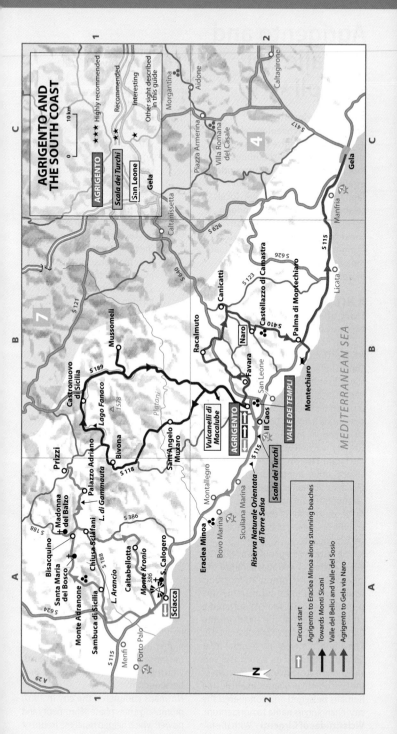

AGRIGENTO AND THE SOUTH COAST

AGRIGENTO ★★★ Highly recommended

Scala dei Turchi ★★ Recommended

San Leone ★ Interesting

Gela ★ Other sight described in this guide

0   10 km

Legend

⬆ Circuit start

➡ Agrigento to Eraclea Minoa along stunning beaches

➡ Towards Monti Sicani

➡ Valle del Belíci and Valle del Sosio

➡ Agrigento to Gela via Naro

MEDITERRANEAN SEA

213

Agrigento and La Valle dei Templi★★★

Although Agrigento is best known for its archaeological site, its historic city centre also has a wealth of impressive buildings and monuments. The city is surrounded by almond trees that bloom in January and February, when locals celebrate the Sagra del Mandorlo in Fiore (Almond Blossom Festival). Sunset is the best time to arrive in Agrigento, as the last rays illuminate the pastel houses and the Temple of Heracles.

A BIT OF HISTORY

Story of Akragas – The **site★★** has been inhabited since prehistoric times, but was not a proper town until 580 BC, when settlers arrived from Rhodes and Crete. Under the tyrant **Phalaris** (570–554 BC), the city was fortified and organised politically. The ancients believed he tortured his enemies by roasting them alive inside a hollow bronze bull. Hated by his people, he was stoned to death. The city reached its Golden Age under the tyrant **Theron** (488–472 BC), who, among other things, forbade human sacrifices. Economic stability and political strength went hand in hand, leading to the construction of the Temple of Zeus and the flourishing of literature and the performing arts.

The philosopher Empedocles *(c. 492–432 BC)*, a citizen of Akragas, praised the city's moderate form of democracy, which proved to be surprisingly successful. In 406 BC, the city suffered a crushing defeat at the hands of the Carthaginians, who all but destroyed it. **Timoleon**, a mercenary general from Corinth, improved its layout and services, which are visible still in the ruins of the Greco-Roman quarter. In 210 BC, the Romans besieged and conquered the city, changing its name to Agrigentum. **Vicissitudes of Girgenti** – With the fall of the Roman Empire, the city passed

- ▶ **Population:** 59,136
- ◉ **Michelin Map:** p211:B2.
- **Info:** Via Empocle 73; ℘0922 20 391. www. regione.sicilia.it/turismo.
- ▷ **Location:**
  The archaeological site is situated in the lower part of Agrigento, facing the sea, while the modern urban centre is perched on the slope.
- Ⓟ **Parking:**
  The archaeological area has two car parks: one in the temple area, the other near the archaeological museum. In the city centre, visitors can park in Piazza Vittorio Emanuele, east of the old town, which is crossed by a busy shopping street: Via Atenea.
- ⊛ **Don't Miss:**
  The temple and garden of Kolymbetra; the incredibly well-preserved **Tempio della Concordia;** the **sarcophagus** of Hippolytus and Phaedra in San Nicola Church; the Ephebus of Arrigento in the museum.
- ⚐ **Kids:** Agrigento's public parks with playgrounds.
- ◕ **Timing:** In summer, visit in the early morning or late afternoon, when the warm tufa stone takes on an attractive golden hue.

first to the Byzantines, then into Arab hands (9C). They built a new centre higher up *(at the heart of what is now the modern town)*, calling it **Girgenti**, which became the capital of the Berber kingdom.

Normans conquered the city in 1087, prompting a new phase of prosperity and power, which helped repel the frequent Saracen attacks.

Tempio di Castore e Polluce o dei Dioscuri and the city of Agrigento in the background

© anzeletti/iStockphoto.com

After a turbulent period, when the population gradually declined, Girgenti enjoyed a change in fortune, most notably in the 18C, when the centre was shifted from Via Duomo to Via Atenea. In 1860, the inhabitants, dissatisfied like the rest of the island with Bourbon misrule, enthusiastically supported Garibaldi's mission.

During the Second World War, Agrigento suffered a number of air raids.

Two famous sons – Agrigento has been home to several famous people, both in antiquity and in more recent times. Among the most renowned are the philosopher **Empedocles** (5C BC), who leapt into Etna's crater to prove his divine powers (the volcano reputedly spat back his shoes, turned to bronze). In the 20C, **Luigi Pirandello**, the playwright and novelist, was born in the small village of Caos.

Bookworms should visit the **Biblioteca Luigi Pirandello** at 120 Via Regione Sicilia, which also contains a vast selection of works by other Sicilian authors.

LA VALLE DEI TEMPLI★★★ (Valley of the Temples)

Allow half a day. Archaeological site: ○*Open daily 8.30am–7pm (the site often stays open until 10pm in summer).*

℘*0922 62 16 11. www.lavalledeitempli. eu. Museo Archeologico:* ○*Open 9am– 7.30pm Tue–Sat, 9am–1pm Sun–Mon.* ○€*8 archaeological site;* ○€*13.50 combined ticket with the Museo Archeologico.* ℘*0922 40 15 65.*

The monuments are divided between the **lower agora**, to the south, which includes the temples, the Giardino della Kolymbetra, the antiquaria and the palaeo-Christian necropolises, and the **upper agora**, to the north, which comprises the archaeological museum, the Chiesa di San Nicola, the Oratorio di Falaride and the Greco-Roman quarter. *The description below starts with the Temple of Zeus.*

▶ To walk from one area to the other, visitors can either follow the busy main road or a quieter route through the park. ☐Car parks are located near the Temple of Zeus and the archaeological museum. Ticket offices stand at both entrances.

Stretched along the ridge – inappropriately called the "valley" – and nestling to its south are the 5C BC temples. Burnt by the Carthaginians in 406 BC, the buildings were restored by the Romans (1C BC) in their original Doric style. Their subsequent disrepair is either due to seismic activity or destructive Christians, egged on by the Emperor of the Eastern Empire, Theodosius (4C). The only intact building is the Temple of Concord, which was converted into a church in the 6C. During the Middle Ages, masons removed stones to use for other buildings. The Temple of Zeus (known locally as the Giant's Quarry) provided materials for the church of San Nicola, for example, and the 18C part of the jetty at Porto Empedocle.

All the buildings face east, respecting the Classical criterion (both Greek and Roman) that the rising sun illuminate the deity's statue, which was housed in the *naos* (or cella). Built of limestone tufa, the temples provide a particularly impressive sight at dawn and even more so at sunset, when they turn a warm gold.

Sacrificial Altar

Just beyond the entrance (on the right) are the remains of an enormous altar. As many as 100 oxen could be sacrificed here at any one time. The Italian word *ecatombe*, which today means "disaster", comes from the Greek "100 (*hecatòn*) oxen (*bôus*)".

Tempio di Zeus Olimpico (Giove)★

Razed to the ground, the Temple of Olympian Zeus (Jupiter) was re-erected following the victory over the Carthaginians at Himera (in about 480 BC). One of the largest temples built in ancient times, it stood 113m/371ft long by 36m/118ft wide, and may never have been completed. The entablature was supported by half-columns 20m/66ft high, which probably alternated with giant male caryatids (*atlantes or* **telamons**); an example may be seen in the local archaeological museum (see below). A reproduction stands in the middle of the temple, giving some idea of its vast scale. Some blocks still bear the marks of lifting: deep U-shaped incisions through which a crane's rope was threaded.

Tempio di Castore e Polluce o dei Dioscuri★★

The Temple of Castor and Pollux (also known as the Dioscuri) is probably Agrigento's most iconic temple. Built during the last decades of the 5C BC, it is dedicated to the twins born to Leda and Zeus, who transformed himself into a swan to seduce her.

Four columns and part of the entablature are all that remain of the temple, which was reconstructed in the 19C.

Under one edge of the cornice is a rosette, one of the typical decorative motifs used.

On the right are the remains of what was probably a sanctuary to the chthonic deities: Persephone (*Proserpina*), queen of the underworld, and her mother, Demeter (*Ceres*), goddess of corn and fertility and patroness of agriculture. On the site are a **square altar**, probably used for sacrificing piglets, and another, **round altar**, with a sacred well in the centre.

GETTING THERE AND AROUND

BY AIR – Visitors arriving by air will land at either Falcone-Borsellino airport in Palermo *(approx.150km/93mi from Agrigento)* or at Fontanarossa airport in Catania *(approx. 160km/100mi)*.

BY BUS – The most direct way to get to the site, bus services operate between Agrigento and the other main cities in Sicily, as well as to Porto Empedocle *(the port for ferries to Lampedusa)*; the bus terminal is situated in Piazza Rosselli.

BY TRAIN – The Palermo–Agrigento service takes approximately two hours. Get off at Agrigento Centrale railway station *(not to be confused with Agrigento Bassa)* on Piazza Marconi. This square is also the departure point for shuttle buses to the archaeological area and the beaches in San Leone.

In the distance are the remains of the **Temple of Hephaestus** (Vulcan). According to legend, the god of fire and the arts had a forge under Etna, where he fashioned thunderbolts for Zeus, assisted by the Cyclops.

Giardino della Kolymbetra★

🕐 Open daily Jul–Sept 10am–7pm; Apr–Jun 10am–6pm; rest of the year 10am–5pm. 🕐 Closed 7–31 Jan. ⌸€4. ☎335 12 29 042 (mobile phone).

This 5-ha/12-acre "basin", dug by Carthaginian prisoners and used as a fish-breeding pond, grew into a fertile grove of fruit and citrus trees.

After years of neglect, the Kolymbetra – now restored and managed by the Italian Foundation for the Environment (Fondo per l'Ambiente Italiano) – is planted with olives, prickly pear, poplar, willow, mulberry, orange, lemon and mandarin trees. A pleasant area for a stroll.

▷ Retrace your steps, leave the fenced area and cross the road on the right to return to the Valley of the Temples.

Tempio di Eracle (Ercole)★★

Built in the Archaic Doric style, the Temple of Heracles (Hercules) is the earliest of the group. The remains reveal how elegant this structure must have been. Today, a line of eight tapering columns stand re-erected.

South of the temple can be seen the mistakenly named **Tomba di Terone**. The monument was not the tomb of the tyrant Theron; in fact, it honours Roman soldiers killed during the Second Punic War (218–202 BC). Made of tufa, it is slightly pyramidal and probably once had a pointed roof. The high base supports a second order with false doors and Ionic columns at the corners.

© puckillustrations/Fotolia.com

Telamons and Atlantes (or Atlas Figures)

These imposing giants from Agrigento, more often referred to as atlantes, are sometimes called telamons (telamone in Italian) after the Latin word derived by the Romans from the Greek, telamo(n), which indicated their function: to carry or bear the structure. Their supporting role is accentuated by their position, with arms bent back to balance the weight on their shoulders. The more common term alludes to the mythological figure Atlas, the giant and leader of the Titans, who struggled against the gods of Olympus and was condemned by Zeus to support the weight of the sky on his head. When the earth was discovered to be spherical, he was often shown bearing the terrestrial globe on his shoulders.

Tempio della Concordia

©Diego Barucco/Dreamstime.com

CENTRO CITTÀ

Via U. La Malfa

Via

Via Petrarca

Via Demetra

AGRIGENTO

S. Biagio

Tempio rupestre di Demetra

PORTA ERACLEA

S 118

★★ MUSEO ARCHEOLOGICO REGIONALE

Oratorio di Falaride

Quartiere ellenistico-romano ★

S. Anna Antica

Via Ann Antica

S. Nicola

AGORA SUPERIORE

V. dei Templi

Via d. Valle d. Templi

PORTA DI GELA

PALERMO, CALTANISSETTA, FAVARA

Efesto

Santuario delle Divinità Ctonie

AGORA INFERIORE

★ Zeus Olimpio

Altare sacrificale

Necropoli paleocristiana

★ Giardino della Kolymbetra (Billetterie)

PTA AUREA

Villa Aurea

CONCORDIA ★★★

◆ Casa Pace

★★ CASTORE E POLLUCE

★★ ERACLE

Billetterie

Casa Barbadoro

Via Sacra

Tomba di Terone

★★ HERA LACINIA

S 115

NECROPOLI ELLENISTICO - ROMANA

RAGUSA

Asclepio

S. Biagio

N

0   300m

AGRIGENTO VALLE DEI TEMPLI

▬▬▬ Ruins of Greek fortifications

🏛 Temple   •• Telamon

SE LOGER   Villa Athena...................②

PORTO EMPEDOCLE   SAN LEONE

Along the path, note the **cartwheel ruts**, the largest of which were later transformed into water channels.

Antiquarium multimediale della Valle dei Templi (Villa Aurea)

This centre is housed in Villa Aurea, residence of Sir Alexander Hardcastle, an archaeology enthusiast who re-erected the columns of the Temple of Heracles. The antiquarium offers a historical, topographical and mythological overview of the site and provides an excellent introduction to a visit to the Valley of the Temples.

Necropoli paleocristiana

The palaeo-Christian necropolis lies beneath the road, dug into the bedrock and not far from the ancient city walls. The tombs include *loculi* (cells or chambers for corpses or urns) and *arcosolia* (arched cavities like niches), a common feature of catacombs.

Before the Temple of Concord there is another group of tombs to the right.

Tempio della Concordia★★★

The Temple of Concord is one of the best-preserved ancient temples anywhere in the world, providing a glimpse of the elegance and majestic symmetry of these buildings. The reason it has survived intact is due to its transformation into a church in the 6C AD.

Inside the colonnade, the original arches can still be made out through the cella walls of the classical temple.

Scholars date the structure to around 430 BC, but don't know what god it honoured *(the name "Concord" comes from a Latin inscription found in the vicinity)*. The temple is a fine example of "optical correction": although the columns taper, curve and slant, an observer at a certain distance sees a series of perfectly straight lines.

Antiquarium di Agrigento Paleocristiana e Bizantina

(Casa Pace) This centre explores part of the city's history, including the Temple of Concord's conversion to basilica.

Antiquarium Iconografico della Collina dei Templi (Casa Barbadoro)

⚷ *Closed for restoration at the time of going to press.*

This modern but sympathetically designed building houses a series of drawings, engravings and prints of the Valley of the Temples as seen by travellers undertaking the Grand Tour.

Tempio di Hera Lacinia (Giunone)★★

Atop the hill, the Temple of Hera Lacinia *(Juno)* honoured the protectress of matrimony and childbirth. The name "Lacinia" derives from an erroneous association with the sanctuary of the same name on the Lacinian promontory, near Crotone.

The temple has retained its colonnade (although not in perfect condition), which was partially re-erected in the early 1900s. Built around the mid-5C BC, it was set ablaze by the Carthaginians in 406 BC (scorch marks are still visible on the walls of the *cella*). To the east is the temple altar, while at the back of the building (beside the steps) is a cistern.

▶ From the Antiquarium di Casa Pace, a small road leads up the hill from San Nicola, crossing fields of prickly pear, pistachio and olive trees. As you approach the hilltop, continue towards a group of ruins, passing under a bridge. The path leads to the Greco-Roman Quarter (entry ticket required).

Greco-Roman Quarter★

This extensive complex contains the remains of houses with fragments of ancient pavements bearing geometric or figurative motifs (protected by roofing and plexiglass).

The streets follow the rules of the Greek town planner Hippodamus of Miletus: broad parallel avenues *(decumani)* bisected at right angles by secondary roads *(cardini)*.

Tempio di Hera Lacinia
© emicristea/Fotolia.com

Chiesa di San Nicola

🕐 *Variable hours.*

Built of tufa, the Church of St Nicholas was erected in the 13C by Cistercian monks in a transitional Romanesque-to-Gothic style. The monks took stone blocks from the "Giant's Quarry", as the ruined Temple of Zeus was known, to build the church.

The façade is dominated by two imposing reinforced buttresses (added in the 16C), which flank a beautiful, pointed-arched doorway.

The interior is enclosed within a single barrel-vaulted nave. Four chapels open off the south side. The second contains the famous 3C **sarcophagus of Hippolytus and Phaedra★** (Goethe was particularly enthused by it). Inspired by Greek prototypes, all four sides are sculpted in high relief. The compositions are animated by clean flowing lines and the figures have delicate features with gentle expressions. The subject is the tragic story of Phaedra's unrequited love for her stepson Hippolytus, who was banished and then killed by crazed horses because of the false accusation that he had tried to seduce her.

Above the altar is a fine 15C wooden crucifix, nicknamed *il Signore della Nave* (Lord of the Ship). This inspired Pirandello's short story of the same name, in his *Novelle per un Anno*.

From the terrace in front of the church there is a beautiful **view★**.

Oratorio di Falaride

According to legend, the oratory occupies the site of the palace built by the tyrant Phalaris, hence its name. The present monument was probably a small Greco-Roman temple, converted in Norman times.

Next to the oratory are the remains of an Ekklesiasterion, a small amphitheatre used for political meetings (from the Greek *ekklesia* – meeting) identified as an ancient agora (marketplace or place of assembly).

Museo Archeologico Regionale★★

Partially housed in the old monastery of San Nicola, the museum contains finds from the province of Agrigento (see entry details above).

Panels provide information on the most important exhibits.

Pre-Greek conquest – Among the prize exhibits is a fine, two-handled cup with a tall base decorated with geometric patterns; its shape may stem from the custom of eating seated on the ground with the cup at chest-level. Others of note include a small, elegant Mycenaean amphora, the mould of a **patera** with six animals *(oxen)* in relief and two signet rings, again bearing animals. The most interesting exhibit is a **dinos** (sacrificial vase) depicting the triskelos (literally "three legs") – the symbol of Sicily.

Colonisation – The superb collection of **Attic vases★** *(Room 3, exhibited in two parallel corridors)* consists mainly of black-figure and red-figure ware, including the *cratere di Dionisio* (or cup of Bacchus): the god of wine, dressed in flowing robes, holds a sprig of ivy in his hand and has a leopard-skin draped over his arm. Among the other vessels, don't miss the *krater* with a white background depicting the proud figure of Perseus on the point of liberating Andromeda from her chains, and a larger *krater* featuring the *Transport of the Warrior* (500–490 BC).

This section also contains a large number of votive statues, theatrical masks, moulds and other terracotta figures found during the excavation of the temples. The lower level of this section is filled by the massive figure of **Atlas★** from the Temple of Zeus, the only one of the 38 male caryatids that once adorned the building to survive. On the left, cased, are the heads of another three such powerful figures, one of whom has well-preserved facial features.

The **Ephebus of Agrigento★★** *(Room 10)* consists of a marble statue of a young man (5C BC), found in a cistern near the Temple of Demeter, and transferred during the Norman period to the Church of San Biagio *(see below)*. Archaeologists believe it depicts a local Olympic victor.

Other archaeological finds – Artefacts retrieved from various other sites in the province include sarcophagi, prehistoric remains and the magnificent *krater* from **Gela★★** *(Room 15)*, attributed to the Painter of the Niobids. The upper half depicts a centauromachia *(battle between Centaurs and Lapiths)*, while the lower section shows scenes from battles between the Greeks and the Amazons.

◗ Visitors may finish their tour of Ancient Agrigento by visiting the Chiesa di San Biagio and the Tempio di Asclepio, both some distance from the other ancient monuments.

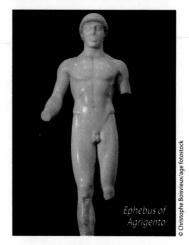

Ephebus of Agrigento

© Christophe Boisvieux/age fotostock

Chiesa di San Biagio
Ⓟ *Park in front of the cemetery.*
The church is down a path on the left.
The 13C Norman church stands on the remains of a **Greek temple** dedicated to Demeter. Just below is another, more rudimentary **temple** to her (the inaccessible *Tempio Rupestre di Demetra*), which bears witness to the popularity of the goddess in ancient Sicily.

Tempio di Asclepio (Esculapio)
Just beyond the Tomb of Theron, on the road to Caltanissetta. Look out for a sign (although obscured) on the right.
The ruins of this 5C BC temple, dedicated to Asclepius *(Aesculapius)*, the Greek god of medicine, sprawl in the middle of the countryside.
The interior is believed to have harboured a beautiful statue of the god Apollo by the Greek sculptor Myron.

👣 WALKING TOUR

The broad **Viale della Vittoria**, shaded by trees, provides beautiful **views** of the Valley of the Temples and leads to a square in front of the station. On the right stands the 16C **church of San Calogero**. The façade has a fine doorway with a pointed arch.
A little farther on is Piazzale Aldo Moro, where the lovely **Via Atenea** begins. Off this thoroughfare, on Via

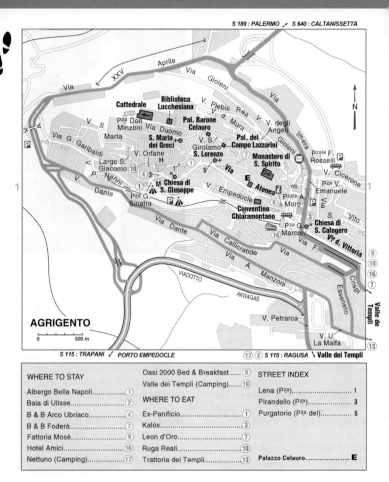

S 189 : PALERMO   S 640 : CALTANISSETTA

AGRIGENTO

0   500 m

S 115 : TRAPANI / PORTO EMPEDOCLE   17 2 S 115 : RAGUSA \ Valle dei Templi

Celauro *(on the right)*, is the **Palazzo Barone Celauro**, where Goethe stayed on his Grand Tour, and the Franciscan Church of the Immacolata *(on the left)*, altered in the 18C.

To the right of the church, beyond the gate, is the façade of the 14C **Conventino Chiaramontano**, so-called because of the style of the portal between the two-light windows.

Return to Via Atenea and continue to Piazza del Purgatorio, overlooked by the splendid façade of 18C **San Lorenzo★** church, its golden ochre tufa in dramatic contrast with the whiteness of the doorway, ornamented with twisted columns.

The **interior** contains stuccoes by **Serpotta** and a painting by Guido Reni.

Nearby, level with Via Bac Bac, stands **San Giuseppe**, dedicated to St Joseph. On **Piazza Pirandello** is the town hall, formerly a Dominican monastery (17C) and an adjacent church with a fine Baroque façade overlooking an elegant flight of steps. Set back, on the left side of the church, is the bell tower.

▶ From Via Atenea, take Via Porcello and follow the steps up Salita di Santo Spirito.

Monastero di Santo Spirito★
Via Santo Spirito 8. ◑*Open on request.* ✆*0922 20 664.*

The church and its dependent convent date from the 13C. Sadly, the state of the buildings is gradually deteriorating. The

Monastero di Santo Spirito

© Michael Owston/Photoshot

façade of the church has a fine Gothic doorway with a rose window above.
The Baroque interior consists of a single nave. The four high **reliefs★** are attributed to Giacomo Serpotta:
The Nativity and *The Adoration of the Magi* on the right; *The Flight into Egypt* and *The Presentation of Jesus at the Temple* on the left.
To the right of the façade is a doorway to the **cloisters**, leading under two of the great supporting buttresses.
The beautiful **entrance★** to the chapterhouse of the monastery consists of an elegant doorway through a pointed arch, flanked by highly decorative Arabo-Norman two-light windows.
The monastery is also home to the **Museo di Santo Spirito** *(opening times vary, call for details; ⌨€2.50; ℘0922 59 03 71)*, housing a collection of objects relating to the rural life and paintings of Francesco Lojacono from Palermo (1841–1915).

Via San Girolamo

This street is lined with elegant *palazzi*: of note is the façade of the 19C **Palazzo del Campo-Lazzarini** at no. 14 *(opposite Santa Maria del Soccorso)* and that of the 18C **Palazzo Barone Celauro** at no. 86.

Biblioteca Lucchesiana

The library, founded in 1765 by Bishop Lucchesi Palli, contains more than 45,000 ancient books and manuscripts. The central hall, dominated by a statue of the bishop, is lined with beautiful wooden shelving. Books on profane subjects are kept to the left of the statue, while religious texts are on the right.
This division is echoed by the two sculpted wooden figures behind the statue: a woman meditating *(left)*, and a woman holding a mirror *(right)*, symbolising the search for truth in the inner self.

Cathedral

☞ *Closed for restoration at the time of going to press.*
The side of the cathedral facing Via del Duomo still bears traces of the Noman original *(notably the 11C windows)*. The main church was rebuilt in the 13C–14C, remodelled in the 17C and then restored after a landslide in 1966.

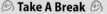

😊 **Take A Break** 😊

Before leaving the Monastero di Santo Spirito, make sure you try the excellent confectionery made by the nuns here *(ring the bell to the right of the cloisters;*
☏ *see Addresses).*

A broad double stairway leads up to the main door, marked by a tympanum and flanked by pairs of pilasters.

On the right stands the unfinished bell tower (1470), which on the south side is marked by four blind arches in the shape of an inverted ship's keel and a series of pointed arches above.

Inside★, the nave has a beautiful **wooden ceiling★** with tie-beams decorated with figures of the saints, painted in the 16C.

The section beyond the triumphal arch is coffered (18C); the great two-headed eagle *(centre)* is the symbol of the House of Aragon.

The Baroque exuberance of the choir, with its angels and golden garlands, is in dramatic contrast to the sobriety of the nave.

Santa Maria dei Greci

The 14C church dedicated to St Mary of the Greeks was built on the foundations of a temple to Athena (5C BC).

🚗 DRIVING TOURS

FROM AGRIGENTO TO ERACLEA MINOA ALONG STUNNING BEACHES

Route outlined in green on map p210. 90km/56mi trip from Agrigento. Allow one day.

▷ From Agrigento, head 6km/4mi W on the Porto Empedocle road (S 115). Turn left after Morandi viaduct.

Casa Museo Regionale (Luigi Pirandello)

Contrada Caos Villaseta. ♿🕐*Open 9am–1pm, 4–7pm (6pm winter).* ⬭€4. ☎*0922 51 18 26.*

This *contrada* on the outskirts of Agrigento was the birthplace of **Luigi Pirandello**, whose **house** stands alone in the middle of the countryside.

The first floor is open to the public. A short film provides visitors with an overview of his life, including the Nobel Prize award ceremony, and the author's funeral. Pirandello last visited the house

in 1934, but only from a distance as it had been sold. The rooms contain manuscripts, theatre plays, novels, family photos and portraits of Marta Abba, the actress to whom he became close late in life. Also on display is a 5C BC Greek *krater*, which once held his ashes. A small path to the right of the house leads to a **pine tree** *(damaged by a storm in 1997)*. At its foot are buried Pirandello's ashes.

▷ Continue along S 115 to Sciacca. From Porto Empedocle, follow the signs to the Madison Hotel.

Scala dei Turchi★★

▷ Follow the signpost to Scala dei Turchi, then right down Discesa Maiata, then walk along the beach to the rock (10min). Alternatively, follow the road for a further 300m/330yd until you come to an electricity transformer hut (left). A small path to the left of the hut leads down to the sea. Arriving from Realmonte, the rock is visible once you have passed the Madison Hotel.

This impressive white rock (made of marl, a mixture of clay and limestone, smoothed by erosion) has gently sloping steps *(scala)* and is a popular place for sunbathing. Narrow and winding wave-like formations mark the other side. The name refers to the local legend that Saracen pirates once scaled the rock after anchoring in the bay.

▷ Continue along S 115 as far as Siculiana Marina, then follow the road to Montallegro for approximately 2km/1.2mi.

Riserva Naturale Orientata di Torre Salsa

🐾*For guided tours,* ☎*0922 81 82 20 or 328 6367584. www.wwftorresalsa.com.*

This World Wildlife Fund reserve covers a wide variety of habitats (dunes, cliffs, marshland and Mediterranean maquis) inhabited by porcupines, crows, birds of prey, waders and sea birds. The reserve also has a fine sand beach.

▶ Take S 115 W towards Sciacca for 5km/3mi and turn left to Eraclea Minoa.

Eraclea Minoa

The remains of the Greek city Heraclea Minoa enjoy a **magnificent setting**★★ on the flank of an isolated hill with a fine **view** of the sea, at the start of **Capo Bianco**. At its feet, the coast opens into a broad bay, lined with a long white sandy **beach**★★ *(from S 115, follow signs to Montallegro-Bovo Marina and Montallegro Marina; a small road on the right leads to the sea).* Before the excavations, on the right, are white "dunes" of marl sculpted by the wind.

The city was probably founded in the 6C BC by Greek colonists from Selinus *(now Selinunte).* Sometime in the 3C BC, the town passed to the Romans; thereafter it embarked on a series of wars and was gradually abandoned. By the 1C BC, it was deserted.

Serious excavation began here in 1950, uncovering the **remains** of rough brick houses, some still containing fragments of mosaic as well as a **theatre** built of a very friable (and not very well preserved) stone.

A small **antiquarium** (🕓 *open 9am– 1hr before dusk;* ⊛ €2) has a display of objects mostly from the necropolis.

TOWARDS MONTI SICANI

175km/109mi round trip from Agrigento. Allow one day.

This tour wends up through **magnificent scenery**★★ from the Agrigento coast to the slopes of Monti Sicani, offering delightful **views** of hills, woods, mountains and meadows. In the spring, the area becomes an explosion of red poppies and yellow broom.

▶ Take S 189 towards Palermo (10km/6mi) and exit at Aragona.

Ritorno (La Via)

A solitary house set amid my native countryside: up here, on this plateau of blue clay, to which the submissive bitter African sea sends a fervour of foam, I see you always, from afar, if I think of that moment in which my life opened up minutely to the immense, vain world: this, this, I say, was where I set out along the path of life.

Luigi Pirandello in *Zampogna*, Rome 1901

Vulcanelli di Macalube★

At the entrance to Aragona, follow signs to Macalube. Turn left at the roundabout, then left again at the next junction and follow the tarmacked road that ends in a clearing. 🅿 *Park and follow the middle path heading up to the top of a small hill (on the right). For information, contact Legambiente-Uffici della Riserva, Via Salvatore La Rosa 53.* 📞*0922 69 92 10. www.macalife.it.*

This hill is dotted with mud cones, known as *vulcanelli* (small volcanoes): a sedimentary, gaseous volcanic phenomenon that produces spurts of cold, white slime.

▶ Return to Aragona and take the road to Sant'Angelo Muxaro (SP 17 then SP 19).

Sant'Angelo Muxaro

Sant'Angelo clings to a craggy mountainside. Some believe this was the capital of the ancient kingdom of Cocalus, the mythical king who received Daedalus on his flight from Minos.

The 18C front elevation of the Chiesa Matrice is divided into three sections by strongly-accented pilaster strips framing the three doorways and rectangular windows *(above).*

Grotta del Principe

By the side of the road, just outside town. P *Leave the car on the verge so as not to obstruct traffic. Although the distance is short, the going is rough.* The Prince's Cavern is a proto-historic tomb (9C BC) consisting of two circular chambers. The first *(larger one with a domed ceiling)* comprised the atrium for the actual burial chamber.

▷ Take the road to Alessandria della Rocca.

The road winds its way uphill through delightful rolling countryside.

Bivona

At the centre of Bivona stands a lovely **Arabo-Norman archway** – the remains of the former Chiesa Matrice. Farther on, **Palazzo Marchese Greco** has a fine, though damaged façade, ornamented with wrought-iron balconies and elegant Baroque stonework.

▷ From Bivona take the road to Santo Stefano Quisquina, then continue to Castronuovo di Sicilia.

The road *(which is in poor condition)* skirting the **Lago di Fanaco** passes through beautiful **mountain scenery★** of meadows, thick woodland, flowers and rocky outcrops.

Castronuovo di Sicilia

The little piazza is overlooked by the Chiesa Madre della Santissima Trinita (1404) and its fine **bell tower**.
From the centre, an attractive paved street leads up to the Chiesa di San Vitale and the castle ruins. A **viewpoint★** at the top of the village offers a magnificent panorama of the surrounding countryside.

▷ From here, the tour heads along S 189 to Agrigento before turning left to Mussomeli. Alternatively, visitors can follow the East of Agrigento tour ⏲*see p232.*

Mussomeli

Mussomeli is squeezed onto a scrubby hillside where houses jostle one another under the watchful gaze of the **Castello Manfredonico★** (⏲ *open Tues–Sun 9am–12pm, 3.30–6.30pm;* ⏲€3; ☎0934 99 20 09) on its lonely rock outcrop. Don't miss the tall front elevation of the Chiesa Matrice (altered in the 17C) and the 16C limestone **Santuario della Madonna dei Miracoli**, with its doorway set between two spiral columns and broken pediment.

▷ Head back along S 189 towards Agrigento. At Comitini, either carry on to Agrigento or join the "East of Agrigento" tour ⏲*see p234.*

ADDRESSES

⭐ STAY

Accommodation options include San Leone, *(a seaside resort 7km/4mi from the city, with a wide choice of hotels and restaurants),* and Villaggio Mosè *(4km/2.5mi east of the Valley of the Temples).*

AGRIGENTO

⊜ **Camping Valle dei Templi** – *Viale Emporium, San Leone.* ☎*0922 411 115. www.agricamping.it.* 🍴. *300 pitches and 15 bungalows.* Camp among olive trees at this flat, well-equipped site, which becomes noisy and crowded in summer.

⊜⊜ **B&B Foderà** – *Via Foderà 11.* ☎*0922 403 079. 5 rooms* ⊐. Located in a quiet little street in the heart of the old town. Rooms sleep 4 for an extra charge of 20 €/day, per person.

⊜⊜ **Arco Ubriaco** – *Via Sferri (near Piazza Municipio).* ☎*0922 594 024. www.arcoubriaco.com. 4 rooms* ⊐. In a former Arabo-Norman villa in the old town, this B&B offers comfortable rooms.

⊜⊜ **Oasi 2000 Bed & Breakfast** – *Via Atenea 45 (first floor), Agrigento.* ☎*0922 27 645. 5 rooms* ⊐. This central guesthouse has five bedrooms with antique furniture and parquet floors.

⊜⊜⊜ **Hotel Amici** – *Via Acrone 5.* ☎*0922 402 831. www.hotelamici.com. 18 rooms* ⊐. A small, central hotel close to the station with small, quiet rooms. Friendly staff and free car park.

🛏️🍴🛋️ **Hotel Bella Napoli** – *Piazza Lena 6.* ℘*0922 20 435. www.hotelbellanapoli.com. 18 rooms (+9 in annexe)* ⊇ *€3.* Choose between the functional hotel rooms or the elegant rooms in the annexe, the Antica Foresteria Catalana (decorated with bricks, wrought iron and wood).

🛏️🍴🛋️ **Villa Athena** – *Via Passeggiata Archeologica 33.* ℘*0922 59 62 88. www. hotelvillaatena.it -* 🛋️ 🅿️ *- 27 rooms.* ⊇ A noble 18C residence inside the archaeological park with astonishing views over the Temple of Concordia.

AROUND D'AGRIGENTO

🛏️ **Camping Nettuno** – *Via Lacco Ameno 3.7km/4mi S of Agrigento.* ℘*0922 41 62 68. www.campingnettuno. com.* After a day in the Valley of the Temples, this campsite is a modest but pleasant outdoor option.

🛏️🍴🛋️ **Fattoria Mosè** – *Via Pascal 4, Villaggio Mos, 4km/2.5mi SE of Agrigento on S 115.* ℘*0922 60 61 115. www.fattoria mose.com. Closed Nov–Feb. 24 rooms.* Not far from the sea and the Valley of the Temples, this farm has a number of comfortable houses for rent with kitchens and outdoor spaces.

🛏️🍴🛋️ **Baia di Ulisse** – *Via Alaimo 22, San Leone, 11km/7mi SE of Agrigente -* ℘*0922 41 76 38. www.baiadiulisse.com.* 🛋️ 🅿️*. 92 rooms.* ⊇ A classic hotel with direct access to the beach. Comfortable rooms with balconies. Restaurant and spa.

🍴/EAT

AGRIGENTO

🍴 **Ex Panificio** – *Piazza Sinatra 16.* ℘*0922 59 53 99.* Local bistro in a former bakery (*panificio*) serving Sicilian food.

🍴🛋️ **Ruga Reali** – *Cortile Scribani 8, Agrigento.* ℘*0922 20 370. Closed lunchtimes (except Sun) and Mon.* The vaulted dining room of this rustic-looking restaurant serves country cooking. Booking advisable.

🍴🛋️ **Trattoria dei Templi** – *Via Panoramica dei Templi 15, Agrigento.* ℘*0922 40 31 10. Closed Sun (Jul–Aug), Fri (Sept–Jun) and one week in Jan.* A friendly trattoria, where traditional Sicilian fish dishes are served in rustic surroundings.

🍴🛋️🛋️ **Kalos** – *Piazzetta San Calogero, Agrigento.* ℘*0922 26 389. www.ristorante kalos.it. Closed Mon.* This elegant restaurant with antique decor offers refined meat, fish and tasting menus.

SAN LEONE

🍴🛋️ **Leon d'Oro** – *Via Emporium 102, San Leone, 7km/4mi S of Agrigento.* ℘*0922 41 44 00. Closed Mon.* Situated in the seaside resort of San Leone, this family-run restaurant also has an excellent wine list to enjoy with local dishes.

LOCAL SPECIALITIES

The Benedictine nuns of the **Abbazia di Santo Spirito** in Via S. Spirito make exquisite almond sweetmeats and the famous *cuscusu* – a semolina pudding with chocolate and pistachio nuts *(available by advance order only)*.

Café Girasole – *Via Atenea 68. Closed Sun except summer.* The place to go for an aperitif in Agrigento. Plenty of snacks, a good choice of wines. Stays open until 4am on Saturdays in season.

Viale della Vittoria – Agrigento's "balcony" is lined with cafés and pasticcerie. At no. 11, the Cafeteria Nobel has a good reputation for its ice creams and chocolate cannoli.

DRINK

Mojo – *Piazza San Francesco 11. Closed Mon.* A good spot for a drink. Live music Saturday evenings in summer.

SHOWS

Stoai – *Via Cavaleri Magazzeni 1, Valle dei Templi.* ℘*0922 60 66 23. Open daily 9am–1pm, 4pm–7pm.* The former covered market plays host to the artisan's market and a theatre show *(reservations required for shows)*.

FESTIVALS

Sagra del Mandorlo in Fiore – The almond blossom festival, the highlight of the year in Agrigento, takes place during the first half of February.

Festa di San Calogero – The Feast of San Calogero is celebrated from the first to the second Sunday in July.

Festa degli Archi di Pasqua *(Festival of the Easter Arches).* Over the Easter period, be sure to stop at **San Biagio Platani**, where this festival is celebrated. The town's citizens, divided into two brotherhoods, erect reed arches decorated with citrus fruit, dates and bread.

Sciacca★

Steeped along a flank of Monte Kronio on the edge of the sea, the port of Sciacca is skirted with colourful houses and fishing boats. Located in one of the island's main thermal regions, it is famed for its sulphurous waters and its remarkable majolica ceramics, which can be acquired from its many local workshops.

HISTORIC CENTRE

The heart of Sciacca is **Piazza Scandaliato** with its broad terrace overlooking the multicoloured harbour packed with boats, and the open sea beyond. Dominating the west side of the square is the 18C **church of San Domenico**; the longer flank accommodates the former **Jesuit College** (complete with fine 17C cloisters), now used as the town hall. Behind lies Piazza del Duomo.

Duomo

The cathedral was founded by the Normans and rebuilt in the 1600s. The Baroque façade remains unfinished. The **interior nave** and **side aisles** feature various works of interest. The barrel-vaulted nave is frescoed (1829) by the local artist Tommaso Rossi, with the Apocalypse and scenes from the life of Mary Magdelene. The chapel (to the right of the chancel) contains a lovely Renaissance marble altarpiece (1581) by **Antonio Gagini**; its walls are hung with evocative paintings of scenes from Christ's Passion.

The central thoroughfare, **Corso Vittorio Emanuele**, runs to the right of the Duomo, past the 15C–17C **Palazzo Arone Tagliavia** (on the right), its fine castellated frontage accommodating three pointed entrances and, above the central arch, a three-light Gothic window. Farther on sits the 19C Imperial-style **Palazzo San Giacomo** (or Tagliavia), with its south-facing façade graced with four sphinx-like hermas. The Venetian neo-Gothic building overlooks Piazza Friscia.

▶ **Population:** 40 929
♿ **Michelin Map:** p210:A1.
🛈 **Info:** Corso Vittorio Emanuele 84.
  ℘0925 21 182.
  www.comune.sciacca.ag.it.
▶ **Location:** Physical stamina is required for a visit to Sciacca; natural terracing divides the town into three sections: the narrow, winding streets of the medieval district of Terravecchia lie to the north of Via Licata; the major monuments lie between Via Licata and Piazza Scandaliato; the port area extends beyond Piazza Scandaliato.
👥 **Kids:** Enquire at the tourist office for activities.
🅿 **Parking:** Sciacca has countless flights of steps and narrow alleyways, so visitors are advised to park their car and explore the town on foot.
🕼 **Don't Miss:** A thermal bath at Valle dei Bagni and a sauna at the Stufe di San Calogero natural steam caves; a walk in the sculpture gardens at Castello Incantato and views from the hilltop towns of Prizzi and Bisacquino.
🕐 **Timing:** Have thermal treatments after you have finished sightseeing, as they can have a very soporific effect.

In **Viale della Vittoria**, which leads off the piazza to the right, stands the **Convento di San Francesco** (generally open mornings except Sun; to confirm call ℘0925 96 1111), which is now a conference and exhibition centre. The monastery cloisters feature sculptures

Port of Sciacca

© Bernhart Udo/Sime/Photononstop

by contemporary artists, including three large *Bathers* by Bergomi (1989).

At the far end of Viale della Vittoria, stands **Santa Maria delle Giummare** *(entrance in Via Valverde)*, founded by the Normans and rebuilt in the 16C. The actual church is contained within the main body of the building; two square "towers" provide residential quarters for the monastery.

A little farther on the right lie the ruins of **Castello della Luna** – built in the 14C, rebuilt in the 16C and almost completely destroyed in the 19C. Now only the perimeter walls and an imposing tower remain.

San Nicolò la Latina

Located below the castle, this church was founded in the early part of the 12C by Giulietta, daughter of Roger I. Its simple façade has a doorway with a heavily moulded frame and three similarly accented single openings above. The interior has a Latin-cross plan with nave, short transepts and three semicircular apses typical of transitional Arabo-Norman prototypes.

Climb back up to the castle ruins and follow Via Giglio to the town gate, **Porta di San Calogero**, to see the remains of the medieval walls. On Piazza Noceto is **Santa Maria dell'Itria**, an annexe to the larger Baroque Chiesa Madre, **San Michele Arcangelo**

(17C–18C). Inside is an 18C gallery and a carved, painted wooden organ case against the back wall; on the right, look for the Catalan Gothic cross and, in the south aisle, a 15C altarpiece of St Jerome.

Continue down towards **Corso Vittorio Emanuele** to the junction with Via Licata, which accommodates two fine 18C buildings: **Palazzo Inveges**, and farther up on the right, **Palazzo Ragusa**. At the next intersection with

Visitor from the Deep

If you were looking out to sea from Sciacca in July 1831, you would have had quite a fright. Within the space of just a few hours, a great land mass emerged from the water and loomed over the horizon. Rather than a monster rising from the underworld, this apparition was a volcanic outcrop that gently settled back into a truncated cone. This precipitated a huge stir and prompted a host of hotly contested theories. The island was christened **Ferdinandea** in honour of the reigning Spanish monarch but it was short-lived: after a mere five months, the island disappeared into oblivion.

Via Gerardi, turn left: on the corner with Corso Vittorio Emanuele is the **Palazzo Steripinto**, a Catalan-style *palazzo* dating from the 15C, whose facade is articulated with diamond-cut rustication.

Via Gerardi opens onto **Piazza del Carmine**, named after the church that stands before the 16C gateway, **Porta San Salvatore**, ornamented by two facing lions.

Santa Margherita

The original church fabric dates from the 13C; the alterations were implemented in the late 16C.

The main front has a Catalan-Gothic doorway, although the Renaissance-Gothic side door on the left side with *St Margaret and the Dragon* by Pietro da Bonitate and Francesco Laurana is more famous. Inside, the coffered ceiling is painted to suggest a starry sky. A monumental 19C organ takes up most of the back wall and a splendid marble altarpiece in the right chapel relates the life of St Margaret.

Nearby is **Chiesa di San Gerlando**. A little farther on the left stands the 15C **Palazzo Perollo:** its façade has three late-Gothic three-light windows and the inner courtyard has a time-worn Catalan staircase.

PALACE AND BATHS
Casa Museo★
(Palazzo Scaglione)

Piazza Don Minzoni (near the Duomo).
🕐*Open daily, 9am–1pm.*

This 18C residence, now a museum, displays objects and works of art collected in the 19C by **Francesco Scaglione**. Rooms are crammed with pictures – the majority by Sicilian painters – engravings, coins, archaeological artefacts, bronzes and ceramics, demonstrating the eclecticism and collecting mania of the period. The last room contains an 18C ivory and mother-of-pearl **crucifix**.

Thermal baths

Via Figuli 2. 🕐*Open Mon–Sat, 8am–1pm.* ℘*0925 96 11 11.*
www.termesciaccaspa.it.

The thermal treatments in the region surrounding Sciacca have been famous since Antiquity, yet it was only in the mid-19C that a spa was opened outside the town centre in the **Valle dei Bagni**. The most modern thermal facilities at the **Nuovo Stabilimento Termale** date from 1938: this extensive complex is surrounded by private gardens near the sea. Here, the natural sulphurous waters are used in mud therapy *(for relieving arthritis)*, balneotherapy *(for osteo-arthritis and skin conditions)* and inhalation treatments.

Other conditions are treated with various therapies also available from the Stufe di San Calogero on Monte Kronio and at the thermal pools at Molinelli. These baths are supplemented by mineral-rich waters issuing from the ground at a constant temperature of 34°C/93°F.

EXCURSIONS
👥 Castello Incantato

2km/1.2mi W. Take Via Figuli out of Sciacca and follow signs for Agrigento (S 115). 🚹🕐*Open Apr–Sept 10am–noon, 4–8pm; Oct–Mar, 9am–1pm, 3–5pm.* 🕐*Closed Mon.* ♿€3. ℘*0925 99 20 64.*

This incredible garden, dotted with sculpted stone heads, was conceived in 1913 by Filippo Bentivegna (1888–1967). Over half a century, *Filippu delli Testi* – as he is known – sculpted these faces in every corner of his extensive estate, with expressions ranging from the worried to the serene.

Monte Kronio

Leave Sciacca along Via Porta S. Calogero. 7km/4mi.

The haul to the summit provides ample opportunity to survey the broad **panorama★★** over the coast, the plain of Sciacca and the bare inland mountains. At the top sits the Franciscan **Santuario di San Calogero**. The naturally-occurring hot vapours in these caves have been used for steam baths since Antiquity. The largest and best known is the **Stufe di San Calogero**. When a vein of hot water within the mountain comes into contact with direct heat, the

Son of the Earth and the Sky

Monte Kronio – The name of this isolated peak *(386m/1,266ft)*, set in a deserted landscape, suggests an immediate association with Cronus *(Greek: Kronos)*, the god of time and one of the oldest figures of the pantheon, born out of a union between Mother Earth (Gaea) and her son, the god of heaven (Uranus).

Banished to Tartarus along with his other siblings (the Titans) by his father, Cronus was assisted by his mother in rising up against Uranus and castrating him; there followed a Golden Age on earth that lasted until his youngest *(oldest in Homer)* son Zeus, assisted by the Cyclops and the Hundred-handed Giants, declared war on Mount Olympus and the other Titans: at this point the myths vary in detail. According to some, the gods were defeated by thunderbolts and falling stones before being imprisoned in Tartarus; other accounts prevalent in Sicily relate how Zeus inveigled the gods by inebriating them with ambrosia and honeyed mead, chaining them up as they slept and relegating them to a group of islands called the Isole dei Beati (Islands of the Blessed).

The other legendary hero associated with this place is Daedalus: being an expert on labyrinths, as is well known, he decided to redirect the boiling vapours that emanated from cracks in the rock in order to harness their power and so the origins of the *stufe vaporose* – the steamy caves – are explained.

water evaporates and escapes upwards through fissures in the rock, breaking into open air at 40°C/104°F.

Italians consider the vapours to have therapeutic powers for treating rheumatism, skin and gynaecological problems.

Stufe di San Calogero

🕐*Open Mon–Sat 8am–1pm, 3–7pm.* 👝€2. ✆0925 96 11 11.

The caves were either inhabited or used for religious purposes until the Bronze Age, then abandoned some time around 2000 BC when steam began to pour into them, possibly as a result of a landslide. They came back into use during the Greek occupation, and the steam may have been interpreted as a mysterious phenomenon. Vases and votive figurines *(some are displayed in the archaeological museum at Agrigento)* are among the artefacts found here. The caves were given their names by a monk in the 4C; having realised the therapeutic potential of the vapours, he set about dividing the caves into rooms with stone benches for his patients. The largest caves include the **Antro di Dedalo** and the **Grotta degli Animali**. The Grotta del Santo nearby, probably sheltered St Calogero, depicted in the majolica icon above the altar (15C).

Today the caves are part of the modern spa complex **Grande Albergo delle Stufe**. A range of artefacts is displayed next to the Stufe in a small **antiquarium** (🕐*open Tue–Sat 9am–1pm, 3–7pm, Mon, Sun and public holidays 9am–1pm;* ✆*0925 28 989*).

🚗 DRIVING TOUR

VALLE DEL BELICE AND VALLE DEL SOSIO
160km/100mi. Allow 1 day.

▶ Take S 115 towards Castelvetrano, then S 188 (dir B) as far as Portella Misilbesi. From here, turn right to Sambuca di Sicilia, still following S 188.

The road skirts around **Lago Arancio**, a man-made protected lake of major environmental importance due to the **storks** that inhabit the area.

Sambuca di Sicilia

The town reclines on a gentle slope. Noble palazzi run along the Corso Umberto I: at the far end, a stairway climbs to a **viewing terrace**.

From Sambuca, follow signs for the Scavi di Monte Adranone *(7km/4mi)*.

Scavi di Monte Adranone

Open Tue–Sat 9am–1pm, 3–7pm. Closed Mon and Sun. ℘0925 946083.
An Ancient Greek settlement (6C BC) overlies another earlier, indigenous one. Perched high on a mountain top overlooking the surrounding countryside, the site is naturally defended on one side and reinforced by strong defensive walls on the other two. The town, loosely identified with Adranon, and mentioned by the historian **Diodorus Siculus**, was probably destroyed in the First Punic War.

Tour

Outside the walls, to the south east, among the hypogea in the **necropolis** is the **Tomba della Regina** made from square tufa rubble stone. Continue to the south gate flanked by large towers. As you walk up towards the **acropolis**, note the large rectangular edifice on the right, probably a public building and, further along, a complex of shops, workshops and residences. **Views★★** from the hilltop take in Sambuca, **Lago Arancio** and the length of the valley. The largest building is the **Carthaginian temple**, flanked on the right by a large cistern. The temple had a central space, open to the sky, which gave onto the cella, to the east.

Continue along the road for a few kilometres and then turn right to Bisacquino.

The road runs through a **landscape★** of rolling hills and steep mountains, passing the abbey of **Santa Maria del Bosco** (16C–17C) on the right, damaged during the earthquake that hit the Belice valley in 1968.

Bisacquino

The birthplace of film director **Frank Capra** (*It's A Wonderful Life*, 1946) is perched on the slopes of **Monte Triona**. Dominated by the impressive dome of

the 18C **Chiesa Madre**, the town has an intricate Arab-influenced layout.
See the **majolica bell tower** of Santa Maria delle Grazie on the church square, as well as the triangular-shaped bell tower of San Francesco, also decorated with majolica.
Typical rural life and trade scenes are recreated in the **Museo Etnografico** in Via Orsini (*open Mon–Fri 8am–2pm, and 3–6pm Tue and Thu; free; ℘091 83 08 047*).

From Bisacquino follow S 188c towards Palermo and take the exit to the 17C sanctuary of the Madonna del Balzo.

A stunning **view★★** of the surrounding area can be enjoyed 900m/2,950ft above the clearing opposite the sanctuary.

Return to S 188. From Bisacquino, head towards Palazzo Adriano.

The road passes **Lago Gammauta**, which can be explored.

Palazzo Adriano

The focal point of this village, in which Giuseppe Tornatore filmed part of *Nuovo Cinema Paradiso,* is the **Piazza Umberto I★**. This elegant square is paved with white stone and lined with fine buildings.
From Palazzo, continue through mountain scenery to Prizzi.

Prizzi

Standing at an altitude of over 1,000m/3,300ft, Prizzi enjoys a charming **site★**, framed by the **Sicani mountains**.
An unusual measurement conversion chart, erected after the unification of Italy, can be admired in the central Corso Umberto I. Further on, the **Piazza Sparacio** is decorated with murals. The oldest part of town, with its narrow streets winding around the Chiesa Madre and the castle, is to the north of **Corso Umberto**.
Return to S 188 and retrace your route for 30km/19mi. Turn left at the junction

to **Chiusa Sclàfani**, an attractive medieval town built around a Benedictine monastery and gardens.

▶ 10km/6mi after Chiusa Sclàfani, follow signs to Caltabellotta.

Caltabellotta

Two roads up to the town offer wonderful **views★**; the route via **Sant'Anna** is especially scenic. Caltabellotta enjoys a fabulous **position★★**, 900m/2,950ft above sea level and was used as a military post. Here, the Angevins signed the treaty ending the War of the Sicilian Vespers (1302).

The tallest point is the chapel and hermitage of **San Pellegrino**, and the ruins of the Norman castle. Next to the castle are the Arabo-Norman **Chiesa Matrice** and **Chiesa del Salvatore** with a late Gothic doorway.

ADDRESSES

🛏️STAY

😑😑 **Verdetecnica** – *Via Monte Kronio 22, Sciacca. ℘0925 81 133. www.verdetecnica.it. 🞕. 6 apartments.* A small hotel on a hill overlooking Sciacca and comprising six apartments, all equipped with bathroom and kitchen. Simple decor. Minimum stay of five days is required in August.

Locanda del Moro – *Via Liguori 44. ℘0925 86 756. www.almoro.com. 13 rooms.* 🛏 Although you need to climb some steep steps to get to this B&B in the centre of Sciacca it's worth it for the warm welcome provided by the owners and the charming surroundings.

🍴EAT

😑😑 **Osteria Cappellino** – *Via Capellino 24. ℘0925 28 179.* In this little family-run place, twin brothers serve up tasty local dishes under mamma's watchful eye. Big plates of *pasta alle sarde* and huge servings of grilled meat.

😑😑 **La Vecchia Conza** – *Via Gerardi 39. ℘0925 25 385. www.vecchiaconza. it. Closed Mon and in Nov.* A welcoming trattoria serving up home-made pasta and tasty dishes with the emphasis on fish and seafood; inexpensive local wines.

😑😑 **Porto San Paolo** – *Via Largo San Paolo 1, Sciacca. ℘0925 27 982. Closed Wed except in Aug.* While savouring fish dishes, choose between the rustic ambience and wooden decor of the dining room and the summer veranda overlooking the port.

😑😑😑 **Hostaria del Vicolo** – *Vicolo Sammaritano 10, Sciacca. ℘0925 23 071. Closed Mon and 14 Oct–1 Nov.* This small, elegant place in the heart of Sciacca serves Sicilian cuisine enlivened with contemporary touches. Good wine list.

😑😑😑 **Villa Palocla** – *Contrada Raganella, 4km/2.5mi W of Sciacca. ℘0925 90 28 12. www.villapalocla.it.* This villa has a truly Sicilian flavour, with its fragrant citrus trees surrounding a mid-18C, late-Baroque style building. It offers accommodation, a fine restaurant, and an excellent range of fish dishes.

TAKING A BREAK

Bar Roma – *Piazza Dogana 12. ℘0925 21 239.* Bar owner Aurelio Licata is famous for his lemon *granita*. Served with a delicious brioche, this is a typical Sicilian summer breakfast.

SHOPPING

Crafts – Sciacca is known for its majolica and ceramics. The shapes and decorations date back to the Middle Ages, when they developed under strong Spanish influence. Specialist shops can be found on **Corso Vittorio Emanuele**.

Food and drink – Sciacca produces white wines such as Sciacca Riserva Rayana. The town is known for its *cucchitella*, a sweet made from almond paste and squash. Anchovies are another speciality, either fresh *(alici)* or salted *(acciughe)*. Don't miss the local specialist **Aligò** – *Via Avellino 25. ℘0925 21 810.*

FESTIVALS

Carnevale – Sciacca's extravagant carnival, with its magnificent procession of allegorical carts, is one of the most famous in Sicily.

East of Agrigento – Naro ★ and Gela

This part of Sicily is one of the least-visited by tourists, largely due to its unfettered postwar industrial sprawl and the installation of a huge petrochemical plant here in 1961. The more intrepid, however, will find every good reason to explore the area. A trip to the Museo Archeologico in the Ancient Greek city of Gela, or a walk around the - sadly neglected - Baroque churches of Naro are well worth the effort.

🚗 DRIVING TOUR

AGRIGENTO TO GELA, VIA NARO
110km/68mi. Allow one day.

▶ Leave Agrigento on the S122 to the east.

Favara
A town of Arab origin, Favara reached its apogee under the powerful Chiaramonte family (13C–14C), who oversaw the building of the massive castle. Piazza dei Vespri is dominated by the imposing façade of the 18C **Chiesa Madre**, its tall dome resting gently on a ring of arches.

▶ Return to S 640. After 7km/4mi, turn left along the SP 13 to Racalmuto.

Racalmuto
Racalmuto was once an important centre for sulphur extraction.
In the centre stand the remains of the **Chiaramonte castle**, marked by two large towers. Racalmuto is the site of Leonardo Sciasia's birthplace, and the literary park here is worth a visit as part of a tour of places which inspired the great writer.

▶ Follow signs to Canicattì (16km/9mi).

▶ **Population:** 72 000
🚲 **Michelin Map:** p211: B/C2
📋 **Info:** Contact the Agrigento (p214) or Gela (p237) tourist offices.
📍 **Location:** The road from Naro and other charming historic hilltowns directly east of Agrigento leads to the coastal road and Gela – one of the most industrialised stretches of coastline in Sicily.
🗺 **Don't Miss:** The archaeological museum.
👪 **Kids:** Enquire at tourist office for children's activities.
🕐 **Timing:** 🚲 *See Agrigento and La Valle dei Templi.*

Canicatti
This important farming centre, with a population of 35 000, exports its Muscat grapes all over Europe.
On **Piazza IV Novembre**, not far from the baroque fountain with a figure of **Neptune** (17C), stands the Chiesa Madre *(San Pancrazio, 18C)*, which was renovated in the early 20C by Ernesto Basile, the architect responsible for Palermo's Teatro Massimo. The church contains an image of the Holy Family by Pietro d'Asaro, a local 17C painter.

▶ Continue south on the S 410d for 14km/18.7mi.

Naro★
The many Baroque buildings testify to the prosperous history of the town, which was probably founded by the Greeks.

The historical centre – Via Dante, the town's central axis, is lined with elegant Baroque buildings. At the western end, **Piazza Padre Favara** is overlooked by the **Chiesa di San Agostino** and its adja-

Minos, Daedalus and Cocalus

In mythology, **Minos** reigned over Crete and the islands of the Aegean. Poseidon sent him a magnificent bull for sacrifice, but the King substituted another animal. Angered, the sea god inspired Queen Pasiphaë with an unnatural passion for the bull. She asked Daedelus to construct her a hollow cow, then hid inside and coupled with the Cretan Bull.

Subsequently, she bore the Minotaur. Daedelus built the Labyrinth to conceal and contain the monstrous creature with a human body and a bull's head. On discovering Daedelus' treachery, Minos imprisoned him and his son Icarus in the Labyrinth. Pasiphaë released them and Daedelus made wings to escape to Sicily (Icarus flew too close to the sun, however, and melted his wings, so plummeting to his death).

Every ninth year, Minos sent the beast seven Athenian youths and seven maidens. When the third tribute was due, Theseus volunteered himself. Minos' daughter Ariadne fell in love with the hero. She gave him a sword to kill the monster and a ball of silk to retrace his path through the impenetrable maze.

Daedalus is said to have taken refuge with Cocalus, the King of Sicily, who killed Minos to protect his guest. In fact, the kingdom of Cocalus was situated on the banks of the River Platani, with a capital called Camico – now identified by some as being the modern Sant'Angelo Muxaro; by others as Caltabellotta.

cent Augustinian monastery, a powerful influence in the 18C. To the left-hand side of Via Dante stands the **Chiesa di San Nicolò di Bari**, preceded by a flight of steps, with its fine early-Sicilian Baroque façade (17C–18C).

The **Chiesa Madre** is immediately visible on the left: built by Jesuits in the 17C, it became the town's main church when the Duomo began to crumble (1867). At the same time, many furnishings and works of art were transferred here from the abandoned cathedral, including the carved wooden sacristy furniture. To the left on entering, don't miss the baptismal fonts (1424).

A right turn after the Chiesa Madre leads into the attractive **Piazza Garibaldi**, enclosed on all sides by gracious buildings. Among the most notable of these is the **façade★** of the **Chiesa di San Francesco**, founded in the 13C, but restored four centuries later. The adjacent former Franciscan monastery

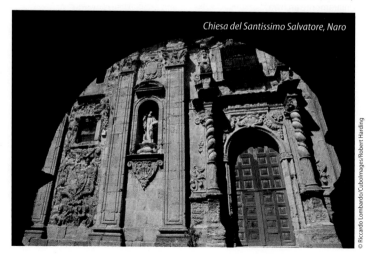

Chiesa del Santissimo Salvatore, Naro

© Riccardo Lombardo/CuboImages/Robert Harding

Leonardo Sciascia

Racalmuto is known as the birthplace of **Leonardo Sciascia (1921–89)**, the Sicilian writer and astute commentator who spent much of his life here and who is buried in the town's small cemetery. Much of Sciascia's inspiration came from this harsh, dry and sun-scorched landscape and from the toil of living and working here. In works such as *The Day of the Owl* and *To Each His Own,* the writer constantly explores themes that have their roots in Sicily and Sicilian identity. A **literary park** in Racalmuto (&*See p232*) is dedicated to the writer.

has attractive cloisters overlooked by municipal offices.

From Piazza Garibaldi, take Corso Vittorio Emanuele and turn right into Via Cannizzaro.

The **Chiesa di Santa Caterina**, which was built in 1366 and altered in the 18C, has subsequently been restored to its original appearance. A bold linearity pervades the interior arrangement, relieved in part by a highly decorative Chiaramonte archway.
Returning to Via Dante, pass the elaborate Baroque façade of the **Chiesa del Santissimo Salvatore** (left).

From Piazza Cavour, turn left into Via Archeologica.

The **Norman Duomo** (12C–13C) stands on the right-hand side of the street. All that remains is a ruin, although fragments of the Chiaramonte doorway still grace the front. The **castle** silhouette can be seen farther along the street. Its irregular form and tufa give it a somber air, although its remarkable gatehouse is worth a detour.

Retrace your steps to Piazza Cavour and walk to the end of Viale Umberto I.

Santuario di San Calogero
Piazza Roma.
From this church founded in the 16C and modified in the Baroque period, there are impressive **views** over the **Valle del Paradiso**.
Inside, against the wall of the stairway down to the crypt, is a **Wounded Christ★** in pink marble, its dark veins suggestive of blood. The crypt is built around the cave where San Calogero, patron saint of Naro, supposedly lived. The black statue is processed on 18 June, his feast day.

Catacombe paleocristiane
In the contrada Canale, south of the town.
This catacomb comprises passageways lined with niches and shallow hollows containing hauls from graves. The main underground chamber or hypogeum is the Grotta delle Meraviglie (Cave of Marvels), which extends 20m/66ft.

Castellazzo di Camastra
2km/1.2mi S along the road to Palma.
This small, ruined castle perches on an isolated rocky outcrop. According to local folklore, this is where Cocalus lived while ruling over his mythical kingdom, hence the popular epithet **Reggia di Cocalo**.

Follow S 410 as far as Palma di Montechiaro.

Palma di Montechiaro
The town was founded in 1637 by the twins Carlo and Giulio Tomasi, one of whose descendants, **Giuseppe Tomasi di Lampedusa** (1896–1957), is author of the posthumously published *Il Gattopardo (The Leopard)* (1958). The town – along with Palermo and Santa Margherita di Belice – is part of the Parco Letterario di Giuseppe Tomasi di Lampedusa, which offers literary walks and tours to discover Sicily through the eyes of the author as well as director Luchino

Visconti, who produced the classic film version (see *www.parcotomasi.it.*)
Standing atop a long flight of steps, the **Chiesa Madre** has a Baroque **façade★** built in white limestone, and framed by two bell towers with onion domes.
Set to one side of the great stairway up to the church is **Palazzo Tomasi**. The building is often referred to as the "Palace of the Holy Duke" in reference to Giulio Tomasi's nickname. The Duke had a strong religious vocation and converted the palace into a monastery.

Castello di Montechiaro

8km/5mi SW along the road to Marina di Palma, then right towards Capreria.
High upon a sea crag (*magnificent* **view★** *of the coast*), the 14C castle has a bleak, proud quality about it. In 1863, its name was incorporated into that of the nearby town of Palma.

▶ Head back to S 115 to return to Agrigento. Or continue east on S 115 to arrive in Gela.

GELA

Viale Mediterraneo 3. *0933 913 788.*
The surrounding plain – which formed the backdrop to the landing of American troops in July 1943 – is one of the more fertile zones of the island.
The oil that feeds the refinery and petrochemical complex contributes to the economy, but not all aspects of the city. Still, it remains noteworthy for its illustrious past.
The colony of Gela was founded by colonists from Rhodes and Crete in the early 7C BC. The town prospered and expanded westwards, leading to the eventual foundation of Agrigentum, which soon surpassed it in importance. Gela reached its height during the rule of two tyrants: Hippocrates and **Gelon** (the latter decided halfway through his reign to move to Syracuse). The city gradually lost its political might, but none of its cultural importance. Indeed, Aeschylus decided to spend the last years of his life here.

Legend claims the tragic poet died when an eagle dropped a tortoise on his bald head, mistaking it for a rock.
Following each successive attack, the town was faithfully rebuilt; until finally, in 1230, Gela was completely reconstructed by Frederick II.

Museo Archeologico★

At the east end of the town in Corso Vittorio Emanuele. 🕐*Open daily 9am–6.30pm.* 🕐*Closed last Mon in the month.* ∞*€4.* *0933 91 26 26.*
The collections are beautifully presented in chronological order and by category.
A fine array of **antefixes** come from the acropolis area; some bear the features of gorgons, others the sneering traits of sileni or satyrs (6C–5C BC).
Recovered from a 5 BC shipwreck is a delicate askos (a globular, spouted vessel), with a silenus (the chief of the satyrs) and a maenad (a follower of Dionysus, the god of wine). The last room (on the ground floor) features a fine selection of **Archaic and Attic vases** from the necropoli at Navarra and Nocera.

Acropolis

Alongside the museum.
The *plateia* (the Roman *decumanus* or main street) divides the town neatly into the sacred south, with its two temples, and the north, which was home to residential quarters and shops.

A Tragic Mistake

The Ancient Greek playwright Aeschylus ended his days in Gela at 456 Av. J.-C after spending most of his life in Athens. Legend has it that Aeschylus was killed in 456 BC when an eagle (or more likely a Lammergeier), mistaking the playwright's bald crown for a stone, dropped a tortoise on his head (though some accounts differ, claiming it was a stone dropped by an eagle or vulture that likely mistook his bald head for the egg of a flightless bird).

Fortificazioni, Gela

© DEA /G DAGLI ORTI/age fotostock

Fortificazioni di Capo Sporano★★
Viale Indipendenza, 4km/3mi to the west of the museum in the district of Capo Soprano. ◷*Open daily 9am–6pm, Sun closes at 1pm.* ⊛€3. ♿.
℘0933 93 09 75.
This stretch of Greek wall *(some 300m/330yd long)* dates from the era when Timoleon restored democracy and rebuilt the town razed by the Carthaginians in 405 BC. A small circular oven dating from the Middle Ages can be found a little further away.

Complesso termale
A short distance from the fortifications, near an almshouse. For information, call ℘0933 91 26 26.
The two rooms of this bath complex date from Hellenistic times. The first is divided into two areas: one circular containing a small basin, the other a pool set in a horseshoe shape. The second room would have been the *hypocaust* (with under-floor heating), used at times as a sauna. The baths were largely destroyed by fire some time towards the end of the 3C BC.

ADDRESSES

⌂ STAY

AROUND NARO
⊜⊜ **Agriturismo Coscio de Badia** –
From Naro, take the SP 12 in the direction of Campobello di Licata and follow the signs.
℘0922 956 365. www.cosciodibadia.it. 7 rooms, half-board available, restaurant ⊜⊜.
A working farm since the 17C, this family of farmers offer these simple but impeccable rooms. Good, cheap family food.

AROUND GELA
⊜⊜ **B&B Villa Erika** – *Via dei Gladioli, Manfria (W of Gela).* ℘0933 921 689 or 3491876073. 3 rooms ⌷. Only 200m/220yd from the beach, this newly built villa is surrounded by a garden and offers immaculate lodgings.

⟟ EAT

AROUND GELA
⊜⊜⊜ **Osteria del Cacciatore** – *Contrada Torre, Castrofilippo (between Favara and Canicatti).* ℘0922 829 824. *Closed Wed. Reservation recommended.* Discover authentic Sicilian cuisine in this "hunting lodge" owned by five sisters. Stews of wild boar, local tripe and fresh game dishes served with jugs of *nero d'avola*.

AT LICATA
⊜⊜⊜ **L'Oste et il Sacrestano** – *Via Sant'Andrea 19, Licata.* ℘0922 774 736. *Closed Mon.* In the old town, this converted church vestry lives up to its reputation. Spaghetti with seafood, swordfish escalope or fillets of seabass with basil.

AT GELA
⊜⊜⊜ **Casanova** – *Via Venezia 89 (road leaving Gela).* ℘0933 918 580. *Closed Wed and afternoons in Aug.* This is *the* gastronomic restaurant in Gela.

Sicily's vast centre is remarkable for its stillness and colour. The high rolling hills, which have been the island's bread basket since Antiquity, turn a deep green reminiscent of Northern Europe in winter and early spring. Later in spring the hills turn gold with wheat, spotted by all manner of wild flowers pushing up from fields and roadsides. By the end of summer, the sun and hot, dry winds turn the landscape the colour of straw. Hawks circle in silent skies and on the ground the occasional magpie *(gazza ladra)* scavenges for lunch. The Sicilian hinterland has been inhabited from prehistoric times and has played an important role ever since. This landscape has even influenced the stories of Greek mythology, including the abduction of Persephone by the Underworld god Hades on the shores of the Lago di Pergusa, near Enna.

Ancient Architectural Treasures

For travellers in search of authenticity – the thick walls of Enna's Norman stronghold standing guard over this vast central plain, the opulent floor mosaics of the Villa Romana del Casale, the home of a wealthy Roman family near Piazza Armerina, or the traditional hand-made majolica and ceramics of Caltagirone – a visit to the "navel of Sicily" is a must.

Highlights

1 Enna's great **castle** (p240)
2 On **Persephone's trail** (p249)
3 Sicily's heart: **Caltanisetta** (p250)
4 The great **mosaics** of Villa Romana del Casale (p256)
5 Climbing the steps of **Caltagirone** (p262)

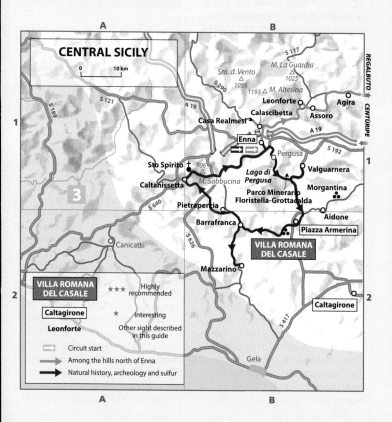

239

Enna★

Situated on a beautiful plateau in the centre of the island, Enna – the highest capital of an Italian province at 948m/3,110ft – is called the "lookout of Sicily". One of the island's oldest towns, it was founded by the Sicani, long before the Greeks arrived. The 13C Lombard Castle built by Frederick II and a plethora of churches hint at the wealth and prestige of their Medieval successors.

A BIT OF HISTORY

The origins of Enna date back to prehistoric times. Its elevated, easily-defensible position was highly valued by each successive occupant. It was probably inhabited by the Sicani, resisting the advances of the Siculi, before becoming a Greek, then a Roman town; in 135 BC the First Slave War erupted here, prompted by the Syrian slave Euno, before spreading across the island for seven long years.

Re-conquered by the Romans, Enna fell again in the 6C, along with the rest of Sicily, to the Byzantines.

Arabs took the city in the 9C and called it "Kasrlànna", which eventually mutated in the local dialect to Castrogiovanni. Enter the Normans, who made it the political and cultural stronghold of their kingdom, followed by the Swabians, the Angevins and the Aragonese. Here, Frederick II of Aragon took the title of King of Trinacria (the ancient name for Sicily) in 1314. Subsequently, the town followed the vicissitudes of the rest of the island, rebelling against the Bourbons and supporting Garibaldi.

In 1927, the ancient name of Enna was restored under Mussolini.

Mythology – In ancient times, the cult of **Demeter** (Ceres to the Romans), earth mother and goddess of fertility, was especially important here. Furthermore, according to Greek mythology, it was on the shores of nearby Lake Pergusa that the God of

▸ **Population:** 28 077
⟐ **Michelin Map:** p237: B1
▣ **Parking:** Park in the upper town.
⊛ **Don't Miss:** The cathedral, Lombard castle and the view from the Pisan tower.
▯ **Info:** Via Roma 464. ℘0935 50 22 14. www.stupormundiviaggi.com
◗ **Location:** The road to Enna is narrow and winding, especially the last stretch. Once in Enna, the Via Roma is the main thoroughfare.
▴▵ **Kids:** Check with tourist office for events.
◔ **Timing:** Allow one day to see the town fully.

the Underworld abducted her daughter Persephone (Proserpina).

🐾 WALKING TOUR

☺ *Bring a jumper or jacket as it's generally cooler here than on the coast.*

TOWN CENTRE

The axis of the town is marked by the **Via Roma**, which starts near the Castello di Lombardia. After a sharp turn, it leads downhill to the Torre di Federico. Most of the monuments and points of interest are located along this road.

Castello di Lombardi★★

◔*Open 8am–8pm (5pm winter).* ⊛*free.* Situated uppermost on the plateau, the **castle** looks out over the town and the valley, including the Rocca di Cerere (Fortress of Ceres), where a temple to Demeter may have stood. This site has been fortified since the earliest times because of its strategic position. The castle was strengthened by the Normans, then made habitable by Frederick II of Aragon, who added a number of rooms to render it suitable for court life. Indeed, he intended it as his summer residence. It was here that he was crowned King of Trinacria and in 1324,

Castello di Lombardia

© Walter Bibikow / age fotostock

convocated the Sicilian parliament. The name of the castle dates from this same period, linked to the presence of a garrison of Lombard soldiers posted there to defend it. The ground plan of the castle, which is roughly pentagonal, hugs the tortuous lie of the land. Of the original 20 towers, only six survive *(some only in part)*.

The most interesting and complete tower is *La Pisana* or *Torre delle Aquile* ("The Pisan Tower" or "Tower of the Eagles"), topped by Guelph crenellations. From the top, a breathtaking **view★★★** stretches over the best part of the Sicilian mountain ranges, **Mount Etna** and **Calascibetta**. Just outside the castle precincts, in the direction of the Fortress of Ceres, stands the statue of **Euno**, a memorial to the slave who began the Slave War.

Rocca di Cerere

From the top of the hill, where the Fortress of Ceres – a temple dedicated to the fertility goddess – once stood, extends an all-encompassing **view★★** that spreads out to include **Calascibetta** opposite, and Enna itself.

Duomo

Although largely rebuilt in the Baroque style in the 16C and 17C, the cathedral has retained its Gothic apses. Its front, preceded by a dramatic staircase, rises above a portico to a bell tower through the three Classical orders. The 16C south door, named after San Martino, has a marble relief panel depicting St Martin and the Pauper; this balances the Porta Santa *(adjacent)*, which is Gothic. The **interior★** is divided into nave and aisles by columns of black basalt, each with finely sculpted bases and capitals. Note, in particular, the reliefs incorporating allegorical creatures, *putti*, serpents and two-headed gargoyles *(second column on the right)* and the corresponding column *(left)*, which are attributed to **Giandomenico Gagini**. The 16C woodwork is especially fine. The coffered **ceiling★** is finely inlaid and graced at the end of each beam by unusual winged figures. At the end of the aisles, the organ loft and choir gallery have elegant inlaid and painted wooden balustrading and niches containing statues of Christ and the 12 Apostles. Behind the high altar, wooden choir stalls display scenes from the Old and New Testaments. Above the altar hangs a fine 15C Christ on the Cross with *(on the reverse)* a painting of the Resurrection known as the *Christ of the Three Faces* because Christ's expression appears to change with the angle from which it is contemplated.

San Michele Arcangelo

Erected in 1658, probably on the site of an old mosque, the church of the Archangel Michael has a blockish square façade and an elliptical plan with radiating side chapels.

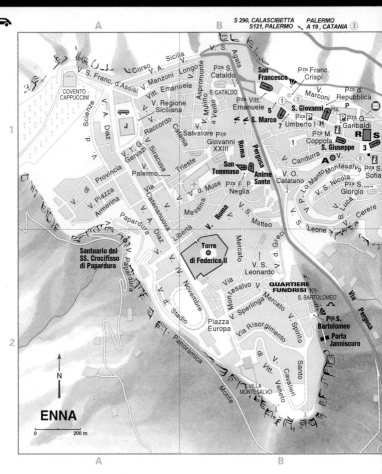

ENNA

S 290, CALASCIBETTA   PALERMO
S121, PALERMO   A 19, CATANIA ③

0   200 m

Follow Via Polizzi out of the square and turn right into Via del Salvatore to **San Salvatore**, an old Basilian church remodelled in the 16C and recently restored. Continue to Piazza Colajanni, which is bordered by fine buildings, including the **Palazzo Pollicarini** and the Church of Santa Chiara.

Santa Chiara

The Church of St Clare, now a memorial to fallen soldiers, has a single nave. The tiled floor is set with two panels: *The Triumph of Christianity over Islam* and *The Advent of Steam Navigation*. Farther along Via Roma is **San Giuseppe**, with its lovely (though rather dilapidated) Baroque façade, complete with bell tower.

▶ From Piazza Coppola, turn left into Via Candrilli.

Campanile di San Giovanni Battista

The elegant bell tower of John the Baptist, with its round-headed arches in the upper storey, is all that remains of the church of the same name.

▶ Return to Via Roma.

San Giovanni

Originally built in the Romanesque style, the Church of St John has been remodelled, decorated with stucco and was completely restored in 1967. Inside is an unusual font: the base is Roman, the central section a Byzantine

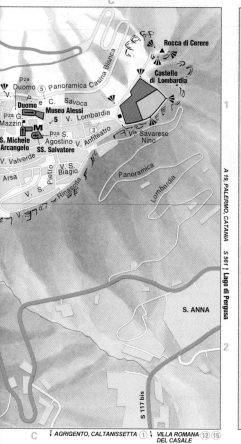

capital made of red marble and the carved basin is medieval (14C).

San Marco

This church, dating from the 17C, was erected on the site of an old synagogue, in what was Enna's Jewish quarter. **Inside**, the spacious hall church is decorated with fine stuccoes of cherubs, garlands of flowers, fruit and shells by Gabriele de Blanco da Licodia (1705). It is also worth noting the inlaid wooden **women's gallery**.

Almost directly opposite the belvedere in Piazza Francesco Crispi, there extends a fabulous **view★** of Calascibetta, Lake Nicoletti and the Lombardy Castle on the right.

The fountain in the garden is graced with a bronze copy of Bernini's *Rape of Persephone*.

Further along is a monumental church dedicated to St Francis **(San Francesco)**. Right on the bend of the road is another church, San Cataldo, with a square façade. Via Roma continues to Piazza Neglia, onto which faces the **Chiesa delle Anime Sante** (All Souls) – with a fine Baroque limestone doorway – and the 15C **San Tomaso**, with its lovely gallery and campanile, intended and used *(around the 10C)* as a watchtower.

▷ Continue along Via Roma.

Good Friday procession

© Bruno Morandi/hemis.fr

The Confraternities

One peculiarity of the residents of Enna is the fact that they are divided into confraternities, each having its "spiritual *contrada* or quarter".
Every confraternity has its own hierarchy of officers, church and traditional costume, all of which are fiercely and proudly defended by its adherents.

The most important popular event is the **Processione della Settimana Santa**, a week-long festival beginning on Palm Sunday when the Collegio dei Rettori *(a council of governors)* processes to the Duomo to begin celebrations in adoration of the Holy Eucharist. In turn, delegations from each confraternity leave their own churches and converge on the cathedral, followed by bands playing funeral marches.

At noon on the Wednesday of Holy Week the church bells are removed and the *troccola*, a special mechanical instrument made of wood, is sounded. The real and proper procession takes place on the evening of Good Friday: hundreds of representatives from the various confraternities, hooded and cloaked in mantles of different colours, process through the streets bearing first the Dead Christ, followed by Our Lady of Sorrows, on their shoulders. On Easter Sunday, the two statues are carried back to their respective churches.

Torre di Federico★

At one time, Enna might have been called the city of towers. Their proliferation is explained by the defensive and strategic role of the town. Many have disappeared, while others have been incorporated into churches as bell towers; only a few survive as free-standing towers today. A case in point is the octagonal tower named after Frederick II of Swabia, which occupies pride of place in a small public park.

▶ This tour can be continued through the Fundrisi Quarter.

QUARTIERE FUNDRISI
About halfway along Via Mercato.

In 1396, King Martin of Aragon quelled a revolt on the island and razed several of the small towns near Castrogiovanni, as it was then, to the ground. The inhabitants of the town called Fundro were transferred here and over the centuries, created an independent community. A walk through the narrow streets, which rise and fall among the typical single-storey houses with their distinctive galleries *(especially along Via San Bartolomeo)*, is particularly recommended.

Frederick's Towers

Frederick II, the Swabian King of Sicily, gave a considerable boost to civic building in the south of Italy. This architecture is characterised by rigorous geometry: buildings rise from a square base, imitating the form of the Roman *castrum*. This shape also appears in the Islamic world, with cylindrical or square towers at the corners and one cylindrical or polygonal tower in the centre *(see the castle at Augusta or Maniace Castle at Siracusa)*. Through time, the octagonal ground plan evolved and was applied here, in Enna.

This choice of plan is in accordance with the mind of medieval man, fascinated as he was by precise geometry and the symbolic significance of such forms. The square – symbolising the Earth and humankind – contrasts with the circle, which symbolised the divine and the heavens. At that time, the octagon represented mediation, the fusion of the two.

From here or Piazzetta San Bartolomeo (which takes its name from the church that presides over the scene), extend various **prospects★** across the northeastern part of the town.

A short way below the piazza stands **Porta Janniscuru**, the only gate to survive of the five that once served the city, and adjacent to this, the Grotta della Guardiola (literally translated as the "Cave of the Guardroom"), perhaps a cult site long before the foundation of the town. Continuing on an axis with Via Mercato, Via Spirito Santo leads to a church of the same name, enjoying a splendid position perched on a rocky spur over a vertical drop.

VISIT
Museo Alessi

Entrance at the back of the Duomo. ℘0935 50 31 65. ⚊Closed for restoration at the time of going to press.

In 1862, the museum was created to house the impressive collections of Canon Alessi, which include 17C and 18C sacred vestments embroidered with gold thread and coral *(in the basement)*. There are a selection of **paintings** *(on the upper floor)*, notably a gentle *Madonna and Child* by an unknown 15C Flemish painter, a 16C *Pietà* with the symbols of the Passion and two panels with John the Baptist and St John the Evangelist from a 16C polyptych attributed to Il Panormita.

Displayed on the first floor is a canvas by Giuseppe Salerno *(known locally as the Lame Man of Gangi)* depicting the *Madonna delle Grazie*, together with the glorious **treasures** from the Chiesa Madre.

The latter consists of sacred relics, a fabulous **Madonna's crown★**, exquisitely enamelled and engraved (17C), a magnificent 17C **pelican jewel★** – symbol of the Sacrifice of the Resurrection for Eternal Life – and the monumental **processional monstrance★** engraved with the spires of a Gothic cathedral, attributed to Paolo Gili (1536–38).

Museo Archeologico Varisano

Piazza Mazzini. ⏱Open Tue–Fri 9am–1pm, 3–7pm. ⚊€2. ℘0935 507 63 04.

Most of the archaeological finds on display are terracotta artefacts recovered from the various necropoli in Calascibetta, Capodarso, Pergusa, Cozzo Matrice and Rossomanno.

▷ Take Via Libertà after the crossroads with Viale Diaz; turn right down a minor road marked with the Stations of the Cross.

Santuario del SS Crocifisso di Papardura

⏱Open Mon–Sat 3.30–6.30pm, Sun 10.30am–noon.

The Sanctuary of the Holy Crucifix of Papardura incorporates the cave where, in 1659, an image of the Crucifix was found painted on a stone slab. This has been attributed to the work of Basilian monks and can now be seen on the high altar.

Inside, the fine **stuccoes** initiated in 1696 by Giuseppe and Giacomo Serpotta, were completed in 1699 by another artist, who also executed the statues of the Apostles. Note also the **silver façade★** of the high altar made by a craftsman from Messina (17C).

DRIVING TOURS

AMONG THE HILLS NORTH OF ENNA
85km/53mi, plus 55km/34mi back to Enna. Allow one day.

▶ Leave Enna as indicated on the map on p237 and follow directions for Calascibetta *(4km/2.5mi N)*.

This tour runs through the gently rolling hills that separate Enna from Catania, passing ancient hill-top villages and providing stunning **panoramic views★**.

Calascibetta
Benefiting from a glorious **setting★** in a natural amphitheatre nestled in a rocky hollow on the side of a hill, this small town was probably founded during the Arab occupation. The **Chiesa Madre**, founded in the 14C, was completely rebuilt following an earthquake in the

17C. Inside, the nave is divided from its aisles by stone columns, which rise from bases bearing carvings of monstrous figures to support the arcades of pointed arches. To the left of the entrance is a fine **16C font**.

The **Norman tower** (11C), standing beside the ruined church of San Pietro, is ornamented with a shallow relief in stone. From the piazza *(left)* extends a marvellous **view★★**, with Enna on the right *(where the castle and belvedere can be seen quite clearly)* and the Lago di Pergusa *(below)*.

Leaving the town in the direction of Villapriolo, the road passes the rock-cut tombs of the **necropolis of Realmese** (4C BC).

▶ Return to the crossroads and take the left turning (S 121) for Leonforte *(20km/12mi NE of Calascibetta)*.

Leonforte
The town perches on a rise enjoying a superb **position★**. The monumental silhouette of Palazzo Branciforte is discernible from a distance, a powerful reminder that Leonforte was founded in the 17C by Nicola Placido Branciforte. Dating from 1611, the palazzo runs along one side of the enormous piazza of the same name. Of particular interest is the **fountain** or **Granfonte** (1651), built by the Branciforte family,

Calascibetta

© Walter Bibikow/Mauritius/Photononstop

View of Agira

© olling/iStockphoto.com

constructed of gold-coloured stone with 24 spouts.

▷ Return to the crossroads and turn left for Assoro *(6km/4mi E of Leonforte).*

Assoro

Located at an altitude of 850m/2,800ft, the town is grouped around the attractively-paved but modest Piazza Umberto I, which has a central fountain and **belvedere-terrace★**.

Beyond the elegant archway linking Palazzo Valguarnera to the town's main church is another small square with **viewing terrace**, which opens onto the Chiesa Madre, or **Basilica di San Leone**. The church, founded in 1186, has been subjected to major alteration: first in the late 14C and again in the 18C. It consists of a nave and aisles and has a doorway on the south side. The **interior★**, enclosed by a fine ribbed vault, is particularly attractive on account of its compactness and profusely gilded Baroque **stucco decoration**. The spiral columns were, in fact, embellished with the climbing plant ornament in the 18C, at the same time as the pelican *(right)* and the phoenix *(left)* were added above the apses. These emblems allude to the Sacrifice of the Crucifixion (according to myth, the pelican plucked flesh from its own breast to feed its young) and the Resurrection of Christ (the phoenix

burnt itself to ashes before emerging rejuvenated).

A **wooden tie-beam ceiling**, painted and ornamented with arabesques (1490) spans the main body of the church; the attractive **wrought-iron chapel gates** (15C) are also worthy of note.

▷ Follow the road past San Giorgio which intersects S 121 again at Nissoria. Turn right towards Agira *(17km/10mi E of Assoro).*

Agira

Spread over the slopes of Monte Teja, at a height of 650m/2,130ft, the town is dominated by its towering **castle**. Built under Swabian rule, this defensive outpost appears to have played an active role in various struggles between the Angevins and the Aragonese, and later, between the Aragonese and the Chiaramonte. From the ruins, there is a beautiful **view★** over Lago di Pozzillo.

Abbazia San Filippo

The abbey is the town's most important religious building. It dates in its present form from the late 18C and early 19C, and the front was completely rebuilt in 1928. Inside, it is decorated with gilded stuccowork; among the works of art is a dramatic wooden Crucifix by Fra' Umile da Petralia *(over the high altar)*, and wooden choir stalls depicting scenes from the life of St Philip by Nicola Bagnasco (1818–22).

▷ Continue along S 121 for 14km/9mi.

Regalbuto

Coming from Agira, the Baroque pink stone façade of **Santa Maria La Croce** (1744) appears on the horizon, graced with columns crowned by an elegant pediment. Turning into Via Ingrassia, immediately on the left-hand side is the Jesuit school and just beyond it, the Liberty-style Palazzo Compagnini. A little farther, the town's main square provides a broad open space before the **Chiesa Madre** (1760), dedicated to St Basil, whose monumental Baroque façade is decorated with pilasters.

▷ From S 121, a narrow road winds to Centùripe (21km/13mi SE of Regalbuto).

Centùripe

This small town, surrounded by olive groves and orange orchards, today seems rather off the beaten track.

Historically, however, it was once a highly strategic outpost between the Catania plain and the mountains inland. This explains why, particularly in Roman times, Centùripe was quite wealthy (in 70 BC, Cicero described it as one of the most prosperous towns in Sicily). Today the town is focused around a central piazza and a terrace nearby, from which there are superlative **views**. Elsewhere, the **Tempio degli Augustali** (1C–2C AD) is a rectangular building raised above a colonnaded street *(alongside the archaeological museum)*. The two monumental tombs with towers are known as *La Dogana (with only the upper floor visible)* and "the castle of Conradin". Down a cobbled side street on the far northwestern side of the town in the *contrada* of Bagni sit the ruins of a **nymphaeum**, hanging above the ravine of the river.

Finally, the vast majority of artefacts recovered from the 8C BC to the Middle Ages are displayed in the **Museo Archeologico** *(Via Giulio Cesare 1; ◷open daily, 9am–7pm; ◷closed national holidays; ☞€4; ✆0935 73 079)* including the statues from the Tempio degli Augustali, representing various emperors and members of their families.

Don't miss the fine head of the Emperor Hadrian which, given its immense size, must have belonged to a statue at least 4m/13ft high; two splendid **funerary urns★** belonging to the Scribonii family (almost certainly imported from Rome); locally produced pottery (3C–1C BC) and an impressive collection of theatrical masks.

Town and Monastery

The story of Agira, home of the ancient historian Diodorus Siculus (90–20 BC), reflects the changing fortunes of the Basilian monastery of San Filippo, which was founded by a Syrian monk some time between the 5C and 6C AD, and which quickly rose to become an important centre of culture and religion. It came to particular prominence when, during the Norman occupation, the resident community was joined by a group of monks from Jerusalem forced into exile by the wrath of Saladin. The monastery also prospered on account of the enormous income generated by its immense holdings throughout Europe. In 1537, Emperor Charles V conceded the title of *città demaniale* upon Agira, providing it with a special "royal" status complete with privileges that included the right to administer its own civil and penal justice system.

The town's decline began in 1625 when King Philip IV of Spain, in a desperate effort to boost the dwindling finances of the monarchy, decided to sell the town to Genoese merchants. Faced with the threat of losing their freedom, the citizens of Agira offered to raise the enormous sum themselves.

Persephone and Hades

Legend describes how the daughter of Demeter and Zeus was once playing here with her companions, the ocean nymphs, when her eye was caught by a particularly beautiful narcissus. As she reached out to pick it, the earth gave way, forming a great abyss from which, with due majesty, **Hades** and his immortal horses emerged. The god forced her to mount his golden chariot before disappearing with her – near Syracuse, by the Cyane Fountain (see Siracusa) – down into the Underworld. Hearing her daughter's piercing cries, her distraught mother set about searching for her. After wandering relentlessly, she finally succeeded in discovering where the girl had been taken and arranged to see her. Before allowing his bride to see Demeter, Hades (or Pluto, as he is also known) made her eat some pomegranate seeds, thus binding her to him for the winter months.

To return to Enna from Centùripe, continue S in the direction of Catenanuova and take the motorway (55km/34mi).

NATURAL HISTORY, ARCHAEOLOGY AND SULPHUR
Approximately 130km/81mi.
Allow one day.

Leave Enna as indicated on the map on p237 and follow directions for Pergusa *(9km/5.5mi S).*

Set between a group of mountains in the Erei chain, the **Lago di Pergusa** is an important migratory stop for many species of bird. Now disfigured by southern Italy's biggest motor-racing track, the *Autodromo di Pergusa*, the lake had a more romantic past – as the backdrop for a Greek mythological story: the abduction of **Persephone** by Hades, Lord of the Underworld.

At the next junction, turn left towards Valguarnera *(18km/11mi SE of Pergusa).* Follow signs on the left.

Parco minerario Floristella-Grottacalda
Contrada Floristella, Valguarnera, 9km/5mi from the lake, signs on the left. Open Mon–Sat 8am–2pm
Guided tours by reservation. 0935 95 81 05. www.enteparcofloristella.it
A sulphur mine until 1984, the park is an important part of the region's industrial history. A dirt track leads to a large, open area and the *palazzina* Pennisi, a small building erected by the barons of Floristella, who had been the long-standing owners of the mine since it opened in 1750. The small white hillocks are the *calcheroni*, round pits lined with inert material, where sulphur was separated from its slag of impurities.
After 1860, domed Gill furnaces replaced the *calcheroni*. Opposite is a sort of gallery with arcades and narrow slits, from where the molten sulphur would flow down to the collection point. There it was allowed to solidify in wooden trapezoidal moulds to produce 50–60kg/110–130lb blocks.
On the far right is the oldest section of the mine, where the shaft-steps used by miners and *carusi* – the young boys employed to carry the ore up to the surface in wooden structures on their backs – can still be seen.

Valguarnera
Until only a few years ago, this small town was inextricably associated with sulphur mining. It has a 17C church with a heavy Baroque limestone front.

Return towards Piazza Armerina *(18km/11mi S of Valguarnera).*

The road winds through a beautiful **valley**★ with gently sloping hills, covered in springtime by a veil of emerald green.

Piazza Armerina
See Piazza Armerina.

Imperial Villa of Casale★★★
See Villa Romana del Casale.

▷ Proceed along S 191 towards Caltanissetta to the fork signposted on the left for Barrafranca *(21km/13mi W of Piazza Armerina).*

Barrafranca
At one time called Convicino *(its current name dates from the 16C)*, Barrafranca simply consists of a collection of ochre-coloured houses clustered on the gentle slopes of a hill.

The entrance to the town is along Via Vittorio Emanuele, which is flanked on either side by elegant town houses, including Palazzo Satariano and Palazzo Mattina. The **Chiesa Madre** (18C) has a bare brick façade and a bell tower crowned with a small dome covered with polychrome tiles.

The **Benedictine Monastery** in Piazza Messina is now virtually in ruins; just beyond it stands a large, eye-catching 18C building that once housed small shops **(i Putieddi)** and the **Chiesa della Maria Santissima della Stella**, marked by its tall campanile topped with a **majolica** spire.

Return to the town's main street *(Corso Garibaldi)*, which leads into Piazza dell'Itria and its 16C church with a brick bell tower.

▷ Continue towards Pietraperzia (10km/6mi) or make a detour (14km/9mi) via Mazzarino.

Mazzarino
This medieval hamlet developed under the patronage of the Branciforte family. Allow time for the main street *(Corso Vittorio Emanuele)* and, alongside the Chiesa Madre, the **Palazzo Branciforti** (17C) and the contemporary Carmelite church. Just outside the little town, perched on top of a small hill lie the ruins of the **castle**. Built on the site of a Roman and Byzantine stronghold, and strengthened under the Normans in the 14C, it was converted into a noble residence at the end of the 15C.

▷ Take S 191 to Barrafranca and continue as far as Pietraperzia.

Pietraperzia
The ochre-coloured houses of Pietraperzia and its ruined Norman castle overlook the valley of the River Salso. On entering the town, on **Piazza Matteotti**, the 16C Chiesa del Rosario stands face-to-face with a fine neo-Gothic Palazzo Tortorici. The 19C **Chiesa Madre** has a square façade crowned with a squat pediment *(for information on admission times, call 0943 40 16 83)*. Inside, above the main altar, is the *Madonna and Child* by Filippo Paladini. Also of interest is the **Palazzo del Governatore** (17C) with its square balcony, supported by grotesque figures.

▷ From Pietraperzia continue to Caltanissetta *(approx. 15km/9mi).*

Caltanissetta
Corso Vittorio Emanuele 109.
0934 53 41 11.
Set between soft hills and valleys, this city stands on a 568m/1,863ft plateau, offering **panoramic views** over the centre of Sicily. Caltanissetta started life as a small Greek town but prospered mainly in the early 1900s, when local mines made Caltanissetta the world's leading sulphur exporter, accounting for four-fifths of the world's supplies. Competition from the New World, however, soon forced the mines to close.

Historic Centre
The town's historic quarter is clustered around **Piazza Garibaldi** at the junction of the town's two main thoroughfares *(Corso Umberto and Corso Vittorio Emanuele)*. Grouped around the square are the town hall *(in a former Carmelite convent)*, the cathedral, the **Chiesa di San Sebastiano** which, like Sant'Agata *(at the end of Corso Umberto)* and Santa Croce *(end of Corso Vittorio Emanuele)*, is painted dark red in marked contrast to the natural stone colour of

the other buildings. In the centre is the 👤👤**Fontana del Tritone** (1956) by local sculptor Michele Tripisciano, based on a 19C model. The bronze work consists of a seahorse being held back by a triton, while under threat from two winged monsters. Beyond the town hall *(in Salita Matteotti)*, stands the 17C **Palazzo Moncada** which, although never completed, has a façade with intriguing carved corbels of human and animal figures.

Cathedral – The cathedral was erected in the late 16C. Its interior frescoes are by the Flemish painter Guglielmo Borremans (1720). An alternation of painted panels and stucco decoration combines to produce a dramatic impact. The 17C wooden figure of St Michael (1615) is by the Sicilian sculptor Stefano Li Volsi *(chapel to the right of the choir)*. The gilded wooden organ in the choir was built in 1601.

Sant'Agata al Collegio – The 17C church has a composite front elevation fashioned in natural stone, red plasterwork and marble *(doorway)*. The inside features inlaid polychrome marble decoration and a beautiful marble altarpiece carved by **Ignazio Marabitti**.

To the east of Piazza Garibaldi stretches the *Quartiere degli Angeli*, which has retained its medieval layout. At its centre stands **San Domenico**, a church with a fine Baroque façade enthusiastically decorated with undulating panels. The painting of the *Madonna of the Rosary (inside)* is by **Filippo Paladini**.

Museo Archeologico

Contrada S. Spirito, Via S. Spirito.
🕙*Open daily, 9am–1pm, 3.30–7pm;*
🕙*Closed last Mon of month.* 🎟️*€4.*
📞*0934 56 70 62.*

The museum explores the town's indigenous civilisation and Hellenistic influences. Finds from the Greek necropolis at **Gibil-Gabib** include an unusual small clay cask from 4C BC, later used as a funerary urn. Other exhibits, such as a *strigil* (the tool used by athletes to scrape away oil, sweat and dead skin, as illustrated in a mosaic at Villa Romana

del Casale), were discovered at the Greek necropolis at **Vassallaggi**.

Among the objects found in the Greek settlement of Sabucina, note the small-scale terracotta model of a **temple★**; the votive object dating from the 6C BC; two large basins *(one on a high pedestal)* for holding drink or oil; and the *krater* bearing a painting of the god Hephaestus, seated in his forge and hammering out hot iron (6C–5C BC).

Finds from the site at **Dessueri** include a fine set of "teapots" used for boiling opium (indigenous culture, 13C BC) and an Attic *kylix* showing Heracles armed with a club.

Abbazia di Santo Spirito

3km/2mi NE on S 122 towards Enna.
The abbey – founded by Roger I (11C) and consecrated in 1153 – is Romanesque in style. It has three typically Norman apses ornamented by decorative blind arcading. Inside is a 15C wooden crucifix and an early Romanesque baptismal font decorated with stylised palmettes.

▶ From Caltanissetta, return to Enna via S 117b, a road providing fine views over the countryside *(33km/20mi)*.

ADDRESSES

♿ *See also "Addresses" for Piazza Armerina, p253.*

🛏️ STAY

🛏️ **C.C. Ly Hostel Enna** – *Via Vulturo 3.* 📞*0935 27 52 77 or 328 28 82 879. www. ccly-hostel.com. 8 rooms and a dormatory.* All the comforts of a hotel with the prices and atmosphere of a youth hostel. The light, spacious dormatories and double and triple rooms have a designer, pop décor. Enviable location.

🛏️🛏️🛏️ **Grande Albergo Sicilia** – *Piazza Colaianni 7.* 📞*0935 50 08 50. www.hotel siciliaenna.it. 76 rooms* 🍽️. Not far from the Castello di Lombardia, this plain-looking hotel offers pleasant rooms and spacious communal areas. Breakfast is served on a terrace with **views** over the old town. Friendly staff.

NEAR ENNA

Cannalotto Agriturismo – *Between Enna and Leonforte, signed on the left. 0935 904 250. www.canalotto.it. 5 rooms, restaurant.* This house, surrounded by cypress and palm trees nestles on a farm growing olives, fruit and vegetables. On the upper floor, the rooms are plainly, tastefully decorated; the restaurant serves farm produce.

Agriturismo Azienda Baglio Pollicarini – *In Pergusa. 0935 54 19 82. www.bagliopollicarini.it. 5 rooms, half-board available, restaurant.* This tastefully-renovated former 17C monastery offers spacious, comfortable rooms. The common areas are well-appointed and the garden is an oasis of calm. The restaurant is highly recommended and offers a good range of regional specialities.

La Casa del Poeta – *Contrada Parasporino, Villagio Pergusa. 0935 54 15 78. www.lacasadelpoeta.it. 7 rooms.* B&B housed in a 19C villa set in lush surroundings. Each room is a work of art. A soothing, streamlined décor, ideal for reading or writing.

Masseria Bannata – *Contrada Bannata SS117 b . 0935 68 13 55. www.agriturismobannata.it. 5 rooms.* *Bannata* means sunkissed in Arabic: ideal for anyone seeking a charming agriturismo between Enna and Piazza Armerina. Stone walls and rustic furniture.

CALTANISSETTA

Hotel Plaza – *Via Gaetani 5, Caltanissetta. 0934 58 38 77. 33 rooms.* After returning tired but happy from a day visiting the little town and its environs, recharge your batteries in this hotel offering spacious, comfortable rooms furnished in a modern style.

ⵙ/EAT

ENNA

Bottiglieria Belvedere – *Via Vulturo 26. 0935 23 396. www.bottiglieriabelvedere.it.* A pleasant, central wine bar opened several years ago serving good food to enjoy with a fine selection of wines.

Divini Sapori – *Via Lombardia 6. 0935 19 80 533. www.ristorantedivini sapori.it. Booking recommended.* Close to Castello di Lombardia, this contemporary restaurant specialises in fish and meat (cured meat or seafood antipasto) and crisp *pizze*.

Trinacria – *Viale Caterina Savoca 20. 0935 50 20 22. Closed Mon.* An excellent choice for lovers of regional cuisine. Serving the best of Sicily, including very filling antipasto, this restaurant is not for dieters!

CALTANISSETTA

Vicolo Duomo – *Piazza Garibaldi 3. 0934 58 23 31. Closed Sun, Mon lunch and Aug. Booking recommended.* A small restaurant on the town square with an unfussy atmosphere serving delicious regional dishes.

TAKING A BREAK

Caffè Roma – *Via Roma 312, Enna. 0935 50 12 12. Open 8am–11pm. Closed Tue.* The Caffè Roma was founded in 1921 and has long been a firm favourite with locals. Rustic decor and exposed stone provide the backdrop for excellent sweets and savouries.

Al Kenisa – *Via Roma 481, Enna. 0935 18 65 05. Open 9am–midnight. Closed Mon.* Don't miss this little literary café, even if you only go to relax on the terrace under the awnings spread out like desert nomads' tents. Inside, the bookshop is perfect for anyone wanting to expand their historic or literary knowledge of the region.

FESTIVALS

Settimana Santa – During the traditional Holy Week festival the confraternities of Enna take part in a hooded and cloaked procession through the town. *For additional suggestions, see Piazza Armerina "Addresses".*

Piazza Armerina★

Overshadowed by the Villa Romana del Casale, Piazza Armerina is a pleasant stop in its own right. This pretty town is dominated by a grand Baroque cathedral that fronts onto a piazza in the historic centre. Every August, the streets of Piazza Armerina come alive with medieval re-enactments of the arrival of the Norman Count Roger to liberate the town from the Saracens.

 WALKING TOURS

MEDIEVAL QUARTER★

The little town, threaded by narrow medieval streets, is visible from a good distance away and dominated by the **Duomo** at the highest point (721m/2,364ft), overlooking Piazza del Duomo. At the heart of the old town, Piazza Garibaldi is lined with elegant palazzi.

Duomo

This monumental Baroque building, crowned with a great dome, towers over its own **piazza**. Commissioned and built with funds donated by Baron Marco Trigona, whose statue overlooks the square, the front elevation of the cathedral contains an elegant central doorway surmounted by a square window.

Above sits the eagle, the heraldic emblem of the Trigona family. Inside, notable works of art include the baptismal font and the **Madonna delle Vittorie★** above the main altar at the far end of the nave. This Byzantine image is popularly linked to the banner given at the Council of Melfi by Pope Nicholas II to his legate Roger I "to go before him and inspire his army in its future campaigns". In the chapel (*left of the chancel*) is a **painted wooden cross★** from 1455. Overlooking the nave are two wooden organ cases; one ornamented with the Trinacria, the ancient symbol

- ▶ **Population:** 20 760
- ⚉ **Michelin Map:** p237: B1/2
- ℹ **Info:** Via Gen. le Muscara 47/A, ℘093 56 80 201. www.comune. piazzaarmerina.en.it.
- ◗ **Location:** The town sits in rolling countryside at an altitude of 700m/2,300ft. Behind a mass of modern constructions, the narrow streets of the historic centre wind uphill to the cathedral at the town's highest point. Piazza Armerina is the closest settlement to Villa del Casale and visitors travelling from Enna or Caltagirone must first drive through Piazza Armerina to reach the villa.
- ◉ **Don't Miss:** Fine art in the Duomo.
- ◷ **Timing:** Piazza Armerina's sights can been seen in a couple of hours and it makes a nice short stop on the way to Villa Romana del Casale.

Duomo, Piazza Armerina

© Philippe Michel/age fotostock

The Palio and its Legend

The Palio festival (&see Addresses) re-enacts the arrival in Sicily of the Norman *Gran Conte* – Count Roger – and the defeat of the occupying Saracens, which was considered a sort of holy war. Hearing of Roger's landing, the inhabitants of Piazza rose in revolt, claiming Roger Guiscard de Hauteville (known in Italy as Ruggero d'Altavilla) as their leader. On arrival, the count's paid mercenaries/*condottiere* gave the town a banner which earned great admiration from the faithful. The banner was then furled and put away until the mid-1300s, when it was recovered and borne with great ceremony to the town church. As if by a miracle, the plague then decimating the town suddenly died out and the banner became a cult object. According to tradition, the standard in question is the one bearing the Madonna delle Vittorie, now in the cathedral.

of Sicily *(left)*, the other showing Count Roger on horseback *(right)*.

 WALKING TOUR

In Via Cavour, behind the Duomo, stands a 17C **Franciscan complex** *(now a hospital)*; its sandstone and brick church are marked by a bell tower with a conical spire covered in majolica tiles. The south face of the convent buildings includes an elegant **balcony** supported by Baroque brackets, and designed by GV Gagini.

Continue to Slargo Santa Rosalia and **Palazzo Canicarao**, now commercial offices *(Azienda di Promozione Turistica)*. Turn down Via Vittorio Emanuele, which opens out before two church façades situated face-to-face: the **Chiesa di Sant'Ignazio di Loyola** is preceded by a staircase that divides into two above the first flight; the **Chiesa di Sant'Anna** has a convex façade. Above, the solid profile of the **Aragonese castle** (1392–96), once the home of Martin I of Aragon, towers protectively. Return to Piazza Duomo and take the Via Monte down to the **Chiesa di San Martino di Tours**, founded in 1163.

ON THE EDGE OF TOWN

On the western side of town, at the far end of Via Sant'Andrea, stands a 12C hermitage, l'Eremo di Sant'Andrea and farther on, the precincts of **Santa Maria del Gesù** (17C). These are now abandoned but the fine portico with a loggia above have remained intact.

EXCURSIONS
Villa Romana del Casale★★★
5km/3mi SW.
&*See Villa Romana Del Casale.*

Aidone
From Piazza Armerina, take the S 228 (7km/4mi NE).
This village, a few kilometres from the ruins of Morgantina, is home to the small **Museo Archeologico Regionale** (&open 9am–7pm; ∞€6; &0935 87 307). Housed in a former Capuchin monastery and accessed through the church of San Francesco, the museum is worth visiting for the **Venere dei Morgantina**, a 5C BC statue of Venus (or Demeter) recently returned to Sicily after being displayed at the Paul Getty Museum in Malibu for the last 30 years. Other items include a unique 3C BC 16-piece silverware set (**Tesoro di Eupolemos**) and some fine antefixes from the mid-6C BC, bearing masks of gorgons, lions and maenads, the female worshippers of Dionysus, Greek god of wine and mystery.

Scavi di Morgantina
From Aidone follow signs for Scavi di Morgantina (approx. 7km/4mi NE of Aidone). &*Open daily 8am to 1hr before sunset.* ∞€6 (€10 combined ticket with the Aidone museum). &0935 87 955, www.aidone-morgantina.it/morgantina.*
The area of **Serra Orlando** has been inhabited since the Bronze Age. Morgantina (probably named after the king of the Morgeti, an Italic tribe

Theatre, Scavi di Morgantina

© Concetta Zingale/Dreamstime.com

from central-southern Italy) enjoyed rapid growth during the Iron Age. In the 5C BC, the town was refounded a short distance from the original, at Serra Orlando. Excavations have uncovered the remains of the Siculi centre colonised by the Greeks, which grew to prominence in the 1C AD and was then abandoned. The **site** extends from one hill, into a small valley, and up the next rise. Excavations here include a large **agora**, a small **theatre**, a marketplace and a trapezoidal stairway with an adjacent senate chamber (*bouleuterion*).

Remains of a **gymnasium** and a sanctuary to the deities Demeter and Kore, as well as the foundations of a number of Hellenistic houses, have also been found. On the northern hill, there are a number of fragments of **mosaic** visible under protective roofing.

ADDRESSES

🛏 STAY

🍴🍴 **Ostello del Borgo** – *Piazza San Giovanni 6, Piazza Armerina. ℘0935 68 70 19. www.ostellodelborgo.it.* ⊿⊑. More of a guesthouse than a hostal housed in a wing of the former monastery of St John. Some of the monks' cells have been converted into spacious, comfortable guest rooms.

La Volpe e l'uva – *Via Santa Veneranda 35. ℘0935 68 07 52. www.volpeuva.it.* ⊿ *3 rooms.* Follow in the footsteps of the poet Aesop in this comfortable, colourful B&B managed by a young, friendly couple. Local specialities for breakfast.

🍴 EAT

Eyexei – *Contrada Morgantina - Aidone. ℘0935 87 341 or 368 71 90 257. www.ristoranteeyexei.com. Closed Sun and Mon eves.* Surrounded by the remains of Morgantina, this country brasserie specialises in fresh, rustic cuisine.

🍴🍴🍴 **Al Fogher** – *S 117 bis, 3km/1.8mi N of Piazza Armerina. ℘0935 68 41 23. Closed Sun evening and Mon. Booking recommended.* Efficiently run by an enthusiastic couple, the Al Fogher is one of the best-known restaurants in Sicily. Traditional, authentic Sicilian fare with a contemporary twist.

FESTIVALS

Palio dei Normanni – From 12–14 August, the town puts on a re-enactment of the legendary arrival of Roger de Hauteville *(Ruggero d'Altavilla)*, followed by jousting and a procession in which the statue of the Madonna and Child with two angels, kept in the cathedral, is carried through the streets. ⓑ*See box opposite, The Palio and its Legend'.*

Villa Romana del Casale ★★★

This splendid and imposing Roman villa, built between the end of the 3C and the beginning of the 4C AD, owes its reputation to the extraordinary and well-preserved mosaic floors that cover much of the site.

A BIT OF HISTORY

This country villa was built between the end of the 3C and the beginning of the 4C AD, possibly by a member of the Imperial family: one of the most likely candidates is Maximian, one of the tetrarchs who jointly ruled the Empire from AD 286–305. Surrounded by large estates, the villa was occasionally occupied until the 12C. It was destroyed by a fire, then buried in mud following floods and a subsequent landslide in 1161. It was only partially rediscovered at the end of the 19C.

The large complex (c. 3,500m2/37,600sq ft) was built on different levels. The main entrance led into a polygonal courtyard, which provided access to the large peristyle overlooked by guest rooms (north) and the owner's private apartments (east). Beyond the guest rooms were the servants' quarters, complete with kitchen. The private apartments used by members of the household were divided in two by a large basilica for meetings and official receptions.

At the rear of these buildings stands a separate octagonal latrine reserved for the family. The living area was situated to the south of the complex and consisted of an elliptical atrium which gave out onto an apsed triclinium (dining room) (**24**), six small rooms and service amenities.

The western part of the complex housed the baths. Water was supplied by two aqueducts connected to a third which, in turn, was fed by the River Gela.

Mosaics – What makes the villa unique is its floors, which consist almost enti-

- ♿ **Michelin Map:** p237 B2.
- ℹ **Info:** Open daily 9am–6pm (4pm winter). €10. ℘0935 68 00 36, www.villaromana delcasale.it.
- 😊 **Don't Miss:** The fascinating **thermal complex** and the amazing attention to detail in the **Corridor of the Great Hunt** and the **Room of the Small Hunt**.
- ▶ **Location:** To get to the villa from Caltagirone or Enna, cross Piazza Armerina and take the Caltanissetta road (no direct links to this road from S 117b).
- 🕐 **Timing:** Visit the villa early in the morning, especially in summer when conditions can be unpleasant due to the large number of tour groups and the heat generated by the plexiglass roofs.
- ✕ **Where to Stay/Eat:** For hotels and restaurants, see Piazza Armerina.

rely of mosaics that survive in excellent condition. The majority of the panels are polychrome and feature mythological scenes, incidents from daily life, special occasions such as a hunt, circus games, feast days honouring the gods and a grape harvest – alternated with geometric decorations. The evocative portrayal of movement is remarkable and has been interpreted as the work of North African craftsmen.

VISIT
Terme

♿ Information on the villa's baths can also be found under Introduction: Art.

Just inside the entrance to the steam baths (on the left) is a section of the **aqueduct** that supplied the villa with water. Immediately beyond is the suite of rooms that makes up the thermal complex. In the first are the great furnaces (praefurnia) (**1**), which heated the water to generate steam, which circulated through cavities below the floors and in the walls, to heat the rooms.

The underfloor heating is visible in the **Tepidarium** (**3**): small brick columns support the floor, leaving a large cavity between the floor and the ground, through which hot air could circulate. This room was maintained at a moderate temperature for use immediately after the **Caldaria** (**2**), where saunas and the hot baths were taken.

Sala delle Unzioni (4)

The function of the small, square anointing room is reflected in the mosaic decoration. Slaves are shown preparing oil and massaging the bodies of the bathers *(the figures at the top left)*, with some of the tools of their trade: the *strigile*, a sort of curved spatula with a handle used for scraping and cleaning the skin, and a jar of oil *(figure at the top right)*.

Frigidarium (5)

The octagonal room set aside for cold baths has a central mosaic with a marine theme: cherub fishermen surrounded by tritons, nereids (sea nymphs) and dolphins. From the *frigidarium*, the **piscina** and the end of the aqueduct can be seen. Beyond the **shrine of Venus** (**6**) is the **polygonal courtyard** articulated by a colonnade. In the centre are the remains of the impluvium – a cistern in which rainwater is collected from surrounding roofs and then channelled towards the great **latrina** (**7**).

The main villa entrance was from the courtyard: on the south side you can see the remains of the entrance (**A**) comprising a central door flanked by two side doors.

Peristilium

Pass through the **vestibule** (**8**). The mosaic features figures bearing a candlestick, a branch of laurel and below, a figure with a diptych *(a book consisting of two panels)* from which he might address the master of the house and any guests. Opposite is the **lararium** (**9**), where statues of the household gods, the *lares*, were kept.

The imposing rectangular portico *(eight columns on the short sides, 10 on the longer sides)* is dominated by a great fountain with a small statue as its centrepiece.

© SCALA

Detail of the mosaic from the Corridor of the Great Hunt

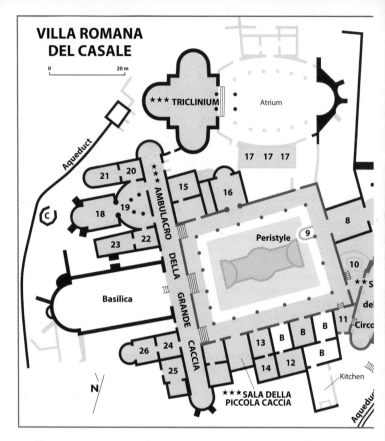

VILLA ROMANA DEL CASALE

0 ——— 20 m

★★★ TRICLINIUM

Atrium

Aqueduct

17 17 17

21 20

★★ AMBULACRO

15 16

18 19

C

23 22

8

Peristyle 9

10

Basilica

DELLA GRANDE CACCIA

★★ S...
del...

11 Circo...

13 B B B

26 24 B

14 12

25

Kitchen

N

★★★ SALA DELLA PICCOLA CACCIA

Aqueduct

The **Peristilium mosaic★★** running along all four sides of the portico is ornamented with round medallions that feature the heads of both wild and domestic animals *(bears, tigers, wild boars and panthers; horses and cows).*

Piccola latrina (10)

The floor mosaic depicts animals, including an ass, cheetah, hare and partridge.

Sala del Circo★★

The long room, apsed at both ends, represents a circus, identified as the Circus Maximus in Rome. The decoration illustrates a chariot race, the final event in the festival honouring Ceres, goddess of plenty and the harvest, whose cult was particularly popular in nearby Enna (&see Enna: Mythology). Above the *spina*, the central line around which the horses are racing, the winner receives his prize, the victory palm, while another character blows a horn to signal the end of the race.

Along the south side of the peristyle are rooms reserved for guests. Access to these was via a second **vestibule (11)**, decorated with beautiful mosaics showing the lady of the house with her children and her servants as they hold lengths of cloth and a box of oils.

Other rooms (**B**) comprised the servants' quarters and kitchen.

Sala della Danza (12)

The mosaic, unfortunately incomplete, shows women and men dancing.

Sala delle Quattro Stagioni (13)

The four seasons, after which this room is named, are personified here by two women *(spring and autumn)*, and two men *(summer and winter)*.

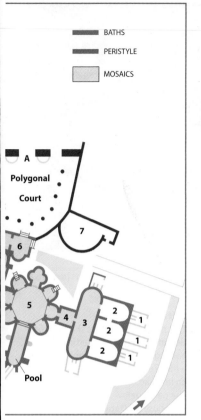

another hunter *(right)* holds up a hare. The central part of the mosaic is dominated by a banqueting scene.

Shaded by an awning, game is being cooked over a fire. There is a pause in the day's activity: the horses are tethered, the nets hung up, and the huntsmen relax around the fire.

All around are hunting scenes: at the top left, two falconers seek out birds hidden among tree branches; on the right a man encourages his dogs to follow a hare. The last panel depicts the netting of deer and a boar being speared.

Ambulacro della Grande Caccia★★★

The fabulous **Corridor of the Great Hunt** *(60m/200ft long with a recess at each end)* is the most engaging and monumental part of the whole villa.

The floor mosaic depicts an elaborate hunting scene. Panthers, lions, antelopes, boar, dromedaries, elephants, hippopotamuses and rhinoceroses are caught prior to being shipped to Roman amphitheatres.

Just beyond the midway point are three figures: the central one is presumed to be the Emperor Maximian, protected by the shields of two soldiers. Farther on, another scene shows a tiger pouncing on a crystal ball in which his image is reflected. Nearby, a controversial scene illustrates a griffin holding a box from which a boy's face peeps out.

Some maintain that the boy is bait to attract the animal, while others interpret the scene as a stark warning against the cruelty of hunting.

In the right recess, Africa is depicted as a female figure with an tusk, flanked by an elephant, a tiger and a phoenix *(&for a description of these rooms, see below)*.

Sala degli Amorini Pescatori★★ (14)

A few cupid-like cherubs aboard six boats concentrate on fishing with lines, tridents and nets, while in the centre of the composition two others play in the water with dolphins. In the upper section a large building stands on the shore, fronted by a columned portico, among palm trees and umbrella pines.

Sala della Piccola Caccia★★★

Here, in the **Room of the Small Hunt**, five panels depict the heat of the hunt. In the top left corner, a hunter releases his dogs to chase after a fox *(on the right)*. To give thanks for favourable conditions and a successful day, a sacrifice is offered to Diana, the goddess of hunting.

Two high-ranking officials burn incense on the altar while behind them, a wild boar is seen in a net *(on the left)* and

Sala delle Dieci Ragazze in Bikini★★(15)

In the **Room of the Ten Girls**, the mosaic shows two rows of girls pictured in underwear, which was commonly worn for gymnastics. The young women perform exercises: weightlifting, discus throwing, running and ball games. In the bottom row, the girl wearing a toga is

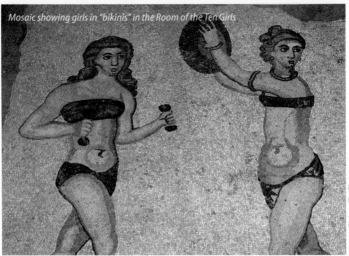

Mosaic showing girls in "bikinis" in the Room of the Ten Girls

© Antonio Zimbone/Tips/Photononstop

about to crown and award the victory palm to a girl performing with a hoop.

Diaeta di Orfeo★ (16)

The Chamber of Orpheus was reserved for playing music. At the centre is Orpheus, seated on a rock, playing the lyre and enchanting the animals that surround him. In the apse behind is a statue of Apollo.

The villa's south wing housed the main reception rooms: a central atrium is flanked by an apsed *triclinium* for meals. Two rooms on the north side (**17**) contain mosaics of cherubs harvesting grapes.

Triclinium★★★

The large central square space extends into three broad apses.

Central area

The main mosaic is dedicated to the **Twelve Labours of Heracles** (*Hercules to the Romans*). On the left is the Cretan Bull, the powerful animal sacrificed to Athene by Theseus at Marathon after it was caught by the hero. Beside it is the Hydra of Lerna, guardian of the Underworld, whose many heads were chopped off by Heracles. At the top *(in the centre)*, is the great Nemean Lion, which was slain by Heracles. Heracles wore its pelt as a cloak and its head as a helmet;

Zeus brought the lion to the heavens as a zodiac constellation.

Left apse

This mosaic represents the **glorification of Heracles**, depicted in the centre holding the hand of his nephew Lolaus, while Zeus bestows a laurel wreath on his head.

The panel below illustrates the metamorphoses of **Daphne** into a laurel *(on the left)* and of Cyparissus into a cypress *(right)*. Daphne was the nymph loved by Apollo; to escape him, she prayed to her father, a river god, and her mother, Earth, to be turned into a laurel tree. In consolation Apollo made himself a laurel wreath, which was henceforth awarded at the Pythian Games.

Central apse

The scene represents a **battle of the giants:** five huge creatures have been struck by Heracles' poisoned arrows. One of the Labours consisted of Heracles stealing the Oxen of Geryon and carrying them back to Greece. In the mosaic below, **Hesione**, daughter of the king of Troy, is threatened by a sea monster sent by Poseidon – the result of the father's failure to pay Poseidon and Apollo for their assistance in building the walls of Troy. The only way to safeguard the city from the sea monster was to sacrifice

Hesione. Heracles undertook to slay the monster on condition that the king give him his famous horses; when he again reneged on his promise, Heracles raised an army against Troy.

Right apse

On the left, three maenads *(women followers of Dionysus)* are depicted attacking Lycurgus, king of Thrace. Continue along the wall of the aqueduct. Just before a small hexagonal latrine (**C**), steps on the left lead to room 18.

Diaeta di Arione (18)

The chamber of Arion was probably dedicated to making music and reading poetry, judging by the mosaic decoration which depicts the poet and musician Arion sitting on the back of a dolphin at sea, holding a lyre and surrounded by sea nymphs, tritons and cherubs astride wild beasts and sea monsters.

Atrio degli Amorini Pescatori★★(19)

The mosaic illustrates various fishing scenes, running all the way around the semicircular portico.

Vestibolo del Piccolo Circo★★ (20)

The Vestibule of the Small Circus in the larger private apartment of the villa takes its name from another circus scene in the thermal baths, this time with children as the protagonists. Racing around the posts are chariots drawn *(working counter-clockwise from top right)* by flamingos, geese, waders and wood pigeons. Each chariot team also has a child on foot beside it, carrying an amphora and chasing the birds.

Cubicolo dei Musici e degli Attori (21)

This *cubiculum* probably served as a bedroom for the owner's daughter. In the apse, two girls sit at the foot of a tree making crowns out of flowers.

Vestibolo di Eros e Pan (22)

Dominating the antechamber is the horned figure of Pan, god of the woodlands, fighting Eros, the god of love. Next to Pan is the judge, bearded and wearing a purple toga and laurel wreath. Behind are satyrs and maenads, who are supporting Pan, and the family of the house, who are supporting Eros. Above the wrestling match is a table carrying prizes for the winner. On another level, the fight symbolises the difficulty for the ugly (Pan) to vanquish love.

Cubicolo dei Fanciulli Cacciatori★ (23)

This *cubiculum* was probably the bedroom of the son of the house-owner. At the top of the mosaic, girls collect flowers; a boy carries two rose-filled baskets on his shoulders. Lower down, a group of children kill a hare, a small antelope and capture a duck.

Walk around the large **basilica**, noting the marble-tiled floor fragments.

Vestibolo di Ulisse e Polifemo★ (24)

These mosaics illustrate the story of Odysseus *(Ulysses to the Romans)* outwitting the Cyclops Polyphemus, who has eaten some of his men, by enticing him with a cup of wine.

Cubicolo della Scena Erotica★ (25)

Surrounded by images of the four seasons, a polygonal medallion enclosed within a laurel wreath shows a man embracing a loosely-clad girl. In his left hand he holds a situla, or jar.

In the room behind the vestibule (**26**) is a luscious fruit **mosaic★** rendered with an exquisite delicacy.

Caltagirone★

Listed as a UNESCO World Heritage site since 2002, Caltagirone, also known as the "city of earthenware", has enjoyed a long love affair with ceramics, which you'll find everywhere – from its shops and homes to its bridges, balustrades, façades and balconies.

◀▪▙ WALKING TOUR

Via Roma, Caltagirone's main street, bisects the town, cutting towards the famous steps to **Santa Maria del Monte**, and continuing up to the church entrance.

Its way is lined with some of the town's most interesting buildings, many with **majolica** decoration. Near its start, on the left, begins the elegant balustraded enclosure of the **Villa Comunale** *(a public garden)* and the **Teatrino** *(housing the Ceramics Museum)*.

Villa Comunale★

This wonderful garden was designed in the late 19C by G.B. Basile, who modelled it on classic English landscapes.

The edge along Via Roma is marked by an ornamental balustrade topped with vases bearing disturbingly devilish faces. These alternate with bright green pine cones and majolica lamp standards. Shaded pathways open into secluded spaces, ornamented by ceramic sculptures, figures and fountains.

A delightful **bandstand** is decorated with Moorish elements and glazed panels of majolica.

Beyond the **Museo della Ceramica** on the right-hand side of Via Roma is the splendid 18C balcony-cum-terrace of **Casa Ventimiglia**. Beyond the **Tondo Vecchio**, the curved stone and brick building, sits the remarkable façade *(right)* of **San Francesco d'Assisi;** this overlooks the majolica bridge, also named after St Francis, which carries the road into the very heart of the town. Beyond the little **Church of Sant'Agata**, the seat of the ceramicists' confraternity,

▸ **Population:** 39 504
⚙ **Michelin Map:** p237: B2
▯ **Info:** Via Volta Libertini 4, ℘0933 53 809, www.comune.caltagirone.ct.it.
▶ **Location:** Most of the major monuments, located in the upper town, are best explored on foot.
Ⓟ **Parking:** There are parking spaces along the ringroads to the east and west of the town.
⊚ **Don't Miss:** La Villa Comunale and La Scala di S. Maria del Monte.
👥 **Kids:** Pottery workshops scattered across the town.
🕐 **Timing:** Allow half a day. The Luminaria festival is 24–25 July.

stands an austere prison block that was built under Bourbon rule.

Museo della Ceramica

Via Roma/Via Giardino Pubblico. 🕐*Open 9am–6.30pm.* ⊛€4. ♿ ℘*0933 58 418.*

The **Teatrino**, an unusual 18C building decorated with majolica tiles, houses this interesting museum. The importance of moulded clay is exemplified by an elegant 5C BC **krater★** showing a potter at his wheel, working as he is watched by a young apprentice. The 17C is particularly well represented, with *albarello* jars (apothecaries' jars) – painted in shades of yellow, blue and green – and amphorae and vases.

Carcere Borbonico

The prison, an imposing square sandstone building, has been greatly improved by recent restoration. It was designed in the late 18C by the Sicilian architect Natale Bonajuto and now houses the town's small municipal museum.

Museo Civico – *Via Roma 10.* 🕐*Open Tues–Sat 9.30am–1.30pm, Tues, Fri–Sat 4–7pm, Sun 9.30am–12.30pm.* ⊛*Free.* ℘*0933 31 590.* The second floor has a

City of Earthenware

Potteries

Sitting on inexhaustible supplies of clay, the city began its rise to prominence as a centre for terracotta pottery, before moving into tableware. Local shapes gave way to Greek influences and, as trade increased, production became more efficient and more precise with the introduction of the wheel *(by the Cretans in about 1000 BC)*.

© Giovanni Bertolissio/hemis.fr

The critical turning point, however, was in the 9C arrival, when the Arabs brought Eastern designs and – most importantly – glazing techniques, which rendered objects impermeable to water. The dominant colours were blue, green and yellow. The significance of the Arab contribution is honoured in the town's name which, according to the most intriguing hypothesis, might be derived from the Moorish word for *castle* or *fortress of vases*. With the arrival of the island's Spanish rulers, tastes and demands changed.

The painted decoration was predominantly monochrome *(blue or brown)* and comprised organic designs or the coats of arms of noble families or religious orders. The town's fortunes were further swelled by the development of other industries, including honey production.

Artisans organised themselves into confraternities, which, in turn helped to build workshops in the town's southern quarter. In addition to ceramic table and kitchenwares, Caltagirone established a reputation for tiles and ornamental plaques for domes, floors, and church and *palazzo* façades. Of all the great
artists to work here during the 16C and 17C, the Gagini brothers and Natale Bonajuti are perhaps the most renowned. With the arrival of the 19C there began a period of decline, arrested in part by the production of figurines often used in Nativity scenes. In the second half of the century, this art form reached new heights of excellence in the hands of such experts as Bongiovanni and Vaccaro.

The art of clay-working – The techniques used in Caltagirone have remained unchanged for centuries. The ductile clay mixture is worked wet, by hand, using a potter's wheel. Otherwise it is turned into a liquid and cast in a mould. The object is then left and placed in an oven to dry at a very high temperature. After firing, it is ready for use.

There are a large range of decorating techniques, including carving, graffito design or moulding with stones, shells or other objects on the unbaked article. Colour may be applied at various stages for different effects *(before or after firing, following a second firing, or cold)*. The simplest product is the porous reddish terracotta, typical of objects made in antiquity. The first *majolica* (terracotta decorated with enamel) appeared in the 16C. Porcelain is produced from a different type of clay: a white paste known as kaolin, usually with a glazed finish.

permanent exhibition of contemporary work in majolica. One room displays the gilded wood and silver litter of San Giacomo (late 16C), which was used in processions until the 1960s.

The third room is devoted to the Vaccaro family: two generations of painters active during the 19C; Mario's *Little Girl Praying* is especially evocative.

The first floor plays host to the municipal art collection of mainly Sicilian painters.

Piazza Umberto I

The most prominent building facing onto the square is the **Duomo di San Giuliano**, a great Baroque edifice that has been subject to much remodelling, including the entire front in the early-1900s. It comes into view from the steps below Santa Maria del Monte, at the foot of which, on the left, stands **Palazzo Senatorio** with the courtyard, **Corte Capitaniale**, behind. This is a fine example of early civic architecture *(1601)* by one of the Gaginis.

To the right, a stairway leads up to the **Chiesa del Gesù**, which is home to a Deposition by Filippo Paladini *(third chapel on the left)*. Behind it nestles the **Chiesa di Santa Chiara** with its elegant façade attributed to **Rosario Gagliardi** (18C) and, beyond again, the early 20C Officina Elettrica, the façade of which was designed by **Ernesto Basile**.

▷ Return to Piazza Umberto I.

Scala di Santa Maria del Monte★

This long flight of steps acts as a conjunction between the old town *(at the top)*, which accommodated the seat of religious authority in the 17C, and the new town, where the municipal administrative offices were located. On either side of this axis lie the old quarters of San Giorgio and San Giacomo; both conceal some fine buildings among their narrow streets (⊙ *see below*). The 142 **lava stair treads** are complemented by highly decorative multicoloured majolica tile uprights, echoing Moorish, Norman, Spanish,

Baroque and contemporary influence. Once a year, the stairway is brought to life by a multitude of small flickering coloured candles. This fabulous spectacle takes place on the nights of San Giacomo, 24 and 25 July. Presiding atop the steps is **Santa Maria del Monte**, formerly the town's main church and headquarters of the religious authorities. The altar is graced with the lovely Conadomini Madonna, a 13C panel painting.

San Giorgio and San Giacomo Quarters

Via L Sturzo, leading off to the right from the foot of the steps, has a number of fine buildings. These include **Palazzo della Magnolia** (no. 74), which is ornamented with exuberant and elaborate terracotta decoration by Enrico Vella. Just beyond the *palazzo* are two 19C churches: **San Domenico** and **Santissimo Salvatore**. The latter contains the mausoleum of the politician Don Luigi Sturzo and a *Madonna and Child* by **Antonello Gagini**.

At the far end of Via Sturzo stands the **Chiesa di San Giorgio** (11C–13C), home to the panel painting of the **Mystery of the Trinity★**, attributed to the Flemish artist Rogier van der Weyden.

The logical extension of Via Sturzo *(opposite side of the steps)*, is Via Vittorio Emanuele. This leads to the **Basilica di San Giacomo**, dedicated to the town's patron saint and housing a Gagini silver casket containing the relics of the saint.

ON THE EDGE OF TOWN

A stroll through the typical back streets of the old quarters on the periphery of town reveals various unexpected surprises, such as the splendid neo-Gothic façade of the **Chiesa di San Pietro**, complete with majolica decoration.

Chiesa dei Cappuccini

⊙*Open daily 9am–11.30pm, 3.30-6.30pm.* ⊛€2. ☏*0933 21 753.*

The Capuchin church on the eastern edge of the town contains an altarpiece by **Filippo Paladini**, which depicts the Hodegetria Madonna *(an icon represent-*

ing the Virgin as a Guide or Instructress pointing to the Way of Redemption, said to have been painted by St Luke).

On the nave's left side is a Deposition by Fra' Semplice da Verona, which has an interesting play on perspective. Additional paintings are displayed in the local art gallery next to the church, with works drawn from the 16C to the present day. There is access from here to the crypt, where an unusual arrangement of figures re-enact different scenes from the life of Christ.

Museo delle Ville Storiche

Villa Patti - Via Santa Maria di Gesu. ○ *Open daily 9.30am–1.30pm, 3.30–6.30pm.* ○ *Closed Tue and Thu afternoons.* ☎ *Free.* ✆ *0933 41 812.*

Housed in the elegant Villa Patti, built in the second half of the 19C, this museum offers an insight into the development of Sicilian second homes in the 18C. The display explores over 62 historic villas and ends with an exhibition of works by the photographer G.Gambino on the villas of the Val di Noto.

ADDRESSES

🏠 STAY

CALTAGIRONE

⊜⊜ **Tre metri sopra il cielo** – *Via Bongiovani 72.* ✆ *0933 1935106* or *392 312 22 38. www.bbtremetrisoprailcielo.it. 2 rooms* ⚏. With **views** of the magnificent Santa Maria staircase, the rooms in this B&B are quiet and comfortable. Breakfast is served on the roof terrace.

⊜⊜ **La Pilozza Infiorata** – *Via SS Salvatore 95-97.* ✆ *0933 22 162. www.la pilozzainfiorata.com. 5 rooms* ⚏. This delightful B&B offers spacious rooms. The terrace has **views** over the town's small streets.

NEAR CALTAGIRONE

⊜⊜ **Il Baglio di San Nicola** – *In San Nicola Le Canne, 6km/3.7mi from Caltagirone on the SP39.* ✆ *339 602 47 46 (mobile). www.ilbagliodisanicola.it. Closed out of season. 4 rooms* ⚏*, restaurant*⊜⊜. This agriturismo stands out for its incomparable, peaceful location

among beautiful hills. The restaurant offers good regional specialities.

⊜⊜ **Colle San Mauro** – *In San Mauro, 5km/3.1mi from Caltagirone on the SP39.* ✆*/fax 0933 53 890. www.collesanmauro.it.* 🅿🛉*. 16 rooms* ⚏*, restaurant*⊜⊜. A farmhouse in the hills offering spacious, comfortable rooms. A good base for exploring the region, with walking paths through the vineyards and olive groves to work up an appetite for the restaurant's local cuisine.

SAN MICHELE DI GANZARIA

⊜⊜ **Pomara** – *Via Vittorio Veneto 84, San Michele di Ganzaria, 14km/9mi NW of Caltagirone on S 124.* ✆ *0933 97 6976. www.hotelpomara.com. 40 rooms.* A rural retreat within easy distance of a town between Caltagirone and Piazza Armerina. The family-run hotel has a swimming pool, spacious rooms and classical decor.

🍽 EAT

⊜ **Non Solo Vino** – *Via V. Emanuele I.* ✆*0933 31 068. Closed Mon.* A traditional, tasteful first-floor restaurant on the corner of Piazza del Municipio. Serves excellent pasta with wild asparagus or fresh fish at the weekends. Copious antipasti buffet. Very friendly service.

SHOPPING

Glazed earthenware is on sale in countless shops in the town centre and on either side of the **Scala di Santa Maria del Monte**. In general, the further up the steps you climb, the lower the prices. For an overview, head for the Mostra Mercato Permanente in Via Vittorio Emanuele, which displays work by the town's craftsmen and women.

FESTIVALS

La Luminaria – Festa di San Giacomo – This festival for the town's patron saint falls on July 24–25, when the steps of Santa Maria del Monte are decorated with small oil lamps (*coppi*).

Festa del Presepe – The art of the *figurinai* – sculptors who created small terracotta statues for Nativity scenes *(presepe in Italian)* – flourished in Caltagirone until the end of the 18C. This tradition is celebrated from November to January, with exhibitions of different cribs held throughout the town.

The history of southeastern Sicily has been shaped by a single natural cataclysmic event: the earthquake of 1693, which destroyed dozens of towns and cities, and killed thousands of people, including two-thirds of the population of Catania. Out of the rubble rose some of the most fanciful and gravity-defying Baroque architecture the world has ever known: churches, palazzi and public squares were reborn in what UNESCO – when designating the area a World Heritage site in 2002 – called "the culmination and final flowering of Baroque art in Europe".

Highlights

The Reimagined Landscape

Although the damage caused by the earthquake differed from town to town and village to village, rebuilding brought a cohesion to the architectural landscape, as many of the same artists and architects experimented with the style of the day.

The overall effect is dramatic – one of princely ornamented towns set against a quiet, traditionally peasant backdrop. This is most poignant in the terraced hills of the green and fertile Iblei Mountains. The towns are small and different enough to make for a road trip that is at once relaxing and exciting.

Each new centre offers something special – its own use of Baroque, combined with local traditions, agriculture and twists on Sicilian cuisine.

Noto

In many ways, Noto looks like the prototypical Baroque town. Walking the straight Corso Vittorio Emanuele between the façades of its grand struc-tures, you sometimes feel as if you've stumbled across an operatic stage set.

Ragusa

In contrast, Ragusa is divided between the modern post-earthquake town and the rebuilt medieval town, Ragusa Ibla. It stretches over three hills connected by a small valley easily walked on foot. Ibla's fantastically imaginative ornamentation, combined with its small medieval streets, makes it a one-of-kind architectural experience.

Siracusa

Set by the sea, Syracuse is the most storied town in this part of Sicily. Cicero described it as the "greatest Greek city and most beautiful of all".

The layers of civilisation, from an impressive collection of Greek remains through to Baroque make for what UNESCO describes as "a unique testimony to the development of Mediterranean civilisation over three millennia".

The landscape is dotted with prehistoric sites, including the Cava d'Ispica, between Modica and Ispica – a natural cave filled with neolithic sanctuaries and burial chambers.

The local cuisine also tends to be very different from the rest of the island. Almonds are used extensively in everything from Pesto Ragusana pasta to the almond milk served for breakfast. The Iblei Mountains produce some of Italy's most fragrant olive oil and a selection of honeys. The region also makes some of Sicily's most noteworthy red wines, including Cerasuolo di Vittoria *(the only wine in Sicily afforded DOCG status)* and the single-grape varietal Nero d'Avola.

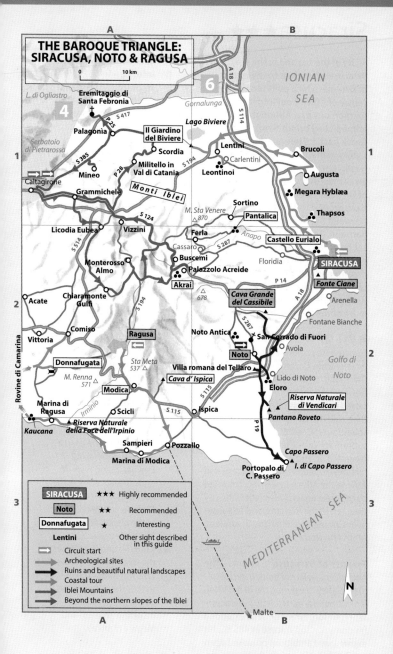

THE BAROQUE TRIANGLE: SIRACUSA, NOTO & RAGUSA

0   10 km

4

6

IONIAN SEA

L. di Ogliastro

Eremitaggio di Santa Febronia

Palagonia

Gornalunga

Lago Biviere

Serbatoio di Pietrarossa

Il Giardino del Biviere

Scordia

Lentini

Carlentini

Brucoli

S 417

P 25

S 385

Mineo

P 28

Militello in Val di Catania

S 194

Leontinoi

Augusta

Caltagirone

Grammichele

Monti Iblei

S 124

Megara Hyblæa

Thapsos

Licodia Eubea

Vizzini

M. Sta Venere △ 870

Ferla

Pantalica

Sortino

Anapo

Castello Eurialo

S 514

Monterosso Almo

Cassaro

S 287

Buscemi

Palazzolo Acreide

Floridia

SIRACUSA

▲ *Fonte Ciane*

Acate

Chiaramonte Gulfi

S 194

Akrai

△ 678

Cava Grande del Cassibile

S 287

P 14

A 18

Arenella

Comiso

Vittoria

Ragusa

Sta Meta 537 △

Noto Antica

✕ **San Corrado di Fuori**

Fontane Bianche

Noto

Avola

Donnafugata

M. Renna 571 △

Modica

Cava d' Ispica

S 115

Villa romana del Tellaro ▲

Lido di Noto

Golfo di Noto

Irmino

Scicli

Eloro

Riserva Naturale di Vendicari

Marina di Ragusa

Ispica

▲ Pantano Roveto

Riserva Naturale della Foce dell'Irpinio

P 19

Kaucana

Sampieri

Pozzallo

Marina di Modica

Capo Passero

Portopalo di C. Passero

▲ *I. di Capo Passero*

Rovine di Camarina

SIRACUSA ★★★ Highly recommended

Noto ★★ Recommended

Donnafugata ★ Interesting

Lentini   Other sight described in this guide

⇨ Circuit start

Archeological sites

Ruins and beautiful natural landscapes

Coastal tour

Iblei Mountains

Beyond the northern slopes of the Iblei

MEDITERRANEAN SEA

N

Malte

Siracusa★★★

A city of the sea and in the sea, Syracuse extends onto the island of Ortygia, which pulls the city's centre of gravity out into its harmonious bay. Although its name immediately brings to mind its Greek past, its tyrant rulers and its rivalry with Athens and Carthage, a lesser- known period of its history awaits discovery in the narrow lanes of Ortygia, where time seems to have ground to a halt somewhere between the Middle Ages and Baroque. Accented by dusty palaces set between characteristic dead ends, the historic centre is a place of dreams and solitude. The restoration of many Ortygian buildings is now finally underway, revealing even more of the island's original beauty.

A BIT OF HISTORY

Syracuse was colonised in the 8C BC by Greeks from Corinth, who settled on the island of **Ortygia**. It wasn't long, however, before this powerbase was seized by a succession of tyrants. Under their rule the city enjoyed success and splendour (5C–4C BC), establishing its supremacy over the rest of Sicily. Between 416 BC and 413 BC, a furious conflict developed between Syracuse and Athens, the Athenian warriors being led by the great general Alcibiades. The city then fell to the Romans, and to subsequent invaders – barbarians, Byzantines, Arabs and Normans.

Tyrants of Syracuse – Tyrants - the Ancient equivalent of modern dictators - played a key role during the island's Hellenistic period, particularly in Syracuse. When **Gelon**, tyrant of Gela, extended his dominion to Syracuse in 485 BC, his expansionist ambitions provoked open conflict with the hostile Carthaginians. Gelon, in alliance with **Theron**, the tyrant of Akragas (Agrigento), succeeded in defeating them at the battle of Himera in 480 BC. He himself was succeeded by his brother **Hieron I** (478–467 BC), and it was during his reign that

▶ **Population:** 124 083

⌖ **Michelin Map:** p265: B2

ⓘ **Info:** Via Roma 31; ✆0931 46 29 46. Via Maestranza 33, Ortygia; ✆0931 46 42 55. www.comune.siracusa.it.

◖ **Location:** The historical centre, situated on the island of Ortygia, is linked to the mainland by the Ponte Nuovo. Just behind Ortygia lies Akradina, the modern and commercial part of town crossed by Corso Gelone. The Neapolis quarter contains the archaeological area. To the east of Neapolis lies Tyche, an ancient residential area named for the goddess of fortune. Dominating the remainder of the city is the Epipolae *("upper town")* – a section of the city once guarded by the strategically positioned castle of Euryalus.

🅿 **Parking:** Leave your car in the Ponte Nuovo area and use the bridge to Ortygia.

⊛ **Don't Miss:** The charm of the historic island of Ortygia, going back in time at Teatro Greco, the acoustics at Orecchio di Dionisio and the collections at the Museo Archeologico Regionale Paolo Orsi.

👥 **Kids:** Testing the echoes at the **Orecchio di Dionisio**.

🕐 **Timing:** Allow one full day to tour the surrounding archaeological sites, including Thapsos and Megara Hyblaea.

Cumae was assisted in averting the Etruscan threat (474 BC).
After a brief period of democracy, punctuated by battles against Athens, **Dionysius the Elder** acceded to the

GETTING THERE AND AROUND

The nearest airport is **Fontanarossa airport in Catania**, which is linked to Syracuse by buses that run daily *(1hr)*. Buses leave from **Piazzale San Antonio to Catania** *(approx. 1hr)*, Palermo *(4hr)*, Ragusa *(2hr)* and a number of other destinations. For further information, contact the following two bus companies: **AST**, *℘840 000 323; www.azienda sicilianatrasporti.it*, and **Interbus**, *℘0931 42 525; www.interbus.it*.

A train service also operates from Syracuse to Catania *(1hr 30min)*, Messina *(3hr)*, Ragusa *(approx. 2hr)* and Taormina *(2hr 15min)*.

Cars are only allowed onto Ortygia at certain times. You are strongly advised to park at Talete (northeast of Ortygia, just after the C1 bridge (€1 8am–2pm, €0.60 2–10pm, €1 10pm–8am). Take the free shuttle to any part of the island (every 10–20 mins).

From Ortygia, a taxi to the Teatro Greco will cost €10 (always negotiate in advance). You can also rent a bike or scooter at Hollywood Rent (Via dei Mille 51; *℘0931 46 13 51; €7/day)*.

SIGHTSEEING

Antico mercato d'Ortigia – *Open Mon– Sat, 7am– 1pm.* Syracuse's old covered market *(Via Trento 2)* built at the beginning of the 20C but abandoned in the mid-1980s is now home to tourist agencies selling excursions, guided tours, tickets for local transport and cultural events, and audioguides.

Syracuse by sea – Boat trips around the Porto Grande and Ortygia by motor launch are operated by Motonave Selene. Excursions along the coast provide a different perspective on the town. Outings last on average 35min, but may be extended on request; they can also include lunch or dinner by prior arrangement. This is also the only means of seeing Castello Maniace.

Trips run Mar–Nov *(and at other times of year, depending on sea and weather conditions)* by appointment only. *℘0931 79 10 33 or 340 05 58 769.*

throne (405–367 BC). He refused the discredited title of tyrant and adopted instead that of **strategòs autokrátor**, meaning "Absolute General".

The shrewd strategist underpinned his government by courting popular opinion, which he secured with gifts and favours, and nurturing his reputation as the defender against the Punic threat – which he did not, however, succeed in eliminating. During his tyrannical rule, Syracuse became an independent and mighty force in its own right.

On a more personal level, Dionysius I appears to have been haunted by suspicions that someone might be plotting against him. His fears developed into manias of persecution and culminated in the decision to retreat with his court to the castle of Ortygia. Writers such as Valerius Maximus, Cicero and Plutarch describe how the tyrant was so distrustful of the barbarians that he entrusted the task of shaving to his daughters, but fearing even they might murder him, he insisted that walnut shells be used rather than razors; he had a ditch dug around his marital bed with a bridge that he could remove when he retired for the night and a sword suspended from a horsehair above the head of an envious member of his court called Damocles (hence the expression "the sword of Damocles" to allude to a looming threat).

Upon his death, he was succeeded on the throne by his son **Dionysius (II) the Younger**, who lacked the political astuteness of his father; he was briefly toppled by his uncle **Dion** in 357 BC, who in turn was assassinated four years later. Dionysius II was expelled a second time following a desperate plea from the Syracusans to the mother-city Corinth; in 344 BC **Timoleon**, a general, was sent to the rescue; a wise and moderate

Palazzo delle Poste and port

© Bruno Morandi / hemis.fr

statesman, he restored peace to Sicily. There followed **Agathocles**, who didn't flinch from murdering members of the aristocracy to secure his grip on power; his attempts to rout the Carthaginians from Sicily were unsuccessful and culminated in his defeat at Himera in 310 BC. The last tyrant to govern Syracuse was **Hieron II** (269–216 BC), a mild and just ruler celebrated by Theocritus (*Idyll xvi*), who oversaw the last Golden Age of Syracuse and entered an alliance with Rome against the Carthaginians in the First Punic War. In 212 BC, despite the clever devices designed by Archimedes, the town fell to Roman rule and became the capital of the Roman Province of Sicily.

Archimedes – No reliable source of information exists for the life of Archimedes, the mathematician, born in Syracuse in 287 BC. It is said that he was so absorbed by his research that he even forgot to eat and drink; his servants were forced to drag him to the public baths, where he continued to draw geometric shapes in the ash. It was while soaking in his bath that he came upon the principle that ensured his fame: a body immersed in a liquid is subject to a force equal to the weight of the volume of the liquid that has been displaced. Thrilled with this discovery, he stood up suddenly and rushed from the house shouting "Eureka!" (I've got it!).

Besides his contributions to the study of arithmetic, geometry, physics, astronomy and engineering, Archimedes is credited with several significant mechanical inventions, notably the Archimedes Screw – a cylinder containing a spiral screw for moving liquid uphill, like a pump; the cogwheel; celestial spheres and burning glasses – a combination of lenses and mirrors with which he succeeded in setting fire to the Roman fleet.

According to tradition, Archimedes was so deeply involved in his calculations when the Romans succeeded in penetrating the city that he died from a sword wound inflicted by a Roman soldier, oblivious to what was happening.

Poetic muses – During Antiquity, the city occupied a major role in the arts. Several of its rulers became so taken with the power of patronage that before long established foreign poets and writers were welcomed to their court. Some, like Dionysius the Elder, tried to establish themselves as writers but without success. The first to take an effective interest was Hieron I, who proclaimed himself protector of poets and invited illustrious figures such as Bacchylides, Xenophon and Simonides, and competitive rival poets **Pindar** and **Aeschylus** to his court.

In contrast, **Plato** endured difficult relations with Syracuse, particularly with its rulers. Dionysius the Elder reluctantly welcomed him, only to expel him shortly afterwards; after his demise, the philosopher returned (under protection of the regent Dion), only to be expelled a second time – by Dionysius II – after failing to persuade the tyrant to accept the principles of his Utopian state (outlined later in his *Republic*).

Theocritus, the protagonist of a kind of bucolic poetry at which Virgil was later to excel, was probably a native of Syracuse.

More recently, **Salvatore Quasimodo** (1901–68) was born in Syracuse. A terse poet obsessed with the malaise of life, he won the Nobel Prize for Literature in 1959.

PARCO ARCHEOLOGICO DELLA NEAPOLIS ★★★

&♿⏲*Open daily, May–Sept 9am–6pm (other months, contact for details).* ✆€10. ☎0931 66 206. *The main entrance is on Viale Paradiso (buses 1, 6, 10, 13 and 19, stop Via Paolo Orsi). Another smaller entrance can be found on Via Rizzo.*

TEATRO GRECO ★★★

This is one of the most impressive theatres to survive from Antiquity. The *cavea*, cut out from the bedrock, took full dramatic advantage of the natural slope of Colle Temenite.

The theatre was modified by Hieron II in the 3C BC, when it was divided into nine wedge-shaped sections, and a passageway was inserted around the *cavea*, about halfway up. The wall in front of each section is inscribed with the name of a famous person or deity. Today, certain letters may still be distinguished, including those spelling out Olympian Zeus in the central section; to the right, facing the stage, appear the letters naming Hieron II, his wife and his daughter-in-law. The theatre was altered in Roman times, possibly to host gladiatorial combats before the amphitheatre (♿*see below*) was completed. Later, the Spaniards installed waterdriven millstones here: the furrows left by mill-wheels in the *cavea* can still be seen, as can the drainage channel.

Behind the cavea is a large, open area with the **Grotta del Ninfeo** (*Nymph's Cave*) in the centre. The rectangular tank set before it was filled with water drawn from the aqueduct that was built by the Greeks. Having fallen into disuse during the Middle Ages, the aqueduct was restored in the 16C by the Marchese di Sortinoto in order to power the watermills erected in the theatre.

To the left extends the **Via dei Sepolcri** (*Street of Tombs*). Marking the rockface on each side are a series of Byzantine tombs and votive niches.

ORECCHIO DI DIONISIO ★★★

The haunting cave known as the "Ear of Dionysius" is situated in one of the most striking former limestone quarries (*latomie*) in Siracusa: the aptly-named

Teatro Greco

© Ventura69/Dreamstime.com

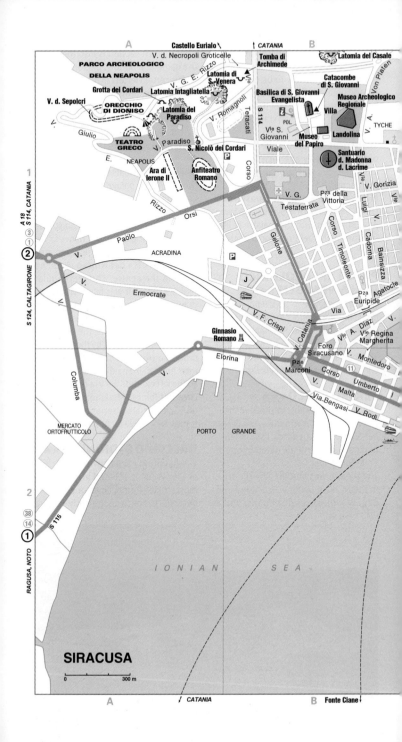

SIRACUSA

Orecchio di Dionisio

© Vito Arcomano / Fototeca ENIT

👥⛰**Latomia del Paradiso★★**, now a delightful garden shaded with orange trees, palm trees and magnolias. As its name suggests, the cave resembles an auricle *(cavity inside the ear)*, both in the shape of the entrance and the winding internal space beyond. It was the artist **Caravaggio** who gave the cave its name during his visit to Sicily in the early 1600s, on hearing the intriguing explanation of how Dionysius the Elder was able to hear his enemies without seeing them, thanks to the cave's extraordinary echo. The cave has amazing acoustics, which both guides and visitors will occasionally test by suddenly bursting into song.

The neighbouring **Grotta dei Cordari** was used until fairly recently as a cool place where rope-makers would work, twisting stretches of twine.

ARA DI IERONE II

This enormous altar, 200m/650ft partly carved out of the rock, was commissioned by the tyrant Hieron II in the 3C BC for public sacrifices. Originally, a large rectangular area may have stretched out in front, probably with a portico and a central pool.

ANFITEATRO ROMANO★

The Roman amphitheatre was built during the Imperial era. The rectangular pit in the centre of the arena is connected to the southern entrance by a ditch. This "technical" area was reserved for the stage machinery that provided special effects during performances.

Opposite the amphitheatre entrance stands the pre-Romanesque Church of **San Nicolò dei Cordari** (11C). To the right, sits a Roman water tank used to flood the amphitheatre for performances of *naumachiae* (re-enactments of sea battles) and for cleaning the arena after the gory fights between gladiators and wild animals.

TOMBA DI ARCHIMEDE

Visible from the outside only from the corner of Via Romagnoli and Via Teracati.

At the eastern end of Latomia Intagliatella are the **Grotticelli Necropolis**. Among the cavities hollowed out of the rock, one is ornamented with Doric columns *(now badly damaged)*, pediment and tympanum. This "Tomb of Archimedes" actually conceals a Roman *columbarium* (a chamber lined with niches for funerary urns).

AROUND THE ARCHAEOLOGICAL PARK

MUSEO ARCHEOLOGICO REGIONALE PAOLO ORSI★★

Viale Teocrito 66. 🕐*Open 9am–7pm, Sun and public holidays 9am–2pm.* 🕐*Closed Mon.* ⬤€8. ♿ 📞*0931 46 40 22.*

Set in the garden of the **Villa Landolina**, the Paolo Orsi Museum provides an unrivalled insight into Sicily's prehistory up to the period of the sub-colonies of Syracuse.

The artefacts are presented chronologically in three main sections. There is also a basement auditorium, where audiovisual presentations are given (♿*See programme schedule at the entrance*).

Section A: Prehistory and protohistory

The displays open with a collection of fossils and minerals, skeletons and prehistoric animal remains, along with information about the island's fauna. The models of two **dwarf elephants** found in the Grotta di Spinagallo in Syracuse (*the originals are in Rome's Museo di Paleontologia*) are of particular interest; these were thought to have been at the root of the Cyclops myth, through a mistaken interpretation of the hole created by the elephant's trunk. Human artefacts representing the Palaeolithic and Neolithic eras are followed by specimens dating from successive phases. Most of the artefacts are pottery fragments, including a simple, yet highly sophisticated red-burnished **vase★** mounted on a very high foot, characteristic of Pantalica.

The section ends with a display of miscellaneous bronze objects (*spearheads, belts and buckles*) not included in the rest of the section.

Section B: Greek colonisation

These objects illustrate the foundation and development of Greek colonies in eastern Sicily. The three Ionic colonies were Naxos, Katane and Leontinoi, from where the beautiful headless marble **kouros** (*Archaic male figure*) came. The two Doric colonies were Megara Hyblaea and Syracuse, both of which are extremely well represented. The singular limestone figure of the **Mothergoddess★** nursing twins (6C BC) was recovered from the necropolis at Megara Hyblaea. Seated and headless, the figure powerfully embodies maternity, extending her arms to embrace and contain two babies that seem to melt into her, as if all three were one.

The Syracuse collection is vast and includes two famous exhibits, which are often reproduced: a polychrome shallow-relief clay panel with a **gorgon**, and the bronze statuette of a horse, the museum's symbol, which was found in the necropolis at Fusco.

At the entrance to this section devoted to Syracuse is the splendid headless statue of **Venus Anadyomene★** or Landolina Venus (*after the man who discovered her*). This Roman copy of an original by Praxiteles is one of many made in Antiquity (*others include the Medici Venus, the Capitoline Venus*) characterised by sinuous lines. The poise with which she holds the drapery is underlined by the delicate way in which the fabric falls into folds to echo the perfect shape of a shell.

Section C: Sub-colonies and Hellenised centres

The first part, devoted to the sub-colonies of Syracuse, contains a selection of various anthropomorphic figures, including a clay *acroterion* representing a **rider on horseback**. The second part details the history of minor centres. Note the tall clay sculpted enthroned figure of **Demeter** or **Kore** dating from the latter half of the 6C BC.

The third and last part of this section is devoted to Agrigento and Gela. The strikingly painted **Gorgon's mask** (*part of a decorative temple frieze*), comes from Gela, as does the fine Attic red-figure *pelike (two-handled vase)* by the painter Polygnotos. Three wooden **Archaic statuettes** are rare examples of votive art: although these were probably widespread, in most cases the wood will have perished with time.

CATACOMBE DI SAN GIOVANNI★★

Via S. Giovanni alle Catacombe
Open Tue–Sun, 9.30am–12.30pm, 2.30–5.30pm; in summer 10am–1pm, 2.30–6pm. €8. 0931 64 694.

The catacombs are situated in the Akradina area, which until Roman times was reserved for the cult of the dead. Unlike the Roman catacombs elsewhere in mainland Italy, which are excavated from fragile tufa, which restricted their size (due to the threat of collapse), these catacombs are cut out from a layer of hard limestone. This meant that they could therefore be safely extended into considerably larger underground chambers.

This complex system of catacombs was developed around the tomb of

St Marcian, one of the early Christian martyrs (4C–5C). The extensive network of rectilinear tunnels depends upon a central axis that probably followed the lines of an abandoned Greek aqueduct. At right angles to this principal artery lead a series of minor vein-like passageways. The chambers vary in size according to whether they accommodated a single person or several *(maximum 20 people)*. Interspersed among these large cavities are a number of smaller and shallower hollows for children.

At intervals, there appear round or square areas used by Christians for interring martyrs and saints. The most significant of these is the *Rotonda di Adelfia*, in which a wonderful sarcophagus was found intact, carved with biblical scenes *(awaiting display, possibly on the second floor of the archaeological museum)*. Note also, beside the main gallery, the Greco-Roman conical cisterns, later used as burial chambers.

Cripta di San Marciano

The Crypt of St Marcian, situated near the necropolis, marks the place where the martyr is alleged to have met his death.

The Greek-cross chamber lies 5m/16ft below ground level. The far wall accommodates three semicircular apses: the right one is the altar where St Paul is supposed to have preached on his return from Malta in AD 60 *(Acts of the Apostles,* Ch 28 v12); against the right wall of the central apse sits the tomb popularly believed to be that of the martyr.

The peep-hole inserted on one side was to enable the pilgrims to see the body and to allow a cloth to be passed over it and then kept as a relic.

Basilica di San Giovanni Evangelista

The church stands over the crypt of St Marcian. This picturesque ruin, open to the sky, is one of the most atmospheric spots in Syracuse, especially at sunset, and even more intensely on saints' days and holidays when Mass is celebrated. Founded in association with the martyr's crypt, the basilica was destroyed by the Arabs, but restored by the Normans.

The main frontage of the Norman church, ornamented with a lovely rose-window, is still visible on the left flank. The main damage was incurred during an earthquake when the roof collapsed. The **interior**, now partly taken over by clumps of tree spurge *(Euphorbia dendroides)*, preserves its original Byzantine main altar.

MUSEO DEL PAPIRO

Via Teocrito 66. ◐*Open daily 9am–2pm.* ◐*Closed Mon.* ✉*Donations welcome.* ✆*0931 61 616.*

The rediscovery of papyrus in Syracuse can be attributed to Saverio Landolina, who in the 18C, reassessed the value

Catacombe di San Giovanni

© Sandro Bedessi / Fototeca ENIT

Papyrus, Fonte Aretusa

© Giovanni Simeone/Sime/Photononstop

Papyrus and the Origins of Paper

The *Cyperus papyrus* plant grows vigorously in Egypt and has thrived in Syracuse since Antiquity along the banks of the River Ciane *(see Excursions)*. A perennial marsh plant, it grows in various forms and sizes, and produces a profusion of tall stems ending with ruffs of bracts. In Ancient Egypt, it was used in all kinds of different ways to exploit its amazing versatility: the stems were bundled together to build lightweight boats or woven to make ropes, baskets and trays, clothes, wigs, and even shoes (such as sandals). The ruff at the top was used to make fans and parasols for civil or religious ceremonies and funeral rites. It has even been suggested that the most tender, spongy part of the stalk may have been eaten.

The most famous product made from papyrus is paper, although this involves a fairly complex process. Selected according to its age (a determining factor), small strips of papyrus, cross-cut from the stems, are placed in basins to strengthen them prior to the bleaching process. The strips are then laid in two perpendicular layers one on top of the other, and pressed and dried. The resulting sheet has a flat surface (with horizontal fibres) suitable for writing, backed and supported by the vertical fibres. It is interesting to note that in many languages the word for paper actually comes from the word "papyrus" (French *papier*, German *Papier*, Spanish *papel*, Welsh *papur* and so on).

The material displayed in the Museo del Papiro covers all possible applications of papyrus. This includes documents from the time of the pharaohs (fragments of the *Book of the Dead*); objects made of rope; fans made from the same variety of plant; and featherweight boats with slightly raised prows and sterns adept for navigating through shallow waters and marshy areas, and still very much in use by hunters and fishermen in Africa. The last section is dedicated to paper, its actual production *(reconstruction of a workbench)*, as well as the pigments and instruments used by scribes.

Santa Lucia

St Lucy, the patron saint of Syracuse, lived here in the 4C, and many local churches are dedicated to her, including the Duomo. Her *dies natalis*, on 13 December, when her earthly life came to an end and her spiritual life began, is celebrated with a procession headed by the silver statue of the saint from the Duomo to the place where she was entombed.

of the plant, which was being used by the local population at that time for decoration. He also succeeded in reinventing the art of paper-making *(several examples can be seen in the museum)*.

SANTUARIO DELLA MADONNA DELLE LACRIME

Via Santuario 3 ⏰*Open daily, 7am–1pm, 3–8pm.* ✆*0931 21 446; www.madonnadellelacrime.it.*

Ortygia

"Sicanio praetenta sinu iacet insula contra

Plemyrium undosum; nomen dixere priores

Ortygiam. Alpheum fama est huc Elidis amnem

occultas egisse vias subter mare, qui nunc ore,

Arethusa, tuo Siculis confunditur undis."

"Stretched in front of a Sicanian bay lies an island, over against wave-beaten Plemyrium; men of old called it Ortygia. Hither, so runs the tale, Alpheus, river of Elis, forced a secret course beneath the sea, and now at thy fountain, Arethusa, mingles with the Sicilian waves."

Virgil, *The Aeneid,* Book III (lines 692–95).

This modern, conical structure in reinforced concrete *(80m/262ft in diameter and 74m/243ft high)* dominates the skyline. Its construction was prompted by what locals believe was a miraculous event that occurred in 1953, when a painting of the Madonna shed tears. Since then, the shrine has attracted large numbers of pilgrims.

SANTA LUCIA EXTRA MŒNIA

Piazza S. Lucia ⏰*Open daily 9.30am–12.30pm, 3–6pm.* ⊜*€8 (guided tours of the catacombs by reservation).* ✆*0931 64 694. www.basilicasantalucia.com.*

This basilica faces onto its own piazza. According to tradition, it was erected to mark the spot where the saint was martyred in 303, as **Caravaggio** suggests in his painting of the subject *(now in Palazzo Bellomo).*

The original Byzantine church underwent considerable changes over the years to arrive at its present form in the 15C–16C.

The oldest extant parts are the front entrance, the three semicircular apses and the two lower tiers of the bell tower (12C). The painted wooden ceiling is 17C. Below the church lie the **Catacombs of Santa Lucia** (⚿ *closed to visitors without an appointment).*

Still in the same square, the small octagonal building contains the tomb of the saint. Her actual relics, however, were transported to Constantinople in the 11C by the Byzantine general George Maniakes, and then to the Duomo in Venice, following the fall of Constantinople during the Fourth Crusade.

GINNASIO ROMANO

The Roman Gymnsasium, situated on Via Elorina just beyond the **Foro Siracusano**, formed part of the market place of ancient Akradina, along with the Forum. It was part of a complex that comprised a *quadroporticus*, with a small theatre – seating is still visible in the cavea – and a small marble temple, which served as a stage set.

ORTYGIA★★★

The island of Ortygia, the city's most ancient settlement, is linked to the mainland by the Ponte Nuovo, a natural extension of one of Syracuse's main thoroughfares, Corso Umberto I.

The sea has a much more powerful presence, and the harbour, filled with colourful boats, stretches to the right and to the left.

Along the seafront lies a lovely neo-Gothic red-plastered *palazzo*, once the home of poet and writer **Antonio Cardile** *(b. Messina 1883, d. Siracusa 1951)*.

The linearity of the **Porta Marina** is interrupted by a Catalan aedicule framing the entrance to Passeggio Adorno, a 19C walltop walkway.

The view also includes the Porto Grande, where several bloody naval battles were fought in Antiquity.

FONTE ARETUSA★

The Fountain of Arethusa played a significant role in persuading the first group of colonists to settle here in Antiquity. Legend relates how Arethusa, one of Artemis' nymphs, tormented by the demonstrations of love from a hunter named **Alpheus**, looked to the goddess for help.

Artemis turned Arethusa into a stream so that she might escape underground and re-emerge on the island of Ortygia as a freshwater spring or fountain. Alpheus, meanwhile, changed himself into an underground river, crossed the Ionian Sea and came up in Ortygia, having mingled his waters with those of Arethusa.

Today, the fountain sustains palm trees and clumps of papyrus, ducks and drakes. Looming on the horizon on the far side sits the **Castello Maniace** *(the castle is generally open to visitors from 9am–1pm; €4; for more information call ☎0931 46 44 20)*, a sandstone fortress built by Frederick II of Swabia in the first half of the 13C. Its name honours the Byzantine general **George Maniakes**, who in 1038 tried to rescue Ortygia from the Arabs and then fortified the island. The massive square structure is a typical Swabian construction: the architectural features are both functional and cosmetic, suggesting the castle was conceived to function as a defensive stronghold and also as a bold visual reminder of Swabian authority.

Cross the tip of the island to reach the eastern shore for **views** of the castle *(the best view, however, is from the sea)*; pass in front of the Church of **Santo Spirito**, with its three-tiered white façade unified by volutes and decorative pilasters. Farther along, in Via **S. Martino**, the **Church of San Martino**, whose origins date back to the 6C, is fronted by a Catalan-Gothic style doorway.

Continue along Via S. Martino to the **Church of San Benedetto**, with its fine coffered ceiling, and the adjacent Galleria Regionale di Palazzo Bellomo.

GALLERIA REGIONALE DI PALAZZO BELLOMO★

Via Capodieci 14–16. ◷*Open daily, 9am–7pm, Sun and holidays 9am–1pm.* ◷*Closed Mon.* ✆*€8.* ♿*.* ☎*0931 61 340.* Palazzo Bellomo, first built under Swabian rule (13C), was extended and raised in the 15C, giving it two different styles: at ground level it has the appearance of a fortress, while the first floor has elegant three-light windows separated with columns. The *palazzo* was built as a private residence before being acquired by the nuns from the adjoining convent of St Benedict in the 18C. Today, it is all part of the same museum.

Museum

The museum is mainly devoted to Sicilian art. However, Byzantine influences can be found in a series of paintings *(Room IV)* by Venetian artists working in Crete (at a time when it formed part of the Venetian Empire). These show *The Creation (six panels)*, *Original Sin* and *Earthly Paradise*. The upper floor is largely devoted to paintings: the most striking – although damaged – is the **Annunciation★** by **Antonello da Messina**. There is an inherent Flemish quality to this picture in its minute attention to detail; the overall formality, spacious composition and precise definition of perspective is more typically Italian. In The **Entombment of St Lucy★** by **Caravaggio**, the artist's characteristically dramatic and provocative style is evident in the arrangement of the crowd: the main figures jostling around the dead saint are the gravediggers, including one in the foreground who has turned his back to the onlookers.

The museum also displays an eclectic collection of objects: furnishings, holy vestments, Nativity figures, furniture and ceramics.

▶ Take Via Capodieci, then turn right into Via Vergini.

PIAZZA DUOMO★★

The attractive irregular square precedes the cathedral, curving at one end to accommodate its majestic front elevation. The open space becomes especially dramatic when the cathedral façade is caught by the setting sun or floodlit after nightfall. The other fine Baroque buildings enclosing the square include the **Palazzo Beneventano del Bosco**, which conceals an attractive courtyard, and opposite, **Palazzo del Senato**, whose inner courtyard displays an 18C senator's carriage; at the far end stands the **church of Santa Lucia**.

Next to Santa Lucia, the former convent and church of **Montevergini** houses the Galleria Civica di Arte Contemporanea.

GALLERIA CIVICA D'ARTE CONTEMPORANEA

⏱*Open during exhibitions only* ♿ ☎*0931 24 902.*
The former convent and Church of Montevergini *(entrance in Via delle Vergini)* houses the municipal collection of contemporary art.

DUOMO★

The area now occupied by the cathedral has been a place of worship since early Antiquity. A temple erected in the 6C BC was replaced by a temple dedicated to Athena, built with the booty taken from the Carthaginians after their defeat at

Himera (480 BC). In the 7C AD, the temple was incorporated into a Christian church.

It was then possibly converted into a mosque by the island's Arab rulers before being restored for Christian use by the Normans. The 1693 earthquake caused the front façade to collapse; it was rebuilt in the Baroque style (18C) by the Palermo architect Andrea Palma. The entrance is preceded by an atrium screening a fine doorway flanked by a pair of twisted columns, the spirals of which are decorated with vines and grapes *(a symbol of the Passion)*.

Inside, the right side of the south aisle incorporates the temple columns; today these frame the entrance into the lateral chapels. The first bay *(on the right)* contains a Greek marble krater font, supported protectively by seven small 13C wrought-iron lions.

The next **chapel**, dedicated to **St Lucy**, has an 18C silver altar front. The silver figure of the saint in the niche is by Pietro Rizzo (1599). Elsewhere, the cathedral is furnished with statues by the various **Gagini**: the *Virgin* is by **Domenico**; *St Lucy (north aisle)* and the *Madonna della Neve* in the north apse are by **Antonello Gagini**. Via Landolina, north of the piazza, accommodates the **Chiesa dei Gesuiti**.

From the church, make your way to the nearby **Piazza Archimede**. This square was constructed more recently. Presiding over the central space, overlooked by fine buildings, is the 19C **fountain of Artemis**.

Arkimedéion – *Piazza Archimede 11.* ⏱*Open 9am–7pm.* 💶*€6.* ☎*0931 611 21. www.arkimedeion.it.* On the square's northern flank, the Palazzo Pupillo is home to a new museum dedicated to Archimedes and his discoveries.

A series of interactive displays provide you with an insight into the mathematician's experiments and discoveries, his helicentric theory and ship-burning mirrors.

PALAZZO MERGULESE-MONTALTO★

Via Montalto.

This superb, though rather dilapidated, *palazzo* dates from the 14C. The upper section is ornamented with highly elaborate **windows★★**, set into richly carved arched settings subdivided by slender, twisted columns.

▶ Return to Piazza Archimede.

VIA DELLA MAESTRANZA★

Via della Maestranza is one of Ortygia's main thoroughfares and also one of the oldest. It threads its way between a succession of aristocratic residences, predominantly Baroque in style. Among the most interesting are: **Palazzo Interlandi Pizzuti** *(no. 10)* and, a little farther on, **Palazzo Impellizzeri** *(no. 17)*, with its sinuously linear arrangement of curved windows and balconies. **Palazzo Bonanno** *(no. 33)*, which now accommodates the headquarters of the tourist office, is an austere medieval building sheltering an inner courtyard and a first floor loggia. At no. 72 stands the **Palazzo Romeo Bufardeci**, with its exuberant frontage and Rococo balconies.

The street opens out into a small square before the **Church of San Francesco all'Immacolata** flanked by a 19C bell tower. The elegant front elevation is gracefully articulated with columns and pilasters. At one time the church used to host a ritual rooted in Antiquity: on the 28 November the *Svelata* (literally, the unveiling) took place, during which an image of the Madonna was unveiled. This event occurred in the early hours before dawn *(so that people could go to work, in an era when the working day started very early)* after a long vigil accompanied by local bands. Almost at the end of the street is the curved façade of **Palazzo Rizza** *(no. 110)*. **Palazzo Impellizzeri** *(no. 99)* dominates the view, rising to its full height through a sumptuous frieze ornamented with human faces, grotesque masks and organic decorations.

The **Quartiere della Giudecca** extends behind this section of the street. During the 16C, a community of Jews settled and thrived in this quarter until expelled. Today the quarter retains its medieval street plan, threaded by atmospheric narrow streets.

At the end of the street the **Belvedere S. Giacomo**, once a defensive bastion, offers a splendid **view★** of Syracuse. The nearby **Forte Vigliena** can be seen on the right.

▶ Return to the centre of Ortygia by Via Minniti, south of the fort, and turn right down Via Alagona.

MIQWÈ

Via Alagona 52, in the Residence Hotel Alla Giudecca. Mon–Sat guided tours every hour from 11am–7pm. ⊚⊛€5. ℰ0931 22 255.

Europe's largest Jewish ritual baths were recently discovered in the basement of this apartment hotel. There is a clear Byzantine style to the architecture.

▶ Return to Via Minniti, then turn right and take the first left, which will take you to Piazza San Giuseppe.

MUSEO ARETUSO DEI PUPI

Palazzo Midiri Cardona, Piazza San Giuseppe. ⏰*Mon–Sat 11am–1pm, 4–6pm (4–6.30pm in summer).* ⊚⊛€2. ℰ*0931 46 55 40. www.pupari.com.*

This modest museum presents the work of local puppet-making brothers, Saro and Alfredo Vaccaro, including their set designs and most famous puppets.

▶ Return to the Belvedere San Giacomo and turn left into Via Vittorio Veneto.

VIA VITTORIO VENETO

This street, once called **Mastrarua**, was the main thoroughfare of Ortygia. The route followed by official parades and royal processions, it is lined with fine *palazzi*. **Palazzo Blanco** *(no. 41)* is graced outside with a niche in which stands a statue of St Anthony; its inner courtyard and staircase are well worth

Tempio di Apollo

© Sandro Bedessi / Fototeca ENIT

seeing. **Casa Mezia** *(no. 47)* has a doorway surmounted by a griffin. Beyond the **church of San Filippo Neri** follows **Palazzo Interlandi** and the badly-damaged **Palazzo Monforte**. This last *palazzo* marks the corner with **Via Mirabella**, which is also lined with fine buildings.

Directly opposite Palazzo Monforte, the doorway of the elegant **Palazzo Bongiovanni** is surmounted by a mask and, above, a lion holding a scroll bearing the date 1772, which in turn, acts as a central support for a balcony.

▷ Continue along Via Mirabella.

Take a small detour to the right to the neo-Gothic **Palazzo Gargallo** *(Archivio Distrettuale Notarile – Records Office)*. Via Mirabella heralds the beginning of the Arab quarter, characterised by extremely narrow streets known as *ronchi*. One of these streets conceals the palaeo-Christian church of **San Pietro**.

A little farther along Via Mirabella stands the church of **San Tommaso**, which was founded in Norman times (12C). Turn back along the Mastrarua; **no. 111** has a doorway decorated with monstrous creatures. No. 136 is the birthplace of the writer, **Elio Vittorini** (1908–66).

TEMPIO DI APOLLO

This temple of Apollo, built in the 6C BC, is the oldest peripteral Doric temple *(that is, enclosed by columns)* in Sicily. According to one inscription it was dedicated to Apollo; according to Cicero, it was dedicated to Artemis, before being transformed into a Byzantine church, then a mosque, and back again into a church by the Normans. The remains of the peristyle columns and the sacred precinct wall are still in evidence.

Corso Matteotti, described as the drawing room of Ortygia, leads off the piazza, flanked on either side by elegant shops.

EXCURSIONS

NEAR THE TOWN
Castello Eurialo ★
9km/5.5mi NW along Via Epipoli, in the Belvedere district. ○*Open daily, 9am– 4pm (7pm in summer).* ⊗€4. ℘*0931 71 17 73.*

The road up to the fortress gives an idea of the scale of the defensive system put in place by Dionysius the Elder. In addition to fortifying Ortygia, the strategist built a wall around the entire settlement, encompassing the districts of Tyche and Neapolis which, until then, had stood outside the city limits. With this in mind, he ordered the construction of the imposing **Walls of Dionysius** (*mura dionigiane* – 27km/17mi) across the Epipolae high plateau enclosing the north side of the town; one section of wall is still visible along the road leading up to Belvedere (*left*).

The ridge provided a strategic position for the castle. Its name, Euryalus, is derived from its headland position, which resembles the head of a nail (*Greek: euryelos*).

The fortress is one of the most impressive Greek defences to have survived from Antiquity. Its heart is ringed with a series of three consecutive ditches linked by a warren of underground passages. The entrance to the archaeological area coincides with the first of these ditches. A little farther on, there is a second deep trench lined with vertical walls, followed by a third, making this a veritable Chinese-puzzle masterpiece of defensive design.

Behind stood the square keep, preceded by an impressive series of defensive towers. The far corner provides a fine **view**★ down to Syracuse (*opposite*) and the plain stretching away to the left.

TEMPIO DI GIOVE OLIMPICO

3km/1.8mi out of town along Via Florina, signposted right.

The 6C BC Temple of Olympian Zeus occupies a suitably commanding position, raised high above the surrounding landscape.

FONTE CIANE★★

8km/5mi SE. ⊙*Visit by request* ℰ*346 15 99 635.*

The River Ciane, which almost merges with the River Anapo, is the main link with the internal area of Pantalica (⎈*See Pantalica*) and a favourite starting point for **boat trips**★★. Shortly after setting off, a splendid **view** of the **Grand Harbour** of Syracuse opens out before you. The boat then continues through lush vegetation: reeds, ancient ash trees and eucalyptus, before entering a narrow gorge and emerging in a papyrus grove. Here, according to the myth transcribed by Ovid (*Metamorphoses: The Rape of Proserpine,* Book 5, l 409–437), Cyane the water nymph tried to obstruct Pluto from abducting Persephone and was transformed into a spring.

PANTALICA★

50km/ 31mi W of Siracusa.

Once the site of ancient **Hybla** (728 BC), Pantalica combines the honeycombed archaeological remains of its necropoli with the dramatic natural surroundings of the Anapo Valley.

Pantalica has been inhabited since the Bronze Age. Towards the middle of the 13C BC, the Sicani moved inland from their original settlements in the dangerously exposed coastal regions to the more defensible river gorges at Pantalica.

Flora and Fauna

The geological formation known as the *cave iblee (or Hyblaean quarries)*, a series of deep canyons cutting through the landscape, harbours a broad range of plants in a concentrated area. The tree varieties that make up the thickly wooded section up the rocky slopes include white and black poplars and willows; there is also a profusion of tamarisks, oleanders, wild orchids and the nettle *Urtica rupestris* – a relic from the Ice Age. Clinging to the slopes elsewhere are patches of Mediterranean maquis: a forest of holm and cork oaks interspersed with, in the more arid parts exposed to the sun, an aromatic scrub of sage, thyme, giant fennel, euphorbia and thorny broom. As regards fauna, the Anapo Valley also accommodates a large number of different species: foxes, pine martens, porcupines, hares and hedgehogs; painted frogs and other amphibians; dippers, stonechats, kingfishers, partridges and a pair of peregrine falcons.

Burial chambers made of honeycombed rocks

©Peeter Viisimaa/iStockphoto.com

ARCHAEOLOGICAL SITE★

◷ *Open access.* ⮞*No charge.*
Dating from successive periods, these five necropoli consist of some 5,000 burial chambers honeycombing the quarry walls. The earliest in the north and northwest necropoli *(13C–11C BC)* are elliptical in shape; the most recent *(850–730 BC)* are rectangular. Unlike most sepultures for larger groups, they are organised into compact family units.

RISERVA DELLA VALLE DELL'ANAPO★

⮞ *There are two entrances to the Anapo Valley, via the Fusco gate.*

▷ Off the Floridia-Sortino road, turn left after 12km/7mi at the fork marked with a sign for Valle dell'Anapo; 700m/770yd farther along, continue left, or via the Cassaro gate (from Ferla, follow signs for Cassaro; at the first fork, turn left and continue to the bridge over the river; the Ponte Diga gate is located thereabouts – 4km/2.5mi from Ferla.

An expedition through the protected area *(soon set to become a nature reserve)* around the Anapo Valley reveals an extraordinary **landscape** that comprises a succession of gorges and cliffs, along which the old Syracuse-Ragusa-Vizzini railway ran.

FERLA

42km/26mi W of Syracuse and 15km/9mi W of Pantalica.
Isolated on a limestone upland plateau crossed by the River Anapo, the town boasts several attractive 18C religious buildings. These include the church of **San Sebastiano**, whose three naves house various chapels and works of art, including a 17C painting depicting the Martyrdom of St Sebastian, and **Sant'Antonio**, which overlooks an attractive square cobbled with geometric designs.
The elegant frontage of this church comprises five convex panels articulated with columns, while inside are some lovely Baroque details.
The road from Ferla to Sortino provides panoramic **views**★ over the surrounding plateau and the deep cleft hewn by water erosion.

SORTINO

32km/20mi NW of Syracuse.
Rebuilt in the 18C atop a hill, the town is laid out on a rectilinear, grid-like plan. The **Chiesa Madre** is fronted by a forecourt cobbled with lozenge-shaped stones and has a fine façade of warm golden stone. The elevation comprises a doorway flanked by spiral columns ornamented with organic decoration; a level above with statues; and along the top, an open balustrade. The interior ceiling and apse are

charmingly frescoed (1777–78) by Crestadoro.

The 👥 **Museo dell'Opera dei Pupi** (🕐 *open Mon–Sat, 9.30am–12.30pm, 3.30–5.30pm, Sun 10am–12pm, 3.30–5pm;* ✆*free;* ✆*0931 91 74 33)* is housed in the former monastery of St Francis. This museum contains the puppet theatre and puppets that once belonged to the renowned puppeteer **Ignazio Puglisi** (1904–86). This fascinating collection is organised by theme, with rooms dedicated to grotesque monsters *(devils, skeletons and giants),* Paladins and Saracens and to the *cartoni,* large sections of cardboard portraying the puppets that were used as a background.

One of the last rooms in the museum is dedicated to the characters of farce, which spoke in Sicilian dialect and traditionally brought the puppet shows to a rousing end.

Sortino is also famous for its thyme, eucalyptus and orange-flower honey The **Casa Museo dell'Apicultura Tradizionale** (*Via Gioberti 5;* ✆*0931 95 29 92;* ✆*€2)* has a display of honey production methods and tools. In October, the best producers sell their honey and other craft products during the Sagra del Miele.

🚗 DRIVING TOUR

ARCHAEOLOGICAL SITES
80km/50mi. Allow one day.

▶ From Siracusa, take the S 114 towards Catania.

Thapsos
🕐*Open daily, 9am–1pm.* 🕐*Closed Sun and public holidays. Visits by reservation; contact the Soprintendenza a few days in advance.* ✆*€6.* ✆*0931 48 11 42.*

The Magnisi peninsula, which separates the Bay of Augusta from the Bay of Syracuse, is tenuously connected to the mainland by an isthmus of sand. Thapsos grew to become one of the most important prehistoric cultures in the Middle Bronze Age (15C–13C BC),

and the recovery of Mycenaean and Maltese ceramics from this area suggest that it continued to be a trading emporium of considerable importance.

Archaeological site
Excavation has revealed remains of a substantial settlement, including round huts from the 15C–14C BC. More sophisticated residential complexes from the 13C–12C BC include rectangular chambers arranged around a cobbled courtyard, reflecting Mycenaean influences. Farther south along the dirt track are some fragments of Early Bronze Age fortifications.

A few hundred metres beyond this extends a vast **necropolis** containing 450 burial chambers. These consist of man-made hollows preceded by a vestibule, which in most cases consists of a small shaft, *dromos* passageway or tunnel *(more evident along the seashore where the sea has eroded the external wall).* The burial chambers are round, with conical ceilings; in some, the walls have shallow niches *(visible in one tomb, where the ceiling has collapsed),* where grave goods were deposited. The chambers were used for whole families and dependants, and designed to serve several generations. Entombment was by inhumation.

Mother-goddess, Megara Hyblaea

Museo Archeologico, Siracusa/SCALA

▶ Return to the coast road and continue in the direction of Augusta.

Megara Hyblaea

The Greek colony of Megara Hyblaea, founded by the Megarians of Greece in 728 BC, was twice razed to the ground: once in 483 BC by Gelon, the tyrant of Gela, and again by the Romans in 213 BC. The archaeological site is situated in a strange setting, stranded between the sea and the chimneys of the Augusta oil refinery.

Excavations

The **necropolis** lies outside the town walls, alongside the older enclosure walls *(before crossing the railway bridge, by the bend take the dirt track off to the right).* Beyond the entrance extends one of the *decumani* that once led to the **agora** *(marketplace).*

The site shows clear evidence of successive building phases as Archaic constructions give way to Hellenistic ones above. On the left of the piazza sits a sanctuary, recognisable by the semicircular north end wall. Follow D 1, a street on the left, which passes alongside a large **Hellenistic house** from the 4C–2C BC *(entrance marked by iron steps)* comprising 20 rooms arranged around two courtyards. Some rooms preserve remains of *opus signinum* floors (an amalgam of clay particles mixed with minute pieces of rubble, bound with lime).

To the left of the agora lie the **Hellenistic baths**. Farther along is a *Pritaneo (where magistrates would meet)* from the Archaic period (6C BC). The *decumanus* continues beyond the square as far as the **West Gate** and fortifications from the Hellenistic period.

▶ Continue north for 15km/9mi.

AUGUSTA

Augusta today is an important Italian commercial port. Founded by Frederick II Hohenstaufen, the town occupied a strategic defensive position overlooking the bay. The **Spanish gate** at the entrance to the citadelle is flanked by two imposing bastions.

BRUCOLI

This small and charming fishing village is clustered around its picturesque little **harbour**, which lies at the mouth of the River Porcaria.

▶ Head towards Lentini *(25km/15mi W of Brucoli).*

LENTINI

The centre of this small town dependent on citrus fruit farming is marked by the **Chiesa Madre** dedicated to Sant'Alfio *(a popular saint in the hamlets around Etna).* Preserved in its palaeo-Christian vault are the alleged relics of St Alfio, St Filadelfio and St Cirino.

A small **archaeological museum** (🕐open 9am–7pm; 🚫closed Mon; ✍€2; 📞095 78 32 962) displays artefacts recovered from the Leotinol excavations.

LEONTINOI

Access is easiest via Carlentini. For information, contact the archaeological museum: 📞095 78 32 962.

Leontinoi, inhabited since protohistoric times *(as the bases of huts to the right of the entrance to the archaeological zone on Collina di Metapiccola testify),* was colonised in 729 BC by the Chalcidians of Naxos. It was here that the philosopher **Gorgias** was born.

Excavations have revealed the remains of pyramidal tombs and walling beyond. The Syracusan gate, which once served as the town's main entrance, frames what may have been an acropolis on the San Mauro hill, where the remains of a temple are to be found. The incline passes in front of the circular base of what was probably a defensive tower. From the top, a wonderful **view** extends over Lentini and an artificial lake, the **Biviere**, beyond. The mound to the left is Colle di Sant'Egidio, where the town's necropolis was located.

IL GIARDINO DEL BIVIERE★

Contrada Case Biviere, VIlla Borghese. From Lentini railway station, turn right and follow the sign for SP 67 to Valsavoia. By the fork in the road, on the right, stands a villa with a large green entrance. ⏰*The garden is open by appointment only; to make a reservation, phone or send a fax at least two weeks in advance. Brunch, drinks, lunch or tea can be booked for groups.* 🍴*€10.* 📞*095 78 31 449.*

According to legend, when **Heracles** came to these parts intending to present the skin of the Nemean lion to Ceres, he fell in love with the area and created a lake that would bear his name.

This was subsequently changed to Biviere *(drinking trough or fish-farm)* during the time of Arab occupation. The gardens were created in 1967 at the behest of the Borghese princes. They comprise Mediterranean species and exotics such as *Encefaloartus horridus* – the blue prickly cycad thought to exist only in fossil form before botanists discovered the plant in Tanzania

ADDRESSES

🛏 STAY

ORTYGIA

🛏 **Tre Archi** – *Primo Ronco Via del Crocifisso.* 📞*0931 483 020. www.trearchi siracusa.com. 4 rooms.* By no. 30 on Via del Crocifisso, take the little passage on the right to find this charming guesthouse tucked away in a courtyard. Its location in the heart of Ortygia is ideal for exploring this most attractive part of Siracusa on foot. The colour schemes in some of the rooms are on the bright side, but the rooms themselves are comfortable and functional.

🛏 **Vittoria** – *Via Mirabella 18.* 📞*0931 462 119. www.vittoriaflorio.it. 6 rooms, 2 apartments* 🍴. Pretty rooms on the first floor of a building next to the church of San Tommaso. The guesthouse is down a small street in an inner courtyard. Breakfast is served on the sunny terrace.

🛏🛏 **Itaca** – *Piazza Archimede 2.* 📞*931 483 021 or 331 33 43 721. www.itacainn.it.* 🍴. *5 rooms* 🍴. The rooms with windows or a balcony overlooking the square have good views, whereas those overlooking the courtyard provide peace and quiet. Rooms are pleasantly furnished with a contemporary or 1970s look. Two of them, which come equipped with a spacious kitchen, can sleep up to 6 people.

🛏🛏 **Aretusa Vacanze** – *Vicolo Zuccalà 1.* 📞*0931 483 484. www.aretusavacanze.com. 10 rooms.* Right by the Arethusa fountain, this modest guesthouse occupies a 17C palazzo that has retained its attractive façade. The building has been fully renovated and contains clean, spacious rooms *(sleeping 1–4 people)*. There is a lift for access and guests enjoy all the creature comforts, with flat-screen TVs, four-poster beds, internet access and well-equipped kitchen areas. Sun terrace on the roof. Guests are looked after very well and a 20 percent discount is available for long stays.

🛏🛏 **Corte degli Angeli** – *Ronco San Tommaso 15.* 📞*0931 461 802. www.lacorte degliangeli.com. 3 rooms* 🍴. In a historic palazzo in the heart of Ortygia, this B&B offers exceptionally comfortable rooms in a friendly, welcoming environment. One of the rooms is relatively dark, however, and the bathrooms are small, if prettily decorated. Rooms facing onto the square are lighter, but also noisier.

🛏🛏🛏 **Gutkowski** – *Lungomare Vittorini 26, Siracusa.* 📞*0931 46 58 61. www.guthotel.it. 13 rooms.* Careful attention to detail is evident throughout this hotel, with its elegant entrance on the ground floor, delightful panoramic sun-terrace and tastefully decorated rooms. Excellent welcome and delicious breakfast.

🛏🛏🛏 **Alla Giudecca** – *Via Alagona 52.* 📞*0931 22 255. www.allagiudecca.it. 26 rooms and suites* 🍴. The lovely apartments in this hotel-apartment complex can be rented for a few nights. Very comfortable, with good facilities, and a magnificent terrace with **views** over Ortygia.

🛏🛏🛏 **Palazzo del Sale** – *Via Santa Teresa 25.* 📞*0931 65 958. www.palazzo delsale.it. 7 rooms* 🍴. Not far from the Arethusa fountain, this building has been very tastefully and simply renovated. An unusual communal area, plus spacious, bright rooms, some of them with small terraces. Very welcoming.

🛏🛏🛏🛏 **Algilà Ortigia Charme Hotel** – *Via Vitt. Veneto 93.* 📞*0931 46 51 86. www.algila.it. 30 rooms.* 🍴. It's hard to imagine a better spot overlooking the *lungomare*. This hotel consists of three palazzi knocked into one. Part-Baroque and part-Moorish, the rooms have been tastefully decorated.

IN THE NEW TOWN

🍽 **Piccolo Hotel Casa Mia** – *Corso Umberto 112.* *☎0931 46 33 49.* *www.bbcasamia.it. 23 rooms.* Elegant and simple, the rooms in this family-run B&B are filled with antiques and period quirks. There's a charming courtyard, where breakfasts of hot rolls, fruit tarts and home-made jams are served in the summer.

NEAR THE BEACHES

🍽 **Dolce Casa** – *Via Lido Sacramento 4, Loc. Isola (take S 115 towards Noto, then turn left to Loc. Isola).* *☎0931 72 11 35.* *www.bbdolcecasa.it. 10 rooms.* Situated halfway between Syracuse and the sea, this private villa has been converted into a friendly B&B. The light, spacious rooms, furnished in rustic style with the occasional romantic touch, and the beautiful garden adorned with palm and pine trees, ensure a relaxed and pleasant stay.

🍽 **Kalaonda Plemmirio Hotel** – *Strada Capo Murro di Porco, SS 115 dir. Noto, turn left towards Isola.* *☎0931 714 829. www.kalaonda.it.* ⛵. *18 rooms.* ⌷ ✕ *€25/35.* An artful blend of rustic architecture and contemporary design, this charming inn, a member of the Relais du Silence, is less than 1km/1000yds from the sea. Tasty cuisine made from fresh local produce.

NEAR CASSIBILE

🍽 **Agriturismo La Perciata** – *Via Spinagallo 77, 14km/9mi SW of Siracusa on P 14 (from Maremonti, head to Canicattini, then take the turn-off to Floridia).* *☎0931 73 66. www.perciata.it. 11 rooms. 3 villas* ⌷, *restaurant* 🍽. This Mediterranean-style villa amid an oasis of greenery is ideal for a relaxing holiday. Activities on offer here include tennis, horse-riding and hydro-massage. Comfortable rooms and apartments with elegant, rustic decor.

🍽 **Agriturismo Limoneto** – *Via del Platano, 9km/5.6mi southwest of Siracusa on the SP 14 towards Canicattini; follow signs for Palazzolo Acreide.* *☎0931 71 73 52. www.limoneto.it.* ♿ ⌷. *Closed Nov. 10 rooms* ⌷, *half-board available.* In the midst of a farm growing organic lemons, you will find complete peace and quiet, and a warm welcome. Wood is a major feature of the spacious, bright rooms, which can accommodate a whole family.

🍽EAT

🍴 **Castello Fiorentino** – *Via del Crocifisso 6, Ortygia.* *☎0931 21 097. Closed Mon.* One of the most popular trattoria-pizzerias with a large, slightly down-at-heel dining room, in which a squadron of waiters perform their own surrealist ball: running, turning, whirling and yelling out orders with gusto to add to the already-deafening hubbub. Succulent pizzas and well-sauced pasta dishes. Always packed, so arrive early.

🍴 **Trattoria Archimede** – *Via Gemmellaro 8, Ortygia.* *☎0931 69 701. www.trattoriaarchimede.it. Closed Sun (in low season) and public holidays.* The street is flanked by two dining rooms with walls covered in photographs and prints. This is one of the most popular places with tourists, but with good reason as the food satisfies the tastebuds without emptying your wallet. Dishes like fish lasagna, pasta with sea urchins and spaghetti with clams form the lion's share of the menu, while pizzas are served in the evenings.

🍴 **Sicilia in Tavola** – *Via Cavour 28, Ortygia.* *☎392 46 10 889. www.sicilia intavola.eu. Closed Mon.* The strong point of this rustic-looking little trattoria is its wide choice of fresh pasta, home-made the way it should be and cooked with love. Go for the pasta over the meat and fish dishes, which are more expensive and less exciting.

🍴 **Do Scogghiu** – *Via D. Scinà 11, Ortygia. Closed Mon. Booking recommended.* Generous portions, succulent antipasti and pasta al dente! Simple, attentive service.

🍴 **Locanda Mastrarua** – *Via V. Veneto 11, Ortygia.* *☎0931 62 084. www.locandamastrarua.com. Closed Wed.* A modern, bright and welcoming restaurant keen to offer the best of traditional cooking. High-quality produce, carefully presented. Try the grilled meats or the *mastrarua*, a dish of almond-encrusted sea bass with spinach.

🍴 **Taverna Sveva** – *Piazza Federico di Svevia 1, Ortygia.* *☎0931 246 63. Closed lunchtimes.* A few colourful tables on a quiet square at the end of the island, serving inventive food with jazz playing in the background. Try the *gnocchi al pistacchio* and the citrus tiramisu.

 Don Camillo – *Via Maestranza 96, Ortygie. ℘0931 67 133. www.ristorante doncamillosiracusa.it. Closed Sun and public holidays.* The town's most famous restaurant serves classic Sicilian cuisine with a creative twist. Good quality fish soup, tuna carpaccio, cassata and cannoli.

 Oinos restaurant – *Via della Giudecca 69/75, Ortygie. ℘0931 46 49 00. www.oinosrestaurant.it. Closed Sun.* Complex contemporary cuisine prepared by two young chefs – one Italian, the other Japanese. Atmospheric dining room decorated in grey and sand hues.

TAKING A BREAK

Enoteca "Capriccio" – *Via dell' Amalfitania 11, Siracusa. ℘0931 46 49 18. Open 10am–10pm.* This wine bar serves a selection of Sicilian wines, as well as local wine-based flavoured liquers such as *Rosolio al mandarino* and *Rosolio alla cannella.*

Gelateria Bianca Salvatore – *Corso Umberto I, Siracusa.* Customers are spoilt for choice at this reasonably priced gelateria, which has a selection of 30 different flavours of ice cream served either in a cup or cone and a pleasant shady terrace from where you can watch the world go by.

Gran Caffè del Duomo – *Piazza Duomo, Ortygie. ℘0931 21 544.* A very pleasant terrace on the pedestrianised square opposite the graceful curves of the cathedral façade… a perfect spot for your morning cappuccino or the city's best *latte di mandorla* (almond milk).

Biblos – *Via Cons. Regionale (just after the intersection with Via Roma), Ortygie. 6pm–10pm. Closed Wed.* A good bookshop that also serves as a dynamic cultural centre and internet café serving a good cup of tea to enjoy while you surf the web.

SHOWS

Teatro dei Pupi del Fratelli Mauceri – *Via della Giudecca 17, Ortygie. ℘0931 46 55 40. www.pupari.com. Open Tue–Sat 10am–1pm, 4pm–7pm; Sun 10.30am–1pm.* This small theatre in the heart of the Ortygia district is run by the Mauceri brothers, whose puppet performances offer an entertaining insight into traditional Sicilian culture. Make sure you also visit the nearby Alfredo Mauceri workshop, where the puppets are made.

SHOPPING

Artesania Design – *Via Apollonion 5, Ortygia. ℘328 78 95 230 (mobile), www.alessiagenovese.it.* Very unusual and highly sought-after lamps by the young designer, **Alessia Genovese**.

Circo Fortuna – *Via Capodieci 15, Ortygia. ℘0931 62 681, www.circofortuna.it.* An enticing range of plates with poetic and amusing decorations, T-shirts and unusual objects created by talented craftspeople.

Galleria Bellomo – *Via Capodieci 15, Siracusa. ℘0931 61 340. www.bellomo gallery.com* This workshop-cum-gallery, opened in 1980, displays a fascinating collection of papyrus items made by the owner, Signora Massara, who inherited her love for papyrus from her father-in-law.

Galleria del Papiro – *Via Ruggero, Settimo 35, Siracusa. ℘339 15 02 337 (mobile). Open Mon–Sat 9.30am–1pm, 3.30pm–7pm.* The artist **Alessandro Romano** uses papyrus as the raw material for his works of art, many of which are exhibited and on sale in this gallery.

SEASIDE RESORTS

The coast to the south of Syracuse has a number of attractive sandy beaches, such as **Arenella**, with its stretches of rocky coastline and picturesque creeks, including Ognina, a paradise for diving enthusiasts. The most beautiful beach in the area is **Fontane Bianche**, *(20km/12mi south of the city).*

FESTIVALS

Classical theatre – In May and June, the Greek theatre provides a wonderful setting for performances of famous **Classical Greek** and **Latin plays**. *(For information on dates and performances, contact: Istituto Nazionale del Dramma-Antico, Corso Matteotti 29, Siracusa; ℘0931 48 72 00; Fax 0931 48 7210; www.indafondazione.org.)*

Festa di Santa Lucia – The festival of the patron saint of Syracuse, St Lucy, is celebrated on 13 December.

Noto and the Coast★★

Noto dates from the time of the Siculi. Completely destroyed by the earthquake of 1693 and then rebuilt on a new site 10km/6mi away from the original town, its streets, laid out on a grid plan, are lined with handsome palaces, churches and other Baroque monuments in the local white limestone, which has mellowed with time to a golden hue. Several Sicilian architects worked together on this project – the most inventive was probably Rosario Gagliardi.

A BIT OF HISTORY

Prior to 1693, Noto stood some 10km/6mi away from its present site (see below, Noto Antica). The earthquake destroyed the old town and a less vulnerable site was chosen for the new town, one that might accommodate a straightforward linear town plan, in line with Baroque ideas. Three of the main streets run on an east-to-west axis and are always bathed in sunshine. Three social categories were catered for: the highest part was reserved for the nobility, the centre for the clergy, while ordinary people were left to fill the rest of the town. Many Sicilian artists cooperated in Noto's reconstruction, conducted under the supervision of the Duke of

GETTING THERE

Noto is 55km/34mi from **Ragusa** and 30km/19mi from Siracusa, from where there are trains (90min and 40min respectively) and buses (1hr to Ragusa and 40min to Siracusa). The bus station is situated in Piazzale Marconi behind the park (Giardino Pubblico), while the railway station is in Viale Principe di Piemonte, a 10min walk from the historical centre of the town. Bus services run between Noto and Fontanarossa airport in **Catania** (approx. 80km/50mi).

▶ **Population:** 23 766
◔ **Michelin Map:** p265: B2
ℹ **Info:** Piazza XVI Maggio (opposite the theatre); ℘0931 83 67 44; www.comune.noto.sr.it.
◑ **Location:** The main monuments in the historical centre are grouped between the central Corso Vittorio Emanuele, which runs through the town from east to west, and Via Cavour, its counterpart to the north.
🅿 **Parking:** Park in the public gardens at the edge of town coming from Syracuse.
◈ **Don't Miss:** A walk through the Baroque city centre, or the eerie atmosphere of Noto Antica. Descend into the Cava Grande Gorge and take a refreshing swim in the natural rock pools at the bottom.
👥 **Kids:** Swimming in the natural rock pools at the Cava Grande.
◔ **Timing:** Allow one day for a tour of the surrounding area. Allow half an hour to descend into the Cava Grande Gorge, but double to walk back up! Early morning and late evening are the best times for bird watching at the Vendicari Nature Reserve.

Camastra, acting representative of the Spanish viceroy; these included **Paolo Labisi**, **Vincenzo Sinatra** and **Rosario Gagliardi**.

The new town was built like a stage set: its perspectives were enhanced with curvaceous forms and curvilinear accents in façades, decorated brackets and keystones, curlicues and volutes, masks, cherubs and balconies with wrought-iron railings. Although Noto

Cattedrale di San Nicolo

© Philippe Renault/Photononstop

was rebuilt by local craftsmen, it fits into a much larger picture, as Italian hands modelled, fashioned and realised expressions of the Baroque movement all over Europe.

🐾 WALKING TOUR

BAROQUE CITY CENTRE★★

The main axis is **Corso Vittorio Emanuele**, which runs through three piazzas, each with its own church. The street extends from **Porta Reale**, a monumental gateway modelled on a triumphal arch and erected in the 19C. Above the entrance is a **pelican**, the symbol of self-denial – a reference to King Ferdinand II, who visited the town in 1838 – flanked by a tower *(a symbol of strength)* and a *cirneco (an old Sicilian breed of dog and symbol of loyalty)*. Beyond, to one side the elegant public gardens *(Giardino Pubblico)* are dotted with bougainvillea, palm trees and marble busts. This is a popular place for townspeople to congregate for the daily social ritual of the *passeggiata*.

PIAZZA IMMACOLATA

The square is overlooked by the Baroque façade of **San Francesco all'Immacolata** (designed by Sinatra). An impressive stairway leads up to a terrace, with a statue of the Virgin in the centre.

The church contains notable works of art removed from the Franciscan church abandoned in the old town of Noto. These include a painted wooden *Virgin and Child* attributed to Antonio Monachello (1564) on the altar and the tombstone of a Franciscan priest (1575) set into the floor of the nave *(right)*.

To the left of the church, by the entrance to Via San Francesco d'Assisi, sits the **Monastero del Santissimo Salvatore** marked by an elegant tower rising above

San Franceso all'Immacolata

© Paola Ghirotti / Fototeca ENIT

the curved frontage. The windows have wonderful pot-bellied wrought-iron balconies, which are echoed across the street at the **Convento di Santa Chiara**, by Gagliardi.

PIAZZA MUNICIPIO★

This is the busiest and most majestic of the three squares, overlooked on the left by the eye-catching elevation of the **Palazzo Ducezio**, and on the right by the flight of steps to the cathedral entrance, flanked by two horseshoe-shaped hedges.

Cathedral★★

The broad façade with its two bell towers does not completely obscure the remains of the dome, which collapsed in 1996, destroying a large section of the nave. The wide stairway appears to sweep up from the piazza, accentuated by two tall, exedra side hedges, each with a paved area above, emphasising their serpentine line. Alongside the cathedral, on the same level, stand the 19C **Palazzo Vescovile** *(Bishop's Palace)* and **Palazzo Landolina di Sant'Alfano**, both sober in appearance in contrast to the exuberant style of the other buildings in the square.
On the opposite side of the square sits the **Palazzo Ducezio** *(◷open daily 9am–1.30pm, 4–8pm; ◙€4)* enclosed by a classical type of portico designed by Sinatra. The upper section was added in the 1950s.
On the east side of the square is the **Basilica del Santissimo Salvatore**.

VIA NICOLACI★

Right off Corso Vittorio Emanuele.
The eye is naturally drawn along the street as it gently rises up to the **Chiesa di Montevergine**, with its concave frontage framed between bell towers. Both sides of the street are lined with Baroque buildings: on the left, note **Palazzo Nicolaci di Villadorata** *(◷open daily 10am–1pm, 3–7pm, ◙€4; ☎0931 83 50 05; www.palazzonicolaci.it)*, with its fabulous **balconies★★★**.
The richly carved brackets are ornamented with fantastical cherubs, horses,

mermaids and lions, grotesque figures including one, in the centre, with an exaggerated snub nose and flaired lips. Returning to Corso Vittorio Emanuele, on the left stands the imposing complex of the **Jesuit Church and College** attributed to Gagliardi.

PIAZZA XVI MAGGIO

The most striking feature on the square is Gagliardi's elegant convex façade for the **Chiesa di San Domenico★**, designed with emphatic use of line and contained by two tiers of columns separated by a high cornice. The interior is predominantly white, encrusted with stucco and graced with polychrome marble altars.
In front of the church lies the delightful **Villetta d'Ercole ★**, a public garden with an 18C fountain named after the mythological hero Heracles. Opposite, stands the 19C **Teatro Comunale**.
The second street on the left off Corso Vittorio Emanuele, Via Ruggero Settimo, leads to the **Chiesa del Carmine**, with its concave frontage and charming Baroque doorway.

▷ Return to Piazza XVI Maggio and up Via Bovio, fringed on the right by a former Carmine convent, the Casa dei Padri Crociferi.

VIA CAVOUR

This noble street runs parallel to, but on a level above, Corso Vittorio Emanuele, between a series of interesting buildings: **Palazzo Astuto** (no. 54), with its bulging wrought-iron balconies, and **Palazzo Trigona Cannicarao** (no. 93).

▷ Beyond the palazzo turn left onto Via Coffa, then left again at the end to pass before the late-Baroque **Palazzo Impellizzeri** and turn right onto Via Sallicano.

Via Sallicano leads right up to the **Chiesa del Santissimo Crocefisso** in Piazza Mazzini. Designed by Gagliard, the church was never completed. Inside, though, it contains a few works of note, including a splendid pair of Romanesque lions and *(behind the altar to the right)* **Francesco Laurana's** sensitive *Madonna della Neve* (Madonna of the Snow), the only statue in Sicily actually signed by the artist.

EXCURSION
Noto Antica
10km/6mi NW.

Along the road to the site of the original Noto is a sign for **Eremo di San Corrado fuori le Mura:** this 18C sanctuary was built beside the cave where St Corrado lived in the 14C.

The main road then continues past the **Santuario di Santa Maria della Scala** to the site where the town of Noto stood before the 1693 earthquake. Stretched along the Monte Alveria ridge, between two deep gorges, it was easily defensible and resisted numerous attacks, most notably as the last bastion of Arab Sicily to fall before the Normans conquered the island.

Beyond Porta Aurea, the gateway to the now-deserted city, which developed along a ridge of Monte Alveria, is bounded by two deep gorges that made the site easy to defend. The street system remains eerily intact.

🚗 DRIVING TOUR

RUINS AND BEAUTIFUL NATURAL LANDSCAPES
85km/53mi. Allow at least one day, including the excursion to Cava Grande and the tour of the Riserva di Vendicari.

▶ Head to Avola and follow signs to Avola Antica *(10km/6mi along a winding road).* After the town, turn right to a viewpoint where you can park the car.

Cava Grande del Cassibile★★
Of particular interest to nature lovers, Cava Grande provides the opportunity to explore a forgotten corner of the Iblei Mountain landscape dominating southeast Sicily. From above, there is a magnificent **view★** over the **Cava Grande Gorge★** plunging between

sheer limestone cliffs. The river winds along the valley bottom, opening out intermittently to make a succession of tiny lakes, which are accessible by a path leading into the gorge. To the left is the **Grotta dei Briganti** (Bandits' Cave), one of the many rock-hewn dwellings in this small settlement.

Descent
It takes half an hour to walk down to the river, or *cava* as it is known locally – allow twice that time to climb back to the top. The track, which at times is quite difficult to follow, cuts its way along the river through luxuriant vegetation. After a few hundred metres, bush gives way to an open clearing around a series of **natural rock pools★★** created by the river, complete with flat, rounded slabs of rock and ideal for whiling away an hour in the sunshine. In summer, the cool water is very tempting. Furthermore, the rock pools are surrounded by idyllic scenery, providing an unusual and highly recommended alternative to a swim in the sea off the Syracuse coast.

▶ Return to Avola. Take S 115 to Noto and then S 19 to Capo Passero. A road to the left leads to Eloro.

Eloro
Ancient Helorus was probably founded by the Syracusans in the 7C BC. It enjoys a splendid **situation★** on a hill over-looking the sea.

Excavations
On entering the site, to the east you see the ruin of a great *stoà* (portico), once the entrance to the sacred precinct where the **sanctuary** dedicated to Demeter and Kore was located. The sanctuary is now buried below the later remains of Byzantine buildings.

Down by the river lie the remains of a **theatre** *(cavea)*, badly scarred after a drainage channel was dug under Fascist rule. Westward is the base of a **temple** thought to have been dedicated to Asclepius (Aesculapius), son of Apollo and god of medicine and healing. Beyond, northern and western sections of the

enclosure walls are still in evidence, as is the **north gate** marking the beginning of the main street, running on a north-to-south axis, rutted by cartwheels. In an area east of the principal thoroughfare lies a large, open space that was most likely used as the *agora* (marketplace).

▷ Return to S 19. After 3km/2mi, turn right towards the Villa Romana del Tellaro.

Area archeologica e Villa Romana del Tellaro

ⓘ*Open daily 9am–7pm.*≈*€6.* ℘*0931 57 38 83. www.villaromanadeltellaro.com.* The remains of a Roman villa dating from the second half of the 4C AD have been uncovered beside the River Tellaro, west of the main Noto-Pachino road. These fragments, found in the 1970s, suggest the internal decoration must have been at least as sumptuous as that of the Roman Villa del Casale, near Piazza Armerina.

Tour

The residence is planned around a square peristyle: excavations of the north wing have revealed **mosaic floors** with geometric designs of diamonds and spirals. Before leaving, note on the right, traces of buildings annexed to the main complex – possibly servants' quar-

ters – and the remains of a wall from the Greek period.

▷ Return to S 19, continue south for a further 4.5km/3mi and then turn left to the Riserva Naturale di Vendicari.

Riserva Naturale di Vendicari★

ⓘ*Open daily Apr–Oct 8am–7pm, Nov–Mar 7am–5.30pm.*≈*Free.* ℘*0931 67 450. Car park €4. This reserve is open throughout the year; the best time of day for bird watching is early morning or late afternoon.*
☺*Bring your binoculars!*

The Vendicari Nature Reserve was created in 1984 and consists of a strip of marshy coastline covering 574ha/1,418 acres. It provides a rare, and now completely protected, habitat for migratory species and a variety of sand-loving Mediterranean vegetation.

In autumn, it is common to see a variety of waders: grey heron, little egret, black stork and greater flamingo. Later, lesser black-backed, slender-billed and Audouin's gulls regularly winter in the area. Between November and March, the swamp attracts many species of wintering duck, including teal, shoveler, pintail, mallard and red-crested pochard. Among the species to breed here are the black-winged stilt – the emblem of Vendicari – Kentish plover, little tern, reed warbler and little bittern.

Go Fish!

During the catch, the fishermen used to signal the number of tuna netted in the various chambers: a white and red flag was flown when there were 10; a red flag meant there were 20; a white one meant 30; a red-and-white one was flown with a white one to signal 40, and so on. If they were unable to estimate the number of fish, they used to wave a sailor's jacket on top of an oar – a gesture known as **u' cappottu**, which meant: "we can't count them any more, there are too many!"

Tour

The track skirts the edge of the **Pantano Grande** before leading off towards the **Torre Sveva** (Swabian Tower) and the ruins of the **tonnara** (tuna fishery), which functioned until the Second World War.

Nearby lie the remains of a Hellenistic **fish-processing plant:** the tanks were used to steep the excess fish before salting them *(tarichos)* or using the by-products to make *garum* or fish paste – a highly lucrative commodity traded across the Mediterranean from Phoenician to Roman times.

▷ Follow S 19 for 18km/11mi.

Capo Passero

The Ionian Sea meets the Canale di Sicilia at this southeastern headland.

The local tuna fishery flourished during the 20C and the now-unused complex comprises a canning works, a house for the *Rais* – the quartermaster overseeing the cruel practice of *mattanza* (the killing of the tuna) – and the owner's house, offering constantly-changing **sea views★★**.

A natural channel separates the **islet** of *Capo Passero* from the mainland, a strategic place to lay nets when the tuna are running. The islet, meanwhile, has been subject to a compulsory purchase to protect the rare dwarf palms that grow there, decimating the once-dominant tuna industry. As a result the area is no longer the bustling centre of activity it once was.

Portapalo di Capo Passero

The harbour is the hub of activity in this picturesque, archetypal fishing village. Its sleepy air is disrupted daily between noon and 2pm, when the fishing boats return and the quays suddenly throng with inquisitive old men and busy housewives come to purchase the fresh catch of the day.

ADDRESSES

🏨 STAY

Terra di Pace – *Contrada Zisola.* ℘0931 83 84 72. www.terradipace.blog spot.com. *5 apartments (with kitchen).* Located 3km/1.8mi out of Noto on the S 115, this very peaceful farm offers prettily decorated studios looking out onto a huge garden. A small swimming pool for a refreshing dip and tasty organic produce from the farm.

Al Canisello – *Via Pavese 1, Noto.* ℘0931 83 57 93. www.villacanisello.it. *6 rooms.* This typical 19C farmhouse has thick, whitewashed walls and simple, rustic decor. The old-world atmosphere is enhanced by plain, elegant furnishings.

Villa Mediterranea – *Viale Lido, Noto Marina, 7.5km/4.5mi SE of Noto.* ℘0931 81 23 30. www.villamediterranea.it. *Closed Nov–Easter. 15 rooms.* This attractive, Mediterranean-style villa, located on the seafront at Noto Marina, offers a friendly, family-run atmosphere. Direct access to the beach.

🍴 EAT

Trattoria del Carmine – *Via Ducezio 1/A, Noto.* ℘0931 83 87 05. www.trattoriadelcarmine.it. *Closed Mon.* A great option after a hard day's sightseeing, this trattoria serves good, home-made cooking in a small dining room with tables covered with paper cloths.

Trattoria del Crocifisso Da Baglieri – *Via Principe Umberto 46/48, Noto.* ℘0931 57 11 51. www.ilcrocifisso.it. *Closed Wed, one week after Easter and two weeks of late Sept.* This simple trattoria takes visitors on an enjoyable trip back in time, with its traditional Sicilian atmosphere, regional dishes and reasonable prices.

TAKING A BREAK

Anche gli Angeli– *Via Arnaldo da Brescia 2.* ℘0931 57 60 23. This concept store with cool, high vaulted stone ceilings is a bookshop, lounge and hardware store. The "in" place to be in Noto.

FESTIVAL

Primavera barocca – This spring festival, held during the third weekend in May, culminates in the famous **Infiorata**, a flower festival which takes place in Via Nicolaci. Towards the middle of May, the locals recreate brilliantly coloured tableaux of flowers composed entirely of petals inside the doorways of the *palazzi*. The cobblestones of the street are transformed into a giant canvas of petals to form designs which vary from year to year.

Ragusa and the Coast ★★

Ragusa, partly rebuilt following the 1693 earthquake, sits on a plateau between deep ravines. The modern town lies to the west, while the old town, Ragusa Ibla, clusters on an outlier of the hills of Monti Ibei, to the east. The Syracuse road offers magnificent **views** of the old town.

🐾 WALKING TOURS

RAGUSA IBLA★★

A visit to the old town logically begins from the long stairway of Santa Maria delle Scale, which leads down from the new *(higher)* part of town to Ragusa Ibla. At certain points, it provides splendid **views★★** of the rooftops, notably the dome of **Santa Maria dell'Itria** *(left)* and the neo-Classical dome of the cathedral.

Santa Maria delle Scale was rebuilt in the 18C; the Gothic south aisle, with its elegant **pointed arches★**, remains from the earlier construction. Below the second archway is a **Gagini School** terra cotta panel depicting the *Dormition of the Virgin*.

▶ **Population:** 72 755
⛲ **Michelin Map:** p265: A2
🚩 Tourist office: Piazza S. Giovanni, Ragusa.
📞 0932 68 47 80.
www.comune.ragusa.gov.it.
▶ **Location:** Ragusa is actually two cities in one: the less-interesting upper, more modern town, built to a regular street plan, and the charming lower town situated to the east.
🅿 **Parking:** Park in the upper town as the narrow medieval layout of the lower town is most suited to exploration on foot.
👁 **Don't Miss:** Ragusa Ibla, fine collections of Antiquity at Museo Archeologico Regionale di Camarina and the elegant gardens at Castello di Donnafugata.

In Ibla itself, as if guarding the entrance to the Salita Commendatore, stands the statue of San Francesco di Paola set against a corner of **Palazzo Cosentini**, with its ornate **balconies★★** carved with caricatured figures and masks. This is one of the most secluded corners

View over Ragusa Ibla with the dome of Santa Maria dell'Itria
© Rene Mattes/hemis.fr

Detail of Duomo di San Giorgio

© Emilio Suetone/hemis.fr

of town, with a warren of intersecting stepped alleyways hiding some evocative buildings.

The church of **Santa Maria dell'Itria** is notable for its campanile, ornamented at the top with floral panels of maiolica from Caltagirone. Just beyond the church is **Palazzo Nicastro**★★ or *Vecchia Cancelleria* (1760) – the old prison: note its ornate doorway and balcony. The steep slope downhill on the left emerges in front of the steps leading up to the elegant convex front of the **Chiesa del Purgatorio**.

▷ Follow Via del Mercato, turn right into Via Solarino and then left into Via S. Agnese, which leads into Via Tenente di Stefano and Via Bocchieri.

PALAZZO LA ROCCA

This Baroque *palazzo* still bears traces of the original medieval building that preceded it. The six **balconies**★★ along the main façade are ornamented with portrait heads depicting real people of the day.

DUOMO DI SAN GIORGIO★★

The most striking feature from a distance is the 19C neo-Classical dome, with its blue lantern articulated with Corinthian columns. From the piazza, the eye is drawn up the imposing flight of steps to the wonderful pink façade. The elegant and harmoniously proportioned front elevation comprises a central, slightly convex bay contained by three tiers of columns, flanked by a side bay surmounted by a volute. Delicately carved decoration ornaments the doorway and cornice. The figure of St George on horseback driving a spear into the dragon, is incorporated into the façade *(above the left volute)*, and as the centrepiece of the beautiful railings at the bottom of the steps. The building was erected in the 18C by **Rosario Gagliardi**.

The interior, divided into nave and aisles, has the same frieze along the nave as the one on the exterior.

PIAZZA

The rectangular space before the Duomo is set at a slight angle to the church, on a slope. The other buildings enclosing it include **Palazzo Arezzi**,

GETTING THERE

There are daily bus services from **Agrigento** *(2hr 30min)*, **Catania airport** *(2hr)*, **Palermo** *(4hr)* and **Syracuse** *(approx. 2hr)*, and a train service from Syracuse. Trains and buses arrive in the modern town. For more information or timetables, contact the **tourist office**.

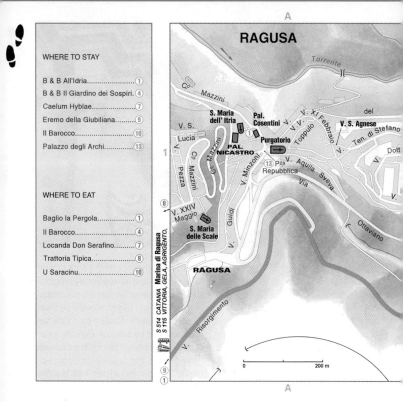

RAGUSA

WHERE TO STAY

B & B All'Idria...................①

B & B Il Giardino dei Sospiri.④

Caelum Hyblae...................⑦

Eremo della Giubiliana..........⑨

Il Barocco............................⑩

Palazzo degli Archi.............⑬

WHERE TO EAT

Baglio la Pergola..................①

Il Barocco............................④

Locanda Don Serafino..........⑦

Trattoria Tipica....................⑧

U Saracinu..........................⑩

with a wonderful balcony projecting over an archway through to the street beyond; farther on, across on the opposite side of the square, is **Palazzo Donnafugata**.

SAN GIUSEPPE★

Silence and modest dress should be observed in the church, which is part of the Benedictine monastery.

The elegant front elevation bears a remarkable resemblance to that of San Giorgio and for this reason has been attributed to Gagliardi. It rises through three tiers of Corinthian columns and figurative statues. The oval **interior** is enclosed below a dome; the floor is a combination of majolica tiles and black pitchstone.

Note the gratings that enabled the enclosed nuns to follow mass out of sight of the congregation.

▸ Follow Via XXV Aprile.

GIARDINO IBLEO

🕒*Open daily 8am–8pm.*

The public gardens containing several religious buildings are laid out at the far end of Ragusa Ibla. Just outside the entrance *(on the right)* stands the elaborate Catalan Gothic portal of **San Giorgio Vecchio** (15C).

The church just inside the gardens, on the left, is **San Giacomo**, better known as "Chiesa del Crocefisso" because of the wooden effigy contained within *(left of the main altar)*. It dates in the main from the 14C *(the 1693 earthquake caused the lateral aisles to collapse; these were never rebuilt)*, and encloses a ceiling painted with historical panels from 1754 – unfortunately, several are missing. The *trompe l'oeil* dome is especially effective.

To the side of the garden stands the **Chiesa dei Cappuccini**. This contains a lovely **triptych★** by **Pietro Novelli** showing the Virgin Mary, St Agatha and St Lucy. The figure left of the central panel looking out of the picture is a

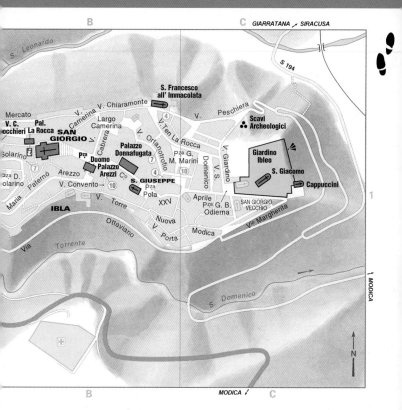

self-portrait. A wonderful **view** from the gardens extends over the Irminio Valley.

Archaeological excavations conducted on a site just beyond the garden have unearthed a street and a residential quarter dating from the Classical period; on top are layers of various medieval constructions.

Farther along Via Pescheria *(on the right-hand side)* note the **Chiesa di San Francesco all'Immacolata**. The church, rebuilt in the 17C, preserves a 13C Chiaramonte doorway *(west flank)*.

NEW TOWN

The "modern" town has been developed on a framework of straight, parallel streets intersecting at right angles to each other, to form a grid-like pattern up the side of the Patro hill. The elegant **Via Roma** bisects the town on a parallel axis to the side of the hill; the perpendicular **Corso Italia** runs down towards Ibla. On the right is Piazza San Giovanni,

overlooked by the church with which it shares its name.

Cattedrale di San Giovanni

The cathedral dates from the early 18C. Its imposing Baroque front elevation, flanked by the campanile, has a broad, raised terrace.

Farther along Corso Italia *(on the left)*, is the 19C Chiesa del Collegio di Maria Addolorata, with **Palazzo Lupis** beyond. Via San Vito *(right)* follows: no. 156 is **Palazzo Zacco**, marked by a great coat of arms supported on decorative brackets on the corner. Note the balcony **brackets** projecting from the lateral façade carved with figures and grotesques. Back in Corso Italia, a short distance farther along on the left, rises the 18C **Palazzo Bertini**. Three **masks★** peer down from the carved window keystones. According to tradition, these personify a hungry and toothless pauper *(left)*; a nobleman, serenely confident of his social status; and a prosperous merchant with the self-satisfied expression of the rich.

Museo Archeologico Ibleo

Via Natalelli 107; under the Ponte Nuovo, on the first floor of a building, above a garage. ○*Open 9am–1.30pm, 4–7.30pm.* ✆€4. ☏0932 62 29 63.
The local archaeological museum displays artefacts recovered from the surrounding area. Among the most interesting is a reconstruction of the Classical necropoli at Camarina and Rito, and one of the kiln at Scornavacche.

EXCURSIONS

COMISO

17km/10mi W.
Originally a Greek settlement, Comiso was destroyed by the Romans. Monasteries revived the area in Byzantine times and it continued to prosper under the Normans and Aragonese. After an earthquake in 1693 shattered its architecture, Comiso was rebuilt in a Spanish Baroque style. During the Cold War, the town housed American missiles, not removed until 1991.

Piazza Fonte di Diana

The central square is graced with a neo-Classical **fountain** dedicated to the goddess Diana. Excavations carried out in the little street directly opposite have revealed parts of the **Ancient**

Origins of "Donnafugata"

The name, which is Arabic in origin, is misleading. It does not, in fact, refer as first appearances might suggest to a woman fleeing some tyrannical husband or father (*fuga* in Italian means "escape" or "flight"), nor to one of the legends that linger in some popular memory, but is a free interpretation and transcription of *Ayn as Jafât* (meaning Fountain of Health), which in Sicilian dialect became "Ronnafuata" and so was corrupted to its modern form.

baths: an octagonal caldarium and a nymphaeum with a black-and-white mosaic featuring Neptune surrounded by nereids (2C AD).

Piazza delle Erbe

The main building overlooking the square is the town's principal church, dedicated to **Santa Maria delle Stelle**. Its front elevation rises through three tiers of Doric, Ionic and Corinthian pilasters. The square is also home to the neo-Classical **covered market** (1871) and the **Museo Civico di Storia Naturale** (○*open Mon–Sat 9.30am–1pm, 4–7.30pm; Sun 9.30am–1pm;* ✆€3.50) with its collection of cetaceans *(whales and other such mammals)* and sea turtles, and the **Biblioteca di Gesualdo Bufalino**, a library bequeathed by the author *(1920–1996)* to his native town.

Chiesa dell'Annunziata

The elegant neo-Classical front elevation of this church, raised high above an unusual flight of steps, comprises two levels linked by a single element: the palm leaf. The airy light interior, ornamented with white, blue and gold stucco decoration, contains two paintings by Salvatore Fiume *(in the chancel)*.

Chiesa di San Francesco (dell'Immacolata)

The Renaissance church contains the great **Naselli Chapel**; this rises from a square ground plan to an octagon, then a ribbed dome. Against the wall stands the funerary monument of Baldassare Naselli, surmounted by a small shrine *(both by the Gagini)*. At the back of the church is a lovely 17C gallery, painted with fruit and flowers.

Piazza San Biagio

The square is graced with the **Chiesa di San Biagio**, a Byzantine church rebuilt in the 18C and the **Castello Aragonese**.

Chiesa dei Cappuccini

Located in the south of the town, this building dates from 1616. Inside is a fine intarsia *(inlaid wood)* **altar★** and a deli-

Carmelo Cappello Sculpture Collection

The collection is located on an industrial estate (ASI) south of Ragusa, in Contrada Mugno, 97100 Ragusa, exit from S 115 at 321 km. ◔*Open Mon–Thu 9am–12.30pm, 3.30–5pm, Fri 9am–12.30pm.* ◔*Closed Sat–Sun.* ☏*0932 66 71 24.*

Carmelo Cappello, a native of Ragusa *(b. 1912)*, began to work in the 1930s. His style, which evolved from being highly figurative in the early years to pure abstraction in his latest creations, is well represented in this small, but interesting collection. *Il freddoloso (Shivering with Cold* – 1938), one of his most famous works, is a realistic figure charged with great expression. In his later works, facial features become abstract by being reduced to a minimum: compare the expressive faces of the two women with well-defined noses and eyes *(though no hair or mouth)* in *Le Prime Stelle (The First Stars)* to the faces of the two athletes in *Acrobati* (1953–54). In this latter work, individual personality and detail has been distilled, abstracted and replaced by a concentration on rhythm and movement of line. Cappello's latest works are austere studies of pure line, clinically cold *(an impression imparted by the polished steel)*, yet which twist and merge, attempting to encapsulate in form the fluid dynamics of the universe.

cate statue of the Madonna (18C). The mortuary chapel preserves the mummified remains of various religious and illustrious men.

NEAR COMISO
Vittoria
Approx. 6km/3mi W.

The town – founded in the 17C on the wishes of Countess Vittoria Colonna, after whom it is named – was partly spared by the 1693 earthquake. Its straight, perpendicular streets are scattered with elegant Liberty-style *palazzi*. The centre is the Piazza del Popolo, where **Santa Maria delle Grazie** stands with its elegant façade next to the neo-Classical municipal theatre. In Via Cancellieri, leading off the piazza, are a number of fine buildings: note the Liberty-style **Palazzo Carfì-Manfré** (no. 71) and the Venetian Gothic **Palazzo Traìna** (nos. 108–116).

Via Cavour provides access to the town's main church and the museum. **San Giovanni Battista** (1695) has a distinctively linear front, with three entrances and two small lateral domes. The interior is richly decorated with neo-Classical stucco friezes picked out in white, pale and dark blue and gold. The **Museo Civico** (◔*open Tue–Sat 9.30am–1.30pm, 4–7.30pm; Wed, Fri, Sun*

9.30am–1pm; ◔*closed Mon;* ⌷€3.50; ☏*0932 72 25 21)* is accommodated in the countess's castle, completed in 1785 on much earlier foundations. The well-restored rooms continue to reflect the fact that they were used as a prison until 1950.

The small museum brings together old machinery for producing special theatrical effects *(wind and hail-producing apparatus)*, a selection of traditional farming tools and various ornithological specimens.

The WWI **concentration camp** located just outside the town centre in **Via Garibaldi** primarily held Hungarian soldiers (who were on excellent terms with the locals); one of the dormitory blocks now contains **Museo Storico Italo-Ungherese** (◔*open Mon–Sat, 9am–1pm;* ◔*closed Sun and public holidays;* ⌷*Free;* ☏*0932 86 59 94).*

Vittoria gives its name to the regional wine Cerasuolo di Vittoria made in the only DOCG *(Denominazione di Origine Controllata e Garantita)* appellation of Sicily. This aromatic cherry-coloured wine is made from a balance of hearty Nero d'Avola grapes and the lighter varietal Frappato. Try it with pasta, antipasti, game or even fish dishes.

ACATE

Approx. 15km/9mi NW.

In the past, the little town was called Biscari; its modern name probably comes from the word for agate, a semi-precious stone found locally.

For generations, it belonged to the princes of Paterno-Castello, hence the massive residence in the town centre. It is also worth seeking out the town's main church (**Chiesa Madre**) and **San Vincenzo**, which claims to preserve the martyred saint's relics.

🚗 DRIVING TOUR

COASTAL TOUR

110km/69mi from Ragusa, finishing in Comiso. Allow one day.

▷ From Ragusa, take S 194 to Modica *(12km/7.5mi SE)*.

Modica

🔆*See Modica.*

▷ Take S 115 to Pozzallo *(20km/12.5mi SE)*.

Pozzallo

This sleepy hamlet lies on the edge of a long beach.

Its most characteristic landmark is the **Torre dei Conti Cabrera**, which was originally built by the local count as a watchtower at a time when pirates frequently attacked the community. Destroyed by the 1693 earthquake, it has since been rebuilt.

▷ Continue along the coast road.

This coast road passes the resorts of **Marina di Modica** and **Sampieri**.

▷ Turn right at the junction to Scicli and continue 10km/6mi to the town (🔆*See Modica)*.

After 6km/4mi the coast road passes through the **Riserva Naturale della Foce dell'Irpinio** before arriving at **Marina di Ragusa**, a popular seaside resort. The **Parco Archeologico di Kaucana** is nearby, between Punta Secca and Casuzze. There are two entrances to the archaeological site: one along the coastal road, the other on the road from Punta Secca to Marina di Ragusa. It encloses the ruins of a residential area and a small palaeo-Christian church.

▷ Continue along the coast road.

Rovine di Camarina

Camarina was founded in 598 BC as a Greek town by Syracuse; it suffered assaults on many occasions, only to be rebuilt and then finally destroyed by the Romans in 258 BC. **Excavation** has revealed part of the walls, as well as the remains of a 5C temple dedicated to Athena and a residential quarter built on a grid street pattern, dating from Hellenistic times *(marked by the fence on the other side of the road)*.

Museo Archeologico Regionale di Camarina

🕐*Mon–Sat, 9am–1.30pm.* ✒️€4.
♿ 📞*0932 82 60 04. In the first room the most recent finds recovered as a result of ongoing work are displayed; these are gradually replaced and transferred to the permanent collection. The layout is therefore subject to reorganisation.*

The ships wrecked off the coast of Camarina have given up a wealth of treasures, including a wonderful **Corinthian bronze helmet★** (6C–5C BC), an Attic-Etruscan helmet (4C BC), an elegant bronze-and-enamel perfume container (2C AD), and a hoard of more than 1 000 bronze coins (AD 275). There is also an unusual set of **lead weights** recovered from the seabed. The museum has a vast collection of well-preserved Corinthian *(older and therefore more crudely made)* and Attic **amphorae★**. Etruscan and Punic amphorae are distinguished by their elongated forms. The section devoted to the Archaic period contains a number of interesting pieces, including a fine **aryballos** *(a small bucket-like vessel used for drawing water from a well)* decorated with two facing lions (T 2281) from the necropolis at **Rifriscolaro**.

▶ From Camarina head inland to Donnafugata *(12km/7.5mi)*.

CASTELLO DI DONNAFUGATA★

○*Open Nov–Mar Tue, Thu and Sun, 9am–1pm, 2.45–4.30pm (Wed, Fri and Sat 9am–1pm); Apr–Oct Tue, Thu and Sun, 9am–1pm, 2.45–5.30pm (Wed, Fri and Sat 9am–1pm)* ○*Closed Mon.* ●€5. ♿ ℘*0932 61 93 33. http://www. comune.ragusa.gov.it/turismo/castello/ 09oraricastello.html.*

The oldest part of the castle *(which includes the square tower)* dates back to the mid-17C when the Donnafugata fiefdom was acquired by Vincenzo Arezzo La Rocca. The building was then continuously altered until the early 20C, when Corrado Arezzo transformed the façade into the one that can be seen today. What is striking about the castle's exterior is the elegant Venetian-Gothic **loggia** that dominates the centre of the façade. Trefoil arches are a recurrent motif here and repeated in the two-light windows throughout the building.

Gardens

The big garden, shaded first by large banyan trees *(Ficus magnolioides)*, then by other Mediterranean and exotic species *(succulents and cluster pines)*, conceals various follies intended to charm and bemuse its visitors, like the round temple and a coffee house *(where refreshments could be taken)*, the stone maze and several artificial caves encrusted with fake stalactites *(below the temple)*.

Villa

The first floor is open to the public. At the top of the black stone *(pietra pece in Italian)* staircase, ornamented with neo-Classical statues, is the **Salone degli Stemmi**, named after the armorial crests of great Sicilian noble families painted on the walls. Among the suites of rooms are some with delicately painted *trompe l'oeil* ceilings. These include the stucco-decorated **Salone degli Specchi** *(the Hall of Mirrors)*, the **Billiard Room** and **Music**

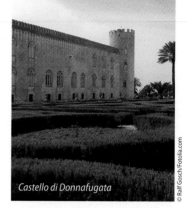
Castello di Donnafugata
© Ralf Gosch/Fotolia.com

Room, each with painted landscapes projecting out beyond the walls, and the bedroom of the Princess of Navarre, paved in black *pietra pece* (a bitumous limestone mined locally, from which pitch is made) and white limestone. The **Stanza del Signore** and the **Fumoir** are beautifully furnished; the decoration of the latter, a smoking room, is perfectly appropriate to its function. It is papered with pipe motifs and the ceiling is painted with medallions filled with playing cards and stunning peacocks fanning their tails at the corners.

The castle has inspired a number of writers and artists. **Guiseppe di Lampedusa** used the name Donnafugata in his famous 1958 novel *The Leopard* as the title of the country house inhabited by main protagonists, the Salina family. It has also been featured in the making of many well-known films, including the *La Giara* scene in the film *Chaos* by the **Taviani brothers**.

▶ From here, continue to Comiso *(16km/10mi N, ♿See Comiso).*

ADDRESSES

🏠 STAY

in your room or on the terrace, which also provides a fine view. Village cuisine on offer.

🍴🛏 **Il Giardino dei Sospiri** – *Via dei Sospiri 24. ☎0932 65 14 18 or 333 217 44 85 - www.ilgiardinodeisospiri.it. 1 room.* Owned by the same person as the Belvedere All'Idria (see above). In the heart of d'Ibla, this studio has a kitchen, with a ground-floor double bed and two twin beds on the mezzanine – perfect for a couple with children. The real bonus is the delightful garden with palm and lemon trees!

🍴🛏🛏 **Il Barocco** – *Via Santa Maria La Nuova 1, Ibla. ☎0932 66 31 05. www.ilbarocco.it. 14 rooms 🍽.* The best of the pleasant, plush rooms in this old palazzo overlook the courtyard.

🍴🛏🛏 **Caelum Hyblae** – *Salita Specula 11, Ibla. ☎0932 68 90 48. www.bbcaelum hyblae.it. 7 rooms 🍽.* There's a charming, peaceful atmosphere in this guesthouse nestling in the shadow of the Duomo. The cosy rooms are simply furnished and breakfast is served on the roof terrace with views over the old town.

🍴🛏🛏 **Palazzo degli Archi** – *Corso Don Minzoni 6, Ibla. ☎0932 68 60 21. fax 0932 68 56 03. www.hotelpalazzodegliarchi.it. 🅿. 10 rooms 🍽.* The colour crimson dominates the exterior and interior of this hotel. Situated close to Ilba, this is a very comfortable place to stay.

🍴🛏🛏🛏 **Eremo della Giubiliana** *Contrada Giubiliana, SP25 towards Marina di Ragusa, after 7.5km. ☎0932 66 91 19. www.eremodellagiubiliana.it. ⚲ ✗ .24 rooms. 🍽.* Between Ragusa and the coast, this charming, elegant former 13C hermitage (*eremo*), once home to the Knights of Malta, offers comfortable rooms, a restaurant and well-being centre.

🍴 EAT

🍴🛏 **Trattoria Tipica** – *Corso 25 Aprile 16. ☎0932 62 12 24. Closed Sun.* A warm welcome and ultra-fresh produce in this little restaurant offering copious portions of local specialities at very reasonable prices. No terrace and slightly ageing decor, but good value for money.

🍴🛏 **U Saracinu** – *Via del Convento 9, Ibla. ☎0932 24 69 76. Closed Sun and 10–30 Jul.* This welcoming restaurant on the cathedral square serves up tasty, fortifying cuisine.

🍴🛏🛏 **Baglio la Pergola** – *Contrada Selvaggio (in the stadium district), Ragusa. ☎0932 68 64 30. Closed Tue.* A varied selection of main courses and pizzas are on the menu in this restaurant in a typical country *baglio* or stronghold. The traditional Sicilian specialities are particularly recommended.

🍴🛏🛏 **Il Barocco** – *Via Orfanotrofio 29, Ibla. ☎0932 65 23 97. Closed Wed and Jan.* This central family pizzeria has a curious decoration that may not please lovers of minimalism - but it certainly merits its name.

🍴🛏🛏🛏 **Locanda Don Serafino** – *Via Orfanotrofio 39, Ibla. ☎0932 24 87 78. www.locandadonserafino.it. Closed Tue.* Seasonal Sicilian specialities served in the stone-vaulted dining room, housed in what was once the stables of an aristocratic mansion. An extensive wine cellar features an unusually diverse selection of wines from Sicily, Italy and the world. The piano-bar in the entryway is perfect for an after-dinner drink.

TAKING A BREAK

Gelati Di Vini – *Piazza Duomo 20, Ibla. ☎0932 22 89 89.* A gelateria offering hand-crafted and truly original ice cream: specialities include carob, pistachio and melon, but you should not miss out on the sweet wine flavours, which are light and refreshing.

SEASIDE RESORTS

Ragusa is situated close to some of the most popular seaside resorts in southern Sicily, characterised by fine sandy beaches, sand dunes and rocky cliffs. **Sampieri**, **Donnalucata** and **Scoglitti** are perfect for a relaxing holiday, while **Marina di Ragusa** and **Marina di Modica**, both of which are exposed to the wind and therefore very popular with surfers and windsurfers, are more suited to outdoor enthusiasts and night owls.

Val di Noto by bike – Mountain-bike excursions available to Donnafugata, Pantalica and in the Val di Noto. **Hybla Bike Touring** – *Via del Bagolaro 9, Ibla. ☎0932 66 74 19.*

FESTIVALS

I Misteri – This parade and torch-lit procession takes place on Good Friday.

Festa di San Giorgio – A re-enactment of the martyrdom of St George is held in Ragusa on the last Sunday in May, ending with a grand firework display.

Modica ★

Modica has suffered two major catastrophies in its history: the earthquake of 1693 and the flood of 1902. Each time, the city - which was listed as a UNESCO World Heritage Site in 2002 - has been rebuilt, and it is now famous for its Baroque churches, palazzi and 120-year old bakery serving delicious traditional pastries.

A BIT OF HISTORY

Before the earthquake of 1693 much of the population lived in troglodyte dwellings cut into the limestone cliffs surrounding the modern town. In the centre stood the castle, isolated on its rocky spur and enclosed on the north side by walls. Two rivers flowed through the valley, converging midway to form the River Scicli (or Motucano). As the threat of attack dwindled, the people moved down into the valley, but it was not until the earthquake that the cave dwellings were finally abandoned. The town clustered naturally into a Y-shape around the confluence of the two rivers, linked by a succession of 20 bridges between the banks, earning it the name "Venice of the South". Then, in 1902, a series of freak storms raised the water level to a terrifying height of 9m/29ft, after which the waterways were sealed off and transformed into wide streets that became the main thoroughfares of present-day Modica.

👣 WALKING TOUR

Since the 19C, the upper and lower sections of the town have been linked by a stairway leading up from Corso Umberto I to San Giorgio, Modica's most beautiful church.

SAN GIORGIO ★★

The flight of almost **300 steps** was completed in 19C and complements the elegant façade, merging with it to produce a dramatic **composition★★**. The design has been attributed to Rosario Gagliardi,

- ▶ **Population:** 54 721
- ⚷ **Michelin Map:** p265: A2
- 🛈 **Info:** Modica Tourist Office, Corso Umberto 149; ℘0932 75 96 34, www.comune.modica.gov.it.
- ◖ **Location:** Modica is divided into the upper town, dominated by the castle, and the lower town, hemmed in by high ground, along the two main streets, Via Marchesa Tedeschi and Corso Umberto.
- 🔖 **Don't Miss**: Climbing the staircase at San Giorgio connecting upper and lower Modica. Contemporary paintings at Palazzo Polara. Artisanal Modica chocolate from a centuries-old process derived from the Aztecs and imported under Spanish rule.
- 👫 **Kids:** The **caves** of Colle di San Matteo at Scicli.
- 🕐 **Timing:** Visit churches and museums in the early morning or late afternoon; most are closed for 2–3 hours midday.

GETTING THERE

The most convenient way to reach the town is by car, although train (20min from Ragusa and approx. 2hr from Siracusa) and bus services are also available (for information, contact the tourist office).

although some claim it resulted from a collaboration of architects, notably Paolo Labisi. The lofty front elevation rises through three levels to a single bell tower; a sense of sweeping movement is imparted by the projecting convex central bay, flanked by twin bays that accommodate the double aisles. Inside, St George's contains a chased silver altar

San Giorgio

©Antonio Brundo/Fotolia.com

front, upon which sits a fine **polyptych** (1513) by Bernardino Niger. The three tiers show in ascendance: St George and St Martin, the Holy Family, and the Joyful Mysteries and Glorious Mysteries. The transept floor is inlaid with a 19C meridian line by A. Perini. The third chapel on the right contains an Assumption altarpiece by Francesco Paladini.

Beside the church stands **Palazzo Polara**, which houses the **Pinacoteca Comunale** (*open daily except Sun, 9am–1pm*), and its collection of contemporary paintings.

On Via Posteria is the **Casa Natale di Salvatore Quasimodo** (*open daily 10am–1pm, Sat 10am–1pm, 4–7pm; closed Mon; €2; 0932 75 28 97*), the house where the 20C poet was born, containing furniture and possessions from the writer's study in Milan.

Continue down to **Corso Umberto I**, the main thoroughfare of the Città Bassa *(lower town)*, lined with elegant 18C *palazzi* and religious institutions. As the street approaches the centre, it passes the undulating façade of **Santa Maria del Soccorso** and, a little farther on, the Church of San Pietro.

SAN PIETRO

St Peter's was rebuilt after the earthquake: the front **façade★** is ornamented with statues of the 12 Apostles.

CHIESA RUPESTRE DI SAN NICOLA INFERIORE

Open Jul–Aug Mon–Sat 10am–1pm, 5–8pm; Sept–Jun Tue–Sun 10am–1pm, 4–7pm. €2. 331 74 030 45.

In the apse of this rock-hewn church is a series of Byzantine-style frescoes dating from the Norman era. Pride of place is given to Christ Pantocrator *(centre)*; at his side stand the Madonna and Child and the Archangel Michael.

San Pietro with statues of the Apostles

©Antonio Zimbone/Tips Images

At the intersection with the other branch of the "Y" (*Via Marchesa Tedeschi*) stands **San Domenico** and beyond, the town hall. This provides a good **view** of the castle above. Almost opposite, the Via De Leva leads through to the *palazzo* that shares its name and a fine **Chiaramonte Gothic** entrance. Before the end of the street stands the Baroque **Chiesa del Carmine**. Continue to the junction with Via Mercé and turn right: ahead is the **Convento dei Padre Mercedari** housing the Museo Civico and Museo delle Arti e Tradizioni Popolari.

MUSEO DELLE ARTI E TRADIZIONI POPOLARI★

Convento dei Padri Mercedari, Via Mercé. ⚊ *Closed for restoration at the time of going to press.* ℘*0932 75 27 47.*
This museum is dedicated to rural arts, crafts and practices.
The convent is also home to the small **Museo Civico** (open Mon–Sat, 9am–1pm; Free; ℘*0932 94 50 81*) displaying a collection of archaeological artefacts found in the region.
Behind the castle in Via Crispi, sits **Palazzo Tomasi Rosso**, with its limestone doorway and balconies; note the stone-carved grimacing masks, acanthus leaves and wrought-iron railings.
Via Marchesa Tedeschi, the other arm of the "Y", climbs steadily to *Modica Alta* (upper Modica).

SANTA MARIA DI BETLEM

This church is notable for its elaborate 19C Nativity scene, comprising 60 terracotta figures modelled by G. Papale.
The street continues uphill past the 19C Baroque-fronted church of **San Giovanni Evangelista**. At the top (*Belvedere del Pizzo*), a splendid **view★** extends over the town encompassing the Jewish quarter known as il Cartellone (*right, beyond Corso Umberto I*), and the Francavilla district (*near side of Corso Umberto I*), the oldest part of town dominated by San Giorgio.

EXCURSIONS
Scicli

10km/6mi SE. The tour starts in Piazza Italia. *For information on opening times of the churches, contact the local tourist office in the Palazzo Spadaro on Via Francesco M. Pena,* ℘*0932 83 96 08.*
Scicli is high up in the hinterland, far from the beaten track. Badly damaged by the 1693 earthquake, it has risen, phoenix-like, from the ashes.
The **Chiesa Madre** shelters the wooden statue of the **Madonna on horseback**. Originally, the figure was kept in its own sanctuary, 6km/4mi west of the town.
Opposite the church stands **Palazzo Fava**, its corbels carved with emblems of chivalry. The balcony overlooking San Bartolomeo is especially fine.
On the corner of the piazza a narrow staircase to the right of the church leads up to Via Duca d'Aosta and **Palazzo Beneventano**. This building, an elegant example of secular late-Baroque architecture (18C), is flamboyantly ornamented with fantastical figures, decorative pilasters, masks of Moors and Muslims, and wild tiger-like animals. Head down to Piazza Italia, follow Via San Bartolomeo to the end of the street.
The façade of **Chiesa di San Bartolomeo** rises through three tiers of columns to a bell tower.
Inside, it contains an 18C **Nativity scene★** by the Neapolitan craftsman Pietro Padula. All 29 carved wooden figures (*originally there were 65*) are especially finely crafted.
To the rear of the church is the **Colle di San Matteo**. The caves that punctuate the side of the hill form part of the **Chiafura troglodyte settlement**, inhabited until the 1960s.
Via Mormino Penna – This elegant street passes between the fine Baroque exteriors of several *palazzi* and three churches. The first is **San Giovanni Evangelista**, a church with a **façade★** with a convex central section. Farther up is a second church, **San Michele**, laid out to the same oval plan. The 19C building opposite, **Palazzo Spadaro**, preserves its original decoration inside and out. The street ends before **Santa**

Bird's-Eye Views

Two spots provide a good overview of Scicli's rooftops: one is **Colle della Croce** in front of the 16C–17C Church of Santa Maria della Croce; the other, offering the marginally better prospect, is **Colle di San Matteo**, set before a church of the same name and now sadly abandoned. Behind rise the ruins of a castle possibly constructed during the Arab occupation.

Teresa, a church with a late-Baroque interior.

Walk back along Via Mormino Penna and turn down Via Nazionale to Piazza Busaccasu. Buildings facing onto the square include a Rococo church, **Chiesa del Carmine**, and its adjacent convent and **Palazzo Busacca**.

CAVA D'ISPICA★

From S 115, follow signs to Cava d'Ispica. *Tours leave from the Ufficio della Sovrintendenza.* ◑*Open Mon–Sat 9am–1.45pm.* ◎€4.

Situated between the towns of Ispica and Modica, this fissure, approx.13km/8mi long, is studded with rooms, sanctuaries and necropoli, which date from the

Chiesa del Carmine, Scicli

© Alessandro Rizzo/Fotolia.com

Neolithic era. The grottos formed naturally and were later modified by humans. The actual Cava d'Ispica contains the **Larderia★** (from the word *ardeia* – with abundant water), which consists of a palaeo-Christian catacomb (4C–5C) lined with an impressive number of burial chambers *(464)*.

The tour follows the contours of a rock wall. Beyond the Church of Santa Maria *(high up in the cliff on the left)* and the Camposanto or Holy Ground, are located the **Grotte Cadute**, which comprise a residential complex on several levels. Holes in the ceiling and cut steps enabled residents to move around with the aid of poles and ropes that could be pulled up in times of danger.

Opposite the entrance to the fenced area, on the far side of the main road, another road leads to the rock-hewn church of **San Nicola** and the **Spezieria**, a little church perched on a sharp rocky outcrop. The name, corrupted from the local dialect, is linked to the myth of a monk-cum-apothecary who prepared herbal remedies. The church interior is subdivided into two parts: a nave and a misaligned chancel with three apses. Return to the car and drive up the main road to the first turning on the left.

Baravitalla – On the plateau stand the ruins of the Byzantine church of **San Pancrati** *(on the left, fenced off)*. Further on, a path leads left to other points of interest *(⊘difficult to find without a guide)*: the **Tomb with decorative pilasters** has a double front entrance and the **Grotta dei Santi** has fresco fragments.

On the main road, continue towards Cava d'Ispica to the **Grotta della Signora**, sheltering a spring considered sacred since ancient times. The walls bear graffiti from prehistoric or palaeo-Christian eras *(swastikas and crosses)*.

Meanwhile, in the opposite direction, further towards Ispica, the central part of the gorge conceals the **"Castello"**, an enchanting residential complex several storeys high and only abandoned in the 1950s *(⊘very difficult to find: consult a local guide for detailed directions)*.

Cava d'Ispica

© DEA A TESSORE / age fotostock

ISPICA

13km/8mi SE of Cava d'Ispica.

The hub of this small town is **Piazza Regina Margherita**, where the Chiesa Madre, San Bartolomeo and Palazzo Bruno (1910), with its distinctive angular tower are situated. Corso Umberto I, running behind the church, passes between a series of fine buildings before leading to the Liberty-style jewel of the town: **Palazzo Bruno di Belmonte** *(now the town hall)* designed by **Ernesto Basile**. Opposite stands the lovely **covered market**. Other buildings of quality lie beyond it, notably **no. 76** and **no. 82**.

Return to Piazza Regina Margherita and turn down Via XX Settembre to the church of **Santa Maria Maggiore**, which forms a **harmonious ensemble★** with the semicircular arcade before the church by **Vincenzo Sinatra**.

Don't miss the cycle of **frescoes★** by Catanian artist Olivio Sozzi (1763) inside. The large central panel depicts scenes from the Old and New Testaments: Adam and Eve, Judith with the head of Holofernes, Moses *(below)*, the Apostles with St Peter *(centre)* and Christ holding the Eucharist *(above)*.

The chapel in the left transept contains a canopy with an unusual carved wooden figure of Christ at the Column.

This statue is carried annually in procession during the Maundy Thursday *(the Thursday before Easter)* celebrations. In the opposite direction, Corso Garibaldi leads to the elegant **Chiesa dell'Annunziata**.

Parco della Forza

Via Cava Grande. ⏱*Open Mon–Sat.* ♿€2. ✆*0932 95 11 33.*

This site has been occupied since Neolithic times and was only abandoned in the 1950s *(♿very difficult to find: consult a local guide for directions).* During the Middle Ages, the plateau above the gorge was fortified with a citadel. This was raised around the **Palazzo Marchionale**, the layout of which may still be made out. Some rooms contain fragments of original painted, fired lime floor tiles. The small fortress also contained several churches, including the **Annunziata**, with 26 graves inlaid into its floor.

The cave known as the **Scuderia**, because it was used as stables in medieval times, bears traces of graffiti horses. The most striking feature is the **Centoscale**, a immensely long underground stairway *(240 steps cut into the rock)*, which descends 60m/200ft at an angle of 45 degrees to emerge on a level with the valley floor, below the river bed. The age of the passage is uncertain, but its function was to ensure a water supply even in times of drought.

A total of 100 slaves (hence the name) collected the liquid as it filtered down from the river bed (at its deepest point, the passageway was 20m/65ft below water level).

Outside the park stands **Santa Maria della Cava**, a little rock-hewn church containing fragments of fresco in layers *(apply to the custodians for access)*.

ADDRESSES

🛌 STAY

🍴🍽 **Bristol** – *Via Risorgimento 8/B, Modica.* ✆*0932 76 28 90. www.hotel bristol.it. 27 rooms* 🛏. Situated in a quiet, residential area in the modern part of the town, this simple, well-kept hotel is ideal for both business visitors and tourists. The rooms here are comfortable and well-appointed, and the staff are friendly and welcoming.

SCICLI

🍴🍽🍽 **Conte Ruggero** – *Piazza Italia 24.* ✆*0932 93 18 40. www.conteruggero.it.* 🅿. *5 rooms* 🛏. In a splendid late-Baroque palazzo, this hotel offers elegant, refined rooms. A very romantic choice!

🍴 EAT

La Locanda del Colonnello – *Vico Biscari 6.* ✆*0932 75 24 23 . www.palazzofailla.it. Closed Wed.* This gourmet trattoria serves local rustic cuisine made the traditional way. Specialities include pasta with sardines and almonds, squid casserole and *cannoli* with ricotta made from ewe's milk.

🍴🍽 **Taverna Nicastro** – *Via Sant'Antonio 28 .* ✆*0932 94 58 84. www.tavernanicastro.it. Closed lunch, Sun–Mon and the week of 15 Aug.* A welcoming, traditional taverna, where you can eat outside when the weather is good. Generous, tasty antipasti.

🍴🍽🍽 **Fattoria delle Torri** – *Vico Napolitano 14, Modica.* ✆*0932 75 12 86. Closed Mon. Booking recommended.* This traditional restaurant, located in an elegant old *palazzo* in the town centre, serves a range of interesting and creative dishes based on local specialities. Meals can also be taken under the shade of the lemon trees in the attractive outdoor courtyard.

TAKING A BREAK

Antica Dolceria Bonajuto – *Corso Umberto I 159, Modica.* ✆*0932 94 12 25. Closed Mon.* This confectioner's, founded in 1880, offers delicacies such as *mpanatigghi* (sweet pastries with an unusual filling of minced meat and chocolate); *liccumie* (filled with eggplant and chocolate); flavoured Modica chocolate made according to the original Aztec recipe; and *riposti* (delicately decorated almond sweets, originally produced for weddings). Also worth sampling are the aranciate and *cedrate* (sweets made with orange and lemon peel) and the *nucatoli* (made with dried figs, almonds, quince and honey).

Caffè dell'Arte – *Corso Umberto I 114, Modica.* ✆*0932 94 58 95. www.caffedell arte.it. Closed Wed.* This café is renowned for its granite (crushed ice drinks), its excellent *cannoli* and *cassate*.

FESTIVALS

Three festivals are celebrated by Scicli. The first, the **Cavalcata di San Giuseppe**, takes place on 18 and 19 March. This essentially commemorates the flight of Joseph and Mary into Egypt, although it also celebrates the rite of spring after the passage of winter with all the affiliated pagan rituals. Colour is the festival's dominant element as flowers are used to bedeck the horses' harnesses and great wood bonfires are lit all along the route followed by the fugitives, lighting up the garish costumes of the onlookers who throng the streets. Meanwhile, the air rings with jingling horse bells and people's voices animated with merriment after the procession, gathering for great feasts partaken in each other's houses. At Easter, the **Festa dell'Uomo Vivo** celebrates life itself with a lively procession of a statue representing the Resurrected Christ, raced along by young men, through the town's streets. At the end of May, the **Battaglia delle Milizie** consists of a statue of the Madonna on horseback being carried in procession, defeating and trampling over Saracen soldiers (long ago, this festival took place on the Saturday before Easter).

The Iblei Mountains ★

The rolling limestone mountain range on the eastern tip of Sicily is dotted with small farming villages clinging onto the wooded slopes. Deep gorges, rivers and country roads cut through these forests, where terraces of almond, citrus and olive trees provide locals with their livelihood. The highest peak, Mount Lauro, is 986m/3,235ft. The region also produces some of Sicily's most flavoursome olive oil and honey.

▷ **Location:** The Iblei Mountains are a low-lying range stretching over the Ragusa, Siracusa and Catania provinces with mountain locales connected by pleasant rural roads.

🕐 **Timing:** Pleasant from spring through to autumn; avoid the heat of August.

🚗 DRIVING TOURS

THE IBLEI MOUNTAINS ★

The round trip of approx 160km/100mi can be completed over two days, starting at Caltagirone and overnighting in Vizzini.

▷ From Caltagirone, follow signs to Ragusa and Grammichele on S 124.

The southeastern corner of Sicily is dominated by the Iblei Mountains, which encircle and protect Ragusa. The little mountain villages have retained their rural aspect, living in close harmony with the fertile land that has sustained them for centuries.

▷ Follow S 124 as far as a junction where both roads are signposted to Grammichele; take the left fork.

The road provides wonderful **views** ★★ over the vast agricultural plain that is intensely cultivated with cereal crops. Beyond the hills which, according to **Tomasi di Lampedusa**, evoke *un mare bruscamente pietrificato* (a suddenly petrified sea), looms the dark majestic form of **Mount Etna**.

Grammichele

After the earthquake of 1693, the new town was laid out according to a singular plan, centred around a hexagonal piazza and six radial axes passing through the centre of each side. A series of orthogonal streets were then arranged in concentric hexagons around the central space.

The buildings overlooking the piazza include the Chiesa Madre and the town hall; the latter, in turn, houses the **archaeology museum** *(first floor)* *(🕐 open Mon–Sat 9am–1pm, 4–7pm Tues and Thu 3–7pm; ✆ €1.50; ☎ 0933 85 92 29).*

Occhiolà

Ufficio Parco Archeologico Occhiolà, Piazza Morello, Grammichele, ☎ 0933 94 48 55.

Occhiolà is situated about 3km/1.8mi from Grammichele along the road to Catania, near a road-maintenance building before a tight bend.

A stone *(on the left)* bearing an inscription marks the beginning of the road to the site where the old town stood, enjoying a **scenic position**.

▷ From Grammichele, take the road up to Licodia Eubea *(11km/7mi).*

Licodia Eubea

This hamlet, occupying a **panoramic situation** ★★ at the head of the River Dirillo, was probably built upon the ancient ruins of Euboia, founded by the colonists of Leontinoi in about 7C BC. It comprises several 18C churches and **Palazzo Vassallo** *(Via Mugnos, at the end of Via Umberto)*, a formal Baroque building with a doorway

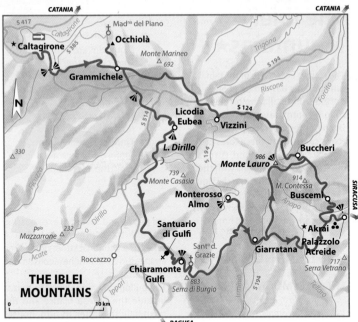

flanked by columns and a balcony laden with masks and volutes.

From the ruins of the medieval castle there is a sweeping valley **view★**.

▷ Return to the junction and the sign towards Lago di Licodia (or Dirillo) then head towards the lake.

Follow the old road to Chiaramonte Gulfi for about 10km/6mi through a stretch of **mountain scenery★**. A little farther on, the **Lago Dirillo** dam comes into view on the left.

▷ Near a bend, just before a road-maintenance *casa cantoniera* (on the right), turn left (the road to the right leads to Vittoria and Chiaramonte Gulfi).

Santuario di Gulfi

Before the earthquake destroyed it, a village occupied this broad site, now home to the Gulfi sanctuary. The sanctuary was built in the 18C on the spot where it is said yoked oxen transporting a statue of the Madonna "emerged from the sea" and knelt down.

The story is illustrated inside by four painted **medallions**.

▷ Continue along the road for approx. 4km/2.5mi.

Chiaramonte Gulfi

The Greek town of Akrillai, renamed "Gulfi" by the Arabs, was razed to the ground in 1296 and immediately rebuilt by Manfred Chiaramonte. Although much of the fabric was destroyed by earthquake, the hamlet preserves its medieval organisation.

The *Arco dell'Annunziata*, an ancient gateway to the old town, is all that survives from the Chiaramonte era (14C). Among the principal Baroque buildings, look out for San Giovanni *(at the top of the hill)* and the **Chiesa Madre**.

The 18C **Palazzo Montesano** on via Montesano *(call for opening times ℘0932 92 80 49)* houses a museum showcasing ethnic instruments, Art Nouveau works *(including those by Lalique and Basilie)* and olive oil, one of the town's principal products.

In the higher part of town, the Santuario delle Grazie sits surrounded by pine trees *(picnic facilities)* and an all-encompassing **view**★ over Chiaramonte and, in the distance, Etna.

The road to Monterosso Almo *(20km/12.5mi)* snakes its way among gentle slopes covered with cultivated fields enclosed by **drystone walls**.

Monterosso Almo

The church of **San Giovanni**★ lends its name to the piazza here: together they provide a focal point for the upper part of this agricultural town.

The front elevation of the church, attributed to **Vincenzo Sinatra**, rises through columns to culminate in a bell tower. In the lower neighbourhood stands a church to rival San Giovanni **Sant'Antonio**. The same square is graced with the neo-Gothic **Chiesa Madre** and the elegant Palazzo Zacco.

▷ Follow S 194 for 7km/4mi.

Giarratana

Three monuments constitute the artistic heritage of this hamlet: the late-Renaissance **Chiesa Madre** and two Baroque churches dedicated to San Bartolomeo and Sant'Antonio Abate. An onion festival, the *Sagra della Cipolla*, is held here every August.

▷ From Giarratana, either continue to Palazzolo or shorten the tour by turning left to Buccheri and following the winding road that leads to the top of **Monte Lauro**.

The road *(10km/6mi)* that winds up the mountain through intense patches of colour from red valerian *(Centranthus ruber)* and deep green carobs and pines provides glorious **views**★ over the high plateau.

▷ To get to Palazzolo from Giarratana, follow the main road for 14km/9mi, then turn right towards the site of Ancient Akrai.

Akrai★

⏱ *Open 8am until 1hr before dusk.*
💶 *€4.* ♿ ☏ *0931 87 66 02.*

Akrai was founded in 664 BC as a defensive outpost of Syracuse. At the top of the hill, where the acropolis once stood, is the orchestra of an ancient white stone theatre.

The **bouleuterion**, a stepped meeting-area, lies to the right. Near the gate is a section of the old *plateia*, paved with slabs of lava stone.

Christians converted two old Greek quarries next to the theatre into catacombs and troglodyte dwellings. Near the entrance to one, the **Intagliatella** is an evocative low relief of a hero banqueting and sacrificing.

I Santoni

1km/0.6mi from the archaeological site.
Tucked into a small valley nearby, a dozen 3C BC rock-hewn figures testify to the existence of a mysterious and bloody cult built around the mother goddess Cybele, depicted seated between two lions or standing with smaller figures.

Palazzolo Acreide

Palazzolo was largely rebuilt in the 18C and has a superlative spread of Baroque buildings lining its main thoroughfares: Corso Vittorio Emanuele and Via Carlo Alberto, which intersect at Piazza del Popolo. The square is dominated by the majestic façade of **San Sebastiano**. At the western end of the *corso* stands the **Chiesa dell'Immacolata**, with its convex frontage, in which is preserved a delicate *Madonna and Child* by **Francesco Laurana**. Via Carlo Alberto passes between a series of *palazzi* with wonderful Baroque details. One of the streets off to the right *(Via Machiavelli)* leads to the **Casa-Museo dell'etnologo Antonino Uccello** (⏱ *open 9am–1pm, 2.30–7pm;* ☏ *0931 88 14 99) a palazzo* once owned by Baron Ferla and later turned into a house-museum by another owner, the ethnologist Antonio Uccello.

At the end of the street, turn right onto Piazza Umberto I to the church of **San Paolo** and its striking façade, possibly designed by **Vincenzo Sinatra**.

On the square with the same name is the **Palazzo Rizzarelli-Spadaro** and

© mirabile / Fotolia.com

Drystone Walling

An ever-present reminder of human impact on the rural landscape are the ribbons of drystone walling that extend in all directions: small, low-lying yet resistant courses of stone, no more than a metre high, enclose the cultivated fields. Interestingly, the very nature of these walls reflects the geological formation of the Iblei. Just as with the bedrock, the surface layer of limestone is impermeable: where this layer is damaged by erosion or fracture, water will penetrate through the underlying layers causing them to crumble and disintegrate into lumps. In the most extreme cases, this can produce whole canyons. The broken lumps of rock litter the ground, requiring farmers to remove them before they can sow their fields; the walls are conceived as a way of re-using the stones so laboriously gathered which, instead of being heaped in a pile, are recycled as building materials. However, this is no haphazard pastime but a skilled art learned from master-craftsmen known in the vernacular as *mastri ri mura a siccu*. The walls segregate different land holdings and enable flocks to graze unsupervised; they also support terraced land.

its **Centro Espositivo Museale delle Tradizioni Nobiliari** (◷open Tue–Sun 10.30–1.30pm, 2.30–7pm; ℘0931 87 58 20), which explores aristocratic life before the unification of Italy. Follow Via dell'Annunziata out of the piazza to the church of the same name; its façade, which remains incomplete, has an interesting **doorway★** flanked by spiral columns.

Return along Via dell'Annunziata and turn left down Via Garibaldi to **Palazzo Iudica** (at nos. 123–131) and its amazingly long balcony supported by console brackets carved with monsters, fantastical figures and other Baroque elements. The road to Buscemi (9km/5.5mi) provides a number of stunning **views★**.

BUSCEMI

This farming hamlet is home to an unusual and intriguing museum dedicated to rural craftsmanship: **I Luoghi del Lavoro Contadinoa**. Its various venues, eight in all, are scattered through-out the town: the blacksmith's forge, the oil press, a farmstead, the houses of a farm labourer (*lo Jurnataru*), cobbler and carpenter, plus a wine press. The tour finishes with the watermill (*Mulino ad acqua Santa Lucia*), situated in the valley of mills (*valle dei mulini*) at Palazzolo Acreide.

The mill now houses the small **Museo della Maccina del Grano** (◷open 9am–1pm; ⊸€5 for the "Luoghi del Lavoro Contadino", €3 for the mill and minibus there, reservation necessary; ℘0931 87 85 28; www.museobuscemi.org). A number of Baroque monuments line the streets, including the lovely façade of the Chiesa Madre, the curvilinear elevation of Sant'Antonio da Padova e San Sebastiano. Immediately after rejoining the main road, glance up at the rockface below the town to see the Siculi excavated tombs (12C–13C BC).

▷ After 6km/4mi, the road reaches Buccheri.

BUCCHERI

Perched at a height of 820m/2,689ft, this hamlet has a church dedicated to Mary Magdalen with a façade (18C) articulated by two tiers of columns and pilasters. Another honours St Anthony Abbot with a front elevation that rises in one sweep to a tall tower, exaggerated by a long, steep staircase.

▷ Continue to Vizzini.

VIZZINI

The town of Vizzini served the novelist **Giovanni Verga** as a backdrop for several books, including *La Lupa (The She-Wolf)*, *La Cavalleria Rusticana* (on which Mascagni based his famous opera), and *The Story of Mastro Don Gesualdo*.

Vizzini has grown up around Piazza Umberto I, on which you'll find the Palazzo Verga and the Palazzo Municipale are located.

Alongside the town hall rises a flight of steps, the **Salita Marineo**, decorated with majolica tiles featuring geometric and floral designs arranged around a central medallion painted with views of buildings in Vizzini. This scheme, completed in 1996, echoes a similar stairway to Santa Maria del Monte at Caltagirone (♿ *See Caltagirone*). The Chiesa Madre preserves a Norman-Gothic doorway *(right side)*, the sole vestige of the original church that survived the 1693 earthquake.

The town's Baroque constructions include the beautiful frontage of **San Sebastiano**. The church of **Santa Maria di Gesù** contains a *Madonna and Child* by **Antonello Gagini**.

▷ From Vizzini, either take the old road to Caltagirone and Grammichele *(S 214 for 30km/19mi)*, or follow the tour described below.

BEYOND THE NORTHERN SLOPES OF THE IBLEI

Tour: 100km/62mi from Caltagirone or 75km/47mi from the end of the tour

described above (Vizzini). Allow one day. ♿ *See above for the Caltagirone-Grammichele section of the tour.*

▷ After Grammichele, follow S 124 for approx. 10km/6mi as far as the turn-off to the left for Militello in Val di Catania *(25km/15mi E of Grammichele)*.

Militello in Val di Catania

The Baroque town of Militello is largely indebted to Joan of Austria (1573–1630), for its prosperity.

When she married Francesco Branciforte, she brought a sophisticated sense of culture with her. As a result, the streets of the old town offer a multitude of fine Baroque buildings.

Start at Piazza del Municipio, home to the **Monastero Benedettino** (1614–41), an imposing Benedictine monastery *(now the town hall)*, which has a highly decorative frontage. The main **façade** of the **church** next door is ornamented with rusticated window surrounds, a common feature peculiar to the Militello style. Inside, it contains Sebastiano Conca's painting of *The Last Communion of St Benedict (third chapel on the left)* and a fine set of carved wooden choir stalls.

▷ Continue along Via Umberto, past the Palazzo Reforgiato, to Piazza V. Emanuele.

Museo di San Nicolò – *Via Umberto 167.* ◷*Open Wed–Sun 9am–1pm, 4.30–7.30pm.* ◷*Closed Tue.* ♿€4. ✆*095 81 12 51.* The museum is housed under the **Chiesa Madre** (1721) and enjoys an impressive **display★**. The last rooms are devoted to pictures: an altarpiece *Annunciation* by Francesco Franzetto (1552), a strongly-lit Caravaggioesque *Attack on San Carlo Borromeo* by the Tuscan painter Filippo Paladini (1612), and a gentle *Immacolata* by Vaccaro.

The church of **Santa Maria alla Catena** on Piazza Vittorio Emanuele was rebuilt in 1652. Its fine **interior★** is encrusted with lovely **stuccowork** by artists from Acireale; scenes from the Joyful Mysteries adorn the upper tier, while the lower tier harbours various Sicilian saints surrounded by cherubs, festoons and cornucopia.

▶ Turn left onto Via Umberto.

Beyond the attractive concave façade of the Chiesa del Santissimo Sacramento al Circolo lies Piazza Maria Santissima della Stella.

Maria Santissima della Stella – This church, with its fine doorway and spiral columns, was erected between 1722 and 1741. Inside is a magnificent glazed terracotta **Nativity altarpiece★** (1487) by the Florentine master **Andrea della Robbia**. The **Treasury** contains a late-15C altarpiece with scenes from the life of St Peter by the Maestro della Croce of Piazza Armerina. **Palazzo Majorana**, one of the few buildings dating from the 16C, extends along the same side of the square. Note its heavily rusticated cornerstones bearing carved lions.

▶ At the far end of the palazzo turn left, then immediately right for Santa Maria la Vetere.

Chiesa di Santa Maria la Vetere – Most of the church collapsed following the earthquake of 1693, leaving only the wall of the south aisle intact. Above the

front's 16C porch sits a **lunette** enclosing shallow reliefs. The overall **impact★** is heightened by the splendid position of the church, nestling in its green valley. Pass back through the town gate and immediately turn left for the Chiesa dei Santissimi Angeli Custodi. The **Chiesa dei Santissimi Angeli Custodi** contains a wonderful majolica **floor★**, laid with tiles from Caltagirone (1785).

Return the way you have come and turn left so as to skirt around the ruins of the Branciforte castle (comprising a round tower and sections of stone wall). Pass through the town gate – Porta della Terra – and reach the piazza beyond.

At the centre of what once constituted the castle courtyard sits a fountain: **Fontana della Ninfa Zizza** was built in 1607 to commemorate the construction of Militello's first aqueduct.

▶ Continue on to Scordia (11km/7mi NE).

Scordia

Scordia is built on a rectilinear town plan, arranged around the palazzo of the Branciforte family, who were the lords during the 17C. The main square, Piazza Umberto, is enclosed by many noble *palazzi* and a church with a lofty elevation.

▶ Continue on to Palagonia (12km/7.5mi NW).

S 385 picks its way through **rolling landscape★** past endless lush groves of lemon and orange trees, for which the area is famous, and the small, rocky hills known as *Coste* to the south.

Palagonia

According to Siculi legend, their gods the **Palici**, were born from the bubbling sulphurous waters of the **Laghetto di Naftia**. Nowadays, the lake is rather prosaically masked from view by natural gas pumping rigs. The name Palagonia is strongly associated with the area's production of superbly juicy blood oranges.

Seeds and Diamonds

One of the most commonly recurring elements in the Iblei landscape is the **carob tree**, a large evergreen growing, often in isolation, in the middle of a field. The broad growth of characteristically shiny dark green leaves provides deep shade. Its beans, which can be used as a thickener or an alternative to coffee when ground into powder, or animal feed, once had a nobler use: the fact that their weight is always consistent, meant they came to be used as units of measurement for precious stones; the term "carat" derives from the Arabic name for the carob, *Qirat*.

○ Follow S 385 from Palagonia towards Catania; take the right fork signposted for Contrada Croce. After 4.5km/3mi, as the road curves to the right, look out for a track on the left closed by a metal barrier.

Eremitaggio di Santa Febronia

A 15min walk up the track, this small hermitage is named after Santa Febronia. It's known locally as a' Santuzza because the saint's relics are brought each year in a procession from nearby Palagonia. The small retreat, carved out of the rock, is Byzantine (7C). Inside, the apse contains a fine, slightly damaged fresco of Christ flanked by the Madonna and an angel.

○ Take S 385 to Caltagirone. After 8km/5mi, turn left to Mineo.

Mineo

The place where the writer Luigi Capuana (1839–1915) was born has been identified as the ancient town of Mene, founded by Ducetius, king of the Siculi. The town's main gateway is the **Porta Adinolfo (18C)**. Beside it sits the Jesuit College and beyond lies the shady main square and **Chiesa del Collegio**. At the top of the town lie the ruins of a castle.

○ Retrace your steps to S 385, from where the views to Caltagirone (25km/ 15mi) are particularly impressive.

ADDRESSES

🏠 STAY

VIZZINI

🍽 **Agriturismo A Cunziria** – Contrada Masera, Vizzini. ☎0933 96 55 07; Fax 0933 96 60 87. www.cunziria.com. Closed Mon. 🍴. 14 rooms 🛏. This farm, not far from the hamlet of the same name, has a restaurant partially built in former cave dwellings. Stay in simple little wooden chalets in countryside dotted with fig and orange trees.

🍴 EAT

CHIARAMONTE GULFI

🍽🍽🍽 **Majore** – Via Martiri Ungheresi 12. ☎0932 92 80 19. www.majore.it. Closed Mon and Jul. A sign on the wall that reads "This place is devoted to the pig" leaves you in no doubt as to the menu. This longstanding restaurant exclusively serves pork-based dishes, all very carefully prepared at good prices.

MILITELLO IN VAL DI CATANIA

🍽🍽 **U'Trappitu** – Via Principe Branciforte 125. ☎095 81 14 47. Closed Mon and lunchtimes. 🍴. This trattoria occupies a former olive oil mill, which has been cleverly renovated with old millstones and presses used in the decor.

PALAZZOLO ACREIDE

🍽🍽🍽 **Valentino** – Via Galeno, on the corner of Ronco Pisacane 125. ☎0931 88 18 40. In a little town dating back to very ancient times you will find this very pleasant, simple eatery serving suitably regional cuisine.

TAKING A BREAK

The **pasticcerie** of **Militello** prepare all kinds of sweet specialities: cassatelline (cakes made of almond paste, chocolate and cinnamon); mastrazzuoli (Christmas treats made of almonds, cinnamon and a wine-based preparation known as vino cotto); and mostarda is prepared with extract of prickly pear cooked with semolina or grape must.

TOURS

Cavalleria Rusticana, the Pietro Mascagni opera inspired by the writings of Giovanni Verga, was set in a town modelled after Vizzini. For fans of opera, an exploration of Vizzini might begin at the hostelry where Turiddo and Alfio challenge each other to a duel, at the church of Santa Teresa or Santuzza's house. Ask about guided tours at the tourist office (Piazza Umberto; ☎0933 193 72 51).

Lapped by the Ionian Sea, the conveniently compact northeastern corner of Sicily has something to offer even the most demanding of travellers. Ancient ruins, a history steeped in Homeric legend, a bustling urban centre, one of the world's most active volcanoes, chic seaside resorts, summer concerts in an Ancient Greek theatre, fertile farmland, a distinctive cuisine and delicious wines – this is Sicily at its very best.

Highlights

The Volcanic Influence

Looming over it all is Etna, often known by its old Arab-influenced name, *Mongibello*, and always visible in the distance. Much of the year the volcano is capped with snow and puffs out a plume of smoke from its summit.

Europe's highest volcano has made its presence felt in everything from the now-cooled hills of black lava *(sciara)* that skirt its flanks to the paving stones of Catania and the terraced walls of its citrus groves, as well as countless portraits and paintings, and thousands of years of myth and legend.

Catania

Sicily's second city, Catania, is less than half the size of Palermo but still packs a powerful cultural punch. It's a town where music, food, art and an ancient cult dedicated to Saint Agatha are still taken very seriously.

It's easy to get around, and you can walk the city in half a day – although getting to know its secrets takes much longer.

Taormina

Sicily's most popular seaside resort, perched about 250m/820ft above the Straits of Messina and topped with an ancient panoramic Greek theatre, still in use, arguably occupies one of the most advantageous positions in the world. Beginning in the late 19C, Taormina became a popular destination for European aristocrats and the bourgeoisie. The German photographer Wilhelm von Gloeden, who photographed local youths and male nudes, paved the way for artists and intellectuals to take up residence here.

Nowadays chic boutiques, tourist shops and summer crowds obscure much of what was Taormina, but its charm remains.

From a prime spot on a clear day you can see past Messina and over the straits to mainland Italy at Calabria.

Etna

Mongibello, 3,300m/11,000ft high, is prone to eruption, earning its reputation as "nature's wildcard". Any trip to the area should include a visit to its towns, flanks and summit.

On summer evenings when the volcano erupts, watching the fireworks from a terrace far away is after-dinner entertainment for locals and tourists alike.

The volcanic soils of Etna and its microclimes contribute to its stunningly fertile and diverse array of agriculture, which can be enjoyed in its pistachio-flavoured Bronte pasta sauces and other savoury and sweet dishes, its abundance of autumnal wild mushrooms, and a variety of sweet lemon called *interdonato*, from the Messina coast, whose skin is so mild it's eaten along with the flesh.

Wine Region

The relatively small farms and vineyards that flank Etna are home to Sicily's most dynamic wine scene.

Though the area has produced wine for millennia, its heyday was the late 19C, when much of the rest of Europe was blighted by phylloxera. In the

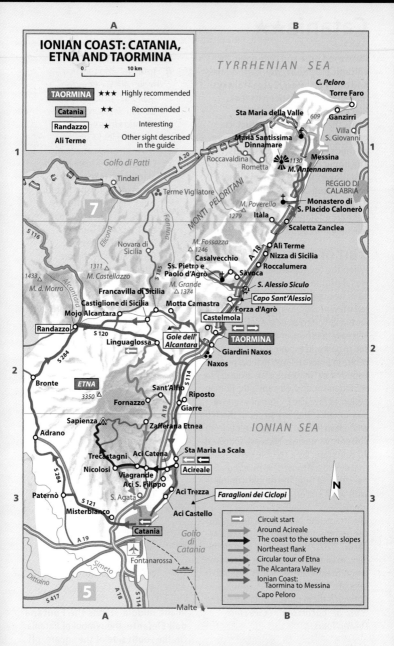

IONIAN COAST: CATANIA, ETNA AND TAORMINA

0 10 km

TAORMINA	★★★	Highly recommended
Catania	★★	Recommended
Randazzo	★	Interesting
Ali Terme		Other sight described in the guide

TYRRHENIAN SEA

C. Peloro
Torre Faro
Sta Maria della Valle
609
Ganzirri
Villa
S. Giovanni
Maria Santissima
Dinnamare
1130
Messina
M. Antennamare
REGGIO DI
CALABRIA
Golfo di Patti
Tindari
A 20
Roccavaldina
Rometta
Terme Vigliatore
MONTI PELORITANI
M. Poverello
1279
Itàla
Monastero di
S. Placido Calonerò
Scaletta Zanclea
Novara di
Sicilia
M. Fossazza
1246
Ali Terme
A 18
Nizza di Sicilia
1311
M. Castellazzo
Casalvecchio
Roccalumera
1433
Ss. Pietro e
Paolo d'Agrò
Savoca
M. d. Morro
M. Grande
1374
S. Alessio Siculo
Alcantara
Francavilla di Sicilia
Capo Sant'Alessio
Castiglione di Sicilia
Motta Camastra
Forza d'Agrò
Mojo Alcantara
Castelmola
Randazzo
S 120
Gole dell'
Alcantara
TAORMINA
Linguaglossa
Giardini Naxos
S 284
Naxos
Bronte
ETNA
Sant'Alfio
3350
Riposto
Fornazzo
Giarre
IONIAN SEA
Sapienza
Zafferana Etnea
Adrano
Sta Maria La Scala
Trecastagni
Aci Catena
Nicolosi
Acireale
Viagrande
Aci S. Filippo
S 284
S. Agata
Aci Trezza
Faraglioni dei Ciclopi
Paternò
S 121
Aci Castello
Misterbianco
N
A 19
Catania
Golfo
di
Catania
Simeto
Fontanarossa
Dittaino
S 417
A 18
S 114
Malte

	Circuit start
	Around Acireale
	The coast to the southern slopes
	Northeast flank
	Circular tour of Etna
	The Alcantara Valley
	Ionian Coast: Taormina to Messina
	Capo Peloro

last decade, dozens of new winemakers have come here – from Tuscany, Northern Italy, France and other parts of the world – to rediscover this volcanic landscape and its local varietals, essential to producing Etna Rosso and Etna Bianco wines.

The countryside and vineyards are dotted with Palmento: stone lava buildings, mostly abandoned or converted to other purposes but once used for fermenting and pressing wine.

319

Catania★★

Destroyed time and time again by volcanic eruptions, war, earthquakes and other disasters, Catania always manages to get back on its feet. Black – the colour of the lava stone that's used to construct its monuments, houses and even pave its roads – dominates its streets. The home town of Vincenzo Bellini and Giovanni Verga, it's an elegant and bustling city, brought into the 21C by its high-tech industry, which has earned it the nickname of the Silicon Valley of Sicily.

A BIT OF HISTORY

When the town planner William Light was designing the city of Adelaide in 1836, he used Catania, which he had visited a few years previously, as his model. Fortunately, its chaotic traffic has proved less easy to export, and visitors are advised to park and explore the pleasant city centre in a more relaxed manner on foot. Founded by Greek colonists around 724 BC, Katane flourished during the Roman period, as revealed by its many surviving monuments. Tragedy struck in the 17C when lava flowed into the streets from volcanic vents near Nicolosi, followed 20 years later by a terrible earthquake that destroyed most of its buildings. But the city rose from the rubble, complete with wide streets, piazzas and monuments.

The brainchild behind this design was the architect **Giovanni Battista Vaccarini** (1702–68). Baroque is so dominant, in fact, that the theatre, odeon and amphitheatre are all hidden behind or beneath 18C *palazzi*.

Catania is the departure point for the "Circular Tour of Etna". See Etna: Driving Tours.

WALKING TOUR

PIAZZA DEL DUOMO★

The town is centred around this square, which is lined with an elegant Baroque ensemble designed by Vaccarini.

- ▶ **Population:** 296 469
- **Michelin Map:** p317: A3
- **Info:** Servizio turistico regionale Via Alberto Mario 32. ℘095 74 77 415. Bureau del tourismo Via Vittorio Emanuele 172, ℘095 74 25 573. www.turismo.catania.it.
- **Location:** The Viale Regina Margherita is lined with a series of impressive historic villas. Flanked by the best shops, Via Etnea runs past the Piazza del Duomo, Piazza dell'Universita, Piazza Stesicoro before arriving at Villa Bellini.
- **Parking:** The undisciplined traffic makes exploring on foot preferable. The port has a large underground parking lot; other sites dot the city.
- **Kids:** The Circumetnea railway that circles Mount Etna from Catania; dolphin watching.
- **Don't Miss:** Piazza Duomo and its elephant obelisk, Palazzo Biscari, the lovely gardens of the Villa Bellini, a morning stroll through the fish market.
- **Timing:** One of the hottest cities in Italy, with summer temperatures often exceeding 40°C/104°F, Catania is best visited in early morning in summer, or in spring or autumn.

In the middle stands the **Fontana dell'Elefante**, the symbol of Catania. On the south side of the square, offset by the Chierici and Pardo *palazzi* behind, sits the more delicate **Fontana dell'Amenano**.

The star is the **Duomo's façade**, flanked to the right by the Bishop's Palace and Porta Uzeda and to the left by the attractive front of the Badia di

GETTING THERE AND AROUND

Getting to Catania – Fontanarossa airport is 7km/4.5mi to the south of Catania (℘095 34 05 05; www.aero porto.catania.it). The Alibus links the airport with the city centre and railway station (departures every 20min from 5pm to midnight); the ticket is the same price as on the city buses. The bus terminal is in Piazza Giovanni XXIII, also home to the main train station. Catania has good rail connections

with Messina (2hr) and Syracuse (1hr 30min); the service to and from Palermo (just over 3hr) is less frequent. TTT Lines runs a ferry between Catania and Naples (about 10hr); ℘095 34 06 44; www.tttlines.it.
City buses – These are operated by AMT (Azienda Municipale Trasporti), Via Plebiscito 747; ℘095 73 60 111; www.amt.ct.it A ticket costs €1 and is valid for 90min; a day pass is €2.50.
🛈 For coin ranges, see the Legend on the cover flap.

Sant'Agata. The square's north side belongs almost entirely to the **Palazzo Senatorio** or **Palazzo degli Elefanti** (now the town hall), another Vaccarini creation.

Fontana dell'Elefante

This fountain, recalling Bellini's famous obelisk-bearing monument in Rome's Piazza Minerva, is the symbol of Catania and was designed by *Vaccarini* in 1735. The lava elephant sculpture dates from the Roman period and bears an **Egyptian obelisk** celebrating the cult of Isis (the Mother goddess, who became the centre of a popular Greco-Roman mystery cult), as well as the emblem of St Agatha.

Duomo★

🕐 Open 7am–noon, 4–7pm.
℘095 32 00 44.
The cathedral is dedicated to St Agatha, patron saint of the city; it was erected in the late 11C by the Norman king Roger I and rebuilt after the earthquake of 1693. The **façade★** is considered one of Vaccarini's masterpieces.
Farther along Via Vittorio Emanuele II, the tall Norman lava apses can be admired from the courtyard of the Bishop's Palace. Its solid outward appearance is relieved in part by tall, single and narrow, slit-like openings that underline its origin as a fortified church. The remains of 3C Roman baths, the **Terme Achilliane** (accessible through a

Fontana dell'Elefante and Duomo, Piazza Del Duomo

© Sime/Photononstop

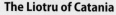

The Liotru of Catania

Locals refer to the elephant in Piazza Duomo as the **Liotru**, which is local dialect for **"Eliodoro"** the name of a learned 8C necromancer from Catania. Legend claims he rode an elephant after bringing it to life. Over the centuries, the magician's name has been adopted for the statue of his steed.

During prehistoric times, **dwarf elephants** did inhabit Sicily – the Museo Archeologico Paolo Orsi in Siracusa has several examples – so perhaps the story isn't entirely fantastical. Some scholars even connect the cyclops of Homeric legend with pachyderms (where the trunk is interpreted as the third eye).

trapdoor) can be seen to the right of the entrance outside the church.

Interior

Restoration of the floor has revealed several column bases from the original Norman church. Against the second pilaster *(right)*, in the nave, stands the funerary monument of **Bellini**. He died at home in Puteaux, near Paris, where he was originally buried.

The transepts both contain chapels, segregated from the crossing by a glorious Renaissance archway. The chapel *(right)*, dedicated to the Madonna, contains the sarcophagus of Constanza, wife of Frederick III of Aragon, who died in 1363.

The southern chapel is dedicated to St Agatha: although Renaissance in spirit, it is encrusted with **gilded stucco** decoration that verges on the kitsch. The elaborate Spanish doorway leads to the reliquary and treasury of the saint.

The sacristy has a large fresco *(badly damaged)* showing a fairly accurate topographical view of Catania before 1669. To the right of the Duomo, the Seminario now houses the Museo Diocesano di Catania.

Museo Diocesano

Piazza Duomo

🕐 *Open Mon–Fri 9am–2pm, Sat–Sun 9am–1pm.* 🎫 €7; €10 includes admission to the Roman baths. 📞 095 28 16 35. www.museodiocesicatania.com.

The Diocesan Museum houses a collection of paintings, ornaments and vestments belonging to the cathedral and the diocese, as well as the **Vara di Sant'Agata** – the float that was used to carry the saint's bust and reliquary during processions. The museum is the entrypoint to the underground **Terme Achilliane** the 4C–5C BC Roman baths under the piazza.

Badia di Sant'Agata★

The church beside the Duomo contributes to the overall splendour of the piazza. The serpentine lines of the **façade★** are contained by a cornice that emphasises the ground level with a triangular pediment at the centre. This is another example of Vaccarini's mastery in design.

Fontana dell'Amenano

The fountain is named after the river that provides its source, which winds its way past some of the main Roman monuments (the theatre and baths or *Terme della Rotonda*). Locally, the foun-

Fish market, Piazza Alonzo di Benedetto

© Bildagentur-Online/age fotostock

© Saffo Alessandro/Sime/Photononstop

Olive glove in Catania, Mount Etna in the background

tain is called *"acqua a lenzuolo"* because the cascade of water resembles a fine veil. The open area behind is Piazza Alonzo di Benedetto, where a bustling and picturesque **fish market** takes place each morning. The covered section once housed the military guard for the **Porta Carlo V**, part of the city's 16C fortifications. Its main frontage can still be seen from Piazza Pardo.

THE SURROUNDING QUARTER

A number of interesting sights lie along the stretch of Via Vittorio Emanuele II behind the Duomo. A small square *(right)* harbours the **church of San Placido** with its gently undulating façade by **Stefano Ittar** (1769). Opposite the right side of the church *(Via Museo Biscari)* is the former convent. The remains of the 15C **Palazzo Platamone** can still be seen in the courtyard *(access from Via Landolina)*. Original features include a decorative balcony in coloured stone, adorned by a series of pointed arches. The courtyard is now used as a venue for concerts and theatre performances.

Palazzo Biscari★

Via Museo Biscari. Guided tours only (20min) by appointment. 095 32 18 18. www.palazzobiscari.com. This is Catania's finest private building. Erected in the early 18C, the palazzo

owes its richness to Ignazio Paternò Castello II, Prince of Biscari – a man of eclectic interests and a lover of art, literature and archaeology. The entrance to the *palazzo (Via Museo Biscari)* is through an elaborate portal. Inside is a splendid room with frescoes by Sebastiano Lo Monaco, complemented by stuccowork, gilded mouldings

---

Catania during the Roman period

Visitors particularly interested in Roman remains can request to be taken by a theatre custodian to visit the **Terme della Rotonda** *(Via della Rotonda)*; little survives of these baths, however, other than a single, circular domed chamber that was converted into a church in Byzantine times (6C). Access may also be arranged to the **Terme dell'Indirizzo** *(Piazza Currò)*, a more extensive baths complex comprising at least 10 domed rooms. Here, the wood-stoked burner that provided heating is clearly visible, as are sections of rectangular hot-air ducting. Guided tours run by the staff of the Ancient Theatre; contact the theatre in advance: 095 74 72 111.

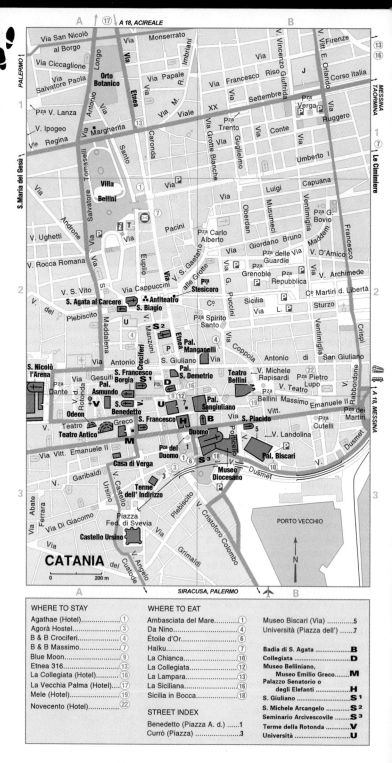

CATANIA

WHERE TO STAY

Agathae (Hotel) .... ①
Agorà Hostel .... ③
B & B Crociferi .... ④
B & B Massimo .... ⑦
Blue Moon .... ⑨
Etnea 316 .... ⑬
La Collegiata (Hotel) .... ⑯
La Vecchia Palma (Hotel) .... ⑰
Mele (Hotel) .... ⑲
Novecento (Hotel) .... ㉒

WHERE TO EAT

Ambasciata del Mare .... ①
Da Nino .... ④
Étoile d'Or .... ⑥
Haïku .... ⑦
La Chianca .... ⑩
La Collegiata .... ⑫
La Lampara .... ⑬
La Siciliana .... ⑯
Sicilia in Bocca .... ⑱

STREET INDEX

Benedetto (Piazza A. d.) 1
Currò (Piazza) 3

Museo Biscari (Via) 5
Università (Piazza dell') 7

Badia di S. Agata .... B
Collegiata .... D
Museo Belliniano,
      Museo Emilio Greco ...... M
Palazzo Senatorio o
      degli Elefanti .... H
S. Giuliano .... S¹
S. Michele Arcangelo .... S²
Seminario Arcivescovile .... S³
Terme della Rotonda V
Università .... U

and mirrors. The ceiling's centre opens into an oval dome, complete with gallery. Musicians once played here, so the notes seemed to descend from the heavens.

A pretty spiral staircase provides access to the small platform, where an admirable **view** extends over the terrace. **Lavish decorations★★** adorn the south wing: figures and volutes, cherubs and racemes fill the window frames.

Teatro Antico and Odeona

Via Vittorio Emanuele II 260. ◷*Open 9am–5.30pm.* ◉€4. ✆*095 71 50 508.*
The theatre's design is Roman. However, scholars suggest it occupies the site of an older Greek structure.

Built of lava stone, its tiered seats would have accommodated 7,000 spectators. As far back as Norman times, the theatre's marble slabs were recycled into the cathedral, while houses and a street were built over the theatre itself.

Nextdoor stands an **odeon**, which served as a more intimate venue for music, poetry and oration. A small **antiquarium** exhibits fragments discovered during excavations.

Casa di Verga

Via Sant'Anna 8. ◷*Open Tue–Sat 9am–1.30pm, 2.30–7.30pm (6pm Wed and Fri).* ◉€4. ✆*095 71 50 598.*
The modest house where the writer **Giovanni Verga** (1840–1922) spent many years is preserved much as he left it.

Museo Belliniano

Piazza S. Francesco 3. ◷*Open Mon–Sat 9am–1pm.* ◉€5. ✆*095 71 50 535.*
The house where the composer **Vincenzo Bellini** (1801–35) was born has a display of documents, mementoes and portraits of the composer, together with a harpsichord and a spinet that once belonged to his grandfather. The last room contains autographed original scores.

Museo Emilio Greco

Piazza S. Francesco d'Assisi 3. ◷*Open daily, 9am–1pm (3–6pm Tue and Thu).* ◷*Closed public holidays.* ◉€3. ✆*095 31 76 54.*
This archive and museum houses the complete **graphic works★** of Catania artist and sculptor **Emilio Greco** (1913–95). The subjects, for the most part, are female heads and nudes, and illustrate his perceptive predilection for Hellenistic art.

VIA CROCIFERI★

▷ Begin at Piazza San Francesco, with its monumental church, and turn down Via Crociferi.

Via Crociferi is regarded as Catania's Baroque street *par excellence*. The magnificent buildings along either side, particularly in the first section, impart a rare graciousness. Through the gateway, **Arco di San Benedetto**, are the Badia Grande and its diminutive Badia Piccola. On the left are the churches of **San Benedetto** and **San Francesco Borgia**; between the two runs a narrow street with **Palazzo Asmundo** at the far end.

Farther along Via Crociferi *(left)* stands a former Jesuit residence that now accommodates the Istituto d'Arte. The first courtyard, attributed to Vaccarini, is graced with a fine two-tier portico: the same bay elevation has also been used in the University courtyard in Piazza dell'Università – also laid with a striking black-and-white cobbled pavement.

The elegant, curvilinear **façade★** of **San Giuliano** *(right)* was probably designed by Vaccarini. Above the elaborate altar of agate and other semi-precious stones sits a 14C painted wooden Crucifix.

▷ Turn left into Via dei Gesuiti.

San Nicolò l'Arena

◷*Open Mon–Fri 8am–8pm, Sat 8am–1pm.* ◉*Free.*
The Benedictine Order built a grandiose monastery (16C–17C) and an imposing **church** alongside it, although the façade

was never completed. Inside the huge and bare church is a lovely 18C organ case behind the altar. The meridian line, laid in the transept floor in 1841, catches the sunlight precisely at 13 minutes past noon *(at one time, this occurred at noon)*.

Monastery★

🕐*Piazza Dante 32.* 🕐*Open Mon–Fri 9am–5pm, Sat and Sun 9am–12pm.* 👓*€6.* ☞*Guided tours.* 📞*095 71 02 767. www.officineculturali.net.*

The present building dates from the 18C. An eye-catching doorway *(left of the church)* provides access to the courtyard, from where the east and south sides of the building, designed by Antonino Amato, may be admired. The **opulent decoration** recalls the Palazzo Biscari. The first cloisters surround a small neo-Gothic arcaded courtyard with majolica. The monastery now houses the university arts school and the magnificent **Sala Vaccarini**.

▷ Return to Via Crociferi.

The street terminates at the gates of Villa Cerami, now the seat of the Faculty of Jurisprudence.

A Composer of Genius

Vincenzo Bellini, creator of "La sonnambula", "Norma" and "I puritani", was a Romantic composer who dedicated himself to his works with "the passion that is so characteristic of genius, convinced that a large part of success depends on the choice of an interesting theme, warm expressive tones and a contrast of passions". He is commemorated in Catania's opera house, the Teatro Bellini, inaugurated with a production of his "Norma" in 1890. The acoustics of this beautiful auditorium are among the finest in the world.

▷ Head towards Corso Vittorio Emanuele and continue with visits to the Museo Belliniano, Museo Emilio Greco, Teatro Antico and Casa di Verga *(see Visit).*

VIA ETNEA★

Catania's best shops and boutiques flank this straight, 3km/1.8mi thoroughfare, which runs through Piazza del Duomo, Piazza dell'Universita and Piazza Stesicoro before arriving at the front of Villa Bellini, Catania's flower-filled public gardens.

Piazza dell'Università

Elegant *palazzi* surround the square on all sides. On the right stands Vaccarini's **Palazzo Sangiuliano**; the **university** *(left)* is arranged around an attractive courtyard surrounded by a portico with a loggia above. In the evening, the piazza is illuminated by four lamps (1957) made by a local sculptor.

Farther down the street rises the concave frontage of the **Collegiata** *(Santa Maria della Consolazione)* by **Stefano Ittar** (18C). A short distance beyond on the left, is the graceful **Palazzo San Demetrio** (17C–18C).

On the right, along Via Antonio di S. Giuliano, stands the richly-decorated **Palazzo Manganelli** used as a setting for scenes in Luchino Visconti's film version of *The Leopard*.

Returning to Via Etnea, just inside the entry to the 18C **San Michele Arcangelo**, a double marble staircase climbs to two Baroque stoups with angels drawing aside a marble drape to reveal a basin.

Piazza Stesicoro

To visit, contact the Teatro Antiquo in advance: 📞095 74 72 268.

The ruins in the square are all that survives of an enormous **Roman amphitheatre** *(105m/344ft by 125m/410ft)* – the second-largest amphitheatre in the Roman Empire, after the Colosseum. Most of the remains are hidden beneath the piazza and the surrounding buildings.

St Agatha

Agatha was a wealthy 3C Christian noblewoman from Catania. A victim of religious persecution and the unwelcome advances of the Consul Quilianus, she was imprisoned, tortured (her breasts were cut off) and burned. She died on 5 February 251. The following year, the saint's veil was said to have saved Catania from a flow of lava, after which Agatha became the city's patron saint. During the festival in her honour, celebrated on 3–5 February, Catania's streets are thronged with noisy and colourful crowds bearing witness to her popularity. She is even remembered in one of the local specialities, the *minni di Sant' Agata* (*minni* is Sicilian dialect for breasts); these small cakes covered with frosted icing and topped with a cherry recall her martyrdom.

San Biagio
(Sant'Agata alla Fornace)

🕐*Open Mon–Sat 7.15am–midday, 5–7pm, Sun 9am–1pm.* ✆*095 71 59 360.* The 18C church was built on the foundations of a chapel dedicated to the patron saint of Catania. In Roman times, the town's lime kilns were concentrated here. A chapel within the church *(far right)* preserves the *carcara* (kiln or furnace), where Agatha supposedly died. Tradition claims the church of **Sant' Agata in Carcere** behind Piazza Stesicoro was built on the site of her imprisonment in 251.

Villa Bellini★

The large, luxuriant park is thick with exotic plants. From the hilltop *(where a kiosk stands)*, there is a beautiful **view** over the city and Mount Etna.

Santa Maria del Gesù

Although built in 1465, this church has undergone considerable alteration. From the original survives the Cappella Paternò, complete with Renaissance archway surmounted by a lunette and inset with a Pietà by **Antonello Gagini**. He is also the creator of the Madonna and Child *(second altar on the right)*.

ADDITIONAL SIGHTS
Castello Ursino

Piazza Federico II di Svevia
🕐*Open Mon–Sat, 9am–1pm, 2.30–7pm, Sun and public holidays 9am–8pm.* ☞*€6.* ✆*095 34 58 30.* Frederick II of Swabia erected this austere, fortified castle on the seafront in the 13C, however a great river of lava extended the shore in 1669. The castle is possibly named after a Roman consul *(Arsinius)* or the Orsini, a Roman family who sought refuge here in the Middle Ages.

The castle is square in plan with a large, round tower at each corner and two additional towers.

Pinacoteca

The art gallery showcases 15C–19C southern Italian artists. Notable works include a polyptych with the *Virgin Enthroned with St Anthony and St Francis* by **Antonello de Saliba** (15C), a pupil of Antonello da Messina. Among the pictures influenced by **Caravaggio** is the expressive *St Christopher* by **Pietro Novelli**.

There are two beautiful studies by **Michele Rapisardi**, an artist from Catania, who was prominent in the 19C; one is a sketched *Head of the Mad Ophelia*. Before leaving, cast an eye over the *Pastorello Malato (The Ailing Shepherd-boy)*, a delicate watercolour by Guzzone and the vivid paintings by Lorenzo Loiacono.

Orto Botanico

Two entrances: Via Longo 19 and Via Etnea 397. 🕐*Open Mon–Fri 9.30am–7pm, Sat 9.30am–1.30pm (Via Etnea entrance).* 🕐*Closed Sun and public holidays.* ☞*€4.* ✆*095 43 09 01. www.dipbot.unict.it.* The botanical gardens were laid out in the 1950s with various indigenous plants as well as more exotic varieties.

LE CIMINIERE

At the eastern end of Via Umberto I (B1-2), the former Ciminiere industrial plant, overlooking the coast, has been turned into an exhibition space and, for the last ten years or so, a museum centre.

Museo del Cinema★

Piazzale Asia, Le Ciminiere (at the eastern end of Via Umberto I). Open *Tue–Sun 9am–12.30pm, Tue and Thu also 3–4.30pm.* Closed Mon and *public holidays. Visits lasting one hour.* €4. 095 40 11 928.

Designed by French architect François Confino, the brains behind the Museo del Cinema in Turin *(see Green Guide to Northern Italy)*, this museum recently-opened in a former sulphur factory offers a fascinating insight into the world of film. The display begins with a series of **magic boxes** showing freeze frames from iconic films and illustrating the arrival of the first film in Sicily *(Messina, 1913)*. The pictures in the **portrait room** come to life as the likes of Sophia Loren and the Taviani brothers share their passion for film. There's also a full reconstruction of an early 20C **cinema★**.

Acis and Galatea

The sea nymph Galatea fell in love with the shepherd Acis. Tragically, she also caught the eye of Polyphemus, the Cyclops and arch enemy of Odysseus (Ulysses). Rejected, the monster left the caves of Mount Etna to kill his rival. Zeus took pity and transformed Acis into a river *(the modern Akis)*, which flows to Galatea's realm, the sea, and reunites the pair.

Another legend claims his dis-mem-bered body became the nine Aci towns: Aci Bonaccorsi, Aci Castello, Aci Catena, Aci Platani, Acireale, Aci San Filippo, Aci Sant'Antonio, Aci Santa Lucia and Aci Trezza. This stretch of coastline is known as the **Riviera dei Ciclopi** *(Cyclops Coast)*.

Next, we enter a typical **courtyard★** of an Italian apartment building, in which the windows are screens showing scenes from films set in courtyards. This is the start of the **themed section★★**, in which the museum shows its most playful side. As if you were in a real house, you go from room to room discovering memorable scenes projected onto cleverly displayed screens, including dining room plates animated with clips of people feasting, a library glowing with a magic lantern, a bedroom with kissing scenes, a kitsch sitting room, a café/bar and an old-time garage straight out of Cinéma Paradiso!

Museo dello Sbarco in Sicilia ★ (Museum of the Sicily Landings)

Piazzale Asia, Le Ciminiere. Open *Tue–Sun 9am–12.30pm, Tue and Thu 3–5pm.* Closed Mon. €4. 095 40 11 929. *Avoid visiting with small children who might find the museum upsetting.*

The visit begins with a film of the American landings on Sicily in 1943, followed by a reconstruction of a small, peaceful Sicilian town square from the pre-war period. Next comes a **bomb shelter**, in which you experience a simulated bombing raid *(sirens, darkness, tremors)* before returning to the same square, this time completely destroyed. The visit continues in a more traditional, but fascinating vein, presenting details of the landing operations over two floors, beginning with "Operation Husky", agreed upon in Casablanca and involving the Mafia.

Films, photographs, a reconstructed bunker and contemporary accounts provide an insight into the operations leading to the 22 July 1943 Liberation of Palermo.

EXCURSIONS
Acireale★

Acireale (17km/10mi) is accessible via the A 18 motorway (Acireale exit) or the S 114 coast road.

This pretty Baroque town is set around the spectacular Piazza Duomo. Its elegant shops include *gelaterie*, serving the renowned local **ice cream**. Acir-

Piazza Duomo, Acireale

© Tommaso di Girolamo/Tips Images

eale is also famous for its ancient **hot springs**, extravagant carnival and puppet theatre.

Corso Umberto I extends to the north; Via Vittorio Emanuele to the south, lined by fine buildings, shops and *gelaterie*.

Piazza Duomo★★ – This finely proportioned space is enclosed by Baroque buildings: the **Duomo**, the **Basilica dei Santi Pietro e Paolo** (17C–18C) and the **Palazzo Comunale** (1659), all graced with elegant wrought-iron **balconies★**. Slightly behind, at the start of Via Davì, sits the 17C **Palazzo Modò**; the façade bearing the name of the long-gone early-20C theatre, the Eldorado.

Duomo – The cathedral is dedicated to the Annunciation and Santa Venera. Its two-tone neo-Gothic façade was designed by GBF Basile (1825–91), architect of Palermo's Teatro Massimo. Standing between two *campanili* with majolica spires, the front is ornamented by a fine 17C portal.

From Piazza Duomo take Via Settimo, then Via Vittorio Emanuele.

Basilica di San Sebastiano – A statue-topped balustrade crowns the **Baroque façade★**, which consists of a harmonious combination of columns, pilasters, niches and volutes drawn together within a frieze of angels.

Inside, the transept and chancel contain frescoes by P. Vasta depicting scenes from the life of St Sebastian, the town's patron saint.

From Piazza Duomo take Via Cavour (in front of the square).

Piazza San Domenico – The fine Baroque façade of **San Domenico** dominates one side of the tiny piazza, also overlooked by **Palazzo Musmeci** (17C), with its elegant wrought-iron balconies and Rococo windows.

Farther along the right-hand road is the **Biblioteca Zelantea**, the town library, annexed with an **art gallery** (◷*open Wed–Sat 10am–1pm, Tue 10am–1pm, 3.30–6.30pm;* ⬭*Free;* ℘*095 76 34 516)*, which has a plaster model of a bust of **Julius Caesar** (1C BC).

From Piazza Duomo, continue to the end of Corso Umberto I.

Villa Belvedere – The lovely peaceful gardens, complete with a panoramic terrace, provide a magnificent **view★** of Mount Etna and the sea. Don't miss the statue of **Acis and Galatea**.

◗ Continue to the south of the town, along the S 114 to Via delle Terme.

Terme di Santa Venera – *Via delle Terme 47;* ♿℘*329 66 27 566; www.terme-acireale.com; reservation only, two days in advance).* This Neo-Classical style spa was opened in 1873 by Baron Agostino Pennisi di Floristella (whose castle still stands behind the spa, near to the station). Acireale then became a popular spa, visited by Wagner and the royal family, among others.

Opened in 1987, the **Santa Caterina** spa uses sulphurous radioactive water, sometimes combined with volcanic clay for mud therapy.

The source of the spa is located in **Santa Venera al Pozzo**, 3km from Acireale, where archaeologists have discovered the remains of a **Roman baths** with two rooms with barrel vaulting, probably the *tepidarium* and *caldarium*.

Grotta del Presepe di Santa Maria della Neve

From S 114 to Messina, turn right at the traffic light by the Villa Belvedere towards Santa Maria la Scala. The Church of Santa Maria della Neve is on the left.

The Grotto of the Crib, adjacent to the church, is a winding lava ravine (a refuge for bandits until the 18C).

In 1752, the first nativity featured 32 sumptuously dressed, life-size figures with wax faces.

Santa Maria della Scala

Follow the same road to Grotta del Presepe di Santa Maria della Neve as far as the coast.

This picturesque village, which grew up around the 17C **parish church**, has an attractive little harbour.

Return to S 114 and continue towards Catania, then take the left fork for Capo Mulinit. About 100m/330ft along this road lies the Museo dei Pupi dell'Opra (Via Nazionale per Catania, 193–195).

🚗 DRIVING TOUR

AROUND ACIREALE
Approx. 15km/9mi.

Aci Catena

The little town, which owes its name to the cult of the *Madonna della Catena* (Madonna of the Chain), centres on the charming square, Piano Umberto.

Aci San Filippo

At the heart of the hamlet stands the church, ornamented with an 18C façade and a campanile with a lava base.

▷ From Aci San Filippo, return to S 114 and continue towards Catania.

Aci Trezza

This small fishing town is known for the **rocks of the Cyclops★** (*Faraglioni dei Ciclopi*) – jagged black lava rising from crystal-clear waters.

The Odyssey relates these were hurled by Polyphemus against Ulysses. Next to the rocks sits the **island Lachea**, now a biology research station.

▷ Continue along S 114.

Aci Castello

This seaside village is on a stretch of coastline dotted with lemon trees

(hence the area's other nickname, **Riviera dei Limoni**).

Faraglioni dei Ciclopi, Aci Trezza

© Sandro Bedessi / Fototeca ENIT

Giovanni Verga

The little harbour of Aci Trezza, bathed in sunshine and dotted with multicoloured boats hauled up onto the beach, seems inhabited by the ghosts of fictitious characters created by the Italian author Verga. How easy to imagine Maruzzi and the other members of the Malavoglia family waiting anxiously here on the shore, ceaselessly searching the horizon for the Provvidenza with its cargo of lupins. Aci Trezza was used by Luchino Visconti in 1948 to shoot his film *La Terra Trema (The Ground Trembles)*, based on Verga's novel, *I Malavoglia*. An organisation arranges tours to the **Parco Letterario Giovanni Verga** (a route that links places mentioned in the works of Verga in Catania, Aci Castello and Aci Trezza). Contact the Museo Casa del Nespolo (Sept–Jun 9.30am–12.30pm, 4–7pm, Jul–Aug 9.30am–1pm, 5–9pm; ℘095 7116638; €1.55).

Castle★ The Norman fortress, built of black lava, stands on a rocky spur. This site has been fortified since Roman times. It served as a prison under the Bourbons.

From the top there is a marvellous **view★** of the **Faraglioni dei Ciclopi** and **Lachea**. The castle houses a small **museum** with a collection of archaeo-logical artefacts. ◷Open Jun–Sep 9am–1pm, 4–8pm, Oct–Apr 9am–1.30pm, 3–5pm. ◉€3. ℘095 73 71 111.

ADDRESSES

🏨 STAY

⬭ **Mele** – Via Leonardi 24. ℘095 312 258, www.hotelmele.it. 🚿. 8 rooms ⛳. You have to pass the entrance to a Goth/Punk pub to access this modest pensione on the first floor run by a friendly mamma. The place is clean and very floral, if a little decrepit. Only one room has a private shower; the rest share bathrooms. Noisy weekend evenings.

⬭ **Agorà Hostel** – Piazza Currò 6, Catania. ℘095 72 33 010. www.agorahostel.com. 🚿 ⛳. This reasonably-priced hostel is situated in a 19C building fronting an old square close to the fish market. It offers two doubles, rooms with bunk beds and a number of communal areas.

⬭ **B&B Massimo** – Via Etnea 290. ℘095 311 343. www.massimobedandbreakfast.it. 🚿. 6 rooms ⛳. Opposite Villa Bellini, this small, charming guesthouse is well-kept and welcoming. Plain but spacious, peaceful rooms, with a few parking spaces in the courtyard.

⬭ **Blue Moon** – Via Collegiata 11. ℘095 327 787. 🚿. 6 rooms ⛳. A very central hotel, where you will be welcomed with a smile. Choose between three rooms with a shared shower on the landing, or three other, more expensive but brand-new rooms with private bathrooms and air conditioning.

⬭⬭ **La Collegiata** – Via Vasta 10 (on the corner of Via Etnea). ℘095 31 52 56. www.lacollegiata.com. 🅿. 12 rooms ⛳. In the heart of the historic centre, this welcoming hotel offers small but pleasant rooms with slightly theatrical decor dominated by red velvet.

⬭⬭ **Crociferi** – Via Crociferi 81. ℘095 715 22 66. www.bbcrociferi.it. 3 rooms ⛳. Huge, bright rooms in a very attractive 18C palazzo. One of them, which can sleep four, has a remarkable painted Art Nouveau ceiling. Two others enjoy a charming **view** over Piazza San Baggio. Free transfer from the airport if you stay more than two nights.

⬭⬭ **Etnea 316** – Via Etnea 316. ℘095 25 03 076. www.hoteletnea316catania.com. 9 rooms ⛳. You will find a warm welcome and honest prices at this hotel just opposite the Villa Bellini. The rooms are large, tastefully decorated and comfortable. Naturally, those facing the courtyard are quieter. A popular spot, so book well in advance. Parking on the square or side streets.

⬭⬭⬭ **Novecento** – Via Monsignore Ventimiglia 37. ℘095 31 04 88. www.hotelnovecentocatania.it. 17 rooms ⛳. Not far from the station and the Teatro Massimo Bellini, this is a cosy, quiet and friendly hotel. The communal areas are inviting and the rooms, although fairly small, all come with fitted carpets.

🍽🛏📺 **Hotel Agathae** – *Via Etnea 229. 📞095 25 00 436. www.hotelagathae.it. 15 rooms* 🔁. This recently three-star hotel takes advantage of its elegantly decorated Art-Nouveau style building, The rear faces the park pf Villa Bellini; breakfast amid the greenery on the splendid terrace. Well equipped with high-tech electronics, lift and parking.

FURTHER FROM THE CENTRE

🍽🛏 **La Vecchia Palma** – *Via Etnea 668, Catania. 📞095 43 20 25. www. lavecchiapalma.com. 11 rooms* 🔁. This family-run, Art Nouveau-style hotel has spacious rooms that offer modern facilities, but retain their original decor.

🍴/EAT

Midday options include the city centre bars, which sell sandwiches and one-course lunches, and the trattorias near the fish market *(behind Piazza Duomo)*.

🍽 **Da Nino** – *Via Biondi 19. 📞095 31 13 19. Closed Sun.* The pastel decor adds little warmth to the welcome, but it's all about the food and once the compliments start flowing, the owner loosens up. He has plenty to be proud of: the place is full of regulars enjoying the tasty antipasti, fish of the day and ripe fruit for dessert. Simple and effective.

🍽 **Étoile d'Or** – *Via Dusmet 7/9. 📞095 340 135. Closed for lunch.* Near the market, this very popular tavola calda cooks up a vast array of appetising dishes: stuffed aubergines, *arancini* (deep-fried balls of rice with meat), marinated pork chops, beef stew, spaghetti with clams, and more.

🍽 **La Collegiata** – *Via Collegiata 3. 📞095 321 230, www.lacollegiata.eu.* The draw of this pub/ restaurant beside the collegiate church is more the relaxed terrace than the food. Economical menus at lunchtime *(6.50 to €15)* and pizza at dinnertime. Lively upstairs bar in the evenings.

🍽🛏 **La Chianca** – *Piazza Duca di Genova 21. 📞095 32 70 22. Closed Mon and lunchtimes.* A wine bar with a good reputation on a quiet little square with an inviting, trendy atmosphere. Good Sicilian wine list. Jazz musicians some evenings.

🍽🛏📺 **Sicilia in Bocca** – *Via Dusmet 35. 📞095 25 00 208. www.siciliainbocca giuseppe.it. Closed Mon.* Nice, rustic dining room under a basalt stone-vaulted ceiling, attracting a varied clientele, from families to young, artistic types. An eccelctic menu combines traditional seafood cuisine with more inventive dishes that vary according to the chef's mood.

🍽🛏📺 **Ambasciata del mare** – *Piazza Duomo 6. 📞095 34 10 03. www.ambasciatadelmare.it. Closed Mon.* "The" fish restaurant in Catania, located just by the market. People come in family groups to enjoy a delicious meal in refined surroundings.

FURTHER FROM THE CENTRE

🍽🛏📺 **Haïku** – *Via Quintino Sella 28. 📞095 53 03 77. www.haiku-ct.it. Closed Mon.* This haven of peace and greenery in the city is well worth the walk! Choose from a selection of tasty, generously portioned organic dishes that revisit the repertoire of Italian classics. You then enjoy them under the fig trees in the large garden. Try the luscious pistachio tiramisu.

🍽🛏📺 **La Lampara** – *Via Pasubio 49. 📞095 38 32 37. Closed Wed.* A simple, family-run restaurant, where the son is the chef and the father serves. The cuisine here is traditional, based on fresh fish and seafood.

🍽🛏📺 **La Siciliana** – *Viale Marco Polo 52/A. 📞095 37 64 00. www.lasiciliana. it. Closed Sun evening, evenings of public holidays and Mon.* This renowned local restaurant is well worth a visit for its traditional Sicilian cuisine served in a rustic setting. The patio is superb to sit out on in summer.

TAKING A BREAK

Una Hotel Palace bar – *Via Etnea 218. 📞095 25 05 11. www.unahotels.it. Open 3pm–1am.* On the 7th-floor roof terrace of the city's most sophisticated hotel, you can enjoy an aperitif or an almond milk in the open air with a **view** of the volcano.

Al Caprice – *Via Etnea 28–34. 📞095 32 05 55. Closed Mon.* This traditional-style café, situated in the city centre not far from the cathedral, is perhaps the most typical in Catania.

Chiosco Vezzosi – *Piazza Vittorio Emanuele, Catania.* The *chiosco* (kiosk) serves a range of healthy and refreshing snacks, such as inexpensive fruit salads and freshly squeezed juices made from lemons, melons and peaches.

Focacceria Turi Finocchiaro – *Via Euplio Reina 13. ℰ095 71 53 573. Open from 7pm; closed Wed.* This establishment has been serving excellent, home-made Sicilian cuisine – such as meat from the rotisserie and delicious fish and seafood dishes – since 1900. Tables inside and out.

Pasticceria Spinella – *Via Etnea 300. ℰ095 32 72 47. www.pasticceriaspinella. it.* Opposite the Villa Bellini, this is one of the best-known pasticcerie in Catania *(1930)*. The elegant atmosphere, excellent service and high quality ensure it remains one of the busiest cafes in town.

I dolci di Nonna Vincenza – *Piazza San Placido 7. ℰ095 71 51 844. www.dolcinonnavincenza.it.* It can be difficult to walk past this delightful shop not far from Palazzo Biscari without being drawn inside by the smell of delicious Sicilian cookies and cakes.

Pellegrino – *Piazza dei Martiri 19.* Take a table to sit outside and enjoy good ice cream with a **view** of the port.

ACIREALE

The town centre is packed with pastry shops and ice-cream parlours and bars with terraces.

SHOPPING

Dagnino – *Via Etnea 179. ℰ095 31 21 69. Closed Mon.* One of the best food shops in town, where you will find the classics of Italian cuisine: cheeses, cured meats, sauces, preserves, honey, biscuits and wines.

Tertulia – *Via Michele Rapisardi 1–3. ℰ095 71 52 603.* This modern bookshop-café offers a relaxed atmosphere and a good selection of books.

ENTERTAINMENT

Le Ciminiere – *Viale Africa 2 (at the Eastern end of Via Umberto I), Catania. ℰ095 73 49 911.* The town's old sulphur refinery, abandoned after the Second World War, has been transformed into a venue for cultural events.

FESTIVALS

Festa di Sant' Agata – During the Festival of St Agatha, from 3–5 February, the bust and reliquary of the patron saint of Catania are paraded through the city to scenes of great jubilation.
🖑 *See St Agatha box, p325.*

ACIREALE

Festa di San Sebastiano – On 20 January, St Sebastian's float is carried through the streets of the small town.

Carnevale – This is one of the most famous carnivals in Sicily, with a magnificent parade.

OUTDOOR FUN

The sea – Il Lido di Plaja, south of the city, is Catania's beach. The River Simeto delivers golden sand here. North, after Le Ciminiere, is the old neighbourhood of San Giovanni li Cuti with a beach of black sand and lava chunks.

👥 **Dolphin watching** – The scientific association **Ketos** has dolphin-watching boat tours from the ports of Catania, Aci Trezza and Riposto. *ℰ347 40 86 749. www.ketos.sicily.it.*

TOURS

By bus – The circular bus route 410 passes the main sights and points of interest. Services run by appointment only. *ℰ095 73 60 111. www.amt.ct.*

Guided tours – For guided tours on a variety of itineraries contact Catania's tour guide association: *ℰ095 331 64 95 334. www.guidecatania.it.*

PUPPET THEATRE

Acireale is renowned for its puppets, which are slightly smaller and lighter than those made in Catania.
The Acireale puppet tradition is kept alive by two companies: the **Centro Servizi Spettacoli E. Macrì** *(via Alessi, ℰ095 60 62 72, www.teatropupimacri.it)* and 👥 **Turi Grasso**.
The latter runs the **Museo dei Pupi dell'Opra** *(Via Nazionale per Catania 193–195, Capomulini)*, which displays a collection of puppets typical of the Aci area. These illustrate the craftsmanship involved in the making of the figures, the intricacy of their costumes and the individuality of the different painted faces. The museum also has a small theatre.
Open summer, Wed, Sat–Sun and 9am–noon, 6–9pm; otherwise Wed, Sat–Sun 9am–noon, 3–6pm. Jun–Sept performances every Sun and Thu, 9pm. Reserve at ℰ095 76 48 035. www.operadeipupi.com.

Etna★★★

Mongibello, the "mountain of mountains", as Etna is also known, is the highest summit in Sicily. Cloaked in snow during winter, it is one of Europe's best know active volcanos. Its height, continuously modified by eruptions, is around 3,350m/ 11,000 ft. With its dramatic volcanic displays, Etna is one of the island's most interesting sites and can be explored on skis or by bicycle, horse, car or by Circumetnea train. The area also has a fascinating artistic, cultural and culinary heritage, which includes Etna wine, pistachio nuts, honey, strawberries, fragrant granite and warm brioche.

VISIT THE VOLCANO

As the volcano is still active, the landscape is constantly evolving. Contact the local tourist office to find out which side of the mountain is currently the most interesting.

The delightful village of **Zafferana Etnea** is a good base for trips to either side of the volcano; because of its altitude of 600m/1,950ft, it has the advantage of offering magnificent **views** of the coast from Acireale to Taormina.

South side★★★

Four-wheel drive excursions operate daily (weather permitting) from the week before Easter to the end of Oct, 9am–4pm. Duration: approx. 2hr there and back. €55, including guide. For further information, contact Funivia dell'Etna, Piazza V. Emanuele 45, Nicolosi; 095 91 41 41; www.funiviaetna.com. For mountain treks on the south side, contact Gruppo Guide Alpine Etna Sud, Piazza V. Emanuele 43, Nicolosi; 095 79 14 755; www.etnaguide.com.

From **Nicolosi** and **Zafferana Etnea** two beautiful roads wind up to **Rifugio Sapienza** *(1,910m/6,262ft)*, the starting-point for all expeditions to the crater. The **route★★** runs through an unnerving and alien landscape dominated by black lava and relieved occasi-

- **Michelin Map:** p317:A2
- **Info:** Centro Visita Parco dell'Etna Via del Convento 45, Nicolosi, 095 82 11 11, www.parcoetna.ct.it. Centro Visite Randazzo Via Umberto 197, 095 79 91 611/00 11.
- **Location:** Etna can be explored from the southern or northern slopes of the volcano. The two routes offer contrasting views and landscapes: the route up the southern side to Rifugio Sapienza passes through a barren, black and desert-like environment, while the northern side via Piano Provenzana wends its way through a lush larch forest.
- **Parking:** Park at the Rifugio Sapienza for trips to both sides of the volcano.
- **Kids:** Tours and hikes to the volcano's crater.
- **Timing:** The best time for a volcano trip is in summer when the roads are accessible. Climb early in the morning. The landscape changes regularly, so ask at the tourist office before setting off.

onally by a white patch of snow or pink and yellow bursts of flowers in spring. Arriving from Zafferana, just before the refuge, a sign points to the **Crateri Silvestri** - craters formed in 1892 and reached by a short walk through a lunar landscape.

Following the 2001–02 eruptions, which seriously damaged parts of the cable car, you must drive or hike *(allow 4hr for the ascent)* to the summit. *Funivia dell'Etna runs four-wheel drive vehicles from Rifugio Sapienza to around 2,700m/8,850ft. The last stretch is purely pedestrian.*

Visitors are strongly advised to avoid the central vent.

Saponaria on the slops of Etna

© Antonio Zimbone/Tips/Photononstop

The **Valle del Bove** – a vast sunken area, split with great crevasses and chasms – extends to the southeast of the central crater. This area is prone to violent eruptions, some of which are highly dangerous, precipitating lava flows that on occasion have reached the towns below.

At the time of going to press, the Valle del Bove can be reached on foot (1hr there and back from the arrival area for four-wheel drive vehicles).

The walk is fairly strenuous and walking boots are essential. Ask local guides for directions.

North side★★★

Four-wheel drive excursions with a guide operate May–Oct 9am–4pm (weather permitting), from Piano Provenzana. Duration: approx. 2hr there and back. €50, including a guide. To book, call S.T.A.R. a few days in advance. 095 37 13 33. To make the climb on foot (6 to 7 hr round trip and about €60 per person) contact Le Gruppo Guide Alpine Enta Nord, Via Roma 93, Linguaglossa; 095 77 74 502; www.guidetnanord.com.

The ascent to the craters can be made either on foot or by four-wheel drive. Visitors can leave their car at Piano Provenzana, where a ski resort was destroyed in 2002. A new observatory stands at 2,750m/9,020ft with a magnificent **view★★**. A shuttle bus runs to 3,000m/9,840ft before a guided ascent is made for those out of breath.

🚗 DRIVING TOURS

FROM THE COAST TO THE SOUTHERN SLOPES

45km/28mi drive from Acireale. Allow half a day (excluding the summit ascent).

On the bleaker, southern slopes, concretions of black lava form a lunar-like **landscape★★**. Little towns ring the edge. All have one feature in common: the dark lava stone that paves the streets and ornaments the buildings.

Acireale★

See Catania.

Aci Sant'Antonio

Several of the town's most important monuments are collected around Piazza Maggiore, most notably the **Duomo** with its imposing façade, extensively rebuilt after the terrible earthquake of 1693. Opposite stands the 16C church of San Michele Arcangelo.

At the far end of Via Vittorio Emanuele, the main street leading out from the

2001 eruption of Etna

© Franco Barbagallo/hemis.fr

History of Etna

The volcano and its story – Etna evolved out of a series of submarine eruptions during the Quaternary Era (c. 500,000 years ago) at the same time as the plain of Catania was formed, originally as a broad bay. Etna erupted regularly during Antiquity – at least 135 times. However, the most cataclysmic event occured in 1669, when a lower vent expelled a river of lava. As it flowed to the sea, it devastated part of Catania.

Violent eruptions took place in 1910, leading to 23 additional craters being formed; in 1917 a fountain of lava spurted 800m/2,500ft into the air. Outpourings of molten lava in 1923 stayed hot for more than 18 months and in 1928, the volcano destroyed the village of Mascali. More recently, the 2001 blast swept

piazza, stands what remains of the Riggio family *palazzo*.

◗ Leave Aci Sant'Antonio and head towards Nicolosi. The following three villages are situated along the SP 4-11.

Viagrande
The centre of the village is paved with huge slabs of lava. The 18C Chiesa Madre is built from the same dark stone.

Trecastagni
According to some sources, the name of this small town (literally "three chestnuts") actually derives from *tre casti agni*, a reference to the three chaste lambs worshipped here: Alfio, Filadelfio and Cirino.

A festival is celebrated on 9–10 May, the highlight being the **procession of wax effigies**, borne by strong, bare-chested *ignudi* to the **Santuario di Sant'Alfio** on the outskirts of town.

Via Vittorio Emanuele, lined by fine buildings, leads to **Chiesa Madre di San Nicola**, with its great central campanile. The terrace provides marvellous **views**.

Pedara
Piazza Don Diego is graced with the Duomo and its unusual spire covered in brightly-coloured majolica tiles.

Nicolosi
♿ *See South side.*

away key components of the cable car, reaching as far as the boundary of Rifugio Sapienza. The black lava around the craters dates from recent eruptions; lichens grow on the older grey stone. The presence of both and their sometimes inconvenient effects (blocked roads and ruined buildings) demonstrate the volcano's constant activity.

Etna has four maws: the southeastern crater that began suppurating in 1978, the immense **central crater**, the northeastern crater at the highest point (which has been dormant since 1971) and the *Bocca Nuova* (literally the "New Mouth"), most active lately. ♿ *See Introduction: Volcanoes in Sicily.*

National Park – The protected area, designated a National Park in 1987, covers some 59,000ha/145,730 acres. The mountain consists of an enormous black cone, visible up to 250km/155mi away. The extremely fertile lower slopes are heavily cultivated with dense groves of oranges, mandarins, lemons, olives, agaves and prickly pears, as well as bananas, eucalyptus, palm trees and maritime (parasol) pines. Vineyards here produce the excellent red, rosé and white *Etna* wines. Probably the most common of the wild plants is *Euphorbia dendroides* (tree spurge). Above 500m/1,640ft, plantations of hazelnuts, almonds, pistachios and chestnuts give way to oaks, beeches, birches and pines, especially around Linguaglossa. The landscape at this altitude is also characterised by a local variety of broom.

At 2,100m/6,900ft, the desolate landscape sustains desert-like plants like *Astragalus aetnensis* (a local variety of milk-vetch), a small prickly bush often found alongside violet, groundsel and other flowers that populate the slopes of the secondary craters. Higher up, snow and, for a long time after an eruption, hot lava, prevent any type of macroscopic vegetation from growing: this comprises the "volcanic desert".

Etna also harbours colonies of small mammals (porcupine, fox, wild cat, weasel, marten and dormouse), birds (kestrel, buzzard, chaffinch, woodpecker and hoopoe), a few reptiles, including the asp viper, and a large variety of butterflies, including the Eastern orange tip *(Anthocharis damone,* more commonly known in Italy as the *Aurora dell'Etna).*

THE NORTHEAST FLANK
60km/37mi drive starting from Linguaglossa. Allow half a day to visit (excluding the ascent).

Linguaglossa
The name "Linguaglossa" derives from the ancient term for "a big tongue of lava". Perhaps this is a reference to its vulnerable "red-hot" position on the slopes of Etna, down which incandescent lava has flowed on several occasions. The **Chiesa Madre**, built of sandstone and lava, looms over the central piazza. Inside, it is furnished with lovely **wooden choir stalls★** (1728).

The scenic **Mareneve** road leads through a wonderful larch and pine wood *(affected by the eruption in 2002)* to **Piano Provenzana**.

Ascent of Etna
The ascent of Etna was difficult, but the view from the top was worth all the effort: "no imagination in the world has had the courage to depict such a marvellous sight. There is nowhere on the surface of the globe that can combine so many striking, sublimely beautiful details. The summit is situated on the edge of a bottomless chasm, as old as the world itself, and it often erupts cascades of fire, thrusting up incandescent stones with a roar that shakes the whole island."

From *Journey to Sicily and Malta* by Patrick Brydone (1773)

Eastern approach★

From Piano Provenzana, the Mareneve road skirts the eastern side of the summit before dropping downhill. On the lower eastern slopes, many farming villages have rallied to exploit the fertile soil, cultivating vines and citrus fruits.

Near **Fornazzo**, just before the road meets the Linguaglossa to Zafferana Etnea road, it passes the incredible lava flow that spared the little **Cappella del Sacro Cuore** (left) in 1979. The molten stone flowed right up to one wall and even slightly penetrated the chapel. Pilgrims leave ex-voto offerings here, believing it was saved by sacred intervention.

From Fornazzo, a road down to the left leads to Sant'Alfio.

Sant'Alfio

This tiny village has a monumental 17C **church**, remodelled in the 19C, with an unusual lava façade incorporating a campanile. From the terrace before the church, there is a splendid **view★** of the Ionian Coast.

Sant'Alfio's main attraction, however, is a famous giant chestnut tree known as the **castagno dei 100 cavalli** (on the main road to Linguaglossa; ⏰open Sat–Sun 10am–12.30pm, 3.30–6.30pm; Mon–Fri, contact Pro Loco; ℘095 96 87 72). This fabulous specimen, over 2000 years old, comprises three distinct trunks with a combined circumference of 60m/196ft. Its name derives from a legend relating how Queen Joan (whether it refers to Joan of Aragon, Queen of Castile or Joan of Anjou, Queen of Naples, is not clear) sheltered under its branches one night during a storm with her entourage of 100 knights.

Go back in the direction of Fornazzo and turn left towards Milo.

Milo

One of the most lively towns perched on Etna with **panoramic views** of the coast, Milo has almost been destroyed by lava flows on three occasions: in 1950, 1971 and 1979.

Continue in the direction of Zafferana Etnea as far as Trecastagni and Nicolosi, then continue along the southern slope towards Catania.

CIRCULAR TOUR OF ETNA

155km/97mi round trip, starting in Catania. Allow one day.

The road runs around Mount Etna, providing a kaleidoscope of different **views** of the volcano as it passes through a number of picturesque little villages. This highly scenic tour is also possible by train (*Ferrovia Circumetnea via Caronia 352/A, Catania ℘095 54 12 50, www.circumetnea.it*). Directions below refer to touring by car.

Catania★★

🕭*See Catania.*

Leave Catania along Viale Regina Margherita or Via Vittorio Emanuele and take the S 121 (*6km/4mi*).

Misterbianco

The imposing 18C church dedicated to **Santa Maria delle Grazie** rises tall above the rooftops, its elegant façade visible from miles away. In the south apse nestles a *Madonna and Child* attributed to **Antonello Gagini**.

Continue on S 121 for 11km/7mi.

Paternò

In 1072, **Roger II** built a castle here atop the crag. Its square form is relieved on one side by a series of two-light windows. The black lava stone provides a strong contrast to the white stone ornamentation. Clustered around the castle are the main religious buildings: the **Chiesa Madre** founded in Norman times and rebuilt in the 14C, and **San Francesco**. The town's other buildings developed below, predominantly in the 17C, and the new seat of Piccolo Teatro houses the **Galleria d'arte Moderna**.

After 7km/4mi, turn right.

Santa Maria di Licodia

Piazza Umberto's slightly raised square stretches before a former Benedictine monastery *(now the town hall)* and the Chiesa del Crocifisso. Down the left side of the church stands its distinctive and attractive **bell tower** (12C–14C).

▷ Continue to Adrano *(8km/5mi)*.

Adrano

Dating back to Neolithic times, this is one of the oldest settlements on the slopes of Mount Etna.

The **castle** (⏱*open Tue–Sat 9am–1pm, 3–6pm, Sun and public holidays 9am–1pm; ⬤free; ✆095 76 98 849)* was built during the Norman occupation and still overlooks the central Piazza Umberto. This unmistakable square edifice of dark lava was built in the Swabian era; inside are three museums.

The **Museo Etnoantrolpologico** collects objects made by local craftsmen. Over three floors, the **Museo Archeo-logico Regionale** displays artefacts relating to the area's history. Of particular note *(on the second floor)* is the *ban-chettante* ("banqueting guest"), an early bronze figurine of Samian workmanship; the terracotta bust of a female Sicilian deity (5C BC), a clay Locrian female bust (5C BC), a figurative group of Eros and Psyche and a splendid **Attic vase★** with small columns (5C BC).

The top floor is devoted to the **picture gallery**, sculptures in wood, alabaster and bronze from the early 17C to the early 20C, and a series of contemporary works.

The piazza extends eastwards into the garden of the Villa Comunale, onto which face the imposing elevation of the monastery and church of **Santa Lucia**. The 18C church façade is by Stefano Ittar.

▷ The Saracen bridge is outside the town, beside the River Simeto. Leave by the road south of Adrano and follow signs for Bronte. A sign at a crossroads indicates the way to the bridge. Follow the dirt track, which continues on to the river and the bridge.

☺ Trekking ☺

Hiking, downhill skiing trips and visits to the extraordinary **volcanic caves** dotted around Etna are organised on request by local mountain guides.

For mountain treks on the south side: *Gruppo Guide Alpine Etna Sud, Piazza V. Emanuele 43, Nicolosi; ✆095 79 14 755; www.etnaguide.com.*

For trekking on the north side: *Le Gruppo Guide Alpine Enta Nord, Via Roma 93, Linguaglossa; ✆095 77 74 502; www.guidetnanord.com.*

Ponte Saraceno

The Saracen bridge was first erected by the Romans, rebuilt under Roger II and altered through successive centuries. The pointed arches spanning the river are marked with contrasting coloured stone. A short walk north along the river leads to the amazing **Simeto Gorge**. Formed by a lava flow, it was then polished clean as water eroded great blocks of basalt *(a visitor centre is located on the S 114 towards Syracuse, near the Ponte Primosole).*

▷ Continue along S 284 for 15km/9mi to Bronte.

Bronte

Pride of place in the centre of this town, which is famous for its pistachios, is given to the Collegio Capizzi. This prestigious 18C boarding school is housed in a fine *palazzo*.

Randazzo★

This small town is dangerously close to the volcano. Randazzo could be called the "black town" due to its lava paving, arches and principal monuments in the attractive historical centre built around the main street, Corso Umberto.

▷ The walk begins at the northeastern end of Corso Umberto.

The 13C **Chiesa di Santa Maria** has undergone considerable modification over centuries.

What survives is the plan, the characteristic tall Norman **apses★** ornamented with blind arcading and the south wall pierced by its two- and three-light windows. The neo-Gothic façade and bell tower are both 19C.

▶ Turn right into Piazza Roma.

A street to the left leads to Piazza San Nicolò. The church after which the square is named was erected in 1594 and has a front elevation enlivened by dark lava stone; the campanile dates from 1783. The other buildings overlooking the square include Palazzo Clarentano (1508), graced with decorative two-light openings, and the 14C Church of Santa Maria della Volta.

To its right opens the delightful **Via degli Archi** ornamented, as the name suggests, with a series of arches.

Via Polizzi, on the right, leads from the piazza to **Casa Spitaleri**, with its fine lava doorway.

▶ Turn down Via Duca degli Abruzzi.

An intersection from the right leads into Via Agonia, where condemned prisoners were led from their castle-prison to the *Timpa*, in front of San Martino.

Only one house conforms to the 14C archetype, with a single large open space on the ground floor and two square rooms on the first floor.

▶ Via Duca degli Abruzzi leads back into Corso Umberto.

An archway on the right marks the old entrance to the **Palazzo Reale**. Only part of the façade, a lovely two-coloured string-course and a pair of two-light windows, now remains. Before the 1693 earthquake destroyed the *palazzo*, it accommodated guests including Joan of England, wife of the Norman King William II; Costanza of Aragon and, in 1535, Emperor Charles V. Continue to **Chiesa di San Martino**

ETNA

(⏱*closed noon–4pm)*, founded in the 13C and rebuilt in the 17C.

The fine **campanile★** *(13C–14C)* has an octagonal spire. Inside, are two Madonnas by followers of the Gagini and

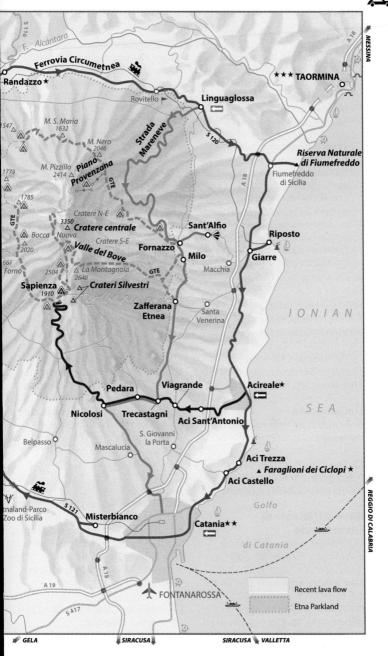

a polyptych attributed to Antonello de Saliba. Opposite the church are the ruins of a 13C castle, once part of the medieval citadel to which the Porte San Martino, once gave access. At the beginning of Via Castello, the Castello Svevo houses the **Museo Archeologico Paolo Vagliasindi**, the **Museo dei Pupi Siciliani** and the **Museo della Civiltà Contadina** (⏱ *open 9am–1pm, 3–7pm;*

Ascent to the Summit

Unpredictable and ongoing eruptions undermine any permanent infrastructure (roads, ski runs, ropeways, refuges). Favourite or recommended itineraries, therefore, should be considered as temporary and subject to closure at short notice. At the start of the season *(normally in May)*, shorter walks that stop well below the top are organised. When the highest sections are cleared of snow, it's possible to reach 3,000m/10,000ft. High summer is the best time, especially in the early morning. At any altitude, temperatures can plummet here. Carry a thick fleece, a light jacket and appropriate footwear *(preferably waterproof hiking boots)*. You can rent jackets and boots locally. Sunglasses and sunscreen are also wise.

On Foot – Opportunities abound for both short and long excursions (the longest and most complex being the **Grande Traversata Etnea**: five days of trekking, with daily 12–15km/ 7–9mi hikes) and marked nature trails.

By Car – For the less agile, see the volcano via a **circular tour of Etna**, either by car or train. The rail line starts in Catania, loops the mountain, and stops at Riposto *(approx. 5hr)*, returning to Catania by bus or train.
For information, apply to the **Ferrovia Circumetnea**, *Via Caronia 352/A, Catania; ✆095 54 12 50; www.circumetnea.it.*

€4 combined ticket; ✆095 92 1861). The display includes the 4C BC **Arpies vase** from the town's Greek necropolis.

▶ Continue on S 120 or the smaller parallel road in the direction of Bronte. After 4km/2.5mi, follow Linguaglossa.

Linguaglossa
See p335 in the section devoted to the northeastern slope of Etna.

▶ Pass through Fiumefreddo di Sicilia *(11km/7mi)* and head for the coast, turning towards Marina di Cottone.

Riserva Naturale di Fiumefreddo
Visitor centre near Masseria Belfiore in Via Marina, Fiumefreddo. For opening hours contact: ✆095 77 69 011. www.comune.fiumefreddo-di-sicilia.ct.it. Free.
The River Fiumefreddo rises from two springs, both 10–12m/33–39ft deep, known as Testa dell'Acqua and Le Quadare (*paioli* in Sicilian dialect). In full sunlight, their depth and clarity are astounding. The pH of the river – which never exceeds 10–15°C/50–59°F even in summer and flows remarkably slowly – provides the right conditions for an unusual range of water-loving plants *(certain members of the Ranunculus family and papyrus)*. Other species include the white willow, aquatic iris and horsetail. The springs also attract migrating birds: herons, oystercatchers and golden orioles. Beside the nature reserve stands the 18C **Castello degli Schiavi** (*private, not open to the public*), designed by the architects Vaccarini and Ittar in 18C.

▶ Continue for 10km/6mi along S 114 to Catania.

Giarre
This small town was bestowed upon the Bishop of Catania by **Roger II** in 1124. Via Callipoli is lined with elegant shops and town houses, including the Liberty-style **Palazzo Bonaventura** (no. 170) and the Moorish motif **Palazzo Quattrocchi** (no. 154).

▶ From Giarre, head for the coast in the direction of Riposto.

Riposto
The town's name means depot and in the 19C, this port town became a major shipping point for wine and other goods; many of its old warehouses survive. The **Santuario della Madonna della**

Lettera (🕐*open by appointment only at least three days in advance, ☎095 77 94 464*) was built in 1710.

Excavations beneath the sanctuary have revealed a funerary chamber from the palaeo-Christian period, coins from the Arabo-Norman era and architectural remains from Aragonese times.

▶ Return to Giarre and head along S 114 for 13km/8mi.

Acireale ★
🕐*See p329*

Aci Trezza
🕐*See p331*

Aci Castello
🕐*See p331*

ADDRESSES

🏠 STAY

FIUMEFREDDO DI SICILIA

◒ **Feudogrande** – *Via Maccarone 84. ☎0956 49 291. www.feudogrande.it. 7 rooms.* ⊒. A perfect base from which to visit Etna and Taormine, close to the Fiumefredo nature reserve. Simple, spacious and comfortable rooms.

LINGUAGLOSSA

◒◒ **Casa Etna** – *Via Trento 4, Linguaglossa. ☎095 64 31 84. www.casa etna.com. 3 rooms and 1 apartment* ⊒. Well located in the centre of the town, this guesthouse offers pretty rooms with all modern comforts, including terraces on the second floor.

NICOLOSI

◒ **Etna House** – *Via Monpilieri, Travessera 7, Nicolosi. ☎095 91 01 88 or 347 11 36 512. www.bedandbreakfast-etnahouse.it.* 🏊⊒. In a quiet location, 15min walk from the town centre, this B&B offers plain, but clean and comfortable rooms. The little swimming pool is refreshing after a hike.

◒◒◒ **Corsaro** – *Loc. Piazza Cantoniera, Nicolosi. ☎095 91 41 22. www.hotelcorsaro.it. Closed 15 Nov–24 Dec. 20 rooms* ⊒. This comfortable hotel at an altitude of 2,000m/6,560ft is popular with skiers and walkers. It has 20 pleasant rooms and a good restaurant.

RANDAZZO

◒◒ **Agriturismo L'Antica Vigna** – *Loc. Monteguardi, 3km/1.8mi of Randazzo on S 284. ☎349 40 22 902. www.anticavigna.it.* 🍴. *10 rooms* ⊒, *restaurant*◒◒. This family-run farm guesthouse with pool serves regional dishes made from organic, home-grown produce.

◒◒ **Ai Tre Parchi** – *Via Tagliamento 49. ☎095 799 16 31. www.aitreparchibb.it. 5 rooms* ⊒. A small hotel in the historic centre with a garden. The owners organise hikes and riding expeditions around Etna.

TRECASTAGNI

◒◒ **Il Vigneto** – *Via Zappalà 1, Trecastagni. ☎095 78 01 029. www. ilvignetobeb.net.* 🍴. *3 rooms* ⊒. *(2 night min.)* Surrounded by greenery, this large villa offers accommodation in period-style rooms with antiques.

◒◒ **Case Zuccaro** – *Corso Buonarroti 10, Trecastagni. ☎095 98 91 295. www.case zuccaro.com. 3 rooms* ⊒. At 600m/200ft altitude, this B&B is surrounded by an ancient garden with a huge, peaceful **panoramic** terrace.

ZAFFERANA ETNEA

◒◒◒ **Airone** – *Via Cassone 67, Zafferana Etnea. ☎095 70 81 819. www.hotel-airone.it. Closed 2 Nov–15 Dec. 62 rooms* ⊒. An elegant hotel and spa with modern, comfortable rooms, magnificent **views** of the coast and complete services.

🍴 EAT

RANDAZZO

◒◒ **Trattoria Veneziano** – *Via Romano 8. ☎095 79 91 353. www.ristoranteveneziano.it - Closed Sun eve. and Mon.* 🍴. This central restaurant serves traditional cuisine made from local produce.

◒◒ **Le Delizie** – *Via Bonaventura 2. ☎095 92 11 26.* This family-run restaurant on the outskirts of town serves traditional dishes.

TRECASTAGNI

◒◒ **Villa Taverna** – *Corso Colombo 42, Trecastagni. ☎095 78 06 458. Closed Mon, lunchtime Tue–Fri and Sun evenings.* 🍴. This highly original restaurant is typical of Catania's old town.

Taormina★★★

From its rocky plateau, 200m/656ft above sea level, Taormina occupies one of the best seats in the house, looking out from its balcony over the sea to Mt Etna. The breathtaking beauty of the landscape and its artistic history – the Greek theatre stands testament to its creative past – have rendered Taormina world-famous. A popular destination for travellers since the 1700s, its popularity soared at the end of the 19C when foreigners, particularly English and German tourists, constructed villas in the city; luminaries drawn here included magnates such as the Rothschilds and the Krupps, and writers such as D.H. Lawrence. In more recent times, Taormina has become a favourite with the international jet set. From April to September, the countless tourists who pour into the town tend to tarnish its beauty a little, but it's still well worth the effort.

A BIT OF HISTORY

Legend relates how the crew aboard a Greek vessel that was sailing along the eastern coast of Sicily were distracted while making a sacrifice to Neptune. The outraged god of the sea sent forth a strong wind that shipwrecked the boat. Just one of the sailors, Theocles, succeeded in reaching a local beach. Fascinated by the area, he returned to Greece to persuade a band of his countrymen to come to Sicily and found a colony.

This was **Nasso**, modern-day Naxos (◔ see Excursions: Giardini Naxos). There is a seed of truth in the legend: a Greek colony was indeed founded here in the 8C BC and its people quietly prospered until 403 BC when Dionysius, the tyrant of Syracuse, decided to extend his territory to include this part of the island; following their defeat, the colonists were allowed to settle on the plateau of Monte Tauro (200m/650ft above sea-level) which had hitherto been occupied by the Siculi. From that time, records

▶ **Population:** 11 096

⏱ **Michelin Map:** p317:B2

▤ **Info:** Piazza S. Caterina (Palazzo Corvaja), ℘0942 23 243, www.comune. taormina.me.it

◗ **Location:** The historic centre is best explored on foot, and the reward for tackling the many flights of steps and steep slopes (avoid the hottest part of the day) is the magnificent **view** from the top of the town.

🅿 **Parking:** As it is extremely difficult to find parking in the historical centre, visitors are advised to leave their cars in one of the well-signposted car parks along the road leading into town and to walk into the centre.

◉ **Don't Miss:** Magnificent panoramas of Mt Etna from the Greek Theatre, the atmosphere of the Old Town with its splendid palazzi, coffee and a stroll along Porta Catania, and a tour of the Alcantara Valley, including the Gole dell'Alcantar.

👪 **Kids:** Cable car rides from Taormina to Mazzaro, and boat rides to grottoes and caves at Mazzaro and Capo Sant'Andrea.

🕐 **Timing:** Apr–Oct. Avoid August crowds.

refer to the settlement of Tauromenion, modern Taormina. At first, the town was allied with Rome and then conquered by Octavian; when the Roman Empire fell, it became the capital of Byzantine Sicily. Shortly after the arrival of the Arabs it was destroyed, only to be immediately rebuilt and, in 1079, conquered by the Norman Count Roger d'Altavilla, under whom it enjoyed a long period of prosperity.

In the centuries that followed, it became a Spanish dominion before succumbing to French and then Bourbon rule until the Unification of Italy.

THE GREEK THEATRE★★★

🕐 *Open 9am–2hr before dusk.* 👁€8.
♿ 📞 *0942 23 220.*

The theatre was built by the Ancient Greeks (Hellenistic period) and then transformed and enlarged by the Romans. What survives today dates from the 2C AD. The amphitheatre exploits the natural lie of the land: several of the *cavea (auditorium)* steps are cut directly from the bedrock.

The Greek theatre conformed with the correct application of the Classical orders; it included a semicircular *orchestra* section reserved for musicians, chorus and dancers. The Romans removed the lower tier of steps when converting the orchestra into a circular arena, a shape better-suited to hosting circus games; they also added a corridor to provide access for gladiators and wild animals.

From the top of the *cavea*, visitors and spectators can absorb the full impact of the **panoramic view★★★** over Mount

GETTING THERE AND AROUND

Trains and buses run to and from **Catania** *(approx. 1hr)*, Messina *(1hr)* and Siracusa *(2hr 30min)*. There is also a daily bus service from the town to **Fontanarossa** airport at **Catania**. **Taormina-Giardini** train station is situated in **Villagonia**, *3km/1.8mi from the centre; the bus station is on Via Pirandello.*

The **CST** *(Compagnia Siciliana Turismo)* bus company offers excursions to places including Syracuse, Agrigento, Piazza Armerina, Palermo, the Aeolian Islands, the Alcantara gorge and Etna. *Corso Umberto 101; 📞0942 62 60 88.*

Etna. This magical sight extends all along the top of the *cavea* as far as the opposite left-hand corner, where the outlook encompasses Taormina itself.

The theatre, which continues to be used, has hosted the *David di Donatello* prize, a prestigious event in the Italian film calendar.

It now hosts *Taormina Arte,* an international festival of cinema, theatre, ballet and music, during the summer.

Greek Theatre with a view to Mount Etna

© René Mattes/hemis.fr

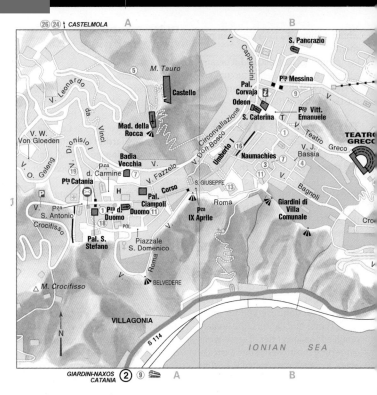

WALKING TOUR

CENTRAL TAORMINA

The centre of Taormina radiates from the main thoroughfare, Corso Umberto I.

Corso Umberto I★

Stroll along this peaceful thoroughfare beginning at **Porta Messina** as it gently climbs up to **Porta Catania**, past elegant shops, restaurants and cafés and into an intricate network of side streets, filled with the scent of almond paste wafting from back-street sweet-shop kitchens. Just beyond Porta Messina, at the entrance to the street, stands the 17C **Chiesa di San Pancrazio**.

This is dedicated to St Pancras who, according to legend, was the first Bishop of Taormina. The church, meanwhile, sits among the foundations of a temple dedicated to Zeus Serapis *(notice the remains of the Ancient wall now incorporated into the building's left flank).* Along the street are three piazzas.

Piazza Vittorio Emanuele

This square occupies the site of the Roman Forum. Behind the **Chiesa di Santa Caterina**, with its Baroque pink marble and Taormina stone doorway, are the red-brick ruins of an **Odeon** – a small covered theatre from the Roman period (1C AD).

Palazzo Corvaja

The heart of the building, which includes the square tower and the central section overlooking the courtyard, dates from the period of Arab domination. The left wing and the staircase up to the first floor were added in the 13C; the right wing dates from the 15C.

Having been abandoned and left to decay over the years, it was restored after the Second World War. It features a succession of styles: the top of the tower is Arab, the windows of the state room (13C) and the front entrance are Catalan-Gothic; the Sala del Parlamento *(in the right wing)* is Norman.

The offices off the courtyard, occupied by APT, the Sicilian Tourist Authorities, include displays of Sicilian puppets and ornate carts.

On the first floor of the palazzo is the **Museo Siciliano di Arte e Tradizioni Popolari** (◔ *open Tue–Sun 9am–1pm, 4–8pm;* ◔ *closed Mon;* ⊜ €2.60; ✆ 0942 62 01 98), housing a collection of carts, puppets, costumes, embroidery, cribs and a series of ex-votos.

Naumachie

In a side-street off to the left.

The name technically refers to the simulated naval battles that the Romans so enjoyed watching. In this case, it refers to a red-brick wall dating from the Roman period, which probably supported a large cistern.

Piazza IX Aprile★

This delightful little square overlooks the sea, offering wonderful **views★★** over the bay and across to Mount Etna.

It is enclosed on the other three sides by the bare façade of San Giuseppe (17C), San Agostino *(now a library)* and the Torre dell'Orologio, which sits on an open loggia that provides a through way to the 15C part of the town.

The extant building dates from the late 17C, when the clock was added, although the foundations appear to date as far back as the 6C AD, when the tower formed an integral part of the town's defences.

The piazza is a popular meeting place, crowded with people sitting at the outside tables of its many bars.

Piazza Duomo

A splendid Baroque **fountain** in Taormina stone rises from a circular base at the centre of the square. The largest basin, facing eastwards, at one time served as a drinking trough. Elevated in the centre, it bears the symbol of the town: a female centaur with two legs and two arms, who holds an orb and a sceptre, the symbols of power.

Duomo

The 13C cathedral is dedicated to St Nicholas of Bari. The front elevation has a starkly simple façade, relieved only by a **Renaissance** doorway flanked by single-light windows, surmounted by a rose window. The crenellations along the roof line have earned it the name of "cathedral-fortress".

The fabric of the building is Gothic; the ground plan is a Latin cross. The nave is separated from the side aisles by an arcade of pointed arches, which spring from column shafts of pink marble. The clerestory above comprises simple single-light windows that illuminate the nave. A fine 16C **polyptych** by Antonello de Saliba sits over the second altar in the south aisle.

TAORMINA'S PALAZZI★

The old town centre is dotted with fine *palazzi*: most are Gothic in style with Arabo-Norman touches and built of black lava stone and white Syracuse stone, set into geometric patterning.

Palazzo dei Duchi di Santo Stefano

Via del Ghetto (left), before
Porta Catania.

This fine building was built for the Dukes of Santo Stefano, part of the De Spuches family, in the 15C. The bold rustication gives it the appearance of a fortified residence.

The most effective decorative element is the two-tone *(black lava and white Syracuse stone)* geometric frieze, which runs the length of the upper storey.

The *palazzo* accommodates the **Fondazione Mazzullo** (🕐 *open daily 9am–12.30pm, 3–6pm; 0942 61 02 73*), which hosts exhibitions of sculpture and drawings by the artist Graniti *(and the occasional temporary show, notably during Advent when a display of terracotta Nativity scenes is arranged)*. A recurrent theme among the works in lava, granite and bronze is the expression of pain: this is especially notable in the series of *Executions by Firing Squad* and in the *Wounded Cat*.

Badia Vecchia

Via Dionisio 1.

This building with a two-tone frieze normally houses the **Museo Archeologico** (⚬ *closed for restoration at the time of going to press; 0942 62 37 00).*

Palazzo Ciampoli

Providing a backdrop to the steps of Salita Palazzo Ciampoli, to the right of Corso Umberto I, just before Piazza Duomo.

Despite its poor condition and an unsightly old discotheque sign, the **façade** of this *palazzo* is a fine one, composed of two levels separated by a decoratively engraved stone panel. The entrance is set into an elegantly pointed arch, surmounted by a shield bearing the date when the palace was built: 1412.

Giardini di Villa Comunale★★

Via Roma.

The gardens are planted with flowering plants and shrubs ranging from the common to the exotic. When the gardens were under private ownership, a series of eclectic **follies** were erected; the most unusual consists of arches and arcades reminiscent of a beehive, hence the name *(the Beehives)* given to it by its owner, Lady Florence Trevelyan, who used it for bird-watching.

The little road that runs along the seaward edge provides a fine **view** of Mount Etna and the south coast.

EXCURSIONS
Beaches

A cable car (2min) links Taormina with Mazzarò on the coast. There is a series of steps also linking the two (allow 25min for the descent and about 40min to climb) through the mountainside of figs, cacti and olive trees.

From Mazzarò, a bus service operates to various beaches. The cable car runs every 15min Apr–Sept 8am–1am and Oct–Mar 8am–8pm; €3 single trip; www.taorminaservizipubblici.it.

The little bay of **Mazzarò** is enclosed on the south side by **Capo Sant'Andrea**, which is riddled with caves and grottoes, including the Blue Grotto *(Grotta*

Rivers of Water and Lava

Alcantara Gorge – Lost in the mists of time, a small volcano north of Mount Etna woke and poured forth enormous quantities of lava, which flowed down to the sea and beyond to form Capo Schisò. The tortuous route taken by the river of lava was followed by a torrent of water, which ploughed a channel through it, smoothing the lava and clearing away the aggregate. Towards the end of its journey, the water encountered more friable ground and sweeping onwards, exposed two sheer cliffs of very hard basalt that had cooled and hardened into fascinating prism-like shapes. This is the gorge, only part of which is now accessible.

The name of the river, and of its valley, *Al Qantarah,* dates back to the period of Arab occupation and refers to the arched bridge built by the Romans to withstand the force of the river in full spate, an impressive sight even today.

Azzurra). The sound of fishermen calling for people to join a boat trip echoes the lengths of the beaches.

Beyond the headland is the delightful **bay★★** that sweeps round to **Isola Bella**, linked to the main shore by a narrow strip of land.

The island, a natural symbol of Taormina, is part of a regional reserve now administered by the University of Catania. The longest beaches, **Spisone** and **Mazzeo**, extend north of Mazzarò.

Castello

4km/2.5mi along the road to Castelmola; a track turns up to the right.
The castle can also be reached on foot by following the signs for "Salita Castello", up a series of broad steps *from Via Circonvallazione (about 1km/ 0.6mi there and back) in Taormina, or by taking Salita Branco, which starts in Via Dietro i Cappuccini.*
Avoid taking this walk in the midday sun or in the height of summer!

The **castle** stands isolated on the summit of Monte Tauro *(398m/1,305ft).*

Just below it stands the **Santuario della Madonna della Rocca**: the little terrace before the church offers a fine **view★★** of Taormina's ancient theatre and town. A footpath continues up to the castle, a medieval fortress built on the foundations of a former acropolis from Antiquity. Little survives other than the old walls and tower fragments.

From here, another splendid **view★★** extends over the theatre and Taormina.

Isola Bella

© unknown1861/iStockphoto.com

Legend of the Alcantara Gorge

At one time the Alcantara River flowed calmly along its course without crags, rapids or sheer drops, making the valley fertile. The people who lived there, however, were evil: they hurt each other and had no respect for nature.

Two brothers lived in the valley and cultivated a field of wheat. One was blind. When the time came to divide up the harvest, the sighted farmer took the grain measure and began to share out the wheat. One measure for himself and one for his brother. Then, overtaken by greed, he decided to keep most of the harvest for himself. An eagle, happening to fly overhead, witnessed what was occurring and reported the incident to God, who hurled a thunderbolt at the cheat, killing him outright. The thunderbolt also struck the heap of grain that had been unjustly set aside, turning it into a mountain of red earth from which poured a river of lava, which flowed down to the sea.

Legend from the book entitled *Al Qantarah* by L Danzuso and E Zinna.

Castelmola★

5km/3mi NW.

This village, occupying a strategic **position**★ behind Taormina, centres on the picturesque Piazzetta del Duomo, from where a network of tiny streets extends outwards.

Magnificent glimpses of the landscape may be snatched from various points, especially from Piazzetta di Sant'Antonino, where the **view**★ opens out towards Mount Etna, the north coast and the beaches below Taormina.

Very little remains of the ruined **castle** other than sections of the 16C walls and a good **view** of Monte Venere *(beyond the cemetery)* and the lesser Monte Ziretto.

The **Chiesa dell'Annunziata**, next to the cemetery, preserves an attractive doorway sculpted in white stone.

Try the regional speciality, a potent almond liqueur that was invented by Castelmola locals.

Giardini Naxos

5km/3mi from Taormina and linked to the city by frequent bus services (departures every 30min from the Taormina stop on Via Pirandello).

The beach on which the first Greek colonists probably landed 2 700 years ago now accommodates thousands of tourists. They are drawn to the charming position, the particularly mild climate, the long beach and the splendid scenery. The seaside attractions only add to the archaeological lustre.

Capo Schisò is a promontory formed by a great lava flow. Here, the first Chalcidian colonisers founded Naxos in 735 BC, making it the oldest Greek settlement in Sicily. The name is borrowed from the Cycladic island, where, according to legend, Dionysus met and then married Ariadne after she was abandoned by Theseus.

From the 5C BC, the domination of Naxos became a prime objective for aspiring empire-builders, notably Hippocrates of Gela and later, Hieron of Syracuse. The latter evicted the inhabitants of Naxos and deported them to Leontinoi in 476. Eventually, the support offered by Naxos to the Athenian expedition against Syracuse (415 BC) led to the city's demise. In 403 BC, Dionysius the Great razed it to the ground, leaving the exiled survivors to found Tauromenion.

For a long time the "garden town" merely served as a sheltered anchorage for nearby Taormina. The epithet originated from the cotton and sugar-cane plantations, eventually replaced by citrus orchards.

A popular resort since the 1950s, it's now one of Sicily's largest tourist centres.

Naxos

The archaeological site is behind the port, not far from the Giardini Naxos exit off the A 18. Access to the site is from

Via Stracina, the continuation of Via Naxos or, during opening hours, via the museum in Via Schisò. ⏱*Open 9am–1hr before dusk.* ✎*€2.* ♿ ☎*0942 51 001.*

The 4 BC town followed the same boundaries as its 7C–6C BC predecessor: all but the old city walls and the **temenos** *(sacred precinct)* were removed and replaced by a regular, orthogonal *(right-angled)* street plan as advocated by the 5C BC architect-urban planner Hippodamus of Miletus.

On entering the site from Via Stracina, follow the path along the boundary walls of the ancient city. On the southwest side, these incorporate the walls of the **temenos**, enclosing the ruins of a large temple dating from the late 6C BC. Nearby sit two kilns: the larger for firing architectural elements in terra cotta, the smaller for vases and votive objects.

Leave the sacred precinct by its northern entrance *(traces of which are still visible)* to emerge onto *plateia B.*

Follow this broad avenue some distance for views of the new city.

At *stenopos 6*, turn left towards the museum: on the left, level with *stenopos 11*, are the remains of a small temple from the 7C BC.

Archaeological museum

Via Schisò. ⏱*Open 9am–1hr before dusk.* ✎*€2.* ☎*0942 51 001.*

Situated alongside a small Bourbon keep, the museum houses artefacts from the excavations.

The ground floor contains pottery that testifies to the existence of settlements on Capo Schisò from Neolithic times and the Bronze Age.

The display includes a range of painted **cymae** *(decorative roof ornaments)*, a figurine of a veiled goddess *(probably Hera)*; a delicately contrived **statuette of Aphrodite Hippias** and a collection of objects from a **surgeon's tomb**. Inside the keep are objects found at sea: anchor shafts, amphorae and grindstones.

🚗 DRIVING TOURS

THE ALCANTARA VALLEY

60km/37mi. Allow one day (including the visit to the gorges and riverbed walk).

Etna looms over the Alcantara Valley, appearing and disappearing between the hills as the road winds its way in an ever-changing kaleidoscope of **views★**.

Giardini Naxos

♿*See opposite.*

Along the road, you will see olive-wood sculptures by **Francesco Lo Giudice**, known as *Il Mago* (the magician) on the left-hand side.

▶ Take the S 185 in the direction of Gazzi.

Gole dell'Alcantara★

The Alcantara Gorge is part of a vast nature area formed by canyons of ancient lava flows traversed by the Alcantara river and dotted with waterfalls and ponds. ⏱*Open 8.30am–7pm.* ✎*€8. Themed tours and classes are organised, including cooking with local foods.* ☎*0942 98 51 10.* *www.terralcantara.it.*

Under normal conditions it is possible to walk upriver May–Sept. There is also a **lift** to take visitors back up to the top of the gorge. At the opening of the gorge, rent boots and waders. *Special camping facilities are available nearby.*

The gorge

👥⌚The descent on foot affords a spectacular **view★** of the entrance to the gorge.

Once level with the river bed, the salt cliffs tower some 50m/165ft above the narrow stretch of water. Their massive bulk, exaggerated by shadow, seems accentuated farther up the gorge, where the world suddenly seems to be composed of three elements: rock, water and sky.

As you walk, the sun casts bright light into the darkness; occasionally refracted into a thousand tiny mirrors by droplets of water thrown out by the **waterfalls** and collected into rivulets that stream down the sheer rockface.

Motta Camastra

A road off to the right leads to this small town at an altitude of 453m/1,486ft.

▶ Return to the S 185.

Francavilla di Sicilia

On 21 June 1719, a battle took place here between the Spaniards and Austrians, an event recorded for posterity by prints preserved in the Capuchin Monastery on top of the hill nearby. Founded in the 16C, the monastery has a few original cells and a small museum about life in this offshoot of the Franciscan Order. In the church there is an 18C wooden aumbry (small cupboard) for Eucharist vessels bearing a **pelican** plucking the flesh from its breast to feed its young; a symbol of the sacrifice of Christ.

▶ Take the SP 7 south.

Castiglione di Sicilia

Castel Leone (now reduced to a ruin) dominates the town from on high, set as it is on its rocky spur of tufa. The **site★** of the castle has been a lookout point since ancient times. From here, magnificent **views★★** stretch over the town and Etna. To the east lie the ruins of a fortress from 750 BC.

The main monuments are clustered around the highest part of the town. The 18C church, **San Antonio**, has a concave façade and a campanile built of lava with an onion-shaped dome.

The **interior**, decked with polychrome marble, has a triumphal arch (1796) and a fine wooden organ in the chancel.

San Pietro preserves some of the primitive Norman original tower in its campanile. **Santa Maria della Catena** has a fine doorway with spiral columns. A right fork off the road to Mojo Alcantara leads to the remains of a **Byzantine chapel** (or cuba) dating from the 7C–9C.

▶ Take the SP 7II towards Randazzo, then turn right onto SP 7III.

Mojo Alcantara

The name of this little town comes from a small volcano, which erupted and gave rise to the creation of the gorge. Today, it is a green, innocuous-looking cone.

▶ Return to the SP 711 and follow it to the right, then turn right onto S 120.

Randazzo★

See Etna.

From Randazzo, it is possible to join the Circumetnea (see Etna) or continue on towards the Nebrodi Mountains (see The Nebrodi Mountains).

IONIAN COAST: TAORMINA TO MESSINA

Approx. 70km/44mi from Taormina. Allow one day.

▶ Leave Taormina via S 114.

Forza d'Agrò

This medieval hamlet caps the furthermost spurs of the Monti Peloritani, enjoying a splendid **prospect★** of the coast. The best **viewpoint** is the terrace of Piazza del Municipio.

Steps lead up to the 16C **Chiesa della Triade** and the remains of a Norman castle.

Capo Sant'Alessio★

This headland is crowned with a round fortress and a polygonal castle on the eastern tip (closed to the public). On the south side is the wonderful **beach** of Sant'Alessio Siculoe.

Santissimi di Santi Pietro e Paolo d'Agrò

The **church**, founded by Basilian monks, is striking not only on account of its unusual use of brick, volcanic stone, lime-stone and sandstone, but also as a synthesis of Byzantine, Arab and Norman influences.

The **exterior** is ornamented with decorative banding, interlaced arcading and herringbone patterns. The **interior** space is divided into nave and aisles by Corinthian columns.

Casalvecchio

This little town enjoys a fabulous panorama: from the terrace before the **Chiesa Madre di Sant'Onofrio**, the **view★** takes in the Ionian Sea lying off Capo Sant'Alessio and Forza d'Agrò, and to the south, Mount Etna.

In a neighbouring former church house is the eclectic **Museo Parrocchiale** (contact Signore Carmelo Crisafulli at the town hall for information: ☎0942 76 10 30), which displays a silver life-size statue of Sant'Onofrio (1745), liturgical furnishings and sacred vestments.

▷ Continue on the S 114. After 2km/1.2mi, take the exit for Sàvoca.

Sàvoca

Approx. 3km/1.8mi inland.

This medieval town is divided into two hilltop ridges, interconnecting with three spurs on which the districts of San Rocco, San Giovanni and Pentefur are built.

Beyond the town hall, but still outside the old town, sits the **Convento dei Cappuccini** (☉open summer 9am–1pm; ☎0942 76 12 45), a Capuchin monastery with a **crypt** that contains the mummified bodies of 32 former town dignitaries and friars from the 17C and 18C. Several of these are displayed in niches, others in wooden sarcophagi. From the area in front of the church there is a **view** of the town, the ruined castle and il Calvario (or "hill of Calvary") in the distance.

▷ Go back the same way and turn up Via Borgo and then immediately left on to Via San Michele.

This leads to the gateway to the old town centre. Beyond the archway stands the 15C church of **San Michele**. As the same street continues, wonderful **views★** extend over the rooftops and the valley and up to the **Norman castle** ruins and the church of San Nicola (or Santa Lucia). At last, the **Chiesa Madre** comes into view, with its 16C portal surmounted by the Savoca coat of arms, bearing the elderberry (sambuco) branch from which the town's name is supposedly derived.

Itàla

The little hamlet of Croce jostles around the **Basilian Church** of **San Pietro e San Paolo**, which was rebuilt in 1093. Continuing back along the coast, the road passes **Capo Alì**, which is topped by a round watchtower, probably from the Norman period. It continues through the seaside resorts of **Alì Terme**, **Nizza di Sicilia** and **Roccalumera**.

▷ After 2km/1.2mi, turn inland.

Scaletta Zanclea

Scaletta Superiore (2km/1.2mi inland) has a **castle** that was originally built to serve as a Swabian military outpost (13C). It was eventually acquired by the Ruffo family, who used it as a hunting lodge until the 17C.

The massive fortress now houses the **Museo Civico** (☉open Mar–Oct 9am–1pm, 4–8pm; for more information, call ☎090 95 967) and its collections of weaponry and historic documents.

Monastero di San Placido Caloneró

On the road to Pezzolo, a short distance before Galati Marina.
✦ Closed for restoration at the time of going to press. ☎090 68 58 00.

The **Benedictine monastery**, now an argricultural technical institute, has attractive 17C cloisters with columns with high dosserets and Ionic capitals.

A fine Durazzo Gothic portal (to the right of the atrium, leading into the first cloisters) provides access to a vaulted chapel with clustered columns.

ADDRESSES

🏨 STAY

Casa Diana – *Via di Giovanni 6.* 📞*0942 23 898.* 🖨. *4 rooms.* With a good location right in the centre, this slightly ageing pensione run by a friendly mamma has the added advantage of a roof terrace. Quite a narrow staircase leads up to the rooms, which are clean but basic, and quite noisy on the street side. No breakfast.

Il Leone – *Via Bagnoli Croci 126.* 📞*0942 23 878. www.camereilleone.it.* 🖨. *19 rooms.* Acceptable, but austere rooms. Some are slightly more expensive and come with a private bathroom and air conditioning. Decent overall, although the communal areas look a bit lacklustre. Ask for a room at the top with a terrace and sea view.

Casa Grazia – *Via Jallia Bassia 20.* 📞*0942 24 776.* 🖨. *6 rooms.* They may not be over-endowed with views and space, but the spotless rooms in this tall, thin pensione each come with a fridge and a balcony. The top-floor room, no 7, even has a terrace while the two cheaper rooms share a bathroom.

Hotel Villa Igiea – *Via Circonvallazione 28. 0942 625 275.* 🖨. *12 rooms.* A fine, late-19C neo-gothic building furnished in the Art Nouveau style with the atmosphere of an old-fashioned family home. The rooms *(cheaper with shared bathrooms)* and the breakfast terrace enjoy a splendid **view** over the bay.

Pensione Adele – *Via Appolo Arcageta 16.* 📞*339 57 23 756. www. pensioneadele.it. 15 rooms.* A large, centrally located building with pleasant rooms, a TV lounge and a roof terrace. In summer, there is a shuttle service for the beach.

Hotel Villa Nettuno – *Via Pirandello 33.* 📞*0942 23 797. www.hotelvillanettuno.it.* 🖨. *13 rooms €4.* This lovely Art-Nouveau style villa opposite the cable car has a wonderful garden with a belvedere offering a superb **view** over the sea. Breakfast is taken on the terrace, or in winter, in the lovely family room with its period furniture. Most of the rooms, which are simple but clean, have a little balcony or terrace.

Villa Fiorita – *Via L. Pirandello 39.* 📞*0942 24 122. www.villafioritahotel. com. closed Nov–Feb.* 🏊. *25 rooms.*

Occupying an 18C villa, this hotel is a particularly peaceful choice, with a lovely **view** and traditional decor. The garden contains a Roman tomb.

Villa Paradiso – *Via Roma 2.* 📞*0942 23 921. www.hotelvillaparadiso taormina.com. 37 rooms.* The villa once belonged to Florence Trevelyan, the English aristocrat who owned the Isola Bella. As a hotel, it has been decorated with great attention to detail and class. The rooms are pretty, if not huge, with balconies offering **views** of Etna or the Bay of Naxos. Tennis courts and free shuttle for the beach, where guests can take advantage of club facilities.

Villa Schuler – *Piazzetta Bastione, Via Roma.* 📞*0942 23 481. www. hotelvillaschuler.com. Closed Dec–Feb. 26 rooms.* Converted into a hotel in 1905, this old house in the historic centre is surrounded by a Mediterranean garden full of tropical flowers and plants. The hotel retains some of its late-19C atmosphere and has old-fashioned, comfortable rooms.

CLOSE TO TAORMINA

Villa Regina – *Punta San Giorgio, Castelmola, 5km/3mi from Taormina.* 📞*0942 28 228. www.villareginataormina. com. Closed Nov–Feb. 10 rooms.* This simple guesthouse has a cool, shady garden and a delightful **view** of Taormina and the coast. Ideal for those in need of a peaceful break.

Villa Sonia – *Via Porta Mola 9, Castelmola, 5km/3mi from Taormina.* 📞*0942 28 082. www.hotel villasonia.com. Closed Nov–Feb.* ♿. *35 rooms.* Situated at the entrance to the charming village of Castelmola, this attractive villa is tastefully decorated with period items and Sicilian handicrafts. Alongside the standard rooms, the hotel also has luxury rooms offering excellent standards of comfort and service, albeit at exorbitant prices *(€180–200 per night)*.

La Riva – *Via Tysandros 52, Giardini Naxos.* 📞*0942 51 329. www.hotella riva.com. Closed Nov. 38 rooms.* A charming family-run pensione on the seafront, with 38 rooms furnished in original Sicilian style and a dining room on the fourth floor that offers superb **sea views**.

🍴 EAT

Al Grappolo d'Uva – *Via Bagnoli Croci 618.* 📞 *0942 625 874.* This little wine bar, with its rustic decor, has a few tables, some of them made from barrels, where you can sample wines from Etna and throughout Sicily with prosciutto, antipasti, bruschetta or grilled vegetables.

Mamma Rosa – *Via Naumachia 10. 0942 243 61. www.mammarosa taormina.com.* This cheerful trattoria has two terraces and serves up succulent plates of fish, grilled or in a salt crust, pasta with sardines, seafood risotto and pizza.

Al Duomo – *Vico Ebrei 11. 0942 62 56 56. Closed Mon, Jan and Nov. Booking advised.* This restaurant does everything right: a lovely terrace with **views** of the cathedral and delicious dishes based on local produce.

Osteria Nero d'Avola – *Piazza San Domenico 2B. 0942 628 874. Closed Mon.* Fans of "slow food" and wine lovers are in their element in this convivial *enoteca*, where owner Turi Siligato holds court. Sample from scores of Sicilian wines and more than a dozen olive oils with a daily-changing menu based on Siligato's finds from local fishermen or his own mushroom forays. Try pasta with sea urchins, "Mediterranean sushi" or a salad of interdonato lemons.

La Piazzetta – *Vicolo F. Paladini 5/7. 0942 62 63 17. Closed Nov–Jan and Mon Sep–Jul .* The cuisine at this friendly, family-run establishment with a typical village-restaurant atmosphere is distinctly Mediterranean, with an emphasis on fish. Pleasant terrace.

Il Baccanale – *Piazzetta Filea 1, Taormina. 0942 62 53 90. Closed Thu Oct– Mar.* This restaurant, serving fine Sicilian cuisine, is popular with foreign tourists and enjoys a rustic atmosphere with outdoor tables on a small piazza.

Al Saraceno – *Via Madonna della Rocca 18, Taormina. 0942 63 2015. www.alsaraceno.it. Closed Mon (except Jul and Aug) and Nov.* On fine days the splendid **view** from the spacious terrace extends as far as the Straits of Messina. Fresh fish and pizza are the specialities.

CLOSE TO TAORMINA

Bagni Delfino – *Via Nazionale, Mazzarò, 5.5km/3.5mi from Taormina on S 114. 0942 23 004. Closed Nov–15 Mar.* Combine lunch with a dip in the sea at this attractive restaurant situated right on the beach.

Sea Sound – *Via Jannuzzo 37/A, Giardini Naxos. 0942 54 330. Closed Nov–Apr.* This sea-facing restaurant serves a range of delicious fish dishes on a delightful terrace.

TAKING A BREAK

Caffè Wunderbar – *Piazza IX Aprile 7. 0942 62 53 02.* Greta Garbo and Tennessee Williams enjoyed meeting for cocktails in this café at the foot of the Torre dell'Orologio, in one of the most attractive corners of Taormina. The interior is elegant in style, while the terrace enjoys magnificent **views** of the Bay of Naxos.

Mocambo Bar – *Piazza IX Aprile 8. 0942 23 350.* "Take a seat at the Mocambo and watch the world go by…" is the advice given by the owners of this bar-pasticceria, which enjoys a superb location overlooking the beautiful Piazza IX Aprile. Open from breakfast to after dinner, the bar has a pleasant atmosphere throughout the day and into the evening.

Bam Bar – *Via DiGiovanni 45. 0942 24 355.* The best *granite* in Taormina, in friendly, colourful surroundings.

Pasticceria Saint Honoré – *Corso Umberto I 208. 094 22 48 77. Open 7am–midnight.* You're spoilt for choice in this pasticceria with its wide selection of cakes, ice creams, pastries and *torrone* (a type of nougat). Alternatively, enjoy a cooling glass of granita on the terrace.

Bar San Giorgio – *Piazza S. Antonio1, 98030 Castelmola, 5km/3mi from Taormina. 0942 28 228. www.barsangiorgio.com.* Established in the early 20C, this traditional café enjoys a wonderful location in the quiet Piazza S. Antonio, with superb **views** of Taormina and the sea. Try the local *vino alla mandorla* (almond liqueur).

SHOPPING

La Bottega del Buongustaio – *Via G. di Giovanni 17. 094 26 25 769.* Set back from the bustle of Corso Umberto, this shop specialises in DOC-label Sicilian produce, including wines, liqueurs, sauces, preserves, honey, pasta and olive oil. An excellent address for those wishing to take home some of the island's specialities.

FESTIVALS

Taormina Film Fest – Last week of June. This film festival includes dance, theatre and music. *For information, 0942 21 142; www.taorminafilmfest.it.*

Taormina arte – This organisation sponsors international film, music, opera and theatre festivals: *Jun–Sept. For information, 0942 21 142; www.taorte.it.*

Messina

After plans to build a bridge linking Sicily with the mainland were abandoned in 2011, Messina remains the main port of entry for visitors travelling to the island by boat. At its narrowest point, the channel between Sicily and the rest of Italy is just 3.3km wide, so passengers don't have to wait too long before discovering this city, which is centred around its bustling port.

A BIT OF HISTORY

Founded as a Greek colony in the 8C BC, Messina was originally called **Zancle** after the sickle-like shape of its harbour. The history of the town is inextricably linked to the sea and to the straits that bear its name.

According to tradition, sailors have long claimed the straits are guarded by two monsters, Scylla and Charybdis. **Scylla** was the daughter of Phorcys and Hecate *(Greek goddess associated with the underworld)* and loved by Poseidon. This aroused the jealousy of his wife Amphitrite, who used herbs to turn her into a monster that devoured mariners sailing too close to her cave on the Calabrian side of the strait. Her victims included six sailors on Odysseus's ship. Under another rock on the Sicilian side of the strait lived **Charybdis**, who would drink and regurgitate sea water three times every day; when trapped by this whirlpool, sailors often fell prey to Scylla *(Odyssey)*.

Messina acted as a trading post for goods, people, and artistic trends and ideas. From this dynamic setting emerged figures such as the 15C painter **Antonello da Messina**.

In more recent times, the town has suffered the effects of devastating earthquakes. In the 1908 quake, 90 percent of the town was destroyed and more than 100,000 were killed. Many of the town's buildings were also destroyed in bombing raids during the Second World War.

▶ **Population:** 243 381

⌖ **Michelin Map:** p317: B1

🛈 **Info:** Piazza della Repubblica, ✆090 67 29 44; Via dei Mille, ✆090 29 35 292.

▶ **Location:** Messina is a modern city that grew up behind the sickle-shaped port that gave the town its name in ancient times. Most of the monuments that survived the terrible earthquake of 1908 and the bombing raids of the Second World War are grouped behind the central port area. To reach the historic centre from the motorway, take the Messina-Boccetta Porto exit and follow Viale Boccetta to Corso Garibaldi, which runs parallel to the seafront.

◉ **Don't Miss:** Panoramas from Monte Antennammare and Casalvecchio, glorious beaches at Capo Peloro and the macabre fascination of the crypt of the Capuchin monastery at Savoca.

👥 **Kids:** The lively mechanical show of the Orologio Astronomico on the Duomo bell tower as it strikes midday.

🕐 **Timing:** Allow half a day for driving tours around Capo Peloro and a full day for a tour from Messina to Taormina.

SIGHTS
Duomo

After the 1908 earthquake, the **cathedral** was almost completely rebuilt in the style of the Norman original.

The façade rises in tiers and is relieved with single-light windows and a small central rose window. The **central doorway★**, one of three, was re-erected using elements of the original fabric (15C). It is flanked by small columns sup-

GETTING THERE AND AROUND

From mainland Italy – Messina handles the principal ferry services from mainland Italy. Ferries run from Reggio Calabria *(45min, Stazione Ferrovie Stato, ☎0965 75 60 99)* and Villa SanGiovanni *(20min, Caronte Shipping, Via Marina 30, ☎0965 79 31 31 and Ferrovie dello Stato, Piazza Stazione, ☎0965 75 60 99).*

For hydrofoil services *(20min)*, contact SNAV, Reggio Calabria, ☎0965 29 568.

For visitors arriving by air, the nearest airports are in **Reggio di Calabria** and **Catania**.

From within Sicily – Messina is linked by train with Palermo *(3hr)*, Taormina *(1hr)*, Catania *(approx. 2hr)* and Siracusa *(3hr)*. A number of bus companies operate services to Palermo, Taormina, Catania, Capo d'Orlando, Patti and Tindari.

Connections with the Aeolian islands – Trains *(approx. 40min)* and buses run from Messina to Milazzo, from where ferries cross to the Aeolian islands. Alternatively, hydrofoil services are operated by Aliscafi SNAV from Messina *(1hr 20min)*, Via San Raineri 22: ☎090 3621 14, *Fax: 090 71 73 58.*

---

ported by lions, and surmounted by a lunette with a *Madonna and Child* (16C). Projecting from the right is a building lit by two-light Catalan Gothic windows. The beamed, painted **ceiling** replaces the older one, which was destroyed by bombing raids. The carved rosettes on the central beams betray Eastern design influences.

Treasury

Access from inside the Duomo. ⊙*Open Mon–Sat Apr–Oct 9am–1pm, 3–6.30pm, rest of the year 10am–1pm.* ●*€5 with bell tower access.* ☎090 67 51 75.

The display is dominated by religious objects and vestments. The oldest exhibit (from the Middle Ages) is the Pigna, a lamp made of rock crystal. Much of the silver plate was made in Messina, including the arm-shaped reliquaries (the one of San Marziano is inscribed with Moorish and Byzantine patterns), candlesticks, chalices and a fine 17C **monstrance** (containing a host) with two angels and a pelican on top presiding over the rays of divine light.

Orologio astronomico★

The **astronomical clock** is the most interesting component of the 60m/200ft high bell tower to the left of the cathedral. The mechanism dates from 1933 and was built in Strasbourg. It comprises several tiers, each bearing a diffe-

rent display with a separate movement. At the bottom, a two-horse chariot driven by a deity indicates the day of the week; above, the central figure of Death waves his scythe threateningly at the child, youth, soldier or old man – the four ages of man – that pass before him. At the third stage, the Sanctuary of Montalto *(turn left to compare it with the real one)* sets the scene for a group of figures which, according to the time of year, represent the Nativity, Epiphany, Resurrection and Pentecost. At the top, the tableau enacts a scene relating to a local legend whereby the Madonna delivers a letter to the ambassadors of Messina, in which she thanks and agrees to protect the inhabitants of the town, who were converted to Christianity by St Paul the Apostle: the same **Madonna della Lettera** *(Madonna of the Letter)*, is patron saint of the city. The two female bell-strikers are the local heroines, Dina and Clarenza, who were alive during the period of resistance against the Angevins (1282). The summit is capped with a lion.

The south side of the bell tower *(starting from the bottom)* shows a perpetual calendar, the astronomical cycle marked by the signs of the zodiac and the phases of the moon.

When the clock strikes midday, all the mechanical figures come to life accompanied by music: the lion *(symbol of the vitality of the town)* roars three times, while the cockerel crows from between the two girls.

Santissima Annunziata dei Catalani

A short way from the cathedral, set among fine *palazzi* in Via Garibaldi, sits the Catalan Church. Built in the 12C when the Normans controlled the island, it is named after its patrons, who were Catalan merchants.

The **apse**★is a fine example of the Norman composite style, incorporating Romanesque elements *(small, blind arches on slender columns)*, Moorish influences *(geometric motifs in polychrome stone)* and Byzantine features *(dome on a drum)*.

Fontana di Orione

In the centre of Piazza del Duomo is a **fountain** designed by the sculptor Montorsoli to commemorate the inauguration of an aqueduct.

Sculpted in a pre-Baroque style (16C), it incorporates allegories of four rivers: the Tiber, Nile, Ebro and Camaro – the River Messina was diverted into the new aqueduct.

Monte di Pietà

Corner of Via XXIV Maggio and Piazza Crisafulli. The front elevation of this late-Mannerist building is ornamented with a massive rusticated doorway framed between solid columns and a broken pediment; above, the balcony rests on brackets carved with volutes. The upper storey, destroyed by the earthquake, has not been rebuilt, giving the building an unfinished air. Today, it is used for concerts and recitals.

Chiesa di San Giovanni di Malta

The west front of this square late-16C building overlooking Via Placida is articulated with white stone pilasters, niches and windows, and in the upper tier, a gallery.

Chiesa di San Francesco d'Assisi o dell'Immacolata

This monumental church was almost entirely rebuilt following the 1908 earthquake and retains original features such as the three austere 13C stone **apses** and fine rose window on the façade.

ADDITIONAL SIGHTS
Museo Regionale

Via della Libertà 465. ◷*Open Mon, Wed and Fri 9am–1.30pm and Tue, Thu and Sat 9am–1.30pm, 4.30–7pm, Sun and public holidays 9am–1pm.* ⊛€3. ♿ ✆*090 36 12 92.*

The chronological arrangement of the displays begins with local history and the artistic climate that prevailed during the Byzantine and Norman eras. The first rooms are dedicated to paintings and sculpture: shallow reliefs and capitals. Among the most notable examples is a fine early-15C polychrome wooden Crucifix *(third room on the right)* and a glazed terracotta medallion from the Della Robbia workshops of a sweet-faced Madonna gazing at her Child.

The works in the next room indicate the strong influence exerted by the Flemish style, as seen in the **Madonna and Child** attributed to a follower of Petrus Christus (15C).

In the striking *Deposition* by Colijn de Coter, in the same room, the scene is heightened by the anguished expressions of mourners and the use of burnt, dull colours.

The adjacent room is devoted to the Messina painter Girolamo Alibrandi. The most striking paintings include the huge *Presentation at the Temple* of 1519 (note the noble expression and gentle features of the woman in the foreground) and *St Paul*. The elegant statue of the *Madonna and Child* nearby is by **Antonello Gagini**.

The Roman painter **Polidoro da Caravaggio** and the Florentine sculptor and architect Montorsoli introduced Mannerism to Messina. Their work, together with that of their followers, is displayed in the next galleries.

Michelangelo Merisi, better known as **Caravaggio**, spent a year in Messina (1608–09); during this time he painted the *Adoration of the Shepherds* and the *Resurrection of Lazarus (Room 10)*. The short time he spent here was sufficient to influence contemporary artists living in the city.

The splendid **Senator's Coach★** *(Room 12)*, dated 1742, incorporates a number of exquisite furnishings, including gilded wooden carvings and painted panels. The top floor of the museum is devoted to decorative and applied arts.

Santa Maria Alemanna

In Via S. Maria dell'Alemagna, which runs across Via Garibaldi.

This sad ruin (there is no roof or façade) still manages to convey something of the original Gothic style, so rare in Sicily, with its graceful pointed arches supported on pilasters and column clusters.

🚗 DRIVING TOURS

CAPO PELORO

Circular tour beginning in Messina. 70km/44mi. Allow half a day.

This excursion starts from Messina and follows a panoramic route around the headland, past glorious beaches that skirt the tip, continuing along the Tyrrhenian shore. The houses that make up the lively little fishing village of **Ganzirri** *(5km/3mi N of Messina along the coast road)* are clustered around two wide saltwater lagoons used for farming shellfish. The road along the "lakeside" hums with restaurants, pizzerias and activity late into the summer evenings. Continuing north for 3.5 km/2mi beyond the Straits of Messina lies **Torre Faro**, a small fishing village overlooked by a lighthouse. Drive through **Lidi di Mortelle** and on to Divieto before turning inland towards Gesso. The road that forks right *(6km/4mi past the town)* leads up to Antennammare.

Monte Antennammare

The road winds up to the San Rizzo pass, where a second road forks right to the **Santuario di Maria Santissima di Dinnammare**, situated on the top of Mount Antennammare *(1 130m/ 3 706ft)*. From here, a spectacular view spans the **panorama★★** of Messina, Capo Peloro and Calabria to the east, the Ionian coastline with the sickle-shaped promontory of Milazzo and Rometta on a hill to the west.

▶ Return to the Col San Rizzo then take the S 113 on the right. This road coasts its way down towards Messina through wooded slopes.

Santa Maria della Valle o Badiazza

The Benedictine abbey also known as Santa Maria della Scala was probably built in the 12C and restored in the 14C. The church is not open to the public. Its **exterior**, however, has windows set into pointed arches finished in volcanic stone. Through these, the interior can be glimpsed, with its two-colour ribbed vault and sculpted truncated pyramid capitals.

▶ Return to Messina.

ADDRESSES

🛏 STAY

MESSINE

🛏 **Nuovo Camping dello Stretto** – *Via Circuito Torre Faro.* ✆*090 32 23 051. www.campingdellostretto.it.* 🅿. A brand-new, well-kept campsite that also rents out small studios.

🛏 **Hotel Cairoli** – *Viale S. Martino 63 (on the corner of Piazza Cairoli).* ✆*090 67 37 55. www.hotelcairoli.com.58 rooms* ⬜. A nice, if slightly faded hotel with its glory days clearly behind it. The staircase and corridors are kitsch. Rooms are spacious and soberly decorated, a little past their best but very well-kept. A decent choice and warm welcome.

🛏🛏🛏 **Hotel Royal Palace** – *Via Tommaso Cannizzaro 224.* ✆*090 29 21 075. http://nhroyalpalace.hotelsinsicily.it.*

Processione della Vara

© avilon/Fotolia.com

P €10/day. 102 rooms ⌷. This luxury hotel, right in the centre, offers bright, very comfortable rooms well equipped with Wi-Fi, satellite TV, etc. The best choices are those on the sixth floor, which have recently been renovated and have a little terrace with a nice **view** of the port. The restaurant serves copious breakfasts, but is not worth visiting for other meals.

GANZIRRI

⊜⊜⊜ **Villa Morgana** – *Via C. Pompea 237, Ganzirri, 5km/3mi N of Messina along the coast road.* ☎090 32 55 75. www.villa morgana.it. *14 rooms* ⌷. Guests will immediately feel at home in this hotel in a private villa, surrounded by a large, well-tended garden. On the coast road, a few kilometres from Messina, the hotel has an attractive lounge and comfortable rooms.

♀/ EAT

⊜⊜ **Don Nino** – *Viale Europa 39, Isolato 59, Messina.* ☎090 69 42 95. Take dried cod, tomatoes, potatoes, olives, capers, pine nuts, sultanas, onion, garlic, oil, celery and carrot, mix well together and you have *ghiotta di pesce stocco,* one of the specialities of Messina cuisine and of Don Nino in particular. *Buon appetito!*

⊜⊜ **Trattoria del Popolo** – *Piazza Lo Sardo 30.* ☎090 671 148. Closed Sun. Under the arcades of the circular Piazza del Popolo, take a seat and enjoy simple, fortifying local cuisine.

⊜⊜⊜ **Piero** – *Via Ghibellina 119.* ☎090 64 09 354. Closed Sun. This centrally-located restaurant with a classic décor serves extra fresh fish dishes, such as grouper tartare and swordfish steaks. Quality service.

⊜⊜⊜ **Le Due Sorelle** – *Piazza Municipio 4, Messina.* ☎090 44 720. Closed Sat–Sun at lunchtimes and in Aug. Booking recommended. This restaurant in the heart of the historical centre serves a range of local home-made dishes. Fish takes centre stage in the evening, although you will still find other traditional Messina dishes on the menu.

TAKING A BREAK

Pasticceria Irrera – *Piazza Cairoli 12, Messina.* ☎090 67 38 23. www.irrera.it. Founded in 1910, this pastry shop is one of the best in Messina. Local delicacies include *pignolata* (a typical Messina speciality made with twists of fried puff pastry with lemon or chocolate icing) and *torrone fondente* – a version of nougat.

Pasticceria F. Gordelli – *Via Ghibellina 86 (the road running parallel to Via Cesare Battisti), Messina.* ☎090 66 29 22. Another excellent pasticceria in which to sample some of the city's renowned cakes and pastries.

FESTIVALS

Venerdì Santo – The *Processione delle Barette,* a procession of wooden sculptures that follow the Stations of the Cross, takes place on Good Friday.

Jazz Festival – Jul–Aug. Open-air concerts in Piazza Antonello from 9.30pm. The festival was held for the first time in 2009.

Passeggiata dei Giganti – On 14 August, the Moor Grifone and Mata – legendary founder of the city – are borne aloft in procession through the streets.

Processione della Vara – The image of the Assumption of the Virgin is carried through the town on 15 August.

The Tyrrhenian coast on Sicily's northern spine is a land of beaches, forests and mountains. It's ideal for spending a morning lazing on an isolated stretch of sand or in a deserted creek, before an afternoon of hiking through a maze of pine forests or across acres of pastureland.

Traditional Mountain Villages

Less than an hour's drive inland from the coast, tradition remains central to the lives of the region's farmers, who make their living by working the land or grazing their flocks in the high, lush meadows below bare outcroppings of rock. The area is crossed by two mountain ranges – the Nebrodi to the east and the Madonie to the west – and covered by Sicily's largest concentration of forests, and offers spectacular **views** of Mount Etna and the Aeolian islands.

Nature Parks

The steep Nebrodi Mountains and the more rolling Madonie – now Regional Nature Parks teeming with flora and fauna – are a favourite of hikers, cyclists and nature lovers. Both parks have made a huge effort to welcome visitors and offer information about hikes, nature walks, sports and other activities for all ages and abilities.

History and art enthusiasts are not neglected either: the coast and hills are home to Norman *(and earlier)* castles that once surveyed the coast and/or the natural mountain passes that connect Catania with Palermo. You'll find well-preserved examples of *castelli* in Caccamo, Milazzo, Castelbuono and Cefalù, along with fascinating ruins in Mistretta, Nicosia and Polizzi.

Museums, culture and art

There are some fascinating museums as well, including the **Museo della Cultura delle Arti Figurative Bizantine e Normanne** – the Norman and Byzantine art museum set in a Benedictine monastery in the hill town of San Marco d'Alunzio. Also not to be missed is the **Museo Siciliano delle Tradizioni Religiose**. High in the Nebrodi, in San Salvatore di Fitalia, this unusual museum explores the blend of local traditions

Highlights

1 The **stunning coastline** of Capo di Milazzo (p366)
2 **Norman and Byzantine art** in San Marco d'Alunzio (p377)
3 **Mountain panoramas** in the Madonie (p383)
4 The "**river of art**" (p393)
5 One of Sicily's finest **castles** in Caccamo (p400)

Madonie Mountains

© Demetrio Carrasco / age fotostock

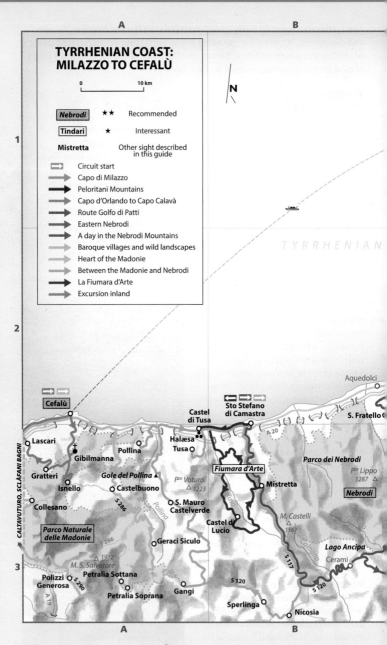

TYRRHENIAN COAST: MILAZZO TO CEFALÙ

0 ——— 10 km

Nebrodi ★★	Recommended
Tindari ★	Interessant
Mistretta	Other sight described in this guide

Circuit start
Capo di Milazzo
Peloritani Mountains
Capo d'Orlando to Capo Calavà
Route Golfo di Patti
Eastern Nebrodi
A day in the Nebrodi Mountains
Baroque villages and wild landscapes
Heart of the Madonie
Between the Madonie and Nebrodi
La Fiumara d'Arte
Excursion inland

TYRRHENIAN

Aquedolci

Cefalù

Castel di Tusa
Sto Stefano di Camastra
S. Fratello

Lascari
Halæsa Tusa
A 20

Pollina
Gibilmanna

Fiumara d'Arte

Parco dei Nebrodi

Gratteri
Gole del Pollina ▲
P.co Voturo △ 1223

Isnello
Castelbuono

P.co Lippo 1287 △

Mistretta
Nebrodi

Collesano
S. Mauro Castelverde

Parco Naturale delle Madonie

M. Castelli △ 156?

Castel di Lucio

CALTAVUTURO, SCLAFANI BAGNI

Geraci Siculo

Lago Ancipa
Cerami

△ 1912
M. S. Salvatore

S 117

Polizzi Generosa
Petralia Sottana

S 120

Petralia Soprana
Gangi

A 19

Sperlinga
Nicosia

---

and religion that typifies Sicily (☺ *see p388*). The churches along this coastline feature many fine examples of art and architecture, from Medieval to Baroque, and include fine examples of work by sculptor and architect **Antonello Gagini** (1478–1536), along with that of his father, **Domenico**. The Madonie Mountains are also home to a rare display of contemporary art in nature – the Fiumara d'Arte (☺ *see p384*) is a 80km/50mi trail of contemporary environmental sculpture in natural settings.

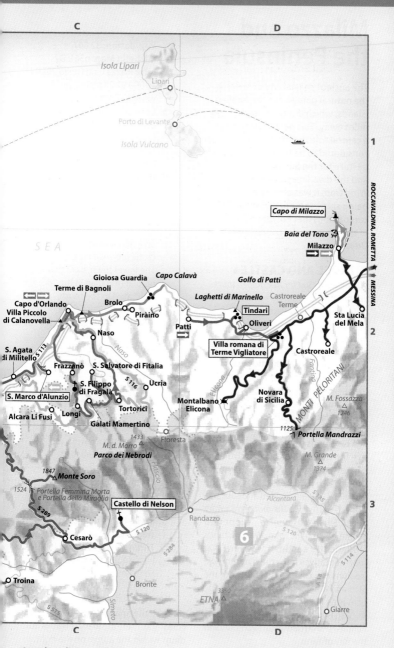

Local traditions and products

The mountain landscapes provide lots of opportunities to explore local traditions and products.

The Nebrodi Mountains are famous for their colourful ceramics, which are produced in Santo Stefano di Camastra. The area is also known for its honey, chestnuts and some of Italy's tastiest prosciutto, cured from black Nebrodi pigs who are fed on a diet of acorns and nuts. It's easy to travel in this part of Sicily – everything is close by, making it ideal for short excursions by car and on foot.

Milazzo and the Peninsula

The ancient coastal city of Mylae is the natural gateway to the Aeolian islands, which dot the horizon a few miles away. This part of Sicily plays a central role in classical mythology: considered to be the grazing pasture for the Sun God's herds and the dwelling place of Eolo, the Wind God, it was also where, after being shipwrecked, Ulysses and his companions met Polyphemus, one of the Cyclopes described in Homer's Odyssey.

CITADEL AND CASTLE★

Open Tue–Sun for free guided tours 10am–noon, 3–5pm (Jul–Aug 7pm). 090 922 28 65. www.comune. milazzo.me.it. At the time of going to press, only the area leading to the Duomo is open to visitors.

The town's main fortification was founded by the Arabs (10C) on the site of a former Ancient Greek acropolis. On the left, through the **Spanish walls**, the **Duomo Vecchio** (1608) is a good example of Sicilian Mannerism. The **Aragonese city walls** (15C) are punctuated by five truncated-cone towers: two flank a gateway bearing the coat of arms of the Spanish monarchs, Ferdinand and Isabella – a shield divided into four sections *(representing the monarchs under which Spain was unified)*, supported by the eagle of St John. Within stands Frederick II's **castle**. It was here that representatives from the five *campate* (regions of Sicily) met to constitute the Sicilian Parliament of 1295. The castle provides breathtaking **views** of the Aeolian Islands *(from left: Vulcano, Lipari, Panarea and on clear days, Stromboli)* and the Bay of Tono.

THE BORGO

The *borgo* is the oldest part of the town: a medieval quarter overlooked by the citadel. The entrance to this district coincides with the beginning of Via Impallomeni *(from Piazza Roma)*, lined on both

> **Population:** 32 647
> **Michelin Map:** p361: D2
> **Info:** Piazza Caio Duilio 20. 090 92 22 865. www.aastmilazzo.it.
> **Location:** Milazzo sits at the base of a promontory jutting into the Tyrrhenian Sea. Despite its modern, industrial appearance, the town has a number of important historical and artistic monuments. The oldest part is the medieval centre, perched on a hill leading to the castle *(north of the city)*. The lower town, built to a regular grid plan in the 18C, is situated to the south, along the eastern coast. Milazzo is the main port for the Aeolian Islands.
> **Kids:** Myths and legends at the **Grotta di Polifermo** cave.
> **Don't Miss**: A stroll in the **medieval quarter** of The Borgo, the **views** from delightful inland hilltop towns **Cristina** and **Rometta**, the **beach** at the **Baia del Tonno** and the quirky **apothecary's pharmacy** in **Roccavaldina**. An **antiques fair** is held in The Borgo on the first weekend of every month.
> **Timing:** Allow one day for inland tours from Milazzo.

sides by the Spanish Military Barracks (1585–95). There are many religious buildings within the *borgo*: on the right, in the steep street of the same name is the **Santuario di San Francesco di Paola**. Inside, in the Gesù e Maria chapel, is an unusual carved wooden altar, decorated with gilt and mirrors, set with a *Madonna and Child* panel by Domenico Gagini (1465).

A little farther up Salita San Francesco is the Viceroy's residence (**Palazzo dei Vicerè**), built in the 16C and altered in the 18C, when the balconies with Baroque brackets were added. Beyond, on the other side of the road, is the **Chiesa del Santissimo Salvatore**, whose 18C façade was designed by Giovan Battista Vaccarini.

Continuing along Via San Domenico, on the right is the **Chiesa della Madonna del Rosario**, which until 1782 served as the main seat of the Inquisition Tribunal.

Erected in the 16C, it was radically alte-red during the 18C, when the interior was given its stucco decoration and frescoed by the Messina painter Dome-nico Giordano. Salita Castello *(on the left)* leads up to the Spanish city walls.

CITTÀ BASSA

The lower part of town is the modern section of Milazzo, built in the 18C.

At the heart is the **Piazza Caio Duilio**. Facing onto the Piazza's west side is *Palazzo* Marchese Proto *(once Garibaldi's headquarters)*; on the eastern side is the **Chiesa del Carmine's** elegant **façade★**, composed of a doorway (1620), with a niche containing the statue of the Madonna della Consolazione (1632).

Continue along the old Strada Reale *(now Via Umberto I)*: on the parallel street *(Via Cumbo Borgia)* is the **Duomo**

GETTING THERE AND AROUND

Milazzo is linked to **Messina** by train *(40min)* and by bus, operated by the **Giuntabus company** *(Via Terranova 8, Messina, ℰ090 67 37 82; www.giuntabus.com)*. **Palermo** *(approx. 200km/125mi away)* can be reached by train *(approx. 2hr 30min)*. Milazzo's railway station is situated in Piazza Marconi *(approx. 3km/ 1.8mi from the historic centre of the town)*.

Nuovo, built in the 1930s. Its interior is hung with a few prized paintings: on the high altar, figures of St Peter and St Paul (1531) frame the wooden effigy of St Stephen; these panels are from a dismantled polyptych by Antonello de Saliba, who also painted the *Adoration of the Shepherds*.

The luminous *Annunciation* painted with vibrant colours typical of the Venetian School and the *St Nicholas Enthroned with Scenes from his Life* are both attri-buted to Antonio Guffrè, a painter of the Antonelli School (end of the 15C).

Posted at the crossroads with Via Cristo-foro Colombo is the Liberty-style **Villino Greco**, with its fine friezes of stylised flowers and organic decoration.

Port of Milazzo with a view to the citadel and the castle

© Jean-Pierre Degas/hemis.fr

🚗 DRIVING TOURS

CAPO DI MILAZZO
Approx. 8km/5mi by car.

Take the **Lungomare Garibaldi** along the seafront, overlooked by the elegant proportions of the 18C façade of Palazzo dei Marchesi D'Amico and cross the waterfront district of Vaccarella, *(which begins with the piazza before the church of Santa Maria Maggiore),* then follow the **panoramic road★** that runs along the eastern side of the Milazzo promontory to the end.

Arriving at **Capo dì Milazzo★**, pause to take in the wonderful **view★★** of the Mediterranean *maquis* extending over the rocky spur to blend with the dazzling blue sea beyond.

From the left side of Piazza Sant'Antonio, steps drop down to the **Santuario di Sant'Antonio di Padova** and the bay. It is said that St Antony of Padua sought refuge in a cave here during a storm in 1221. Since then, it has been a place of pilgrimage; it was transformed into a sanctuary in 1575 under the patronage of a nobleman, Andrea Guerrera. In the 18C, it was further endowed with altars and decoration of polychrome marble as well as panels depicting scenes from the saint's life.

To return by a different route, take the road along the ridge of the little peninsula and fork right along the road to **Monte Trino**, the highest point on this strip of land, unfortunately marred by telecommunications transmitters.

From the little piazza before the **Chiesetta della Santissima Trinità**, there are wonderful **views★** over Milazzo, its citadel and the sickle-shaped promontory.

To the west, the coastal road leads to the **Grotta di Polifemo**, mythical meeting place of Odysseus and the Cyclops. In front of the cave is a broad beach that lines the glorious **Baia del Tono** (known locally as *Ngonia*, from the Greek word for bay).

PELORITANI MOUNTAINS
180km/112mi round trip from Milazzo – allow one day.

*This excursion follows the S 113, occasionally heading inland up the slopes of the **Monti Peloritani** – the Sicilian extension of the Calabrian Apennines.*

▷ Follow S 113 to Patti as far as San Biagio *(for information on the Villa Romana di Terme Vigliatore, see Driving Tour route Golfo di PATTI),* then take S 185 to Novara di Sicilia. After 5km/3mi, turn right to Montalbano Elicona *(44km/27mi from Milazzo).*

Montalbano Elicona
Perched at 900m/3,000ft on the eastern spur of the Nebrodi Mountains, this town is ideal for woodland walking *(Bosco di Malabotta)* and rambling among the crags of Argimosco. Its most impressive feature is the great **castle** *(🕐open Tue–Sun 10am–1pm, 3–6pm; ◉€3; ♿, ✆0941 67 80 19)* erected by Frederick II of Swabia and destroyed by him following the Guelph uprising of 1232. It was rebuilt by Frederick II of Aragon in the early 14C and is surrounded by sloping medieval streets.

Walk around the ramparts *(⚠special care required climbing up)* for **views** in every direction.

▷ Return to S 185 and turn right to Novara di Sicilia *(36km/22mi from Montalbano).*

Novara di Sicilia
This small mountain town, between the Peloritani and Nebrodi ranges, is laid out on medieval lines, complete with a towering Saracen castle, now in ruins. In the centre, the **Duomo** shelters a carved wooden altar and lecterns, sculpted with unusual figures with primitive features.

The road continues inland on S 185 to a mountain pass, **Portella Mandrazzi** (1,125m/3,690ft), with wonderful **views** over the Alcantara valley to Mount Etna. From here, it is possible to carry on to

Francavilla di Sicilia and explore the Valle dell'Alcantara (♿see Taormina).

▶ Continue inland and return to S 113. Head towards Milazzo and after 5km/3mi, turn right to Castroreale (33km/21mi from Novara di Sicilia).

Castroreale

The ancient town of **Cristina**, perched upon spurs among the Monti Peloritani, became a dominion of considerable jurisdiction following Frederick II of Aragon's concession of sovereignty in exchange for loyalty during the war against the Angevins. Re-christened Castroreale, it retains many medieval features: interconnecting streets that open onto delightful little piazzas and many churches, several containing art testifying to the town's glorious past.

▶ The visit starts in Piazza del Duomo.

Chiesa Madre

An elegant **Baroque portal** graces the façade of the main church in stark contrast to the massive 16C campanile. **Inside** hang a charming **St Catherine of Alexandria** (1534) and Mother and Child (1501) by Antonello Gagini and in the north aisle, Andrea Calamech's St James the Great (St James the Apostle). From the east terrace outside there is a fine **view★** over the plain of Milazzo. Continue along Corso Umberto I and turn left towards the 15C **Chiesa della Candelora** – a church dedicated to Candlemas, the feast commemorating the purification of the Virgin Mary and the presentation of Christ in the Temple. Proceed along Salita Federico II to a round **tower**, all that survives of the castle built by Frederick II of Aragon in 1324. From the top there is a fine **view★** over Castroreale, the little Moorish dome of the church of the Candelora and the countryside beyond.

Head down to Piazza Peculio, flanked by the 15C church of the Holy Saviour (**San Salvatore**), damaged in the 1978 earthquake. Its semi-collapsed bell tower

(1560) once formed part of a chain of watchtowers with those of the cathedral and castle.

▶ Continue along Via Guglielmo Siracusa.

Pinacoteca di Santa Maria degli Angeli

🕐Open by appointment only. ✆090 97 46 534. ➱€2.

This art gallery houses **rare paintings and sculptures**, including a panel of St Agatha (c. 1420) in the Byzantine style, a Flemish triptych depicting The Adoration of the Magi with St Marina and St Barbara, a fine polyptych of The Nativity from the Neapolitan studio of G.F. Criscuolo, a marble statue of St John the Baptist by Calamech (1568) and a silver altar-frontal by Filippo Juvarra (18C).

Museo Civico

Via G. Siracusa. 🕐Open Jul–Aug daily 9am–1pm, 4–7pm. 🕐Closed Wed afternoon. ✆090 97 46 534. www.castroreale.it.

The municipal museum, in a former oratory dedicated to St Philip Neri, contains sculptures in wood and marble, including the splendid **funeral monument★** of Geronimo Rosso (1506–08) and a fine work by **Antonello Gagini**. Along the same street is **Sant'Agata**, containing an Annunciation by Antonello Gagini (1519), a statue of St Agatha (1554) by the Florentine sculptor Montorsoli, and a 17C plaster and papier-mâché image, the **"Cristo Lungo"**, carried in procession on a 12m/39ft pole so as to be visible from every corner of town.

▶ Return to S 113 and continue along the road as far as Olivarella, then turn right to Santa Lucia del Mela (20km/12.5mi from Castroreale).

Santa Lucia del Mela

The little town is overshadowed by the **castle**, built in the 9C by the Arabs and altered during the Swabian and Aragonese occupations. Little survives other than a massive round tower fortifying the main gateway, part of a triangular bastion, and sections of defensive walls sheltering the **Santuario della Madonna della Neve** (1673). Take a look at the *Madonna of the Snow* by **Antonello Gagini** (1529) inside.

On the way down into the town there is an elegant Renaissance **doorway★** leading into the **Chiesa Madre di Santa Lucia** (17C): note the lunette containing a relief of the Madonna attended by St Agatha and St Lucy, with the eagle, symbol of regal patronage. To the left of the church is **Piazza del Duomo** and the **Bishop's Palace**. The façade of the **Chiesa dell'Annunziata** *(Via Garibaldi)* has a fine 15C bell tower with sculptured low-reliefs surrounding a lunette depicting the Annunciation, decorated with plant motifs.

▶ From Santa Lucia, return to Olivarella and then turn right onto S 113. Follow the road as far as Scala, then turn right to Roccavaldina *(20km/12.5mi from Santa Lucia).*

Roccavaldina ★

The main attraction of this small town is the extraordinary **apothecary's pharmacy★** *(○opening times vary, contact for details ℘090 99 77 741/736; www.comune.roccavaldina.me.it).*

The shopfront consists of a 16C Tuscan-style doorway flanked by a stone counter from which members of the public were served. Inside is a rare **collectio-**

n★★ of majolica drug jars *(albarelli).* All the pieces come from the famous Patanazzi family workshop in Urbino, having been commissioned by the Messina herbalist Cesare Candia *(whose coat of arms, consisting of a dove and three stars, is found on each of the 238 jars).* The collection has been in the town since 1628; it includes typical long-necked vases, jugs and *albarelli* (pharmacy jars) bearing scenes from the Bible, Classical mythology or Ancient Rome.

Overlooking the same piazza is the 16C **castle**, an imposing transitional building that is at once both a fortress and an aristocratic residence.

On the edge of the town, in the tranquil gardens of the former Capuchin monastery, stands a **municipal villa**, enjoying a panoramic **view★** over the Milazzo promontory.

▶ Follow the scenic road for a further 6km/4mi.

Rometta

Strategically positioned at 600m/ 2,000ft, Rometta earned its place in history by courageously resisting the Arab invaders: it was the last town to fall into their hands in 965. Little remains of the city walls other than the gateways, Porta Milazzo and Porta Messina.

From the ruins of Frederick II's **castle**, there is a wonderful **view★** of Capo Milazzo and the Aeolian Islands.

Apothecary's pharmacy, Roccavaldina

© Federico Meneghetti/Cubo Images/Robert Harding

▶ From Rometta, either return to Milazzo *(22km/14mi)* or head towards Villafranca and follow the tour around Capo Peloro (🖝 *see Messina).*

ALONG THE COAST FROM CAPO D'ORLANDO TO CAPO CALAVÀ

Approx. 20km/12.5mi along S 113 in the direction of Messina.

Villa Piccolo di Calanovella

Marked by the 109km/68mi distance marker on the S 113 between Messina and Palermo. ⏰*Open Mon–Sat 9am–noon (4–6pm Mon, Wed, Fri).* ⏰*Closed Sun and public holidays.* 🗗 €4. ♿. ✆*0941 95 70 29. www.fondazionepiccolo.it.*

In keeping with the wishes of the last members of the Piccolo family, a museum-foundation was set up in the late-19C villa, where they had lived since the 1930s. The Piccolos were an artistic family: in particular Lucio (who died in 1969), an acclaimed poet, and Casimiro, an enthusiastic painter and photographer, and scholar of the occult. They were often visited by their cousin **Giuseppe di Lampedusa**, drawn by the peace and quiet of the villa, who wrote a large part of his masterpiece *(The Leopard)* here. In the room he once used is one of his letters to the Piccolo family, as is the bed in which he slept. This is ornamented by a beautiful ivory and mother-of-pearl **bedhead** depicting the Baptism of John *(made by Trapani craftsmen in the 17C).*

Elsewhere in the villa a series of fantastical **watercolours★** by Casimiro Piccolo line the walls. He enjoyed painting scenes from a fairy-tale world suffused with light and populated with amiable gnomes, elves, fairies and butterflies.

Before leaving, take a stroll under the pergolas in the villa gardens and seek out the **canine graveyard** for the family pets.

Capo d'Orlando

Tourist Office, Via Andrea Doria. ✆*0941 91 81 34. www.aastcapodorlando.it.*

As one of the more important seaside resorts on the northern coastline, this pleasant town offers beautiful pebbled and rocky beaches, along with the delightful Lido San Gregorio to the east.

🗗 The centre of the town falls between **Via Piave**, which is lined by smart shops, and the promenade that parallels the beautiful **beach**.

At the promontory tip is a purpose-built **viewpoint★** accessed up a flight of stairs. It overlooks the ruins of the castle of Orlando and the 17C **Santuario di Maria Santissima di Capo d'Orlando**, where pilgrims flock each year on 22 October.

▶ Leave Capo d'Orlando via S 116. On exiting the town, take S 113 towards Messina.

Following the coast beyond the cape towards San Gregorio, the road offers beautiful **views★** of the blue sea and coast, dotted with rocks and small, characterful seaside resorts.

Terme di Bagnoli

⏰*Open daily 9am–2pm.* ✆*0941 95 54 01.* 🗗*Free.*

On the outskirts of Capo d'Orlando at San Gregorio are the remains of a bathing complex attached to an Imperial-era Roman villa.

They include the **frigidarium** *(marked 1-2-3)*, the **tepidarium** *(4)* and the **caldarium** *(5 and 6)*. In rooms 4, 5 and 6 are fragments of mosaics displaying geometric decoration.

Brolo

A flourishing port until the late 17C and now a seaside resort, the town has a fine medieval castle *(private)* built by the Lancia family in the 15C.

▶ Beyond Brolo, turn right at the next junction for Piràino.

Piràino

Stretched strategically along the spine of a hill, Piràino retains much of its medieval form and is scattered with religious

The Legend of Capo d'Orlando

The history of Capo d'Orlando is intertwined with the legend of its foundation at the time of the Trojan War by Agathyrsus, son of Aeolus. The legend also relates how the ancient settlement of Agathyrnis came to be renamed Capo d'Orlando by Charlemagne, who was passing through these lands on a pilgrimage to the Holy Land and decided to call the place after his heroic paladin.

In 1299, the town witnessed the pivotal naval battle between James and Frederick of Aragon over the throne of Sicily.

buildings. Its legendary origins *(supposedly founded by the Cyclops Piracmon)* are probably rooted in the discovery of large bones in several nearby caves. All the **churches** are strung along the main street of the town *(when the churches are closed, contact the tourist office for the key: ☎0941 58 63 18)*.

The **Chiesa del Rosario** *(the easternmost church)*, dedicated to the Madonna of the Rosary, was rebuilt in 1635, while retaining its 16C campanile. Inside, it has a fine coffered wooden **ceiling** set with Byzantine-Norman rosettes and an unusual wooden **high altar** painted with floral motifs *(first half of the 17C)* decorated with wooden medallions representing the Mysteries of the Rosary. The wooden figures in the centre of the altar represent the Madonna with saints.

Farther along is the **Chiesa della Catena**, erected in the latter half of the 17C, where the first elections were held after the Unification of Italy. It contains some fine Byzantine-type **frescoes** from another church, the Chiesa della Badia. Beyond is Piazza del Baglio, named after the complex of low-level workers' houses and workshops arranged around the **Palazzo Ducale**, built by the Lancia family (15C–16C).

Proceeding westwards, the high road passes the beautifully preserved **Torre Saracena** or *Torrazza* (10C). From its terrace extends a magnificent **view★** across the rooftops and beyond to Capo d'Orlando. The tower was part of a defensive chain system that would have transmitted signals from the 16C **Torre delle Ciavole** on the coast, via the **Guardiola** situated to the north of the town, to the *Torrazza*.

On the western edge of town is **Santa Caterina d'Alessandria**, the church dedicated to St Catherine of Alexandria and built in the 16C, but altered in the 17C. Inside, the wooden altar is decorated with floral motifs. A low relief *(right of the altar)* depicts St Catherine of Alexandria overcoming the infidel.

▷ Turn back towards the coast.

Note, on your left, the **Torre delle Ciavole** (👣 *see above*).

▷ Continue on to the small seaside resort of **Gioiosa Marea** and follow the signs for San Filippo Armo and San Leonardo *(about 9km/5.5mi)* to Gioiosa Guardia.

Rovine di Gioiosa Guardia

The ruins of this medieval town, abandoned by its inhabitants in the 18C for Gioiosa Marea, are situated at 800m/2,625ft above sea level and surrounded by a romantic landscape. The idyllic serenity of the place is enhanced by the splendid **view★**.

▷ Return to the coast.

A little farther on is **Capo Calavà**, a spectacular rocky spur.

ROUTE GOLFO DI PATTI
40km/25mi. Allow half a day.

From Capo Calva to Capo Milazzo, the sweeping Golfo di Patti is a ribbon of undulating scenery, pretty beaches, charming towns and archeological sites.

Tindari archaeological site

© Sandro Bedessi / Fototeca ENIT

Patti

This small town in the hinterland extends down to the sea at Marina di Patti, where the remains of a Roman villa were recently discovered (&*see below*). The old town centre still retains its medieval network of narrow streets, spanned by arches.

Elevated to a bishopric by Roger II in 1131, then nominated a royal town by Frederick III of Aragon in 1312, Patti received the title of *magnanima* (generous) from Charles V for a generous tribute to the Crown. Little remains of this glorious period, Patti having succumbed to repeated earthquakes.

The present **cathedral** building (🕐*for admission times contact* ℘*0941 84 08 13*) dates from the 18C, its 15C **portal** having been restored to the main façade. Small clusters of columns flanking the main entrance have magnificent capitals, carved with fantastical monsters.

Inside, the **sarcophagus of Queen Adelasia** (*in the right transept*) – wife of Roger I – is a 16C restoration of the 1118 original.

On the northern side of the town (*beside the River Montagnareale*) is Porta San Michele, the only fragment of the Aragonese defensive town walls to survive. Beyond the gate sits the church of **San Michele**, with a marble ciborium by Antonello Gagini (1538) and a **triptych** featuring angels flanked by St Agatha and Mary Magdalene.

Villa Romana di Patti

In Patti Marina, near the underpass of the motorway on the right.
🕐*Open 9am–2hrs before dusk.* ✍€2.
℘*0941 36 15 93.*

The Imperial Roman villa was discovered during motorway construction. The complex is arranged around a peristyle with a portico from which lead various rooms, including one paved with mosaics featuring geometric motifs and depictions of domestic and wild animals.

▷ Follow S 113 for 9km/6mi, then turn left to Tindari.

Tindari★

Tourist Office - Via Teatro Greco 15.
℘*0941 36 91 84.*

From the east, **Tindari** sits against a succession of hills that emerge from the sea and rise to form a land mass resembling a dragon slumbering peacefully. Perched high on its head stands the sanctuary, a discernible landmark from afar. As the road winds down the dragon's back, wonderful **views★** open out over the

City of Castor and Pollux

The Greek colony of **Tyndaris** was founded by the tyrant of Syracuse, Dionysius the Elder, in 396 BC to accommodate refugees from Sparta at the end of the Peloponnese War (404 BC). The name refers to the Dioscuri, **Castor** and Polydeuces/**Pollux**, sons of Leda and Zeus and brothers of Helen (whose abduction was the catalyst for the Trojan War) and Clytaemnestra. Leda was the wife of the mythical hero Tyndareus of Sparta, who was said to have fathered Castor, while Pollux was believed to have been fathered by Zeus. Consequently, the Dioscuri are also known as the *Tyndaridi*. The link between the town and the heavenly twins is taken up on coins and mosaics.

The new town, occupying a raised, yet naturally defensible position, developed its strategic importance in policing the sea between Messina and the Aeolian Islands. Despite its impressively solid defensive fortifications on the landward side, the town fell into the hands of the Carthaginians. Later, under Roman dominion, it flourished through a period of great prosperity, prompting a range of public buildings such as schools, markets and public baths to be constructed or redeveloped. The theatre, which was built by the Greeks, was modified so as to accommodate the demands of its new audience.

Thereafter, Tyndaris progressively declined: a landslide destroyed part of the city, including its most important features, and further damage was then incurred by the Arab conquest in the 9C.

bay of Patti and the **beaches** that sweep round to Capo Milazzo.

The **sanctuary**, a relatively recent addition to the landscape, shelters a Byzantine Black Virgin, which attracts large bands of pilgrims around the Marian feasts of the Visitation *(31 May)* and the Birth of the Virgin *(8 September)*.

At the foot of the rockface are the **Laghetti di Marinello**. (⚑*See below*).

Archaeological Site★

🕐*Open 9am–1hr before dusk.* ✆€2.
𝓟*0941 36 90 23.*

The path up to the top of Capo Tindari passes alongside sections of the defensive **walls** built during the reign of Dionysius. The walls were only built around the vulnerable parts of the town, laid out on a grid system with three wide *decumani* (main thoroughfares) interconnected by *cardini* at right angles.

An **antiquarium** *(beyond the entrance to the site on the left)* displays artefacts recovered from the excavations.

The **Insula romana** comprises an entire block to the south of the main axis or *decumanus superiore*, with baths, taverns and houses, including a patrician house with fragments of mosaic.

The arcaded remains of the **basilica** give some suggestion of the scale and elegance of the original building. Even though the ruin has been classified a basilica or public meeting house, its true function is still uncertain: it may possibly be a part of some monumental *propylaeum* (gateway) for the agora or main square of the city.

▷ Turn left onto *decumanus superiore*.

The **theatre** was built by the Greeks (late 4C BC) to take advantage of the lie of the land, with the *cavea* (auditorium) facing the sea and the Aeolian Islands. It was adapted for staging gladiator fights in Imperial times.

▷ Follow S 113 for 3.5km/2mi, then turn left to Oliveri.

▲▲ Laghetti di Marinello

This is the name given to the pools of water left by the tide on the wide, sandy strip below Capo Tindari, some of which contain a rich variety of aquatic plants. The area also attracts a selection of birds: gulls, grebes, coots and little egrets. According to legend, these rock pools appeared to save a little girl who would otherwise have fallen to her death from the headland; she was saved when the sea supposedly withdrew to leave a soft landing pad of sand. In 1982, one of the rock pools seemed to assume the profile of a veiled woman, interpreted by local people as the Madonna of the sanctuary. The pools can be reached on foot *(about 30min)* from Oliveri. The beach tails off into a glorious **bay**★★.

In summer, this is a paradise for bathers, although the beach is rarely crowded *(swimmers are strongly recommended not to bathe in the pools as the water is stagnant: it is preferable to swim in the bay)*.

▶ Return to the main road, continuing along it for 6.5km/4mi to the district of San Biagio.

Villa Romana di Terme Vigliatore★

Open 9am–1hr before dusk. *090 97 40 488.* €2.

The 1C AD suburban residence has not been fully excavated. The villa comprises the residential quarters *(left)* and a small bath complex *(right)*.

To the left is a square **peristyle** with eight columns down each side. Ahead is a **tablinum** (archive room) with an *opus sectile* floor of geometric patterns. The most interesting part of the complex, however, is the private baths *(right of the entrance to the site)*. To the left of the semicircular bath is the **frigidarium**. The baths' heating system is visible. Hot air from a furnace circulated by convection through the wall cavities and between the ground and the floor, raised by brick columns *(suspensurae)*.

▶ From Terme Vigliatore continue to Milazzo *(See Milazzo)*.

THE EASTERN NEBRODI

Approx. 85km/53mi. Allow at least half a day.

This itinerary snakes its way inland from Capo d'Orlando located on the eastern slopes of the Nebrodi Mountains.

▶ Leave Capo d'Orlando by the coastal road towards Sant'Agata Militello. At Rocca di Capri Leone, turn left towards Frazzano *(17km/11mi S of Capo d'Orlando)*.

Frazzanò

The **Chiesa Madre della Santissima Annunziata** (18C) has a fine Baroque façade ornamented with giant pilasters and an elegant portal with spiral columns.

The **Chiesa di San Lorenzo** has a plainer façade relieved by a fine portal with spiral columns and a flurry of sculptural motifs. Inside is a fine wooden statue of the church's patron, St Lawrence (1620).

▶ Proceed to the next right turning, signposted for the Convento di San Filippo di Fragalà *(4km/2.5mi S of Frazzanò towards Longi)*.

Convento di San Filippo di Fragalà

This imposing Basilian abbey was built by Roger I d'Altavilla in the 11C. Though abandoned and crumbling, it is still worth viewing: note the three apses in the Arabo-Norman style articulated by brick pilasters and the octagonal drum over the intersection of the transepts. Remains of Byzantine frescoes can be seen on the church walls. The adjoining monastic buildings are open to the public.

▶ The road continues to Portella Calcatizzo. At the fork carry on to San Salvatore di Fitalia *(approx. 20km/12mi from San Filippo di Fragalà)*.

San Salvatore di Fitalia

Perched high in the Nebrodi, this small town has a fine church (1515) dedicated to **San Salvatore**.

The **capitals** are sculpted with plant and anthropomorphic motifs typical of medieval decoration. The capital of the first column *(right)*, bearing the name of the stonemason who carved it, features an unusual mermaid with a forked tail. In the right aisle hangs Antonello Gagini's

Madonna of the Snow (1521) and on the high altar, a **wooden statue★** of Salvator Mundi (Saviour of the World, 1603) at the moment of the Transfiguration.

Museo Siciliano delle Tradizioni Religiose

Call tourist office for hours.
0941 486 027.
This **museum** documents local cults with displays of amulets for protection against the Evil Eye, votive objects and *pillole* (pills) – tiny squares of paper designed to be swallowed by the faithful while they recited prayers requesting divine intervention. The collection also includes **engravings** and **lithographs** depicting sacred images (17C–20C), dress robes worn by the confraternities and more.

▶ Return to Portella Calcatizzo and Tortorici, then head towards Castell'Umberto. From here, follow S 116 to Naso *(28km/17mi from San Salvatore di Fitalia).*

Naso

This small town, translated as "nose", is situated inland on a strategic headland at an altitude of 500m/1,640ft. As such, it enjoys superb **views ★** of the Aeolian Islands. Founded by the Normans, it was subsequently controlled by the Cardona family before becoming a lordship of the Ventimiglia family. The central Piazza Garibaldi, with its magnificent **view** of Etna, runs into Piazza Dante and Piazza Roma. The **Chiesa Madre** on Piazza Roma is notable for its *Madonna and Child*, painted in the distinctive Gagini style.

▶ Follow the right side of the Chiesa Madre into Via degli Angeli.

This street leads to the **Chiesa di San Cono**, founded in the 15C and restored two centuries later. A crypt housing the relics of the church's patron saint can be seen in the catacombs.

▶ Return to Piazza Roma and take Corso Umberto.

After Piazza Parisi, turn right on Via Belvedere for another superb **view★★** of Etna and the Aeolian Islands.

Follow Via Convento to the Convento dei Minori Osservanti and the **Chiesa di Santa Maria del Gesù**. Inside the church, note the splendid funerary monument of Artale Cardona, in Gothic-Renaissance style.
The route back to town *(on Via Cibo)* passes the **Chiesa del Salvatore**, adorned with a Baroque façade, double bell tower and a splendid parvis in locally-fired brick.

▶ Continue along S 116 for another 15km/9mi as far as Capo d'Orlando.

From Naso, visitors can continue on to Randazzo (approx. 55km/34mi) to link up with the circular tour of Etna (See Etna).

ADDRESSES

BOATS TO THE AEOLIAN ISLANDS

Ferries and hydrofoils operated by SNAV and NGI depart daily from Milazzo to the Aeolian Islands.
Taranto Navigazione runs mini-cruises, both during the day and in the evening.
For further information, see Isole Eolie.

STAY

Jack's Hotel – *Via Colonnello Magistri 47, Milazzo.* *090 92 83 300.* *www.jackshotel.it. 14 rooms €5.*
This small hotel, conveniently located for both the port and the town centre, is simple and well maintained, with well-furnished rooms. Good value for money.

CAPO D'ORLANDO

Nuovo Hotel Faro – *Via Libertà 7, Capo d'Orlando.* *0941 90 24 66. www. nuovohotelfaro.com. 31 rooms €5.*
As its name suggests ("lighthouse" in Italian), this family-run hotel is situated near a beacon. The communal areas are simple but pleasant and although the bedrooms are not the most modern, they are clean and well-kept. The biggest

draw is the location – the beach is only a stone's throw away.

😊😊 **La Tartaruga** – *Lido San Gregorio, Capo d'Orlando, 2km/1.2mi E of Capo d'Orlando. ℘0941 95 54 21. www.hotel tartaruga.it. Closed Nov. 53 rooms ⬜.* In the heart of the tourist area *(2km/1.2mi from Capo d'Orlando)* this imposing hotel overlooking the beach offers comfortable, modern rooms and a swimming pool. The restaurant *(closed Mon)* is reputed for its fresh fish.

SAN SALVATORE DI FITALIA

😊😊**Casali di Margello** – *Strada Provinciale 155, 6km SE of San Salvatore di Fitalia. ℘0941 48 62 25. www.casalidi margello.it. 8 rooms.* This agriturismo close to Nebrodi makes an ideal base for exploring the nature park. Its colourful maisonettes with rustic bedrooms are set between olive and orange trees. The restaurant serves local specialities made from produce grown on the site. Swimming pools and hiking trails.

⍲/EAT

😊😊 **Il Covo del Pirata** – *Via San Francesco 1, Milazzo. ℘090 92 84 437. www.ilcovodelpirata.it. Closed Wed (except Aug).* Situated on the seafront, this locally popular spot serves excellent pizzas, baked in a wood-fired oven.

😊😊 **Al Castello** – *Via Federico di Svevia 20. ℘090 92 82 175. Closed Wed.* If you're looking for an original place to eat, this restaurant serving dinner at the foot of the castle walls is a must.

CAPO D'ORLANDO

😊 **Il Gabbiano** – *Via Trazzera Marina 146, Capo d'Orlando. ℘0941 90 20 66. Closed Tue.* Unanimously considered to be the best pizzeria in the area, this simple, well-run restaurant also has a spacious veranda.

😊😊 **Trattoria La Tettoia** – *Contrada Certari 80, Capo d'Orlando; 2.5km/1.5mi S of Capo d'Orlando on S 116. ℘0941 90 21 46. Closed Mon (except Jul–Sept).* 🍴. This family-run trattoria has a friendly, informal atmosphere; genuine regional cuisine, and a **panoramic** terrace that's delightful in the summer.

😊😊😊 **Bontempo "Il ristorante"** – *Via Fiumara 38, Naso. From S 113 to Milazzo, turn right to Sinagra, just before Ponte Naso. ℘0941 96 11 88. www.bontempoil ristorante.com. Closed Mon and Nov.* This restaurant is housed in a modern, white building surrounded by greenery *(10km/6mi to the southeast of Capo d'Orlando)*. It has three spacious dining rooms and serves a range of local dishes.

MARINA D'PATTI

😊😊 **Il Casaro** – *Via Luca della Robbia 3, Marina di Patti. ℘0941 36 74 75. Closed Mon, Dec and Jan. Booking recommended.* This popular eatery enjoys a good reputation in the area. There is an attractive bar, wooden veranda and a small garden for summer dining. Good-quality cuisine at reasonable prices.

TAKING A BREAK

Bar Washington – *Lungomare Garibaldi 95, Milazzo. ℘090 92 23 813.* A perfect place for a lunchtime snack, this bar also serves *pignolate* (a local speciality made with twists of fried puff pastry with lemon or chocolate icing), a selection of pastries and ice cream.

FESTIVALS

CAPO D'ORLANDO

Vita e paesaggio di Capo d'Orlando
Since 1955, this summer competition, backed by the Messina painter Giuseppe Migneco, has asked artists from Italy and abroad to explore the life and countryside of Capo d'Orlando. Some works are acquired by the local art gallery.

Capo d'Orlando in Blues – For information on this summer festival of Blues music, see *www.capodorlando blues.it* or call ℘392 66 38 053.

TINDARI

The Tindari Estate festival is held in the theatre at Tindari from the last week in July to the third week in August. The programme includes prose readings, dance performances and classical and contemporary music concerts.

The Nebrodi Mountains ★★

The Nebrodi mountains are carpeted with the largest swathe of woodland in Sicily (50 000ha/123 500 acres). Named after a now-extinct species of Siclian deer, the area has been a regional nature park since 1993. Traditions run deep here and you'll soon find yourself in villages where a rare ancient dialect is spoken. The highest peak is Monte Soro, outside San Fratello.

🚗 DRIVING TOURS

A DAY IN THE NEBRODI MOUNTAINS
*Approx. 200km/125mi. Allow one day. This circuit may also be done from Sant'Agata Militello, though it is worth doing in a counter-clockwise direction to enjoy the **views** of Mount Etna, notably from Lago Ancipa. For the first part, from SantoStefano di Camastra to Mistretta (14km/9mi), see itinerary ②.*

▶ From Mistretta, follow S 117 to the Nicosia/Troina fork; turn left to Troina.

⚜ **Michelin Map:** p360: B3
ℹ **Info:** Piazza Duomo Sant'Agata di Militello, ☎0941 40 25 24, www.parcodeinebrodi.it.
▶ **Location:** The Nebrodi extend between Santo Stefano di Camastra and Capo d'Orlando.
🕐 **Timing:** Allow the better part of a day.

Troina
The medieval citadel is perched high above the town's rooftops, standing shoulder to shoulder with Troina's main church. Sadly, only the bell tower survives from the original Norman building (11C).

▶ From Troina, return towards Cerami and turn right to Lago Ancipa (approx. 8km/5mi).

Lago Ancipa
This man-made lake, formed when the San Teodoro dam *(120m/394ft)* was built, lies in a glorious stretch of countryside. The road skirts the lake before leading on to Cesarò *(25km/16mi)*. Although narrow and badly rutted, it picks its way through woods and along valleys, providing unforgettable **views★★** of Mount Etna.

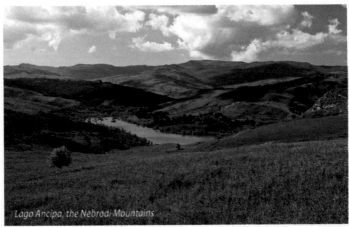

Lago Ancipa, the Nebrodi Mountains

© Sandro Bedessi / Fototeca ENIT

Cesarò

Follow signs just outside the town to Cristo sul Monte, from where a haunting **view★★** extends across to Mount Etna. However, the best panorama is from the Christo Signore della Montagna, a huge bronze statue in the cemetery above the town.

▶ Take the S 289 up the narrow pass, Portella della Miraglia and Portelle della Femmina Morta, through mountain scenery and beech woods.

At the top, a dirt track leads to the summit of **Monte Soro**, the Nebrodi's highest peak *(1,847m/6,058ft)*.

▶ Take the steep, winding SS120 to Maniace *(17.5km/10mi from Cesarò)*.

Maniace-Castello di Nelson★

🕐*Open Apr–Sept Tue–Sun 9am–1pm, 2–7pm, Oct–Mar Tue–Sun 9am–1pm, 2–4.45pm.* 🕐*Closed Mon.* 🚶*Guided visit (45min).* ⬥€3. 📞*095 69 00 18.*
The Benedictine Abbey, founded in the 12C at the behest of Queen Margaret, wife of William the Bad, sat on a key communication route into the Sicilian hinterland. This prosperous monastery underwent various modifications before being finally handed over to Admiral Horation Nelson in 1799 *(for his role in suppressing anti-Bourbon rebellions in Naples)*, along with the title Duke of Bronte. Although the British naval hero never visited the building, his descendants lived there until 1981 and transformed it into a magnificent private residence.
The adjacent abbey **chapel** is graced with an elegant doorway.
Inside, it houses a Byzantine icon, supposedly carried by the Byzantine *condottiere* George Maniakes, who inflicted a crushing defeat on the Saracens in 1040. The main house, surrounded by a park *(4ha/10 acres)* and an attractive garden, has some beautifully furnished rooms.

▶ Return to Cesarò and continue along the road to San Fratello.

San Fratello

In this perched shepherding village, founded by a group of Lombard settlers, you can still hear locals speak a Siculo-Gallic dialect that even locals from neighbouring towns won't understand. San Fratello is linked by name to the *sanfratellani*, a fine breed of horse that can occasionally be spotted roaming freely on the edge of town.
On the north side, *(by the cemetery)*, there is a track to a Norman church, the 11C–12C **Chiesa Normanna dei Santi Alfio**, **Filadelfio e Cirino**. A marvellous **view★★** extends over the surrounding landscape.

▶ From San Fratello, follow the road back to the coast and turn right for Sant'Agata di Militello *(18km/11mi)*.

Sant'Agata di Militello

This seafront resort skirts a long stretch of beach. The main buildings, the Castello dei Principi Gallego and the adjacent 18C Chiesa dell'Addolorata, are both located on Piazza Crispi. The town has a small natural history museum, the **Museo Etnoantropologico dei Nebrodi** *(Via Cosenz;* 🕐*open 8.30am–1.30pm;* 🕐*closed Sun;* 📞*0941 72 23 08)*.
Close to the mountains and other coastal sights, Sant'Agata is an ideal base from which to explore the area.

▶ From Sant'Agata, follow S 113 to Capo d'Orlando, then turn right to San Marco d'Alunzio *(10km/6mi)*.

San Marco d'Alunzio★

This delightful small town, situated 550m/1,800ft above sea level and 9km/6mi from the coast, enjoys **magnificent views★★** of Cefalù and the Aeolian Islands. Each phase in Sicilian history has left its mark here. Occupied by the Greeks, it became *Municipium Aluntinorum* under the Romans, then renamed San Marco dei Normanni in memory of the first town conquered by the Normans in Calabria. The locally quarried red marble is seen in many of town's buildings. Just outside the town

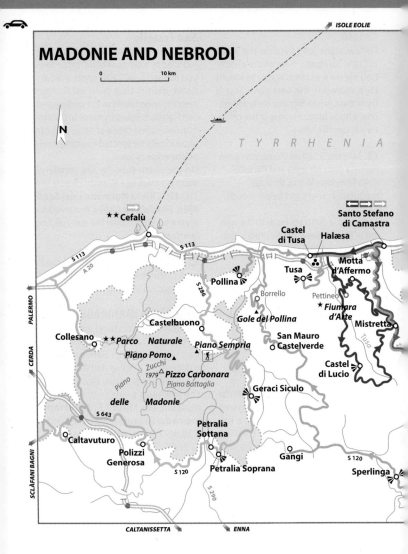

MADONIE AND NEBRODI

ISOLE EOLIE

0   10 km

N

T Y R R H E N I A

Cefalù ★★

S 113

S 113

A 20

Santo Stefano di Camastra

Castel di Tusa   **Halæsa**

Tusa

Motta d'Affermo

S 286

Pollina

Borrello

Pettineo

★ **Fiumara d'Alte**

Mistretta

Castelbuono

Gole del Pollina

PALERMO

Collesano

★★ **Parco**   *Naturale*

San Mauro Castelverde

CERDA

Piano Pomo ▲

Piano Sempria

Zucchi
1979 △ **Pizzo Carbonara**

Piano Battaglia

Castel di Lucio

Piano

delle   *Madonie*

Geraci Siculo

S 643

Caltavuturo

Petralia Sottana

SCLAFANI BAGNI

Polizzi Generosa

S 120

Petralia Soprana

Gangi

S 120

Sperlinga

S 290

CALTANISSETTA   ENNA

centre is the **church of San Marco**, built on the foundations of a **temple** dedicated to Heracles (4C BC), of which a few tufa stone blocks remain. The open-air church preserves its stone walls and a re-erected doorway.

San Teodoro (or Badia piccola)

San Teodoro was built in the 16C *(on the site of a Byzantine chapel)* using a Greek-cross plan with each square arm enclosed by a little dome. The interior is ornamented with magnificent Serpotta-style **stuccowork★** depicting *Judith and Holofernes, Manna falling from Heaven in the Desert (at the sides of the altar)*, scenes from the parable of the prodigal son. Hellenistic cisterns and the remains of 2C–3C AD paving can be seen in the churchyard.

Museo della Cultura delle Arti Figurative Bizantine e Normanne

&. ⏰Open 9am–1pm, 3.30–7.30pm *(3–6.30pm in winter)*. ⏰*Closed public holidays.* ⊛€1.55. ✆0941 79 77 19. www.comune.sanmarcoda lunzio.me.it.

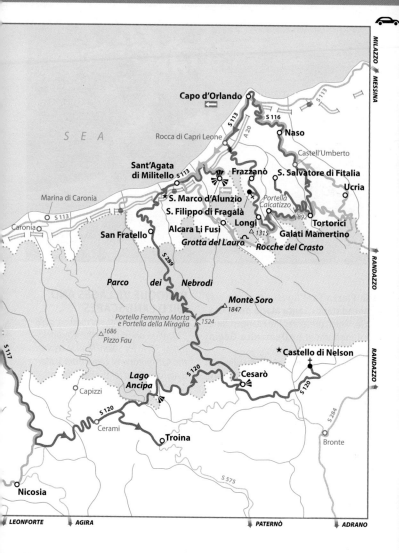

SEA

Capo d'Orlando

Rocca di Capri Leone

Naso

Castell'Umberto

Sant'Agata
di Militello

Frazzanò

S. Salvatore di Fitalia

Ucria

Marina di Caronia

★ S. Marco d'Alunzio

Portella
Calcatizzo

Caronia

S. Filippo di Fragalà

Longi

Tortorici

San Fratello

Alcara Li Fusi

△ 1315

Galati Mamertino

Grotta del Lauro

Rocche del Crasto

Parco   dei   Nebrodi

Monte Soro
1847

*Portella Femmina Morta
e Portella della Miraglia*   1524

△ 1686
Pizzo Fau

★ Castello di Nelson

Lago
Ancipa

S 120

Cesarò

Capizzi

Cerami

Troina

Bronte

Nicosia

MILAZZO   MESSINA

RANDAZZO

RANDAZZO

LEONFORTE   AGIRA   PATERNÒ   ADRANO

Next to San Teodoro, the former 16C Benedictine convent houses the **museum** of Byzantine-Norman art. On the ground floor, interesting 11C **frescoes★** have been uncovered. Those on the right are well preserved: the Madonna *(in the vault)* has beautifully delicate hands; in the tier below, the four Doctors of the Orthodox Church – St John Chrysostom, St Gregory of Nazianzus, St Basil the Great and St Athanasius – are shown against a blue background. Frescoes from other churches are also displayed on the ground floor,

while objects discovered in local necropoli are on the first floor.

In the Chiesa di San Giuseppe is the Parish Museum **Museo Parrocchiale** (*⊙open summer 10am–1pm, 4–7pm, ⊙closed Mon; by appointment rest of the year;* ⊗€2.60; ℘0941 79 70 45) with collections of sacred furnishings and wooden reliquaries.

The main street *(Via Aluntina)* runs through the **historic centre** of San Marco past the Chiesa Madre dedicated to **San Nicolò**.

Black Nebrodi pigs in the Nebrodi mountains near San Teodoro

© Sandro Bedessi / Fototeca ENIT

In Piazza Sant'Agostino, some way ahead stands **Santa Maria delle Grazie**, which preserves the Filangeri funeral monument by **Domenico Gagini** (1481).

Note the 18C **Church of San Basilio** with its arcade of pointed arches *(right)*, and then continue on to the 17C **Church of Ara Coeli**, graced with a doorway ornamented with volutes and floral elements, whose **Cappella del Santissimo Crocefisso** houses an expressive 17C Spanish wooden **Crucifix★**.

San Salvatore

Also known as the **Badia Grande**, San Salvatore once adjoined an important Benedictine convent; now it stands in ruins. Its elegant Alunzio marble **doorway★** is ornamented with columns, angels and cherubs. **Inside**, visitors are greeted by a band of serenading angels playing trumpets, allegorical figures, playful cherubs and more exuberant **stucco decoration★**.

▷ Leave San Marco and head back to S 113. Turn left to Santo Stefano di Camastra.

Look out for signs to **Caronia** *(4km/2.5mi inland)*, where there is a Parco dei Nebrodi visitor centre.

BAROQUE VILLAGES AND WILD LANDSCAPES

Approx. 65km/40mi, see map on p378-379. Allow one day. On the way back follow SS116 for 30km/18mi to rejoin the A20 motorway. Leave from S. Marco d'Alunzio. Head for the coast then Sant'Agata di Militello, then take the left fork towards Alcara Li Fusi.

Alcara Li Fusi

Founded in the 12C, this pretty village derives its name from the Arabic Al-Quariah-al, and from fusi, a locally-made spindle.

▷ Start your visit on Piazza San Pantaleone

The central square is dominated by two churches **San Pantaleone** *and* **Chiesa Madre**. Inside the Chiesa Madre, a chapel is dedicated to the town's patron saint: San Nicoló Politi. Enclosed by a beautiful wrought iron balustrade, it is decorated with stucco and a painting by Filippo Tancredi.

▷ Take Via Don Gusmano to the medieval quarter.

Motta still has its original pattern of narrow alleyways. Only a tower - the **Torretta di Castel Turio** - built on a rock remains of the Castel Turio. Below, the huge Fontana Abate, also known as the Sette Cannoli, built in the 18C, is renowned for its chilled water.

▷ Take the secondary road, Alcara-Bazzana, towards Longi, to Grotte del Lauro.

Grotta del Lauro and Rocche di Crasto

One of the most fascinating natural features in Alcara Li Fusi is the Grotta del Lauro. Surrounded by the imposing Rocche di Crasto, a rocky dolomictic amphitheatre that stands at an altitude of 1 300 m/4 265ft, this grotto is filled with spectacular limestone formations, stalactites and stalagmites.

This site is also the nesting place of the golden eagle, which was recently reintroduced into the Nebrodi (*see Addresses p383*).

▷ Travel up the hill towards Longi.

Longi

This small town is dotted with bell towers clustered around a former medieval castle. At the centre, the Chiesa Madre *(16C and 17C) has a rich collection of religious art and a beautiful carved Baroque presbytery.*

▷ From Longi, head towards Galati Mamertino and cross the mountain stream. Look out for the shepherds' shelters.

Galati Mamertino

This typical Nebrodi village is centred around **Piazza San Giacomo** and its 18C palaces. Their unique arrangement is called La Palazzata. One of them houses the **Palaeontology department** of the Gemellaro Geological Museum in Palermo (*℘ 328 77 76 401 or 329 58 84 106)*, which has a large collection of fossils and a copy of a skeleton of Elephas Antiquus. On the south side of the square, at no. 28, the palace occupied by the local noble family, **Palazzo De Spuches**, features the family crest over the carriage entrance. Opposite,

the Renaissance-style **Chiesa Madre** houses some fine marble statues and a remarkable wooden statue of Saint Sebastian.

▷ From Piazza San Giacomo take Via Toselli.

The northern half of the town has kept much of its medieval appearance. The most interesting churches include the **Rosario** with its statute of the Virgin of the Snow by Antonello Gagini. The church of **San Luca** is fronted by a large marble staircase, while the church of **Santa Caterina** has a movingly life-like wooden Christ sculpted by Frà Umile da Petralia, a marble statute of Saint Catherine of Alexandria by Gagini and paintings from the same period.

🐾 Galata Mamertino offers an ideal base from which to explore the Nebrodi. The Area del Capriolo, for example, is a 50 ha/123acre wooded area where deer have been introduced to see how well they adapt to the environment (see Addresses p382).

▷ From Galata Mamertino take the main road down the valley towards Tortorici.

Tortorici

This small town sprawls along the foot of Monte San Pietro (1 089 m/3 500ft). It was once renowned for its bronze foundries and bell-making workshops, a fact reflected in its rich artistic heritage. Although its historic quarter is peaceful and quiet, the main square, **Piazza Faranda**, is usually humming with life. The church that gives onto the square, San Nicoló di Mira, was rebuilt in 1682 and today follows the Orthodox liturgy.

▷ Walk up Vittorio Emanuele and Via Roma to **Piazza Duomo** at the heart of the medieval quarter.

The imposing church of San Francesco has a stunning 15C portal perched at the top of a monumental staircase. The Baroque church of Santa Maria closes the western side of the square.

The small bridge across the Calagni stream leads to the town's last **bronze foundry** which still makes church bells. It has been in the Trusso family since the second half of the 20C *(free visits by reservation ℘0941 430 475 or 328 65 90 199)*. A bell founded in 1676 greets visitors at the entrance to the garden.

From the road that leads up to Tortorici and Ucria, admire the views over the valley and the sea in the distance. Traditional peasant houses can be seen among the hazel trees.

Ucria

▶ Park on the central Padre Bernardino square and continue on foot to the Chiesa Madre.

A small town to the east of the Nebrodi park, Ucria has retained many of its medieval streets. The **Chiesa Madre** has an elegant three-nave design and many works of art, including marble statues, paintings and a 15C wooden crucifix.

In the lower half of the town, don't miss the church of the Annunziata and Santa Maria della Scala, and the church of Rosario with its beautiful 17C wooden ceiling. The collections housed in the **Museo Etnostorico A. Gullotti** *(Scuola Media Statale Novelli, Via Crispi; ℘0941 66 4021; Tues–Sun 8.30am–1.30pm, Thurs 2-6pm; €1.50)* shed light on rural life in the region.

▶ Head back towards the coast via Naso.

ADDRESSES

🏠 STAY

SANT'AGATA DI MILITELLO

🍽🛏 **Villa Nicetta** – *Contrada Nicetta, Acquedolci, 6km/4mi SW of Sant'Agata di Militello.* ℘0941 72 61 42. www.villa nicetta.it.🖨.10 rooms🛏. This 18C house, surrounded by old barns, olive presses and other farm buildings, is now transformed into tastefully decorated accommodation. Horse-riding and mountain biking is available.

SAN MARCO D'ALUNZIO

🛏 **La Tela di Penelope** – *Via Aluntina 48.* ℘0941 79 77 34. www.lateladipenelope-vacanze.com. 4 rooms. 🛏. Located on the main road in San Marco d'Alunzio, this simple, smart B&B is owned by the same person who runs the town's woven textile shop (⚭*see Shopping*). Breakfast served in the local bar.

🛏🛏🛏 **La Collina dei Nebrodi** – *Contrada Asa.* ℘0941 79 76 22 or 333 114 39 81. 🏊.www.lacollinadeinebrodi.it. 10 rooms.🛏. Perched on a hill at an altitude of 650m/2 000ft opposite San Marco d'Alunzio, this pretty agriturismo enjoys stunning views of the surrounding landscape running down to the sea. It's an ideal starting point for hikes in the nature park, including guided hikes to the Rocche di Crasto (6hr walking) every Sunday.

TORTORICI

🛏 **Fontanapietra** – *Contrada Colla 8, 8km/4mi south west of Tortorici towards Floresta.* ℘0941 49 7001 or 339 76 78 428. 🖨 🍴. 5 rooms. 🛏, 1/2 board €50 per person per day. Located at an altitude of 850m/ 2 788mi, this agriturismo lost in the middle of the wilderness is surrounded by beech and hazel trees. The charming, historic stone building has three bedrooms. Another, more recent building, has two bedrooms with a shared bathroom. Mushrooms and grilled meat feature highly on the menu.

🍴 EAT

SANT'AGATA DI MILITELLO

🛏🛏 **Antica trattoria Za Pippina** – *Via Cosenz 197 (lungomare).* ℘0941 70 27 23. One of the last restaurants along the sea front. Unfortunately, it is across the road from the beach but that is its only fault. Specialising in grilled fish and seafood cooked over the coals on the terrace. Graze on the well-stocked antipasti buffet.

GALATI MAMERTINO

🛏 **Antica Locanda** – *Contrada Parrazzi, Galati Mamertino.* ℘0941 43 47 15. *Closed Wed and mid-Jan to mid-Feb.* A welcoming trattoria with a rustic décor serving quality regional cuisine. Excellent value for money.

SAN MARCO D'ALUNZIO

⊜⊜⊜ **La Fornace** – *Via Cappuccini 115, San Marco D'Alunzio.* ℘*0941 79 72 97. www.casemedievali.com. Closed Mon (in winter).* Popular with gourmets, this restaurant is renowned for its *maccheroni al ragù* and chargrilled meat.

ACTIVITIES

Parco dei Nebrodi – Information about excursions and guided walks can be found at park information points. *www.parcodeinebrodi.it.*

SHOPPING

SAN MARCO D'ALUNZIO
La Tela di Penelope – *Via Aluntina 40.*
This shop sells delightful handcrafted woven textiles produced on old restored looms. Well worth a visit.

Madonie★★

With its green rolling hills, deep woodlands, fast-running mountain streams, soaring summits and rich diversity of plants, animals and birds, the Madonie Regional Nature Park is popular with nature lovers, hikers and mountain bikers for its spectacular and ever-changing landscape.

A BIT OF HISTORY

The Sicilian Apennines form a natural geological extension of the Calabrian Apennines. The range comprises the **Monti Peloritani** *(above Messina)* together with the **Nebrodi** and **Madonie** mountains, which enjoy the same landscape, flora and fauna.
The two latter areas have been designated regional parks to preserve their natural heritage.
Rivers and mountain streams flow through valley gorges cut by erosion: one of the most spectacular is the **Gole di Pollina**, near Borrello.

Flora

The vegetation varies with the altitude: the coastal strip, up to 600–800m *(2,000–2,600ft)*, is covered with oaks *(cork and holm)* and scrubby shrubs typical of the Mediterranean maquis (tree spurge, myrtle, *Pistacia lentiscus*, wild olive, strawberry tree/arbutus, juniper); above, at 1,200–1,400m *(4,000–4,600ft)*,

◔ **Michelin Map:** p360: A3
ℹ **Info:** Corso Palo Alliata 16, Petralia Sottana, ℘0921 68 40 11, www.parcodelle madonie.it.
▷ **Location:** The gently undulating hills of the Madonie are replaced to the north by the wilder scenery of Piano Battaglia and Battaglietta, the Pizzo Carbonara *(1,979m/6,491ft, the highest peak in the range)* and the Serre di Quecella; the latter are often referred to as the "Sicilian Alps" on account of their resemblance to the Dolomites.
👥 **Kids:** Outdoor activities for all ages at Sicily's first adventure park, The Parco Avventure Madonie.
🅿 **Parking:** Car parking is available at Rifugio Sempria for the Giant Holly Trail.
👁 **Don't Miss:** The lofty outlooks of **Petralia Soprana** and **Polizzi Generosa** and gorge walks in **Le Golle di Pollina**.
🕐 **Timing:** Allow one day for round-trip driving.

grow various species of oak; over 1,400m/4,600ft, the slopes are covered with glorious beech woods.

Between Vallone Madonna degli Angeli and Manca li Pini *(northern side of Monte Scalone)*, grow 25 Nebrodi spruce, the only examples of this endemic – and now rare – species *(one other stands by the ruined castle at Polizzi)*.

One of the most interesting places for plants is Piano Pomo, where giant holly grows: a few, thought to be over 300 years old, reach over 14m/46ft in height and have a circumference of 4m/13ft.

Fauna

The area has a variety of indigenous birds and animals, although the growing presence of humans – and an increase in hunting and poaching – has virtually annihilated many of the larger species: red and fallow deer, wolf, lammergeier and griffon vulture.

Those still found, however, include porcupines, wild cats, foxes, martens and some 150 or so species of bird, such as hoopoes, buzzards, kestrels, red kites, peregrine falcons, ravens, golden eagles and grey herons.

Among the area's most interesting residents are the many species of butterfly (some 70 or more).

🚗 DRIVING TOURS

The itineraries suggested below follow scenic routes, which, depending on the direction in which they are travelled, provide a completely different set of **views**.

THE HEART OF THE MADONIE

160km/100mi round trip starting from Cefalù. Allow one day.

Cefalù★★

👣 *See Cefalù.*

▷ Take the road out of Cefalù along the coast eastwards, enjoying the views of the lookout tower on the promontory. A signpost a little farther on indicates the road (right) for Castelbuono *(22km/14mi)*.

Castelbuono

This charming town, laid out across the lower undulations of the surrounding mountains, grew up in the 14C around the **castle** built by the **Ventimiglia family**. The massive square construction with towers has undergone many alterations over the years.

The town itself is a charming jumble of winding streets, many on a steep incline, that converge on shady piazzas.

At the heart of the town is Piazza Margherita, overlooked by the **church of**

Castelbuono

©durisi63/Fotolia.com

Madrice Vecchia and the old **Banca di Corte**.

Madrice Vecchia

Built in the 14C on the ruins of a pagan temple, the church has a 16C Renaissance portico and a splendid central portal in the Catalan style. On the left side rises a campanile with a fine Romanesque two-arched bell opening, culminating in an octagonal spire covered with majolica tiles. The interior preserves several rare works of art, including a **polyptych★** above the high altar depicting *The Coronation of the Virgin,* attributed to Pietro Ruzzolone (or possibly Antonello del Saliba). Note the unusual figure of a saint wearing spectacles *(bottom right)*. To the right is a statue of the *Madonna delle Grazie* by **Antonello Gagini**. Below the north aisle, the fresco of the *Sposalizio delle Vergini* (Betrothal of the Virgins) shows a strong Sienese influence in the elegant features and pleasing symmetry of the composition. A few of the columns separating the aisles are painted with frescoes; among these is the figure of St Catherine of Alexandria, characterised by her poise and delicate features. The crypt is entirely decorated with 17C frescoes depicting scenes from the Passion, Death and Resurrection of Christ.

▷ Take Via Sant'Anna up to the castle.

Castello di Castelbuono (Museo Civico)

🕐 *Open daily 8.30am–2pm, 2.30–8pm.* 🕐 *Closed Mon.* ✆ *€3.* ✆ *0921 671211.* *www.museocivico.eu.*

The massive form of the **castle** appears through the Gothic arch, with a square tower at each of its corners.

The **Cappella Palatina** *(second floor of the castle)* is decorated with **stuccowork★** picked out from a gold-leaf background and attributed to **Giuseppe Serpotta** (1683), brother of Giacomo. The collections include treasures and furnishings from the **Cappella Palatina** and a fine selection of contemporary paintings, mainly by Italian artists.

▷ Via Roma leads off from Piazza Margherita.

Museo Francesco Minà-Palumbo

Via Roma 52. 🕐 *Open 9am–1pm, 3–7pm.* 🕐 *Closed Mon.* ✆ *€2.* ✆ *0921 67 18 95. www.museominapalumbo.it.*

Housed in a former Benedictine convent, the **museum** evolved from the botanical passion of **Francesco Minà-Palumbo**, a local 19C doctor. The result is a lifetime's systematic collection, classification and representation on paper of the botanical species, reptiles and insects of the Madonie Mountains, some of them now extinct.

A little farther on is the **Church of San Francesco**, together with its extension, the **Mausoleo dei Ventimiglia**, a late medieval octagonal structure known as **La Madrice Nuova**, which contains a fine *Deposition from the Cross* by Giuseppe Velasco and Baroque altars with spiral columns by Vincenzo Messina. In Corso Umberto I is the **Fontana di Venere Ciprea** *(reconstructed in 1614),* with Andromeda *(at the top),* Venus and Cupid *(central niche)* and four bas-reliefs depicting the myth of Artemis *(Diana)* and Actaeon.

▷ Leave Castelbuono and follow the signs for San Guglielmo and Rifugio Sempria, where the car can be left.

Il Sentiero degli Agrifogli giganti

🥾 *3.5km/2mi – allow 2hr 30min.*

This beautiful walk along the **Giant Holly Trail** leads from **Piano Sempria** through woods of holm and young oak to **Piano Pomo**. The giant holly trees here are 15m/50ft tall and some are more than 300 years old.

▷ The road continues onwards towards Geraci Siculo *(22km/14mi).*

Geraci Siculo

Lose yourself in the maze of narrow, cobbled streets that spider this hamlet, particularly the upper part. The castle was originally built for the Marchesi Ventimiglia *(accessible by road – turn right by the entrance to the town)*. It's now a sad ruin but from here, marvellous **views★** extend out in every direction.

At the town centre stands the Gothic **Chiesa Madre**, whose highlight is the *Madonna and Child* by **Antonello Gagini**, found in the second chapel of the north aisle.

The road from Geraci to Petralia *(14km/9mi)* proceeds through a glorious, sweeping landscape with lovely **views★** of the mountains, Enna and Mount Etna.

Petralia Soprana

To visit the Chiesa Madre and other churches, contact 0921 68 41 20.

Upper Petralia stands at 1,147m/3,762ft, making it the highest town in the Madonie and blessing it with **spectacular views**. Narrow streets weave between austere *palazzi* and churches, all built of local stone, occasionally opening out onto picturesque little squares and breathtaking scenery. The **Belvedere** *(by Piazza del Popolo)* provides the best vantage point from which to survey the **panorama★★** of Enna *(far left)*, with Resuttano, Monte Cammarata and Madonna dall'Alto *(on the right)*.

The focal point of the town is the **Piazza del Popolo**, where the town hall is located, occupying the former premises of a Dominican convent. The street to the Chiesa Madre leads through the delightful **Piazza Quattro Cannoli**, past its stone fountain. The right flank of the **Chiesa Madre**, preceded by a lovely portico, has a **view** that extends over Piano Battaglia, Polizzi, Mount Etna and Enna. **Inside**, look for the fine wooden crucifix by the master craftsman **Frà Umile da Petralia** *(right of the altar)*, who was born here, and a lovely wooden altar carved by Bencivinni in the Cappella del Santissimo Sacramento *(left of the main altar)*. The rear wall is taken up by an 18C organ case.

The **Church of Santa Maria di Loreto** stands on the site of a former Saracen fortress. Its convex front elevation was designed by the Serpotta brothers. The large altarpiece inside, depicting the Madonna and Child, is attributed to Giacomo Mancini (15C).

A splendid **panorama★★★** extends behind the church with views over the jagged **Madonie e Nebrodi Mountains** and **Mount Etna**.

Another church, dedicated to the Great Redeemer **(Santissimo Salvatore)**, conforms to an elliptical plan and has an 18C decoration. It contains a wooden figure of St Joseph by Quattrocchi and in the sacristy, two works by **Giuseppe Salerno**: *St Catherine of Alexandria* and the *Madonna with a Cat*. Both pictures display an intimacy and gentleness unusual for this painter.

Petralia Sottana

Despite the name, Lower Petralia is perched on a rocky spur 1,000m/3,300ft above sea-level in a lovely position overlooking the River Imera valley.

Corso Paolo Agliata, where the headquarters of the Madonie Park Authority *(Ente Parco delle Madonie)* are located, leads past the **church of Santa Maria della Fontana** with its lovely 15C doorway. Farther along the same street stands **San Francesco**, with its fine bell tower rising from a pointed arch. Inside, it contains a number of paintings by Giuseppe Salerno.

As the street curves round to the right, the eye is drawn to the bell tower-cum-archway of the Chiesa della Misericordia, inlaid with a meridian line. A little farther on lies Piazza Umberto I and the **Chiesa Madre** (17C), an imposing building overlooking the valley, holding various paintings by **Giuseppe Salerno**, including a *Triumph of the Eucharist (first altar on the left)* and *The Five Wounds of Our Lord* (once erroneously thought to be a *Deposition*). Look for the delicate rendering of the *Nativity* by **Antonello Gagini** in the chapel to the right of the high altar. The church also holds an 11C bronze Islamic candelabra in its sacristy: it is generally locked away for most of the year, but brought out for certain religious ceremonies.

Continue uphill to the 16C **Chiesa della Trinità** (la Badia) (to visit the church, contact the parish priest).

The Popular Epithet: Zoppo di Gangi

The last work of **Gaspare Vazzano** (or Bazzano), a cycle of frescoes in the Chiesa Madre at Collesano, is clearly signed "Zoppo di Gangi". Vazzano was born in Gangi in the latter part of the 16C and, despite being trained as a painter in Palermo, always gravitated towards the towns of the Madonie Mountains in search of work. The other painter with whom he shares his nickname (which translates as "The Lame Man of Gangi") was a contemporary, also from Gangi: **Giuseppe Salerno**. It remains difficult to ascertain the relationship enjoyed by the two artists despite a recent theory that suggests Salerno collaborated with Vazzano, at least during his early career as a painter.

The common pseudonym might possibly be explained as an act of homage by the pupil, who was a few years younger than Vazzano. The two painters fit into the same artistic movement, yet their styles are quite different. Vazzano's use of tonal colour, gentle facial expression and softer line endow his paintings with a certain sentimentality that contrasts sharply with Salerno's bolder style achieved by strong use of line and precise draughtsmanship. His intention is to produce a cruder kind of work that dogmatically embodies a concept, a message or a doctrine. These different personalities and distinctive means of artistic expression are the hallmarks of two Sicilian painters who have each granted an important legacy to their native land.

A fine Gothic doorway leads into the church, which gives pride of place to a large 23-panel **marble altarpiece★** by **Giandomenico Gagini**. The central section shows the Mystery of Easter; this is surrounded by the Trinity *(above)*, the Crucifixion, the Resurrection and the Ascension. The lateral panels *(top left to bottom right)* relate scenes from the life of Christ.

⬆ Excursion on foot
Allow 3hr 30min to the top.
On the northern edge of Petralia, a track worn by pilgrims leads up to the **Santuario della Madonna dell'Alto** (1,819m/5,966ft). This houses a painting of the Virgin and Child from 1471.

▶ Continue to Polizzi Generosa *(20km/12mi).*

Polizzi Generosa
Polizzi enjoys a splendid **situation★** on a limestone spur dominating the northern and southern slopes of the Imera Valley. From here, the surrounding mountain tops appear to float on low cloud when it collects around the valley floor on crisp mornings.

Despite the town's elusive origins, it seems to have played an active role in ejecting the island's Arab invaders: **Roger II** had a castle built here to defend against an attack from the infidels. Later, Frederick II was so impressed by the hospitality extended to him on his visit that he bestowed the title of Generosa on the little town.

Begin a tour from the main piazza, marked by the ruins of the castle on the highest point *(917m/3,008ft)*.

Also located on the piazza is the Palazzo Notarbartolo (16C), which houses the **Museo Ambientalistico Madonita** *(contact for opening times: ✆0921 64 90 93; www.mam.pa.it; www.polizzigenerosa.it)*, a natural-history collection presented as a series of reconstructed natural habitats (the preserved animals died of natural causes or were retrieved from poachers).

Via Roma leads downhill past Palazzo Gagliardo (16C–17C) and, opposite, the **Chiesa Madre** *(opening times vary: ✆0921 64 90 94)*, which contains a Flemish triptych *(presbytery)* and a lovely *Madonna of the Rosary* by **Giuseppe Salerno** – one of the two Zoppo di Gangi (⟳ *see page 387*).

Piazza Umberto I lies beyond. From here, Via Garibaldi leads to San Girolamo with its fine Baroque doorway before ending at Piazza XXVII Maggio. This square offers a dramatic **view★★★** across the highest peaks of the Madonie: in the centre is the northern valley of the River Himera; to the left sits Rocca di Caltavuturo, Monte Calogero *(right in the middle, in the far distance)* and Monte Cammarata; the far right is marked by the Dolomite-like profile of Quacella, followed by Monte Mufara and Pizzo Carbonara. Almost directly opposite is the lower section of the Massicio dei Cervi, known as the *Padella* (meaning a frying pan). According to local tradition there is a secret entrance to a cave full of treasure here, the whereabouts of which may only be revealed during Easter Mass. Below lies the Valle dei Noccioleti.

▷ Continue on down to the coast along S 643 for approx. 15km/9mi; at the fork, turn left towards Caltavuturo *(25km/15mi from Polizzi)*.

Caltavuturo

Clinging to the foot of the Rocca di Sciara, the "Fortress of the Vulture" – derived from the Arabic *(qalaat,* fortress) and the Sicilian vernacular *(vuturo,* vulture) – preserves a few prized 16C works of art in the **Chiesa Madre★**. These include an attractive *Madonna of the Rosary surrounded by the Mysteries,* executed by followers of Pietro Novelli and at the back of the church, a fine Baroque organ by Raffaele della Valle.

▷ Leave Caltavuturo by S 120 towards Cerda. At the fork, turn left for Sclafani Bagni *(10km/6mi)*.

Sclàfani Bagni

Crouched on the edge of a rocky crag in a wonderful **position★**, the entrance to this hamlet is marked by the **Porta Soprana**, a gate surmounted by the Sclàfani family coat of arms. On the left sits the *castelletto,* a defensive tower and beyond lies the **Chiesa Madre**, graced with a decorative Gothic doorway (15C).

Highlights inside are *L'Agonizzante* by the Zoppo di Gangi **Giuseppe Salerno** (⚅*see below)*, and a sarcophagus carved with a bacchanal from the ancient city of Himera (⚅*see Termini imerese)*. The beautiful organ *(currently under restoration)* at the back of the church is by Raffaele della Valle (1615).

Up to the right of the church, the 14C tower offers a wonderful **view★★** over the sea below Himera and Caltavuturo and across to the Madonie mountains.

▷ Return to S 643, following the road to Collesano *(30km/19mi)*.

Collesano

The heart of this small holiday resort still has many of its original medieval buildings, including the **Chiesa Madre**, theatrically placed at the top of a great flight of steps. An enormous 16C *Crucifixion* hangs above its nave. Look out too for *St Catherine* (1596) in a bay in the south aisle completed by Giuseppe Alvino, also known as *Il Sozzo* (literally translated as the Soak!) and for works by Zoppo di Gangi **Gaspare Vazzano**, such as the **Santa Maria degli Angelia** *(north aisle)*.

The way up to Piazza Gallo, in the oldest part of town, leads past the ruins of the castle, from where a splendid **view** opens out over the valley bottom and the coast.

▷ From Collesano, turn down towards the coast signposted for Cefalù *(17km/10.5mi)*.

BETWEEN THE MADONIE AND THE NEBRODI

180km/112mi round trip, starting from Santo Stefano di Camastra – allow one full day.

Santo Stefano di Camastra

Santo Stefano is famous for its colourful **hand-painted ceramics★★** and the streets are lined with small gift shops offering pots, vases and plates to buy. Gentle haggling for the best price is acceptable.

At the **Palazzo Sergio** you will find the **Museo della Ceramica** (⏰ *open 9am–1pm, 3.30–7.30pm;* ⏰ *closed Mon and festivals;* 🎗 *donations welcome;* ♿ 📞 *0921 33 70 96)*, where pride of place is given to S Lorenzini's *Andare (Departing)* comprising of five warriors "sinking" into the ground. Upstairs, several beautifully restored *palazzo* rooms have original **tiled floors★**, frescoed ceilings and 18C furnishings.

Outside the town *(beyond the Ceramics Institute)*, lies the **Cimitero Vecchio**, a cemetery containing graves ornamented with majolica.

Mistretta

This small hamlet *(located 950m/3,000ft above sea-level)* is one of the departure points for excursions into the Nebrodi Mountains. The town is a collection of simple stone houses grouped around the ruins of a feudal castle, with a clutch of striking buildings including the **church of San Giovanni** (1530) and the 16C **Chiesa Madre**, dedicated to St Lucy *(the popular saint martyred in Syracuse)*. Inside, a chapel dedicated to the Madonna shelters a *Madonna of Miracles* attributed to Giorgio da Milano; a larger side chapel honouring St Lucy contains a fine altarpiece by **Antonello Gagini**, with statues of St Lucy, St Peter and St Paul (1552). Mistretta's Saint's Day festivities are one of the biggest events of the year here, held on the 7–8 September, when the Madonna delle Luci is paraded through the streets, along with statues of the village's legendary founders, Mytia and Kronos.

At the top of the town stands the Renaissance **church of Santa Caterina**.

▶ From Mistretta, continue along S 117 as far as the junction with the Troina/Nicosia road, then turn right to Nicosia *(30km/19mi)*.

Nicosia

Around the castle ruins in the upper part of Nicosia, the city's stone roads rise and fall in an irregular pattern to reveal churches, palaces and dwellings cut into the cliff. These caves represent the remains of a troglodyte movement once prevalent in southeastern Sicily.

Founded during the Byzantine era, Nicosia managed to resist subordination for centuries largely as a result of the rivalry between the upper and lower parts of town, with each faction fiercely clinging to its respective church *(San Nicolò and Santa Maria)*.

The social heart of town is **Piazza Garibaldi**, especially wonderful in the evening when it is suffused with artificial light. It is lined with distinguished buildings, including the 19C **Palazzo di Città**, which encloses an elegant courtyard.

View to Nicosia

© John Frumm/hemis.fr

The **Cattedrale di San Nicolò** was originally built in the Gothic style as seen on the main **doorway**★ decorated with flowers, acanthus leaves and palmettes. The ceiling, completed in the 19C, is crowned in the dome by an unusual statue of St Nicholas "suspended" from on high. This 17C figure is by Giovan Battista Li Volsi, who also built the decorated walnut **choir stalls**★ (1622). The roof of the church holds a secret: above the vault spans another earlier trussed and painted wooden ceiling from the 14C–15C. Attached to the inside wall of the main façade is an organ by Raffaele della Valle. The church features examples of Gagini workmanship in the font and pulpit, and a sculptural arrangement of *Christ in Glory between the Virgin and John the Baptist* attributed to Antonello Gagini *(second chapel on the left)*.

The **chapter house** is hung with fine 17C paintings including a **St Bartholomew**★ by *Lo Spagnoletto* (José de Ribera).

Santa Maria Maggiore is strategically placed with glorious **views** of the hills. In 1757, a landslide swept away the church with the upper part of the town. Soon afterwards, work began on a replacement.

The noble La Via family gave a delightful 17C doorway from their palazzo for the church entry. Inside, the **Cona**, a large marble composition in six tiers, illustrates scenes from the life of the Virgin, crowned with a figure of St Michael: a work by **Antonello Gagini** and his pupils.

Atop the steep rocks behind the church stood the **castle** *(accessible by car along Via San Simone, leading uphill from just outside the town centre)*. From the ruins, a fabulous **view**★ extends over the mountains.

▶ Returning towards Piazza Garibaldi, take Via Fratelli Testa. On a rise off to the right sits the Chiesa del Santissimo Salvatore.

The **Church of Santissimo Salvatore** enjoys a fine **view**★ over the town.

▶ Continue along Via Fratelli Testa, then Via G.B. Li Volsi. At the intersection with Via Umberto I, turn left uphill.

Chiesa dei Cappuccini

Inside is a fine 18C wooden tabernacle attributed to **Bencivinni**.

8km/5mi farther on, the road reaches Sperlinga, a little town overlooked by its castle fortress, backed up against a vertical cliff face.

Sperlinga

The compact hamlet stretches along a spur of rock shaped like an upturned ship's keel.

It seems to have started life as a troglodyte community contemporary with the Sicani; several cave dwellings are open to view below the town. At the highest point the strategic **castle fortress** stands rooted to the bedrock.

This castle is built on several levels. The caves excavated from the rock *(to the left of the entrance)* were used for stabling animals, as prison cells and as forges. Two of the caves now house a small **anthropological museum** (🕐*open daily 9am–1pm, 4.30–7pm)*. At the front of the castle is the Prince's reception room. The chapel and residential quarters lie opposite: the undercrofts in this section of the castle served as granaries. Between the two wings, a steep staircase cuts up into the bedrock to the lookout tower: from here, the **view**★★ pans 360 degrees over the Gangi plateau with the Madonie range behind, the Nebrodi to the north, Mount Etna to the east and the Erei Mountains to the west. To the right an undulating ridge runs from Monte Grafagna to San Martino and links up with the Nebrodi mountain chain.

A scenic road snakes its way towards Gangi, the largest of the towns in the Madonie area *(20km/12.5mi)*.

Gangi

At one time Gangi was identified with the ancient Engyum, a Greek town founded by colonists from **Minoa**; the town that survives today has largely evolved since the 14C, scattered over the crest of Monte Marone. Best known as the birthplace of the two 17C artists, both known as Zoppo di Gangi (look out for the beautifully rendered *Last Judgement* by one of them in the church of San Nicola), today's Gangi is a curious mix of modern concrete houses interwoven with picturesque narrow streets and old stone-built houses.

Città alta

The tree-lined **Viale delle Rimembranze**, commemorating soldiers killed in the Second World War, leads to the entrance to the upper town. The most obvious point of reference on **Piazza San Paolo** is the simple stone front of the church of St Paul (16C). The later Chiesa della Badia (18C) has a similar, bare stone, front elevation. **Corso Umberto I** is lined with a number of *palazzi*, including the 19C **Palazzo Mocciaro**, and leads to the town centre. The imposing 18C **Palazzo Bongiorno★** (*⊙open 9am–1pm, 3–7pm; ⊙closed Mon; ☞free; ℘0921 50 20 17*) has elegant *trompe l'oeil* **frescoes★** in the rooms on the piano nobile. These are by Gaspare Fumagalli, a Roman painter active in Palermo around the mid-18C and comprise a series of allegorical subjects.

The town's main square is the **Piazza del Popolo**, overshadowed by the **Torre Ventimiglia★** – a 13C watchtower transformed into a bell tower in the 17C.

In a corner of the piazza is a charming grotto with the **Fontana del Leone** (1931) fountain.

The **Chiesa Madrice** was erected in the 17C on the foundations of an older oratory; inside are several significant works of art including **The Last Judgement★** (1629), on the left side of the chancel. The main masterpiece of Giuseppe Salerno, it was modelled on Michelangelo's Sistine Chapel in Rome (*⟲ See The Green Guide Rome*). Common elements include the standing figure of Christ, the skin of St Bartholomew, a self-portrait of the artist, and the figure of Charon, the devil's ferryman. The level beneath is divided into two: to the left stand the Elect with the Archangel Michael; to the right, the Damned, with the jaws of Leviathan. The church also contains fine wooden sculptures by Quattrocchi, among them a **San Gaetano★** *(far end of the south aisle)*.

From the church forecourt, there is a good **view** of the lower part of Gangi *(including the Torre Saracena, left)* and the Capuchin Monastery.

The street leading on from Corso Umberto I, Corso Fedele Vitale, is lined with "Roman shops" **(botteghe romane)** that date from the 16C and are so-called because goods are sold through a small window and counter next to the doorway.

Further on, the Palazzo Sgadari houses the local **Museo Civico** (*⊙open 9am–1pm, 3–7pm; closed Mon; ☞€2.50;*

Sperlinga

© Fototeca ENIT

Madonie mountains, San Mauro Castelverde village in background

© Saffo Alessandro/Sime/Photononstop

℘0921 68 99 07) with archaeological finds from Mount Alburchia. At the end of the road is the square mass of the Castello dei Ventimiglia.

Città bassa

Return to Piazza del Popolo and turn down Via Madrice to the **Chiesa del Santissimo Salvatore**. This contains a wooden Crucifix by Fra' Umile da Petralia and a painting by Giuseppe Salerno entitled *On the Road to Calvary*, reflecting the influence of Raphael's *Spasimo di Sicilia* in the Chiesa dello Spasimo of Palermo.

Farther downhill is the **Chiesa di Santa Maria di Gesù**, which originally housed a Benedictine Hospice (15C). Inside, are several works by Quattrocchi, notably a wooden group depicting *The Annunciation*.

Santuario dello Spirito Santo

About 1.5km/1mi S of Gangi on the Casalgiordano road.

A local story relates how, in the 16C, a deaf-mute labourer was working in the fields when he came across an image of Christ painted on a rock, which miraculously began to speak.

A sanctuary was built on the site of the miracle, which continues to attract pilgrims. Today, the image on the rock is masked by the painting behind the altar attributed to Vazzano.

▶ From Gangi, it is possible to continue along S 120 to link up with itinerary 'The Heart of the Madonie', extending it with a drive to Petralia Sottana *(15km/9mi)*.

▶ Alternatively, if proceeding with this itinerary , make your way back for about 3km/2mi to the fork and turn left towards San Mauro Castelverde *(30km/19mi from Gangi)*.

San Mauro Castelverde

This little hamlet enjoys bird's-eye **views★** to the Aeolian Islands and across the Nebrodi and Madonie Mountains. The town plan is typically medieval, with a web of narrow streets. The 13C **church of Santa Maria dei Franchi** (contact ℘0921 67 40 83 to arrange a visit) contains a Madonna by **Domenico Gagini** and a font by **Antonello Gagini**. The bell tower is 18C.

▶ Follow the road to Borrello. After Borrello Alto, follow signs to Gangi-San Mauro (left). After approx. 1km/0.6mi, a signpost on the

right indicates the Case Tiberio
U' Miricu.

Le Gole di Pollina
*Follow the small road to a fork, then
turn left. The asphalt peters out at this
point, so park here and proceed on foot.
A little farther on, follow the paved road
on the right to the flight of over 400
steps leading to the gorge.*
The **gorge**★★ is particularly impressive
in summer, when dry conditions make
the river bed accessible, allowing visitors
to walk between the cliffs.

◗ Head back to Borrello and
continue down towards the coast:
at the fork, turn left, following the
coast road. Turn right along the road
signposted for Pollina.

Pollina
This hilltop town is in a perfect **position**★ to enjoy postcard **views**★ of the
coast below. The **Chiesa Madre** (16C),
sitting at the heart of a complicated
network of medieval streets, shelters
an engaging **Nativity**★ by **Antonello
Gagini**. In the Middle Ages, the town
was dominated by a castle: today, only
a square tower remains.
A Greco-Roman style theatre has
recently been built alongside, complete
with spectacular panoramic mountain
and sea **views**★★; a winding road leads
to the coast.

◗ Continue back down towards
the coast and Cefalù. Signs on the
right indicate the way to Tusa and the
archaeological site of Halaesa, lying
before the village itself.

Halaesa
◷ *Open 9am–1hr before dusk.*
⊙€2. ☎0921 33 45 31.
The remains of Halaesa are found just
beyond the chapel of Santa Maria
di Palate. This little town was originally
founded by the Siculi in the 5C BC;
it passed into Greek and Roman hands,
before being destroyed by the Arabs.
Excavations have revealed a Roman

forum, a patrician house and sections
of bastion from the Greek era.

Tusa
8km/5mi S of Halaesa.
This modest town was probably founded
by the people who escaped Halaesa as
it was being razed. The medieval upper
area through the main gateway is where
the most interesting churches are found.
The **Chiesa Madre**, with its entrance set
in a decorative pointed arch, is home
to a delicate marble Annunciation from
the Renaissance (1525), ornamenting
the altar. The wooden choir stalls carved with dragons, cherubs and masks
are 17C; the *Madonna and Child* is by
followers of Gagini.
Nestling among other narrow streets is
the little stone **church of San Nicola**
with its tile-topped campanile.

◗ Return to the coast road. At this
point continue the tour by following
the itinerary described below, or
return to Santo Stefano di Camastra
(9km/5.5mi).

LA FIUMARA D'ARTE★
*80km/50mi, starting at Santo Stefano
di Camastra. Allow at least half a day.*

Fiumara d'Arte translates as **River of
Art**★★ and is an open-air sculpture park
following the the River Tusa. The brainchild of **Antonio Presti**, founder of the
Atelier sul Mare (◖*see below*), the River
of Art provides an interesting symbiosis
of art and landscape.

◗ From Santo Stefano di Camastra,
follow S 113 towards Palermo.

The first large sculpture looms into sight
on the right, standing on the beach of
Villa Marigi. Tano Festa's *Monument to
a Dead Poet* (1990) is as blue as the sea
and sky, and was conceived as a window
to infinity.

◗ Continue a few kilometres along
S 113, then turn left to Pettineo.

The Hidden Work of Art

One other work of art in nature is **The Room of the Golden Boat** by Hidetoshi Nagasawa – set in a cave on the bed of the River Romei *(near Mistretta)*. Inside, the rock is entirely faced with plates of polished steel. Within the enclosed space, a pink marble tree has been "planted" in the ground, but this cannot be seen because the shell of an overturned boat covered in gold leaf has been built on top of it. As such, we are encouraged not to go and see the tree, but to imagine it.

On the right, the second work stands in the middle of the almost permanently dry river bed: Pietro Consagra's *Matter Could Have Not Existed* (1986) consists of two reinforced concrete sections on two levels: one white, the other black, creating a complex line. The **scenic road**★ climbs up into the Nebrodi Mountains, providing **good views**★ over the landscape. **Pettineo** crouches on the top of a small hill. Beyond it on the left, just before Castel di Lucio, stands Paolo Schiavocampo's *A Curve Thrown After Time* (1990). As **Castel di Lucio** comes into view, a sign on the left points to Italo Lanfredini's *Ariadne's Labyrinth* (1990) standing lonely on a hill *(as the road turns in a hairpin bend to the left, keep straight on)*. This cement-and-clay maze enclosed by a succession of towering mountains enjoys a fabulous **location**★.

At the Carabinieri station note Piero Dorazio and Graziano Marini's **Arethusa** (1990), made from large polychrome ceramic panels.

Back down on the main road, follow the winding route to **Mistretta** *(see above)* to *The Ceramic Wall* (1993), a collaboration of 40 artists.

After Mistretta, a road forks left towards **Motta d'Affermo**, where Antonio di Palma's blue wave entitled *Mediterranean Energy* (1990) dominates the landscape. Head back towards the sea

to **Atelier sul Mare**, the hotel-cum-museum of Antonio Presti *(Via Cesare Battisti 4, Castel di Tusa;* guided tours *11am–noon;* €5; 0921 33 42 95; www.ateliersurmer.it; Addresses).

ADDRESSES

STAY
CASTELBUONO

Agriturismo Masseria Rocca di Gonato – *Località Eremo di Liccia, 8km/5mi S of Castelbuono.* 0921 67 26 16. www.roccadigonato.it. 11 rooms, half board. Restaurant. This isolated mountain agriturismo enjoys **panoramic views**. The spacious rooms are furnished with basic creature comforts and the restaurant serves local cuisine, including meat produced on the farm.

CASTEL DI TUSA

Albergo Atelier sul Mare – *Via Cesare Battisti 4,* 0921 33 42 95. www.ateliersulmare.it. 40 rooms. This hotel-cum-museum features a series of guest rooms decorated by artists of international renown.

GANGI

Tenuta Agrituristica Gangivecchio – *Contrada Gangi Vecchio, 4km/2.5mi from Gangi.* 921 60 21 47. Closed Jul. 9 rooms. This 14C Benedictine monastery was converted into a hotel in 1978. Guest rooms are housed in the main building, as well as in the converted stables.

Villa Rainò – *Contrada Rainò, Gangi.* 0921 64 46 80. www.villaraino.it. Closed first week of Jul. 15 rooms. Restaurant. Access to this delightful hotel is via an awkward descent along a narrow road. The effort is worth it, as the hotel has 15 tastefully decorated rooms and a restaurant serving regional cuisine made from fresh produce.

EAT
CASTELBUONO

Vecchio Palmento – *Via Failla 2.* 0921 72 099. Closed Mon. This simple, family-run restaurant has a number of dining rooms and a garden *(unfortunately by the road)*. The menu features typical Madonie specialities.

People walking in Italo Lanfredini's Ariadne's Labyrinth (1990)

© John Frumm/hemis.fr

⊖⊜ **Nangalarruni** – *Via delle Confraternite 5. ℘0921 67 14 28. www. hostarianangalarruni.it. Closed Wed.* Delicious regional cuisine is served in a dining room from the mid-18C, with an attractive blend of exposed brickwork and old wooden beams.

⊖⊜ **Palazzaccio** – *Via Umberto I 23. ℘0921 67 62 89. www.ristorante palazzaccio.it. Closed Mon and 15-30 Jan.* This charming little town-centre restaurant serves regional cuisine made from locally-sourced produce in an historic vaulted dining room with exposed stonework.

⊖⊜ **Romitaggio** – *Loc. San Guglielmo, 5km/3mi S of Castelbuono. ℘0921 67 13 23. www.romitaggio.it. Closed Wed and from mid-Jun–mid-July.* 🍽. Housed in a former 14C monastery, this restaurant has retained the simple style of its original building. Traditional local cuisine is served in a courtyard in summer.

TAKING A BREAK
CASTELBUONO
Extra Bar Fiasconaro – *Piazza Margherita 10. ℘0921 67 12 31.* This bar sells delicious panettone (Christmas cake), *colomba* (dove-shaped Easter cake) and, in summer, *ciambelle* (almond doughnuts). Also available to order is the local *testa di turco* ("Turk's head"), made from bread dough stuffed with pork, ricotta cheese, eggs, cocoa and cinnamon.

POLIZZI GENEROSA
Pasticceria al Castello – *Piazza Castello 10. ℘0921 68 85 28.* This *pasticceria* produces excellent *sfoglio polizzano* – a type of local millefeuille made with *soft cheese*, sugar, chocolate and cinnamon – traditionally eaten during the third week of July as part of the **Sagra dello sfoglio**.

SHOPPING

Manna – Small, whitish and slightly sweet stalactites hanging from ash trees, when dried manna is used as a sweetener and laxative. Once one of the town's sources of income, it is now more of a curiosity and can be found at the tobacconist's shop at the end of Corso Umberto I.

ACTIVITIES

👥 **The Parco Avventure Madonie** – *www.parcoavventuramadonie.it.* Adventure park fun for all ages.

FESTIVALS

Madonna della Luce – Mistretta celebrates the *Madonna of Light* on 7 and 8 September, when a Madonna is borne aloft, escorted by two giant figures representing Mythia and Kronos (*legendary founders of Mistretta*).

San Marco d'Alunzzio – Processione dei babbaluti – On the last Friday in March, in celebration of the Passion, the wooden cross of Ara Coeli is borne aloft through the town by hooded men singing and praying, known as the *"babbaluti"*.

Cefalù★★

Deriving its name from the Greek "kephaloidion", meaning "head", this charming fishing village with a stunning natural setting and beautiful cathedral has everything you need to enjoy a relaxing holiday – including a surprising number of wine shops and wine bars.

●●● WALKING TOUR

Arriving from Palermo, visitors catch their first **sight**★★ of the town from a distance, with the impressive bulk of the cathedral set against the Rocca. Cefalù is an excellent base for excursions into the Madonie (●*see Madonie*).

Piazza del Duomo, stretching below the cathedral, is lined with splendid *palazzi*: Palazzo Piraino *(on the corner of Corso Ruggero)* with its late 16C portal, the medieval Palazzo Maria with a Gothic portal, possibly once a royal residence and, to the left of the cathedral, the 17C Palazzo Vescovile or Bishop's Palace.

Duomo★★

●*Open 8am–6pm (5pm in winter).*
The golden-hued cathedral, a Romanesque jewel set behind a series of palm trees, appears to merge into La Rocca - its backdrop of limestone hills. It was built by the Norman **King Roger II** between 1131 and 1240, after making a vow during a near-shipwreck. Towers frame the Moorish-style façade, divided into two storeys by the portico, rebuilt in the 15C by the Lombard architect, Ambrogio da Como.

The upper section is beautifully ornamented with blind arcading. The central doorway, known as the **King's Gate** (*Porta dei Re*), at one time served as the main entrance.

Interior

The church, with a Latin-cross floor plan, consists of a single nave flanked by aisles, subdivided by columns with fine **capitals**★ carved in the Sicilian Arabo-Norman style.

▶ **Population:** 13 771
⚅ **Michelin Map:** p360: A2
▤ **Info:** Corso Ruggero 77 ℘0921 42 10 50. www.comune.cefalu.pa.it and www.cefalu-tour.pa.it
◉ **Location:** The town clusters on the west side of the majestic outcrop.
P **Parking:** The motorway exit leads easily to Via Roma, where you can park, then head towards Via Matteotti and Corso Ruggero on foot.
👥 **Kids:** Puppet shows at Corte delle Stelle.
◉ **Don't Miss:** The cathedral and its mosaics, *Portrait of an Unknown Man* by Antonello da Messina at the Museo Mandralisca; a stroll on the Lungomare.
◉ **Timing:** Take your time in the summer months. Otherwise, plan a half day for the town. Summit excursions are best in the morning.

GETTING THERE AND AROUND

Buses runs from **Palermo** to **Cefalù** *(the terminal is in front of the railway station)*. The train takes just over 1hr. Train connections are less frequent from **Messina** and the journey takes approx. 3hr.

The railway station is about a 10min walk from **Corso Ruggero**, following **Via Aldo Moro** and **Via Matteotti**. Boats leave **Cefalù** for the **Aeolian Islands** *(approx. 90min)*.

For further information, contact *Aliscafi SNAV, Corso Ruggero 82, ℘0921 42 15 95; Aliscafi SNAV; www.snav.it.*

In summer, hydrofoils speed to the **Aeolian Islands** *(2hr)*: **Ustica Lines**, *℘0923 87 38 13 and 0909 889 949; www.usticalines.it.*

Mosaic of Christ Pantocrator, Duomo

© René Mattes / hemis.fr

The fabulous **mosaics★★** (1148), executed in a spectacular array of colours *(emerald green, in particular)* on a gold background, adorn the chancel.

The eye is immediately caught by the enormous majestic image of the **Christ Pantocrator** gazing down from the apse, his right hand raised in benediction. His left holds a text from St John's Gospel *(Chapter 8, Verse 12)*: "I am the light of the world: he who followeth me shall not walk in darkness, but shall have the light of life." Below, on three different levels, the Virgin, attended by four Archangels and the 12 Apostles, is imbued with sensitivity and gentleness unusual to poker-faced Byzantine art.

The side walls of the choir are covered with more mosaics dating from the late 13C, depicting prophets, saints and patriarchs; the angels in the vault date from the same period.

The stained-glass windows designed by Michele Canzoneri depict biblical themes and date from the 1990s.

The cloister, part of which was being restored as this guide went to press, is lined with columns and capitals of the same style as those in Monreale (◷*open 10am–1pm, 3–6pm, €3, ✆338 81 75 498*).

Corso Ruggero

Cefalù's main street, lined with a wide range of boutiques, overlies the ancient Roman *decumanus,* which bisects the town on a north–south axis. The two resulting halves are quite different: to the west lies the medieval quarter, a labyrinth of narrow streets dotted with steps, arches and narrow passageways; to the east, a network of regular streets at right angles.

From Piazza Duomo, take the left road. Farther along on the left, stands the **Chiesa del Purgatorio** *(for opening times contact ✆0921 92 20 21)*, its front graced by an elegant double staircase leading up to a Baroque doorway. Just inside is the sarcophagus of Baron Mandralisca.

Osterio Magno★

⚯*Closed to visitors.*

On the right of the *corso* stands the residence of King Roger, later the property of the Ventimiglia family, and comprising two parts dating from different periods. The older, two-coloured part of lava and gold-coloured stone faces onto Via Amendola and has two elegant **two-light windows**; it dates from the 13C. The adjoining square tower, on the corner of Corso Ruggero, and built in the 14C, has a fine three-light window set into an elaborate Chiaramonte-style arch. The **palace**, now completely restored, is used for temporary exhibitions. Corso Ruggero leads into **Piazza Garibaldi**, site of one of the town's four gates. Facing the piazza is the Baroque **church of Santa Maria alla Catena**

Christian Symbols

The Greek word for fish, *Ichthys*, is composed of the initial letters of the Greek words *Iesoûs Christòs Theoû Hyiòs Sotr,* which translates as "Jesus Christ, Son of God, Saviour". This is why the image of a fish is often used as a symbol of Christ.

(Saint Mary of the Chain). Its bell tower incorporates parts of the ancient megalithic town walls.

From Piazza Garibaldi, take Via Spinuzza and then Via Vittorio Emanuele.

A little farther along on the left is the **medieval wash house**, known to the locals as *u ciumi* ("the river"), used until comparatively recently. The road ends in Piazza Marina. Just before, note **Porta Pescara** on the left. This is the only surviving medieval gateway of the original four and currently has a display of fishing equipment.

Turn right into Via Ortolano di Bordonaro. Towards the end of the road, a street *(left)* leads directly into Piazza Crispi where the **Chiesa della Idria** (Church of the Hydria) stands, flanked by the Bastion of Cape Marchiafava, with its sweeping **view**.

Retrace your steps and continue as far as Via Porpora, where there is a tower with a postern (an opening allowing only one person to pass at a time). Behind Via Giudecca, the ruins of ancient fortifications can still be seen.

Return to Piazza Duomo and take the picturesque **Via Mandralisca**, leading to the museum of the same name. Set into the paving *(towards the beginning of the street before Piazza del Duomo)* is the Cefalù coat of arms: three fishes with a loaf of bread, all symbols of Christianity, while also referring to the town's economic resources.

Museo Mandralisca
Via Mandralisca 13.

Open 9am–7pm (11pm in Aug).
€5. 0921 42 15 47.
www.fondazionemandralisca.it
The museum was founded at the request of one of Cefalù's most generous benefactors, Baron Enrico Piraino di Mandralisca, a 19C art collector. The museum houses a collection of coins and medals; a series of paintings including **Antonello da Messina's** wonderful **Portrait of an Unknown Man★** from c. 1470; and archaeological artefacts, including an unusual bell-shaped *krater* depicting a tuna seller (4C BC).

EXCURSION
La Rocca
20min to the Temple of Diana; another 40min to the top.
A path leads uphill from Corso Ruggero and Via dei Saraceni to the summit. The first part of the route leads past ancient crenellated walls before rising steeply. During summer, this stretch is best tackled in the early morning or at dusk. From such height, the magnificent **view★★** pans across from Capo d'Orlando to Palermo. On a good day, the Aeolian Islands are visible. Finds on this rocky outcrop confirm it as the one of the earliest settlements in the area, with evidence from different periods in history, including the ruins of an Ancient Greek megalithic building, popularly called the **Temple of Diana**. On the top are the remains of a 12C–13C castle, recently restored.

DRIVING TOUR

EXCURSION INLAND
60km/37mi. Allow half a day.

From Cefalù, follow signs to the Santuario di Gibilmanna, 12km/7mi along a scenic road.

Santuario di Gibilmanna
Open 8am–1pm, 3pm–7pm (5.30pm in winter).
The **sanctuary**, dedicated to the Madonna, is perched high on the Pizzo San Angelo (800m/2,600ft above sea

level), surrounded by oak and chestnut woods. Its name refers to its position (from the Arabic *Jebel*, a mountain) and the old tradition, now obsolete, of making manna. Of ancient origins – founded at the behest of Gregory the Great in the 6C – it passed into the hands of the Capuchin Friars Minor in 1535. The present building is the result of remodelling, especially in the Baroque period. The façade was rebuilt in 1907 while the shrine is the object of a devout pilgrimage on 8 September, the festival of the Madonna.

The building adjacent to the monastery, once used as a stable and guest rooms, has been converted into an interesting **museum** about the Capuchin Friars of the Demone Valley. Of particular interest are a **polyptych** by Fra' Feliciano *(at the time he was known as Domenico Guargena)*, a 16C alabaster rosary belonging to Fra' Giuliano da Placia and a small 18C reed organ.

Down in the catacombs there are rare reliquaries in painted tin or wood made by the friars.

▶ Return to the road and continue for a further 10km/6mi.

Isnello

This little holiday resort, the starting point for many walks into the surrounding area, stands in a **spectacular position★** clinging to the rock amid a gorge of high limestone walls. Its narrow streets have a typical medieval layout.

Take the road back towards the sanctuary; at the junction *(signposted to Piano delle Fate)*, turn left to continue along the **panoramic** road.

This leads through two small villages, **Gratteri** *(the centre still has a medieval feel)* and **Lascari**, before continuing on down to the coast and Cefalù.

TERMINI IMERESE AND AROUND

65km/40mi. Departs from Termini Imerese, 35km/22mi from Cefalù. Off region map p362.

Termini Imerese

🅸 *Cortile Maltese, ℰ091 81 28 505.*
Termini has been famous since Antiquity for the hot, sulphurous thermal waters that gush from its rocks, believed to have therapeutic properties. Modern Termini is also an important port with a large and bustling industrial area. The town is further energised by an annual **carnival**, during which a procession of allegorical floats and events fills the streets with spectacle.

A good place to start exploring the town is Piazza Duomo, overlooked by the Palazzo del Comune, containing a former Council Chamber decorated with frescoes by Vincenzo La Barbera (1610) depicting the history of the town.

Duomo

The cathedral was largely rebuilt in the 17C. Inside, it has a fine **marble relief** Madonna del Ponte *(fourth chapel on the right)* by Ignazio Marabitti (1842). A lovely wooden statue of the Immacolata by Quattrocchi (1799) adorns the chapel dedicated to the Immaculate Conception, while the chapel of San Bartolomeo is furnished with a Venetian-style Rococo sedan chair once used for taking communion to the sick.

Museo Civico

In Via Museo Civico, on the opposite side of the piazza to the Duomo.
🕐*Open daily 9am–1pm, 4–7pm; Sundays 8am–12.30pm.* 🕐*Closed Mon and public holidays.* ♿ *℘091 81 28 550. www.comuneterminiimerese.pa.it.*

The museum is well laid out, with helpful information boards; it comprises an archaeological collection and a section dedicated to art. The first rooms display material from **Palaeolithic** and **Neolithic** times recovered from local caves; excavated artefacts from Himera, including two fine red-figure Attic craters (5C BC); coinage from the Ancient Greek, Roman and Punic periods. Finally, a large room is dedicated to **Hellenistic** and **Roman pottery**: grave goods such as oil lamps, small receptacles and ointment jars; figurines dressed in togas found in the forum and the House of

Stenius (1C AD); portraits, including one of Agrippina (mother of Caligula), which still bears traces of paint; terracotta piping from the aqueduct of Cornelius and Roman inscriptions.

The chapel of San Michele Arcangelo, frescoed by Nicolò da Pettineo, leads off the **Archaeology** department. It also contains a *Madonna and Saints* triptych by **Gaspare da Pesaro** (1453) and an interesting 15C wooden composition, unusual in its depiction of the Trinity as a *Pietà* (with the Holy Spirit personified). On the floor above, the **art gallery** is hung with paintings from the 17C–19C. Notable works include a Flemish *Annunciation* (16C), several pieces by the local painter Vittorio La Barbera (*Crucifixion*, 17C), a *St Sebastian* by Solimena and in a small room at the far end, a tiny portable Byzantine-style **18C panel triptych**.

From behind the Duomo, Via Belvedere leads up to a terrace with **views** of the coast. A little farther on *(to the left)* is an attractive little church dedicated to **Santa Caterina d'Alessandria** (14C). Just beyond lie the shaded gardens of **Villa Palmeri**, where the remains of the **Roman Curia** can still be seen. From the park, follow Via Anfiteatro down to the ruined **Roman amphitheatre** (1C AD). Return to Piazza Duomo and follow Via Mazzini; on the right stands the 17C **Chiesa del Monte**, long used as the town's Pantheon.

Città bassa

Return to the car and drive down to the lower part of town along the Serpentina Balsamo. A lane leading off a left bend provides an opportunity to stop and take in the lovely **view** of the blue-tiled dome of the **Chiesa dell'Annunziata**. **Piazza delle Terme** *(at the bottom)* is dominated by the Grande Albergo delle Terme, built in the 19C to designs by the architect Damiani Almeyda.

Acquedotto Cornelio

Take the road to Caccamo and turn left *(yellow sign)*; after 300m/330yd, on a bend, the Roman aqueduct can be seen on the left, spanning the width of the River Barratina valley.

▷ Leave Termini Imerese on the A 19 (towards Catania), then follow the signs *(18km/11.2mi drive)*.

Scavi di Himera

Open Mon–Sat, 9am–dusk, Sun and public holidays, 9am–1pm. €2. ☏ 091 81 40 128.

Himera was founded in 648 BC by colonists from Zancle *(modern Messina)*. The Carthaginians suffered a crushing defeat here in 480 BC at the hands of the allied forces of Agrigento and Syracuse. Its demise came in 408 BC, however, when a second wave of invading Carthaginians first conquered and then razed the town to the ground.

The ancient town is situated at the top of a hill south of the Messina-Palermo road. Here, sections of wall and part of the sacred area with three temples have been excavated. Farther along the road is the **antiquarium**, displaying artefacts found on the site.

However, the most significant and best-preserved structure is the **Temple of Victory** (5C BC), which stands at the bottom of the hill. It seems probable that the Greeks forced the Carthaginians to build this temple to celebrate their victory in 480 BC. Vestiges of columns, the *cella*, the *pronaos* and the *opisthodomus* are clearly visible.

(The eaves were once decorated with sculpted lions' heads, now in the Palermo archaeological museum.)

▷ Return to Termini Imerese, then head out of town on the SS 285 (Via Giovanni Falcone) and drive for 10km/6.2mi.

Caccamo

Clinging to a rocky precipice among the lower spurs of Monte San Calogero, this pretty little town is overlooked by its impressive castle.

Castle★

Entrance from Via Termitana.
Open Mon–Fri 8.30am–12.45pm, 3–7.15pm, Sat–Sun 10am–12.15pm, 3–5.15pm. Closed public holidays. €4. ☏ 091 81 49 252.

This is one of Sicily's best preserved castles, arranged over several levels as a result of spiralling 14C, 15C and 17C extensions. The main unit probably dates from the 11C. The defensive elements of the castle were reinforced by the Chiaramonte, while in the 17C, these were relaxed under Amato ownership, as it was transformed into a noble residence. Beyond the first gate a 17C ramp leads up to a second gate. The broad, paved courtyard provides access to the Torre Mastra, where magnificent **views★** include Termini Imerese, Mongerbina, Capo Zafferano, Rocca Busambra and the Vicari Castle. An 18C doorway leads through to the Sala delle Armi or Salone della Congiura where the rebellious barons gathered before confronting William the Bad.

The apartments to the left of the Weapons Hall give access to the Torre Gibellina; rooms to the right include the Salotto dei Nobili, before leading onto a terrace with a **panoramic view**.

▶ Return to Corso Umberto I and turn right to Piazza Duomo.

Piazza Duomo★

This square provides an attractive open space split between two levels. The elevated northern side is fronted by a harmonious group of buildings, namely the **Palazzo del Monte di Pietà** (17C) flanked on the left by the **Oratorio del Santissimo Sacramento** and the **Chiesa delle Anime Sante del Purgatorio** (right).

This very special arrangement constitutes a sort of theatrical stage from which to survey the lower part of the square. The balustrade, which separates and links the two levels, is surmounted by four statues representing the Blessed Giovanni Liccio, Santa Rosalia, San Nicasio and San Teotista.

Chiesa Madre

The main church, dedicated to St George, is on the west side of the piazza. **Inside** hangs a dramatic painting of *The Miracle of Sant'Isidoro Agricola* (1641) by Mattia Stomer, while in the chapel of the Holy Sacrament, a ciborium sits above the inlaid marble altar with reliefs by the Gagini School (15C).

Down Corso Umberto I and off to the right is Piazza San Marco, lined with the buildings of a former Franciscan monastery, the Church of the Annunciation, with its twin bell towers, the Chiesa della Badia, and what was the 14C church of **San Marco**.

San Benedetto alla Badia

The single-nave church has a superb **majolica floor** attributed to Nicolò Sarzana from Palermo (18C), although this is badly damaged in places and mostly covered by carpets. It is worth climbing up to the women's gallery, once the preserve of nuns of a closed order from the convent that stood adjacent to the church.

Admire the **stuccoes** in the apse by Bartolomeo Sanseverino (18C): the lunette *(above)* depicts *The Supper at Emmaus;* the statues flanking the altar are allegories of *Chastity* and *Obedience*.

▶ Return to Corso Umberto I. Just before Piazza Torina, turn left uphill.

Santa Maria degli Angeli (San Domenico)

The two-aisled church has a trussed **wooden ceiling** with paintings of Dominican saints.

In the chapel dedicated to Santa Maria degli Angeli *(right)* is a lovely *Madonna and Child* by Antonello Gagini (1516) and on the underside of the main arch, a series of small paintings by Vincenzo La Barbera depicting *The Mysteries of the Rosary* (17C).

Before leaving Caccamo, it is worth walking to the far side of town and turning right *(signposted "Centro Storico")*. At a point along this route there is a great **view★** over the town.

▶ Take the same route back to Termini Imerese, then the A 19 (towards Palermo) or the SS 113 to return to San Nicola l'Arena via the coast.

San Nicola l'Arena

A **castle** with three round towers overlooks the picturesque harbour of this resort. In the distance *(west)* stands a lookout tower on strategic Capo Grosso.

ADDRESSES

STAY

⊜⊜ **Congregazione Suore Collegine della Sacra Famiglia**– *Piazza Marina 3. ℘329 14 11 371. www.conventisicilia.it.✍. 20 rooms.* The sisters of the convent have been here since the 17C and offer rooms without frills – monastic, but impeccably clean. Some rooms have fantastic sea **views**. Roof terrace.

⊜⊜⊜ **Riva del Sole** – *Lungomare Giardina 25. ℘0921 421 230. www.riva delsole.com. 28 rooms. ✍.* Located on the seafront, a few steps from the town centre, this modern hotel offers comfortable, recently-decorated rooms.

⊜⊜⊜ **La Plumeria** – *Corso Ruggero 185. ℘0921 92 58 97. 12 rooms. ✍.* A tastefully-renovated 16C residence in the centre of Cefalù, a short walk from the cathedral. Spacious, bright rooms and friendly service.

EAT

⊜⊜ **La Botte** – *Via Veterani 6. ℘0921 42 43 15. Closed Mon and in Jan.* This centrally located, family-run trattoria serves fresh, traditional Sicilian cuisine in a simple, rustic atmosphere.

⊜⊜ **Porticciolo** – *Via C.O. di Bordonaro 66. ℘0921 92 19 81. Closed Wed. Booking recommended.* In the heart of town, this pleasant restaurant serves seafood, local specialities and pizza.

⊜⊜ **Ti Vitti'** – *Via Umberto I 34. ℘0921 92 15 71.* This family-run brasserie serves hearty dishes, including homemade *pasta*, fresh fish and pistachio nougat.

TAKING A BREAK

Bar del Molo – *Piazza Marina 4–5. ℘0921 42 23 39.* This popular bar with a splendid terrace enjoys lovely **views** of the surrounding area.

Bar Duomo – *Piazza Duomo 19. ℘0921 42 11 64.* Next to the town's magnificent cathedral, this bar is well known for its excellent ice cream.

Pasticceria-Gelateria Pietro Serio – *Via Giuseppe Giglio 29. ℘0921 42 22 93.* This recommended pasticceria serves a range of cakes, pastries as well as traditional confectionery.

TERMINI IMERESE
Try the exquisite home-made ice creams and water-ices *(granite)* made by **Gelateria Cicciuzzu** on the Belvedere terrace behind the Duomo.

GOING OUT

Le Petit Tonneau – *Via V. Emanuele 49. ℘0921 42 14 47.* This excellent rustic-style wine bar overlooking the marina in the medieval heart of Cefalù has a balcony, plus a good list of Sicilian wines.

SHOPPING

A Lumera – *Corso Ruggero 180, Cefalù. ℘0921 92 18 01.* This shop sells a range of traditional Sicilian ceramics, famed for their quality and beauty.

ENTERTAINMENT

Teatro dei Pupi a Cefalù – *Corso Ruggero 92. ℘0921 92 38 82. Shows at 6pm and 9pm. Closed Fri.* The Girolamo Cuticchio puppet company from Palermo recounts the extraordinary exploits of Orlando, Rinaldo and Carlo Magno (Charlemagne) in this splendid theatre.

FESTIVALS

Festa di San Salvatore – The festival of Cefalù's patron saint is held 2–6 Aug and includes the *'nntinna 'a mari*. During this competition, volunteers must crawl along a horizontal pole suspended above the water in order to reach the statue of the Saviour *(the event starts at 5pm on 6 August!).*

Madonna della Luce – On 14 August, a procession of boats makes its way from Kalura to the old harbour and back.

TERMINI IMERESE

Carnevale – The towns' traditional carnival includes a procession of allegorical floats plus other events around the town.

THE ISLANDS AROUND SICILY

Sicilians proudly refer to their massive, diverse island as "the continent" and its satellite islands and archipelagos as "the islands". These islands – wilder, less developed and more sparsely populated – are fragments of Sicily in various stages of volcanic activity, from active to long dormant. They bear the marks of Sicily's many influences, from prehistoric to Greek to Byzantine to Arab.

Island Hopping

The islands offer astonishingly different natural perspectives on the Mediterranean – each with its own landscape, beauty, moods and traditions. They are easily accessible from April to October by ferry and hydrofoil (and, in some cases, airplane). All sorts of visitors make the journey: honeymooners find romantic spots in the countryside, history buffs explore the ancient and prehistoric remains on land and in the sea, divers discover a rare bounty of marine life, nature lovers enjoy excursions on foot to see volcanoes as well as rare species of sea turtle and migratory birds, and gastronomes delight in the unique sweet white wines, fresh capers, seafood and fish dishes.

The string of seven Aeolian islands off Sicily's northeastern coast in the Tyrrhenian Sea is the most popular – with chic resorts poised among the rugged cliffs that plunge to the sea. Generally, the longer the ferry trip, the more isolated the island. You could spend weeks hopping among the Aeolian islands alone; from the charming and bustling Lipari, to the darkly powerful active volcanic

Highlights

1 Climbing to the **active crater** of Vulcano (p411)

2 An **Evening Boat Trip** around Stromboli (p413)

3 **Views** from the top of Pantelleria (p424)

4 Hatching **rare sea turtles** on Lampedusa (p431)

5 Diving to explore the **undersea marvels** of Ustica (p437)

islands of Vulcano and Stromboli, and the gentler caper- and vine-covered slopes of Salina to the remote heather-covered Alicudi.

Pantelleria

In the Mediterranean sea, to the southwest, and closer to Tunisia *(84km/52mi)* than the Sicilian main island, Pantelleria is the largest satellite and perhaps the most contradictory.

It is a chic summer destination for European film stars, albeit one possessed of a savage nature typified by

Island of Lipari

©Danin Tulic/iStockphoto.com

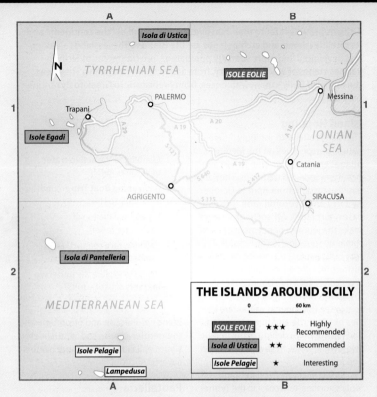

THE ISLANDS AROUND SICILY

0   60 km

ISOLE EOLIE	★★★	Highly Recommended
Isola di Ustica	★★	Recommended
Isole Pelagie	★	Interesting

fierce winds that whip round its shores and slopes. The dark soils and traditional Arab-influenced homes known as *dammusi* (thick-walled cubic lavastone structures with domed roofs) evoke another time far from the European mainland.

The unique nature of Pantelleria is also evidenced by the traditional *giardini Arabi*: high, circular, stone-walled structures built to protect citrus trees and other plants from the wind.

Lampedusa

The southernmost islands, also near Tunisia, are the Pelagie, including the near-barren island of Lampedusa.

Once the fief of the Tommasi line of princes (the most famous of whom was **Giuseppe di Tomasi di Lampedusa**, author of the 1958 Sicilian classic, *The Leopard*), Lampedusa is surrounded by **white sand beaches** and **turquoise sea**. The Pelagie are known for sea sponges and the egg-laying refuges of the endangered **Loggerhead sea turtle**. In recent years, Lampedusa has increasingly become an immigration point for North African asylum seekers.

The Egadi Islands

Just a few kilometres off the coast of Trapani, **Favignana** and its smaller sisters, **Levanzo** and **Marettimo**, traditionally revolved around tuna fishing but have in recent years become a favourite beach destination for Italians to explore its inlets and coastal grottoes.

Ustica

Though inhabited since the Neolithic period, Ustica *(about 50km/31 miles off Palermo)* is best known for its scuba diving. Its pristine waters are home to Italy's first Marine National Park – an attraction for numerous scuba divers who fan out around the volcanic island and its coves. In recent decades, archaeological excavations have found a large **Bronze-Age village**.

Isole Eolie★★★

The seven sisters lie in a long arc along the northeast coast of Sicily. The "home of the winds" in mythology, this archipelago has extremes of weather even in summer, ranging from still and hot to stormy. The Greek ruins at Lipari attract visitors, but the main draws are sun, sand and sea. The rocky shores are teeming with rich aquatic life: anemones, sponges, algae, crustaceans and molluscs, as well as flying fish, turtles and hammerhead sharks. Boat trips provide good views of the indented coastline, hidden coves and bays.

A BIT OF HISTORY

The Greek myths ascribe the islands to **Aeolus**, the son of Poseidon, whom Zeus made guardian of the winds. He ruled over an island encircled by walls of bronze. The hero **Odysseus** (Ulysses) temporarily sheltered on the Aeolians during his travels, where he met the monster Polyphemus. These islands were created by shifting tectonic plates that ripped open a giant chasm on the bed of the Tyrrhenian Sea. The released magma hardened into a great volcanic outcrop, some 1,000m–3,000m/3,000ft–10,000ft from the ocean floor, of which only a minute proportion emerges above the water. According to the most recent theories, this happened during the Pleistocene Era, just under a million years ago. The first islands formed were **Panarea, Filicudi** and **Alicudi**.

The youngest islands – **Vulcano** and **Stromboli** – are still active today. Each successive eruption over the millennia threw up everything from pumice stone, a material so light that it floats on water, to great streams of black obsidian, a glassy and friable rock that was made into cutting tools.

The islands' sparse population subsists on fishing, farming (especially vines and the harvesting of capers for salting), quarrying pumice *(as on* **Lipari**, *although this is a dying trade)*, and most of all, albeit for a short season, tourism.

▷ **Population:** 12 000
◔ **Michelin Map:** p398: B1
▤ **Info:** Corso Vittorio Emanuele 202, Lipari ℘090 98 80 095, www.aasteolie.191.it.
▷ **Location:** The two most remote islands, Filicudi and Alicudi, are wild and untamed; Salina is secluded; Lipari and Panarea are popular with tourists. Vulcano and Stromboli are active volcanoes.
⊛ **Don't Miss:** The castle, archaeological museum, boat trips and belvedere Quattrocchi on Lipari; the crater, black beaches and healing mud on Vulcano; the volcano and night-time boat trips on Stromboli; Pollara Beach at Salina; the Bay of Cala Junco on Panarea.
👪 **Kids:** Beaches at Cave di Pomice a Porticello and Canneto.
◕ **Timing:** Plan several days to explore the stunning string of islands. Summer is the best season, barring August. Inter-island trips can take 10 minutes or four hours, depending on your transport and route.

SIGHTS
LIPARI★

This is the largest and most densely populated of the Aeolian Islands. Its physical relief, with areas of gentle lowland, have provided a haven to settlers over the centuries. Inhabited since Antiquity, when it was famous for obsidian, the island has enjoyed several periods of great prosperity, interrupted by frequent incursions and attacks.

In 1544, the Turk **Kaireddin Barbarossa** razed **Porto delle Genti** *(a small hamlet*

GETTING THERE AND AROUND

The **Aeolian islands** are linked to the mainland by hydrofoil *(aliscafo)* and ferry *(traghetto)*. On average, the hydrofoil *(foot-passengers only)* costs twice as much and takes half the time.

Ferries run regularly from **Milazzo** on the main island *(1hr 30min–4hr)* and are operated by **Siremar**; the same agency runs a hydrofoil service *(40min–2hr 45min)*. SNAV also operates a daily hydrofoil service from **Messina**, **Reggio Calabria**, **Palermo** *(Jun–Sept)* and **Cefalù** *(Jun–Sept only; not daily)*. Ferries *(14hr; twice a week)* and hydrofoils *(4hr, Jun–Sept)* also leave from Naples. The former are operated by Siremar and the latter by SNAV. For information and reservations, contact: **Siremar** *(Gruppo Tirrenia)*;

☏*090 92 83 242 (from Italy) or 081 017 1998 (from mobiles and abroad)*, *www.siremar.it*; **SNAV**, Stazione Marittima, Napoli, ☏*081 42 85 555, www.snav.it*; **N.G.I.**, ☏*090 92 83 415, www.ngi-spa.it*; **Ustica Lines**, ☏*090 92 87 821, www.usticalines.it*.

VISITOR INFORMATION

Banking facilities – Banks are available on **Lipari**, **Vulcano** *(in Porto di Levante)* and **Salina** *(in Malfa)*. Visitors should note that the only **cashpoint facilities** in the Aeolians are on Lipari, in Corso Vittorio Emanuele, and that credit cards are NOT universally accepted.

Post offices – Corso Vittorio Emanuele 207, Lipari; Via Risorgimento 130, Santa Maria di Salina; Via Roma, Stromboli.

---

near Lipari), killing or deporting most of the population as slaves to Africa.

The main moorings are in the town of Lipari, served by two ports: the charming and constantly bustling **Marina Corta** is used by the hydrofoils and by smaller craft, and **Marina Lunga**, where the ferries moor *(it is also the site of the town's bus terminal)*.

From here, it is easy to reach the island's other towns: Canneto, Acquacalda, Quattropiani and Pianoconte.

🚗*The best way to explore is by car or moped.*

Boat trips★★ leaving from Marina Corta to Canneto survey the roughly-hewn, indented coastline of the southwestern corner of the island.

Fish port of Lipari

© Jean-Marie Liot/hemis.fr

Città di Lipari★

Lipari is also the name of the main town on the island. At its crest is a fortified citadel and behind, the former Franciscan monastery that now accommodates the town hall.

Two bays sprawl far below. **Marina Corta** is watched over by a little church dedicated to souls in Purgatory – **"Anime del Purgatorio"** *(once isolated on a rock, but now linked to the mainland)* – and by the 17C **Chiesa di San Giuseppe**. Marina Lunga is the larger of the two inlets. The lower town or *città bassa* provides the perfect backdrop for the traditional *passeggiata* or early-evening stroll.

Castle★

Head up to the castle from Piazza Mazzini. The citadel was constructed on a Greek acropolis before being surrounded by walls (13C); it was reinforced by Emperor Charles V (16C) after the town was sacked by Barbarossa. Approach from **Piazza Mazzini**, by the most ancient route. Beyond the Spanish fortifications and the Greek tower (4C BC), with its great medieval portcullis (12C–13C), lies the heart of the citadel.

On the right is a church, Santa Caterina, and beyond it, an **archaeological area** spanning the Bronze Age *(Capo Graziano culture)* through to Hellenistic and ancient Roman times.

Behind sits the **Chiesetta dell' Addolorata** and the 18C **Chiesa dell' Immacolata**. To the left of these, in the centre, stands the cathedral dedicated to the patron saint of the Aeolian Islands, **San Bartolomeo**. Medieval in plan, it was rebuilt under Spanish rule; the façade is 19C.

Museo Archeologico Eoliano★★

Via del Castello. ⏰*Open daily 9am–1.30pm, 3.30–7pm.* ✆€6. ♿ ✆*090 98 80 174.*
Housed in several of the castle buildings, the exhibits of this excellent museum range from prehistoric to classical times. The museum is laid out chronologically and special displays also explore marine archaeology and vulcanology. Most of

Pumice

White, sponge-like and light enough to float on water, pumice stone is used in pharmaceutical processes, cosmetics (it has delicately abrasive properties), buildings (to make earthquake-proof breeze-blocks) and most recently for stone-washed jeans and denim. The pumice from Lipari is of particularly high quality.

the artefacts have been recovered from excavations since 1949.

The section devoted to the **prehistory of Lipari** starts with a room of obsidian artefacts. The glass-like volcanic stone was highly prized for its strength and razor-sharp cutting edge; although fragile, it was crafted into tools and exported widely in antiquity.

The Capo Graziano culture (1800–1400 BC), which takes its name from a site on Filicudi and the ensuing Capo Milazzese culture from Panarea, marks a particularly prosperous period for the islands *(Rooms V and VI)*. The large Mycenean vases – probably traded here for raw materials – support this notion.

The following period (13C–9C BC), known as the Ausonian, is illustrated with one-handled bowls with horn-shaped appendages (probably to ward off evil spirits), which later evolved into stylised forms of animal heads *(Rooms VII–IX)*.

The buildings opposite contain rooms devoted to the prehistory of the smaller islands and to **vulcanology** *(building on the left)*.

The **Greco-Roman period** begins in Room X. After being abandoned for many years, the Lipari acropolis was colonised by Greeks from Knidos and Rhodes (6C BC). Don't miss the cover of the *bothros* (votive pit) dedicated to Aeolus with its handle in the shape of a stone lion.

The chronological displays continue in the building to the north of the cathedral *(the room numbers are reversed in the first three rooms, passing from XVIII*

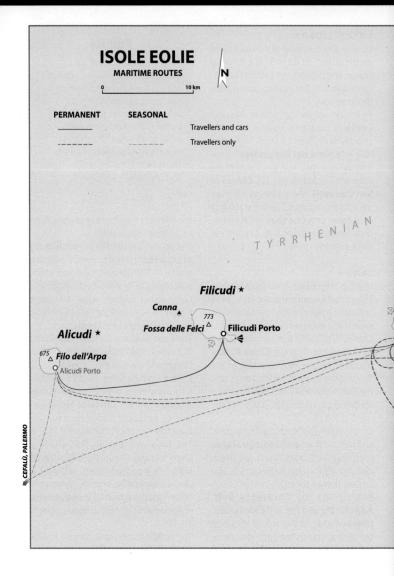

ISOLE EOLIE
MARITIME ROUTES
N
0   10 km

PERMANENT   SEASONAL

Travellers and cars

Travellers only

TYRRHENIAN

Filicudi ★

Canna ▲

Fossa delle Felci △ 773   Filicudi Porto

Alicudi ★

675 △ Filo dell'Arpa
Alicudi Porto

CEFALÙ, PALERMO

to XVII then XVI). The **reconstruction of the Bronze Age necropolis★** (12C BC), which compares burial techniques over a period of time, is particularly interesting. The museum also displays cargo from some 20 trading shipwrecks, including **amphorae★**. Among the fine examples of **red-figure ware★** is a highly unusual scene (360 BC): a naked acrobat balances in a handstand before Dionysus and two comic actors with

exaggerated features. The same case contains three vases by the **"painter of Adrastus"** (King of Argos).

The cult of Dionysus, god not only of wine but also of the theatre and celestial bliss, explains the inclusion among the grave goods recovered from votive pits of **statuettes of actors** and **theatrical masks**.

The museum has an extremely rich, varied and early **collection★★** of such

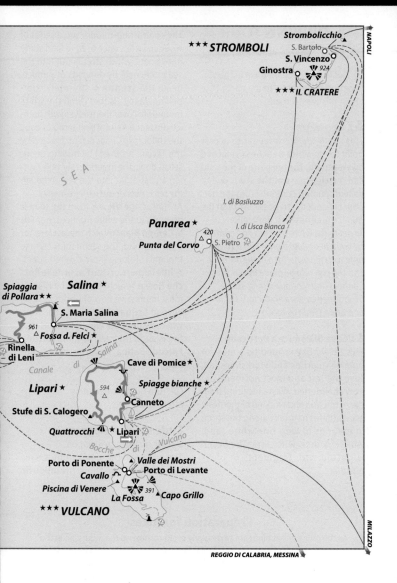

***STROMBOLI**

Strombolicchio
S. Bartolo
S. Vincenzo
Ginostra 924
***IL CRATERE**

NAPOLI

S E A

I. di Basiluzzo

Panarea ★
I. di Lisca Bianca
Punta del Corvo 420 S. Pietro

**Spiaggia
di Pollara** ★★
Salina ★
S. Maria Salina
961 △ **Fossa d. Felci** ★
**Rinella
di Leni**
Canale *di Salina*

Cave di Pomice ★
594 **Spiagge bianche** ★
Lipari ★
Stufe di S. Calogero **Canneto**
Quattrocchi ★ **Lipari**
Bocche di *Vulcano*

Porto di Ponente ▲ **Valle dei Mostri**
Cavallo **Porto di Levante**
Piscina di Venere 391 **Capo Grillo**
La Fossa
***VULCANO**

MILAZZO

REGGIO DI CALABRIA, MESSINA

objects *(Room XXIII)*. Among the masks are those used in productions of plays by **Euripides**, **Sophocles** and **Aristophanes**.

The last part of the museum explores the Hellenistic and Roman periods, with a remarkable quantity of clay lamps, each with its own unique decoration. Several items of earthenware illustrate the Norman, Spanish, Renaissance and Baroque periods.

Parco Archeologico
On the far side of the citadel, on the right.

In the archaeological gardens are aligned numerous sarcophagi. From the terrace there is a lovely **view**★ over the little Church of the Lost Souls, jutting out into the sea opposite Marina Corta, and Vulcano.

🚗 DRIVING TOUR

27km/17mi round trip. Allow half a day.

▶ Set out from Lipari town in the direction of Canneto, to the north along the coastal road.

🧍🧍 Canneto

This small town is a favourite access point for its **white beaches★**, reached by a footpath. The brilliance of the sand and the **clearness of the sea** is due to its high pumice content. From the harbour of Canneto, it is possible to visit the pumice quarries near Porticello.

To get to the white beaches and quarries by boat, negotiate a price and return time with the fishermen at the harbour. This trip can also be made by bus from Canneto and Marina Piccola; ask to be dropped by the only factory still in operation (5min by foot).

🧍🧍 Cave di Pomice a Porticello★

This lovely bay is lined by a mass of pumice quarries and workshops; all, save the last and most northern, are now abandoned. Waste resulting from the extraction and working of the stone accumulates naturally along the shore in mounds of very fine white sand, which hardens with time. The beach is dotted with fragments of black obsidian.

The contrasting colours and a series of wooden jetties once used to load stone onto boats, which stretch out into the sea made pale by deposits of pumice, make the **scene★★** strangely compelling. Many visitors climb the white mounds to cover themselves with pumice dust for a natural skin scrub or copy the children in *Chaos* (a film directed by the Taviani brothers) by hurling themselves down the mounds, roly-poly fashion and straight into the sea *(although the sea is now about a metre away!)*.

At sunset, the **view★** from the road is dramatic as the white pumice pyramids in **Campo Bianco** catch the last rays: for a split second, the scene might evoke thoughts of alpine snow-covered slopes. A little farther on is the **Fossa delle Rocche Rosse**, which features the island's most impressive flow of obsidian.

Beyond **Acquacalda** is Puntazze, from where a wonderful **view★★** opens over five islands: from left to right, **Alicudi**, **Filicudi**, **Salina**, **Panarea** and **Stromboli**.

▶ Turn right immediately after Pianoconte.

Stufe di San Calogero

Site closed for renovation.

The waters of these hot springs have been famed for their therapeutic

---

Preparation for Hikes

As the eruptions at night are particularly exciting, hike up the mountain in the late afternoon and return in the evening *(don't forget to take a torch)*, or the following morning. Allow three hours for the climb up and two hours for the descent. Although the climb is not particularly taxing, it is not recommended for those who suffer from heart problems, asthma or vertigo and should not be undertaken by the faint-hearted, especially in rare cases of bad weather. **Qualified guides** are available on Stromboli; they offer guided walks of the island and afternoon or evening excursions to the crater.

For the ascent, be sure to bring sturdy shoes, a flashlight, a light jacket, water, a pair of long trousers, a spare T-shirt and, if opting to stay the night, a good sleeping-bag and heavier clothing to wear at the top, where the temperature can drop quite dramatically. Though this excursion can be completed year-round, the best time is in late spring when the weather is mild and temperatures are not too high. A night excursion during the summer months can also be very rewarding.

Island of Vulcano seen fron Lipari, Isole Eolie

© Michał Krakowiak / iStockphoto.com

properties since Greco-Roman times. Among the ancient ruins *(alongside a modern spa which, alas, is closed)* is a **domed chamber**. Since recent studies revealed it to be from the Mycenean period, it may be considered the oldest thermal complex and indeed, the only Ancient Greek building still in use today. Here, people splash themselves with water that springs from the ground at a temperature of 60°C/140°F.

Quattrocchi

This viewpoint offers the most spectacular **panoramas**★★ in the archipelago, with Punta di Jacopo and then Punta del Perciato in the foreground. Behind sit treacherous crags of rock known locally as *faraglioni*, while the profile of **Vulcano** interrupts the skyline. As Lipari looms back into the picture, a fine **view**★ opens out onto the town.

VULCANO★★★

According to Greek mythology, it was on this island, with a surface area of 21sq km/8sq mi, that Hephaestus, the god of fire, worked as a blacksmith in his forge with the assistance of the Cyclops. His Roman name (Vulcan) became synonymous with the island

and indeed, with vulcanology: the scientific study of volcanoes.

The very existence of the island results from the fusion of four volcanoes: the largest and most dominant peak, **Vulcano della Fossa**, is a 391m/1,282ft mountain of reddish rock; it is also the most active. Beside it sits the diminutive Vulcanello *(123m/403ft)*, which erupted on the north side in 183 BC to form a round peninsula. The peculiar way these volcanoes behave – spewing acid lava and setting off a series of explosions until the plug is catapulted skywards, thereby releasing large incandescent masses of molten rock – has been classified as **Vulcanian**.

Although the last eruption occurred in 1890, Vulcano is still active; even today, phenomena continue to occur, including *fumaroles* (steam plumes) and sulphurous mud, highly prized for its therapeutic properties. The jagged shoreline resembles tentacles plunging into the sea.

The rock's hue ranges from red to yellow ochre. Together with desolate, lonely scenery, all this gives the island a strangely unnerving, yet outstanding, beauty.

Porto di Levante e Porto di Ponente

The island's main town sits midway between these two ports and borrows both their names. A compact place and full of small shops, it is decorated with contemporary **sculptures** made of lava (Hephaestus and Pandora's Box at the harbour and Aeolus at Rest in the main square).

Ascent to the Crater★★★

Allow 2hr from the end of the main road leading out of Levante.

The road offers fabulous **views★★★** over the archipelago in the foreground and the Vulcanello peninsula.

Lipari lies opposite: on the left is **Salina** – recognisable by its two humps – while in the distance sits **Filicudi** (on a clear day, Alicudi may also be visible). Off to the right, surrounded by its flock of islets, sits **Panarea**, with **Stromboli** some way beyond.

The higher the path climbs, the stronger the smell of sulphur, accompanied by the occasional cloud of steam. At the top, the **sight★★★** is unforgettable: Cratere della Fossa's huge bowl stretches below, its southern rim blurred by clouds of boiling, sulphurous vapours. These fumaroles escape from cracks in the crust with a whistle. The rock is stained yellow ochre and red by the fumes that condense into the most delicate crystals while still hot.

A **tour of the crater★★★** (about 30min) reveals the southern part of the island and, from the highest point, stunning **views★★★** of the archipelago below.

Beaches★

Beware of being scalded in the steam vents.

There are two beaches near the main town: black beaches **(spiagge nere)** – so-called because of the dark lava sand – line the lovely bay of Porto di Ponente, although these tend to become very crowded in summer. The other **(spiaggia delle Fumarole)** has waters that can reach very high temperatures, heated by bubbles of sulphurous steam.

On the opposite side of the island is the remote, and therefore less frequented, **spiaggia del Gelso** (Mulberry Beach), accessible by sea, by bus from Porto del Levante (check timetables as services are highly restricted), or by car along the road from Porto Levante to Vulcano Piano that forks for Gelso and Capo Grillo.

Grotta del Cavallo e la Piscina di Venere

Departures by boat from the black beaches. Take swimwear for Venus' Pool.

The boat skirts around Vulcanello, with its **Valley of Monsters**, before circumnavigating the most jagged part of the coast, then stops at a grotto named after **seahorses** once found in large numbers here. On the left is **Venus' Pool**, a shallow pool of clear water and an idyllic place for an unforgettable swim. (Those who wish to stay for a few hours can go with one of the early boat trips, which run fairly regularly throughout the day, and return on one of the later ones; check with the fisherman for details.)

I Fanghi★

Mud is one of Vulcano's specialities. Leaving the port on the right, behind a rock of incredible colours ranging from every shade of yellow to red, there is a natural pool, the **Laghetto di Fanghi**, sitting in what looks like a pale moonscape. The pool itself contains sulphurous mud with renowned **therapeutic** properties for the skin and circulation, if not for the putrid smell that lingers in the air.

La Valle dei Mostri

On Vulcanello.

A trip at dawn or sunset is particularly recommended when the evocative shapes of the rocks, caught by the sun's rays, are at their most eerie and impressive.

The **Valley of Monsters** consists of a downwards slope of black sand dotted with blocks of lava. These strange shapes suggest prehistoric animals, monsters and wild beasts (including a

View of Stromboli from the sea

© Danin Tulic/Dreamstime.com

bear reared up on its hind legs and a crouching lion).

Capo Grillo

Approx. 10km/6mi from Porto Levante.
The local road to **Vulcano Piano** and beyond to the cape offers a variety of prospects of Lipari and the great crater. From the promontory, there is a splendid **view★** of the archipelago.

STROMBOLI★★★

This island-volcano possesses a sombre, disquieting beauty: the coastline of steep crags is forbidding. The almost total lack of roads, the untamed scenery and most particularly, the volcano – that methodically makes its presence felt with outbursts of fire and brimstone – all have a strange and awesome power of attraction.

Rossellini's 1950 film *Stromboli, terra di Dio* (Stromboli, Land of God) highlighted the difficulties of living in such an elemental place. The volcano plays the main role, while the island is portrayed as the most fascinating and atmospheric of all the Aeolians.

There are two villages: on the northeastern slopes, surrounded by a green mantle, stand the small square white houses of **San Vincenzo** *(where the landing stage is located).*

On the southwestern side is **Ginostra**, which consists of a huddle of about 30 houses clinging to the rock in desperate isolation. It has no roads, just a mule track that winds along the side of the hill. The town is accessible by sea *(although not all year round)* via the smallest port in the world.

The arid, precipitous northern flank, which separates the two villages, is the most impressive, scarred by the **Sciara del Fuoco** – down which the burning lava flows each time the volcano decides to erupt. On 30 December 2002, new vents opened in the volcano and a huge section of the mountain fell into the sea, causing a tidal wave that engulfed boats and houses, fortunately without any loss of life.

Opposite San Vincenzo is the tiny islet of **Strombolicchio**, a single spur of rock resembling a horse's head and topped by a lighthouse.

The Crater★★★

The hike up to the crater of Stromboli makes for a unique and fascinating experience. The route itself is beautiful, opening up unforgettable **views★★** in all directions, before emerging at the top of one of the very few active volcanoes in the world. The crater comprises five vents. A certain feeling of restlessness pervades the place. This atmosphere is charged and heightened by what is going on some few hundred metres away, as with each explosion, incandescent stones are thrust skywards. The spectacle more than compensates for the steep and arduous climb.

Ascent

5hr round trip: From the ferry jetty at San Vincenzo, head for the village centre and follow the tarred road to San Bartolo.

The typical white houses quickly fall away as the mule-track winds up the hill *(follow the signs)*, at first paved with slabs of lava, then, after a few bends, narrowing into a well-worn footpath. After 20min, it reaches an observation point called Punta Labronzo *(refreshments available here and a good view of the craters)*.

Beyond this point, the real climb begins. The path picks through lush vegetation, meandering upward at a moderate incline to a ledge *(✋avoid going too close to the edge)*. The **view★★** of the **Sciara del Fuoco** includes its great black slope, where lava chunks crash from the crater into the sea. The footpath is reduced to a steep track cut deeply into the side of the mountain. This veritable trench, excavated by water erosion, leads to a reddish lava section, where care should be taken in the awkward scramble upwards. After the next easy bit, a fine **view** opens to the left, taking in the town and **Strombolicchio**, now almost 700m/2,300ft below.

At this point, the path climbs onto a broad, steep and sandy ridge up to the summit. Level with the craters, safely tucked behind low, semicircular walls, are the first eruption-viewing points. At this altitude, the craters appear between intermittent clouds of vapour.

A final stretch of ridge leads to the highest point and the **observation point** closest to the crater vents. On days with a favourable light wind, the **view★★★** from here can be truly exceptional, providing an unforgettable experience.

Evening Boat Trip★★★

A night-time excursion is perhaps the most dramatic introduction to the island. Under normal conditions, the rocky **Sciara del Fuoco** makes for an impressive sight; at night the impact is exaggerated a hundredfold. The volcanic eruptions thrust fountains of luminous stones into the black night sky with incredible regularity in nature's most magnificent firework display (in daylight, the emissions merely look grey).

SALINA★

Recognisable by its distinctive two-humped volcanic profile *(hence Didyme, its name in Antiquity, meaning "twins")*, this island is remote and lonely, despite its central location in the archipelago. At one time it comprised six volcanoes, but four have since disappeared. Their historic eruptions have, however, left Salina with a welcome legacy – some of the most fertile soil in the islands. Salina itself derives its modern name from the salt works (a small lake) – now abandoned – at Lingua, a town situated on the south coast.

Today, the island is renowned for two specialities: **capers** that are gathered locally and the famous sweet and strong golden-coloured wine *Malvasia delle Lipari*, made from the island's grapes. The carpet of vines that carry the Malvasia grapes and the profusion of caper flowers both give the island a very fertile feel.

There are two landing stages: **Santa Maria Salina** and the smaller **Rinella di Leni** *(where there is also a campsite that gets extremely crowded during the second and third week of August)*.

Trips Inland

By car or moped (available from small car-hire firms on the island). There is also a local bus service: timetables are displayed at the port of Santa Maria Salina.

A panoramic road offering many **views★** of the jagged coastline links the harbour with the island's other hamlets. From the main town, **Santa Maria Salina**, the road heads northwards, past Capo Faro, on its way to **Malfa**. The coast road climbs above **Punta del Perciato**, a beautiful natural arc visible only from the sea or from the beach a little farther on at

Pollara. Before descending to this stunning **beach**, peep through the vegetation for a glimpse of the house (*private*), where parts of the film *Il Postino (The Postman)* were made. It was here that the meetings between Neruda (*Philippe Noiret*) and the postman (*Massimo Troisi*) took place.

Spiaggia di Pollara★★

There are two paths down to this beautiful bay. One leads to a small anchorage enclosed by its own miniature shoreline of rocks. The other provides access to a broad beach overshadowed by a striking white semicircular cliff wall, a desolate remnant of a crater.

On the way back to Malfa, the road forks inland to **Valdichiesa**, with its popular pilgrimage site – the sanctuary dedicated to the Madonna del Terzito – as well as the town of **Rinella di Leni**.

Fossa delle Felcia

Nestling inside the dormant crater of the taller of Salina's two mountains is a beautiful **fern wood** (known as *Fossa delle Felci*). This protected nature reserve is accessible on foot (*about 2hr at a leisurely pace*) by a path from the Santuario della Madonna del Terzito in Valdichiesa. There is a second track that runs from Santa Maria Salina.

PANAREA★

The smallest Aeolian Island rises to its highest point with **Punta del Corvo** (*420m/1,378ft high*), the western flank of which plunges almost vertically into the sea. The gentler slopes on the eastern side accommodate Panarea's small resident community before terminating in a high black lava coastline, skirted by small pebbled beaches.

The island was settled by the Romans, but archaeological evidence dates back to Mycenaean and earlier inhabitants. In the southeast, around **Punta Milazzese**, lie the remains of a prehistoric village set high above the bay of Cala Junco.

Around the island are scattered islets and rocks, the most notable being the dreaded *formiche*. Hidden just below the

surface, they have been responsible for a large number of shipwrecks along this coastline since earliest times.

FILICUDI★

Fringed by steep slopes and a coastline of mostly basalt rock, this small island consists of a group of craters, the highest being the **Monte Fossa delle Felci** (*773m/2,535ft*), traversed by a few faintly-cut paths. About 250 souls reside here, mainly in three sleepy hamlets.

From the island's landing stage at **Filicudi Porto**, it is easy to reach the **prehistoric village** situated on the promontory of **Capo Graziano** (*about 40min there and back*). This contains the remains of about 25 roughly oval huts. The settlement dates from the Bronze Age and was transferred from its original site closer to the shore for better defence (*see also the Archaeological Museum at Lipari, where finds from this site are displayed*).

From here, there is a beautiful **view★** of the bay, the summit of **Fossa delle Felci** and **Alicudi** (*in the distance on the left*). If approaching by sea, stop at the huge cave called **Grotta del Bue Marino**, whose lava red walls are barely visible in the pitch-black interior.

The tall volcanic chimney-stack formation (*faraglioni*) just offshore is known as **La Canna** (stick or cane) on account of its shape.

ALICUDI★

The most isolated of the Aeolian Islands, Alicudi consists of a round cone covered with purple heather (*hence its ancient name, "Ericusa"*).

Tombs from the 9C were uncovered here by archaeologists in 1904, but there is little else to suggest the island was permanently settled in ancient times – one possible suggestion is that it was used purely as a burial ground by some of the other Aeolian islands. Today it is inhabited by no more than 140 people, living a remote way of life that has remained virtually unchanged for centuries. Here, with the bustle of mainland Italy a world away, life continues at an easy pace – there are no real navigable roads, instead the network around the island consists of variously challenging volcanic stone paths. Walking – along with mules (invariably overloaded with people and their goods) – are the only real means of getting around.

A single village, **Alicudi Porto**, groups one small church and a handful of white and pastel-coloured houses at the foot of the mountain; its slopes rise up past the **Timpone delle Femmine** - fissures in the rock where local women used to hide from pirates – to the **Filo d'Arpa** (literally, "Harp String"), the indentation of an ancient crater.

The rather taxing hike up to this point rewards you with a **magnificent view★** out over coastline that drops precipitously to the sea. Marked with caves on the way (✎ follow the footpath as it snakes from Chiesa di San Bartolo up through the cultivated terraces; the walk takes about 1hr 45min to the summit and back at a brisk pace).

There is little shade on this walk, so take a sunhat, plenty of water and sunscreen with you during the summer months.

ADDRESSES

STAY

The price of accommodation follows the seasons and is quite high on the islands, where everything closes from November to March. A double room in low season costs €60–80, but prices double at Easter and in August. In addition to traditional hotels, more moderately priced accommodation is available in rented rooms and flats (contact the tourist office for a detailed list of what's available).

LIPARI

Baia Unci Campeggio – Via Marina Garibaldi, Loc. Canneto, Lipari. ℘090 98 11 909. www.baiaunci.com. Closed mid-Oct–mid-Mar. For visitors who enjoy the outdoors, this campsite is ideally placed by the sea, in one of Lipari's delightful bays. Fully equipped with modern facilities, the campsite also has a beach, where deckchairs, parasols and boats are available for hire.

Hotel Oriente – Via Marconi 35, Lipari. ℘090 98 11 493. www.hoteloriente lipari.com. Closed Nov–Easter. 32 rooms. This small, family-run hotel in the centre has simple rooms and a pleasant garden. The owner's interest in ethnography is reflected in his large collection of traditional Aeolian artefacts.

Hotel Poseidon – Via Ausonia 7, Lipari. ℘090 98 12 876. www.hotelposeidon lipari.com. Closed Nov–Feb. 18 rooms. This central hotel is built in typical Mediterranean style with vivid blue and white tones. The fully-equipped rooms are spotless, with modern, practical furnishings. Service is polite and there's a pleasant sun terrace.

Villa Augustus – Via Ausonia 16, Lipari. ℘090 98 11 232. www.villaaugustus. it. Closed Nov–Feb. 34 rooms. Hidden among the alleyways of the historical centre, this hotel is situated in an old patrician villa, with a pleasant reception area, spacious lounge and well-appointed rooms. Breakfast is served on an attractive patio brimming with plants and flowers.

VULCANO

Hotel Conti – Loc. Porto Ponente, Vulcano. ℘090 98 52 012. www.contivulano. it. Closed 21 Oct–Apr. 67 rooms. This Mediterranean-style hotel is situated near the thermal baths. Housed in a number of different buildings, the rooms are simply furnished and all have their own private entrance. All lie just a stone's throw from the famous black sandy beaches.

Hotel Orsa Maggiore – Via Porto Ponente, Vulcano. ℘090 98 52 018. www.orsamaggiorehotel.com. Closed Nov–Mar. 25 rooms. A delightful garden and a refreshing swimming pool are two of the highlights of this bright white hotel. Situated near the port, it has comfortable communal areas and simple, but well-maintained rooms. The hotel restaurant specialises in fish dishes.

STROMBOLI

B & B Ginostra – Località Ginostra. ℘090 98 11 787 or 338 04 26 790. www. ginostrabb.com. 4 rooms. This B&B overlooking the sea is dominated by hues of white and blue. The breakfast buffet is served in a delightful garden. Friendly and quiet.

Locanda del Barbablù – Via Vittorio Emanuele 17/19. ℘090 98

61 18. www.barbablu.it. Closed Nov–Feb.
6 rooms. 🍽 €30/50. Travellers enjoy
a friendly welcome in this inn with very
pleasant rooms where modern art has
been artfully paired with a selection
of antiques. The daily menu includes a
range of dishes to suit all tastes.

SALINA

⊖⊜🍴 **Hotel Santa Isabel** – Via
Scalo 12, Malfa. 4.5km/2mi NE of Pollara
beach. ☏090 98 44 018. www.santaisabel.it.
Close Nov–Apr. 12 rooms 🍽 €25/35.
Ideally situated with panoramic views
over the crystal-clear sea and the beach.
The spacious rooms each have a living
room and sloping ceilings. The restaurant
serves fish dishes and local specialities.

FILICUDI

⊖⊜🍴 **Hotel La Canna** – Contrada Rosa.
☏090 98 89 956. www.lacannahotel.it.
🅿 🛋. 8 room. 🍽 (Jul–Aug, double room
halfboard €214). Overlooking the port
and the sea, this series of Aeolian-
style buildings blends perfectly into
its surroundings. Two romantic rooms
with small terraces are reserved for
newlyweds; a sundeck and swimming
pool are available for the use of all guests.

ALICUDI

⊖⊜🍴🍴 **Hotel Ericusa** – Via Regina
Elena. ☏090 98 89 902. www.alicudihotel.it.
Closed Oct–May. 20 rooms. 🍽 Halfboard
and full board. This small hotel – the only
one of its kind in the area - gives directly
onto the beach. The menu is prepared
using fresh vegetables and the catch of
the day. Great for anyone who enjoys sun,
sea and solitude!

🍴EAT

LIPARI

⊖⊜🍴 **La Ginestra** – Loc. Pianoconte,
5km/3mi NW of Lipari. ☏090 98 22 285.
Fish and antipasti are displayed in the
dining room and meals are generally
served on the covered terrace.

⊖⊜🍴 **Filippino** – Piazza Municipio,
Lipari. ☏090 98 11 002. www.filippino.it.
Closed Mon (except Jun–Sept), mid-Nov–
mid-Dec.🖿. Compulsory 12% service
charge. This centuries-old restaurant
is renowned throughout Sicily for
its wonderful fish, which is prepared
according to traditional recipes. It has
a relaxed atmosphere, friendly service
and a delightful **view** of Piazza della
Rocca.

⊖⊜🍴🍴 **E Pulera** – Via Isa Conti,
Lipari. ☏090 98 11 158. www.pulera.it.
Closed lunchtime and Nov–May. Booking
recommended. Compulsory 12% service
charge. E Pulera has a garden for dining.
In July and August, a menu of typical
Aeolian dishes is accompanied by
music and folk dancing.

VULCANO

⊖⊜ **Don Piricuddu** – Via Lentia 33.
☏090 98 52 039. Closed Tues, Mar and
Oct–mid-April. Reservation recommended.
This friendly restaurant offers quality
service and dishes made from fresh fish,
served in the dining room or on the
spacious terrace overlooking one of the
town's main streets.

⊖⊜🍴 **Il Diavolo dei Polli** – Loc.
Cardo, Vulcano. ☏090 98 53 034. Closed
Oct–Mar. Booking recommended. This
family-run establishment has a spacious
dining room adorned with decorative
plates and maritime paintings. The
restaurant serves specialities from the
Aeolian interior, which are beautifully
presented with great attention to detail.

STROMBOLI

⊖⊜🍴 **Punta Lena** – Via Marina, Loc.
Ficogrande, Stromboli. ☏090 98 62 04.
Closed Nov–Apr. The Punta Lena is
renowned for its high-quality fresh
fish and delicious seafood specialities
served under an arbour with
magnificent **sea views**.

SALINA

⊖⊜🍴 **Da Franco** – Via Belvedere 8,
Loc. Santa Marina Salina, Salina.
☏090 98 43 287. Closed Dec. This simple
restaurant is easy to find in the upper
part of the village. Its delightful terrace
and veranda with wonderful **views** are
the setting for cuisine that relies heavily
on the sea.

TAKING A BREAK

LIPARI

Pasticceria Subba – Corso Vittorio
Emanuele 92, Lipari. ☏090 98 11 352.
Since 1930, this *pasticceria* has been
making fabulous cakes and pastries, such
as *cannoli* (filled with ricotta cheese),
cassate (brimming with candied fruit),
pasta paradiso (almond cake with fine
strips of citron peel), *nacatuli* (puff pastry
made with Malvasia wine and filled with
almond paste and mandarin juice), as
well as delicious ice cream.

VULCANO

Bar Ritrovo Remigio – *Via Vulcano 1, Porto Levante, Vulcano. 090 98 52 085.* This café offers an enticing selection of typical local specialities such as **cannoli**, **cassate** and **granite**, as well as delicious profiteroles.

SHOPPING

The famous *Malvasia delle Lipari* is a strong, sweet, golden wine made from grapes that have been left to wither on the vine. Its smooth, aromatic flavour makes it an excellent dessert wine. The DOC-endorsed variety, produced only on the islands, must bear the words *"Malvasia delle Lipari"* in full.

OUTDOOR FUN

Diving – To rent snorkels or scuba gear, take a guided dive or join a PADI course, contact the Diving Center La Gorgonia, Salita San Giuseppe, Lipari; *090 98 12 616; mobile 335 57 17 567; www.lagorgoniadiving.it*

Mud therapy on Vulcano – Vulcano's muds are renowned for their rich sulphurous content and special treatments are recommended for those with rheumatic ailments and dermatological conditions (greasy skin, acne, psoriasis). Mud baths are NOT recommended for expectant mothers or those suffering from tumours or with fevers, heart conditions, osteoporosis, gastrointestinal upsets, diabetes or hyperthyroidism.

If you have any doubt as to whether you should have a mud treatment, consult a doctor beforehand. Recommendations for use are short immersions (never more than 20min at a time), taken in the coolest hours of the day and then followed by a hot shower. Do not apply mud to the eyes. In the event of mud getting into the eyes, rinse liberally with fresh water. If you develop any ailments as a result of the mud, consult a doctor immediately.

FESTIVALS

Festa di San Bartolomeo – The festival of St Bartholomew is held on Lipari from 21–24 August, finishing at Marina Corta with a magnificent display of fireworks set off from the sea.

TOURS

SNAV and **Siremar** operate regular services between the islands. Departure times are usually posted up at the port.

Taranto Navigazione runs mini-cruises day and night, with departures from Milazzo, Capo d'Orlando, Patti and Vulcano. *Contact Tar.Nav., Via dei Mille 40, Milazzo; 090 92 23 617; www.minicrociere.com.*

Gruppo di Navigazione Regina also organises excursions from Milazzo with climbs up Stromboli. *Contact 090 98 22 237 or 339 74 86 560 (mobile); www.navigazioneregina.com.*

Boat trips – The easiest and most congenial way to explore the islands is by rubber dinghy. However, given the exorbitant cost of hiring one, there is always the option of joining an excursion to **Stromboli** from **Lipari** or **Vulcano** *(from the other islands, the boats are smaller and the services less frequent)*. Even at night, the "Strombolian explosions" can be watched from the sea. Tours also leave from **Filicudi** and **Alicudi**, **Panarea** and **Salina**.

The trips usually take in all the islands; they sometimes include stops for swimming and for brief visits to the main towns. Excursions can last a whole day *(departing around 9am and returning between 5pm and 7pm)* or half a day *(departing early afternoon and returning late in the evening, as for the Stromboli evening trip)*.

On land – The best way to explore the islands is to rent a bicycle or moped. *Contact the tourist office for info.*

Excursions on Stromboli – Visitors to the volcano are charged a tax of €3 and must be accompanied by a guide *(ensure the leader is qualified)*. *Contact the CAI-AGAI, Porto di Scari e Piazza San Vincenzo, Stromboli. 090 98 62 11. Another option is **Magmatrek**, Via Vittorio Emanuele, 090 98 65 768, www.magmatrek.it.*

Isole Egadi★★

Isole Egadi is made up of three tiny islands at the western tip of Sicily. Favignana is famed for its tuna fishing and a favourite with tourists. Levanzo, with its smattering of hotels, is more remote but still in touch with civilisation. Marettimo, virtually tourist-free, is perfect for indulging in desert island fantasies.

A BIT OF HISTORY

The islands have been inhabited since prehistoric times *(Levanzo and Favignana may even have been part of the main island in the Palaeolithic era)*. Here, the treaty ending the First Punic War (241 BC) was signed when Carthage assigned Sicily to the Roman Empire. After changing hands many times over the centuries, the islands were sold in 1640 to the Pallavicino-Rusconi family. The Florios purchased them in 1874.

SIGHTS
FAVIGNANA★★

The nearest of the Egadis to the Sicilian mainland, this island is often referred to as *La Farfalla* on account of its shape, likened to a butterfly.

Its proper name is, in fact, derived from *favonio*, the prevalent local wind. In times past, the principle profession here was tuna fishing and the **mattanza** (the traditional, but bloody ritual of syste-

▶ **Population:** 4 358
◔ **Michelin Map:** p398: A1
▯ **Info:** Piazza Madrice 8, Favignana, ℘0923 92 00 11, www.favignana.com.
◖ **Location:** Favignana, the largest of the three islands and the most accessible, is popular with holidaymakers. Levanzo, the smallest island, and Marettimo, the most inaccessible, have fewer traditional tourist facilities and appeal to visitors looking for a simpler holiday, surrounded by peaceful landscapes.
⊘ **Don't Miss:** The quarries of Favignana, the superb cave paintings in the Genovese grotto on Levanzo and sea caves of Maretimo.
♟ **Kids:** Sandy beaches at Cala Azzurra and Lido Burrone.
◷ **Timing:** Avoid August, when all Italy goes on holiday. In May and June, crowds fill Favignana for the tuna rituals. A small ferry connects this island to Levanzo (10–25min) and to Marettimo (30min–2hr).

Cala Rossa, Favignana

© Maniapixel/Dreamstime.com

GETTING THERE AND AROUND

Several hydrofoil and ferry services *(especially during the summer)* operate every day out of **Trapani** and **Marsala** *(20–60min by hydrofoil and 1hr by ferry)*.

For information, contact: **Siremar**, *℘091 74 93 111 (from Italian land lines)* or *081 017 1998 (from mobile phones)*; www.siremar.it; or **Ustica Lines**, Via Amm. Staiti 23, Trapani, *℘0923 87 38 13; www.usticalines.it*.

The same company runs services between **Trapani–Favignana–Levanzo–Ustica–Naples**.

The **Favignana–Naples** crossing takes approx. 6hr.

matically killing the tuna trapped in the nets, known as the *camera della morte* – "room of death").

Favignana covers an area of about 20sq km/12.4sq mi. The west "wing" is dominated by **Montagna Grossa**, which, despite its name, rises to a mere 302m/991ft. The eastern part, on the other hand, is flatter and harbours the island's main town. The jagged coastline is interrupted, here and there, with short stretches of sandy beach.

Tufa caves

Quarrying was the island's secondary source of employment. Once cut, the blocks were transported elsewhere in Sicily and exported to North Africa. These quarries, a characteristic feature of the island's eastern flank, give the landscape a disturbing quality.

Great gaping, rectangular, stepped cavities mar the cliffs. These are often overgrown, used as refuse dumps or transformed into secret small gardens, sheltered from the marauding winds. Along the east coast, some sites have been partly flooded by waves to leave behind small, geometric pools of water. The most spectacular quarries are those grouped around **Scalo Cavallo**, **Cala Rossa** and **Bue Marino**.

Favignana città

The main town of the island – indeed, of the archipelago – is built around a small port that nestles in a large bay. On the skyline, perched up on its very own hill, sits the **Fort of Santa Caterina** *(now under military control),* which began life as an ancient Saracen warning station. It was rebuilt by the Norman King Roger II and subsequently enlarged before serving as a prison under Bourbon rule (1794–1860).

Down by the seafront, Favignana boasts two buildings from the **Florio** family, a

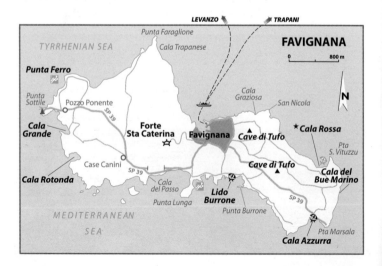

La Mattanza

The complex and ritual method of catching tuna follows – or rather *used* to follow – very precise rules, timings and strictly disciplined practices.

These were established by the **Rais**, head of the tuna fishermen and at one time, also the head of the village: a sort of shaman who specified when it should begin and what procedure should be followed. The methods date back to ancient times, indeed possibly even to the Phoenicians. However, it was not until Arab domination that the most fundamental elements of the "rite" were firmly established. For the *mattanza* was a ritual, complete with its own songs (the *scialome*), concluding in a cruel struggle with these powerful creatures at very close quarters. The outcome, however, was a foregone conclusion and rarely, if ever, in the tuna's favour.

In late spring, the tuna collect in great shoals off the west coast of Sicily where conditions are conducive to breeding. The fishing boats used to lay the nets in a long corridor, which the tuna were forced to follow. The last nets were dropped like barriers to form antechambers, thus averting the risk of overloading and tearing the nets, and losing fish. Beyond these antechambers was laid the *camera della morte* – the "room of death" –an enclosure of tougher netting, often closed along the bottom. When an appropriate number of fish arrived, the Rais would order the *mattanza* to begin. The tuna, exhausted from escape attempts and panicked, injured each other in the press. One by one, they were speared or hooked and heaved aboard.

The term *mattanza* comes from the Spanish word "matar", to kill, which derives from the Latin *mactare*, meaning to glorify, or immolate.

wealthy dynasty involved in the production and export of Marsala wine before it developed its tuna fishing business. These comprise the **Palazzo Florio**, built in 1876, and the great **tonnara** or tuna fishery, now being transformed into a multi-use centre.

The modest town centres around two piazzas: Europa and Madrice, linked by the main street, perfect for a *passeggiata* (evening stroll). On the northeastern edge of town lies the historic district of San Nicola *(behind the cemetery)*, which remains private property and closed to visitors.

Bathing and beaches★

There are two main beaches: a small, sandy bay south of the town, below the lighthouse, in **Cala Azzurra**, and to the southwest, the popular, and more inviting, broad sandy stretch known as the 👥 **Lido Burrone**. *(A bus runs there hourly.)* The rocky bays on this side of the island are more exciting and thrilling to visit, notably those under the towering tufa cliffs at the spectacular **Cala Rossa★** and **Cala del Bue Marino**

nearby. Once quarries, these cliffs are still riddled with a network of long, dark and mysterious passages, where the roof has not collapsed.

The other half of the island contains lovely bays such as the **Cala Rotonda** *(where local legend has it Odysseus was washed up after doing battle with the Cyclops)*, **Cala Grande** and **Punta Ferro**, also a popular area for diving.

The caves

The west side of the mountain slopes into the sea, forming a number of evocative caves and grottoes. On calm summer mornings, local fishermen vie with each other to whisk visitors off to see the most picturesque: **Grotta Azzurra** *(Azure Grotto)*, **Grotta dei Sospiri** *(The Grotto of Sighs, which sounds its laments in winter)* and **Grotta degli Innamorati** *(Lovers' Grotto)* – two identical rocks standing side by side.

LEVANZO★

Tiny Levanzo *(pronounced with an emphasis on the first syllable)* has a surface area of 6sq km/2sq mi, and undulates with pastoral charm. Goats and sheep graze quietly on the sides of its many hills. The tallest of these, Pizzo del Monaco *(278m/912ft)*, tumbles its jaggedly rocky terrain down into the sea; it's a particularly beautiful section of the southwest coast.

Only one road bisects the island from south to north, making this a veritable haven of peace and serenity. The northern part of the island consists of a succession of sheer drops, rocky outcrops and secluded little creeks. Between Levanzo and the coast of Sicily lie two minute islets, **Maraone** and **Formica** *(on which you will find the remains of an old tuna fishery)*.

Cala Dogana

The only hamlet on Levanzo is little more than a clutch of houses overlooking a bay of the clearest water on the south side of the island. From here, a well-kept path snakes to the bays of the southwestern coast, each tightly embracing its own miniature pebbled beach, as far as the *Faraglione* (a large rock). Beyond you'll find a rocky path that leads north up the coast to the **Grotta del Genovese**.

Grotta del Genovese★

Accessible on foot (approx. 2hr there and back), by jeep and then on foot along a steep slope, or by sea. To visit the cave, contact Signore Castiglione in Levanzo. ℘0923 92 40 32 or 339 74 18 800. www.grottadelgenovese.it.

Discovered in 1949, this excavated hollow in the side of a tall cliff bears the marks of prehistoric man. Remains of wall-painting here have been identified as dating from the Upper Palaeolithic era, while the incised drawings may be from the Neolithic period. The *graffiti*, now located behind glass near the entrance, completed when the island was still attached to the island of Sicily, represent bison and a **deer★★** of the most pleasing proportions and elegance. The charcoal and animal fat paintings represent early attempts at fishing *(stylised representations of both tuna and dolphins are discernible)*, animal

husbandry *(a woman leads a cow with a halter)* and ritual images of men dancing and women with wide hips.

MARETTIMO★

This steep, rocky mountain with tall limestone cliffs is the remotest of the Egadi islands. Curious visitors arriving at its tiny harbour have only one option if they wish to stay on the island: simple rooms rented out by local fishermen. *(See www.marettimoresidence.it.)*

At the foot of the mountain nestles the hamlet of Marettimo, a compact collection of square, flat-roofed white houses and terraces interspersed with splashes of colourful bougainvillea. Behind the Scalo Nuovo *(the main dock)* stands the Scalo Vecchio reserved for the local fishermen. To one side extends **Punta Troia**, topped with the ruins of a Spanish castle (17C) that served as a prison until 1844. A series of rugged paths *(manageable most easily astride a donkey)* lead to the remote and wild upland.

Boat Trip Around the Island★★

In the harbour, many local fishermen offer excursions to the numerous caves that hide among the precipitous cliffs along the coast. The most striking include the **Grotta del Cammello**, sheltering a small pebble beach, **Grotta del Tuono** (Cave of Thunder), **Grotta Perciata** and the **Grotta del Presepio**. Many will leave you to swim and pick you up later for an extra fee. The island's clean and clear waters are popular with both snorkellers and divers.

ADDRESSES

🏠 STAY

In addition to several traditional hotels, a number of **rooms** are also available for rent *(apply to the Pro Loco for names and addresses)*.

FAVIGNANA

🛏 **Camping Villaggio Egad** – *Contrada Arena, Favignana. ℘0923 92 15 67. www.egadi.com/egad/. Closed Oct–Apr.* This beautiful campsite just 1km/0.6mi from the centre of Favignana is surrounded by pine, eucalyptus, acacia and oleander. A number of small apartments with modern bathrooms and kitchens are also available for rent.

⌖ **L'Oasi Viillaggio** – *Contrada Camaro 32, Favignana. ℘0923 92 16 35. www.loas ifavignana.it. Closed Oct–mid-Apr. 25 rooms* ⌸. This family-run hotel is located in a peaceful setting in close proximity to the town centre. The recently renovated rooms are comfortable, well-appointed and arranged around a garden with tropical plants, pines and other Mediterranean vegetation.

⌖⌸⌸ **Egadi Hotel** – *Via Colombo 17, Favignana. ℘0923 92 12 32. www.albergo egadi.it. Closed Oct–mid-Apr. 12 rooms* ⌸. This hotel is one of the best-known and most popular on the island. The staff here are friendly and helpful, and the rooms simple, attractive and well-maintained.

⌖⌸⌸ **Aegusa** – *Via Garibaldi 11/17, Favignana. ℘0923 92 24 30. www.aegusa hotel.it. Closed end Oct–Mar. 28 rooms* ⌸. *Restaurant* ⌸⌸⌸. The Aegusa hotel has bright, airy rooms with simple wicker furniture and a friendly, sunny holiday atmosphere. The restaurant, set in a pleasant garden-courtyard, offers a reasonably priced menu, with a wide selection of great fish dishes and traditional cuisine.

LEVANZO

⌸⌸⌸ **Pensione Paradiso** – *Via Lungomare 6. ℘0923 924080. 14 rooms* ⌸.*Restaurant* ⌸⌸. Welcome to "Paradise": this small, traditional pensione offers quiet rooms, most of them with sea **views**. Good meals available.

⌸⌸⌸ **Pensione dei Fenici** – *Via Lungomare. ℘0923 924 083/056. 10 rooms.* ⌸. Large, bright spacious rooms in a small hotel close to the port. Family cooking.

⌖EAT

FAVIGNANA

⌸⌸⌸ **La Bettola** – *Via Nicotera 47, Favignana. ℘0923 92 19 88. Closed Thu (winter) and Jan.* ⌸. This typical trattoria serves traditional Egadian cuisine using fresh, local ingredients. The ambience is simple and typical of the islands.

⌸⌸⌸ **Amici del Mare** – *Piazza Marina. ℘0923 922596.* Huge restaurant with a sea-themed decor and terrace on the harbour. You'll find a very well-stocked

antipasti buffet, along with fish and pasta dishes at reasonable prices. Be sure to check the bill.

MARETTIMO

⌸⌸⌸ **Il Timone** – *Via Garibaldi 18. ℘0923 92 31 42. Closed mid-Oct–Mar.* ⌸. *Booking recommended.* Located in a narrow street, this small restaurant with a traditional blue and white décor serves fresh fish dishes with homemade pasta.

LEVANZO

⌖ If you are only spending a day on the island, bring a picnic or stock up at the grocery store *(Erina – Via Calvario 1)*. There is a picnic area at **Cala Minnola**.

SHOPPING

Favignana's most popular specialities are *bottarga* (dried tuna-fish roe) and *bresaola* (cured or smoked) tuna and swordfish.

ACTIVITIES

Mopeds and bicycles – The two most convenient ways of exploring Favignana are by bicycle or moped. You'll find plenty of hire options walking around town. Cycling is especially popular on this flat and easy terrain.

Diving and snorkelling – The best areas for diving and snorkelling are **Punta Marsala**, **Secca del Toro**, the submerged cave between **Cala Rotonda** and **Scoglio Corrente**, and the rocks off **Punta Fanfalo** and **Punta Ferro**. For **scuba diving** in Favignana, there are two clubs in Punta Lunga: **Posidonia Blu Diving Center**, *Punta Lungo, ℘0923 921 302 or 339 862 01 16, www.posidoniablu. com*, and **Progetto Atlantide**, *℘347 517 83 38 or 347 978 62 15, www.progetto atlantide.com*. In Marettimo, contact **Marettimo Diving Center** – *Via Cuore di Gesù, ℘0923 923 083 or 333 79 94 017, www.marettimodivingcenter.it*.

TOURS

Elyos – *Piazza Madrice 37, Favignana. ℘0923 92 25 87. www.arcipelagoegadi.it.* This tourist cooperative organises tours and boat excursions, as well as airport transfers and more.

Medi@tour – *℘ 0923 923196 or 339 77 29 404. www.marettimoweb.it.* Organises boat excursions, walks and diving trips.

Pantelleria★★

With its meandering coastline, strong winds, steep black terraced slopes and *dammusi* – centuries-old domed, cubic houses of Arabic origin with thick lavastone walls – the island of Pantelleria, also known as the "black pearl of the Mediterranean", is simply exceptional. Montagna Grande, the highest point on the island at 836m/2 743ft, is planted with vineyards whose partially sun-dried grapes are used to produce the sweet Passito di Pantelleria. Enjoying a rich and complex history, Pantelleria suffered invasion by the Phoenicians, Carthaginians, Greeks, Romans, Vandals, Byzantines, Moors and Normans, who united the island with Sicily in 1123.

🚗 DRIVING TOURS

ISLAND CIRCUIT★★
Approx. 40km/25mi round trip.

A scenic road winds its way around the coast, providing glorious **views** of the landscape at every turn.

Pantelleria

The houses of the island's main built-up area are clustered around the harbour. As one of the main German bases in the Mediterranean during the Second World War, the town of Pantelleria was flattened by Allied bombs. Post-war reconstruction done without any formal planning replaced the idyllic, original layout with a mish-mash of charmless concrete cubes.

As a result, the town is a slightly dis-appointing introduction to this beautiful island. The main landmark is the brooding black **Castello Barbacane**, probably founded in Roman times. Since then it has been demolished and rebuilt on a number of occasions. Its partially-restored interior is sometimes open to visitors *(check at the tourist office for the current access).*

▶ **Population:** 7,736
🕐 **Michelin Map:** p398: A2.
ℹ **Info:** Tourist office - Vicolo Leopardi 5. ℘0923 91 17 98. www.pantelleria.com.
▶ **Location:** Pantelleria is the largest of Sicily's satellite islands *(83sq km/32sq mi)*; it is also the most westerly, lying 84km/52mi from the African continent at the same latitude as Tunisia. Its warm climate, however, is constantly tempered by strong winds blowing in from the sea, hence the island's Arabic name *Qawsarah* or *Bent el Rion*, meaning "Daughter of the Wind".
👪 **Kids:** Island boat trips, picnics at La Montagna Grande.
🅿 **Parking:** Parking is available near the official picnic sites at La Montagna Grande and on the outskirts of Nika *(walk into the town)*.
👁 **Don't Miss:** Dramatic views at Scauri, Nika and La Montagna Grande, boat tours of the island, Panteschi gardens at Rekhale and the Grotta Benikula.
🕐 **Timing:** A round trip of the island by car is just 40km/25mi. Leave half a day to a whole day to explore, depending on your schedule.

Look out for the plaque on the wall facing the harbour, dedicated to the anti-Mafia judge Paolo Borsellino, who was assassinated in Palermo in 1992.

▶ Follow the west coast, heading south.

A Unique Landscape

Dammuso house and low-lying plantations

© Lifeinapixel / Fotolia.com

Volcanic land – The highest point on the island is **Montagna Grande** *(836m/2,742ft)*, an ancient crater. Its rocky black lava coastline is riddled with caves and small headlands projecting into the sea. Being volcanic, the land mass is extremely fertile and well-drained, and therefore suited to the cultivation of the vine. Solimano, a sparkling wine with a delicate bouquet, and sweet Passito di Pantelleria, made with sun-dried *zibibbo* (Muscat of Alexandria) grapes are the island's principal specialities.

Salted capers are another local delicacy, harvested from plants abundant with exquisitely delicate flowers.

Various features caused by volcanic activity are still much in evidence on Pantelleria: hot springs emerge from the sea floor just off the coast, sulphuric vapour emanates from natural caves and jets of steam (known locally as *favare*) intermittently escape from the rock, especially in the vicinity of the craters.

Evolution of a house style – The first residents of Pantelleria may have come from Africa in Neolithic times to extract obsidian, which at that time was highly sought-after. Near to a village dating from this period are a number of megalithic funerary structures that are distinctive to the island, known locally as **sesi**, although similar in shape to the *nuraghi* of Sardinia.

Next came the Phoenicians: they called the island "Kossura" and provided it with a large harbour on the spot occupied by the modern main port. Waves of Carthaginians, Romans, Vandals, Byzantines and Arabs followed, who boosted local agriculture by introducing cotton, olives and figs, and improving the cultivation of the vine. Many of the island's farming communities still preserve their original Arab names: **Khamma**, **Gadir**, **Rakhali**, **Bukkuram**, **Bugeber** and **Mursia**.

During World War II, Pantelleria's strategic position in the middle of the Canale di Sicilia separating North Africa from Italy, earned it the attentions of the Fascist government, which began to fortify it. As a result, it was subject to systematic bombing raids in 1943 by the Allies based on the Tunisian coast.

The traditional house found on Pantelleria is the **dammuso**, which is Arab in origin. Built with square stones and a undulating roof that doubles as a terrace, many have been bought up and converted into summer homes.

The inhabitants of Pantelleria, who traditionally tend to be farmers rather than sailors, have found ingenious ways of dealing with the area's strong winds and restricted tree heights (even the olive trees have been adapted to grow at ground level by pruning them into a circular fan of low-lying espaliers). The **Pantesco garden**, a circular or square enclosure with high stone walls, is a sanctuary for citrus trees, which are protected from the wind. Sometimes these gardens are attached to a house, while others are situated in the centre of a field.

GETTING THERE

The quickest and easiest way of getting to the island from mainland Italy is by **air** (Aeroporto di Pantelleria, ☏0923 91 11 72, www.aeroportodipantelleria.it; 5km/3mi south of Pantelleria town). There are direct flights from **Trapani** and **Palermo**; during the summer, services also operate from **Rome** and **Milan**. A shuttle bus links the airport to **Piazza Cavour** in **Pantelleria**. Those already in Sicily, ideally near Trapani, might consider the **ferry** travelling overnight on the outward journey (6hr) and returning by day (5hr). For information contact **Siremar** ☏090 92 83 242 (from Italy) or 081 01 71 998 (from abroad and mobile phones); www.siremar.it. **Ustica Lines** (Via Amm. Staiti 23, Trapani, ☏090 92 83 415, www.usticalines.it) operates a **hydrofoil** service (2hr 30min) from June to September.

Villaggio Neolitico

The archaeological site is situated some 3km/1.8mi beyond **Mursia** and the **Kuddie Rosse**, ancient craters of a reddish colour.

The only discernible feature among the low stone field boundary walls and scattered piles of rubble is the **Sese Grande**★ just beyond the quarry, which rises from an elliptical base of large blocks of lava into a kind of tower. It is surrounded by an ornamental ledge that spirals its way up to the top.

The base has 12 entrances serving passages that interconnect the same number of funerary chambers. Here, the dead were entombed in the foetal position, with the head pointing towards the west and surrounded by their personal grave goods.

A little farther on, the rocky black **Punta Fram** points out to sea. Past the tip of the headland, a flight of steps leads down from the right side of the road to the **Grotta di Sataria**, which contains pools of water fed by hot springs.

Scauri★

High on the cliff edge, enjoying a spectacular **position**★, the tiny village of Scauri sits above its picturesque harbour (20min walk) and is fed by **hot springs**. The village itself is little more than a clutch of houses and a couple of small shops, but the cemetery is worth visiting for the marvellous sweeping **views**★ it offers out to **Cape Mustafa** in **Tunisia** on a clear day.

▶ After continuing some way along the coast, park the car and walk into Nikà.

Nikà

30min on foot there and back.
This minuscule fishing port is situated in a **lava gorge**, with a number of **hot springs** emerging from the nearby rocks.

Back on the coastal road, turn left at the junction for **Rekhale**, one of the few villages with **dammusi** and Pantelleria **gardens** in their original state.

Return to the coast, which at this point drops steeply down to the sea. There is a notable sea cave along this stretch (best reached by boat), called the **Grotta di Nika**, where a hot spring rises up.

Saltalavecchia (literally translated as the "old lady's leap") appears after a bend in the road.

The village, perched on the cliff at one of the highest points, has a dramatic **view**★★ down a sheer face to the sea, 150m/500ft below (☏be careful here as the ground can give way).

Balata dei Turchi

This wild and remote **beach** was reputedly where the Saracens used to land on the island unseen. It is one of the few sheltered coves with access to the sea and, protected from the wind, it is handily overgrown with tall vegetation to hide in, notably wild juniper and sweet-smelling pines.

Dietro Isola

The road around the southeastern part of the island provides some splendid coastline **views**★★ dominated here by the jutting headland.

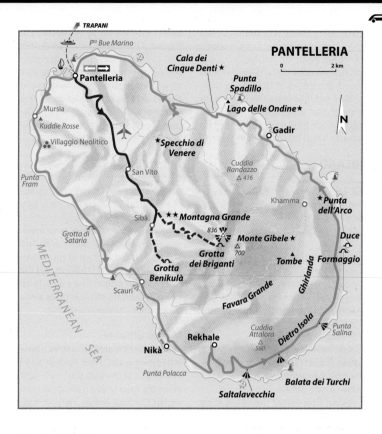

PANTELLERIA

TRAPANI

P^{ta} Bue Marino

Pantelleria

Mursia

Kuddie Rosse

Villaggio Neolitico

Punta Fram

Cala dei Cinque Denti ★

Punta Spadillo

Lago delle Ondine ★

Gadir

★Specchio di Venere

Cuddia Randazzo △ 416

San Vito

MEDITERRANEAN SEA

Grotta di Sataria

Sibà

★★ Montagna Grande

836

Khamma

★ Punta dell'Arco

Duce

Monte Gibele ★

Grotta dei Briganti

△ 700

Tombe

Ghirlanda

Formaggio

Grotta Benikulà

Scauri

Favara Grande

Dietro Isola

Punta Salina

Rekhale

Cuddia Attalora △ 560

Nikà

Punta Polacca

Balata dei Turchi

Saltalavecchia

0   2 km

N

Punto dell'Arco★

At the far end of the promontory sits the **Arco dell'Elefante★**, a spectacular natural archway of grey lava, which resembles the head and trunk of an elephant lying down to take a drink from the sea.

Gadir

The small, picture-perfect harbour bubbles with **thermal spring water** *(in the harbour hollow)*. It's a favourite spot with sunbathers, who take it in turns to wade in small, thermal pools and to relax and recline on the concrete harbourside when the weather is balmy.

A short way beyond, a path leads off to the right of the road to the **lighthouse** on **Punta Spadillo** *(when the lighthouse comes into view, branch left along a second track towards a collection of abandoned houses, then climb up to the batteries).*

Follow the path behind the white one downhill between low lava walls; it eventually opens out by the tiny **Lago delle Ondine★** (lake of waves).

Almost completely surrounded by cliffs and volcanic rock boulders, this lava hollow collects water from the breaking waves to form a small, emerald-green pool of stillness.

After the **Cala dei Cinque Denti★** *(the inlet with five teeth)*, where the craggy lava rock formations look as if they are about to bite a chunk out of the scenery, *(take a left-hand turn at the fork in the road)*.

Specchio di Venere★

"Venus' looking-glass" is a delicious lake of aquamarine water in a former volcanic crater, fed by a **sulphur-rich spring** on its western flank. Its name comes from the myth that tells how Venus studied her reflection in this lake when comparing her beauty to that of her rival, Psyche. Modern visitors in search of similar aesthetic satisfaction apply the rich, muddy mineral deposits found round the edges of the lake to their bodies and then leave this covering to dry in the sun. When baked to a shell, the home-made mud wrap is then washed off with a final dip in the warm waters.

INLAND★★

▶ Leave the town of Pantelleria by the airport road and continue to Sibà. Beyond the village is the Benikulà Cave or Bagno Asciutto (natural sauna).

Grotta Benikulà

Coming from the direction of Sibà, there are no signs to this site: access to the cave is down a road on the left (sign-posted from the other direction). Leave the car and proceed on foot. It takes 10min to walk there and back.
⊛Take swimwear and a towel for the sauna. ⊛Don't spend too long inside the cave, where the heat can be intense: 10min is long enough for a first visit.
Looking down over the valley from above, you'll see two pretty **Pante-schi gardens**. Inside the cave, entered through what looks like a crack in the rockface, is a hot natural sauna. Here, the temperature of the steam rises, the deeper in one goes and the ceiling becomes so hot that it's impossible to keep your hand pressed against it for longer than a couple of seconds. It is worth pausing at the cave entrance to acclimatise yourself, entering only once you are accustomed to the heat. The intense subterranean temperature and darkness of the cave can be a little overwhelming for some visitors.

La Montagna Grande★★

The road up to the Montagna Grande offers magnificent **views★★** over the surrounding landscape. The mountain's sides are pitted with volcanic vents (*Stufe de Khazen*), which can be spotted by the escaping vapour trails, and the terrain is covered with **pine forest** *(there are a number of designated picnic sites*

here). Leave the car by the building at the end of the road and continue on foot past two other buildings (a *dammuso* and a chapel); on the left, a gentle walk up a series of stone steps leads to the **Grotta dei Briganti**, a large cave where the temperature is constantly warm. The cave once served as a refuge for outlaws (hence its name).

Ghirlanda

Costa Ghirlanda *(on the east side of the island)* conceals a number of tombs of indeterminable age. Access is by a bumpy dirt track for which a four-wheel drive vehicle *(or a horse)* is recommended. In a tranquil oak forest *(on the left)* lies a notable collection of rock-hewn **tombs**, which local tradition says are Byzantine in origin. The exceptional beauty of this mysterious place alone makes the excursion worthwhile.

Monte Gibele★

This extinct volcano offers some interesting walks. From Rakhali, head inland and at the junction, fork right along the road until a path appears on the left. Continue on foot. The path leads to the crater, now covered in vegetation. On the way, the track skirts past the dramatic **Favara Grande**, a powerful geyser that shoots jets of steam into the air.

TOUR OF THE ISLAND BY BOAT★★

What better way to enjoy the opaque blackness of the lava rocks, standing in sharp contrast to the deep blue and emerald green sea, than by boat? Or the coastline dotted by secluded creeks, ravines and intriguing **caves** - many of which can only be reached by water? Starting out from **Pantelleria**, a clockwise tour of the island reveals the jagged, low-lying north coast and, in the area of **Cuddia Randazzo**, rocks with strange black profiles resembling animals. A series of inlets and caves follows, many of which are perfect spots for swimming. Then comes the **Arco dell'Elefante★** *(see above)* and a further succession of **caves** and **hollows** divided by pillars of lava. The most dramatic of the grottoes are situated on the coastline between Punta Duca and Punta Polacca, however **Grotta del Duce**, **Grotta del Formaggio** and **Grotta della Pila dell'Acqua** can only be fully explored by the smallest craft. This is the most spectacular stretch of the island's shores. Once past the towering cliffs that reach far into the sky and the large, monolithic rocks jutting sharply out of the sea, visitors are treated to a **view** of **Saltalavecchia**. After brushing past a series of ever-taller rocky outcrops *(along sections of coastline around Scauri)* the coast flattens again in the vicinity of **Cala dell'Alga**.

Capers

© S. Sauvignier / MICHELIN

ADDRESSES

🍽 STAY

If you are planning to stay one or more nights on the island, it is well worth renting a *dammuso*, one of the typical local Arab-style square houses. The tourist authorities will be happy to provide information on where to find houses to rent, as well as terms and conditions.

🍴🍴 **Albergo Papuscia** – *Contrada Sopra Portella 28, Tracino. ℘0923 91 54 63 or 346 12 50 45 76 (mobile). www. papuscia.com. Closed Dec–Apr. 11 rooms.* This small family-run hotel in the upper part of the village offers comfortable rooms housed in typical dammusi. Simple bar and restaurant with a summer veranda. No breakfast.

🍴🍴🍴 **Mediterraneo Hotel** – *Via Borgoltalia 71, Pantelleria. ℘0923 911299, www.pantelleriahotel.it. 43 rooms.* A simple, comfortable hotel by the sea, near the harbour. The rooms are pleasant and fresh, if not very large, with a blue-and-white colour scheme.

🍴 EAT

🍴🍴 **La Favarotta** – *Località Khamma Fuori, Khamma. ℘0923 91 54 46. Open daily for dinner. Closed lunchtimes and Oct–Mar. Booking recommended.* This restaurant offers welcome respite during the heat of summer. Located inland at an altitude of 400m/1,300ft, the hearty menu here nevertheless includes a number of excellent fish dishes.

🍴🍴🍴 **La Nicchia** – *Scauri Basso, Scauri. ℘0923 91 63 42. Open Sat–Sun only. Closed at lunchtime and Jan–Feb.* At La Nicchia, guests can choose between dining on an outdoor terrace with tables and wooden chairs or in the indoor dining room, where the pizza kitchen is open to view, or beneath a delightful pergola at the end of the garden, surrounded by colourful flowers and plants.

🍴🍴🍴 **I Mulini** – *Kania 12, Tracino. ℘0923 91 53 98. Closed Nov–Easter.* This picturesque restaurant housed in an old mill has been tastefully restored in traditional style. The restaurant specialises in simple, local cuisine.

SHOPPING

Visitors should not leave the island without buying some salted capers and a bottle of sweet **Passito di Pantelleria** wine. Buy at shops in built-up areas or from local farms.

SIGHTSEEING

The best way to explore Pantelleria is by car. The road running around the island is asphalted, but very narrow. Bus services from **Piazza Cavour** link **Pantelleria** with other parts of the island. Several tour operators *(some private)* provide information on the types of accommodation and facilities available. Most can also arrange holiday packages, car and boat rentals. Information from the **Pro Loco** and the **Associazione Turistica di Pantelleria** (*℘0923 91 29 48*).

To explore the coast from the sea, rubber dinghies may be hired; organised boat trips are also available.

Lampedusa★

The island of Lampedusa is a limestone plateau that sweeps into an impressive **cliff★★★** in the north, and plunges into long capes, deep coves and sandy beaches to the south. Closer to Africa than Italy, it is surrounded by a **spectacular sea★★** that shifts in colour from turquoise to emerald green to deep blue.

▶ **Population:** 6 170

🎯 **Michelin Map:** p398:A2.

ℹ️ **Info:** Via Vittorio Emanuele 87. ℘0922 97 11 71. www.lampedusa.it

▶ **Location:** The port is in the southeastern section of Lampedusa, an area that is also home to the island's beaches and hotels. The north is mountainous; best explored by boat. Most roads are located to the east, although one heads west inland from the town of Lampedusa to Capo Ponente. The Riserva Naturale Isola di Lampedusa covers the southeastern section of the coast between Cala Greca and the Vallone dell'Acqua, and includes the Isola dei Conigli.

👥 **Kids:** The sea turtles (apply for viewing).

😊 **Don't Miss:** The Isola dei Conigli bay, Tabaccara bay, the view from Albero del Sole in Lampedusa, Pozzolana in Linosa.

🕐 **Timing:** Plan three days. Avoid July and August, when the sea turtles lay their eggs and tourism spikes.

GETTING THERE AND AROUND

The simplest way to get to the islands is by air (*Aeroporto di Lampedusa, ℘0922 97 07 31*): **flights** operate from **Palermo** (*approx. 1hr*), with additional services in summer from many Italian cities. There is also a **hydrofoil** service in summer from **Porto Empedocle** to **Lampedusa** and **Linosa** (*4hr and 3hr*). Contact Ustica Lines, ℘0923 87 38 13, *www.usticalines. it*. Overnight **ferry** services operate from Agrigento (**Porto Empedocle**) to **Linosa** (*6hr*) and **Lampedusa** (*8hr*). Contact Siremar, ℘091 74 93 111 (*from Italy) or 081 017 19 98 (mobiles and international), www.siremar.it*.

VISIT

The town of Lampedusa shares its name with the island itself. Apart from the odd house scattered here and there, this is the only town as such and it hinges on **Via Roma**. The main street comes to life in the morning at breakfast time and again in the evening at sunset until late into the night. It hosts a cluster of small shops and cafés that sprawl onto the pavement. In summer, these bars offer low-key entertainment (*sessions of karaoke or live music*).

Boat Trip Around the Island★

In summer, many a boat owner will tout his or her business down in the harbour, happy to take visitors out and round the island for a reasonable sum. Excursions usually take a whole day, departing at about 10am and returning at approx. 5pm.

The low, jagged coastline is laced with creeks and inlets, including **La Tabaccara★★**. Only accessible by boat, it is washed by a stunning turquoise sea, which also laps the shores of the **Baia dell'Isola del Coniglio★★★**. At Capo Ponente, the most westerly point of the island, the landscape suddenly changes.

The northern **coastline★★** consists of a single, tall cliff that plunges straight down into the sea, indented here and there by a number of intriguing caves and grottoes. Immediately after the **Baia della Madonnin★★** (*so-called because one of its rock formations resembles the Virgin Mary*) are the impressive

Marine World

The islands of the "high sea" – The archipelago of the **Isole Pelagie**★ *(approx. 200km/125mi south of Agrigento between the island of Malta and Tunisia)* comprises the large island of **Lampedusa** (surface area 33sq km/12.7sq mi) and two small islands, **Linosa** and **Lampione**. The inhabitants of Lampedusa have little agricultural experience: the interior of the island is stony and arid, like a miniature desert. Instead they depend on fishing for a livelihood as the large fleet anchored offshore in the well-sheltered bays testify. A few finds confirm that the island was inhabited as early as the Bronze Age. In 1843, the island belonged to the illustrious Lampedusa family (of which **Giuseppe**, author of *The Leopard*, is the most famous member). When it was acquired by King Ferdinand II, he had a prison built on the island and sent a handful of people to reside there.

View of the harbour, Lampedusa

© marie_dufay / Fotolia.com

Marine underworld – Snorkelling is excellent along the rocky coastline, which teems with brightly coloured rainbow wrasse, scorpion fish, blenies *(lurking in small crevasses in the rock)*, sea stars, slender needlefish, octopus, sea cucumbers, sea hares and sponges. The sea floor is a jigsaw of rocky and white sandy patches. At intervals these are suddenly monopolised by dark green underwater meadows of *Poseidonia oceanica* – the seaweed nicknamed "the lung of the Mediterranean".

Divers will discover abundant groves of coral, sponges and madrepores populated with shoals of colourful **parrot fish** and off **Capo Grecale** *(at a depth of 50m/165ft)*, lobsters.

Tabaccara Bay, Lampedusa

© Gianvincenzo Sparacia/Tips Images

Isola dei Conigli

© Chiara Lozzi/Dreamstime.com

Loggerhead Turtle (Caretta caretta)

The Mediterranean's most common sea turtle is a docile, solitary being – other than during the mating season. They live in temperate waters, except when the females haul onto dry land to lay their eggs, every two or three years.

The mother-to-be chooses a sandy beach undisturbed by lights or noise. With enormous effort, she heaves herself from the water (deprived of all her natural dignity, agility and grace) and, using her hind flippers, digs a deep hole in the sand *(40–75cm/16–30in deep)*. Here, she passively lays and then buries her eggs. Her task now over, she turns round and shuffles back to the sea.

Hatching takes place six to eight weeks later. The baby turtles emerge from the sand and instinctively scuttle towards the sea, a threatening and dangerous world

Scogli del Sacramento rocks onto which open a deep cave and its neighbour, the **Grotta del Faraglione**.

The northeastern tip of the island, **Capo Grecale**, is capped with a lighthouse that sweeps its beam across some 60 nautical miles (110km/68mi) offshore. Immediately after Cala Pisana, by the *Grotta del Teschio* (Cave of the Skull), is a 10–15m/30–50ft long beach *(accessible down a path on the right)*.

Exploring the Island on Land

▶ The circular coast road is not asphalted all the way round the island; you are therefore recommended to hire a moped or small four-wheel drive vehicle for the day. From the town of Lampedusa, head east towards the airport.

The dirt track parallel to the runway skirts round many of the creeks and small rocky bays on the south coast. Beyond **Cala Pisana**, it continues to the tip of **Capo Grecale**, where the lighthouse is situated.

From this lofty position, the fine **view★** pans in either direction along the coast and down to the sea, stirring dizzily below.

The road then links up with another that traces the south side of the island. Turn right towards the telecommunications signalling station.

Albero del Sole

These steep cliffs are the highest point on Lampedusa *(133m/436ft)*.

The small, round building contains a wooden crucifix. On the other side of the stone wall (*be careful, as it conceals*

– at least until they grow to any size. Only a few survive to adulthood. In fact, even before they hatch, the eggs easily fall prey to birds and man. As newly-hatched turtles, their greatest threat comes in the shape of fish, greedy for their tender meat. This is why it is important to protect and safeguard both the nesting sites (eliminating noise, light and disturbance) and the seas the turtles inhabit. Visitors should respect a few fundamental rules, notably disposing of their plastic bags with care. In the water, these take on the appearance of a tasty jellyfish for a turtle – a mistake that can cost it its life.

Turtle conservation

The Pelagie – notably Lampedusa's bay of Isola dei Conigli with its long stretch of sand – have been chosen by the loggerhead turtles as suitable sites for laying eggs. A special conservation-cum-education centre, *Centro Recupero, Marcaggio e Tutela delle Tartarughe Marine*, has been set up on **Lampedusa** to monitor and protect the turtle population, with a programme involving local children under the supervision of Dr Daniela Freggi.

On Linosa, the black *(and therefore warm)* sands of **Cala Pozzolana di Ponente** seem to favour the birth of female turtles. Scholars say the sex of a turtle is determined by the temperature: below 30°C/86°F males predominate, temperatures in excess of this favour females. By the beach the *Assocazione Hydrosphera* runs its *Centro Studi sulle Tartarughe Marine*: this displays information concerning the life cycle of the turtles, complete with illustrations provided by enthusiastic volunteers. The centre also has a small "Casualty department" for turtles found sick and exhausted, or brought in by fishermen who have inadvertently caught them on a hook.

The two centres *(on Lampedusa and Linosa)* are part of an Italian project run by the Department of Animal and Human Biology of La Sapienza University in Rome. *Open mid-Jun–mid-Sept 10am–1pm, 4–7pm. The rest of the year only 4–7pm. Closed holidays.* 0922 97 20 76.

a treacherous drop), there is a dramatic **view★★** of the **Faraglione** – or *Scoglio a Vela* (shrouded rock) as it is also called – and cliffs plunging steeply into the sea *(one way to enjoy the view without fear of falling is to lie flat on the ground, not too near the edge)*.

Return the same way and fork right along the partially asphalted road that runs past a tree plantation *(right)*. At the far end of the enclosure wall, continue along the vague dirt track leading to a small iron cross. The headland *(right)* provides a glorious **view★★** of the **Scoglio del Sacramento★** *(right)*. In the distance *(on the left)*, can be seen the little island of Lampione.

Return to the main road and head south towards the bay around *Isola dei Conigli* (Rabbit Island).

Baia dell'Isola dei Conigli★★★

In this broad bay, with its petticoat of white cliffs and the most beautiful beach on the island, sits a little islet. It could almost be a corner of the Caribbean: the whitest sand slopes gently down to the water's edge, and delicate clear tints of turquoise and emerald green stretch out to sea. Annually, a colony of **loggerhead turtles** makes its way up the beach to lay its eggs.

Today, this exciting event is threatened by an ever-increasing number of spectators who linger here until sunset *(turtles lay their eggs at night, but their extreme shyness means the slightest disturbance will frighten them away)*. This is also the only place in Italy inhabited by an unusual species of stripey lizard of the Large Psammodromus *(Psammadromus algirus)* variety, more usually

433

found in North Africa *(Tunisia, Algeria and Morocco)*.

Madonna del Porto Salvo

This small, ancient shrine of uncertain date is surrounded by a pretty garden, bursting with colour in the summer.

EXCURSIONS

LINOSA★

The untamed beauty of the northernmost island, Linosa resides in the blackness of its volcanic rock and its four great lofty cones pitched dramatically against the blue sky. This island, the tip of a submerged volcano, has evolved in different stages and this is strikingly evident. The gaping maws of the volcano craters *(now extinct)* and bleak laval beaches with their crystal waters leave the visitor with a lasting, if haunting, impression. The only town huddled around the little harbour consists of a collection of houses attractively painted in pastel shades, with strongly-accented coloured corners, doors and windows. From here, there is a variety of possible excursions on foot into the mountains, or by boat around the coast. The few hundred inhabitants of this peaceful islet, who once depended on rearing cattle, now eke out a living from tourism.

The tallest peak is Monte Vulcano *(186m/ 610ft)* – a volcano, as its name suggests, though now extinct.

The interior of the island is predominantly desert-like, but still supports a few areas of cultivation (notably the *Fossa del Cappellano*, which is particularly well sheltered from the wind).

Fringed with a jagged lava coastline, Linosa is considered to be a veritable paradise by **scuba-divers** and snorkelling enthusiasts.

The land-based fauna includes large colonies of Maltese wall lizards and **Cory's shearwaters** – the seabirds that shatter the quiet summer nights with their plaintive cries. Loggerhead turtles still lay eggs on the black **beach** in **Cala Pozzolana**.

A number of popular footpaths lead to the summits of the island's three main peaks: **Monte Rosso** – the crater of which shelters various garden allotments, **Monte Nero** and **Monte Vulcano**.

Boat Trip Around the Island★★

Excursions by boat can be arranged down at the harbour.

The boat skirts the **Fili**, a group of rocks surrounding a sort of natural swimming-pool, enclosed on the landward side by sheer walls of **rock★**, polished and moulded by the rain and wind into wave-like forms. The restless sea and a handful of caper plants complete the landscape. Beyond the *Faraglioni* rocks that stand guard outside the "natural pool" or *Piscina Naturale (also accessi-*

Linosa

© marco cesari / age fotostock

ble on foot), the **lighthouse** comes into view on a stretch of particularly jagged coastline.

Just before the circular trip draws to its conclusion, the boat steams across **Cala Pozzolana★★**; this shelters the only beach on the island, which is backed by a wall of incredible colour that ranges from sulphur yellow through to rust red. The hydrofoils from Lampedusa moor here.

LAMPIONE

Occupied only by a lighthouse, this small, uninhabited and sparsely vegetated island rises vertically from a depth of 60m/196ft as a series of sheer cliffs. The deep, and therefore relatively unpolluted, sea provides ideal conditions for scuba divers to glimpse groupers, lobsters, **yellow and pink coral** and the occasional **grey shark** on the reefs around the island.

Offshore fishing is also popular *(ask around at the harbour in Lampedusa town for a boat and skipper for hire).*

ADDRESSES

🛏 STAY

Various types of apartment are available to rent, in addition to the usual array of expensive traditional hotels. Book well in advance for the summer months. For further information, contact the tourist office.

⊜ **Campeggio La Roccia** – *Via Madonna, Cala Greca, Lampedusa.* ℘0922 97 00 55. *www.laroccia.net.* ⤸. Right on the seafront, this campsite offers a selection of accommodation: bungalows, mobile homes and caravans, as well as large shady pitches for tents. Facilities include a restaurant and supermarket.

⊜⊜⊜⊜ **Dammusi di Borgo Calacreta** – *Contrada Calacreta, Lampedusa.* ℘0922 97 03 94. *www. calacreta.com.* The traditional *dammusi (white-domed buildings with stone walls)* offer a picturesque alternative to staying in a hotel. This complex also includes small white villas rented out by the week.

⊜⊜⊜⊜ **Cavalluccio Marino** – 3, *Contrada Cala Croce.* ℘0922 97 00 53. *www.hotelcavallucciomarino.com. Closed Nov–Easter.* ⤸. *10 rooms, half board only.* This small, elegant family-run hotel with restaurant, situated near one of the island's prettiest bays, offers 10 comfortable, well-maintained rooms. Fresh fish is caught daily by the hotel owner, Signor Pietro.

🍽 EAT

Lampedusa has a wide choice of small restaurants and trattorias all serving a wonderful variety of fresh fish. The *cuscus di pesce* (often made with grouper), a local speciality based on a Tunisian dish, is particularly recommended.

⊜⊜ **Da Nicola** – *Via Ponente, Lampedusa.* ℘0922 97 12 39. *Closed Thu (in winter) Booking recommended.* For excellent seafood and home cooking typical of Lampedusa, this family-run restaurant is well worth a visit. Meals are served in a simple rustic dining room full of small paintings.

⊜⊜ **Al Gallo D'Oro** – *Via Ludovico Ariosto 2, Lampedusa.* ℘0922 97 12 97. *Closed Dec–Feb.* This restaurant is renowned for its fresh fish and good value for money. The decor is rustic, with a wooden gallery, exposed beams, plus numerous prints and paintings. Meals are served outside in summer.

⊜⊜⊜ **Lipadusa** – *Via Bonfiglio 6, Lampedusa.* ℘0922 97 16 91. *Closed at lunchtime, Nov–Easter.* This friendly, family-run restaurant in the centre serves regional cuisine with an understandable emphasis on fresh fish. The decor is simple.

SHOPPING

Natural **sponges** are collected from all around Lampedusa making them one of the most popular purchases available to visitors.

A word of advice – the whiter sponges, although more attractive, have been treated with bleach, which makes them less durable. The slightly brown sponges, on the other hand, last longer.

The locally-grown produce available on Linosa includes lentils and miniature tomatoes; reed baskets are also on sale in the town centre.

Ustica★★

This small volcanic island, with its inky rocks and arid landscape, was called Ustica by the Romans, after the Latin word for 'burnt'. Its dramatic coastline hides beautiful coves and inlets, while the waters around it, including a Marine National Park, are popular scuba diving areas. Tourism is the island's main source of income, although vegetables and cereals are grown on the island.

A BIT OF HISTORY

Ustica was continuously inhabited from the late Neolithic until the end of the Classical period, when it was left to serve as a pirate refuge.

Until the 1950s, it was used as a penal colony, the most famous prisoner here being **Antonio Gramsci**, the prominent Italian Communist. A new identity for the island began to develop in earnest with tourism, as a result of the international divers, who came here to explore the surrounding clear waters. In 1987, the waters around Ustica were designated a Marine National Park.

▸ **Population:** 1 335
- **Michelin Map:** p398:A1.
- **Info:** Piazza Umberto I. ☎091 84 49 237. www.comune.ustica.pa.it; www.ustica.net.
- **Location:** Situated 60km/37mi from Palermo, this tiny island is dotted with rocky inlets and is best discovered by boat. A road and several footpaths allow visitors to explore the island's interior. The western coast is now part of a Marine National Park.
- **Don't Miss:** Sea-watching, boat trips and scuba diving in the Marine National Park and views all along the beautiful path from Torre di Santa Maria.
- **Kids:** Boat trips to the Marine National Park and swimming in the Piscina Naturale.
- **Timing:** June-July and September. Avoid the hoards of tourists in August.

Ustica's beauty may be admired from a boat

© Roberto Rinaldi / Tips Images

GETTING THERE

Direct services operate out of **Palermo**. Crossings by ferry *(2hr 30min)* and hydrofoil *(1hr 10min)* are provided by **Siremar**, *(Gruppo Tirrenia)*, ✆*091 74 93 111 (from Italy)* or *081 01 71 998 (mobiles and abroad); www.siremar.it.*

During the summer season, a hydrofoil service calling at **Trapani–Favignana–Levanzo–Ustica–Naples** is operated by Ustica Lines. *(The* **Ustica–Naples** *leg takes approx. 4hr.)* Contact **Ustica Lines**, Via. Amm. Staiti 23, Trapani; ✆*0923 87 3813; www.usticalines.it.*

SIGHTS
Marine National Park

The nature reserve, Italy's first, was created in 1987 to preserve and protect the natural diversity of flora and fauna off Ustica's coastline. The National Park comprises three zones. **Zone A**, classified as **riserva integrale**, extends along the island's west flank from **Cala Sidotti** to **Caletta** and as far as 350m/1148ft offshore *(marked with special yellow buoys)*: swimming is permitted; fishing and boating are prohibited.

Zone B, classified as **riserva generale**, extends beyond Zone A from **Punta Cavazzi** to **Punta Omo Morto**: here swimming is permitted, as is underwater photography, hook-and-line fishing and commercial fishing *(with a permit from the Commune).*

Zone C, classified as a **riserva parziale**, applies to the rest of the coast: here, national fishing regulations apply and speargun fishing is permitted.

The Submerged World

The sea around Ustica is especially clean and pollution-free *(lying in the middle of an inward current from the Atlantic Ocean).* It provides ideal conditions for different species of aquatic flora and fauna to proliferate. One striking sight is the vast meadow of *Poseidonia oceanica,* a beneficial **seaweed**, nicknamed the "lungs of the Mediterranean" *(because it oxygenates the water),* found up to a depth of 40m/131ft. Just below the surface, the water shimmers with shoals of white bream, two-banded bream, voracious-looking grey mullet *(at the very worst, they only tickle),* saddled bream, salpas, and **rainbow wrasse**. The patches shaded by overhanging rock attract cardinal fish; the rock face itself shelters colonies of beautiful orange "flowered" **madrepore**, which sometimes cover vast sections at a time with colourful **sponges**.

At greater depths lurk larger fish – notably, **grey mullet**. Here, the underwater landscape also harbours moray eels, lobsters, **mantis prawns** and shrimps.

Guided tours

The west coast, designated **riserva integrale** *(highly restricted),* harbours two secret, pink-hued grottoes: **Grotta Segreta** and **Grotta Rosata**, coloured by algae.

The reserve authorities also lay on **sea-watching trips** *(with commentary)* in the *riserva integrale:* a guide will point out specific organisms and fish as they appear – accustomed to the presence of man, they appear almost tame.

Scuba-diving

Highlights for any scuba-diving enthusiast include the **Grotta dei Gamberi**, near Punta Gavazzi, where delicate fan-like red gorgonians thrive *(at a depth of approx. 42m/138ft)* and the **sub-aqua archaeological trail** off the lighthouse-topped headland Punta Gavazzi *(depths of 9–17m/30–56ft, marked by an orange buoy),* where many artefacts – anchors and **Roman amphorae** – can be admired *in situ.*

Another popular haunt is the **Scoglio del Medico:** an outcrop of basalt riddled with caves and gorges that plunge to great depths and whose crystal-clear waters provide a spectacular underwater **seascape★★** of sponges, shoals of colourful fish and weed. **Secca di Colombara** *(40m/131ft below)* is spectacular in a different way, populated as it is by rainbow-coloured spreads of sponges and gorgonians.

Exploring the underwater world of Ustica

© Roberto Rinaldi / Tips Images

USTICA TOWN★

A single road and various flights of steps *(flanked with magnificent hibiscus bushes)* lead up from the harbour to the main town above. A characteristic feature of the houses peculiar to Ustica is the practice of painting their exteriors with artistic murals: bright landscape scenes, *trompe l'oeils,* portraits, still-life paintings and any other fanciful compositions that might spring to mind. The most eye-catching building is the **Torre di Santa Maria**, which houses the **Museo Archeologico** (○open 9am–1pm, 3–8pm in summer; ⊜€2.50; for information on opening times for the rest of the year call ☎091 66 28 452) and its collections of artefacts recovered from shipwrecks, the **prehistoric village** at I Faraglioni and **Hellenistic** and **Roman tombs** found on Capo Falconiera.

Capo Falconiera

At the far end of the central piazza where the **Chiesa Madre** is situated, turn right past the Stations of the Cross. From here, a stepped path *(left)* climbs to the top, where the ruins of a Bourbon fortress and a **3C BC settlement** are located. Naturally short on space and fairly inaccessible, the area was extended by cutting terraces into the rock: as

a result, three tiers of housing are stacked one above the other. At the foot of the fortress, remnants of a contemporary **hypogeum necropolis** have been discovered, together with a second necropolis dating from palaeo-Christian times (5C–6C AD). From here, you get a good **view★** of the harbour and the centre of the island, including **Monte Costa del Fallo** and **Monte Guardia dei Turchi**.

VILLAGGIO PREISTORICO★

This settlement can be seen through a fence.

An extensive **Bronze-Age settlement** has been discovered at Colombaia, in the vicinity of **I Faraglioni**. This comprises a collection of foundations for circular huts that were re-used later for square-based constructions of a type similar to prehistoric houses found on the island of Panarea.

Coast

The jagged coastline has a number of caves that can be explored either by boat *(fishermen in the harbour will volunteer their services for a small fee)* or by land. Small beaches *(Cala Sidoti, Punta dello Spalmatore, al Faro)* succeed lovely rocky bays – including one beneath the lighthouse that encloses the **piscina** naturale★ *(a natural pool immensely popular with swimmers and sunbathers)* along the island's west coast. Conversely, the east coast shelters magnificent caves such as the **Grotta Azzurra**, **Grotta Verde** and **Grotta delle Barche**, which are best explored with a snorkel; the **Grotta delle Barche** can also be reached by a lovely **path★** that threads its way through forests of fragrant pine trees from Torre di Santa Maria, providing marvellous **views★** of the sea and the coast along its length.

ADDRESSES

🏨 STAY

⊖🛏🛏 **Hotel Clelia** – *Via Sindaco I°29, Ustica.* ℘*091 84 49 039. www.hotelclelia.it. 14 rooms.* Once a small pensione, this hotel has expanded over the years. The rooms are pleasant and airy, and offer all the necessary creature comforts.

⊖🛏🛏 **Hotel Diana** – *Contrada San Paolo.* ℘*091 84 49 109. www.hoteldiana-ustica.com. Closed Nov–Feb. 30 rooms.* This circular hotel enjoys a quiet location outside Ustica town, with impressive **panoramic views**. The only disadvantage to the irregularly shaped rooms is the space taken up by the beds. Accommodation is complemented by a good restaurant.

🍴 EAT

⊖🍽 **La Luna sul Porto** – *Corso Vittorio Emanuele II 11, Ustica.* ℘*091 84 49 799. Closed Sun (in winter). Booking recommended.* This pleasant restaurant is run by an Italian woman from Piedmont who fell in love with Ustica over 10 years ago. Simple service, reasonable prices and a lovely **view** of the port from the out-door terrace.

⊖🍽 **Mario** – *Piazza Umberto I 21, Ustica.* ℘*091 84 49 505. Closed Mon (in winter) and Jan.* Dine outdoors in summer and in the trattoria's cosy dining room in winter. A firm favourite for genuine, simple Sicilian cuisine in this delightful corner of the Mediterranean.

ACTIVITIES

🐚Those who love the sea and enjoy swimming should not forget to bring a mask, snorkel and fins: snorkelling and diving will introduce the visitor to a spectacular underwater experience, considered by divers to be one of the top spots in the world, and add a new perspective to their appreciation of the natural beauty of Ustica.

As well as the natural wonders of the marine reserve, the area is also rich in subterranean archaeological wonders, with anchors, amphorae and ancient objects resting *in situ* at many dive sites.

Every year, a special week-long sub-aqua course is organised, including theoretical and practical diving lessons *(marine archaeology, marine biology, modern recovery techniques for lifting artefacts from the sea bed)* and guided tours. *For further information, apply to the Riserva Marina or to Archeologia Viva,* ℘*055 50 62 303.*

EVENTS

Rassegna Internazionale delle Attività subacquee – An International Review of Underwater Activities is organised annually during the summer *(usually in May, June or September)*. This gathering includes a range of different events, such as exhibitions, tastings of local seafood and other activities. There are also special organised dives and courses for divers of all levels – from beginners to advanced – who come from all over the world to explore the depths around this tiny island. *For detailed information and to contact the organisers, visit the website: www.riasustica.it.*

SIGHTSEEING

The standard means of transport available includes hired **mopeds** and a regular **minibus** service around the island in both directions on the one circular road. Extremely good-value bus passes, valid for a week, two weeks or a month, are available from the town hall.

Walking is one of the most popular ways to cover the sights. The island is small enough *(9km/5.5mi)* to circumnavigate by foot in around four hours.

If you are keen to explore the coastline and marine reserve, pick up **boats** at the quay or buy a ticket for the glass-bottomed boat tours, run by Centro Accoglienza *(ask at the tourist office for more details)*.

INDEX

INDEX

INDEX

INDEX

INDEX

INDEX

🛏 STAY

🍷 EAT

MAPS AND PLANS

MAP LEGEND

	Sight	Seaside resort	Winter sports resort	Spa
Highly recommended ★★★	★★★	⚏⚏⚏	✳✳✳	⚕⚕⚕
Recommended ★★	★★	⚏⚏	✳✳	⚕⚕
Interesting ★	★	⚏	✳	⚕

Additional symbols

🄱	Tourist information
═══ ═══	Motorway or other primary route
❶ ❶	Junction: complete, limited
⊐⊏ ═══	Pedestrian street
I═══I	Unsuitable for traffic, street subject to restrictions
⊐⊐⊐⊐ ----	Steps – Footpath
🚆 🚉	Train station – Auto-train station
🚌 S.N.C.F.	Coach (bus) station
⊢⊣	Tram
⊙	Metro, underground
P R	Park-and-Ride
♿	Access for the disabled
✉	Post office
☎	Telephone
✉	Covered market
⋅✕⋅	Barracks
△	Drawbridge
∪	Quarry
✗	Mine
B F	Car ferry (river or lake)
🛥	Ferry service: cars and passengers
⛴	Foot passengers only
③	Access route number common to Michelin maps and town plans
Bert (R.)...	Main shopping street
AZ B	Map co-ordinates

Sports and recreation

🏇	Racecourse
⛸	Skating rink
⚊ ⚊	Outdoor, indoor swimming pool
🎥	Multiplex Cinema
⛵	Marina, sailing centre
⌂	Trail refuge hut
⬤▬■▬▬⬤	Cable cars, gondolas
⬤┼┼┼┼┼⬤	Funicular, rack railway
🚂	Tourist train
◇	Recreation area, park
⛲	Theme, amusement park
Ψ	Wildlife park, zoo
✾	Gardens, park, arboretum
◉	Bird sanctuary, aviary
🚶	Walking tour, footpath
☺	Of special interest to children

Map Legend continued overleaf

MAP LEGEND

Selected monuments and sights

	Tour - Departure point
	Catholic church
	Protestant church, other temple
	Synagogue - Mosque
	Building
■	Statue, small building
	Calvary, wayside cross
◎	Fountain
	Rampart - Tower - Gate
	Château, castle, historic house
	Ruins
	Dam
	Factory, power plant
☆	Fort
∩	Cave
	Troglodyte dwelling
	Prehistoric site
	Viewing table
Ⱳ	Viewpoint
▲	Other place of interest

Special symbols

◆	Gendarmerie (Carabinieri)
	Temple, Greek and Roman ruins
	Beach

Abbreviations

H	Town hall (Municipio)
J	Law courts (Palazzo di Giustizia)
M	Museum (Museo)
P	Local authority offices (Prefettura)
POL.	Police station (Polizia) (in large towns: Questura)
T	Theatre (Teatro)
U	University (Università)

COMPANION PUBLICATIONS

REGIONAL AND LOCAL MAPS

Michelin map 365 Sicilia, which covers the island of Sicily and includes an alphabetical index of towns, as well as maps of **Agrigento, Catania, Messina, Palermo** and **Siracusa**. Scale 1:400 000.

♦ Michelin map 735 Italia, a practical map which provides the visitor with a complete picture of Italy's road network. Scale 1:1 000 000.

♦ Michelin Road Atlas Italia, a useful, spiral-bound atlas with an alphabetical index of 70 towns and cities. Scale 1:300 000.

INTERNET

Michelin is also pleased to offer an online route-planning service, Michelin maps and town plans, and addresses of hotels and restaurants featured in the *Michelin Guide Italia* through the website at:

www.viamichelin.com
www.travel.viamichelin.com

Choose the shortest route, a route without tolls, or the Michelin recommended route to your destination; you can also access information about hotels and restaurants from *The Red Guide*, and tourist sites from *The Green Guide*.

YOU ALREADY KNOW THE GREEN GUIDE, NOW FIND OUT ABOUT THE MICHELIN GROUP

The Michelin Adventure

It all started with rubber balls! This was the product made by a small company based in Clermont-Ferrand that André and Edouard Michelin inherited, back in 1880. The brothers quickly saw the potential for a new means of transport and their first success was the invention of detachable pneumatic tires for bicycles. However, the automobile was to provide the greatest scope for their creative talents. Throughout the 20th century, Michelin never ceased developing and creating ever more reliable and high-performance tires, not only for vehicles ranging from trucks to F1 but also for underground transit systems and airplanes.

From early on, Michelin provided its customers with tools and services to facilitate mobility and make traveling a more pleasurable and more frequent experience. As early as 1900, the Michelin Guide supplied motorists with a host of useful information related to vehicle maintenance, accommodation and restaurants, and was to become a benchmark for good food. At the same time, the Travel Information Bureau offered travelers personalised tips and itineraries.

The publication of the first collection of roadmaps, in 1910, was an instant hit! In 1926, the first regional guide to France was published, devoted to the principal sites of Brittany, and before long each region of France had its own Green Guide. The collection was later extended to more far-flung destinations, including New York in 1968 and Taiwan in 2011.

In the 21st century, with the growth of digital technology, the challenge for Michelin maps and guides is to continue to develop alongside the company's tire activities. Now, as before, Michelin is committed to improving the mobility of travelers.

MICHELIN TODAY

WORLD NUMBER ONE TIRE MANUFACTURER

- 70 production sites in 18 countries
- 111,000 employees from all cultures and on every continent
- 6,000 people employed in research and development

Moving
for a world

Moving forward means developing tires with better road grip and shorter braking distances, whatever the state of the road.

CORRECT TIRE PRESSURE

RIGHT PRESSURE

- Safety
- Longevity
- Optimum fuel consumption

-0,5 bar

- Durability reduced by 20% (- 8,000 km)

-1 bar

- Risk of blowouts
- Increased fuel consumption
- Longer braking distances on wet surfaces

forward together
where mobility is safer

It also involves helping motorists take care of their safety and their tires. To do so, Michelin organises "Fill Up With Air" campaigns all over the world to remind us that correct tire pressure is vital.

WEAR

DETECTING TIRE WEAR

The legal minimum depth of tire tread is 1.6mm. Tire manufacturers equip their tires with tread wear indicators, which are small blocks of rubber moulded into the base of the main grooves at a depth of 1.6mm.

Tires are the only point of contact between the vehicle and road.

The photo below shows the actual contact zone.

If the tread depth is less than 1.6mm, tires are considered to be worn and dangerous on wet surfaces.

NEW TIRE

WORN TIRE
(1,6 mm tread)

Moving forward
means sustainable mobility

INNOVATION AND THE ENVIRONMENT

By 2050, Michelin aims to cut the quantity of raw materials used in its tire manufacturing process by half and to have developed renewable energy in its facilities. The design of MICHELIN tires has already saved billions of litres of fuel and, by extension, billions of tons of CO_2.

Similarly, Michelin prints its maps and guides on paper produced from sustainably managed forests and is diversifying its publishing media by offering digital solutions to make traveling easier, more fuel efficient and more enjoyable!

The group's whole-hearted commitment to eco-design on a daily basis is demonstrated by ISO 14001 certification.

Like you, Michelin is committed to preserving our planet.

Chat with Bibendum

Go to
www.michelin.com/corporate/en
Find out more about
Michelin's history and the
latest news.

QUIZ

Michelin develops tires for all types of vehicles.
See if you can match the right tire with the right vehicle...